Comments from the Field

As someone who looks at IT from the business owner's perspective, I believe that this book should be on the reading list of every VAP and VAR. The industry is experiencing a shakeout and only those who know how to build fast, flexible businesses with the customer at the center will survive. It's great to see a book written by an MCSE who obviously understands business and the importance of partnering with customers and others in the industry.

Kathleen Allen Ph.D., Professor of Entrepreneurship
Marshall School of Business, University of Southern California
Author of Launching New Ventures *and* Growing and Managing an Entrepreneurial Business

---

This book really hits home, describing VAPs and the challenges of providing profitable solutions for clients with SBS, material that has *never* been available previously. I got technical information from chapters that I haven't found in any other training materials. This should be an invaluable tool for helping VAPs provide, sell, and implement successful and profitable solutions with SBS 4.5. I actually enjoyed reading a computer book!

Dennis Anderson, Technical Service Manager
Net\Works Inc., Fridley, Minnesota

I read volumes of technical dogma daily trying to stay current with the latest products and services on the market. Rarely do I find the information to the point and written in a manner that the writer projects being in the trenches right along with me. Chapter 11 was one of my favorites: what do you do now that you landed that contract? It's in there! The material is on the money. Microsoft should have you write their user manuals! Kudos, Josh.

Scott L. Ayon, Owner
Office-Anywhere, Willamina, Oregon

Great stuff!!! The information is very clear and straightforward. It goes to show that no matter how much experience you have with a product, it is always great to get someone else's point of view. The advice given in Chapter 2 is invaluable and I can't wait to write my next proposal.

Ed Berger, MCP, Senior Network Consultant
Livingston, New Jersey

There is a vast market for technology consulting among small businesses. This book should prove to be a valuable resource for these independent technology providers. It compiles best practices from top SBS consultants around the world.

Jeff Cate, President
PC Serv, Nashville, Tennessee

Finally a book about SBS, written for VAPs, that goes beyond technical information and explains how to use it to be profitable in the real small business world. A must read for anyone servicing the small business marketplace.

Lou Ciarlo, Jr., Technical and Customer Support Manager
DMA Data Industries, Inc., Fair Lawn, New Jersey

It was refreshing to read a book that's not just about the technology, but also about the business of selling the technology. It's definitely a market that doesn't attract enough attention. Small business owners in the computer-consulting field have few books tailored to their specific sales needs—your book changes that. It will definitely be required reading for anyone I know who is getting into the business of providing computer services to small businesses.

Brian DeMarzo, MCSE, President
Top Down Design, Staten Island, New York

Not one aspect of how to become an SBS VAP is overlooked in this comprehensive volume: even partnering with other VAPs and learning to make good money along the way. Josh understands SBS technology, three-tier distribution and its nuances, and offers all the information you need on both from the inside out. This resource is certainly the most valuable compilation of real information that I have ever found on these topics in *one* place. It would take many months on one's own to research and experience only a fraction of the wealth of information offered here.

Michelle Graziose Webb, Owner
IWebb, Lafayette, Colorado
Editor emeritus, Selling Windows NT Solutions *magazine*

Building Profitable Solutions addresses not only the technical aspects of becoming a successful SBS VAP, but shows the importance of identifying key talent as part of that successful plan!

Ray Holley, CEO & Managing Partner
Austin Group International, Austin, Texas
Marlar International Search Network

This book contains a wealth of information and resources for small business VAPs. The growth of the small business market offers huge potential for VAPs with the skills and tools to move small business owners into the technology era. To stay competitive today, small businesses rely on outside sources for their technology; this is the opportunity for VAPs to provide robust, yet easy-to-use solutions, such as VERITAS Backup Exec. Key to taking advantage of technology is the ability to protect and manage user information that provides additional opportunities for VAPs' up-sell of complementary solutions dedicated to the small business market.

Mike Ivanov, VERITAS Backup Exec Product Line Manager
VERITAS Software, Heathrow, Florida

Most "computer" books are written for technology users and focus on how to implement a particular product. There is certainly an element of this in *Building Profitable Solutions*. But Josh has gone beyond that to focus on the business purpose of SBS, not only for the end user, *but* for the VAP. Josh shows the VAP how to position SBS to best fit the end user's business, overcome objections, and get that critical buy-in from the proper players. Josh provides tools for building a professional computer consulting business. A first of its kind book.

Larry Lentz, MCSE+I, Owner
Lentz Computer Services, San Antonio, Texas

Josh really hit the nail on the head in Chapter 4 on Staffing Challenges. It's extremely extensive and doesn't miss a beat. This book will not only help you start your own business, but it will help you maintain and grow it.

Stacey Landau, Director of Recruiting
SetFocus, Parsippany, New Jersey

Josh has written an incredible book! He says what needs to be said. As 1999 President of the Association of Microsoft Solutions Providers (AMSP), I'm delighted with his remarks on partnering. As a project management consultant, I can attest to the "real world" nature of his comments on the potential pitfalls of managing a rollout. He has written a most readable book. Members of small consulting firms should read this book. Those who wish to build SBS solutions must read this book. It will be required reading here.

Harry McClanahan, President
Pragmatic Solutions, Saint Louis Park, Minnesota
1999 President of the Association of Microsoft Solution Providers

---

If you're a consultant that is focused on small business or you're thinking about becoming one, this is a must read. Not only does it cover product benefits and provide a technology road map and project plan, Feinberg also helps you outline a successful selling process.

David W. Parker, President & CEO
License Online, Inc., Kirkland, Washington

Josh has captured the essence of every VAP in this book. As I read each chapter, I kept thinking, "He's talking about my business!" An interesting blend of computing history, self-help/therapy, and technical manual, this book offers practical knowledge on how to be a VAP and actually *make money*. It also offers realistic, commonsense solutions to VAP-related problems, *not* some "pie-in-the-sky make you rich" scheme. It gives the VAP the knowledge and tools to make selling and supporting SBS easy and profitable. This book will help my business to grow and succeed, and better yet, it is enjoyable reading—a rare gem in a sea of boring training manuals! I loved it!

Susan C. Zimpel, President
Simple Office Solutions, Eau Claire, Wisconsin

Building Profitable Solutions

with Microsoft® BackOffice®
Small Business Server 4.5

JOSHUA FEINBERG

PUBLISHED BY
Microsoft Press
A Division of Microsoft Corporation
One Microsoft Way
Redmond, Washington 98052-6399

Copyright © 2000 by Joshua Feinberg

Library of Congress Cataloging-in-Publication Data
Feinberg, Joshua.
    Building Profitable Solutions with Microsoft BackOffice Small Business Server 4.5 /
    Joshua Feinberg.
        p. cm.
    Includes index.
    ISBN 0-7356-0849-0
    1. Microsoft BackOffice.   2. Client/server computing.   I. Title.
    QA76.9.C55 .F45   1999
    005.7'1376 21--dc21   99-045526

Printed and bound in the United States of America.

1 2 3 4 5 6 7 8 9   QMQM   4 3 2 1 0 9

Distributed in Canada by Penguin Books Canada Limited.

A CIP catalogue record for this book is available from the British Library.

Microsoft Press books are available through booksellers and distributors worldwide. For further information about international editions, contact your local Microsoft Corporation office or contact Microsoft
Press International directly at fax (425) 936-7329. Visit our Web site at mspress.microsoft.com.

Macintosh is a registered trademark of Apple Computer, Inc. Intel is a registered trademark of Intel
Corporation. ActiveX, BackOffice, FoxPro, FrontPage, Microsoft, Microsoft Press, MS-DOS, MSDN,
NetMeeting, Outlook, Visual Basic, Visual Studio, Windows, and Windows NT are either registered
trademarks or trademarks of Microsoft Corporation in the United States and/or other countries. Other
product and company names mentioned herein may be the trademarks of their respective owners.

The example companies, organizations, products, people, and events depicted herein are fictitious. No
association with any real company, organization, product, person, or event is intended or should be inferred.

Acquisitions Editor: Christey Bahn
Project Editor: Kim Fryer

To Mom, Dad, my sister Karen, and my fiancée Jennifer

Contents at a Glance

Table of Contents

Part 3

Planning the Project and Cementing the Client Relationship

Part 4

Managing the Rollout

Part 6

Maintaining Client Satisfaction and the SBS 4.5 System

Foreword

During a recent conversation, I was asked, "What's the single most important thing small businesses can do to use technology successfully in their business?" My response was, "They should find a good technology provider and build a business relationship that puts the technology provider on par with their accountant, lawyer, and other key advisors." The elevation of the technology provider to this professional status level is a clear reflection of the strategic importance of your services.

As you know, this is an amazing time to be involved in the small business technology services market. Demand for your services has never been higher. At the same time, you face a number of challenges, including how to stay up-to-date on the latest technologies while you are trying to run a profitable business.

Microsoft realizes the challenges that you face and is committed to delivering the products and programs that you need to be successful. To help you accomplish this, we've created innovative products like Microsoft BackOffice Small Business Server 4.5. We have also invested tens of millions of dollars to create the Microsoft Direct Access program, a one-stop resource where you can get the latest technical information about Microsoft products, as well as key business information to increase your profitability.

To ensure that we continue to deliver these and other types of products and programs, we are always gathering as much feedback and information as we can.

Building Profitable Solutions with Microsoft BackOffice Small Business Server 4.5 is an outgrowth of our desire to better serve your needs and those of your small business customers. A little over a year ago, I invited Josh Feinberg to come to Microsoft and provide us with some direct input on our products and services. Our conversations during that visit were very wide ranging and had a direct impact on the features that you see in BackOffice Small Business Server 4.5, as well as changes in other Microsoft programs.

One of the other items we discussed was the lack of any practical guides that focus on the business side of running a technology consulting business. Given Josh's incredible can-do spirit, it is not surprising that he took this idea and ran with it. His background as a very successful technology provider, author, and recognized guru in the small business technology marketplace makes him uniquely qualified to write such a book.

Building Profitable Solutions with Microsoft BackOffice Small Business Server 4.5 offers practical information derived from real-world experience. I'm sure it will prove an invaluable resource for your business.

I also want to reiterate Microsoft's commitment to delivering the products and programs you need. Your feedback is always welcome and appreciated and can be sent to me at: *stevebro@microsoft.com.*

Sincerely,
Steve Brown
Product Manager
Microsoft Small Business Group

Acknowledgments

Writing a 700-page book in four months while continuing to maintain an active local small business client base is no easy task. And frankly, this never could've happened on schedule without the support of so many terrific people.

First and foremost, I want to thank my fiancée Jennifer A. Rossler for inspiring me to keep this project on track, despite the many 80-hour weeks and sacrificed evenings, weekends, and even a few days of vacation. As an internal guru for an investment advisory small business, Jennifer also was a terrific sounding board for developing chapter content and a superb internal proofreader.

My parents, Myra and David Feinberg, and my sister Karen Feinberg have also been tremendously supportive of both my local VAP business and various writing projects. I still remember disassembling and reassembling an IBM PC/XT computer on their kitchen table one Sunday winter morning back in 1989 to prove we were ready to open a retail computer store, selling what are now known as white box desktop PCs.

It's one thing to be a computer consultant or an MCSE. Writing about technology, and in particular the channel opportunities surrounding a platform, is a whole other ball game. I'm particularly grateful to Michelle Graziose Webb, former senior editor of *Computer Reseller News* (*CRN*) and founding editor-in-chief of *Selling Windows NT Solutions* (*SWNTS*) magazine, for getting me started writing the "Small Business Smarts" and "Cha-Ching" columns for *SWNTS* and even more importantly for being a truly awesome mentor. Two of Michelle's former *SWNTS* staff members, Michele Crockett (Managing Editor) and Christy Wolfe (Assistant Editor), were also immeasurably helpful in shaping my growth as a writer and contributing editor.

SBS Product Manager Steve Brown was also instrumental in making this book happen. Last December, Steve and his Waggener Edstrom public relations team—then Jeff Denenholz and Megan Kidd—invited me out to Redmond to give them input and feedback on substantive changes coming down the pike in SBS 4.5. On that trip, I was actually in the Seattle area for just one day.

However, Steve, Jeff, and I did manage to get together for a now historic dinner in Bellevue. And it was during that meeting that we first discussed the ideas for the book you are about to read. During that same trip, Kim Davis of Waggener Edstrom also facilitated several key introductions.

Special thanks also to Kim's colleagues Brandy Bishop, Liz Haas, and Karamy Muessig for putting me in touch with various people at Microsoft.

I also want to express my sincere gratitude to Katy Hunter, SBS Product Manager, for her enthusiastic support of this project and for reviewing chapter content to make sure the book's scope was on track for our intended audience. Julie Briselden, also of the SBS Product Group, assisted by evaluating early chapters as well.

SBS Program Managers Ryan Waite and Erin Dunphy were immensely helpful in guiding my efforts to make this book an essential companion volume to the *Microsoft BackOffice Small Business Server 4.5 Resource Kit* and researching advanced technical inquiries.

Despite the unique nature of this book, Microsoft Press assembled a terrific team of editors to support every facet of the book's development. Acquisitions editor Christey Bahn, content manager Barb Ellsworth, associate publisher Ed Belleba, acquisitions manager Casey Doyle, and managing editor Laura Sackerman were all instrumental in jump-starting this project. An even greater thanks goes out to Kim Fryer, my project editor. Besides being an incredibly organized, remarkably efficient, hugely supportive, and insightful editor, Kim was largely responsible for keeping this project on track despite an extremely aggressive writing, editing, and production schedule.

From the Direct Access team, I'm particularly grateful to Nigel Burton, Julie Hill, and Erin Hiraoka for their ongoing support of this project and my VAPVoice column. Also, special thanks to former Direct Access staffer Vivian Scott, who ran the 1998 SBS VAP Roundtables and helped assemble the details for writing the related roundtable content on the CD-ROM. Vivian also helped "recruit" a few of the SBS VAPs who joined in the focus group for this book.

Thanks also to the active focus group members who shared their wisdom throughout various chapters: Dennis Anderson of Net\Works, Scott Ayon of Office-Anywhere, Jon Bachtold of FAP Inc Advanced Communications, Jon Balch of LR Data, Steve Baus of Baus Systems, Ed Berger, Jeff Cate of PCServ, Lou Ciarlo, Jr. of DMA Data, Brian DeMarzo of Top Down Design, Joe Hackman of Managed Solutions, Ray Holley of Austin Group International, Ray Hord of CompTronics Inc., Kevin Hourican, Haris Jung of Compass Computer Assistance, Stacey Landau of SetFocus, Larry Leffler of Innovative Computer Concepts, Larry Lentz of Lentz Computer Services, Doug Ludens of About.com, Mehul Mehta of Pulse Business Systems, Bob Sievewright of Corporate Technology Solutions, Jaap Smit of UniSPeqs,

Mike Tibbs, Bill Walker of ServiceSolutionS, Peter Williams of The Computer Guys, Jeff Willis of Cmw Merchandising, and Susan Zimpel of Simple Office Solutions.

Special thanks to Alex Orosz of Equus Computer Systems (*www.equuscs.com*) for providing the testbed server for this book. Also thanks to Professor of Entrepreneurship Kathleen Allen, Ph.D., at the Marshall School of Business, University of Southern California, for reviewing Part 2 of this book to ensure the book had sound advice for VAPs and MCSPs.

Thanks also to Jan Jahosky of VERITAS, Howard Butler and Jobee Knight of Executive Software, and Richard Sheng of Trend Micro for providing additional information used for writing various chapters.

Last but certainly not least, thanks to the editors at Siechert & Wood: Carl Siechert, Thomas Williams, and Blake Whittington, for their meticulous attention to detail and reader-advocacy insight, and for sharpening the details of each chapter.

Introduction

Most small business owners want the same technology advantages as their Fortune 1000 counterparts. The challenge has always been how to build a solution for these wants and needs on a small business–friendly budget and with ease-of-use appropriate for a company without a large on-site Information Technology (IT) department.

Microsoft BackOffice Small Business Server (SBS) 4.5 provides the building blocks for technology providers to deploy a variety of server-based applications, which were until very recently available to only Fortune 1000 IT organizations. Small businesses, in most cases, rely on local technology providers to install and support these SBS networks.

This presents an enormous business opportunity for value-added resellers (VARs), value-added providers (VAPs), and consultants. In order to implement these Fortune 1000 class technologies and capture local small business market share, however, you'll need a thorough understanding of both the technical features of SBS, and even more importantly, its unique rules of client engagement.

Who This Book Is For

Because the overwhelming majority of SBS installations involve a technology provider, *Building Profitable Solutions with Microsoft BackOffice Small Business Server 4.5* has been tailored specifically for the channel. And when I say "channel," I'm referring to technology providers who offer or plan to offer solutions built on the SBS platform.

Many small business technology providers have had to adapt their business model rapidly from being driven by product margin and supplemented by service margin to being driven almost entirely by service revenue and supplemented by product margin. In effect, this forces a 180-degree shift in focus.

More established solution providers have typically serviced medium and enterprise-sized clients and are now looking to branch out into small business to diversify their revenue stream. However, many of these more established and larger technology providers need concise tools to help them manage engagements under tighter budgetary constraints than to which they're typically accustomed.

Note

Recognizing a large percentage of SBS installations are located outside the United States, I wrote chapters in this book so that they're largely applicable to both domestic and international technology providers.

Many of the technology providers who are delivering SBS solutions are small or mid-sized businesses themselves. As a result, VAPs and VARs often need to wear multiple hats, including those of technology consultant, salesperson, and project manager.

Many are also active participants in and share similar demographics to participants in Microsoft channel programs such as Microsoft Direct Access (MSDA) and Microsoft Certified Solution Provider (MCSP). These technology providers include:

- Computer consulting firms
- Distributors
- Independent software vendors (ISVs)
- Internet service providers (ISPs)
- System builders
- System/network integrators
- Training providers
- VAPs, VARs, and value-added dealers (VADs)

Tip

Throughout this book, the acronym "VAP" is used to refer to technology providers in the more generic sense.

Why This Book Is Different

Although most of the applications in the SBS 4.5 suite are identical or, at the minimum, very similar to those found in the more enterprise-focused Microsoft BackOffice Server 4.5 suite, technology providers working with smaller organizations face different business challenges. These include tighter deployment cycles, smaller budgets, staffing dilemmas, the need to wear many hats, profitability issues, overcoming the myopia of small business owners, avoiding becoming commodity service providers, and assuming the role of virtual IT organization.

Most SBS books to date strictly deal with SBS training as a technical, how-to feature guide. While readers learn how to properly install, configure, and administer an SBS-based network, they are on their own when learning how to build and run a business based on SBS. In contrast, *Building Profitable Solutions with Microsoft BackOffice Small Business Server 4.5* delivers the tools to grow and sustain a successful technology provider business. These tools will help you understand:

- Making money with SBS
- Setting up shop as a VAP and planning the project
- Establishing your company as a virtual IT department
- Managing the rollout and testing the installation
- Training and retaining your clients
- Further growth opportunities

Because this book is just as much about best practices for running a technology provider business as it is about SBS 4.5, I established a virtual focus group for this book, which incorporated the collective wisdom of over two dozen small business technology providers worldwide. The group as a whole included:

- Over 139 years of experience as small business technology providers
- More than 200 SBS installations, including SBS 4.0 and SBS 4.5; spanning 3,075 client workstations, including Windows 95/98 and Windows NT Workstation 4.0
- $6.6M in projected 1999 annual sales, 73 percent of which was service revenue

- Staffs that included 27 Microsoft Certified Professionals (MCPs) and 22 Microsoft Certified System Engineers (MCSEs)
- Average hourly billing rate of $97

How This Book Is Organized

Much like a franchise kit, *Building Profitable Solutions with Microsoft BackOffice Small Business Server 4.5* illustrates how technology providers can make money with SBS.

In Part 1, "Making Money with SBS," you'll learn why SBS is your platform for opportunity (Chapter 1) and the steps Microsoft took to make SBS 4.5 consulting more profitable for technology providers (Chapter 2).

Part 2, "Setting up Shop as an SBS VAP," delves into four issues that every small business technology provider needs to grapple with at one time or another, including how to maximize your SBS training investment (Chapter 3), handle staffing challenges for SBS projects (Chapter 4), deal with profitability challenges (Chapter 5), and arrange partnering opportunities (Chapter 6).

In Part 3, "Planning the Project and Cementing the Client Relationship," you'll learn about the up-front work involved in an SBS rollout (Chapter 7). This ensures that the proposed solution (Chapter 8) protects your client's existing technology investments while achieving their immediate and future business and technology goals (Chapter 9). In addition, Part 3 helps to solidify the VAP/client relationship and makes sure everyone is on the same page (Chapter 10).

Part 4, "Managing the Rollout," marks a shift from the primarily business-oriented content in Parts 1 through 3 to the more technically oriented solutions content. This includes: learning project management techniques (Chapter 11), automating the desktop rollout (Chapter 12), handling post-installation server configuration tasks (Chapter 13), customizing the SBS Console (Chapter 14), adding value with the Server Status Tool (Chapter 15), extending the Set Up Computer Wizard (Chapter 16), setting up desktop clients (Chapter 17), and configuring Internet access, Web publishing, and e-mail (Chapter 18).

Building on the planning and installation sections, Part 5, "Testing the Installation and Training Your Clients," discusses disaster recovery preparation (Chapter 19), training for administrators and end users (Chapter 20), leveraging Microsoft Office applications (Chapter 21), maintaining software (Chapter 22), and testing the data protection mechanisms (Chapter 23).

Part 6, "Maintaining Client Satisfaction and the SBS 4.5 System," deals with developing the service contract (Chapter 24) and implementing a proactive maintenance program (Chapter 25).

Then in Part 7, "Further Growth Opportunities," I wrap up the book with a hands-on look at adding value to Exchange Server (Chapter 26), implementing RAS and Fax Services (Chapter 27), and elevating your company from service provider to strategic business partner (Chapter 28).

By the end of the book, you'll understand not just the technical administration details of managing SBS, but also what it takes to be a successful and profitable SBS-focused technology provider business.

Using the Companion CD-ROM

Many times computer books contain CD-ROMs that are supplemental in nature to the book's contents. With *Building Profitable Solutions with Microsoft BackOffice Small Business Server 4.5*, however, the CD-ROM is one of the most important elements of the book.

The CD-ROM contains six different categories of files:

- Supplemental chapter information

- **Excel workbooks**—checklists to plan various facets of the SBS rollout

- **Word templates and documents**—forms to help you work with clients, including sample agreements and proposals

- **Microsoft Direct Access VAPVoice column archives**—advice on how to run a business based on SBS, written by yours truly

- **Microsoft Product Support Services (PSS) white papers**—technical solutions provided courtesy of the SBS product group

- **Evaluation software**—useful products to extend SBS systems from VERITAS, Trend Micro, and Executive Software

Feedback

I hope you enjoy reading this book as much I enjoyed writing it. My even greater hope is that you use the advice and tools in this volume to take your SBS VAP business to even more successful levels than you ever could've imagined.

Best of luck and keep in touch! Like you, I'm an SBS VAP and I'd love to hear from you. Drop me a line at *buildingsbs@kisweb.com* and let me know how your SBS VAP business is doing.

Joshua Feinberg, MCSE
KISTech Communications
Red Bank, New Jersey, USA

Part 1

Making Money with SBS

Chapter 1

SBS: Your Platform for Opportunity

Small businesses want and need the same technology that Fortune 1000 companies have had for years. This wish list typically includes a Web site, secure Web browsing and e-mail on every desktop, rich collaborative groupware applications and intranet sites, custom database applications, and centralized security and administration. What's the biggest challenge for consultants? All of these solutions need to be delivered on a small-business friendly budget. What's the silver lining? Nearly all of these small businesses will need help from consultants and resellers.

Like you, I'm a technology provider. I face many of the same obstacles that you face every day: keeping up with an avalanche of software upgrades, juggling dozens of projects and tasks across multiple clients, paying the bills, trying to make it home in time for dinner, calming down panicky clients, and deciding which products and platforms to support. When Microsoft Small Business Server (SBS) came out in late 1997, I saw it as an opportunity to develop my consulting practice for building and maintaining networks for small businesses. What led me to SBS? After all, small businesses already had many networking alternatives available. These options included peer-to-peer networks using Windows for Workgroups 3.11 and Windows 95, client/server networks using Windows NT 3.51, and well-known peer-to-peer products from Apple and Artisoft. Some small businesses had also made substantial technology investments in Novell NetWare-based networks. While all of these options were centered on file and printer sharing, small businesses needed many more tools and services than the crop of products then on the market could provide cost effectively. SBS was developed to address this need, and I saw it as a good solution for my clients.

Until SBS was released, Microsoft BackOffice and Windows NT were the major small business information technology (IT) solutions Microsoft offered. They were being deployed mostly in large Fortune 1000 organizations, which had dedicated IT staff that could handle the complexities of the software and corresponding well-funded budgets for the large initial purchases of hardware and software. Much like the overwhelming success of the integrated family of

What Do Small Businesses Want?

What are some of the key technologies widely implemented by Fortune 1000 IT organizations that small businesses often want?

- Secure and extensible file and printer sharing
- A messaging backbone that can support not only e-mail but groupware and scheduling
- Shared, secure Internet access through a proxy server/firewall solution
- Web development and publishing capabilities
- Enhanced communication services through modem pooling, fax serving, and remote access
- Reliable, secure, scalable database applications

These are all services provided by SBS 4.5, at a fraction of the cost of purchasing the individual applications a la carte.

Office desktop applications, companies worldwide found the comprehensive BackOffice Server suite very appealing. Microsoft wasn't focusing on small businesses in its early BackOffice efforts; it had envisioned the original BackOffice release to be most attractive to larger organizations with IT departments. So the BackOffice product team was surprised to find that a small percentage of the installed base was actually in the small business arena. From that finding, the first version of Small Business Server, SBS 4.0, was born.

Note

When the first version of SBS was released in 1997, its cousin product in larger enterprises, BackOffice Server, was numbered as a "4.0" version. To promote the connection and alignment between the two products, the first version of SBS was also numbered as a "4.0" release. For more information on the background of SBS, see "Roots of SBS," a Word document on the CD-ROM.

Unfortunately, when SBS 4.0 was first released, relatively little training material was available for prospective consultants, although Microsoft did have a few things available. Even when other books and training courses surfaced, I found they all stopped short of telling me how to make money with SBS. I felt as if readers were being trained to be SBS administrators working in a Fortune 1000 IT department, as opposed to principals and managers in small consulting and value-added-reseller (VAR) companies. To be fair, most training products did teach me the basics of what I needed to know to install and support SBS, but I was no longer working as a system administrator for a big IT department. I needed concrete advice on how to manage a consulting practice for networking small businesses. Many of the gaps in my knowledge, such as training, partnering, and project management, I filled in through trial and error. Other areas I filled in by attending seminars, talking to other value-added providers (VAPs), and religiously scouring the trade rags and a host of Web sites and newsgroups.

I found no single source for this information. I knew that many of my fellow VAPs worldwide were in the same situation and learning some painful lessons about how to be successful SBS consultants. I even tripped a few times myself. Many of you also saw some shortcomings in SBS 4.0. Microsoft knew that making good on these problems in SBS 4.0 was the key to succeeding with the next version of SBS.

The Reaction to SBS 4.0

Microsoft had laid out three broad goals for SBS 4.0:

- Deliver easy access to Windows NT Server and BackOffice functionality for administrators and users who aren't trained in Windows NT Server.

- Provide modem sharing, network-based faxing, e-mail, and Internet connectivity—going beyond basic file and printer sharing to leverage Windows NT Server's core application services.

- Offer all this functionality at a price-point appropriate for even the smallest of small businesses.

SBS 4.0 was code-named "SAM" for the late Sam Walton (1918–1992), the legendary retailing pioneer, billionaire, and founder of the Wal-Mart chain of stores and SAM'S Club warehouse stores. Microsoft had envisioned that SBS would be simple enough so that the shrink-wrapped product could be sold at SAM'S Club stores. SBS underscored Microsoft's vision to have a solution so simple that a small business could buy the product and implement it without an IT organization.

Microsoft's basic marketing premise for SBS 4.0, however, was off-center. While Microsoft was doing some marketing aimed at VAPs, small business owners were a primary target. Even though small businesses were comfortable buying and installing software like Microsoft Money and Microsoft Publisher, small business owners weren't about to install their own networks. Industry analysts and columnists may have also misjudged whether small businesses were ready to buy and roll their own networks. At launch time for SBS 4.0, pundits were still forecasting that small business owners would drive down to the local warehouse club and purchase SBS the way they had purchased MS-DOS 6 and Windows 95 version upgrades.

In reality, VAPs were, and continue to be, the main influence on small business networking decisions. Microsoft saw that SBS would need to be retooled to cater directly to VAPs, as opposed to small business end users. Many VAPs don't actually resell products. Rather, these VAPs make product recommendations to their small business clients, who in turn purchase the specified products through retail stores or mail-order firms. Marketing and support for SBS needed to be strengthened to meet the needs of VAPs.

SBS 4.0 also had some shortcomings on the software side, including lack of flexibility in setup, hardware detection, and Internet access. Chapter 2 covers how SBS 4.5 remedies these problems.

The Boom in Small Business Networking

In August 1997, CNET (*www.cnet.com*) published a special report entitled "Boom in the Middle Market" that predicted that the next big technology adoption wave for software, hardware, and networking wouldn't occur as a result of Fortune 1000 spending. This report also looks at the "why" factor for all this sudden interest among leading vendors in positioning small business networks. The 8–10 million U.S.-based small businesses have traditionally been off the marketing radar screen.

The report's conclusion was that small businesses are now more open to investing in networks for two primary reasons. First, the technology available to small businesses for networking has improved markedly over the past few years. Second, small businesses see networks as a necessary efficiency that they must adopt to stay competitive.

ZD Market Intelligence (*www.ci.zd.com*) released results in October 1998 from a study focused on the penetration of local area networks (LANs) in small business (businesses with 100 employees or fewer). Highlights of the study include:

- The larger small businesses (more than 20 employees) have 55 percent LAN penetration.

- The smallest small businesses (fewer than 10 employees) have 10 percent LAN penetration.

- The installation of a small business LAN leads to the creation of some type of IT department.

- The installation of a small business LAN means the small business has graduated from solely using PCs as word processors.

A 1998 GartnerGroup Dataquest (*www.dataquest.com*) report discussed additional small business networking trends. This study analyzed how small businesses are moving rapidly toward adopting Internet usage and peer-to-peer file sharing. These same small businesses, however, have been moving much more cautiously toward the idea of buying into small business server hardware. The report concluded that although "small businesses benefit from small doses of technology that help them keep pace with larger competitors," their budgets don't allow them to move ahead as rapidly as many would like with installing small business networks. Thus the challenge continues to be how to deliver what small businesses want and need in a cost-effective manner.

What VAPs Need

SBS 4.0 appealed to many VAPs for several reasons:

- It allowed VAPs to deploy a comprehensive single-box solution at a fraction of the cost of the individual components.

- It eliminated the inherent risks of integrating software from multiple vendors.

- It provided a quick and easy way to install and manage the server.

- It freed up VAPs to focus on higher-end innovative solutions.

To understand what VAPs need to be successful with SBS, Microsoft invited 40 VAPs representing the average Joe from all over the United States, to Microsoft headquarters in Redmond, Washington, for two 2-day meetings in 1998. Our fellow VAPs spoke, actually more like vented, and Microsoft listened. These VAP roundtables drove many of the cool enhancements in SBS 4.5, such as the addition of the Server Status Tool, the integration of NetMeeting into SBS as the preferred remote administration tool, and the complete overhaul of the Internet Connection Wizard. These improvements to SBS 4.5 will be covered in more depth in the next chapter.

Tip

Although SBS 4.5 ships with NetMeeting 2.11, you can download a free upgrade to NetMeeting 3 from *www.microsoft.com/netmeeting*.

Based on the roundtable feedback, Microsoft also decided to fortify the bridge to VAPs through the Microsoft Direct Access program and focus on most of the marketing efforts for SBS on VAPs rather than end users. The program reached out to VAPs focused on SBS and other strategic products and platforms in eight key areas:

- Local events including seminars held almost every business day of the year in local Microsoft field offices, as well as larger, more general quarterly events

- Special promotions and incentives such as mail-in rebates for cash and free products

- Exclusive online offerings including Microsoft-moderated technical support newsgroups

- Special presales tools such as proposal templates, deployment guides, and best practices advice

- Free and heavily subsidized training available through the Web, CD-ROM courses, and one-day introductory classes offered at Microsoft Certified Technical Education Centers (CTECs)

- Free exclusive phone support in North America for VAPs whose clients have business-down emergencies (Business Critical Phone Support was added in March 1999.)

- Two free telephone support incidents with each retail purchase or free version upgrade of Small Business Server

- Dedicated SBS Product Support Services (PSS) team of system engineers, as opposed to having to speak with multiple technicians about component products (This avoids the need for your call to be transferred between different groups within PSS.)

Unique Small Business Climate

Before you start planning how you'll build an SBS-focused consulting business, it's important to understand some of the idiosyncrasies of small businesses. Unlike medium-sized and large corporations, a small business staff often takes on a variety of functions that would be the domain of multiple people or departments in larger firms even within the same industry. For example, in a small law firm the office manager may be charged with handling purchasing, human resources, accounts receivable, accounts payable, and payroll. In a small advertising agency, the sales manager may oversee such diverse areas as technology, marketing, public relations, and asset management.

Clients Wearing Lots of Hats

Small business owners tend to focus on what they do best. Whether it's selling houses, running restaurants, manufacturing specialty chemicals, practicing law, or preparing tax audits, small business owners generally devote nearly all their attention to their core business objectives and rarely leave time or energy to think about how technology fits into the competitive landscape. Many small business owners still perceive technology spending as expenses as opposed to investments. You as the VAP will need to introduce them to SBS.

What SBS 4.5 Offers a Small Business

SBS 4.5 offers small businesses an integrated suite of server-based applications, including:

- Microsoft Windows NT Server 4.0
- Microsoft Exchange Server 5.5
- Microsoft Proxy Server 2.0
- Microsoft SQL Server 7.0
- Microsoft Internet Information Server 4.0
- Microsoft Modem Sharing Service 4.5
- Microsoft Fax Service 4.5
- Microsoft FrontPage 98
- Outlook 2000
- Microsoft Internet Explorer 5.0

Among the many services that SBS 4.5 can offer to a small business are:

- Secured, shared Internet access, including e-mail and Web browsing
- File and printer sharing
- Easier collaboration with employees and partners
- Modem sharing
- Ability for employees to telecommute using remote access
- Fax from the desktop
- Group scheduling
- Central management of customer contacts
- Intracompany e-mail
- Web site authoring and hosting for an intranet, an extranet, and the Internet
- Greater capability to share information within a company
- Back-end processing of scalable, secure relational database applications

Because small business owners are usually more resource-constrained than Fortune 1000 CEOs, small businesses look to get immediate return on investment (ROI) on their technology projects. So when implementing SBS, you need to provide some tangible, instant gratification. For many small businesses, this means e-mail, Web browsing, and network-based faxing.

When the small business owner does have first hand experience with computer or networking issues, the owner tends to only see a very small piece of the whole puzzle. For example, the small business owner may be familiar with how to use a checkbook management program such as Microsoft Money. Installation of this kind of program is very simple: just run the setup program and you're recording transactions 15 minutes later. Because that might be the full extent of the owner's experience with computers and networks, the small business owner often overlooks such hidden, soft costs that contribute to total cost of ownership (TCO). This includes testing, training, deployment, downtime, knowledge transfer, and ongoing support.

The small business owner also often tries to equate hourly billing rates from technology providers with those of his own internal staff. Part of your challenge is to educate the small business owner on why continual investments in training and retraining are such a critical component of making the best use of small business networks. Ultimately, it's this training and the scarcity of those with similar skills that drives the levels of hourly billing rates for technology providers. Keeping current also is a big part of building a successful SBS-consulting practice.

Most small businesses generally don't have the resources or the need to hire a full-time staff person dedicated to installing, upgrading, and maintaining their office PCs or network. Also bear in mind that clients generally don't tell you the whole story. It's your job to ask open-ended questions about the state of the technology used by the small business. Before you call on a small business prospect, it's important to understand some of the key players in small business technology—the people you'll likely run into providing day-to-day computer support. Generally these technology support functions are taken care of in one of three ways.

- **The Volunteer**—The owner or manager has a spouse, relative, or friend, who may be a teenager, plumber, actuary, or teacher (or any other conceivable profession for that matter), who dabbles in computers as a hobby, and who volunteers to help with occasional computer support needs after-hours.

- **The Moonlighter**—The owner or manager hires a moonlighter who has a day job in a related field with a larger organization. This person may be a SQL database administrator for a large brokerage house or a help desk manager for a hospital. Although the main difference between the volunteer and the moonlighter is compensation, moonlighters will often charge hourly rates substantially below market rates because they perceive the income to be supplemental. In addition, the lower hourly rate often offsets the small business' inconvenience of having access to the moonlighter only after-hours, just like the volunteer. Small businesses generally hire moonlighters only when they can't find a qualified volunteer who can step up to the plate for their support needs.

- **The Internal Guru**—Someone on staff knows just enough to handle many of the basic daily computer support needs. Usually this owner, manager, accountant, sales rep, or other staff member feels comfortable with routine tasks like updating antivirus software definitions, recovering lost Office toolbars, or creating user logon accounts. This same person, however, often lacks formal or on-the-job training on intermediate to advanced level topics and generally shies away from more complicated tasks like configuring Proxy Servers, DHCP scopes, or Exchange Server public folders. (If you need more reinforcement in any of those areas, fear not. There's a lot of drilldown on those three topics in Chapters 18, 23, and 26.)

Sizing Up the Client's Internal Guru

Regardless of the specific small business accounts that you're servicing, the person who is currently providing network or computer support to these businesses probably doesn't make his or her living servicing small business networks. This is where your firm comes into the picture. You're the expert, or at least armed with this book you're the expert-in-training when it comes to installing, customizing, and supporting small business networks.

Although you may be the undisputed expert when it comes to TCP/IP, database-driven Web sites, or virtual private networks (VPNs), it's important to tread lightly when first beginning your engagement with the small business. Although your new client's internal guru may have limited or in some cases totally inaccurate or inadequate knowledge of small business networks, the client's guru has been the trusted technology advisor so far. Before you get too far along in sizing up whether the internal guru knows what he or she is talking about, you'll want to subtly determine whether your firm is being brought in to supplement the internal guru or replace the guru.

If your firm will be supplementing the internal guru and your efforts will be collaborative in nature, you'll want to spend some time getting to know this key internal resource person. As you get further along in discussions, the guru will be able to tell you how the technology was installed, the history behind the implementation, and how the technology was supported before you arrived. You'll also want to find out what the guru's real job is.

While each small business is unique, the following guidelines should help you gain a better understanding of the role of the internal guru.

- Is the guru a decision-maker? A techie? Or both?

- Does the guru feel threatened by your firm? How does the guru feel about external IT vendors?

- Does the guru have aspirations to someday assume a full-time IT position?

- How strong is the guru's technical knowledge in various areas? Does the guru feel comfortable asking for help when overwhelmed?

- Does the guru's boss make the computer-support part of the guru's job a priority? Or is it just a task that the guru gets to when time permits?

- Has the guru ever had any formal training?

It's also extremely important to find out the relationship between the internal guru and the owner(s) of the small business. Often the internal computer guru is a family member, relative, or longtime personal friend of one of the principals in the business. Regardless of whether you'll now be providing all of the computer or network support to this small business or just serving as an escalation point, it's important for you to get the political lay of the land before voicing any controversial opinions, such as "That guy Bob is a total idiot when it comes to routers." Otherwise, you'll be downloading the "remove foot from mouth" wizard from the Microsoft Direct Access Web site. (This wizard doesn't really exist, but it seems like a nifty idea.)

The Role of the VAP in Small Business

Before you can understand the role that technology providers or VAPs play in small businesses, it's important to get a handle on the wide range of occupations and business types that qualify as VAPs. These include:

- Microsoft Direct Access participants

- Microsoft Certified Solution Provider (MCSP) members and partners

- Value-added resellers (VARs) and value-added dealers (VADs)
- System/network integrators
- Computer consulting firms
- Independent software vendors (ISVs)
- Internet service providers (ISPs)
- System builders
- Training providers
- Distributors

Independent research commissioned by Microsoft Direct Access has confirmed that small businesses tend to outsource many of their computer and network support functions to local technology providers. This most often occurs when one or more of the three types of technology support people (the Volunteer, the Moonlighter, or the Internal Guru) either is in way over his or her head technically or just doesn't have adequate time to devote to the increased computer and network support needs of the small business. Even though the guru needs to be replaced or supplemented, that same small business is not yet ready, from a budgetary or needs perspective, to make the big commitment to hire a full-time IT manager.

When Microsoft began researching the idea of developing the small business version of BackOffice Server, they spoke with Microsoft Certified Solution Providers. At the time, many within Microsoft felt that anyone interested in small business networks would either be the small business end users themselves or Microsoft Certified Solution Providers. In 1995 and well into 1996, Microsoft had not yet discovered what they now have an excellent grasp of—that there are over 300,000 VAPs in North America and over 1,000,000 worldwide, many of whom are servicing small networks.

VAPs Wearing Lots of Hats

Small businesses often prefer to work with small, local VAPs. The VAPs that service small businesses are often small businesses themselves. The owners of VAP businesses are often very hands-on from a technical standpoint, either as developers, systems administrators, or some allied field. The owner also oversees sales, marketing, finance, accounting, recruiting, operations, and management, at least during the early years of the VAP's business.

The VAP's staff also has to be extremely versatile. For example, a staff consultant who specializes in messaging applications for a larger VAP may be responsible only for developing front-end groupware forms for collaborative applications. Other colleagues handle the balance of the related tasks for the client engagements.

In contrast, if that same staff consultant with a messaging specialty got fed up with life in the cubicle and were to change jobs to go work for a smaller VAP, the consultant would now add multiple responsibilities to the daily routine. In addition to developing groupware forms, the consultant is now charged with project management, back-end server design, testing, infrastructure, integration, deployment, and training for both administrators and end users. Like their small business clients, system engineers on staff with small VAPs must, by necessity, become quite strong technically in many different subject matters.

Staff members at small VAPs are expected to have a lot of knowledge in many different areas. Essentially, small business clients are paying VAPs and their staff for expertise. Because your resources are finite and constrained just like your small business clients, you need to be especially selective in how you allocate your training budget. This presents many recruiting, staff retention, and training challenges for smaller VAPs, and Chapters 3 and 4 are devoted exclusively to this "it'll make you or break you" topic. Even if you're a one-person VAP, don't even think about betting your business on SBS until you fully understand the dynamics and challenges of training and staffing.

At the beginning of this new century, VAPs are also facing more profitability challenges than ever before. The competition for selling products, in most markets, is nothing short of brutal. Because of plummeting product profit margins, even traditional retailers are rushing to bolster their service capabilities. Lately, it seems everyone, including the office supply superstore down the street, is hanging out a shingle that reads "we install networks." So in addition to a multitude of other hats that small VAPs wear, you'll need to keep a razor-sharp focus in your service business to maintain your billing rates and to keep your staff busy enough on projects with ample margin. This topic is explored further in Chapter 5.

Many times, a new potential client will have service needs that are exactly what your firm provides every day. Perhaps, however, this client might need two or three small projects or tasks that your firm is not quite geared up to provide. Rather than hiring additional staff for short-term needs or investing in steep learning curves or expensive training courses, many VAPs choose to partner with other firms. In Chapter 6, we'll drill down into what every small business VAP needs to know about the perils and the great potential for partnering on SBS-related projects.

During the early stages of the client engagement, you'll likely be donning your sales and marketing hat. You'll need to open a dialogue and address your prospect's concerns one by one. Here are examples of what those concerns might be:

- Many small businesses feel that they're too small to need a network.

- Many small businesses will allow apathy and inertia to postpone perpetually their decision to implement a network. "After all, if we've gone this long without one…"

- Many small businesses have been exposed to a tremendous amount of hype and now have unrealistic expectations about how computers and the Internet can make their firms the next Amazon.com. It's your job to temper those expectations with an ample dose of reality.

- Many small business owners are also in total denial when it comes to data protection and security needs. They may tell you that they trust their employees to be very careful with a database of confidential information that hasn't been backed up since MS-DOS 5 was in vogue.

Because the sales and marketing realm of your VAP business is so broad (at least it is during the earlier stages in the prospect/client life cycle), Chapter 8 will prepare you to respond thoroughly to some of the more commonly heard questions and objections.

Note

The prospect/client life cycle begins the moment that the initial contact is made with the small business client. It then progresses through an initial meeting/consultation, needs analysis and recommendations, project planning, implementation, testing, training, and ongoing support. Your ultimate goal in the life cycle is to transcend the service provider relationship and be elevated to a trusted advisor/business partner relationship. In fact, the topic is so central to theme of this book, the final chapter is devoted entirely toward helping you achieve this aspiration.

The VAP's staff is usually the only full-time expert for implementing and supporting technology who comes into contact with the small business. As a result, the VAP's staff often becomes the virtual IT department for the small business.

Much like an IT department in a medium-sized or Fortune 1000 company, small business VAPs often take on a variety of roles that are usually handled by many different departments in larger technology provider companies and end-user organizations.

This responsibility for being the virtual IT department almost always includes being the IT visionary for the small business. Often the small business owner is accustomed to thinking about technology in terms of small purchases of shrink-wrapped products such as desktop publishing software, antivirus utilities, and laser printers. As the IT visionary for small businesses, you need to help them think of the big picture and guide them through the process of shaping their short-term, intermediate, and long-term IT strategies. In fact, these topics are so fundamentally important to small business VAPs and their clients that Chapters 7 and 9 are largely devoted to the needs analysis and planning required for successful and profitable SBS client engagements.

Because you as the small business VAP are responsible for so many different areas of the client engagement, you have enormous exposure to potential problems, including everything from minor speed bumps to major catastrophes. In essence, you're required to stay on top of dozens of different client projects with dozens of interrelated tasks and potential failure points. Chapter 11 drills down on some of the more popular project management techniques that you'll need if you want to have a be able to amass a portfolio of successful SBS installations.

The Bottom Line

Small businesses want the same technology advantages as their Fortune 1000 counterparts. Their biggest challenge is how to implement these technology solutions on a small business friendly budget. That's where we come into the picture. We, as the consultants and resellers, are the driving forces behind small business technology adoption. Microsoft has completely redesigned SBS 4.5 to give us the tools to make the installation and ongoing support of SBS a *very* compelling business opportunity. My goal is to give you the tools to build a highly successful and profitable VAP business around SBS.

Chapter 2

Profit-Boosting Enhancements in SBS 4.5

In redesigning Microsoft BackOffice Small Business Server to be more VAP-friendly, Microsoft looked at what really defines the concept of value-add and how that definition changes over time. Perceived value-add is relative to how your small business clients perceive your services compared to what they're capable of providing on their own.

Note

To learn about the process Microsoft used to determine how to make SBS more VAP-friendly, see "History of the SBS VAP Roundtables," a Word document on the CD-ROM at the back of the book.

For example, if you're a VAP servicing a Fortune 1000 IT department with several Microsoft Exchange Server experts, you probably won't be called upon to add value by just installing the server and configuring Microsoft Outlook clients. If you have a unique skill, however, such as integrating PROFS or cc:Mail with Exchange Server, a Fortune 1000 IT department may call on you to add value to the in-house Exchange Server expertise, which perhaps is limited to Lotus Notes integration.

As a VAP servicing small business clients, you'll find that equation changes dramatically. Most small businesses have an internal guru who tends to know more about computers and networks than his or her peers. Yet the guru often doesn't have much Microsoft Windows NT Server expertise, let alone Exchange Server knowledge. For small businesses, your knowledge of how to install an Exchange Server and configure Outlook clients would be a welcome addition because you'd be adding value beyond what they can provide for themselves.

Tip

To learn more about the internal guru and the role he or she plays in small business technology adoption, see Chapter 1.

Adding value also becomes relative over time. Suppose one or two versions from now, Exchange Server becomes so simple to install that anyone who can install Microsoft Word feels comfortable configuring Exchange Server. Guess what? You've just become obsolete for that client's purpose, and you now need to reevaluate where you can add value. If, however, your skill set included experience with VBScript and Outlook forms design, you'd be in a great position to once again add value by creating an instant groupware solution.

What does this mean for you the VAP? Adding value is about staying one or two steps ahead of the curve, in particular ahead of your clients' internal gurus. Much of your success in staying current has to do with how proactive you are in identifying next year's hot trend and then allocating the time and budget toward becoming proficient in it.

You can begin to measure how much value you add by comparing your relative expertise to your clients' expertise, much the same way that Fortune 1000 IT organizations determine the salary hierarchy. Think of one of the more senior-level people in a large IT department: a wide-area network (WAN) engineer or a SAP systems architect. In late 1999, no one disputes that these skills are hard to acquire, relatively few people have significant hands-on experience in either area, and the enticing offers from headhunters abound. Next down on the totem pole are the more intermediate level people: a PC support manager or a LAN administrator. Finally, consider some of the more entry level positions such as help desk operator levels 1 and 2, desktop support specialist, and mainframe operator. Salaries will be dependent both on levels of experience and how scarce the skills are relative to the market demand.

Applying the same logic, VAPs providing services that nearly anyone can offer will be at the lower end of the food chain. (This means commodity VAPs dine at establishments where plastic lids come on the soft drinks served in paper cups.) They also don't leave themselves much time or energy for higher margin services or value-added opportunities. For example, if the bread-and-butter service of a VAP's business is in a commodity area such as warranty service on laser printers or teaching introductory Windows 98 classes, that VAP will be forced to keep hourly billing rates low to stay competitive in a highly crowded market. It's a low-margin, high-volume business.

At the other end of the spectrum are VAPs who accurately forecast next quarter's and next year's hot technologies. They keep their skills sharp year after year and accordingly maintain high service margins. Because these VAPs are far ahead of the curve, they never struggle to add value to their clients' solutions. Based on what small businesses require for SBS-centric solutions, today's hot value-added skills include developing groupware or other collaborative solutions, creating electronic-commerce enabled Web sites, building

The Changing Face of Value-Added Services

Value-added services for small businesses 10 years ago (1989/1990) included:

- Deploying servers for file and printer sharing
- Installing hardware such as network cards and drive arrays into servers
- Building MS-DOS-based relational database applications
- Writing MS-DOS-based spreadsheet macros and add-ins
- Rewriting MS-DOS-based applications for 16-bit Windows 3.0

Value-added services for small businesses five years ago (1994/1995) included:

- Configuring routers for Internet and branch office e-mail connectivity
- Migrating 16-bit Microsoft Windows 3.x applications to 32-bit
- Building first generation groupware applications, intranets, and Web sites
- Rolling out remote access servers

Value-added services for small businesses three years ago (1996/1997) included:

- Rolling out Windows NT Server and Workstation
- Building first generation database-driven Web sites

knowledge management solutions on relational databases, and implementing remote access servers and wide area connections.

If you take the view that a skill takes a few years to move from leading edge to a dime a dozen commodity, you'll understand that all hot skills have a certain shelf life after which they get reduced for clearance. That's all the more reason to plan your training investments carefully in your schedule each year.

Assessing Your Knowledge and Background

Many VAPs servicing small businesses come from a Fortune 1000 IT background where they may have been a developer, database administrator, Web content manager, LAN administrator, or project manager. Often these former Fortune 1000 IT staffers end up in the VAP world as a result of their departments being outsourced or their companies being downsized. Or perhaps, they were fed up with a life that was starting to resemble *Dilbert*. If you've recently entered the VAP business, you probably have one of the following types of backgrounds: IT specialist, retailer, Windows NT novice, or Windows NT specialist.

The IT Specialist

Coming from a much larger environment, Fortune 1000 IT staffers are by necessity specialists. While it's common for the owner of a small business VAP to use many diverse skills every day, big IT organizations usually want staff to pick a distinct career path. A consultant for a small business VAP may install a firewall at 9 A.M., write a bunch of SQL Server queries at 11 A.M., build a remote access server by noon, and then spend the remainder of the day teaching an Exchange Server class. If this same consultant were to take a job with some big bank, pharmaceutical company, or brokerage firm, that consultant would be in for a major culture shock. Five different departments handle that consultant's old daily routine. The consultant's new job encompasses just one aspect of the consultant's old job.

The Retailer

In sharp contrast, many small business VAPs have never seen the inside of a cubicle or heard the terms *reorg* or *TCO*. Instead, they evolved into VAPs by owning retail computer stores. Some of these were former, or still continue to be, system builders or resellers of branded systems and software licenses. Several years ago, service margin supplemented these storefront retail businesses. Today, service margin is the basis for their bottom line because reselling products is barely profitable. Their major challenge is how to beef up (no offense to the vegetarian readers) their skills quickly enough so that they can get involved in adding value with solutions based on platforms like SBS. If you're comfortable building and tearing down every imaginable kind of hardware but need an extra jump start in data protection (Chapters 13, 19, and 23), Web sites and e-mail (Chapters 13, 18, and 26), or remote access servers (Chapter 27), this book will put you well on your way to becoming an SBS guru extraordinaire.

The Windows NT Novice

Regardless of whether their previous IT career was programming or negotiating the best price on imported motherboards, many small business VAPs are new to Windows NT. Perhaps they've had some experience supporting a variant of UNIX or a NetWare server, but many VAPs are basically starting from ground zero in terms of their knowledge of Windows NT, BackOffice Server applications, and SBS.

The Windows NT Veteran

Some small business VAPs are Windows NT veterans. Members of this group might have started with Windows NT back in the 1993/1994 timeframe and are extremely comfortable with the native Windows NT Server administration tools and related Microsoft BackOffice Server products. For this group of small business VAPs, SBS is a version of BackOffice customized for small businesses.

Tip

If you're a new VAR or are thinking about becoming one, you need to think about profitability (Chapter 5), partnering (Chapter 6), project management (Chapters 7, 9, 10, and 11), and service contracts (Chapter 24) to have a successful business.

Wizards in SBS 4.5

Considering the widely divergent profiles of these four different small business VAPs, the SBS product group had quite a few challenges when it came time to figuring out what VAPs know about Windows NT Server, BackOffice Server applications, and SBS. In essence, Microsoft needed to reach a common ground that would satisfy both the VAP who is completely new to SBS as well as the seasoned Windows NT Server and BackOffice Server VAP who wants to diversify into small business networks. One way SBS reaches all these VAPs is through the newly redesigned SBS 4.5 Setup program and accompanying wizards.

Changes and Improvements in Setup

SBS 4.5 carries forward and enhances many of the installation wizards and preconfiguration choices that make it possible for a small business VAP new to SBS to get up to speed quickly. Improved flexibility in setup options helps more experienced VAPs spend less time on installation so they can concentrate on providing value-added services.

Software Integration

Service Pack 4 (SP4) for Windows NT Server 4.0 is fully integrated into the largely unattended setup for SBS 4.5. This was done so novice small business VAPs and administrators need not be concerned with installing the service pack.

Tip

Maintaining software version control and service packs is explained in detail in Chapter 22.

SP4 provides four main benefits to SBS 4.5 users:

- Year 2000 compliance for Windows NT Server 4.0
- Control over user profiles stored on the server
- Support for the Euro currency symbol
- Upgrade of the point-to-point tunneling protocol (PPTP) used for secure remote access over the Internet. Chapter 27 explains PPTP in more detail.

Note

The SBS 4.5 setup begins with the installation of Windows NT Server 4.0 and Service Pack 3 (SP3). Several SBS 4.0 server components that have system file dependencies on SP3 were carried forward into SBS 4.5, so SP3 is still needed. Although SBS 4.5 applies SP4 both before and after the BackOffice Server applications are installed, SP3 is installed immediately following the Windows NT Server 4.0 installation.

In SBS 4.5, the Windows NT 4.0 Option Pack (NTOP) was integrated into the unattended installation so that Microsoft Internet Information Server (IIS)

4.0 is installed as part of the standard SBS 4.5 setup routine. IIS is required for, among other things, the HTML-based SBS Console in SBS 4.5. SBS Console is covered later in this chapter. SBS 4.5 also includes Microsoft Proxy Server 2.0, Exchange Server 5.5, and SQL Server 7.0, which have also been integrated into the unattended SBS 4.5 setup.

Redesigning SBS to Be More VAP Friendly

By spring 1998, SBS didn't have huge success stories. Microsoft knew that it was time to get its act together with VAPs and get it together fast. The VAP roundtables, a gathering of VAPs who were interested in talking about SBS, were conceived as a way to get feedback. The VAPs who participated in the roundtables have since impacted several high-level efforts regarding major SBS improvements, including the decision to make the SBS 4.5 version upgrade available free of charge to SBS 4.0 end users. In addition to improvements in the software, other improvements to SBS included:

- Two free technical support incidents with Microsoft Product Support Services (PSS) engineers for each retail SBS SKU sold.

- A dedicated team of over 20 PSS engineers to handle SBS calls in a one-stop-shopping fashion.

- Several password-protected Microsoft Direct Access newsgroups, so VAPs could ask questions of Microsoft PSS engineers and other VAPs. The offerings covered every major channel-supported product including Office, SQL Server, SBS, Windows 95, and Windows NT Server.

- Business Critical Phone Support. This was created specifically for "business down" or emergency issues that weren't conducive to the several-hour delays inherent with the newsgroup approach to technical support.

- More marketing and advertising assistance from Microsoft. VAPs wanted to leverage Microsoft's product marketing efforts through customizable marketing tools. Some of the VAP marketing recommendations that Microsoft has implemented included the creation of product-specific sales centers; downloadable, customizable brochures; and the top 10 things to know about a specific product.

Security Defaults

To help ensure that novice small business VAPs and administrators keep their SBS system as secure as possible, SBS 4.5 includes two defaults that dramatically enhance the server's security. First, the Remote Access Service (RAS) is not configured to be a RAS gateway. When RAS is installed by the SBS 4.5 unattended setup, a default is preselected that causes RAS clients connected to the server to see only the server and not the workstations on the network. See Figure 2-1. If SBS end users connecting over RAS need access to workstations on the SBS network, this default can always be changed. The preselected default, however, greatly increases network security.

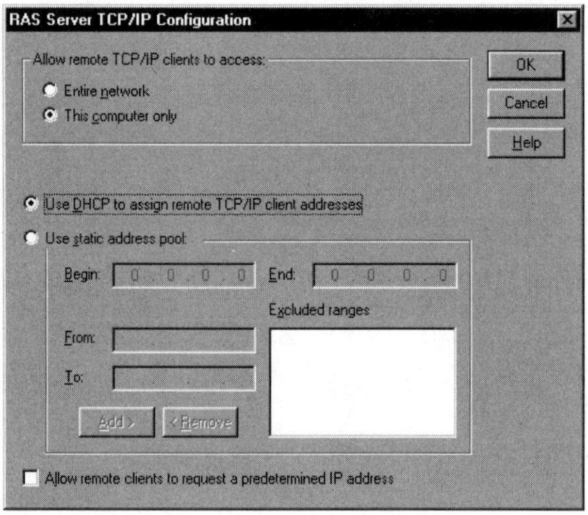

Figure 2-1
With SBS 4.5, the Remote Access Service is preconfigured to enhance network security.

Another security feature of SBS 4.5 is the default IP address of 10.0.0.2, as shown in Figure 2-2. This address is nonroutable and is secure from the Internet. (Microsoft strongly cautions against changing this default.) SBS 4.5 provides additional protection from the Internet through dynamic packet filtering in Proxy Server 2.0. IP addresses, Proxy Server, and Internet connectivity are described in detail in Chapter 18.

Tip

For more information on why SBS internal IP addresses are nonroutable and secure, see the *Microsoft TCP/IP Training*.

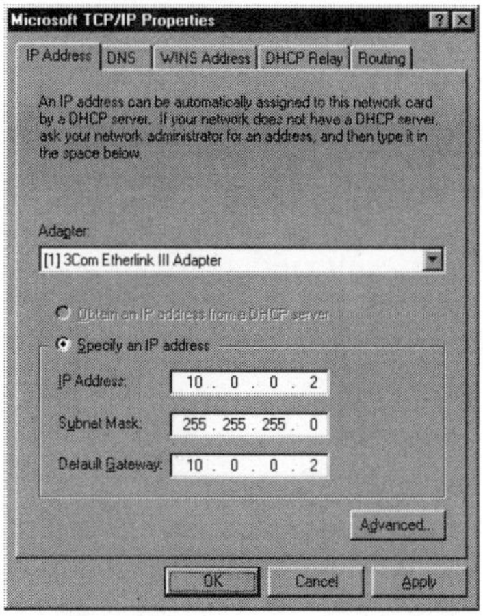

Figure 2-2

In SBS 4.5 the server's default IP address is 10.0.0.2, which is nonroutable and secure.

Exchange Server Defaults

SBS 4.5 also eases setup and administration for novice small business VAPs and end users by making certain desirable Exchange Server 5.5 settings the defaults. Like its predecessor, SBS 4.5 is designed to operate as the sole Exchange organization and site, and so it disables directory replication and synchronization. By making this choice the default, SBS 4.5 conserves memory and drive space.

Note

The SBS VAPVoice column, which I write monthly, is one of the major cornerstones of the Microsoft Direct Access SBS Sales Center. The column includes a "sound off" section that allows readers to voice their opinions on the topic. For your convenience, several of my earlier SBS VAPVoice columns are included on the CD-ROM with this book.

Other Setup Defaults

Several other SBS 4.5 default settings make it possible for less experienced small business VAPs to properly install an SBS 4.5 network. These defaults include:

- Video screen resolution is 800×600 (required by the SBS Console).

- TCP/IP is installed. It's the only protocol that's needed on a pure SBS network, but additional protocols can be added. For example, if the SBS network needs to coexist with a Novell NetWare server, NWLink (that is, IPX/SPX) can be added as an additional protocol suite.

- WINS is installed. It's used for client name resolution.

- Installation folder is WINNT.SBS.

- NTFS file system is installed.

- Server type is primary domain controller. Additional Windows NT Servers can be added as either backup domain controllers or stand-alone servers.

- Domain trust relationships are disabled.

Note

One of the biggest misconceptions about SBS 4.0 concerned the ability to have multiple Windows NT Server 4.0 systems on the same network. SBS 4.5, like SBS 4.0, fully supports having several additional Windows NT Server 4.0 systems on the same LAN. The only limitation is that the SBS 4.5 system can be the only primary domain controller (PDC) because trusts are not supported.

Setup Enhancements

One of the chief complaints about SBS 4.0 was the lack of flexibility in setting up drives, folders, user account information, and hardware. Because SBS 4.0 was supposed to be simple enough to install that small business owners could purchase it in SAM'S Club stores, the SBS product team had to make certain flexibility concessions in order to maintain absolute ease of use.

Target Drives and Folders   With SBS 4.0, you had very little choice about target drives and folders during the integrated setup—basically a take it or leave it deal. Under SBS 4.5, a new powerful Custom Installation feature was introduced to the setup program that allows you to alter target folder locations of all the SBS applications. The only exception is Windows NT Server 4.0, which installs prior to the SBS 4.5 setup program. The following SBS applications allow you to alter the target volume and folder locations at the time of setup, as shown in Figure 2-3:

- Internet Explorer
- SQL Server
- Windows NT Option Pack
- Proxy Server
- SBS Console

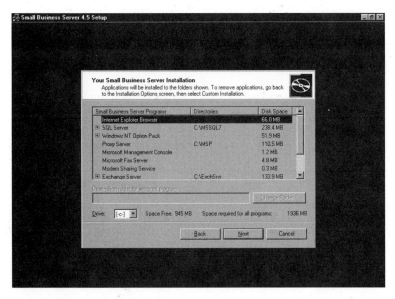

Figure 2-3

The SBS 4.5 setup program provides flexibility for determining target volumes and folders for SBS applications.

- Microsoft Fax Service

- Microsoft Modem Sharing Service

- Exchange Server

- Client applications (These include the installation files for programs such as Microsoft Proxy Client and Microsoft Fax Client.)

The Custom Installation feature also lets you review individual disk space requirements and allows you to make more informed decisions about where to install each SBS application. For example, if you purchased the SBS 4.5/Office 2000 Professional bundle, Microsoft recommends that you have a 4-GB drive or larger for a successful installation. Even though SBS only occupies about 2 GB of drive space once the installation is complete, the setup program requires a substantial amount of headroom or overhead for expanding compressed files during individual SBS application setups. Through creative use of this dialog box, however, you could successfully install the SBS 4.5/Office 2000 Professional bundle across two 2-GB drives. All you'd need to do is to point 500 to 700 MB of applications to your second hard drive, and you'll have more than adequate free space for completing the SBS 4.5 unattended setup.

Tip

The Custom Installation feature also allows you to segment features across volumes such as using the C partition for the OS, D partition for the applications, and E partition for data.

With the Custom Installation feature, you can also minimize the number of files that have to be installed on the primary hard drive. With the SBS 4.5 setup program that runs following the installation of Windows NT Server 4.0 and SP3, you can install all of the remaining SBS applications on a drive other than the primary one.

You can also point the data folders for both _company_ and _users_ to a nondefault volume or path when you perform a fresh installation of SBS 4.5.

Importing User Accounts The Migrate User Wizard, which is new in SBS 4.5, imports a variety of user account information from an existing Windows NT Server 4.0 system. See Figure 2-4. This can be especially useful if your small business client has an existing Windows NT Server 4.0 box that is being replaced by SBS 4.5.

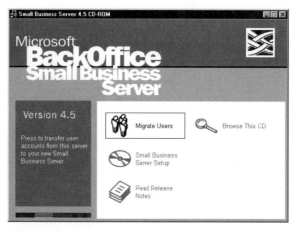

Figure 2-4

The new SBS 4.5 Migrate User Wizard imports existing Windows NT Server 4.0 user account information into an SBS 4.5 system.

The Migrate User Wizard creates a text file that's stored on a floppy disk and sent through _sneakernet_ (that is, you walk the disk from one machine to another) from the Windows NT Server 4.0 system to the SBS 4.5 system. The exported information includes the following data from user accounts on that server:

- User ID
- Full name
- RAS permissions
- Exchange mailbox
- Global Address List information
- Group information and permissions

Tip

The Migrate User Wizard doesn't allow you to export user passwords, Internet access permissions, or Exchange distribution lists. You also can't use the wizard to capture user information from another SBS 4.0 or 4.5 system.

The wizard is run from SBS 4.5 CD-ROM 1 on a Windows NT Server 4.0 system. If you've disabled autorun, you'll need to launch the SBS setup program on the CD-ROM. The exported data is stored in a text file, which can be edited if you wish to remove certain user accounts prior to importing them into the SBS 4.5 system.

From the SBS Console, launch the Import Users Wizard from the To Do List. The user accounts from the Windows NT Server 4.0 system are then imported from the disk into the registry of the SBS 4.5 system. Once complete, all of the imported user account information will be visible within both the SBS User Account Wizard and the Windows NT Server 4.0 User Manager for Domains.

The Timing of SBS Components

Many VAPs often wonder why certain SBS suite components are one version behind. Because SBS is an integrated suite of server components, the development team faces a unique set of timing challenges. As with any integrated suite of applications, the release date of SBS could be thrown off completely by development delays in dependent components. As a result, difficult decisions have to be made in terms of which component versions to wait for and which to incorporate in future suite level service packs or version upgrades. For example, when SBS 4.5 was released to manufacturing in early April 1999, FrontPage 98 was included, even though FrontPage 2000 was very close to completion.

Flexible Hardware Installation

Just as SBS 4.5 brings improved setup flexibility for specifying target directories and folders and for importing user accounts, SBS 4.5 provides much greater flexibility for installing hardware devices through a series of hardware confirmation wizards.

Modem Confirmation Page

Under SBS 4.0, many support problems with the Microsoft Fax Service were traced back to mismatches between modem firmware, unimodem ID, and the .inf driver file. New to SBS 4.5, the Modem Confirmation Page makes an effort to confirm that there is in fact a match between the modem firmware and the device driver that you select. (See Figure 2-5.) While SBS 4.5 is still designed for integrated installation, the SBS product team wanted to provide more flexibility for testing and reconfirming the modem configuration and device driver selection.

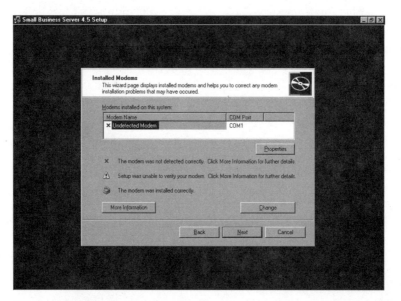

Figure 2-5

New to SBS 4.5, the Modem Confirmation Page helps prevent potentially troublesome mismatches between modem firmware revisions and device driver versions.

The Modem Confirmation Page allows you to view which modem or modems were detected during the unattended installation of Windows NT Server 4.0. From there, the wizard compares the selected device driver and corresponding unimodem ID with the firmware of the modem and alerts you through a yellow or red flag to any suspicious compatibility problems that may arise between the .inf file and firmware. If a yellow exclamation point appears, the wrong modem driver may have been installed. The wizard is advising you to double-check your modem driver version against your firmware version to insure that the proper device driver is selected. If a red *X* appears, SBS 4.5 has determined that your modem was installed during Windows NT Server 4.0 setup as an undetected modem.

Caution

The Microsoft Fax Service won't install properly unless the undetected modem device driver is replaced by the proper device driver for the modem. In addition, the Remote Access Service won't be installed.

Hardware Confirmation Pages

SBS 4.5 also introduces Hardware Confirmation pages that you let you review and modify, if need be, the hardware selection and device drivers for the disk controller(s), video adapters, network card(s), and other mass storage devices that were detected during the unattended installation of Windows NT Server 4.0. See Figure 2-6.

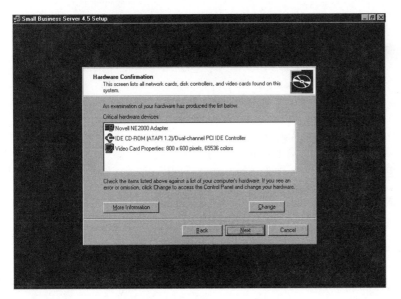

Figure 2-6

New to SBS 4.5, the Hardware Confirmation pages allow you to review and modify the hardware selection and device drivers.

The Hardware Confirmation page appears just after you complete the Modem Confirmation Page. Both steps are completed after Windows NT Server 4.0 and Service Pack 4 have been installed, but before the installation of core SBS applications.

How SBS Wizards Differ from Windows NT Tools

SBS 4.5 administration is built on the foundation of an HTML-based server console that consolidates all the main SBS administrative functions in one place. The SBS Console is also quite flexible and extensible. Chapter 14 provides details on how you can add value to your small business clients' SBS installations by customizing the SBS Console.

In many ways the SBS Console replaces or at least greatly lessens the need to use many of the classic Windows NT Server 4.0 administrative tools. (The underlying executables for the wizards are located in the SmallBusiness folder on the SBS installation CDs.) See Table 2-1.

Caution

You might think that you have two distinct ways to accomplish a task: the SBS way and the Windows NT Server 4.0 way. At times, you might be tempted to experiment and test your Windows NT Server 4.0 knowledge to see if you can outsmart the SBS Console. I cannot stress enough, however, that when a function is present in both SBS and in Windows NT Server 4.0, you always want to use the SBS-specific wizards provided within the SBS Console. Using the Windows NT Server 4.0 or BackOffice Server administration equivalents is risky and, more often than not, will lead to undesirable results. The SBS Console instructions are crystal clear about when you should utilize the Windows NT Server 4.0 or BackOffice Server administration equivalents. The bottom line: when in doubt, use the SBS Console.

File name & size	Function(s)	Comparable Windows NT Server 4.0 tools
Change Password Wizard		
Cpwiz 120 KB	Change a user's password	User Manager
E-mail Distribution List Wizard		
Dlwiz 259 KB	Create an e-mail distribution list, which allows you to send e-mail to a group of people as if you were sending e-mail to a single address	Exchange Administrator
Internet Access Wizard		
Rezwizi 72 KB	Select the users who can access the Internet	Internet Service Manager (Proxy Server)
SBS Internet Connection Wizard		
SBSICW 208 KB	Connect to the Internet by signing up with an ISP or by using your existing ISP	1. Internet Service Manager (Proxy Server) 2. Exchange Administrator
Move Folder Wizard		
Mvfldr 83 KB	Move a shared folder and preserve user access to that shared folder	Windows Explorer
Printer Access Wizard		
Rezwizp 119 KB	Provide access to network printers Usage: rezwizp /p *printername* or rezwizp /f *faxname*	1. Printers folder for network printers 2. No direct comparison for network faxing (unique to SBS)

Table 2-1

Wizards in the SBS Console   *(continued)*

Table 2-1 *(continued)*

File name & size	Function(s)	Comparable Windows NT Server 4.0 tools
Set Up Computer Wizard		
Scw 14 KB	1. Create a floppy disk to connect a client computer to the SBS network 2. Select applications to install on the client computer	No Windows NT Server equivalent; closest in function to the software distribution mechanism in SMS
Share A Folder Wizard		
Shrpubw 179 KB	1. Share a new or existing folder on the server 2. Control which users have access to the shared folder and define the type of access each user has to the shared folder	1. Windows Explorer 2. Server Manager
Shared Folder Access Wizard		
Rezwizf 120 KB	Change access to a shared folder Usage: rezwizf /e *sharename*	1. Windows Explorer 2. Server Manager
User Access Wizard		
Rezwizu 150 KB	1. View or change a user's network access 2. Grant access to a shared folder (the opposite of the Shared Folder Access Wizard from the user perspective)	1. Windows Explorer 2. Server Manager
User Account Wizard		
Addusrw 159 KB	1. Create a user account 2. Give access to network resources 3. Set up a user's computer	1. User Manager 2. Server Manager 3. Windows Explorer

Some functions aren't present in SBS Console, and you'll need to use the tools in Windows NT Server 4.0. See Table 2-2.

Function(s)	Windows NT Server 4.0 tool
Configure account policies and roaming profiles	User Manager
Configure printer auditing	Printers folder
Enable and manage public folders	Exchange Administrator
Set up file auditing	Windows Explorer

Table 2-2

Functions for which you need Windows NT Server 4.0 administration tools

Improved SBS Internet Connection Wizard

The Small Business Server Internet Connection Wizard (ICW) or sbsicw.exe has been greatly enhanced to support cable modems, xDSL, and ISDN routers. ICW now runs in either one of two modes: automated or manual. The automated ICW setup is used to establish a new account with an ISP who fully supports SBS Internet access, e-mail, and Web hosting. The manual ICW setup is used to configure all Internet related services in SBS 4.5 so that they use existing ISP accounts. See Figure 2-7. Both wizards have been completely rewritten for SBS 4.5 and are discussed in great detail in Chapter 18.

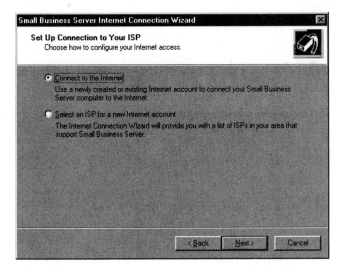

Figure 2-7

The SBS Internet Connection Wizard supports both the creation of a new ISP account and the use of one or more existing accounts.

Set Up Computer Wizard

The Set Up Computer Wizard, shown in Figure 2-8, allows novice small business VAPs and administrators to connect a PC running Windows 95/98, Windows NT Workstation 4.0, or Windows NT Server 4.0 to the SBS network with almost no configuration choices or intervention required. The Set Up Computer Wizard configures the computer and domain names, detects and installs the network card, installs TCP/IP support with DHCP enabled, installs the preselected client applications, and creates shortcuts on the desktop for company and users shared folders. Chapter 17 drills down on these topics to give you a thorough understanding of which steps are required and which are optional at each user's desktop PC.

Figure 2-8

The Set Up Computer Wizard helps you to quickly, correctly, and consistently set up the Windows 95/98 and Windows NT client desktops on an SBS network.

Tip

Chapter 16 looks at how to customize the Set Up Computer Wizard.

User/Workstation Limit Increase

SBS 4.5, like its predecessor, supports an unlimited number of user accounts. That means you can create as many user accounts as desired. The real limiting factor, however, is the number of workstation connections.

With SBS 4.0, you could purchase a license for as few as 5 or as many as 25 workstations. With SBS 4.5, the maximum number of workstations that you can license doubles to 50 workstations. The rationale for this was based on new information regarding small business technology adoption. Microsoft found that almost all small businesses need to hire a full-time IT person when they have 50 PCs or more, or approximately 100 employees. Most small businesses with fewer than 50 PCs tend to use a VAP as their virtual IT department.

SQL Server Storage Capacity Increase

As with the issues of setup flexibility, hardware detection, and Internet access, Microsoft listened very carefully to all of the VAP criticisms of SBS 4.0. VAPs wanted to take advantage of the built-in SQL Server 6.5 database in SBS 4.0; however, many found the limitations too confining for practical use. Under SBS 4.0 with SQL Server 6.5, you were limited to total database space of 1 GB including transaction logs. SBS 4.5 dramatically increases the maximum size of the SQL Server databases. With SQL Server 7.0 running under SBS 4.5, each database can now grow to a total of 10 GB with an unlimited number of SQL Server databases per SBS system.

SBS Distribution Options

When purchasing SBS 4.5, small business end users and VAPs really have two choices in how they procure the server license, CD-ROM media, and documentation.

VAPs in the Three-Tier Distribution Model

One way that SBS 4.5 is sold is through the traditional three-tier distribution model, which can be seen in Figure 2-9 on the next page. In this scenario, Microsoft as the manufacturer decides that it wants to deal with only a handful of direct accounts. So it establishes relationships with distributors, who are authorized to sell Microsoft products to bonafide computer resellers.

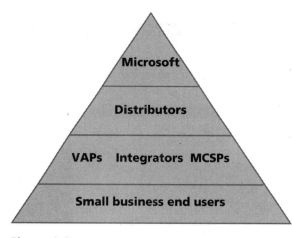

Figure 2-9

The three-tier distribution model.

This means that if the owner of a local florist shop calls up one of these Microsoft distributors to buy SBS 4.5, he or she will be turned away and referred to a local reseller because the florist shop is not a computer reseller. Microsoft sells to distributors, who in turn sell to VAPs, who then resell the SBS 4.5 license to the small business owner. See Table 2-3 for a list of distributors in North America who sell Microsoft products. An updated list of authorized Microsoft distributors can be found on the Microsoft Direct Access Web site (*www.microsoft.com/ directaccess*). Lists of international authorized Microsoft distributors can be found on each Microsoft subsidiary's local Web site.

U.S. distributors	Canadian distributors
Gates/Arrow Distributing	Beamscope Canada
Inacom	EMJ Data Systems Ltd
Ingram Micro Inc.	Ingram Micro Inc.
Merisel	Merisel Canada Inc.
Nascorp	MultiMicro
Pinacor	Tech Data
Tech Data	

Table 2-3

North American distributors

Authorized Microsoft distributors offer a variety of different SBS 4.5 SKUs. A full guide to SBS licensing can be found on the SBS Web site (*www.microsoft.com/smallbusinessserver*). SBS 4.5 version upgrades are being provided free of charge to SBS 4.0 end users and being fulfilled directly through Microsoft. Table 2-4 shows the primary ways that SBS 4.5 is being offered through distribution.

SBS SKU	Part number	U.S. estimated retail price (ERP)
SBS 4.5 with 5 client access licenses (CALs)—base offering	723-00339	$1,499
SBS 4.5 with 5 CALs and 5 Office 2000 Professional licenses	B58-00002	$2,899
SBS 4.5 add-on pack (bump pack) with 5 CALs	807-00036	$299
SBS 4.5 add-on pack (bump pack) with 20 CALs	807-00037	$999
SBS 4.5 competitive upgrade with 5 CALs	723-00342	$929
SBS 4.5 competitive upgrade with 5 CALs and 5 Office 2000 Professional licenses	B58-00009	$2,329

Table 2-4

SBS 4.5 SKUs

Tip

SBS SKUs and prices are subject to change. For the most current products and pricing, always check the SBS Web site at *www.microsoft.com/smallbusinessserver* or the Microsoft Direct Access Web site at *www.microsoft.com/directaccess*.

OEMs Replacing Distributors

The second way that SBS 4.5 is sold is through original equipment manufacturers (OEMs). Many other VAPs and small businesses purchase SBS 4.5 indirectly through hardware OEMs who are authorized to bundle SBS 4.5 with their servers.

In some cases the hardware OEM takes the place of the distributor. The VAP will purchase the server hardware bundled with SBS 4.5 and then subsequently resell the bundled offering to their small business client.

In other cases the hardware OEM takes the place of both the distributor and the VAP. In this situation, the small business end user purchases the server hardware bundled with SBS 4.5 directly from the hardware vendor, effectively bypassing both the distributor and the reseller.

With SBS 4.0, hardware OEMs were able to bundle a special 10 CAL SBS 4.0 SKU with their server hardware. That, however, was the only SKU available for hardware bundling. Under SBS 4.5, hardware OEMs still have one special SKU available, but it now contains only 5 CALs.

Some of the hardware OEMs who have bundled SBS include:

- Compaq
- Dell
- Equus
- Gateway
- HP
- NEC

Smaller system assemblers, many of whom are also VAPs, can bundle SBS 4.5 with their white box server offerings through the Microsoft OEM System Builder Program. A variety of benefits are given to participants in this program, including very low volume commitments. Details can be found on the System Builder program Web site (*www.microsoft.com/oem*).

Tip

A white box server, otherwise known as a clone, is assembled from brand name components but typically doesn't bear a brand name sticker on the outside of the case.

SBS 4.5 also became part of the Microsoft Open License program in June 1999. This provides VAPs and their small business customers' increased licensing flexibility for SBS 4.5 and most other Microsoft products. In many cases, the Open License program also reduces the acquisition and asset management costs of software licensing. Details can be found on the Microsoft Open License Web site (*www.microsoft.com/mlo*).

Office 2000 Integration

Due to strong VAP demand, Microsoft created two special SBS 4.0/Office 97 Professional packages in December 1997. Both of the packages have been updated for Office 2000 and continue to be available through distribution for new installations of SBS 4.5. When either of these two SBS 4.5/Office 2000 Professional packages is purchased, the Office 2000 Professional setup is tightly integrated into SBS 4.5's Set Up Computer Wizard. This allows for easy deployment of Office 2000 on your client's desktop PCs at the same time that all the other SBS 4.5 client applications are set up through an unattended point-and-click installation. Details on the Set Up Computer Wizard are presented in Chapters 16 and 17.

Tip

In Chapter 16, you'll learn how to integrate Office 2000 into the Set Up Computer Wizard, even when Office 2000 has been purchased separately from SBS 4.5.

Redesigning SBS to be More Responsive to Industry Trends

The idea for SBS 4.0 was conceived in August 1995. Over the next two years, several major developments took place in the PC industry that would dramatically impact SBS. The pace of industry change accelerated even more following the release of SBS 4.0 and there's no sign of any slowdown in the pace of innovation and price/performance improvements for small business networks.

The Explosive Growth of the Internet

When SBS 4.0 was released in October 1997, small businesses were already growing accustomed to dial-up ISP accounts, POP3 e-mail, and Web browsing. Proxy Server and Exchange Server in SBS 4.0 were a natural extension of what small business PC users were already accomplishing on a stand-alone basis.

VAPs supporting SBS 4.0 found that their small business customers were more interested in working with local ISPs and maintaining existing ISP accounts than signing up for new ISP accounts from large national ISPs through the SBS Internet Connectivity Wizard. So for SBS 4.5, Microsoft reshaped the SBS Internet Connectivity Wizard to give VAPs and small businesses more options. The wizard now can either launch a highly automated procedure for creating new ISP accounts or provide the flexibility to easily configure existing e-mail, access, and publishing accounts through a set of new wizards. In addition, Microsoft created a set of worksheets that could be sent to the ISP to help with the planning of key Internet configuration data. These worksheets are detailed in Chapter 18.

Internet Usage by Small Businesses

According to the market research firm IDC/Link, small business Internet usage in the United States grew from 19.7 percent in 1996 to 40.7 percent in 1997. Even more interesting in the study is the finding that among these small businesses, the primary Internet access method was a single-user dial-up account for retrieving mail from a single POP3 mailbox. Despite a huge increase in the number of small businesses getting connected to the Internet, most small businesses were getting online through analog modems and single-user dial-up accounts, as opposed to shared secure Internet access and company-wide e-mail through a centralized file and application server, such as SBS. This leaves a huge opportunity for SBS VAPs to implement solutions that deliver secure, high-speed Web browsing and e-mail to every client on the LAN.

Plummeting Hardware Prices

During the same time that SBS 4.0 was being developed, consumers began to see the proliferation of the sub-$1,000 PC, which in turn forced business desktop PC prices downward as well. In addition, hardware OEMs like HP, Compaq, IBM, and Dell were aggressively touting a new product: the workgroup server, optimized for small corporate departments and small businesses.

Following the release of SBS 4.0 in late 1997, PC hardware prices continued to plummet throughout 1998. Consumers saw the emergence of the sub-$500 PC and businesses saw commercial-grade network-ready desktop PCs in the sub-$1,000 price range. Many server vendors even began offering fully configured entry-level workgroup-class servers priced below $2,000.

While the hardware requirements really haven't changed between SBS 4.0 and 4.5, small businesses can better afford to invest in a server-class box to run their SBS network. See Table 2-5 for hardware requirements for SBS 4.5.

> ### *Tip*
>
> For more information on hardware requirements, check out the *Microsoft BackOffice Small Business Server 4.5 Resource Kit* or the SBS Web site at *www.microsoft.com/smallbusinessserver*.

	Minimum	Recommended
Processor	Pentium 120 MHz	Pentium 200 MHz or higher
RAM	64 MB	96 MB or more if SQL Server or Exchange Server will receive moderate usage
Hard drive	2 GB without Office 2000 Professional bundle 4 GB with Office 2000 Professional bundle	Depends on data storage requirements for company shared folders, users shared folders, Exchange Server, and SQL Server
Other	3.5-inch drive configured as A: Video adapter and monitor that supports 800×600×16 CD-ROM drive Network card from Windows NT hardware compatibility list One or more modems from Windows NT hardware compatibility list	Tape backup drive or equivalent One or more phone lines to support dial-up networking, modem sharing, fax serving, and Internet access Uninterruptible power supply (UPS) Fault tolerant hard drive configuration: RAID 1 (mirroring or duplexing) or RAID 5 (stripe set with parity)

Table 2-5
SBS 4.5 server hardware requirements

Key Networking Components as Commodities

The 1995–1997 era also saw the emergence of small business networking product lines from vendors, such as 3Com and Intel, which were specifically targeted at small businesses. By mid-1997, most network-ready PCs were coming with built-in 10/100 Ethernet network cards. During 1998 networking vendors continued their push into small business as 100Base-T Ethernet hubs and switches became cost-effective for even the smallest of small businesses.

The rapid adoption of Internet access through cable modems, DSL, and ISDN also caused the SBS team to make sure that SBS 4.5 was ready to handle these configuration issues with ease.

Mitigating Y2K Concerns

SBS 4.5 was being developed at a time when small businesses were finally starting to become aware that year 2000 (Y2K) was their problem, too. From 1995–1997, most of the media and IT attention was focused on assessing the Fortune 1000 exposure to Y2K problems. In particular, early Y2K efforts were geared toward remediating COBOL programming and legacy mainframe software packages.

By 1998, however, PC/LAN Y2K issues were starting to garner attention among VAPs. In September 1998, Microsoft Direct Access launched a new Y2K Web site specifically geared toward helping VAPs get their clients ready for the year 2000. In doing the integration work for SBS 4.5, Microsoft also made sure that each component within SBS 4.5 would be year 2000 compliant.

Windows NT Workstation 4.0 as the Small Business Desktop of Choice

As prices on business grade, network-ready PCs continued to drop throughout 1997 and early 1998, many of the larger, mail-order PC OEMs began offering Windows NT Workstation 4.0 as an inexpensive, time-of-purchase upgrade on many of their nonconsumer desktop and laptop PC brands. With most vendors, this meant that you could upgrade the desktop operating at the time of purchase from Windows 95 or 98 to Windows NT Workstation 4.0 for under $100.

While Windows NT Workstation 4.0 was initially implemented only by large, well-funded IT organizations during 1996, rapidly falling desktop PC prices led to more widespread adoption of Microsoft's high-end desktop operating system. By early 1997, the major mail-order PC vendors all had network-ready desktop PCs, complete with monitor, that could be bundled with Windows NT Workstation 4.0 for about $1,500.

In August 1995, when Windows 95 was released, Microsoft had positioned the desktop OS as the mainstream corporate OS, while Windows NT Workstation was the high-end corporate OS. Just prior to the Windows 98 release in June 1998, however, Microsoft began a campaign to promote the benefits of Windows NT Workstation 4.0 for small businesses. By the time

Windows 98 was released, Microsoft positioned Windows 98 as the consumer OS and Windows NT Workstation 4.0 as the core business OS.

Enhanced Support for ISDN, xDSL, and Cable Modems

SBS 4.0 was originally designed for small business end users, as opposed to VAPs. Because of that, Microsoft made certain assumptions about levels of expertise. The SBS Internet Connection Wizard was intended to help businesses get from start to finish in creating an online presence in a matter of minutes. To reach this level of simplicity, however, Microsoft had to sacrifice some of the power and flexibility.

Without VAP involvement in the development SBS 4.0, full-time and higher-speed connectivity options were an afterthought. After all, how many small business owners know enough around 1996 to order a T1 line, could afford the overwhelming price tag, and could configure a router and CSU/DSU? (If any of these terms are foreign to you, Chapter 18 will help you fill in the gaps with you may have with Internet connectivity.)

By 1998, however, VAPs were becoming frustrated by Microsoft's decision to build SBS 4.0 Internet connectivity on the premise of dial-up analog modems. Small business clients were demanding higher speed, broadband Internet connections. With SBS 4.5, Microsoft completely redesigned the SBS Connection Wizard to fully support routers delivering ISDN, xDSL, and cable modem Internet access connections.

Upgrades That Ease Support Burdens

Now that Microsoft knew all about VAPs and the critical link they provided to the success of SBS, SBS 4.5 was redesigned from ground up for VAPs. In fact, there's even a new wizard in SBS 4.5 that has the underlying file name of vaprpt.exe. (In case you're curious, it's located in the SmallBusiness directory.) Microsoft knew that VAPs faced a constant challenge to elevate their perceived value-add and to serve more clients . Microsoft also knew that small businesses would not be willing to pay big hourly rates to VAPs for just performing mundane functions like user account administration, retrieving log files, and installing client applications. So Microsoft included tools in SBS 4.5 that would allow VAPs to get out of low-level, low-margin activities so that they could focus more on adding real value to the SBS solution.

Redesigning the SBS Console

Based on feedback from VAPs and Microsoft PSS technical support engineers, Microsoft made a few key enhancements in the SBS 4.5 server console. The SBS Console is still based entirely on HTML and Active Server Pages. Many VAPs had difficulty with console performance and response time when remotely administering the console over dial-up analog and ISDN lines. The SBS 4.0 console pages have a fair amount of graphics to supplement the HTML pages. Although the SBS 4.0 console pages were aesthetically pleasing, the size of the graphics files ultimately made the console difficult to administer remotely. Under SBS 4.5, the large image files are removed from the console and replaced with simpler, smaller image files. The SBS 4.0 Manage Server console has also been renamed the SBS Console in SBS 4.5.

The SBS Console also has a new indicator that displays how much total space is on each drive volume as well as a graphical representation of how much free disk space is remaining, as shown in Figure 2-10. This keeps critical information right in front of VAPs and small business end user administrators.

Figure 2-10
You can tell at a glance approximately how much disk space is remaining on each volume by looking at the newly redesigned SBS Console Home page.

The SBS Console Home page also helps you stay on top of any critical services that may have stopped. Rather than having to examine the Event Viewer logs and the Control Panel Services applet, the SBS Console Home page now displays an X with the name of any of the key Windows NT Server 4.0 services that are stopped. You no longer have to visit the Services applet or run net start commands just to restart a stopped service. Simply click the X, as shown in Figure 2-11. Just like the new drive space indicators on the console, the stalled services indicators also help keep this critical information front and center. No more digging around in two places just to figure out that a service is stopped.

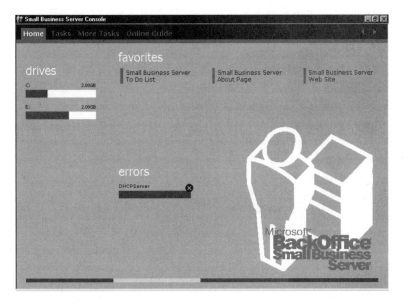

Figure 2-11
The newly redesigned SBS Console Home page makes it easy to identify any critical services that have stopped.

Microsoft's design goal on the SBS Console Home page is to give SBS VAPs and small business clients quicker diagnostics. For example, a nontechnical end user may be on the phone with the VAP. The end user can read a few things on the Home page and the VAP can decide quite rapidly whether they need to cancel the rest of their day to go on site immediately, dial in later for remote administration with Microsoft NetMeeting, or wait for the regularly scheduled preventative maintenance service call. So in effect, the new diagnostic tools on the SBS Console Home page help SBS VAPs to manage their often hectic schedules better.

The SBS Console also gives VAPS a great opportunity to add value to their SBS 4.5 installations by customizing the console pages. This topic is explored in Chapter 14.

Proactive Management Through the Server Status Tool

When a Fortune 1000 IT organization implements a BackOffice Server solution, there's generally an entire department charged with babysitting those servers. In a small business environment, there's typically no one on hand to watch over the server's health.

For many small businesses, that means they generally don't know there's a major problem developing until it's too late. That's when you glance down at your pager and see the code words "911!!!" next to the client's phone number. Quick. Drop everything and run over to put out the fire.

Microsoft knows that most VAPs would rather avoid most of this reactive mode fire fighting and concentrate on building more reliable, innovative solutions for these small business clients. These clients would also rather avoid the difficulties and downtime as well. I can't remember the last time one of my clients remarked, "Gee, Josh, I'm kind of nostalgic for a server crash."

To help you stay on top of the well-being of the client's SBS installation, Microsoft designed the Server Status Tool for SBS 4.5. With the Server Status Tool, you can configure SBS to fax or e-mail you specific log file reports at prescheduled time intervals, as shown in Figure 2-12. The available logs include:

- Percentage of disk space available on all volumes
- Status of all server services
- Winsock proxy logs
- Proxy Server logs
- IIS logs

Chapter 15 provides additional information on how you can customize the Server Status Tool for your clients' specific needs.

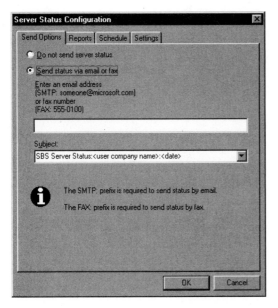

Figure 2-12

The Server Status Tool can fax or e-mail selected log files to you at predetermined time internals.

Remote Management Through NetMeeting

With SBS 4.0, remote management needed to be run either through some type of third-party remote control solution or by a dial-up networking (DUN) connection. The remote control solution solved some of the large image file problems described earlier in the SBS Console section. Because the remote control packages weren't designed and tested under SBS 4.0, the products often created more problems than they solved. The alternative was a low-performance DUN connection. Neither way was ideal. VAPs needed a better way to administer their clients' SBS networks remotely.

With SBS 4.5, Microsoft added NetMeeting 2.11 for remote administration. See Figure 2-13 on the next page. NetMeeting solves many of the performance problems and integration issues that VAPs had to grapple with previously when trying to run SBS Console wizards remotely. In particular, it provides an acceptable performance level. Chapter 25 details the configuration of NetMeeting for remote administration.

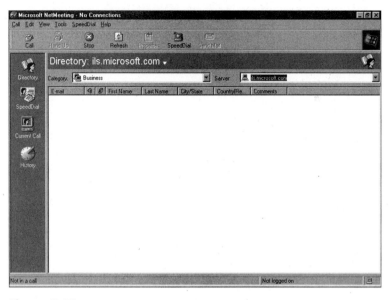

Figure 2-13

SBS 4.5 provides an integrated remote control solution for remotely administering the SBS Console.

The Bottom Line

As a VAP servicing small business clients, you'll find that perceived value-add is relative to how your small business clients perceive your services compared to what they're capable of providing on their own. Adding value is all about staying one or two steps ahead of the curve. Much of your success in staying current has to do with how proactive you are in identifying next year's hot trend and then allocating the time and budget toward becoming proficient in it. You can begin to measure how much value you can add by comparing your relative expertise to your clients' expertise, then by looking at the features in SBS 4.5. Several major new feature enhancements in SBS 4.5 extend the value you can provide to customers. Improvements in SBS also help you come up to speed in deploying it at client sites.

Part 2

Setting up Shop as an SBS VAP

Chapter 3

Maximizing Your SBS Training Investment

Part 1 looked at how Microsoft Small Business Server 4.5 can help you tap into the huge demand for installing and supporting small business networks. In Part 2 you learn about how to set up shop as an SBS VAP. The section begins with this chapter, which covers the critical importance of getting trained and keeping your skills sharp. The next chapter looks at how to overcome some of the staffing challenges associated with being an SBS VAP, including recruitment, protecting your training investment, staff retention, certification, competitive pressures, and compensation.

As an SBS VAP, you need to decide early on whether to be a product reseller and service provider or just a service provider. Chapter 5 looks at profitability challenges and offers guidelines on how to identify your core competencies, how to choose the products and services on which to focus, and how to recognize which products and services your clients should find from another source. Chapter 6 concludes the section with a drilldown on the potential perils and opportunities of partnering with other technology providers.

The Critical Importance of Training

So why am I beginning a section entitled "Setting up Shop as an SBS VAP" with a chapter on SBS training? After all, the focus of this book isn't on setting up a training center or getting trained on SBS technical features. This book is about helping your firm be profitable and successful by offering SBS-centric solutions.

Why should learning about training options figure so prominently in your plans to become an SBS VAP? Isn't having satisfied clients and successful, profitable client engagements more important? Yes, it's important to have a strong, viable following today; the proper training, however, ensures that your firm remains relevant in the future. Much of your value to clients is tied ultimately to how sharp your skills are. So training becomes an important driver for your marketability, competitive positioning, rate setting, and staff utilization. Training is one of the most, if not *the* most, important facets of being an SBS VAP. Your knowledge and expertise are a very big piece of the value-add that you bring to the table. After all, if you knew only as much about small business networks as your small business clients, why would small business owners hire you to be their VAP? Why wouldn't small business owners or their internal "gurus" just run the setup.exe program and install a network the same way they install Microsoft Word 2000, Microsoft Internet Explorer 5, or a new laser printer?

The answer's quite simple: although networks have gotten much simpler to install and administer, setting up a LAN still requires a specialized knowledge of hardware, software, peripherals, protocols, security, applications, and a host of other topics.

Some skills have become commodities, while others are still amazingly difficult to acquire. Much of the consulting work that you'll do for an SBS implementation requires expertise at an intermediate level. Think of the skills you need for being an SBS VAP in the "Goldilocks" framework. The skills you have and the training you seek shouldn't be too basic (you're not being paid the big bucks for knowing how to copy files or plug in a mouse) nor should they be too advanced (small businesses generally don't have the budget for six-figure data warehousing or enterprise resource planning applications). Your skills need to be "just right." The low tech, high tech, and just right tech definitions keep changing over time, in much the same way as your value-add.

Note

To learn more about how your value-add changes over time and how it's all relative to your clients' level of in-house expertise, see Chapter 2.

Training is very expensive. And I'm not just talking whip-out-the-corporate-Amex-or-checkbook expensive. I'm talking about enormous time investments as well. The hard and soft expenses associated with getting trained and keeping up-to-date might be, in fact, your second greatest annual overhead item, only outpaced by salaries of your staff. These somewhat overwhelming time and monetary costs for training are also a big part of reason for the huge shortage of IT workers in many industries, in many parts of the world.

For example, to become a Microsoft Certified Systems Engineer (MCSE), most Certified Technical Education Centers (CTECs) in the United States charge in excess of $10,000 for tuition. The costs, however, just begin to ring up with tuition. Factor in at least $600 for exam fees—assuming you pass all six exams on the first attempt. Most students will also buy additional books and software to supplement the classroom instruction and then set up a lab environment in their home or office to become more familiar with the products (estimate $3,000).

Now what about the nonmonetary costs? What about the cost of being away from clients for 200 hours of classroom time plus commuting? Then consider the 100–200 hours of self-study to supplement classroom learning.

Regardless of whether you choose to pursue the traditional instructor-led classroom training route, use self-study materials, or some combination of the two, training costs aren't trivial. Also bear in mind that training isn't a one-shot deal. As your small business clients request newer applications and operating systems, you'll be hitting the books or heading back to the classroom like clockwork.

Microsoft Official Curriculum Classes

One way to get trained on SBS and the related BackOffice applications is through classes based on Microsoft Official Curriculum (MOC). As the MOC name implies, Microsoft creates these courses—specifically, the Microsoft product groups in Redmond, Washington, typically develop MOC classes. With SBS for example, the same program managers who led the development of SBS 4.5 were on the team of writers and instructional experts who created the two MOC courses for SBS 4.5.

IT professionals also often use MOC courseware as preparation for Microsoft exams and certification. So if you wanted to become a Microsoft Certified Professional (MCP) on Exchange Server, you could take a MOC course on Exchange Server as preparation for the certification exam.

Like BackOffice Server, SBS has no certification exams at the suite level. Several certification exams, however, exist for SBS suite components and related products, such as SQL Server 7.0, Windows NT Server 4.0, Windows NT Workstation 4.0, Windows 95, Windows 98, Exchange Server 5.5, TCP/IP on Windows NT 4.0, IIS 4.0, and Proxy Server 2.0.

Tip

For a full list of certification exams, see the Microsoft Training and Certification Web site at *www.microsoft.com/train_cert*.

MOC courses are available at Microsoft CTECs and Authorized Academic Training Program (AATP) institutions and are taught by Microsoft Certified Trainers (MCTs). In addition to providing classroom instructor-led training, many CTECs offer a variety of flexible options, including online training over the Internet, custom training at customer locations, and self-paced training materials. AATPs are high schools, colleges, and universities offering the same MOC instruction by MCTs to full-time and part-time students. MCTs are MCPs who are technically *and* instructionally certified to train IT professionals on specific Microsoft products.

Tip

You can search for AATPs and CTECs worldwide on the Microsoft Training and Certification Web site at *www.microsoft.com/train_cert*.

You can also purchase self-paced training kits from Microsoft Press based on MOC that cover the BackOffice family of applications such as Windows NT Server, Exchange Server, SQL Server, Proxy Server, and IIS. Specific courses are detailed in "Training Options for Related BackOffice Applications" on the CD-ROM at the back of this book.

In addition to the MOC classes on the related BackOffice family of applications, two distinct one-day instructor-led MOC classes are available for SBS 4.5, as shown in Table 3-1. The first course, *Microsoft BackOffice Small Business Server 4.5 Fundamentals*, covers basic concepts at the beginner to intermediate level. The other course, *Implementing Microsoft BackOffice Small Business Server 4.5*, is intended for VAPs who are more experienced with SBS.

MOC course #1398, *Microsoft BackOffice Small Business Server 4.5 Fundamentals*	MOC course #1399, *Implementing Microsoft BackOffice Small Business Server 4.5*
Delivery method	
Instructor led	Instructor led
Length	
1 day	1 day
Prerequisites (or equivalent knowledge)	
Knowledge of an operating system such as Windows 95, Windows 98, or Windows NT 4.0 Networking concepts Hardware concepts	MOC course #1398 MOC course #685, *Installing and Configuring Windows NT Server 4.0* MOC course #1045, *Overview of Microsoft Exchange Server 5.5*
Syllabus	
Introduction to SBS 4.5 Installing SBS Managing Shared Resources Setting Up User Accounts and Configuring Client Computers Managing E-mail Services Connecting an SBS Network to the Internet	Examining SBS Setup Examining and Extending Client Setup Process Implementing Internet Services Implementing Internet E-mail Services Building Custom Administration Solutions
Highlights	
Installing SBS Configuring shared folders and printers Creating user accounts Configuring client PCs Creating e-mail distribution lists and shared public folders Using the Internet Connection Wizard	Resolving hardware detection issues Changing the SBS default IP address Planning hardware requirements Troubleshooting and extending the Set Up Computer Wizard Configuring firewall, Web hosting settings, and Internet e-mail Customizing the Server Status Tool and remote administration

Table 3-1

MOC SBS Fundamentals course vs. Implementing SBS course

Self-Study Tools

Self-paced training becomes a very appealing choice when:

- You're "maxed" out on time or budget for taking instructor-led classes during the day, evenings, or weekends.

- You don't always have time to attend the Microsoft Direct Access quarterly briefings or seminars.

- You or your boss is concerned about losing out on prime-time billable hours.

- You learn best in a nonconventional training setting, such as at 2 A.M. while you're relaxing in a sweat suit or jeans in your home office.

- You have substantial experience with computer networking and are already familiar with most of the classroom course materials.

The distinction between traditional instructor-led training and self-study tools used to be clear. Before the rise in popularity of online training through the Web, self-study was limited to reading books, computer-based training (CBT), and the online help tutorials accompanying the software. As the demand for skilled IT professionals has soared and the accompanying skill shortage has accelerated, training vendors have become a lot more creative with their self-study programs.

With demanding client project schedules and business models based on staff utilization and hourly billing, you'll quickly learn that the course tuition is only one component of the cost of daytime instructor-led training. Because of this, many VAPs ultimately pursue training in one form or another after-hours.

Many CTECs, AATPs, and other training centers worldwide have responded by offering evening and weekend classes. The pros and cons of instructor-led training are shown in Table 3-2.

While the scheduling flexibility of evening and weekend classes for instructor-led training certainly helps many, other VAPs prefer anywhere, anytime training and forgo the many benefits of instructor-led training. The pros and cons of self-paced study are covered in Table 3-3.

A new hybrid self-study option has emerged more recently: online training with mentoring. This is often an attractive middle ground between going it alone and being spoon-fed because it provides many of the benefits of both self-paced and instructor-led training. An increasing number of online training offerings are being built specifically around MOC.

Pros	Cons
Instructor available for questions and clarifications	If course not carefully researched, pace may be too slow or too fast
Learning enriched by instructors and classmates relating personal field experience to supplement the MOC	If classmates don't meet prerequisites, instructor may end up spending more time on basics and less time on advanced material
Exposed to lots of different approaches and questions from classmates	Only offered at prescheduled times
Interruptions from work and personal routine minimized	Tuition cost often a barrier for small VAPs
Provides structured approach, minimizing the hazards of self-study procrastination	If course only offered during daytime hours, loss of prime-time billable hours
Classroom equipped with required hardware and software	

Table 3-2

Pros and cons of instructor-led training

Pros	Cons
Get trained anytime, anywhere	Need to be highly motivated to make time to study
Almost always lower out-of-pocket costs	No immediate feedback mechanism
Often used to supplement instructor-led training	No immediate peer interaction
Can be selective on which modules to take within the course. Because of this modularity, often used for introductory material, before taking an instructor-led course, or for review purposes before a certification exam.	Subject to business interruptions if tackled during the day and personal/family interruptions if tackled after-hours
	No immediate real-world reality check
Set your own pace	Need to equip your own lab with hardware and software for hands-on practice

Table 3-3

Pro and cons of self-study

Tip

You can find lists of online training with mentoring options on both the Microsoft Training and Certification and Microsoft Direct Access Web sites at *www.microsoft.com/train_cert* and *www.microsoft.com/directaccess*.

Online training with mentoring is Web-based training that's supplemented through live chats with an instructor and peers. The course also usually comes with a guaranteed e-mail response time from the instructor. So if you're really stuck on a concept that can't wait until your weekly live chat with the class, your instructor is required to reply to you within a certain time frame.

Online training with mentoring still allows you to pursue training with great flexibility. Unlike the unstructured self-study options, however, you'll likely need to stick with some type of schedule. For example, if your virtual study group meets online on Tuesdays at 6 P.M. Pacific Standard Time and is scheduled to discuss a specific lesson, the chat won't do you much good if you're three chapters behind the rest of the class.

Because online training with mentoring includes an instructor who moderates the live chats and responds to your e-mails in a timely fashion, this training option is typically more expensive than solo self-study but substantially less expensive than traditional instructor-led courses at training centers.

If you're new to SBS and looking for a quick way to get started with self-study, the Microsoft Web site has a few free self-study options. *Microsoft BackOffice Small Business Server 4.5 Fundamentals* (MOC course #1635) is a six-module self-study course downloadable from the Microsoft Training and Certification Web site at *www.microsoft.com/train_cert*. Microsoft Seminar Online (*www.microsoft.com/seminar*) has two brief SBS 4.0 animated slide shows available, in addition to a more recently added SBS 4.5 online seminar at the 200 level. Both of the SBS 4.0 mini-seminars at the 100 level provide a very basic overview of SBS, and are geared primarily for SBS end users. (Seminar Online uses the 100/200/300 designation the same way that colleges and universities use the terms.) Because they give a high-level overview, these seminars can also be a good way to introduce a potential small business client or prospective new hire to the benefits of SBS.

The first seminar, *Improving Your Small Business with Microsoft BackOffice Small Business Server*, is 18 minutes long and was released in November 1998. It discusses how to build an enterprise-class network on a small business–friendly budget and provides an overview of e-mail, group scheduling, and faxing over a network.

Building a Client Server Network with BackOffice Small Business Server is also 18 minutes and was released in October 1998. It covers the basics of a client/server network and how SBS fits that model, defines what's included with SBS, and introduces you to the SBS Console, fax and modem serving, and SBS limitations.

Microsoft Small Business Server version 4.5 Setup and Overview runs 46 minutes and was released in July 1999. It provides an overview of SBS 4.5 setup and the version upgrade from SBS 4.0 to 4.5.

Tip

To keep abreast of new online seminars for SBS and other related BackOffice Server applications, visit the Microsoft Seminar Online Web site at *www.microsoft.com/seminar*.

Although not designed as a training kit per se, the *Microsoft BackOffice Small Business Server 4.5 Resource Kit* has detailed technical documentation. The book was developed internally at Microsoft by SBS program managers and has sections on planning, deployment, administration, maintenance, performance optimization, integration, security, migration, solutions, tools, utilities, and troubleshooting.

The CD-ROM included with the *SBS 4.5 Resource Kit* also has several utilities, which are helpful:

- **Faxmon**—displays live status of each fax device and job history; and provides logging by job and by device.

- **Faxperf**—shows inbound and outbound bytes, faxes, pages, minutes, failed receipts and connections; data is logged and updated each minute that the utility is in use.

- **SBS Customization Tool**—adds entries and tasks to the SBS Console and custom log reports to the Server Status Tool.

- **TAPI tools**—monitors the status of TAPI lines for modems.

Tip

Several chapters in this book, including Chapters 14 through 16, discuss how you can build sophisticated, small business solutions with tools included with the *Microsoft BackOffice Small Business Server 4.5 Resource Kit.*

Regardless of whether you pursue traditional instructor-led training, self-study, or some combination of the two, you might find it extremely helpful to set up a simulated lab environment in your office or home office. You'll become more familiar with SBS 4.5 and test various configurations and applications.

The Microsoft Direct Access and Certified Solution Provider programs provide many methods for VAPs to obtain a single, not-for-resale (NFR) SBS 4.5 product for internal use only. NFR software is offered at deeply discounted prices, which are below the estimated retail price (ERP). You're restricted, however, to purchasing only one NFR copy for each available product.

By setting up a lab or a test-bed network with an NFR of SBS 4.5, you can install and reinstall SBS 4.5 at your leisure. By the time you perform a client installation of SBS 4.5, you'll be more familiar with each configuration option, choice, and wizard. Table 3-4 shows the recommended minimum configuration for a basic SBS 4.5 tested network for learning purposes.

Tip

For details on configuring a dual boot workstation, see the *Microsoft Windows NT Workstation 4.0 Resource Kit* or the Microsoft Knowledge Base at *support.microsoft.com/support*.

How to Get NFR Software for SBS 4.5 and Other Microsoft Products

NFR software can be ordered through Microsoft authorized distributors. (The Microsoft Direct Access Web site at *www.microsoft.com/directaccess* has a list, as does the Web site of your local Microsoft subsidiary.) From time to time, Microsoft Direct Access has also made NFR software available for various products through other bundles and promotions such as Action Packs and HOT Kits (hands-on-training). (For details on ordering procedures and contents of the Action Packs and HOT Kits, check out the Microsoft Direct Access Web site.) Microsoft Certified Solution Providers (MCSPs) receive NFR software as part of their annual enrollment fee. For details on applying for the MCSP program, check out *www.microsoft.com/mcsp*. In addition to NFR software for VAPs and MCSPs, many Microsoft products are also available on an evaluation basis. Most evaluation copies are effectively crippled at the end of the 120-day period.

Client workstation (desktop PC)	Server
Software	
Dual boot with Windows 95 (or Windows 98) and Windows NT Workstation 4.0	SBS 4.5
Processor	
Pentium 120 MHz or higher processor	Pentium 200 MHz or higher processor
RAM	
32 MB RAM or more	64 MB RAM or more
Hard Drive	
2-GB hard drive or larger	4-GB hard drive or larger (IDE drive adequate for learning purposes)
Other	
3.5-inch disk drive	3.5-inch disk drive
Video adapter and monitor that supports at least 800 × 600 × 16 colors	Video adapter and monitor that supports at least 800 × 600 × 16 colors
Mouse and keyboard	Mouse and keyboard
Ethernet network card from Windows NT hardware compatibility list	Ethernet network card and class 1 business modem from Windows NT hardware compatibility list
	CD-ROM drive
Networking components	
4-port 10Base-T Ethernet hub	
Two category 3 or category 5 UTP network cables	
Optional: tape backup drive (Travan type adequate for learning purposes)	
Optional: server UPS with a serial interface and power monitoring software	

Table 3-4

Recommended minimum configuration for a basic SBS 4.5 tested network

> ### Other Less Conventional Ways to Get Trained on and Keep up with SBS 4.5
>
> Keep abreast of resources from the Microsoft Direct Access program by visiting the Web site frequently (*www.microsoft.com/directaccess*), subscribing to their free weekly e-mail newsletter, and attending free local seminars and quarterly briefings
>
> - Visit the Microsoft Personal Support Center (*support.microsoft.com/support*) and search for SBS 4.5 Knowledge Base (KB) articles.
>
> - Check out the Microsoft TechNet Web site (*www.microsoft.com/technet*) and subscribe to the free weekly e-mail newsletter.
>
> - Subscribe to the Microsoft BackOffice free weekly e-mail newsletter (*www.microsoft.com/backoffice*).
>
> - Review posts on the SBS newsgroups through an NNTP-compliant newsreader. The public SBS newsgroup is located at *microsoft.public.backoffice.smallbiz*. The private SBS newsgroup, which is for VAPs only, is also free but requires registration and confirmation of VAP status. To sign up for the private Direct Access SBS newsgroup, visit the Support page on the Direct Access Web site.
>
> - Look at the readme file located on SBS 4.5 CD-ROM 1. This file contains a wealth of last-minute technical information.
>
> - Invest in a Microsoft TechNet CD subscription (*www.microsoft.com/technet*).

SBS Generalists vs. Area Specialists

Chapters 1 and 2 covered how VAPs servicing small business clients with SBS 4.5 need to wear lots of hats. This means on a typical Friday, you might start the day by finishing a proposal for an Outlook 2000/Exchange Server 5.5 groupware application, later in the morning head out to a client across town to install a multiport serial board for a remote access server, then drive to another client in the afternoon to open up ports on a Proxy Server 2.0 firewall, and finish the day at yet another client who needs you to write a new SQL Server 7.0 query for a lead-tracking application.

If you're fortunate enough to have your calendar packed with clients requesting just one specific skill set, such as messaging or database design, more power to you. Small business owners, however, often don't want to have three or four different VAPs' business cards in their Rolodex. For a small business, a single point of accountability for its computer systems is also often critical.

Specializing does allow your firm to build up proficiency in one particular area. This often leads to higher hourly billing rates, as your firm becomes the be-all, end-all local expert on some niche such as migrating Lotus Notes to Exchange Server.

Focusing on just one solution, however, or just one piece of your client's business, does come with some inherent risks. You are allowing a potential competitor into your account. Let's say your firm has had a successful two-year relationship with a local law firm. You helped them migrate from Lotus Notes to Exchange Server and continue to build new groupware applications for them every few months. During these same two years, another hardware-centric VAP has focused on their hardware, software, desktop support, training, and network administration. This hardware-centric VAP senses greater opportunity in providing services at a higher level for her existing clients and recruits a seasoned developer proficient in both SQL Server and Exchange Server. Your loyal client, enticed by a lower rate structure and one-stop shopping, gives your firm the boot.

Applications and upgrade cycles make it basically impossible for you to know everything about each application in SBS. Most small business VAPs, however, strive to be well rounded. Typically, VAPs need to develop expert proficiency on file and printer sharing and the core SBS specific services, applications, and wizards such as the modem server, fax server, Set Up Computer Wizard, Internet Connection Wizard, SBS Console, and Server Status Tool. Many VAPs will then take time to learn, at least to an intermediate level, two or three of the core BackOffice applications (SQL Server, Exchange Server, Proxy Server, IIS), in addition to Windows NT Server.

Seasoned VAPs then often choose to become experts in a single specialty based on one of the BackOffice applications. These specialties may include messaging and groupware, relational database applications, Web site design, Internet access and firewalls, or wide area connections and remote access.

Many veteran VAPs also come to SBS with a strong technical background in other platforms such as Macintosh, NetWare, UNIX, or mainframe. The years of experience with another operating system often makes this VAP a natural for becoming a migration or interoperability specialist.

Comparing Training Options

Because making informed training investments is so critical to being a successful and profitable SBS VAP, I've devoted an entire chapter to the topic. On the CD-ROM in the back of this book I've also included two Excel templates: "Courseware Comparison Matrix," which will help you evaluate training options, and "Internal Skills Inventory," which will help you keep tabs on your training assets or, as economists say, investments in human capital.

Courseware Comparison Matrix

The courseware comparison matrix, shown in Figure 3-1, is designed to make sure you ask enough questions so that you can properly evaluate various SBS training options. Although I designed the template primarily to evaluate MOC offerings at CTECs and AATPs, many of the items on the spreadsheet can be readily adapted for evaluating non-MOC classes and various self-study options.

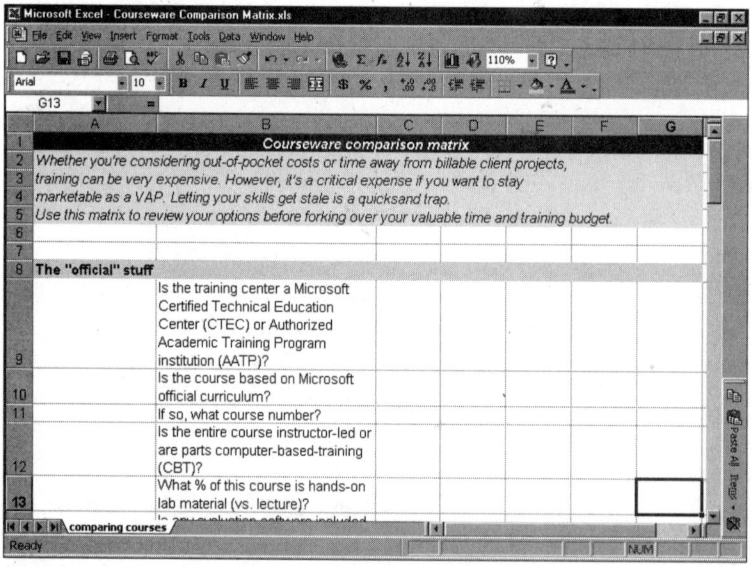

Figure 3-1

"Courseware Comparison Matrix," included on the CD-ROM in the back of this book, can be used to review your options before you spend valuable time and your training budget.

Internal Skills Inventory

Because training is so expensive, you'll find it helpful to create and maintain an internal skills inventory, as shown in Figure 3-2. Chances are, you're already keeping track of your firm's aggregate skills in one form or another. You may have this information in your staff members' resumes.

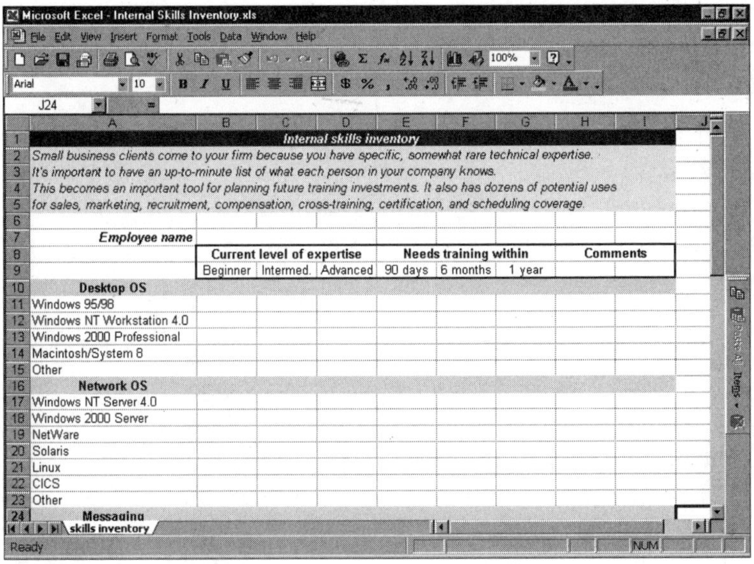

Figure 3-2

Small business clients come to your firm because you have specific, somewhat rare technical expertise. Use this matrix to keep track of what skills your firm has and what skills you need to acquire.

Tip

If you sense that your staff is keeping their resumes a little too current, you won't want to miss Chapter 4.

The laundry list of skills for your firm may also be found in your direct mail pieces, sales letters, sales presentation slides, press releases, brochures, and Web site. The key part of the inventory is to gather all the information in one place, apply the criteria across all staff members, and then update the inventory at least once a quarter. To help you get started, I've included an Excel template, "Internal Skill Inventory," on the CD-ROM in the back of this book.

Caution

Think about what a hay day a headhunter would have with your internal skills inventory if it were to fall into the wrong hands. Don't let this be a deterrent to creating the internal skills inventory, but think carefully about how and where you store this file.

Building a Training Budget Around the Comparison Matrix

Now armed with a detailed inventory of who knows what within your firm, you'll be able to put your courseware comparisons side by side with your staffs' skills inventory when making training investment decisions. Just as important, your staff needs to understand that training is expensive and as such, that you take the commitment to keeping their skills current very seriously.

Each time staff members want to take an instructor-led course or purchase a self-study program, they should use the courseware comparison matrix to interview the training vendor and evaluate various options. Once your staff members have more complete information on the available courses, you can evaluate how the specific course request fits into the current internal skills inventory and how the course will help the individual and company meet its skills acquisition goals.

If individuals on your staff want to pursue more training than you're able to pay for as their employer, make sure they check out the Microsoft Training & Certification program (_www.microsoft.com/train_cert/itcr_). Through Training & Certification, Microsoft has partnered with Key Bank USA and Servus Financial Corp. to arrange for low-cost financing for people who want to take MOC training courses at CTECs or AATPs.

The Microsoft/Key Bank USA IT Career Loan covers training and certification costs, books, hardware, software, and living expenses. The loan is provided at competitive interest rates and has no application fees and no prepayment penalties.

In addition, the Microsoft/Servus IT Career Loan Program from Servus Financial Corp. also can be used for tuition, books, fees, and living expenses. Special packages also exist for computer loans for hardware, software, and peripherals; as well as consolidation loans that allow students pursuing MOC training and certification to refinance existing education debt. Like the Key Bank loan, the Servus financing has a simple online application, no application fee, and no prepayment penalty.

Microsoft Training & Certification also has a variety of other financial aid programs available for use with MOC-based training. For Training & Certification financing programs outside the United States, see the International portion of the Training & Certification Web site.

Getting Up to Speed on the Entire Solution

Being a technically effective VAP with SBS 4.5 requires a command of many different applications. If you choose to specialize in one or more areas, however, you'll need more application-specific training.

The MOC instructor-led and self-study options for SBS 4.5 focus on the unique features of SBS. These topics typically include working with the setup program, Hardware Confirmation pages, Set Up Computer Wizard, SBS Console, Server Status Tool, Microsoft Fax Server, and Internet Connection Wizard.

SBS 4.5 training typically doesn't dive too deep into the BackOffice family of applications in SBS: SQL Server 7.0, IIS 4.0, Proxy Server 2.0, and Exchange Server 5.5. By acquiring in-depth knowledge and expertise on one of more of these applications, however, you'll be in a much better position to add value at a higher level.

On the CD-ROM, I've included a document, "Training Options for Related BackOffice Applications," that has pointers to MOC courses, Web sites, and implementation white papers for learning more about specific BackOffice applications included with SBS and how they fit into the solutions that you can deliver to your small business clients.

The Bottom Line

You have many ways to get up to speed on SBS 4.5. Most small business VAPs highly recommend that you acquire an evaluation license for the SBS 4.5 and set up a simulated lab environment. In addition to hands-on interaction with the product on your own, two instructor-led SBS 4.5 classes are available. You may also choose to go on and learn more about one or more of the bundled SBS 4.5 applications, such as SQL Server 7.0, Proxy Server 2.0, IIS 4.0, or Exchange Server 5.5. "Training Options for Related BackOffice Applications" on the CD-ROM at the back of the book has numerous course listings and pointers to help you get started in learning about the related BackOffice family of applications.

Staffing Challenges for SBS Projects

If your experience is typical of most technology providers in the United States, you'll quickly discover that two of the greatest challenges for endurance and growth (and generally the two greatest expenses) are keeping up with an onslaught of new products and maintaining your staffing at optimal levels to meet client scheduling demands.

Chapter 3 looked at how you can get a better handle on the training component of being a Microsoft BackOffice Small Business Server VAP. As the book continues to look at "Setting up Shop as an SBS VAP" in Part 2, Chapter 4 delves into another crucial area of concern for VAPs: how to build your army of talent.

You might be wondering why a chapter on issues typically germane to a headhunter has ended up in such a prominent spot in a book about SBS. As your business flourishes, staffing may end up being *the* most formidable growth inhibitor that you'll face.

Whether you're a solo-practice technology provider or you're responsible for a staff of dozens, you'll find something of value in this chapter. Sooner or later even a one-person shop might need to understand what some of the slightly larger local competitors do to woo and hold onto their best and brightest system engineers and developers.

This chapter begins with tips on hiring and retaining staff and then continues with a discussion of the pros and cons of getting your staff trained and certified. Next, the chapter covers developing creative compensation strategies, informally assessing staff performance, and keeping your staff from jumping ship to join your competitors. Finally, the chapter wraps up with advice on how to assess your competitive position in the local market for project staffing.

Best Practices for Recruitment

Because the perfect candidate probably is an unattainable ideal or, at very best, is not actively on the job market, it pays to develop a sound recruiting strategy if you're serious about filling the ranks of your staff. Such a strategy includes making use of all available recruiting methods, writing compelling job descriptions, and using the interview process to select candidates and sell your company to them.

Recruiting Methods

Given the rapid surge in popularity of the Internet over the past few years, recruiting employees with technical backgrounds has become a totally different ball game. No longer are you limited to such traditional, career recruiting strategies as classified ads in the Sunday newspaper or contracting with IT recruiters. Today, Internet-based employee-recruitment services are experiencing unbelievable growth.

Note

Recruiting is truly a ball game on many levels. If your local labor market is typical of many areas in the United States, a highly skilled MCSE or MCSD is at least as desirable to you as a major league baseball player who was the MVP in the All-Star Game and has a .350 batting average. So if your pitches, or job offers, don't make the grade, you run the risk of striking out. With a carefully crafted staffing strategy and the proper execution, however, your firm will have much better odds of consistently hitting home runs in recruitment.

Web-Based Recruiting Tools

Recruiting staff through various online jobs banks on the World Wide Web provides some enormous cost advantages compared to conventional means of advertising. Some of the more popular Web-based career-oriented sites where you can advertise for rather modest listing fees include:

- Monster.com (*www.monster.com*)

- CareerMosaic (*www.careermosaic.com*)

- CareerBuilder (*www.careerbuilder.com*)

Many of the popular search engine portal sites, such as Yahoo! (*www.yahoo.com*), allow you to post classified ads for job openings free of charge. Also don't forget to post job listings on your own company Web site.

Many VAPs have moved nearly exclusively to online recruiting. Web-based recruiting also helps to weed out some less desirable candidates. One British VAP even goes so far as to assert that if candidates don't have an e-mail account or Web pages by the year 2000, they're probably not worth employing. Although the exclusionary idea may seem a bit radical at first, isn't your company in the business of providing solutions such as secure Internet access, Internet-enabled e-mail, and browser-based Internet, extranet, and intranet applications?

Note

Although rather extreme recruiting measures are beyond the reach of most small business VAPs, some Fortune 1000 IT organizations have had to resort to them to attract the right talent in certain hard-to-fill positions. These efforts, such as including a new luxury car, have transcended the normal signing bonuses and stock options.

Newspaper Classified Ads

In many parts of the world, IT job shortages are so severe that it's difficult to envision any moderately effective recruiting tool going by the wayside. For example, although help wanted classified ads in the Sunday newspaper are often less descriptive, more costly, and less effective than online recruiting, the employment classified ads for IT positions won't go away anytime soon. For your particular business, newspaper classified ads may be a great tool to supplement online recruiting. Your success with them, however, depends a lot on the demographics of the local newspaper readership.

> **_Note_**
>
> If you're advertising on Web-based career sites or placing classified ads in the local newspaper, you're only going to attract candidates who are actively looking to change jobs. Many of the best candidates for a given position are already gainfully employed with another firm. Connecting with these type of potential candidates is generally much more challenging. Although you certainly didn't hear it from me, certain recruiting firms are notorious for raiding IT talent from other firms.

Employee Referral Programs

Many VAPs also report great success in setting up employee referral programs to boost their recruiting efforts. With this type of program, the staff gets compensated for their word of mouth candidate referrals that result in new hires. Typically, a firm pays some type of predetermined fixed-amount bonus to the referring employee once the new hire has completed a certain length of service with the firm.

College Interns

If your firm happens to be located near a college or university, interns or less formal part-time college hires can also provide a big boost on the staffing front. Employing college students provides a myriad of benefits. You get your company's name out on campus as an employer of choice. Students get to build their real-world skills while in school. Your firm gets to work with students, who are generally highly motivated and are great potential full-time staff members during their semester breaks and ultimately on a permanent basis following graduation. In addition, every semester or two you'll get access to a new group of first-year students who may be quite eager to learn the ins and outs of being a system engineer or developer for a small business VAP.

> **_Note_**
>
> Local high schools and vocational schools can also be excellent sources for recruiting an eager-to-learn, part-time work force.

Traditionally, college students have been willing to work for relatively low hourly pay, in return for getting significant hands-on experience. With the IT job market in its present bull market state, however, college students aren't likely to join and stay on your SBS rollout team for minimum wage.

Tip

College students often need time off to study during midterms and final exams. Make sure you have adequate backup staff so that your small business clients aren't left in a lurch three or four times a year.

IT Recruiters

While many IT recruiters tend to service larger system integrators and Fortune 1000 IT organizations, some small business VAPs do turn to IT recruiting firms to bolster their staffing efforts. IT recruiters in the United States generally work on a contingency basis, so they're only paid their fee if and when they find a candidate who joins your firm. Many recruiting firms will prorate their recruiting fee if the newly hired candidate leaves within a certain time frame (usually one year). Because recruiting fees can range from 20 to 50 percent of the candidate's first year salary, IT recruiting firms are often beyond the financial reach of most small business VAPs.

While examining costs that may be prohibitive, you also need to consider the salary ranges that you're able to pay potential hires. The salaries that you, as a small business VAP, can pay staff will generally be driven by the hourly billing rate that you think a potential hire will be able to sustain with your current and future client projects. You'll also need to factor in such expenses as overhead and benefits, as well as anticipated weekly utilization rates (how many hours a week you can bill for staff members on average).

In addition to planning carefully and making generous or competitive job offers, you need to understand the nature of the job market for skilled IT professionals. When a candidate is interviewing with you, the candidate is likely to be interviewing simultaneously with other competing firms. Candidates with hot skills will typically see multiple job offers and counter-offers from prospective employers. You and the candidate often discover that the IT job market is more akin to the free agency concept seen by sports stars. As a result, you may be outbid by other technology providers with deeper pockets. This failure doesn't necessarily point to any weakness in your recruiting process. Rather, it might be indicative of a competitor having a roster of clients who are willing to pay higher hourly billing rates.

Job Fairs

Job fairs are another recruiting tool used by VAPs with varying levels of success. Depending on the scope of the job fair and whether it's industry-specific or just geographic in nature, your booth may be beside other technology providers or next to other local firms in a variety of industries. Because job fairs tend to be staffed by human resources (HR) recruiters from much larger companies than a typical small business VAP, get a grasp on the scope and demographics of the job fair before sending in your deposit and signing on the dotted line. Some qualifying questions that the organizers should be able to answer based on past events include:

❑　What percentage of candidates at this job fair are anticipated to be IT professionals?

❑　Of these IT professionals, what percentage are entry level? What percentage have one to three years of experience? What percentage have five years of experience or more?

❑　What percentage of the these IT professionals have four-year degrees? What percentage have vendor certification?

❑　What's the breakdown between exhibitors? What percentage are Fortune 1000 employers and what percentage are local, small businesses?

❑　Who are some of the other technology providers that typically exhibit at this job fair?

Speaking Opportunities

Speaking opportunities are an interesting indirect recruiting method. Although not a recruiting opportunity per se, speaking engagements let you keep your name and expert status in front of trade groups, chambers of commerce, and user groups and build your reputation as an employer of choice in the local community.

Writing Job Descriptions

Writing a clear job description is also a very important part of the recruiting process. Make sure to detail the job requirements, scope, and responsibilities and thoroughly cover important areas such as the required business, communication, and technical skills. If tackled properly, the job description becomes an invaluable screening tool that helps you shorten the recruitment cycle and find higher caliber candidates.

Summary of Common Recruiting Avenues for Small Business VAPs

❑ Web-based recruiting tools, such as CareerMosaic and Monster.com, as well as some search engine portal sites, such as Yahoo!

❑ Newspaper classified ads

❑ Employee referral programs and associated bonuses

❑ College interns

❑ IT recruiters

❑ Job fairs

❑ Speaking opportunities

What Should Be in a Small Business VAP's Job Descriptions?

Ray Holley, president of the Austin Group International, an Austin, Texas-based IT recruiting firm and the author of the "Head Hunting" column for *Computer Reseller News* (CRN), has developed a document to assist technology providers in writing more complete job descriptions. The document deals with topics such as:

• Duties

• Qualifications and experience, dividing them up into columns for "must have" and "a plus"

• Personality traits

• Short-term problems and long-term challenges

• Compensation, including base salary and other forms of compensation such as bonus, commission, auto allowance, corporate credit card, cell phone, and home office setup allowance

Holley also takes great pains to point out that an ad offering "a competitive package" is not nearly descriptive enough and actually can be misleading if you haven't taken the time to research your local competitors' compensation packages.

"Job Description," a Word document, is included on the CD-ROM in the back of the book.

The Interview Process

Once you've used your portfolio of recruiting tools to attract candidates and crafted a detailed job description, you'll need to begin the interviewing process. To help you approach interviewing with some degree of consistency across candidates, the CD-ROM in the back of the book contains "Interviewing Checklist," a Microsoft Word template. The template helps you organize your criteria for evaluating the candidates' qualifications, such as technical, problem solving, and interpersonal skills.

While the checklist does offer some basic structure for developing the interview content, the topics for this area of the interview will vary tremendously across companies. In compiling the technical interview questions and scenarios, you should review your client files to determine the typical day-to-day problems that candidates will face in the field.

For example, if you envision that candidates will spend much of their time on basic SBS infrastructure installs, you'll probably want to ask about topics such as recovering a server from a "blue screen of death" (BSOD) or configuring well-known ports on Microsoft Proxy Server. If these candidates are interviewing for a Web-site design position, you'll likely want to assess their expertise on topics such as Active Server Pages (ASPs), Open Database Connectivity (ODBC), Microsoft SQL Server query construction, and design tools. Remember to make sure your tech questions really capture the essence of the position's daily scope and responsibilities.

In addition to hiring full-time, salaried staff, you may also choose to supplement your SBS team with consultants or independent contractors for specific project needs. By hiring independent contractors on an as-needed basis, you'll also keep overhead down, while keeping your core team of full-time employees more fully utilized. In today's red hot job market, hiring independent contractors gives you one more way to tap into the pool of labor that's beginning to shun the one-company allegiance model.

Tip

The United States has some very specific IRS guidelines and tax and liability ramifications for employers who use an independent contractor, as opposed to a full-time salaried employee. Regardless of where your business is located, make sure to speak with government labor representatives, as well as your accountant and attorney, before engaging the services of an independent contractor.

A Novel Approach to the IT Staffing Dilemma

SetFocus, an MCSP and Certified Technical Education Center (CTEC) in Parsippany, New Jersey, was founded in 1997 under the basic premise that the demand for highly skilled IT developers greatly exceeds the available supply. In addition, this firm believes that you can't effectively train someone to be a developer just through a series of random three or five day classes.

SetFocus offers a small group of candidates—who are selected through a rigorous screening process and who sign a binding one-year contract—three months of *free*, intensive, hands-on training in object-oriented, client/server, and Internet/intranet development. Once the training is completed, SetFocus then places students on nine-month, on-site, paid consulting projects for their clients in positions that utilize their newly acquired skills in Visual Basic, SQL Server, and Visual InterDev. At the end of the one-year SetFocus Masters program, students have acquired a strong technical background, MCSD certification, and nine months of on-the-job experience. For more information on SetFocus and how you can hire a SetFocus graduate, see *www.setfocus.com*.

Best Practices for Staff Retention

You've recruited and hired exceptional individuals to join your SBS deployment and support team, completing half your battle. Now comes the even more challenging part: retaining your staff. How do you keep your staff happy enough to keep them from seeking out the next big thing?

In October 1998, G2R Inc., a market-research firm in Mountain View, California, published a report called "HR Best Practices for IT Services: Recruiting and Retention Strategies," based on research with 21 IT service companies. The findings were particularly applicable to SBS VAPs, who really cannot afford to make any recruiting or retention *faux pas*. These findings included:

- The average company spent 2 percent of its annual revenue on recruiting. (Smaller companies spent even greater percentages.)

- Most companies experienced about 20 percent annual turnover. (The percentages were even higher at pure system integration firms.)

- The strongest source of new employees was employee referrals.

The G2R report also identified five primary motivators for recruiting and retaining staff:

- Raw compensation

- Working environment

- Type of work assignments

- Training and career growth path

- Recognition of efforts

Staff members that leave so quickly that they don't make a contribution can be very expensive to your company and your small business clients. So what do small business VAPs typically do to try to manage the enormous turnover challenge and its associated costs?

- **Develop well-defined career paths.** No one, especially your highly-motivated staff members, wants to feel like his or her career is being held back or that career options are being blocked. Make sure each person on staff has a well-defined career path *within* your company. You may also want to supplement this with some type of mentoring program. (This can be as simple as pairing up a new hire with a more senior staff member for doing lunch at the company's expense, once every month or two.) You may also want to have each staff member and his or her direct supervisor mutually revise the staff member's job description at least twice a year.

- **Insist on an open-door policy.** Each staff member should have a direct pipeline into the top brass in the company. Nothing is more frustrating than a small company with big-company bureaucracy and politics.

- **Provide regular feedback and compensation increases.** Most IT service firms, both large and small, have recognized that an annual review is no longer frequent enough for industries moving at Internet speed. The review process should also include frequent merit and competitive adjustments to salary. Make sure to be pro-active about this process. Often, small gestures go a long way toward showing your staff that you're truly on their side.

- **Set the right goals.** A fine line exists between scheduling aggressively to utilize your staff fully and burning them out with long weeks and excessively high pressure. You need to set realistic goals and deadlines, as well as some type of relief valve to combat the demands of long hours.

- **Provide training and encourage learning.** For technical staff, staying trained and working with leading-edge technology often tops the list for what drives job satisfaction. In looking at how choice assignments are doled out and how training resources are allocated, you need to stress teamwork, cross training, and camaraderie in the continual peer-to-peer learning process. Staff members are frustrated when one person has the keys to the kingdom and that person refuses to share his or her knowledge with others. Make sure to reward employees, not just for what they know, but also for how effectively they share their knowledge with others.

- **During tough times, keep the channels open.** Make sure to keep your staff in the loop during tough financial times and during potential buyouts and takeovers. Be honest about what's going on and let them know what steps you're taking to protect their interests.

- **Reward loyalty.** Reevaluate bonuses and benefits you give to employees and increase their levels substantially based on length of service. Fortune 1000 companies traditionally have increased the paid-vacation benefit after five years. For your firm, it may be more appropriate to increase the amount of paid vacation after two or three years, rather than waiting for five. Also, develop bonus programs that are tied to staff staying on to complete certain predefined strategic projects. (These types of bonus programs can actually save your company a great deal because staff downtime during the middle of a major project can be extraordinarily expensive.)

- **Make your company a fun place to work.** When the workload pressure gets intense, or when the excitement level begins to dwindle during repetitive rollouts, remember the need to make your firm a cool place to work. While staff members might have fun receiving big bonus checks, they might really enjoy playing on company-sponsored softball or bowling teams, paintball outings, or bring-your-dog-to-work day.

Getting Your Staff Certified

Get a group of 40 small business VAPs together in one room and you're likely to hear 40 different opinions on the pros and cons of getting certified. While many of their arguments could easily be extended to other vendors' certification programs, for the purposes of this book, I'll limit our discussion to the Microsoft Certified Professional (MCP) program.

What are some of the main arguments in favor of getting your small business VAP staff certified?

- Certification gets you a closer working relationship with the vendor for technical support and marketing purposes.

- Certification provides brand-name credibility to add to your signage, marketing materials, and proposals.

- If you're already providing technical product training for your staff, the marginal effort to pass certification exams is relatively minimal.

- You can often recoup the expenses associated with certifying staff through higher hourly billing rates.

On the flip side, what are some of the main drawbacks for getting your staff certified?

- Your staff may command, or just outright demand, big bonuses and raises.

- Your staff will have a lot more potential mobility. As a result, many small business VAPs have to refresh their MCP talent constantly to retain their MCSP status.

Tip

In order to maintain MCSP member status, you need to have at least two MCPs on staff full-time. For more details, see *www.microsoft.com/mcsp*.

- Once your staff is certified, headhunters will likely begin circling like buzzards.

- Certification has a limited shelf life. After a certain amount of time, the core requirements and electives for different certifications change.

In balancing these benefits and concerns, look at the forces driving your firm to get individuals certified. Is the main impetus coming from the vendor or are your clients requesting certified staff? For each small business VAP, the answer and individual set of circumstances will be quite different.

If your small business clients are requesting that you staff their projects with certified individuals, you have some alternatives to meeting this demand. You can recruit staff that is already certified, you can get some or all of your existing staff certified (home-grown talent), or you can subcontract with independent consultants who are already certified.

In examining whether to invest in certifying your staff, you need to consider the popular sentiment about a "paper" MCP/MCSE, which is someone who has passed the certification exam or exams, but has little if any practical real-world experience. As the demand for certified individuals has skyrocketed, many training firms have sprung up that teach to the test. These firms, some of whom are MCSPs and CTECs, operate in a similar fashion to well-known test-preparation companies such as Kaplan and Princeton Review. The basic idea is to teach the students what they need to know to pass the test, while relegating understanding the underlying concepts and skills to a secondary or distant third priority.

Tip

Some small business VAPs have responded to "paper" MCP/MCSEs by devising their own sets of exam questions to determine the value of the candidate's real-world knowledge.

Many VAPs have staff members who are highly skilled, but the VAPs see no need for ever certifying them. To these VAPs, their years of success as VAPs and their glowing personal client referrals speak volumes about their abilities that a certificate could never replace. On the other hand, many small business VAPs pursue certification aggressively and feel having their full staff certified is a top strategic priority.

For me personally, by the time I pursued Microsoft certification, I had already spent nearly two years installing and supporting the Microsoft Windows NT platform and had over seven years of experience supporting MS-DOS and Microsoft Windows operating systems, desktop applications, PC hardware, and a variety of network platforms.

I generally considered myself a good test taker, based on my experience with standardized tests such as the SAT and GMAT and going to a college that thrived on multiple-choice exams. I never would have been prepared to pursue my MCSE and MCP+I (Microsoft Certified Professional + Internet), however, if I hadn't had at least some hands-on experience. I also felt strongly that my certification credentials would be kind of suspect without the real world experience to back them up.

Regardless of which camp you fall into, now that you know some of the pros and cons of certification you'll be in a much better position to evaluate when getting your staff trained is most cost-effective.

How to Avoid Training Your Competitor's Next Hire

Recruiting, training, and certifying your system engineers and developers can be a very expensive proposition. For details on managing the enormous outlays for training, make sure to see Chapter 3. As we saw in the previous section of this chapter, certain downside risks are associated with getting your staff certified. Many of these are centered on your staff taking their newly minted certificates and heading across town to work for a competitor with deeper pockets.

How can you stop or prevent this from happening? Can you keep the poachers away from your best and brightest staff? I wish I had a better answer for you, but in reality you can't block your staff from getting trained and leaving your firm. In most free markets around the world, staff member are hired at will and are free to come and go as they please.

So does this mean you should totally discount the idea of investing in your staff's training and certification? Not really. Abandoning training and certification wouldn't prove too practical as most of your small business clients hire your firm for projects because your in-house expertise is substantially greater than theirs.

So how can you make a reasonable attempt to protect the substantial investments you make in staff certification and prevent those efforts from being a benefit solely for a staff member's next employer? Before answering this question, you'll need to determine whether certification is just an expense or investment for you or whether your staff perceives company-funded certification to be a fringe benefit.

Some small business VAPs, as well as Fortune 1000 IT organizations, have had limited success in using legal measures, such as handcuff clauses in employment contracts, to soften the blow of the departure of newly certified staff. While such measures aren't an effective deterrent to prevent staff from leaving in a hot job market, these types of contracts generally require that departing staff members repay the company for their training and certification expenses if they leave immediately. Because training and certification can often cost upwards of $10,000 per employee per year in the United States, the costs are clearly not trivial.

These types of agreements are also generally tiered. If the staff member leaves immediately after receiving the benefits of company-sponsored certification, the staff member is liable for 100 percent of the training and certification expense. If the staff member leaves after one year, the liability drops to 50 percent. After two years, the contract liability dissolves.

I haven't heard many accounts of small business VAPs or Fortune 1000 IT organizations taking their former employees to court to collect on these contracts. I have, however, heard anecdotes of the new employer paying the old employer's tab for certification to prevent the outbreak of a local World War III among VAPs.

One New York-based compensation consultant has advised a few larger VAPs to use a similar approach that has more teeth (stronger potential for enforcement). In this case, the employee who wants to participate in employer-sponsored training and certification signs a note with a local bank. As long as the employee remains on staff with the VAP, the VAP picks up the tab for the monthly payments on the loan. If the employee leaves the VAP before the predetermined time period, however, the bank will transfer liability solely to the departing employee and enforce collection as if it were any other personal loan.

When looking at how to avoid training your competitor's next hire, the best medicine is often an ounce of prevention. If you give your staff plenty of reasons to discount offers from competitors, you'll have a happy staff and no need to pursue defensive strategies, such as determining who pays the tab for certification. You may want use the eight staff retention tips outlined earlier in this chapter as the basis for making this fear over the loss of staff certification investment a moot point.

Benchmarking Staff Performance

So with highly valued and sought-after system engineers and developers on staff, should you just let them be to do their own thing or should you be concerned about tracking their performance? As the owner of a small business VAP, you'll likely need to strike a balance somewhere in between being a hands-off manager and being a micromanaging fanatic.

Most small business VAPs find that letting their staff know how they're doing on a regular basis is helpful. By providing more immediate feedback on a monthly or even weekly basis, you'll be able to help them learn from mistakes and grow. You'll also be able to catch potential problems and bad habits before they snowball into major problems that could cause rifts beyond repair. Although the employer will always be the employer, recognize when skill sets in staff are rare and tread accordingly.

If you find it helpful, by all means track the number of billing hours each person completes in a given week. Or perhaps you'll keep tabs on the number of help desk tickets each person completes. Or maybe you'll even chart the results from customer satisfaction surveys.

But don't forget that you still need highly trained, talented staff to survive and grow. If your company culture instills fear of the boss as a ranter, raver, yeller, or screamer, now may be an appropriate time to evaluate how you manage your staff.

The year-end review definitely shouldn't be relied on as the primary performance evaluation tool. With small business VAPs experiencing in excess of 20 percent annual turnover and functioning on Internet speed, the year-end or mid-year review should function more as a recap of past events that have already been *mutually* noted.

Creative Compensation Strategies

As we've seen so far in the chapter, small business VAPs intensely compete to recruit and retain a limited pool of talented system engineers and developers. To cope with these staffing challenges, many offer fairly conventional monetary compensation, above and beyond salary, such as signing bonuses, stock options, and retirement plants. Many small business VAPs also offer bonuses for early completion of projects. Short of handing your staff members blank checks every other Friday, what can you do to motivate them creatively to exceed, grow, and stay with your firm—while at the same time maintaining a budget that your firm can afford to sustain?

Fortune 1000 IT organizations are generally located within sprawling corporate campuses, or similar facilities, where staff has access to a myriad of on-site conveniences. These soft benefits often include on-site dry cleaners, exercise facilities, convenience stores, and subsidized employee dining rooms and cafeterias. What can you do as a small business VAP to compensate your staff more creatively?

- **Get your staff physically fit.** While you may be too small to set up an on-site exercise facility, consider purchasing a few shared memberships at a nearby gym so that your staff can work out before or after hours to relieve stress and stay in shape.

- **Make sure their wallets are full.** Although you may be too small to have an on-site ATM, you don't want your staff wasting time in line at the bank, either. Be creative: look into direct deposit options or have your bank arrange for someone to come on-site on payday for check cashing.

- **Keep the kitchen well stocked.** One way to lessen the negative feelings of having to work long hours or forgoing a lunch break is by keeping your staff fed. Don't just have a break area in the office with a refrigerator and microwave. Keep it stocked with drinks and snacks courtesy of the company. Also don't miss out on the opportunity to show you care by bringing in bagels, donuts, and or even pizzas on a set day of the week or during special company meetings.

- **Provide tax relief.** Arrange for (and pick up the tab for) a local accountant, perhaps the same one who does your firm's books, to come on site for an hour or two each week during tax season to help your staff prepare their own personal tax returns and design some basic financial planning strategies.

- **Help keep your staff looking sharp.** While your firm is probably too small to have a facility on site, you can arrange for a local dry cleaner to provide regular pickup and delivery service to your office, as well an exclusive discount for your staff.

- **Keep the cars running smoothly.** Why should your staff be wasting time with auto repairs? You can arrange for a local auto repair facility to provide pickup and return service, as well as loaner cars to your employees. In addition to special discounts for your staff, why not negotiate or pay outright for the cost of the vacuum and wash whenever they get their car serviced. If you firm is typical of most small business VAPs, your staff relies heavily on their personal cars to get to client engagements. Any unplanned downtime due to car problems could cost your firm big bucks. Anything you can do to help prevent it is a win/win/win for you, your staff, and your clients.

- **Help them have a life, too.** Instead of just buying season sports tickets for your sales reps to schmooze clients, buy a set of season tickets to rotate among staff to enjoy with their friends and families.

- **Don't overburden them with old-fashioned dress codes.** If your clients wear corporate casual—or at least have casual dress on Fridays—make sure your staff gets to take advantage of this perk as well.

- **Allow job flexibility whenever possible.** Think about creative ways to implement, even to a limited degree, job sharing, comp-time, flextime, and telecommuting.

Assessing Your Competitive Position

In much the same way that you market yourself to potential small business clients, you'll need a cohesive marketing plan to convince candidates to join your firm. You might find it bizarre at first, but to a large degree the tables are truly turned. No longer will you receive dozens or hundreds of resumes from qualified applicants for each open position. In most parts of the United States, it's definitely a candidate's market.

Consider developing a list of points to cover in an interview as you prepare to pitch candidates on why they should tie their career plans to your firm. The following checklist isn't a complete list of topics for an interview, but rather it's a number of topics to discuss in the portion of the interview where you sell the candidate on coming to work for your firm:

- Describe what your company does, who you are, who you sell to, and what you represent.

- Tell candidates why they would want to build their career at your firm, what the available career paths are, about your training philosophy, and your involvement with leading edge technologies.

- Describe what others who have held the position for which the candidate is interviewing have gone on to do.

- Discuss why current employees like working at your firm.

- Talk about how your firm differentiates itself competitively.

- Describe the firm's current financial position and overall stability.

- Talk about the firm's visibility in the local community and reputation with groups such as chambers of commerce, user groups, and Association of Microsoft Solution Providers (AMSP).

- Discuss your firm's performance and salary review procedures and compensation packages.

The Bottom Line

As a small business VAP, you might find it very difficult and expensive to recruit and retain staff. This chapter covered the problems you might encounter and offered solutions for getting your staff certified, preventing your certified staff from leaving the firm, keeping tabs on your staffs' performance, compensating your staff, and marketing your firm to job seekers.

Chapter 5

SBS Profitability Challenges

If you were just a Microsoft BackOffice Server administrator on staff in a Fortune 1000 IT organization, you could concentrate on keeping your network up and running, maintaining packet harmony, and warding off blue screens of death. As a Microsoft BackOffice Small Business Server VAP, however, you have a lot more to contend with in your daily routine than just being technically proficient at administering servers and desktops PCs or having a strong technical knowledge of Microsoft Windows NT Server and BackOffice family applications. You're not just a network administrator. You're running a business—and a very challenging business at that.

Every year or two, all your highly marketable skills become somewhat obsolete. For example, if the hottest item on your calling card in early 2000 is knowing how to configure file and printer sharing networks, you'll see a lot less demand for your skills as more power users at your small business clients figure out how to map network drives themselves. In addition, those small businesses that do call upon you for commodity skills will likely have many alternatives available to them. This puts pressure on you to keep your hourly billing rates down.

You'll also likely face a constant onslaught of small business clients and prospects who are looking for something for nothing. While you're a lot more apt to see this type of behavior with prospects rather than your established clientele, you can't let your guard down. You constantly need to ask yourself, "Are we running a business or are we volunteers?" I consider myself fairly adept at maneuvering through the shark-infested challenges of a small business VAP, and rarely does one month go by that I don't get at least one request for a sales call, when in reality the small business client is trying to push for a free consultation. You'll need to diffuse these requests and turn their mild ignorance of industry practices or outright *chutzpa* into a billable needs analysis or IT audit. Chapter 7 deals with this topic in great detail.

The present chapter gets at the heart of the matter: how to make money in a highly-competitive market as an SBS VAP, where all your hottest skills and solutions fade into the woodwork every twelve to eighteen months.

The chapter begins with an in-depth look at product decisions. First and foremost, you'll need to decide whether you want to be a pure service provider (that is, a consultant) or whether you want also to get involved in reselling hardware, software, and peripherals. If you do decide to resell product, you'll need to learn how to cope with razor-thin profit margins, manage software licensing, and position your role in the procurement cycle.

The second part of the chapter examines profitability from the service standpoint. In particular, that section covers pressure on service margins, strategies to help you avoid becoming a commodity service provider, and pointers to information later in this book on how you can pick up incremental service revenue by customizing SBS and Office family desktop applications.

Product Decisions

It's funny how much difference a decade can make. If I were writing this chapter in mid-1989, advising you on how to become a successful technology provider to small businesses, I'd consider it a no-brainer that you'd want to become actively involved in reselling hardware and software products. After all, in the days before Dell and Gateway dominated the mail-order PC industry and the widespread expansion of superstores such as CompUSA, Costco, Staples, OfficeMax, and Best Buy, you could be highly competitive and still see 40–50 percent gross margin points on desktop PCs and off-the-shelf productivity applications.

In fact the margins were so rich and the manufacturer price-protection and stock balancing programs so liberal that you could stock inventory and run an entire retail business with service margin being just an afterthought— an interesting sideline to supplement your core product revenues and fat margins. If you did have a substantial mix of service offerings for small businesses in your marketing literature, it would mainly be services that by today's standards are pretty rudimentary. These might have included extended maintenance contracts on the PC hardware, introductory classes on word processing and spreadsheet applications, or on-site installation of desktop PCs. Around this time, many local resellers were even bundling free unlimited phone support when a desktop PC was purchased with an application. After all, with $2,500 of margin on a fully configured $5,000 PC, resellers had plenty of margin to provide free services to small businesses. Alas, those days are long, long gone for the vast majority of small business VAPs around the world.

Coping with Razor-Thin Product Margins

Many small business VAPs still rely on product sales as a major part of their profit model. Of those who resell product, however, they rarely survive on single-digit profit margins. These VAPs have substantial service income to help pay the bills.

While small business owners are indeed price sensitive, once you've established a relationship with small businesses as their trusted technology advisor, the owners tend to become less concerned about saving the last dollar. They tend to focus on the "will it work?" factor. Remember, small business owners hire your firm to provide a technology solution for a business problem. You should convey that purchase decisions based on solely on price often create many ongoing reliability and support problems.

Small business owners also look to make best use of their time. As a result, they usually recognize that buying and installing networks is not their core competency. They generally also want a single point of contact for all of their computer-related needs, and they'll have little time or patience for dealing with finger-pointing between a hardware provider and a computer consultant. If the small business owner has been burned before, he or she becomes less concerned about getting the absolute lowest price on product purchases.

While product profit margins tend to be razor thin on branded products from top-tier manufacturers, many small business VAPs bypass this dilemma entirely by reselling white box desktop PCs and servers. Many small business VAPs also prefer to resell white box hardware because it provides more configuration flexibility, gives them more control over component selection, and leaves more money on the table for value-added services.

Tip

A white box PC is a computer that's assembled from brand-name components, as opposed to being mass manufactured by a large PC OEM. It's named as such because the front of the computer case rarely has a brand name sticker on it but rather is left "white." White box PC is generally synonymous with the term "clone PC."

A January 1999 report from *Aaron Goldberg's InfoBead Insider*, "Computer Makers Focus on Small Businesses," also reaffirms the booming popularity of white box desktop PCs among small businesses.

- Small business owners tend to be less brand-loyal and more price sensitive.

- The white box computer category of small business PC purchases outpaces each of the top five small business PC brands (Compaq, Dell, Gateway, IBM, and Hewlett Packard).

- Levels of interest in white box computers vary among different-sized small businesses. Small businesses with 5 to 20 employees tend to have stronger interest in clones than larger small businesses. (This segment of the market, the small businesses with 5 to 20 employees, represents about one-third of the total PC unit sales to small businesses.)

Aaron Goldberg's InfoBead Insider also published a September 1998 report, "Small Business Server Markets—The Branded Vendors Fight Back," that discusses the huge popularity of white box servers among small businesses.

Given that even the white box desktop and server profit margins aren't all that stellar, should small business VAPs resell any products to small businesses that aren't purchasing more profitable value-added services? The jury is still out on this issue. Much of the answer to this question is determined by a VAP's individual business and marketing strategy.

Many small business VAPs sell products to clients who don't purchase services from them with the idea that they eventually will contract for more profitable services (just like the classic marketing slogan, "Sooner or later, *you'll* break down and join AAA"). At the other extreme, many small business VAPs flat out refuse to expend their firm's resources providing product-reselling services to small business clients who aren't under contract for other consulting services.

Regardless of whether you choose to resell hardware and software to product-only clients or to your soup-to-nuts clients, you need to manage their expectations about what you can provide given the threadbare profit margins. Small business VAPs often have a difficult time dealing with clients who make a large product purchase and then expect dozens of hours of free service.

Explaining your service and billing policies at the outset is important. If a client purchases $10,000 worth of desktop PCs and software from your firm and you barely cleared $1,000 in net profit, you'll be hard pressed to include free service. The uninitiated small business owner, however, might feel entitled to have you on 7 × 24 leash for the profit on a $10,000 purchase. Even if communications skills and negotiation are not your *forte*, discussing this issue very early on is important so that you can explain to your client why your firm needs to charge for related services and not just throw them in.

If you encounter or anticipate resistance in this area, another alternative is to be a pure service provider for this particularly troublesome client. Under this scenario, you could advise the small business owner what to buy and where to buy it and then provide *a la carte* services once the hardware, software, and peripherals have arrived. You do run some risks with this approach. For starters, the small business owner might really want one-stop shopping. Second, even if this small business owner is not thinking of one-stop shopping at the outset, a trip down to the local superstore to purchase $10,000 of products might prompt a phone call from the superstore's sales manager to pitch a service contract.

If you decide to resell product, you'll also need to figure out what kind of payment terms to offer small business clients. Because so much pressure is on product profit margins already, small business VAPs rarely offer net 30 payment terms to clients. VAPs typically keep their payment terms on product sales very tight, if they're made available at all. Many small business VAPs also insist on a substantial deposit at the time of the product order, with the balance due on delivery. Very few offer credit cards for product purchases, as the 2–3 percent fee for usage often impacts the meager profit margin on product sales.

Some small business VAPs offer progress payment schedules. The biggest challenge under these types of arrangements is how to define what's in and out of scope, as well as how to define clearly what constitutes project completion.

Tip

A progress payment breaks up the total payment on the project into smaller installments, which are invoiced and paid based on completion of certain predefined project milestones.

Sometimes the product profit margin is so thin that the freight charges can make or break the sale. As a result, you need to consider freight on both sides of the equation. Many mail-order PC vendors and software resellers charge in the neighborhood of 5 percent of the total sale for freight and handling. Because out-of-pocket costs for carriers such as UPS, FedEx, or Airborne Express rarely approach half that amount, the freight and handling component of a product sale becomes an important profit center to offset a threadbare net margin. Don't overlook this fundamental issue when preparing product price quotes for small business clients. You should also be aware that the large PC hardware mail-order OEMs, such as Dell, Gateway, and Micron, routinely charge about $100 or more in the United States for freight on *each* desktop PC. In this situation, if your firm delivers a dozen desktop PCs to your small business client (and doesn't charge for delivery), your client has saved effectively $1,200 right off the bat.

So that's the story with freight on the sales side. On the purchase side of product reselling is another interesting angle for freight charges. Most of the major distributors in the United States don't charge for freight if an order hits a certain minimum amount or is placed over the Internet. Thus, if you place an order for a 19-inch monitor or a laser printer or five CALs of SBS 4.5 from a major distributor *and* drop ship the item directly to your small business client, you could conceivably pay nothing for freight and still recoup an extra five margin points through freight and handling. Even if you're not comfortable with this type of business practice, you need to be aware that many of your potential competitors adopt similar billing and price positioning strategies.

Deciding Whether to Sell, Procure, or Advise

Now that you understand the relevant issues surrounding the razor-thin margins in today's market for reselling hardware and software, it's time to look at some other roles that you can assume if you decide that reselling product isn't for you.

Some small business VAPs steer clear of reselling product for reasons other than too much potential for aggravation and too little upside profit potential. Pure service providers, or consultants, often like to keep a separation between their objective fee-based recommendations and the profit margin potential. This is similar to the accountants or portfolio managers who might have ethical problems accepting a commission for recommending an annuity to a fee-based client. Their general feeling is that potential for abuse exists when they recommend to clients what to buy, where to buy it from, and how much to pay for it.

Most small business VAPs, however, dismiss as trivial the potential conflict of interest between being both the one who recommends purchases and the reseller. After all, most of their small business clients want a single point of accountability. Remember that the business of reselling hardware and software is so competitive that it'd be extremely difficult for VAPs to reap windfall profits on reselling product. Because small business VAPs tends to be in the position of the virtual CIO, small business owners trust their VAPs to select the best-value products to use as building blocks in their businesses.

Small business VAPs also routinely dismiss the notion of any potential conflict of interest in reselling products because VAPs have to live with the consequences of their recommendations. Small business VAPs ultimately have to implement and support the recommended products, so they're motivated to select products that are both reliable and simple to install and service. In addition to providing a sort of limited checks and balances, this whole idea of eating your own dog food reinforces the small business desire for a single point of accountability.

Even if you decide to throw your hands up in the air and proclaim, "I will never resell another piece of hardware or software," you have other reasons to stay involved in the small business' asset acquisition process. Many small business VAPs help write the specs for the project to make sure that the acquired products will ultimately help the small business achieve the goals identified in the fee-based needs analysis (Chapter 7).

In addition to advising the small business owner on what to buy in terms of hardware, software, and peripherals, some small business VAPs also take on the role of purchasing agent for the small business. In many cases, the small business owner or the designated person at the client who does purchasing might be totally *unaccustomed* to purchasing PC-related products. Often the person who orders office supplies such as toner, pens, paper, and letterhead is well-intentioned and wants to help with ordering the recommended products for the planned network installation. In reality, you're likely to end up with that person placing an order for a server with 17 GB of RAM, a 4-MB hard drive, SBS version 97, and a 1.7-inch super VGA monitor. Chances are that what's delivered to your small business client will be quite different from the specs you initially provided. As the virtual CIO or IT manager for the small business, you can provide a tremendously valuable service to your clients by getting price quotes, placing the order, and following the order through to installation and implementation.

> ### *Tip*
>
> Procurement services, that is, wearing the hat of the purchasing manager for your small business client, is definitely a billable service.

Software Licensing: SBS and Office

Until recently, small businesses really only had two options for acquiring off-the-shelf Microsoft software. They could either purchase full package product (FPP), which included media and documentation, from retail stores or mail-order firms. Or they could buy popular off-the-shelf software that was bundled with hardware from various OEMs. While those avenues are still widely used, Microsoft made volume discount licensing more readily available to small businesses with as few as five PCs in February 1999.

Under the Microsoft Open License Program, software licenses are sold independently from the media and documentation. Thus a small business with 10 users of Microsoft Office 2000 Professional might only need to incur the expense of purchasing one set of media and documentation to be shared among the 10 licensed users. Not only does this save on initial acquisition costs (generally a 20–30 percent discount off FPP), Open License makes it easier to store and track media. This cuts down on unauthorized software loading that could cause potential support and license compliance headaches. Because the Open License asset inventory is centrally managed, tracking how many licenses are owned is easier.

Qualifying Open License products are divided up into three product family pools:

- **Applications**—such as the Office family products (desktop applications)

- **Systems**—such as Windows 98 and Windows NT Workstation 4.0 (desktop operating systems)

- **Servers**—such as BackOffice Small Business Server 4.5; Windows NT Server 4.0; Windows NT Server 4.0, Terminal Server Edition; SQL Server 7.0; and other BackOffice Server family applications

Because Open License ordering procedures have been simplified and the pricing made quite attractive, small businesses can more easily steer clear of piracy and inadvertently purchasing illegal gray market, counterfeit, or unbundled OEM products. SBS 4.5 and SBS 4.5/Office 2000 Professional became available through Open License with five client access licenses (CALs). The initial Open License agreement, which can be for as few as five PCs, locks in the volume discount on reorders for up to two years. By adding Upgrade Advantage, your small business clients can get free upgrades to the latest versions of the licensed products during the term of the agreement.

Note

When buying SBS through the Open License program, remember to purchase media. Unlike most software, SBS requires software media to install not only the server, but to increase client license capacity.

If you've never looked into volume license agreements for your small business clients, I should warn you that the details and terminology can be somewhat confusing. The design of the Open License Web site (*www.microsoft.com/mlo*), however, has made it much easier for you to offer open licensing to clients without having to become an expert on Microsoft volume licensing. To simplify the licensing process, Open License is also connected to corporate volume resellers. One of these Open License-connected resellers, License Online of Kirkland, Washington (*www.licenseonline.com*), has programs specifically designed to help small business VAPs stay actively involved in reselling software. Additional details on software licensing and how to participate in Open License are available on the Microsoft Direct Access Web site (*www.microsoft.com/directaccess*).

With FPP software sales, small business VAPs find that competing directly with mammoth superstores and mail-order firms is hard. When software is bundled with hardware on an OEM basis, the small business VAP really doesn't see the software sale as an independent profit center. The OEM software license is just treated as another component cost of assembling a white box server. Through Open License, however, small business VAPs can actively and profitably deliver the many benefits of volume licensing to their clients.

Despite the many benefits of the Open License program to both small businesses and VAPs, many VAPs still haven't fully embraced it. Despite the low initial purchase of five licenses, many small business VAPs still perceive that their smallest clients are too small to take advantage of Open License. Because many small business VAPs are actively involved in assembling systems from branded components as mini-OEMs (that is, the white box market), their small business clients generally see most of their Microsoft shrink-wrapped software coming through the Microsoft System Builder program (formerly known as the Microsoft DSP program). For more details on the Microsoft System Builder program, see the Microsoft Direct Access Web site (*www.microsoft.com/directaccess* or *www.microsoft.com/oem*).

Alternatively, if the small business already has PCs running earlier versions of Microsoft Office applications or competing products such as Corel WordPerfect or Lotus 1-2-3, small business VAPs will typically recommend and resell the competitive/version upgrade SKUs for Microsoft Office family applications when their small business clients require Microsoft Office 2000 licenses.

If you anticipate reselling a lot of Open License agreements to your small business clients, you might want to have one of your sales or account managers take the Microsoft Sales Specialist training. The Microsoft Sales Specialist program is all about becoming an expert in software presales functions. One of three main areas of the curriculum is on becoming proficient in recommending appropriate Microsoft license purchases. Although the courseware is delivered through Certified Technical Education Centers (CTECs) and on a self-study basis, the Microsoft Sales Specialist program is *not* certification in the same sense as the MCP program. Once you've earned the Microsoft Sales Specialist designation, you get access to an exclusive password protected Web site. Details are available at *www.microsoft.com/salesspecialist.*

Service Decisions

As price competition between various PC distribution channels becomes more intense, many of the largest retailers, superstores, and hardware OEMs have moved to supplement their bottom line by promoting their firms' service capabilities. Everyone wants to be in the service business in one way or another. Many are even pursuing the rapidly evolving market for installing and supporting small business networks. So where does that leave the small business VAP? Just as always, the small business VAP needs to keep investing in training and retraining to stay a few steps ahead of the curve.

Declining Service Margins— The Big Guys Are in Your Backyard

So how can you cope with the trend toward much larger competitors trying to pursue your bread and butter core small business clients? For starters, begin by learning more about what some of your local, smaller competitors are up to. Then, you'll want to find out more about the larger competitors' weaknesses, so that you can look to exploit any of the more immediate opportunities.

Begin by examining phone support. Many of the larger firms who want to pursue your core clients do offer some limited, free introductory telephone support. After a certain honeymoon period, however, most begin to charge handsomely for in-depth technical phone support on leading applications.

Some small business VAPs provide a limited amount of free technical phone support to their best clients. Others charge for every minute of every call. A third group of small business VAPs say that the choice to charge for phone support depends largely on how profitable the client is.

Small business VAPs feel pressure on their service margins through requests for freebies. Many small business owners have achieved their fame and fortune by being relentless negotiators. Knowing that your firm is small, many also will try to see what they can get away with. By the time you get done reading this book, my goal is for you to know how to turn a request for free services into a billable opportunity and when necessary, as sacrilegious as it sounds, recommend that a prospect take its business elsewhere.

You should also be particularly careful to estimate costs properly, because a major bungle in this area can kill your reputation and service margins. In particular, think carefully about who should pay for overruns when projects exceed estimates or when unforeseen circumstance crop up. Larger competitors can often afford to write off billable hours, in much the same way that major hotels comp frequent-staying guests when a night's stay is not quite up to snuff. As a small business VAP, however, you can ill afford to write off large blocks of hours for disgruntled customers. Chapters 7 and 9 will help you hone your estimates, project plans, and proposals to lessen greatly the possibility of such tragic financial misfortunes.

Many larger competitors tier their hourly billing rates. For example, a PC technician, capable of installing most hardware devices and desktop operating systems, might have a $90 per hour billing rate. At the next level of expertise, a network technician, charged with configuring drive arrays, file permissions, system policies, and Proxy Server ports, might command $125 per hour. A network specialist, such as a SQL Server administrator or Visual InterDev programmer, might command upwards of $175 per hour.

Small business VAPs usually don't tier their rates. They tend to charge a single rate across the board, which is usually within the low-end of the range of larger competitors. MCSE-level (or equivalent) consultants from small business VAPs are often billed out in the same range as PC hardware technicians from larger firms. So which is the best value for small businesses? By reading this book, you'll be able to explain the answer to this question more effectively to a small business prospect so that your firm can profit from this enormous competitive advantage.

Deciding the Amount to Bill

Hourly billing rates are not just driven by expertise and size of your firm. The largest discrepancies in hourly billing rates tend to be geographic in nature. Regardless of where you are, small business VAPs in major cities tend to bill out at much higher rates than their counterparts in suburban or rural areas. Some of these differences might be attributable to a higher cost of doing business, with overhead items such as salaries and office rentals. That you do your homework in this area is important. Make sure to figure out a way to learn what your local and national competitors are charging for comparable services. Most veteran small business VAPs already have a handle on this data.

One way to compare billing rates is *VARBusiness* magazine's free online e-mail newsletter, *VARBusiness Insider*, which has a feature called Price Point that frequently gives a sampling of different hourly billing rates for different types of network services around the United States. Each rate quote is generally prefaced with the geographic region of the country, size of the VAP, size of the client, and technical specialty. You can subscribe to *VARBusiness Insider* at *www.varbusiness.com/insider/listform.asp.*

Many service providers, regardless of whether they're small business VAPs or national competitors, charge rate premiums for certain types of special accommodations. These often include a 50 percent rate premium for after hours evening work, say between 6–10 P.M., and a 100 percent rate premium for overnight work between 10 P.M.–6 A.M. Many small business VAPs and the large national technology providers also charge some geographically proportionate amount for travel time.

Is there ever a good time to notify a small business client of a pending rate increase? Yes and no. Most small business VAPs reevaluate their rate structure once or twice per year and will typically implement changes once a year. Only you can gauge how your specific small business clients will react. Most small business VAPs, however, find that although their clients sometimes complain or resist at first, small business owners ultimately see rate increases as a necessary cost of doing business. If your small business clients are very happy with your services and the relationship is healthy, you should be able to sustain modest 5–10 percent rate increases each year. If the relationship is on the rocks, an unexpected rate increase might cause a rift between you and your client.

If you're a one-person small business VAP, don't be surprised to find an occasional small business owner who tries to equate your billing rate to that of an employee. They will try to grasp at straws like this to control your rates.

Everyone Wants to Be in the Service Business

Although many of the large superstore retailers and mail-order PC hardware OEMs want to be actively involved in servicing small business networks, most established small business VAPs seem to be weathering this challenge to their survival quite well. Because small business VAPs can respond to special requests much more quickly and can be infinitely more flexible than the big guys, small business VAPs should rarely feel threatened by a national competitor on service opportunities.

Tip

If you still are billing out at premium rates for modem and memory installations, now might be a good time to recognize their commodity status and move on to bigger and better service opportunities to bolster your bottom line.

Small business VAPs also often tap vertical markets, such as real estate, legal, or accounting, that are simply too narrow to be sought after nationally by a large competitor. One-on-one hand holding is another big area where small business VAPs tend to excel and large national competitors tend to flounder.

So you're not caught off guard, here are a few specifics on efforts by national competitors to establish a position in servicing local small business clients:

- Dell has partnerships with Wang, Unisys, and other national service providers for installing small business networks.

- Compaq offers authorized resellers the ability to resell prepackaged services, such as prepaid cards for technical support by phone, as well as consulting services for in-depth, on-site projects such as Lotus Notes to Exchange Server migrations.

- Computer superstores such as CompUSA have never been shy about promoting their service capabilities.

- Gateway Country retail stores have recently begun promoting small business service offerings.

- In my local geographic market, well-known office supply superstore Staples advertises the availability of carry-in PC hardware service for $69 per hour and special fixed-price labor rates on items, such as the $29 modem or memory installations.

Tip

To help keep tabs on national superstores, retailers, and hardware OEMs that are moving into small business services, subscribe to *Computer Reseller News* (CRN) or visit the Web site at *www.crn.com*.

How to Avoid Becoming a Commodity

If your only value-add is setting up and supporting stand-alone PCs, now's a great time to learn how to branch out into more lucrative services. By reading this book, you're on the right track. As was covered in Chapter 2, value-add is definitely a moving target. You constantly need to recognize when different services that you provide become commodities so that you can refocus your training efforts and service capabilities.

Remember, a lot of value-add is about perception. For a large national systems integrator, installing a Hewlett Packard JetDirect printer server onto an SBS network would be considered a fairly low tech commodity service. That categorization, however, exists primarily because large national system integrators tend to service medium-sized and enterprise accounts with sizable internal IT departments.

For a small business with no full-time IT staff, the small business VAP becomes the virtual IT department. If a small business is just experiencing first-hand the benefits of a true client/server network, something as basic as installing a printer connected directly to the network (Ethernet as opposed to LPT1) is a value-added service for which most small businesses would gladly pay.

If you're in doubt about the printer server example above, think about how many of your small business clients' internal gurus would be able to obtain the hardware MAC address of the printer server and properly match this up to a DHCP lease reservation on the server within an SBS network.

Whenever you're in doubt about whether a specific service is still truly a value-add or whether it's gravitating toward commodity status, consider the small business internal guru. Ask yourself: is it possible for hobbyists or power users to tackle this specific task with wizards or minimal training? If they perform the task by rote memorization without understanding the underlying technical details, will they still get the job done?

Because so much of your success is driven by perception among local small business owners, many small business VAPs thrive on word of mouth advertising. A small business VAP rarely reports overwhelming success with a print media advertising or direct mail campaign. Unlike retail computer superstores, small business VAPs aren't selling apples and oranges such as laptops or laser printers. Small business VAPs are selling their professional services, similar to the way accountants or attorneys tactfully market their services.

To help maintain high profiles in the local community as an expert, many small business VAPs become active in user groups, civic groups, and chambers of commerce. Many also write computer-related columns in local newspapers and will jump at any public speaking opportunities.

If you have a particularly marketable background or biography from your prior career, don't be shy about publicizing that as well. You can elevate your firm many times above commodity service provider status and brutal service margins if you have a unique credential such as an MBA, an accounting degree, or experience working for a big-six consulting firm. If applicable, make sure to mention these credibility boosters prominently in all of your marketing activities.

In steering clear of commodity service provider status, you should have a concrete goal for your firm's weekly capacity utilization. For example, if each person in your firm is expected to bill out 80 percent of their 40 hour workweek, that leaves one day a week for other activities. As the owner you might choose to use that time for marketing and business development. You'll likely want, however, your technical staff members to use that one day each week for research and development for new solutions or for sharpening their technical skill sets with various training options. Regardless, everyone in your company that comes into client contact, from your receptionist through to the CEO, should always be on the lookout for problems crying out for solutions that your firm can provide.

Software Customization: SBS and Office 2000

The installations of off-the-shelf, shrink-wrapped software such as SBS 4.5 and Office 2000 provide tons of opportunity for training and customization. Sometimes this customization is based on gaps that your firm perceives in the product across the board. Other times, you'll be tailoring these products for a specific vertical industry solution. Regardless, Microsoft has implemented various tools, resource kits, and templates to help you rapidly, easily, and cost-effectively customize your small business clients' solutions. Make sure you leave time in your hectic schedule to learn how these opportunities can elevate your firm from network installer status to solution provider.

To learn more about customizing SBS 4.5, see Chapters 14–18 and 26–27. To learn more about customizing Office 2000, see Chapter 21.

The Bottom Line

This chapter looked at how to survive and thrive given the tremendous financial and market competition challenges facing small business VAPs. The pros and cons of reselling products such as hardware, software, and peripherals were covered. The second half of the chapter focused on how to position your value-added services to avoid being outfoxed by large, national competitors.

Partnering Opportunities

Chapters 3 and 4 covered the importance of carefully planning your training and staffing investments for Microsoft BackOffice Small Business Server projects. Chapter 5 was dedicated to helping you decide how to offer various products and services profitably to your small business clients.

Chapter 6, the final chapter in Part 2, "Setting up Shop as an SBS VAP," covers SBS partnering opportunities. Because most SBS VAPs are often small businesses themselves, we often find it impossible to provide the entire solution without partnering with other technology providers. This chapter will help you prepare for successful and profitable partnering.

When Flying Solo No Longer Makes Sense

Most SBS VAPs thrive because their firm is widely regarded as extremely resourceful generalists. Often a small business VAP will pick one or two specialties; their core competency, however, really is knowing a little bit about everything. What happens when a small business client whom you've worked with for years needs your firm to know a lot about one particular area, and it happens to be outside your area of expertise? How do you know when proceeding with the just the staff and resources from your own firm no longer makes sense? How do you know when it's time to find partners?

Knowing when is not exactly cut and dry. Your small business clients usually want your firm to act as their virtual IT department. Even your clients who have no idea what a corporate IT department does or what "IT" means generally ask for this type of arrangement. Often the small business owner hires or contracts with you or your firm to be their single point of contact for everything and anything that's even remotely related to supporting their PCs and network.

In a large IT organization, separate departments typically exist for functions such as help desk, network administration, desktop support, software development, standardization, research and development, and security. Most SBS VAPs, whether operating as a one-person company or with small staffs, are generally expected to don the vast majority of these varied hats on any given day. Because the small business generally does not have the need or resources to hire full-time IT staff, you in essence become their virtual IT department.

In addition to being a huge help to your small business clients, becoming their virtual IT department is highly beneficial for your firm as well. When small business clients are interested in building a long-term relationship, you gain a predictable, recurring revenue stream, great reference accounts, a client who's generally not as price sensitive as someone looking for a one-time purchase, and spectacular insight into what drives their business needs. Chapter 7 drills down on how to position your company as the virtual IT department and yourself as a small business IT visionary.

Clients put plenty of pressure on your firm to be the SBS super VAP. They expect your firm to be knowledgeable on every conceivable technology problem under the sun. Along the same lines, your clients get a great many benefits and you get a happy, profitable client base when you can provide clients with the complete solution.

As Chapter 3 drives home, however, getting trained and maintaining a level of expertise with every SBS and Microsoft BackOffice application is impossible. If you were to take every training class I mentioned in that chapter and in the "Training Options for Related BackOffice Applications" white paper on the CD-ROM in the back of this book, you'd need at least 14 weeks just to get through the course material. If you're like most SBS VAPs, you have a limited amount of time you can devote to training, and accordingly you need to be selective to be a highly productive, successful, and profitable SBS VAP. Making the most effective use of your training investments is important—which you can't do if you're spread too thin.

Although your small business clients may want you to be their virtual IT department, this doesn't mean your firm has to do all of the work on every single project. Even large Fortune 1000 IT departments are forced to pick what their core strengths are, in what areas they want to staff up and train, and then accordingly contract or partner with other vendors to supplement their internal resources. They'll frequently outsource many functions such as hardware maintenance, custom software development, Web site design, and Internet access.

Many small businesses also like to see that their virtual IT directors are willing to bring in outside experts, rather than paying them to learn as they go. Let's say, for example, that you've developed a simple Web site for your client using Microsoft FrontPage 2000. Although the Web site looks highly professional, averages 10,000 hits each month, and even makes use of several interactive forms, your client is eager to set up an e-commerce site to offer secure shopping cart to customers around the world. Your client wants this Web site overhaul implemented within 60 days. Your firm, however, typically doesn't handle advanced Web site design, and your client is very concerned about scalability, fault tolerance, load balancing, and security. This is a perfect example of when you should partner with a firm that specializes in e-commerce sites so you can provide a complete solution for your client.

By partnering and retaining account control as the virtual IT department, your firm is able to be bigger than it really is in terms of varied skill sets and resource pooling. The decision to partner vs. trying to keep the project in-house usually boils down to the size of the project and the expertise required. In the case of the e-commerce site, assuming your client has a budget commensurate with its wants and needs, your firm may be outmatched in terms of required time to turn around the project relative to staff levels, scheduling availability, and, even more fundamentally, a major skill gap.

In this case, your skills may be very complementary. The e-commerce firm may have relatively little experience with either your client's industry or small businesses in general. The e-commerce firm also may have little, if any, desire to arrange for contracts with ISPs for Web server co-location, to procure and build a Web server, to customize the security and permissions, and to perform ongoing, day-to-day Web server administration. These latter functions may very well be your firm's core competencies, resulting in an excellent marriage of partners.

ISP Web Site Co-Location Service

For a simple small business Web site with static pages—basic ISP Web site hosting—where the small business client shares a Web server with dozens of other Web sites, is usually sufficient. For a high-traffic, database driven e-commerce Web site; however, sharing a Web server is pretty risky from a security and reliability standpoint.

Usually companies with e-commerce Web sites need a dedicated server. Since the small business client doesn't have the 7 × 24 monitoring that a larger IT department would have, the client's best bet usually is to have a dedicated Web server reside at the ISP's facilities. This service is called co-location and generally includes round-the-clock monitoring, tape backup operations, and reboot requests.

In fact, once you've successfully managed a partnership for a single project, you'll probably partner with the e-commerce firm sooner or later to work on a similar high-end Web site project for another client. You can also expect the e-commerce firm to partner with your firm when one of their clients needs more basic network infrastructure design, deployment, training, and ongoing support.

An SBS rollout, like most IT projects, can either be an incredible success story, a harrowing failure, or somewhere in between. The end results will depend on how well the project was planned at the outset. Chapters 7 and 9 focus on how to plan thoroughly for an SBS rollout.

When a project is outside your primary area of expertise, you might not know what questions to ask during the project planning. The line of questioning you follow, however, is often the difference between being able to predict and prevent a future problem or not. Needs analysis is another major area where partnering makes sense. In the case of the e-commerce firm, its project manager or account executive most likely has field-proven checklists and templates to tackle thoroughly the entire needs analysis up front.

Tip

The worksheets and templates on the CD-ROM will allow you to conduct thorough, well-organized needs analysis for an SBS rollout.

Tips on How to Decide When to Partner

If you answer yes to one or more of the following questions, you might wish to partner with another firm:

- ❑ Are you totally at a loss for knowing how to estimate how long a task should take to implement, both in terms of estimated hours of labor and scheduling dependencies?

- ❑ Is the expertise needed way beyond a small stretch of your firm's abilities—to the point where someone would need weeks of intensive training just to achieve beginner-level proficiency on the project?

- ❑ Is it a bad time for your firm to take on a totally new area of specialization?

- ❑ Are you unsure about the technology in question?

- ❑ Would you rather bring in a partner so you can maintain control and still concentrate on your core business segment?

- ❑ Have you ever implemented the technology in question?

Different Ways to Partner

Just as many different types of VAPs implement SBS, many creative ways exist to partner with different types of technology providers. At the end of the day, stay focused and remember partnering is all about being able to leverage your firm's strongest competencies.

Partnering with Other Local Small VAPs

Many SBS VAPs choose to partner with other local small VAPs. Because an SBS rollout tends to be easily managed by a one-person VAP or relatively small VAP, the project would rarely be too large to handle in-house.

You often see SBS VAPs, however, partnering with other small local VAPs when a specific client's technical needs are beyond their immediate reach. The potential partner may be intimately familiar with one BackOffice family application, such as Exchange or SQL Server, or one vertical application, such as a SQL Server–based accounting package for hotel management. By the nature of the specialization, the potential partner would rarely get involved in basic network infrastructure design and would likely never be the main contact for an

Partnering vs. Outsourcing

Before looking at the varied ways to partner, you need to understand how partnering differs from subcontracting or outsourcing. In a partnership, each firm retains its own corporate identity as credentials are presented to the client. For example, if my firm partners with the e-commerce Web site design company, my client is fully aware that there are two distinct consulting companies involved in the development and implementation of its newly redesigned, high-end Web site.

Instead of partnering with the e-commerce design company, I may choose to outsource or subcontract the work to them. Under the outsourcing arrangement, you may choose not to disclose to your client that the bulk of the project is being farmed out. With outsourcing or a subcontractual arrangement, the e-commerce design company functions more as an extension of your firm. As a result, the e-commerce design company usually gets paid by your firm, as opposed to getting paid by your client and ultimately interacts much more with your firm than with your client. Outsourcing or subcontracting also helps to keep the client focused on your firm as the single point of contact, as opposed to blurring the fundamental account control issue.

Nevertheless, partnering has many benefits. Savvy small business VAPs typically try to arrive at some kind of hybrid agreement where they make an arrangement somewhere between a true partnership and a subcontracted job. Because partnering requires a lot more planning between partners than subcontracted work, partnering tends to be more practical on larger projects.

Under a subcontracted or outsourced relationship, you'll likely draw up a formal contract that spells out all the terms, conditions, deliverables, deadlines, and expectations. With an informal partnership that's hastily assembled, you may tend to gloss over some of the more fundamental planning details. Skipping this discussion with your partner, however, can be deadly to the relationship. Establishing clearly defined rules and objectives prior to entering into the partnership is crucial. Each partner also needs to have adequate incentives to get their part of the project completed on time and on budget. A later section in this chapter, "Defining the Rules of Engagement," will cover this area in greater detail.

SBS rollout. So many potential synergies can exist between the SBS VAP and the VAP who just supports a single SQL Server–based hotel management application.

In this case, the SBS VAP partner picks up unique skills to add to a solutions portfolio. Now when you meet the controller of the local hotel and conference center at a chamber-of-commerce breakfast, you can talk about how your firm has a special partnership with another local firm for installing end-to-end SBS networks with a turnkey, hotel-specific accounting package. And because your services are being offered within the context of and in concert with a relatively rare specialty, you can often sustain much higher rates than if you were just providing an off-the-shelf SBS installation.

Tip

To find out about Microsoft Direct Access events in your local area, see _www.microsoft.com/directaccess_. To locate the local Microsoft field office in your area, see _www.microsoft.com/worldwide_.

Many SBS VAPs recommend that you learn who's the cream of the crop in your local geographic area when it comes to various specialties. While user groups and vendor seminars are often great places to meet local VAP colleagues, many SBS VAPs who focus on Microsoft platforms have met potential partners at local Microsoft Direct Access events. Local Microsoft field offices hold free Direct Access half-day workshops for VAPs on variety of topics. For example, at the time this chapter was written, the New Jersey field office was holding Direct Access workshops on:

- Microsoft Exchange 5.5 and Outlook 2000 Solutions

- Windows 2000: Learning the Basics

- Internet/Web 101

- Microsoft Office 2000 Basics

- Microsoft Small Business Server 4.5

In addition to the generally small-scale (20 to 50 attendees) workshops typically held at Microsoft field offices, Direct Access quarterly briefings are usually held at a local hotel and almost always attract hundreds of local VAPs. The free quarterly briefings are full-day or half-day events that feature a main or keynote session as well as more targeted breakout sessions. At the time this chapter was written, the quarterly briefings focused on:

- Using Microsoft Office Customer Manager to Drive Revenue

- Upselling Your Customers to Small Business Server 4.5

- Migrating Customers from NetWare to Microsoft Windows NT Server

In addition to providing a great way to learn about multiple topics in a short period of time, Direct Access workshops and briefings are a highly effective way to meet your local Microsoft representatives. Just as important, though, there's almost always a breakfast or lunch break where you have plenty of time to network with other local VAPs.

Tip

I always make sure I bring plenty of business cards when attending Microsoft Direct Access events. Even if working the room is not exactly your *forte*, don't miss out on this great opportunity to exchange business cards with at least a handful of local VAPs.

When approaching other local VAPs about potential partnering opportunities, make sure you have a good fit. A lot of this comfort level comes from assessing how complementary your skills are. If both of your firms are going for the exact same target market and little if any differentiation exists, you'll find it hard to justify partnering. From a purely practical standpoint, both of you will probably be terrified of the other stealing clients. So when shopping for potential partners, make sure you take the time to learn about their real specialty—often absent from standard marketing materials, business cards, and Web sites.

Partnering with Local Large VAPs

At first glance, partnering with a large VAP may have many benefits. After all, its staff is likely to have in-depth expertise on various topics, plenty of backup staff, and instant credibility with your clients.

Many small business VAPs, however, typically shy away from partnering with larger technology providers. For starters, many SBS VAPs are inherently fearful of losing account control to the larger VAP's sales manager. Even if the small business VAP is comfortable bringing in a larger, more versatile technology provider, often some financial issues need to be addressed.

Larger VAPs in most major markets tend to work with larger accounts (medium and enterprise-sized accounts) and can charge much higher hourly billing rates accordingly for consulting services similar to those offered by smaller VAPs. As a result, many SBS VAPs report that their small business clients couldn't afford the higher rate structures that would come along with the partnership. SBS VAPs are in the best position to realize this. After all, if their small business clients were willing to pay substantially higher billing rates, SBS VAPs would certainly increase their rates across the board.

In addition, large VAPs with staff on medium and enterprise-sized accounts tend to remain on-site for much longer durations. An SBS VAP will rarely be on-site for more than two or three days in a given month. With larger VAPs, staff may be given a desk at the client site and literally work on-site for months at a time because of the nature of the contracted projects and client demands. Thus when small business VAPs approach larger VAPs, often the larger VAPs are concerned the project either isn't adequately budgeted or is too short in duration.

Partnering with ISPs

Turn the clock back five years and you'd find scores of small business VAPs who wanted to sign up for their own T1 or T3 high-speed Internet connections, purchase some routers, modem banks, servers, and then sell dial-up accounts, Internet e-mail, and Web hosting services to their clients. As ISPs such as America Online (AOL) and AT&T WorldNet began offering unlimited access at rock-bottom prices, however, the low-end of the dial-up access market became much less attractive to small business VAPs. Around the same time in 1995–1996, Web site hosting prices plummeted for basic, noncommercial-grade hosting.

Recognizing that high-volume multinational companies drive the low-end side of the ISP market today, many small business VAPs have very little interest in trying to be ISPs. Instead they'll typically partner with a local ISP to offer dial-up and dedicated-access accounts, POP3 e-mail, and Web hosting. In essence, SBS VAPs don't want to be ISPs unless that is in fact their core competency.

In addition, being an ISP today requires substantial investment in telco lines, hardware, software, and staffing. While some local ISPs do successfully function as 9-to-5 companies, the vast majority of ISPs have 7 × 24 monitoring on-site. This kind of staffing and capital investment is often beyond the reach of SBS VAPs. In addition, the SBS VAP would have to first go out and sell enough accounts to cover the costs of their ISP operations. Chapters 7 and 9 include a detailed discussion on planning for ISP accounts during an SBS rollout. Chapters 13 and 18 discuss implementing Internet access accounts, e-mail, and Web site hosting.

Table 6-1 on the next page has a list of more companies or individuals with which a small business VAP could partner.

Technology providers	Non-IT professionals
Cabling installers	Accountants
Hardware providers/ PC OEMs	Attorneys
	Financial Advisors
Independent software vendors (ISVs)	Graphics designers
	Marketing consultants
Phone system dealers	Public relations agencies
Software training centers	
Web site designers	

Table 6-1

Potential partners for small business VAPs

Defining the Rules of Engagement

Now that you know how to decide if you need to partner and to identify potential partners, let's shift our focus toward ensuring a successful relationship. As mentioned earlier, you need to craft your partnerships carefully to ensure the following three parties involved are well served by the arrangement:

- You

- Your partner

- Your mutual client

In addition to exploring how each party benefits from the partnership, you need to make sure you find a partner you can trust. As even the most thorough attorneys will concede, covering every single contingency and scenario in a partnership agreement is impossible. Therefore, gut feel and trust are major elements that must be considered before proceeding any further in talks. Many small business VAPs also prefer to start partnerships with small projects and gradually progress to more substantive endeavors.

You should also consider the potential synergies. If one plus one only equals two—that is, the sum of your skills and your partner's—you may not have found a strong potential partner. Think about how the client will perceive your joint efforts and the value that partnering adds to the project.

Next, you'll need to sit down and develop a plan for how you'll work together. The document should include:

- Discussion of goals of the project and specific tasks
- Which party is responsible for which tasks
- Timeline and scheduling constraints
- Procedures for dealing with change orders and project deviations
- Clarification of compensation for each party
- Responsibility for billing and collection
- Sign-off procedures and responsibilities
- Checkpoints to ensure close communication is maintained
- Primary contingencies and dependencies on the project as a whole and on individual tasks
- Measures to counter potential conflicts of interest and account encroachment
- Confidentiality and nondisclosure agreements
- Identification of *the* primary decision maker in each company

The CD-ROM in the back of the book includes "SBS VAP Partnership Planning Worksheet," a Word template, shown in Figure 6-1 on the next page. While your tendency may be to rush off and get your attorney involved in drafting a formal partnership agreement, you should use the worksheet to capture the relevant information when you meet with a potential partner. By putting many of these items out for discussion, you'll go a long way toward demystifying the entire partnering process.

By using the worksheet as your guide, the two of you can iron out all the technical details and use your attorney just to formalize the arrangement after you've completed your homework. The worksheet should also be used as a planning tool before either of you submit a formal proposal, bid, or project plan to the small business client. By using the worksheet as the foundation for approaching partners about joint projects, you'll be applying a consistent set of criteria across all of your client projects that require technology provider partners.

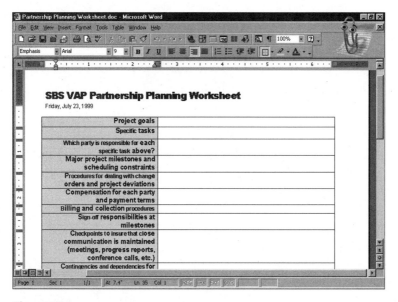

Figure 6-1

The "SBS VAP Partnership Planning Worksheet" on the CD-ROM in the back of the book will help to define the rules of the partnering engagement.

Identifying Complementary Skills

As you work through defining the rules of engagement in the "SBS VAP Partnership Planning Worksheet," you should begin to get a sense for how you and your partner's skills mesh together. The goal is for both you and your partner to each be working on the exact part of the project in which you specialize.

You need to gain a more complete understanding of what specific skills the partner's staff brings to the table. If you've reached this stage already, you probably know what the firm's strongest core competency is; you also need to get a grasp on what the staff members assigned to the project know about different applications and platforms.

To get a better understanding of your partner's skills inventory, you can use the "Internal Skills Inventory" Excel worksheet, first presented in Chapter 3. See Figure 6-2. The "Internal Skills Inventory" worksheet is on the CD-ROM and helps capture information on an individual's level of expertise on desktop and network operating systems, messaging, relational database design, Web site design, Internet connectivity, and security. As you go through each area of specialization for each individual on your partner's staff and mark whether a person is beginner, intermediate, or advanced, you'll begin to get a better sense for which skills are core ones and which skills are ancillary.

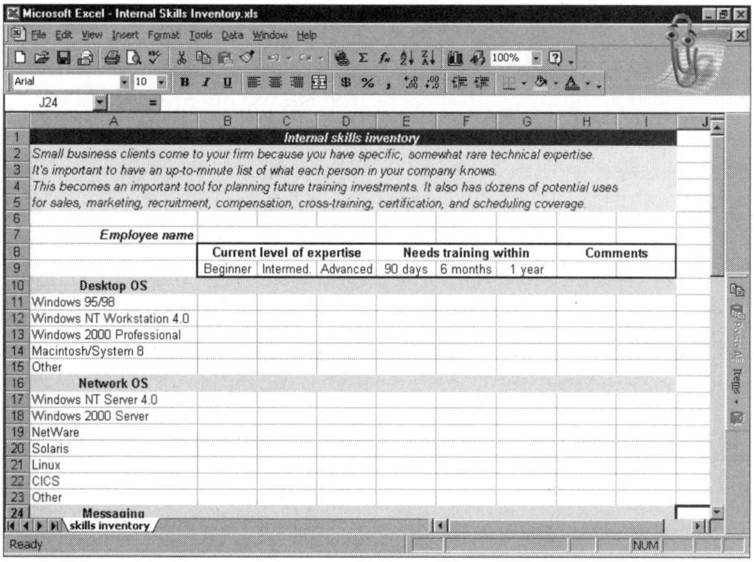

Figure 6-2

The "Internal Skills Inventory" worksheet can help you get a grasp on what your partner's staff knows about specific applications and platforms.

Skills in the Marketing Pitch vs. "Real" Skills and Specialties

Most small business VAPs' marketing materials convey they have the exact same skill set: networks, hardware, software, training, Web sites, and so on.

In reality, most VAPs aren't all that similar. Many have a hook—something special that differentiates them from the pack. Uncovering your partner's unique hook is important so that you can go to your client with a full set of "real" skills—not just marketing hype.

In addition, you'll likely have a hard time finding potential partners if they perceive you're competing directly with them. If you're serious about partnering, perhaps you'll want to print up a second set of business cards targeted specifically at potential partners. (Something to the effect of: "I live, die, and breathe NetWare interoperability with SBS networks.")

The point is to make sure you both drill down beneath the glossy marketing brochure.

Evaluating the Role of the AMSP

If partnering has such a huge potential to grow your SBS consulting business, why not form local groups of technology providers all around the world who are interested in partnering with each other? That's exactly what the Association of Microsoft Solution Providers (AMSP) set out to do when the initial chapter was founded as a Texas nonprofit corporation in 1994. The purpose of the AMSP is to be a facilitator for partnering. Local AMSP chapters around the world promote alliances among Microsoft Certified Solutions Providers (MCSPs) and look to develop virtual corporations that expand individual members' service capabilities.

Tip

The Microsoft Certified Solution Provider (MCSP) program is open to any technology provider worldwide that employs at least two Microsoft Certified Professionals (MCPs). For more details on benefits, program requirements, and membership fees, see *www.microsoft.com/mcsp*.

The basic premises of the AMSP include:

- Most major markets around the world don't have nearly enough MCSPs to fill clients' needs for services.

- Because client needs often cross multiple areas of expertise, individual MCSPs can't fulfill the needs of individual clients by themselves.

- By partnering with other local technology providers and MCSPs, AMSP members can offer a complete solution to clients.

Note

At time of writing, the AMSP had about 1,000 members across 50 chapters in 26 states, 6 chapters in Canada, and 5 chapters outside of North America. For more information on the AMSP, see *www.amsp.org*.

In early 1999, the national AMSP organization conducted a Web-based member survey and found:

- Ninety percent of respondents felt their membership in the AMSP had resulted in a better relationship with Microsoft (partnering with vendor).

- Seventy-three percent of respondents felt their membership in the AMSP had resulted in new business opportunities (partnering with other local MCSPs).

The AMSP Code of Ethics and Professional Conduct

AMSP members are expected to abide by the following codes of conduct:

- Keep high educational standards for skills and knowledge
- Maintain confidentiality, nondisclosure, and discretion
- Disclose fully any conflicts of interest
- Hold themselves accountable for the results of their work
- Uphold social responsibility and public safety regarding their profession
- Differentiate between factual conclusions and subjective opinions in their field of expertise
- Have integrity
- Discourage unauthorized duplication of software

Evaluating the Role of Local User Groups

Similar to the way AMSP members gather at regular local and national meetings with fellow MCSPs, many small business VAPs choose to participate actively in local user groups. Before getting involved with local user groups, you should understand what the group is all about. Some groups are made up of hobbyists; other groups are made up of IT professionals.

The hobbyists in some user groups may be well-respected gurus in their own right and often volunteer to help their friends, such as local small business owners, with computer-related problems. When hobbyists become stumped or realize the need to make a living in their day job or real job, however, they can become a great source of referrals to small business owners. By all means stay on their radar screens, but don't count on hobbyist types of user groups to bring you business. The members in these types of user groups are often notoriously frugal when it comes to paying for computer support. In fact, user groups are often formed to help bypass the need for professional IT assistance.

Distinguishing Between
User Groups for Hobbyists and IT Pros

You'll know you're at a user group for IT professionals when you see business cards being exchanged during networking breaks. If you're still suspicious, check out peoples' titles on the cards. As long as you don't see plumber, used car salesman, sanitation engineer, or hairdresser, you'll know you're on the right track.

The next step is to separate the corporate types, the network administrators, and developers from the local VAPs.

Also, don't discount the IT professionals at large firms. Although you might not have a snowball's chance of getting on the approved vendor list at a Fortune 1000 firm, these IT professionals often freelance with firms like yours during their evenings and weekends.

You're much more likely to meet other potential partners, such as local VAPs and MCSPs, at user groups targeted for IT professionals. Although not expressly designed for VAPs or partnering per se, user groups can be a great way to promote your technical background and unique expertise in the local community. By attending user group meetings, you'll also get to hear others from similar local businesses strut their stuff.

Tips for User Group Decorum

I was very active in the New Jersey Windows NT User Group for quite a long time. If you've never been to a user group meeting, I have a few tips for tactful conduct.

Don't push hard for sales leads—or anything else, for that matter. Never make a blatant pitch, no matter how tempting. It will backfire. Guaranteed.

If you're going to get involved in running the group, be prepared to make a major time commitment.

Don't look for immediate payback. As with most groups, whether they are chambers of commerce, AMSP chapters, or user groups, you need time to plant the seeds and build the requisite trust, bonds, and relationships.

If you fail to pick up on the subtle nuances and dynamics of the group, you might just be banished by the pocket protector groupies. If they change the meeting time or location and don't bother to inform you, you've probably made a major *faux pas*.

Tip

To find information on starting a user group or to locate an existing Windows NT–focused user group in your local area, see the *Windows NT Magazine* Web site at *www.winntmag.com*. Microsoft also offers a user group program for its products called Mindshare. To get more information or locate a user group in your area visit the Mindshare Web site at *www.microsoft.com/mindshare*.

The Bottom Line

Partnering is a flexible, cost-effective way to broaden your skill base and available solutions. Partnering, however, is not without potential pitfalls. In this chapter you learned how to identify potential partners and clarify responsibilities to prevent misunderstandings.

Part 3

Planning the Project and Cementing the Client Relationship

Chapter 7

Building an SBS Technology Roadmap

In a Fortune 1000 IT organization, the chief information officer (CIO) or IT director is usually responsible for being the visionary, spotting trends, and keeping projects on track. In a small business, this responsibility falls entirely upon the VAP.

Small businesses often want this single point of contact for computer support. Your firm will typically be the hardware provider, software reseller, network integrator, application developer, Web site designer, and IT manager. In essence, you become the virtual IT department for companies too small to hire their own full-time IT staff.

Microsoft BackOffice Small Business Server becomes the set of tools, the centerpiece or foundation, if you will, allowing your firm to establish itself as the virtual IT department for local small businesses. Virtual IT is one of the major themes of this book that you'll continue to see in each chapter.

Part 3, "Planning the Project and Cementing the Client Relationship," begins with this chapter, which shows you how to assume the role as the virtual technology manager for a small business.

Chapter 8 teaches you how to sell SBS more effectively as the solution to the technology needs of a small business and compare it to other common, competing networking platforms. Chapter 9 takes the information you gathered in this chapter and the informal buy-in you secured in Chapter 8 and solidifies the details into formal project planning documents. Chapter 10 concludes this section of the book with tips on the discussions and miscellaneous steps that should take place before the rollout is officially started.

Planting the Seeds

How do you get to the highly elevated status where your firm becomes a natural extension of your clients' staff? How do you get appointed as the de facto, part-time CIO for each of your small business clients? How do you get your clients to buy into the whole idea of proactive technology planning and data security? Finally, how does your firm manage to do all this without stepping on the toes of the internal guru?

These goals usually take time, patience, and very careful planning and execution. Unless you're very lucky or have a rather unusual specialty, you're unlikely to achieve your goals solely by accident. The more you know about the process of building an SBS technology roadmap for your clients, the more successful your firm will be.

Tip

Qualifying the small business prospect very early in the process is important. If the small business owner is not prepared to spend at least several thousand dollars between product purchases and retained services, you'll need to rethink whether this prospect is really a candidate for an SBS network. Every once in a while, I run into a prospect who mistakenly thinks an entire network can be rolled out in eight or ten billable hours and the server run on an $800 PC, with a $19 modem. Unless you really enjoy chugging antacids by the dozen and buying Rogaine by the case, steer clear of the frighteningly frugal small business prospect.

At the outset, you'll want to get to know clients on an individual basis. Take some time to learn about their businesses and computer skills, desires, backgrounds, wants, and needs. Learning about the factors that drive their businesses from different angles is crucial. Discuss with them their approaches to marketing, finance, operations, sales, and research for new opportunities, and the challenges they face with each.

Assembling the Technology Roadmap

Small business clients often tend to describe their technology needs in terms of broken or unreliable hardware and software, as well as wish lists. In order to get a handle on the big picture needs of your small business clients, you'll need a method to evaluate how their needs, at the most superficial level, map to various technology solution components.

"Roadmap Template for SBS Network," an Excel workbook on the CD-ROM with this book, defines the scope of the SBS rollout. See Figure 7-1. In addition to helping you get an idea of how many desktop PCs, laptops, servers, and network users will be involved, "Roadmap Template for SBS Network" assesses needs for solutions such as file sharing, network faxing, Web browsing, remote access, and groupware applications.

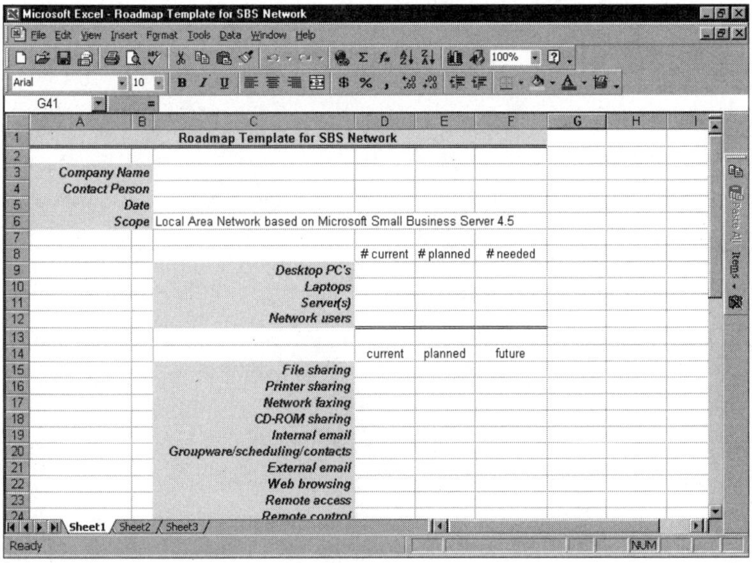

Figure 7-1
Use the "Roadmap Template for SBS Network" to help evaluate the client's needs.

Tip

The small business client gets tremendous value from the "Roadmap Template for SBS Network," your customized line of questioning and subsequent analysis. Resist the temptation to give this highly marketable service away for free, even if the small business prospect persists. This type of work should all be folded into a billable initial consultation, as discussed later in this chapter.

Establishing Yourself as an IT Visionary

Small business clients tend to think of technology as buying a bunch of PCs and software at the lowest possible price. One of the most basic responsibilities of being their virtual IT organization is educating clients on the benefits of different solutions. This includes helping them understand the value of planning, consistency, standardization, testing, training, ongoing maintenance, and regular reevaluation of needs.

Small business owners might also be under the impression that installing an SBS network is a one-shot deal. If you want to be perceived as a true IT visionary, take time to explain how SBS lays the groundwork for a very powerful, customizable, and scalable IT infrastructure. The way that works best for most VAPs is to give examples of how other small businesses have "grown up" technologically with SBS. This often includes a multiphase approach, such as implementing file and printer sharing first, Internet e-mail and secure Web browsing within 60 to 90 days, and finally a scalable contact management relational database within six months.

While many small business owners are inclined to make small impulse purchases for computer hardware, software, and peripherals, they'll benefit if you can get them to think of the big picture. Planning should become a normal part of their technology acquisition and implementation process. Without proper planning, small business owners run a risk of making haphazard purchases. In a vacuum, buying each employee an inkjet printer, tape backup drive, or modem might have seemed like a good idea at the time. The purchases might have depleted the annual budget for computer products, however, and locked the small business into high relative costs, slow performance, and high-maintenance when an SBS network could have been just weeks away.

Quarterly update reports and meetings should be encouraged to review past, current, and future IT projects. Fortune 1000 IT managers or CIOs who're serious about their careers see this type of planning as mission critical. If you're taking on a similar role with your small business clients, planning should *never* be pushed to the back burner.

The CD-ROM in the back of this book includes a Microsoft Word template, "Quarterly Update Report." See Figure 7-2. This template is designed to be used as a report and meeting agenda for reviewing the small business client's standards, projects completed in the quarter, projects in progress, and projects planned to start in the quarter.

Tip

You might want to include the quarterly update report and review meeting in the price for your ongoing service contract with the small business client.

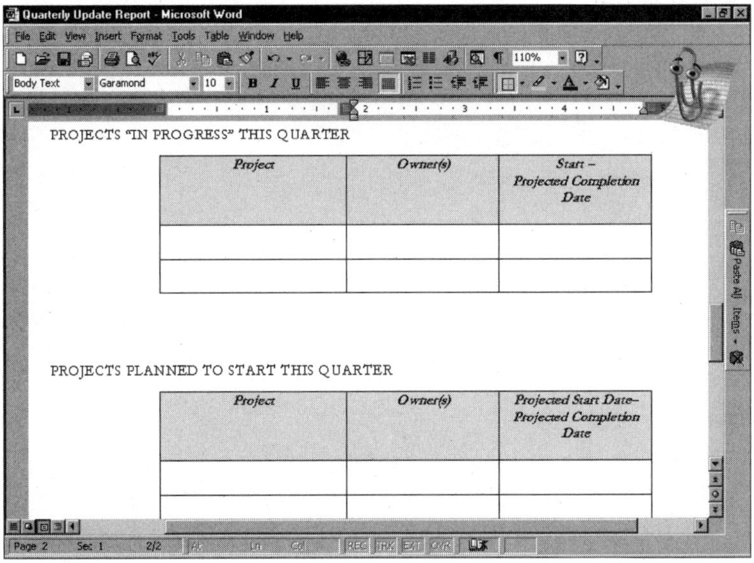

Figure 7-2
Use the "Quarterly Update Report" template to keep your small business clients on track for planning technology projects proactively.

Will a new small business client really be open to setting up quarterly progress reports immediately and authorizing a full-blown IT audit? Sometimes yes, sometimes no. Many VAPs recommend that you hold off on broaching the virtual IT department discussion until your third or fourth meeting.

During your initial meeting with a new client, you're likely to hear about major problems, some of which need to be addressed immediately. Often you'll want to take a gradual approach and concentrate on solving one or two simple problems ASAP. Once you've established credibility and trust with the small business client, you'll be in a much better position to begin talking about long-term goals. You'll also be in a better position to sell the small business owner on the benefits of a fee-based IT audit, as opposed to letting the client cajole you into providing a free estimate.

Other Tips for Getting Started as a Small Business IT Visionary

- Show motivation. Be on the look out for new ways to enhance your clients' business.

- Be dedicated to the task and relentless in your pursuit to improve the status quo. Just installed, an SBS network isn't a one-shot deal; planning requires tremendous staying power and perseverance.

- Don't be afraid to be creative. Small business technology solutions often need to stay within relatively modest budgets. Don't be afraid to think out of the box when appropriate.

- Keep up with advances and new versions. Summarize and share that information with your clients.

- Evaluate how the clients' systems—paper and computer based—function today. Look at how these systems are meeting or not meeting present and future needs. (Most of this work will be done during IT audit.)

- Put yourself in your clients' shoes and think about what *their* clients need from them.

Positioning Your Company as a Virtual IT Organization

Now you're armed with the skills and *the* template necessary to catapult you into the status of a small business technology visionary. Before you call up CNN or ZD Events to get lined up as the preeminent SBS expert for "Larry King Live" or Fall COMDEX, consider how you'll position your firm as a VAP.

The next step is for you, the virtual CIO or IT manager, to figure out how to leverage your newfound, unique expertise to elevate your firm from average Joe-VAP to virtual IT organization. For starters, your staff needs to understand the role your firm has with your clients. At the most basic level, this understanding begins by having your staff refer to the small businesses that your firm services as clients, as opposed to customers. Whenever interacting with a client, your staff should always be thinking about ways to learn more about the client's business needs and how to implement end-to-end solutions.

Just as business unit technologists in a Fortune 1000 company understand the needs, timelines, tolerance for downtime, and budgetary requirements of the department and organization, your staff needs to assume similar, but much less formal roles within your clients' companies. Small business owners often want many of the same technologies as Fortune 1000 companies. Your challenge then becomes how to deliver what they need and want on a small business–friendly budget.

For example, if your small business client wants to talk about getting a Web site, your on-staff Webmaster (or equivalent partnering VAP) should be on hand to discuss how your firm can extend its services to the client. In addition, an account or project manager should also participate in the talks to ascertain the available budget and begin anticipating how needs can be met.

Customers vs. Clients

Just as a five-star French restaurant takes great pains to elevate the dining experience above that of a fast-food establishment, veteran SBS VAPs also make sure that their clients know that the VAP's staff members are certainly not amateurs. SBS VAP's staffs are generally highly skilled service professionals (as opposed to mere computer techies or snake-oil salesmen).

One not so subtle nuance to this marketing and positioning strategy is how you refer to those organizations that pay your bills. The term "customer" implies a transactional nature, where the small business client constantly seeks out the lowest price. Customers rarely engage the services of SBS VAPs. Customers are too busy scouring the aisles of the local computer superstore looking for the rock-bottom price on a laptop, taking their technology adoption advice from a $6/hour part-time clerk.

Clients, on the other hand, look to build long-term relationships with technology providers, who guide the clients by preparing and implementing solutions that are both business-pragmatic and technologically sound.

Tip

Chapter 6 shows how to partner with other VAPs to fill gaps in your firm's skill set. This allows you to achieve your true role as virtual IT department more fully by coordinating the complete solution.

Small business VAPs engaged as virtual IT departments always look to provide a complete solution. Even when your firm cannot provide the product or services directly, you should be willing to take on the role of IT manager. Sometimes this involves partnering with another VAP to meet the client's needs. Other times delivering the complete solution involves interviewing vendors with your client and coordinating outsourcing.

Note

I've found a real niche in being able to help small business clients evaluate various industry software applications. Many times, I've saved my clients from spending thousands of dollars on technologically obsolete applications based on dated technologies such as MS-DOS 6.x and Microsoft Windows 3.x. Often an application that sounds great in the glossy brochure doesn't fare all that well when the SBS VAP puts the technology to the test in their lab environment. Be wary of ISVs who refuse to provide live trial versions of an industry application.

For example, your client needs Internet access to complete an SBS installation. Your firm, however, is not an ISP, nor is your firm the local telephone company. You can add tremendous perceived value to the portfolio of services and solutions by helping your client locate and select from various ISP and telco alternatives.

Tip

Chapter 18 explores the differences between dial-up, router-based, and broadband Internet access, all of which are supported by the completely redesigned Internet Connection Wizard (ICW) in SBS 4.5.

In addition, you could help your client develop the ISP selection criteria by writing the technical requirements, anticipating future needs, and incorporating budgetary constraints. Your firm should also be prepared to assist with ordering any required phone lines (or other circuits) from the local phone company.

Tip

Chapter 18 also discusses the "ISP Selection Matrix," an Excel workbook included on the CD-ROM with this book, which will help you compare various ISP alternatives for your client.

Many small business VAPs shy away from crawling around in ceilings and walls to install data-grade cabling. Because proper installation and category 5 certification is so critical to the network's reliability, assisting your client in vendor selection and project management for this task becomes very important.

You can also add value by talking to vertical industry software vendors with your client. For example, if your client is an attorney, realtor, or accountant, appealing industry-specific software can commonly be found in trade publications and at trade shows. By serving as the technical tire kicker, however, you can help prevent your clients from investing large sums of money in outdated, incompatible, or unstable software platforms. Because the SBS VAP will almost always be charged with implementing and supporting the vertical application, it's in both your and your client's interest for your firm to be totally immersed in the selection process.

Tip

Helping clients select industry-specific software properly is in your best financial interests as well. If your clients make expensive blunders, they'll ultimately have less of a budget available for other strategic networking projects.

Explaining the Value of Proactive Technology Investments

Your small business clients might be fairly reactive in their approach to computer support. Sometimes technology by the seat of your pants doesn't pose any problems. Other times, the lack of planning can be catastrophic.

What are some of the reasons it pays for your small business clients to take a proactive approach to planning their technology investments?

- **Protect investments.** Proactive planning can prevent small businesses from wasting money on technology that will either be obsolete within months after implementation or outgrown too quickly.

The proactive approach puts present and future needs in the context of technology investments.

- **Make more informed decisions.** Rather than taking a haphazard keep-your-fingers-crossed approach to implementing technology, small business owners can be educated on the benefits of constantly changing and evolving technology solutions through proactive planning.

- **Identify dependencies and interrelated projects.** Proactive planning might red flag crucial relationships among projects that were previously transparent. Often tasks might seem unrelated at first, but later prove to be crucial to plan them simultaneously. For example, if one of your client's vendors has a browser-based, bandwidth-intensive application due for release within six months, this *must* be taken into account when planning required bandwidth for Exchange Server and Proxy Server.

- **Protect against the hazards of over- and underbuying.** When you make purchase decisions for hardware, software, and peripherals in isolation, you stand a strong chance of either buying too much or too little. A proactive approach to planning helps to lessen this risk dramatically. When you underestimate needs with a plan-as-you-go approach, you run a big risk of having to spend much more money in the long run. Often when systems are inadequate or lack a cost-effective upgrade path, complete replacement becomes the only viable alternative.

The suite of applications included with SBS 4.5 goes a long way toward helping your small business clients adopt a more proactive technology investment policy. Several SBS-specific and BackOffice family applications are included in the box. Because several applications, such as Exchange Server, SQL Server, Proxy Server, and IIS, are already licensed, you can help your clients respond to rapidly changing requirements without having to purchase additional software.

For example, in the course of developing a proactive technology plan, you learn the small business owner has some serious reservations about the long-term viability of an existing custom order-tracking program based on an Access database. The client anticipates an increased need for security, reliability, and performance as the data storage requirements grow exponentially. Because SQL Server 7.0 is included with SBS, adding the database upsizing to the client's future project plans is a natural lead-in.

Talking Up Data Security

Many of your clients might have lost valuable data and experienced significant downtime when one of the following happened:

- Hard drive crashed

- Virus infected the office PCs

- Sudden power outage caused a database to become corrupted

- Unverified tape backup set proved worthless

- Recently terminated employee erased vital files

- Disgruntled customer hacked into the server and compromised confidential data

Tip

Chapter 19 helps you prepare your small business client for data disasters before they happen.

Unfortunately, planning for data security is a lot like forecasting doom and gloom. After all, if a small business owner has never personally experienced or doesn't know someone who has experienced these data security problems, he or she might not be aware of the potentially devastating effect on the bottom line. As the head of the virtual IT department, you need to make sure these risks are effectively conveyed and your client's data is adequately protected.

Small business owners don't often actively seek better data security until they've been burned. You can usually tell when small business owners have been traumatized by data loss because they're likely to come right out and ask, "How does your proposed plan protect my computers from _____ (fill the blank)?"

Many small business VAPs compare data security to a burglar alarm or an insurance policy. You hope you never need to rely on the data security solutions, but you can sleep better knowing they're in place. In assessing the amount of insurance or protection that should be implemented, talking to your clients about the worth of their business information is critical.

When broaching data security planning, other VAPs have told clients about experiences that similar businesses have had (without naming names). Giving explanations of how various solutions protect against different types of risks also helps. As you explain each solution, estimate and quantify for your client the potential for downtime and data loss that skimping in that area might ultimately cause.

Tip

The beginning of Chapter 15 includes a very simple formula for calculating your small business client's daily and hourly cost of downtime.

Data security solutions you may wish to suggest to clients include use of the following:

- **A firewall**, such the one included with SBS 4.5 through Proxy Server 2.0, to protect against hackers on the Internet

- **Third-party antivirus software programs** to protect against computer viruses, such as the well-known Melissa virus epidemic propagated in early 1999

- **Tape backup solution** to protect against accidental (or even deliberate) file deletion, data corruption, and server hard drive failure

- **Built-in security permission and auditing features in Microsoft Windows NT Server 4.0** to protect confidential data, such as payroll, bonus information, credit card numbers, internal P&L statements, proprietary databases, and company trade secrets

- **System rights and policies in Windows NT Workstation and Server 4.0** to protect against unauthorized system tampering

- **Uninterruptible power supplies (UPSs) and power management software** to protect against data loss and data corruption during power fluctuations

- **A redundant array of inexpensive drives (RAID)** to protect against a single point of hard drive failure on the server

Why Small Businesses Think Their Data Is Safe

Many small business VAPs find they constantly need to remind small business owners about the need for data security. For small business owners, thinking about security isn't intuitive...until it's too late. If there's a silver lining, once small business owners have even a minor brush with data disaster, they will generally get serious about the topic very quickly.

Small business owners often think their data is safe because they place enormous trust in their staff. You'll hear objections such as, "Most of my staff has been with me for years. We're like a family. I trust them completely—and they're all very careful." To which, I almost always have to fight the temptation to roll my eyes and mutter, "Yeah, right!"

Winning Over the Internal Guru

So at this point you've successfully established yourself in your clients' eyes as a small business IT visionary. In addition, you've retooled your firm to serve as your clients' virtual IT department. You've even been able to get your small business clients to commit to proactive technology planning and data security assessments. Now how do you make sure, with all these new, radical steps, that you've still maintained open communication and the support and trust of the internal computer guru? It's not easy. The following tips from my personal experience and other SBS VAPs worldwide, however, will help you stay on the right side of the internal guru:

- Make sure the guru doesn't feel threatened by you.

- Take great pains to work with the guru, not against. This includes informal cross-training whenever time permits.

- Whenever possible, try to make the guru look good in front of management and peers. Conversely, be very careful not to step on toes.

- Avoid finger pointing at all costs. Figure out how to fix the problem at the least cost to the client.

- Let the guru know his or her opinions and input are valued.

Packaging Your Virtual CIO Services

Some small business owners might be accustomed to dealing with multiple providers of computer-related products and services. Others are more comfortable working with a single provider that can serve nearly all of their company's needs. Regardless of which camp the small business is from, it can benefit from consolidating all of its computer support needs under your firm's umbrella. Most importantly, as the small business' single point of contact, you can craft a cohesive strategy that transcends all of its computer-related needs and projects. To be most effective as an SBS VAP, you'll need to build the relationship to the point where you truly are *the* trusted advisor for all technology related issues.

Pricing the Initial Consultation

Because most small businesses are constrained by budgetary limits, many SBS VAPs receive enormous pressure to provide the initial consultation work for free.

Sometimes the pleas for freebies might have little to do with the small business owner's lack of resources or frugality. Rather, the small business owner

Alternate Technology Providers

Small businesses might be using one or more of the following before you propose a virtual IT department arrangement:

- Mail order firms, local superstores, or warehouse clubs for computer hardware

- Computer-savvy friends and family members (the volunteer approach) for technical support by phone

- An employee, who tackled the project as a hobby, for Web site design

- Continuing education courses at a local community college or adult school for training

has no idea how much up-front planning time goes into designing an efficient, reliable, and cost-effective network.

At other times, the small business owner doesn't see the purchase of a network as being much different than buying a known commodity, such as a PC, VCR, photocopy machine, or office furniture. The small business owner just wants to see bottom-line prices—bids—as if the small business was awarding a contract worth in excess of $10 million.

One of your greatest challenges at the outset is how to price the initial consultation work. Nearly all SBS VAPs are forced to navigate this fine line between giving away too much information for free and scaring prospects away with sticker shock.

Some SBS VAPs will provide a fairly comprehensive initial consultation for free as a cost of doing business. Others who provide these services for free consider the initial consultation a necessary presales activity or fact-finding mission. Even those who don't start the meter running at this stage are in strong agreement that you need to bill the client if you do any work while on-site. For example, if following the sales call the small business owner asks for assistance installing a modem, that service *is* billable.

One school of thought advocates recouping the costs associated with free advice. These SBS VAPs, who are also product resellers, recommend providing the initial consultation for free with the idea that they'll load more profit margin into the hardware and software sale to make up for the free consulting.

I'm quite skeptical of this last approach, however. Is the complimentary initial consultation really free and objective when costs need to be recouped through other means? What happens when the curiosity seekers or cherry pickers take up several hours of your time and don't ultimately purchase the products from your firm? In the highly cutthroat environment of razor-thin margins on hardware and software, how many savvy small business clients would be willing to pay inflated hardware and software prices to offset the free consultation they received? If you do take this approach, you'll need to take great pains to make sure you don't compromise business integrity or hardware, software, and peripherals standards.

While some small business VAPs strongly believe in providing some type of free initial consultation, others insist that everyone's best interest is served when the small business client has a fee-based initial consultation. This is similar to the way that fee-based investment advisors manage stock portfolios for fixed fees, as opposed to relying on individual stock trades to generate commissions.

By charging for an in-depth initial consultation, the SBS VAP can take time to learn more about the prospect's problems and challenges. The SBS VAP can then prepare a thorough needs analysis report, as opposed to just a quickly assembled price quote. Depending on the complexity of the project and the depth of the report, SBS VAPs in the United States often charge a fixed fee somewhere between $500 and $1,000. Although if the needs are substantially more complex, or if the SBS VAP brings unusual expertise to the table, I've seen initial consultations priced around $2,000.

Other SBS VAPs who shun the idea of working for free bill for initial consultations at their standard hourly billing rates within the confines of a ballpark estimate. This type of approach might be helpful if you perceive that the small business is in such a state of disarray or has such complex needs that you'll need several meetings just to get to the point where you can write a cohesive needs analysis report and detailed recommendations.

How to Prevent Giving Away the Planning Deliverables

Given that many small business owners tend to feel entitled to free initial consultations and planning for SBS network installations, how do you avoid giving away several hours of planning time that might only benefit a competitor?

Some SBS VAPs aren't overly concerned with giving this time away at the beginning of a new client relationship. These VAPs will generally rely on a gut feel to assess a prospect's sincerity in being interested in a *mutually* beneficial long-term relationship. If you're not comfortable relying on a firm handshake or goodwill or trusting instincts or intentions, you still have at least two ways to reach a certain degree of compromise with the prospect.

> ### Tip
>
> Although you might be tempted to provide ballpark estimates to the prospect based on projects your firm has recently completed, remember that every client situation is unique. By providing unqualified estimates, you might ultimately back yourself into a rather uncomfortable position.

Because you can't prevent your prospect from getting different opinions (and sometimes you'll even want to encourage this), you don't want to spend time doing free work that will ultimately benefit your competitors. To avoid falling into this trap, you might not want to disclose detailed information about product costs or labor estimates until an agreement has been reached with client. Sometimes this agreement is simply negotiating a small fee to prepare the written report. Other times, if your gut feeling is that this client will move forward, you might wish to just finish up the consultation, prepare the report, and hope for the best. Pricing initial consultations is an individual decision that you can only reach properly by examining your firm's marketing message, unique attributes, competitive position, and local reputation.

> ### Tip
>
> If your staff is consistently booked up at 90 percent or higher utilization rates (that is, over 36 hours each week), you probably don't need to provide "free" consultations.

By tackling a small task first, you can lessen the risk of spending hours of free consultation time with prospects that never materialize into clients. During your first meeting, you'll likely uncover at least one major problem crying out for immediate attention. The key to this approach is identifying a task that you feel *extremely* confident in completing successfully within a short period of time.

For example, if during your first meeting you're asked for immediate assistance with a relatively simple, low-risk task, such as updating antivirus software definitions, performing a mail merge in Microsoft Word, or installing a printer, seize the opportunity. While you certainly didn't go out of your way to meet with the client just to get an hour or two of billing, this client's urgent request can be a huge help to you.

By proving your expertise and loosening up the small business owner's wallet for billable services, you'll be in a much better position to convince the small business owner successfully that the next logical step is a comprehensive, fee-based audit of all of the company's IT needs. On another level, the small business owner might now feel more comfortable in eventually signing on for a complete network implementation project once the small business owner has seen your technical know-how and problem-solving skills firsthand.

The most basic strategy to avoid giving away the planning deliverables is to:

- Position yourself (or your firm) as someone who can solve the prospect's most immediate problem.

- Then work your way into being that firm's preferred technology provider.

Rolling Up Your Sleeves

If you haven't started the meter running yet and you're still providing a free consultation, it's time to pull back. Raise the red flag, retreat, and rethink your strategy.

If you start rolling up your sleeves, dishing out professional advice, and getting your hands dirty with site surveys, individual user interviews, and sorting through mountains of dusty documentation and license agreements, it's high time you secured a signed letter of engagement for the initial consultation. The CD-ROM for this book includes a Word template for a "Letter of Engagement for Initial Consultation." See Figure 7-3 on the next page.

Once you've secured the client's written authorization for a relatively low-cost, fixed-price consultation, schedule your next client meeting. I generally allow between 90 minutes and 2 hours to cover the items specifically listed in the section "Scope of Initial Consultation," in the "Letter of Engagement for Initial Consultation."

Make sure that you stay focused during the meeting and don't stray into the section "Items Beyond Scope of Initial Price Fixed Consultation," which is also in the "Letter of Engagement for Initial Consultation." The steps listed in that section should be reserved for subsequent meetings. These steps will require a lot more in-depth information from the client and several hours of additional work on your part and will generally benefit from being split up over two or three distinct on-site visits. That way as you and the client review your notes after meetings, you'll both have ample time to discuss any newly discovered action items. You'll also want to limit the scope of work in the fixed-price portion of the initial consultation, which is why your "Letter of Engagement

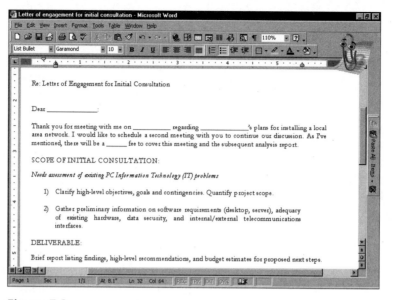

Figure 7-3

Use the "Letter of Engagement for Initial Consultation" template to draw the line between the initial consultation report and the more in-depth "Letter of Engagement for Network Design."

for Initial Consultation" needs to be *crystal clear* on what's in scope and what's beyond scope.

"Summary of Findings from Initial Consultation Meeting," a Word template, is also included on the CD-ROM with this book. See Figure 7-4. Use this template to help you stay focused and organized in preparing the limited-scope deliverable following the initial consultation meeting. Once the template is filled in with the findings from your meeting, the letter should be around two to three pages in length. If your letter is substantially longer, you're probably including too much detail in this preliminary part of the client engagement.

The "Summary of Findings from Initial Consultation Meeting" template has a section titled "Quantify Project Scope." After the initial consultation meeting and preparation of a summary of findings, you should be able to write a more detailed network design proposal based on your initial findings. This new engagement letter should detail the next steps required to design the client's network. Most SBS VAPs bill out for this type of analysis at their standard networking consulting hourly rates. The CD-ROM includes a Word template for the "Letter of Engagement for Network Design." See Figure 7-5.

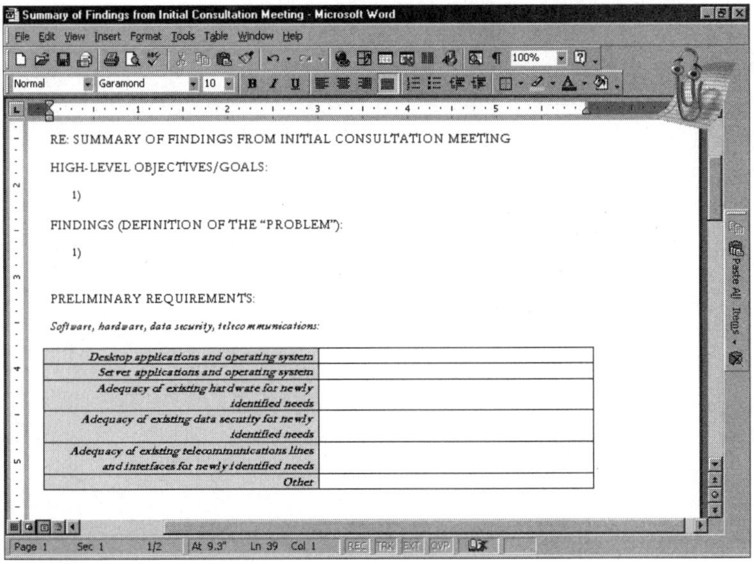

Figure 7-4

Use the "Summary of Findings from Initial Consultation Meeting" to organize after meeting with the client.

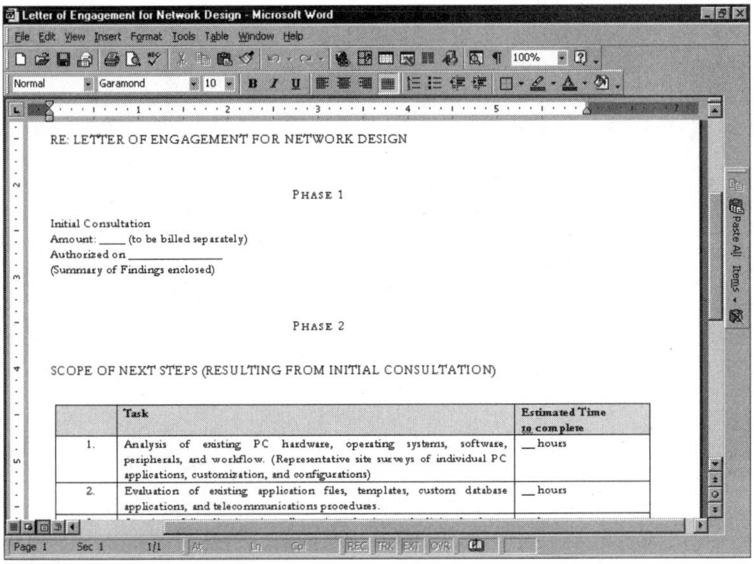

Figure 7-5

Use the "Letter of Engagement for Network Design" template to show the next steps you'll take for the client.

Tip

You'll need to think through carefully how you want to handle billing, rates, and scope. These templates aren't meant to be the be-all and end-all for managing the early part of your SBS rollout, but rather are meant to give you tools for successfully and profitably managing expectations in the early parts of the client engagement.

Conducting the IT Audit

Once you have secured the client's signature on the "Letter of Engagement for Network Design," you'll start moving into the IT audit phase of the engagement. This is where you begin looking at everything and anything that might impact the SBS network that you will likely be proposing.

Tip

Staying objective and keeping an open mind is important. The "Letter of Engagement for Network Design" and IT audit might uncover that this small business isn't a great candidate for SBS.

Microsoft Direct Access on Elevating a Microsoft Windows NT Server Sales Call into an IT Audit Opportunity

In my "VAPVoice: Notes from the Field" column for the May 1999 Microsoft Direct Access Windows NT Server/Windows 2000 Sales Center, I wrote about how small business clients tend to ask for sales calls when they really need an in-depth IT audit. The column, which was titled "Elevating a Microsoft Windows NT Server Sales Call into an IT Audit Opportunity," covers ten key areas to examine with small businesses to help them get a handle on what they already own and what they need.

Although the column was originally conceptualized for a Windows NT Server 4.0 sales call, the core content, message, and checklist are all applicable to SBS. The file for the column, "IT Audit Opportunity.htm," is on the CD-ROM for this book. The Microsoft Direct Access Web site is located at *www.microsoft.com/directaccess*.

Since the small business owner has now authorized your firm to proceed with a much more in-depth study of their needs, your prospect has matured into a client. This is a great sign.

Don't get too excited yet, however. Small business owners tend to think too small when talking about technology. They fixate on individual pieces of the puzzle, rather than the big picture. You'll often see this manifest when the small business owner brings in a circular from the Sunday newspaper advertising a sale or special promotion on antivirus software or a scanner or some other relatively low-cost item and suggest that the item should be purchased. While you should take into account these well-intentioned suggestions in your IT audit, you need to convey a definitive message: "Let's put this all down on paper and figure out where you're going before you start purchasing more hardware, software, and peripherals."

Your job is to help the small business assess what it already has, where the owner wants to be, and how to get there. Once you've gathered all this information, summarize your analysis in a detailed written plan. Chapter 9 details the preparation of these network design and project plan documents.

For now, you need to get the small business owner to start thinking about the big picture. Most SBS VAPs also sit with end users at the small business to learn how they are using their PCs and software today and what they'd like to be able to do in the future. You'll want put on your consultant or business analyst cap and move beyond just the dialog boxes and hardware specifications. This will include extensive discussions on:

- Where the client is at today from a technology standpoint (a snapshot)

- How PCs and software applications are being used

- How technology and computers fit into the strategy of the small business

- With what types of bugs and workarounds end users have learned to live

- What the history is of each workstation (installations, upgrades, crashes, etc.)

The CD-ROM for the book also includes a "30-Point PC Security Check-Up" Word template. See Figure 7-6. By using this checklist, you can help your clients evaluate their adequacy in five major data security areas:

- Data backup
- Disaster recovery/business continuity planning
- Overall security
- Power protection
- Virus protection

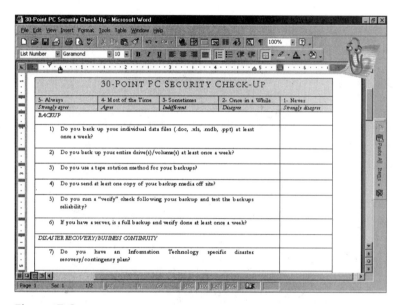

Figure 7-6

Use the "30-Point PC Security Check-Up" template to discuss with your clients how they protect their data.

Capturing the Asset Inventory

Because most of the small businesses you'll work with on SBS projects will generally have no more than a few dozen PCs, SBS VAPs usually capture the asset inventory or site surveys by hand. This is in sharp contrast to enterprise VAPs who would likely use an automated inventory solution such as Microsoft Systems Management Server (SMS). The basic goal during a site survey is to record all relevant information pertaining to the client's existing hardware, software, and peripherals.

Tip

For all of these templates included on the CD-ROM, you should customize each template to fit your firm's unique needs. For example, if you are an MCP or MCSE or your firm is an MCSP, you might want to include the appropriate logos with your customized document templates. For details on proper logo usage, see *www.microsoft.com/mcp* or *www.microsoft.com/mcsp*.

The CD-ROM for this book includes two templates to assist you in completing your client asset inventories. The first template, "Site Survey Inventory (Word)," allows you to print out a hard-copy worksheet, or form if you will, to take with you to the client for the site survey. See Figure 7-7.

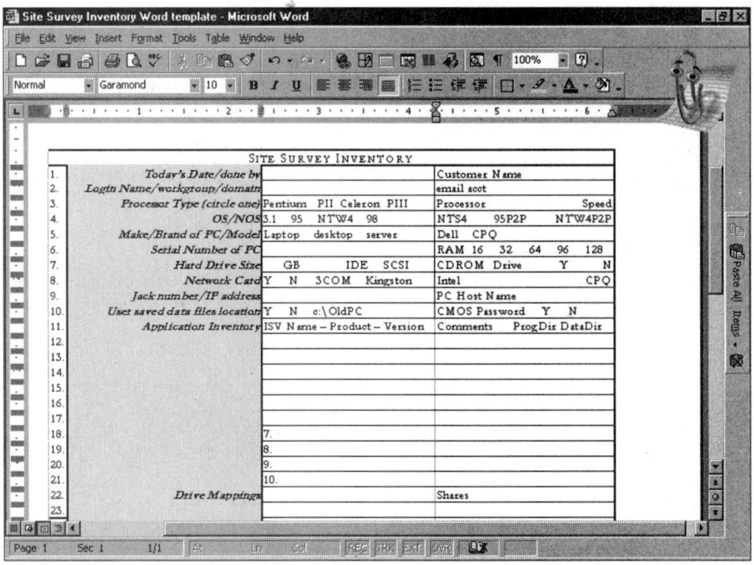

Figure 7-7

You can print out the "Site Survey Inventory (Word)" to use as a paper-based worksheet for client site surveys.

Using the other template, "Site Survey Inventory (Excel)," you can take a slightly more high-tech approach to recording the inventory details. See Figure 7-8 on the next page. With Microsoft Excel running on a laptop, you can capture the site survey information electronically for easier report preparation, querying, sorting, charting, and document merging. The Excel approach also provides the added advantage of being able to update the data easier.

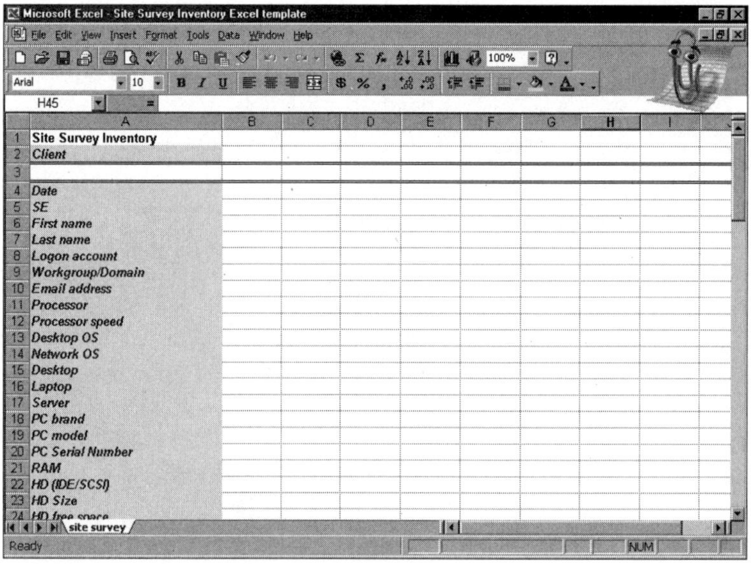

Figure 7-8

You can load the "Site Survey Inventory (Excel)" template onto a laptop to capture basic information electronically at the client site.

Regardless of whether you write down the asset inventory on paper or type the same information into a laptop, you'll want to watch for a few common trends during small business site surveys:

- **Nonstandard hardware.** Typically, you'll find that among 10 desktop PCs, there are 8 different video cards, 7 different sound cards, 4 different network cards, and 10 different CD-ROM drives. This can be especially challenging when it comes to locating device drivers to use for future OS upgrades or rebuilds.

- **Multiple versions of the same application on the same PC.** You'll often find individual PC users with multiple versions of Word or Excel or other applications installed. Also, don't be surprised to find three or more versions of America Online software on small business desktop PCs.

- **Version mismatches across users.** Typically you'll find various PC users running not only different version numbers, but also different maintenance or service releases. This lack of standardization will make it difficult to share files when the SBS network is installed.

Identifying Custom Applications

During the site surveys, how do you unearth software that either should be upgraded or is in desperate need for replacement? Some methods include:

- Find out how the software is being used (or not used).
- Talk about how well the software is meeting their current needs (and anticipated future needs).
- Ask about the software vendor's availability for support, customization, and upgrades (as well as the costs).
- Check to see if the application is 16-bit or MS-DOS-based.

- Learn about the application's function to determine if it can be replaced by an off-the-shelf application.

Solidifying Business and Technology Goals

No matter how thorough your security audit, site surveys, and discussions are, no small business technology recommendations should be made until you and the small business have reached a meeting of the minds on business and technology goals. All too often SBS VAPs and small business owners make rapid purchase decisions that they later regret. The goal with all of the proactive planning is to rise above impulse purchases.

What issues should you discuss with the small business owner as you prepare and deliver your network design report? Some suggestions include:

- Review where they are today and where they're going tomorrow.

- Evaluate the costs and benefits of maintaining existing systems vs. the costs and benefits of replacement.

- Compare the costs of different relative options.

- Discuss how the proposed technology adoption fits into the small business' plans across departments: marketing, sales, finance, operations, and so forth.

- Create a set of concrete, attainable goals with milestones and anticipated timeframes.

Establishing Scope and Priorities

Now that you and the small business owner have jointly decided to move forward, you'll need to decide how to structure the dozens of interrelated tasks, steps, and various phases. You need to establish the scope of what's included during each part of the project, as well as the underlying business and technology priorities.

Some tips for fleshing out these issues include:

- Make sure you have a single point of contact, or an internal tie-breaking authority to make the tough calls when the client's employees have conflicting opinions.

- Encourage the primary decision maker to help you assign measures of relative urgency.

- Assess which part or parts of the project will have the biggest impact on the bottom line.

- Identify the power users and work to meet their needs first. If the power users are satisfied, the remainder of the project will be much easier to tackle.

- Red flag problem areas early and address them. Procrastination will usually only make the problems worse.

Discussing Internet Issues

Although Chapters 9 and 18 will address planning and implementing Internet access, e-mail, Web site production, and bandwidth in much greater detail, your small business clients should be thinking about their online presence early on.

If your small business clients are Internet newbies, you might need to start with some really basic examples. When I have a client who's a newbie, I usually take out my business card and a few business cards from other companies and compare these with the client's business cards. I then ask without trying to sound arrogant, "What would you think of a business card you received to-day without a fax number? What message are you sending to clients when you don't have an e-mail or Web site address on your business card? How are your competitors addressing this?"

On the other hand, many small businesses are already sold on the need for Internet access, Web browsing, e-mail, and a Web site of their own. These small business owners, however, are often thinking of Internet usage as if they were consumers as opposed to business owners. They'll typically have one PC in the office connected to a local ISP through a dial-up analog modem. Without their own domain name, their published company e-mail address is something like *bobby@mycompanyusesfreemailservice.com* (and that single e-mail address is used by everyone within the company).

A lot of how you'll implement clients' Internet requirements depends upon individual client's budgets for these expenses. To help the small business owner put some of these decisions into context, talk about what other local small businesses are doing with the technology. The examples will be even more resounding if you can relate the companies to your client's own industry.

The Bottom Line

Not every small business is a good candidate for a technology roadmap or for SBS. Many small businesses might not be able to get beyond the single-transaction, lowest price mindset. If these problematic small businesses do ultimately retain your firm to implement an SBS solution, you might have a lot more aggravation than you could have ever imagined. By using the checklists, templates, and discussion pointers in the chapter, you can actively seek out those small business clients that want to build a long-term relationship with your firm.

Chapter 8

Pitching SBS as the Solution

Part 3 focuses on how to plan the Microsoft BackOffice Small Business Server rollout project and cement the small business client relationship. Chapter 7 looked at how you can build an SBS technology roadmap by positioning your firm as the virtual IT department and yourself as the virtual CIO. The chapter also explained the value of proactive technology planning, data security, and performing the initial consultation, IT audit, network design, and site survey.

Because small businesses are often resistant to change, SBS VAPs must be able to discuss effectively and persuasively the differences between SBS and the status quo solution. This chapter begins by helping you sell to small business decision-makers, speak to their hot buttons, overcome common objections, and relate your message to bottom-line savings. The second part of Chapter 8 covers how you can position SBS 4.5 in various small business environments where the entrenched, competitive solutions might include sneakernet, peer-to-peer Microsoft Windows 95/98, NetWare, or Macintosh.

People have many different views on whether selling skills can be taught. Some think you can't be trained to sell—either you're born with the gift or you're not. Others are adamant that anyone can sell more effectively with the right training. My personal view is that owners of small business VAPs, as well as their staff to a certain degree, have to adopt some type of sales style that they're comfortable with even if they find selling painful. My goal in this chapter is to give you the tools to succeed, regardless of whether or not you're a great schmoozer.

Selling to the Small Business Decision-Makers

What's involved in selling a small business owner on the benefits of hiring your firm to install and support an SBS 4.5 network? At the most basic level, this involves analyzing your client's requirements and crafting a cost-effective solution. From the initial consultation, IT audit, and site survey meetings, you should already have an excellent idea of what your small business has and what it needs.

As you might have learned in building the technology roadmap, however, the small business owner might not be your primary decision-maker. The small business owner might hold the ultimate check-signing or veto power, but in many small businesses the primary decision-maker is an office manager, a controller, a vice president, or the owner's spouse. Learning who's interested in the bits and bytes discussion and who's purely interested in how much it'll cost is as crucial as finding out what the small business does and what it needs.

When proposing the installation of an SBS network, be aware that many times the small business decision-makers won't be interested in the nitty-gritty details of what kind of NOS suite you'll be installing. They're just looking for

Simplifying the SBS Sales Cycle

Scott L. Ayon, president of SBS VAP Office-Anywhere in Willamina, Oregon, and a 1998 Microsoft Direct Access VAP roundtable participant, offers a five-step checklist to simplify the sales cycle for an SBS network:

1. **Qualify**—First and foremost, make sure the client needs SBS and can afford the project.

2. **Define**—Determine what's included in the scope of the project, being careful to include everything. (See Chapter 7 for tips and templates to capture this vital information more easily.)

3. **Educate**—Talk to the client about how SBS will automate business processes. (This is the thrust of Chapter 8.)

4. **Propose**—The proposal should reflect their software needs, unique challenges, and budget. (Chapter 9 covers writing the project plan.)

5. **Close**—Get the client's sign-off to start the project.

concrete benefits such as centralized file storage and security, Web browser and Internet e-mail access from each desktop, and the ability to send and receive faxes over the network.

Small business decision-makers might show some resistance when they see the price tag of $1,499 (estimated retail price) on SBS 4.5 with five client access licenses (CALs). The key to overcoming this type of objection is finding out if decision-makers are sincerely interested in the answer to their concern, or if they just want to focus on bottom-line costs, ignoring the potential benefits. Having become accustomed to purchasing most of their desktop applications for a fraction of this price, they might need a more detailed explanation on what comes with SBS 4.5. Start by pointing out that SBS is part of the Microsoft BackOffice Server family. Next find out how familiar the decision-maker is with Microsoft Office, and then ask if they remember how most people used to purchase Microsoft Word and Microsoft Excel separately. As Word and Excel became more popular, Microsoft created the Office Professional suite with tight integration between Word, Excel, Microsoft PowerPoint, Microsoft Access, and Microsoft Outlook.

In the same way Office provides a tightly woven bundle of desktop productivity applications, SBS offers small businesses an integrated suite of server-based applications. SBS 4.5 includes:

- **Microsoft Windows NT Server 4.0** for file and printer sharing

- **Microsoft Exchange Server 5.5** for back-end processing of e-mail, messaging, group scheduling, and contact management

- **Microsoft Proxy Server 2.0** for secure, shared Internet access

- **Microsoft SQL Server 7.0** for back-end processing of scalable, secure relational database applications

- **Microsoft Internet Information Server 4.0** for serving Web sites

- **Microsoft Modem Sharing Service 4.5**

- **Microsoft Fax Service 4.5**

- **Microsoft FrontPage 98** for authoring Web pages without programming

- **Microsoft Outlook 2000** for messaging on the client side (Outlook is the preferred client for Exchange Server.)

- **Microsoft Internet Explorer 5.0** for Web browsing

After I've completed a basic rundown and explanation of all the server and client software included with SBS 4.5 for the small business owner, I repackage the message a little differently. Small business owners want the same kind of technology advantages that their Fortune 1000 counterparts enjoy. The big challenge for small business owners and their VAPs, however, is implementing this need on a small business–friendly budget and with small business–friendly ease-of-use. Delivering the applications affordably is crucial. The aggressive pricing on SBS, relative to purchasing either applications *a la carte* or BackOffice Server, makes a Fortune 1000 IT infrastructure a reality for even the smallest companies.

Understanding the Hot Buttons

If you sense resistance during the sales cycle, listen very carefully to the client's objections. SBS might still be a great solution for this particular small business; many times, however, small business owners need to hear three or four different opinions in order to bolster their confidence. If the ball is left in your court, knowing what topics to discuss with the small business owner to understand exactly what's driving the investment in a network is important.

SBS VAPs often find that many of their prospective SBS clients have similar application needs. In most small businesses, one person in the office has a dial-up ISP account, a modem, and an analog phone line. With this primitive setup, this one privileged person can send and receive e-mail and browse Web sites. Whenever anyone wants to send an e-mail to a customer or vendor, receive an e-mail, or visit a Web site, they have to displace this person from his or her PC. Because the office has only one e-mail account, little if any confidentiality exists for e-mail messages.

For example, most small business end users have similar experiences when sending faxes. When the document that needs to be faxed is complete, the end user prints the document and cover sheet, gets up from the desk, walks over to the fax machine, and waits on line until the fax machine is available. Once again, this creates a productivity bottleneck.

To understand the cost of not addressing the single Internet access account or fax machine dilemma, you'll need to talk with the small business owner. Ask the following questions to shed light on the real costs and limitations of sending faxes through a fax machine:

❑ How many people in the office send faxes?

❑ What's the average number of pages in each person's fax?

❑ Does each person typically create a cover page to go along with each fax?

❑ How many faxes a day are sent out?

❑ Given the speed of the fax machine and the fact that the fax machine is also receiving faxes, how many average-sized faxes can be sent out in a given eight-hour workday?

❑ Is the fax machine operating at more than 25 percent of its eight-hour workday capacity? If so, how many times a day is someone forced to wait by the fax machine for it to become available?

❑ How often are people sending the same fax to multiple recipients?

❑ How far away is the fax machine from most people's desks?

❑ What's the productivity impact of people walking over to the fax machine, waiting until the machine is available, and then waiting until their fax goes through?

❑ How many hours are wasted on a daily basis with people waiting around to send outgoing faxes? How many hours does this translate into annually? What's the average hourly wage of the people affected by this productivity issue?

❑ With this information, what's the annual labor cost of sending outgoing faxes?

Hint: If the cost is substantial, Fax Service in SBS and one or two modems dedicated to outgoing faxes will have an enormous impact on the client's bottom line. (Installing and customizing Fax Service 4.5 is the focus of Chapter 27.)

Tip

The Fax Service in SBS can also receive incoming faxes and do any one or more of the following: route the incoming faxes to a designated e-mail account such as the receptionist's account, print incoming faxes on a designated local or network printer, or store the faxes in a folder on the server for retrieval at a later time.

By engaging the small business decision makers in these types of discussions, you can help your client focus on how automating services like faxing will save the company on manual labor. Accordingly, this will also result in salary savings over the course of the year. At the very least, the Fax Service will free up staff to focus on higher-level activities, rather than babysitting the fax machine.

As you get to know more about the client's business, you might be able to spot additional areas where Internet access for each desktop seems to be a no-brainer. For example, if several people frequently send packages through freight carriers such as FedEx, UPS, or Airborne Express, make sure they know how much time they can save when checking on the status of a delivery. So information obtained through a phone call that used to take five to ten minutes, followed by waiting for a faxed copy of a tracer report, can now be retrieved in just seconds through real-time database-driven Web sites.

Make sure that the small business decision-maker is aware of popular Web site resources. For example, if the business does a lot of local deliveries and service calls, is the small business owner aware of Web sites that automatically generate custom maps and door-to-door driving directions? If people frequently travel, are they aware of the dozens of Web sites that will allow them to shop rapidly for great deals on hotels and airline flights?

Tip

Small business owners may be concerned about proper usage of Internet access. Chapter 10 shows how to help your client draft a policy statement on appropriate use of the Internet and e-mail. Chapter 18 covers how to specify the authorized users for Internet access, as well as grant and deny access to specific Web sites.

Besides the advantages of over-the-network faxing, Web browsing, and Internet e-mail for each desktop, SBS also provides centralized storage of information that might be scattered in dozens of places around the office. By setting up folders and share points on the Windows NT Server 4.0 and shared Public Folders accessible through Outlook 2000 on Exchange Server 5.5, the small business will be forced to become more organized and will be able to operate much more efficiently.

In addition to sharing information, protecting and securing information becomes easier as well. Through permissions and auditing, small business owners can insure that only those authorized have access to sensitive information. By centralizing the storage of data, small businesses can also protect data with a tape backup drive, antivirus software, and an uninterruptible power supply (UPS).

Tailoring your message for different audiences and interests is also critical. If you're discussing the SBS project with the president or owner, the hot buttons might include costs, the value of proactive technology investments, industry trends, competitive factors, and lower labor costs through more auto-mation. (With more automation, the company can take on a lot more projects and customers without adding additional clerical and operations staff.)

Tip

If you have small business decision-makers and end users of different levels in the same conversation, always speak to the lowest common denominator. Nothing is more frustrating to the small business owner than feeling like the guru and the VAP are conspiring to speak in the secret code language of blue screens and well-known ports.

If you're discussing the upcoming SBS project with end users in middle management or end users in the trenches, make sure to shift gears. Staff and the internal guru will likely want to talk about ease of use and administration, how the network will make their job easier, and the amount of training required to become proficient. The internal guru often is additionally charged with investigating and testing new products and sometimes has the authority to make decisions that involve small amounts of money.

Because the guru typically has more of a history with the small business and will be the first one on the scene when problems arise, the small business owner will almost always want the guru's buy-in before proceeding. In addition to fixing simple problems, part of the guru's job is to affirm and reinforce the final decision about getting a network. Most new SBS VAPs might think the internal guru could be a potential threat to closing the deal and servicing the small business. The guru in most cases, however, will become an important ally of yours during the sales, installation, and ongoing support phases.

Gurus often are the only ones in organizations who understand the limitations of the current technology and whose eyes don't glaze over when you ask if all applications are 32-bit or not. Interestingly enough, when gurus are asked to evaluate your project plan and proposal, they're usually anything but a hindrance. In a quest to show that they're keeping up with the latest advances in hardware and software, gurus will often push the small business owner to add even more capacity to the system. Don't be surprised if the guru's recommendations include an even bigger product sale for you or the hardware provider—perhaps adding a faster processor, bigger hard drives, or more RAM. Because gurus often have an outside interest in PCs that extends well beyond the workday, gurus will often be quite enthused about the opportunity to trail along and work side by side with the experienced system engineer from the VAP.

**Tip**

You might be inclined to think that whatever the small business owner says goes. If you sense a major difference of opinions between the owner and the guru or other staff, however, meet with both parties to reach some kind of consensus on how to proceed. Even with the owner's blessing, the project will be a nightmare if the guru or other staff members are constantly putting up roadblocks.

Overcoming Obstacles

No matter how thorough your initial consultation, IT audit, site survey, and network design reports, some unforeseen client objection will pop up just before project approval. Because one relatively minor concern might threaten to derail the entire rollout, knowing how to overcome some of the biggest SBS deal-closing obstacles intelligently and successfully is important. With some concrete ideas on how to turn around these objections, you'll be much less apt to get emotional, defensive, or just plain annoyed. You can then stay focused on figuring out the best way to solve the client's problems.

Apathy

You need a powerful force to overcome apathy. If small business decision-makers have an apathetic outlook toward the prospect of implementing a network, they might take weeks, months, or perhaps years before feeling a sense of urgency about network implementation. When you understand the roots of this apathy, you have a great opportunity to push the approval process along.

A typical example of apathy is when small business owners see no problem with their existing peer-to-peer networks. One or two seemingly innocuous foul-ups, however, can cause the small business owner to see the light. With a Windows 98 peer-to-peer network, the "server" seems reliable until the person working on the PC functioning as the server inadvertently hits the reset button with his knee. Network reliability could also get called into question when the user of the server performs an unannounced, unscheduled shutdown and restart because a software setup program prompted a reboot.

Perhaps the server wasn't protected because it lacked fault tolerant drives, a reliable tape backup drive, a server-class UPS, and updated antivirus software. So now the small business owner is scrambling with the internal guru at 2 A.M. trying to restore the company's corrupted contact management database, which contains 25,000 records and three years of data. Situations such as catastrophic data loss are great motivators for combating apathy. All of a sudden, the small business owner becomes very receptive to your suggestions about the centralized security and data protection model that SBS offers.

Note

Make sure you practice what you preach. I found it quite bizarre when a local white-box retail store where some of my clients *used to* buy their boxes lost over two years of customer invoice files. Here's a company whose sole purpose is to sell PC-related products to local consumers and small businesses. This firm should be leading by example to show their customers how to protect data. When I spoke with some of the store's staff, I learned the owner had gone cheap: no fault tolerant drives, no tape backup drive, and no UPS. All it took was one 30 second power-blip and thousands of hours of data entry work were gone. Kaput.

Software vendor technical support and upgrade policies are another powerful counterforce for apathy, especially in regard to vertical, industry-specific software, such as niche applications designed for accountants, attorneys, physicians, realtors, auto body shops, and restaurants. After a certain point, the independent software vendor (ISV) selling vertical, industry-specific software draws a line in the sand and stops providing technical support, annual updates, and patches for old versions of the software. So if an accounting firm needs updated tax tables (and they'd basically be out of business without them), it's forced to upgrade the tax software, which in turn forces an upgrade of the server. This generates a call to your firm to implement SBS, which is a result of an ISV for the industry calling the shots.

One final way to overcome the obstacle of apathy is by talking about the competition. Let's say your client is one of six mortgage brokers in a small town. Interest rates have been low, unemployment remains low, and housing inventory is in short supply in the market. Because the housing market is hot, mortgage brokers keep coming up with creative ways to undercut the competition and lure applicants.

Three out of six of these local mortgage companies purchase a mortgage processing application that runs on SBS. This new package, based on SQL Server 7.0, cuts processing time from three hours to five minutes. Because processing is so much simpler now, the three companies with the new software begin waiving the standard $500 application fee.

Your new client, who doesn't have the software, sees a 90 percent drop in monthly business by the time you get the call. This firm was on the fence about upgrading its network. The new mortgage processing application, which is being used as a wedge by local competitors, is the apathy-buster that pushes along the SBS project sign-off.

Hype

Just when you thought there was no such thing as the client being too enthusiastic about jumping headfirst into a major software implementation, think again. Hype is basically the opposite problem of apathy. Although hype isn't exactly a sales obstacle, you need to manage client expectations regarding unjustified optimism at the earliest opportunity.

In SBS projects, I see the need to combat hype most often with vertical industry solutions. The small business owner returns from a trade show with glossies for an industry-specific application. Thinking the application is the best software since VisiCalc; he or she is ready to open up the firm's checkbook—but wants to run the application by the internal guru and VAP first. Although the ISV's marketing literature and Web site seem quite professional, upon further investigation you learn this $5,000 per seat package is built on an MS-DOS-based Clipper database engine (circa 1991).

Although the client might have been impressed initially with the demo at the trade show, you overcome the hype surrounding the application and save your client from making a sizable investment in an application that should've been retired or supplanted years ago. This application also probably would've been quite problematic to configure for a SBS environment.

Denial

"Why do I need something as big and powerful as SBS? We're just a seven person company."

"My staff has been with me for years. They're very careful with sensitive data and I trust them all completely."

Those are just two of the more common objections rooted in denial that you might hear when proposing the installation of an SBS network. When small business clients say they think SBS is overkill, they might not be thinking of the big picture. That's all the more reason to take the small business through a comprehensive initial consultation, needs analysis, IT audit, and site survey. Many times a small business owner might ask just for file sharing or e-mail. If you press further, however, you'll discover they could also use a contact management system, group scheduling, network faxing, a company Intranet, and secure, high-speed Web browsing from each desktop.

If small business clients insist they have no need for data security, you probably haven't probed deeply enough. Find out where the company stores its client lists, proprietary pricing models, payroll forecasts, bonus calculations, credit card data, and social security numbers. Is everyone in the firm supposed to have access to everything? Does the staff never turn over? Does no possibility exist that someone might inadvertently delete five years worth of sales forecasting with one keystroke? External security breaches or virus contamination aren't risks? While a small business might not be as attractive a target to a hacker such as a large multinational bank, hackers know that small businesses usually leave the front door wide open.

Risk Aversion

Risk averse small business owners are similar to small businesses that are apathetic about installing SBS. Apathetic small business owners know they have a need—they'll just putting the SBS project on the back burner.

Risk averse small business owners also keep shuffling the implementation phase to the back burner, but for totally different reasons. They're truly terrified of what might happen if everything falls apart during the network installation. Fear of SBS being painful prevents the sign-off from taking place. This will often lead them to as such questions as "Won't it be hard to learn how to use? What if we become dependent on SBS and it stops working?" The SBS Console and administration wizards go a long way toward mitigating concerns about ease of management. In addition, Microsoft Product Support Services (PSS) has 7 × 24 telephone support available for SBS.

Some small business owners become risk averse because they think they might eventually outgrow the NOS suite. To help address this concern, Microsoft has a number of upgrade options available. (Full details are available at *www.microsoft.com/smallbusinessserver.*)

- **BackOffice Server 4.5**—If your client grows beyond the 50-PC limit of SBS 4.5, a growth path is available at discounted prices to licensed SBS 4.5 owners.

- **Full application upgrade**—If needed, your client can take advantage of special discounts for SBS 4.5 owners who need to upgrade to full versions of Exchange Server 5.5, SQL Server 7.0, and Windows NT Server 4.0.

- **Retaining special SBS 4.5 features**—If you upgrade any of the individual suite components or upgrade to the full version of BackOffice Server 4.5, your client's server will still retain the SBS-specific applications such as the SBS Console, Modem Sharing Service, and Fax Service.

- **Interoperability**—In addition to being able to add Windows NT Server 4.0 systems to an SBS 4.5 network, clients can add servers for NetWare, UNIX, and Microsoft Windows Terminal Server as well.

Other Tips for Overcoming Obstacles

- Don't jump to any conclusions without talking through your clients' concerns.

- If you're concerned that you might have missed a subtle nuance, ask for clarification.

- Show that you care and understand by repeating their questions as you address each issue.

- Take time to listen carefully to any objections. Think of it as an opportunity to provide additional information about your proposed solution.

- Be careful not to step on their toes as you work to overcome the obstacles.

Framing SBS in Terms of Return on Investment

You might be tempted to invoke some of our industry's favorite IT buzzwords such as total cost of ownership (TCO) and return on investment (ROI) to try to get some of your passionate points across. SBS VAPs, however, generally need to remember that their clients aren't Fortune 1000 IT managers, steeped in the lingo of GartnerGroup, Dataquest, and Forrester. Don't get me wrong. Small business owners are *very* interested in trying to keep their ongoing computer support costs as low as possible. They also expect to get an almost immediate big bang for the buck on their network investment. As their VAP, you need to get the small business owner thinking about these topics. Your challenge is how to do so without resorting to acronyms or analyst-speak.

"Understanding the Hot Buttons," an earlier section in this chapter, listed a number of leading questions you could ask to help a small business owner figure out what outgoing faxes really cost. On the most superficial level, the small business owner probably thinks the only cost of an outgoing fax is the purchase of the fax machine and the message unit or toll calls billed by the telephone company. With these questions in hand, you can guide the small business owner to a more complete understanding of the company's real expenses. Once you've established a ballpark estimate, you'll be in a much better position to tout the benefits of Fax Service in SBS 4.5.

Other discussion points can help your clients understand better their real costs of the status quo. When small business clients get a handle on some of these hidden costs or at least start to think in this framework, they'll find ultimately SBS to be a natural solution. Some of the possible discussion points include:

- How much do you spend each month on overnight letters with carriers such as FedEx, Airborne Express, and UPS?

- Who opens, sorts, and distributes the hundreds of orders you get each day mailed by customers? Who does the data entry? Of these typical customers, how many call in to check if their order was received? How many of them have PCs at home with Internet connections?

- Beside memos and price lists, what else do you need to get out on a regular basis? Newsletters? Bulletins from vendors? Competitive data? Vacation schedules? Benefits information? Company awards and meeting announcements?

- How many people in the company generate fax documents that go out to multiple recipients? Do you ever wonder why a crowd always gathers by the fax machine?

The answers to these questions will help you guide your talks. The important thing to keep in mind is that the answers to nearly every one of these questions will be telltale signs for the need for company-wide and Internet e-mail, network-based faxing, an intranet, and an extranet or a more basic Web site.

Because the SBS solution includes Outlook 2000 and Exchange Server 5.5, you should ask other questions that will give clients tip-offs on how badly their firms need SBS. With the answers the clients give, you'll be in a much better position to discuss the benefits of shared Calendars, Contacts, and Tasks. Examples of questions you can ask include:

- How do people in the office keep track of each other's schedules? How do they schedule meetings, vacation time, or training sessions? How do you get that same information to your 10 field reps?

- Does each person have his or her own personal Rolodex file? How do staff members locate contact information for clients, leads, or vendors when someone's out of the office traveling or on vacation? Do multiple copies and versions of these contact lists exist in different programs on different PCs? How do you keep track of which one

What Does It Really Cost to Send Out 100 or 500 Copies of a Price List?

You might also want to ask the small business owner about the true costs of disseminating documents. Here's an excerpt from a typical conversation:

Josh (the SBS VAP): "What does it cost to distribute your price lists internally today? Externally?"

Pat (the small business owner): "Well, gee, Josh. There's toner and paper for the laser printers and photocopy machines. Then if we're sending the information out to vendors or customers, there's envelopes and postage."

Josh: "Okay. But when a memo is printed out that needs to go to the entire company, how do you get that document to the 25 employees in the main office and the other 10 in the field?"

Pat: "Ohhh. Well my assistant, Leslie, walks around and passes out the memo to each person. Then she'll fax the document right away to all 10 reps in the field. It couldn't possibly take more than a half hour, maybe one hour tops."

Josh smiles to himself, thinking, *Hmmmm. Time for the Exchange Server/Outlook 2000 pitch.* "And what if the same letter or announcement needs to go out to your top 100 customers?"

Pat: "Well, we do that about once a month. Leslie will run a set of labels from her Microsoft Works database. Then she'll collate the various mailing pieces and insert the contents into the big envelopes. She adds mailing labels and postage. Then she'll drive them right over to the post office. It maybe takes her four to six hours tops. Sometimes the vendors give us co-op dollars to send out other mailers during the month. Many months we send the same type of mailers out to our 500 largest international customers. If we're really busy getting mailings ready, Leslie has my *carte blanche* to get the inside sales reps and managers to pitch in with the envelope stuffing."

Josh: "Have you ever taken a survey to see how many of your customers have e-mail and Internet access?"

Pat: "Oh, yeah. We've never done a survey per se. But we do get those requests every so often. I usually tell customers that we're too small for that stuff."

Josh makes a mental note: *Customers might prefer to get these bulletins by e-mail and Web site extranets, but Pat thinks this all costs too much or is too complicated. I'll wait to talk about e-mail and database-driven Web sites until I find out how many tens of thousands of dollars a year in clerical time is being spent just on envelope stuffing.*

is more current? How do you get up-to-date information to everyone in the office? How do the field reps get access to the information?

- How do you know what major project tasks each person and department is working on at any given time? How do you know what's on each plate? How do you revise existing tasks and add new ones to each list? How do you keep track of what's pending and what's been completed?

Common Selling Scenarios

What are some common preexisting network solutions that you're likely to encounter in small businesses? What are the entrenched NOS products that you'll be forced to compare with SBS? How can you position SBS relative to these alternatives?

Sneakernet Environment

Unlike Fortune 1000 companies, many of the SBS prospects you encounter will still be lacking even the most basic networks. They're running Nikenet. In case you haven't heard the terms Nikenet or sneakernet before, they refer to the way data is passed between computers. In this type of setup, when my boss wants a copy of the Word document that I'm working on, I save it to a disk and literally walk it over the boss. So in a way, the speed of the network is dependent on how fast you can run or how good your sneakers are.

Many SBS VAPs compare small businesses without networks that are moving to SBS to third-world countries that are just getting phone service for the first time. In many parts of the world, remote areas that never had telephones are getting service delivered wirelessly, totally bypassing the infrastructure needed for copper lines and local loops. Thus, the first phones the people in those areas have are cell phones.

In much the same way, someone who's never experienced the inherent limitations of a peer-to-peer network might have difficulty truly appreciating what SBS brings to the table. For companies without preexisting networks, focus on pitching the main benefits of SBS as outlined in earlier sections of this chapter. Depending on the technical level requested by the small business decision-maker and the internal guru, you might also want to bring up some of the pro-SBS arguments used in peer-to-peer Windows 95/98 environments.

Peer-to-Peer Windows 95/98 Environment

What are some of the biggest ways SBS shines in comparison to an existing Windows 95/98 environment? For starters, a peer-to-peer Windows 95/98 network means that someone will be using the server as his or her primary PC. Even when usage is light or the PC is dedicated to being the server, small businesses often use peer-to-peer networks to keep costs down.

As a result, the hardware is almost never server class. This means the original implementer was likely to cut corners in terms of the size and reliability of the power supply; the fault tolerance, performance, reliability of the RAM and hard drives; the tape backup solution; and the power protection and the antivirus solutions.

When a small business has a Windows 95/98 PC as its server, you'll often see a single IDE hard disk being used instead of a RAID array of SCSI hard disks. This means if the single hard disk fails, all data will be lost. The system has zero fault tolerance. Because IDE is designed to be a low-cost PC-based technology, performance will suffer as usage scales and more disk-intensive applications are introduced.

With a peer-to-peer network, you have essentially an entire office of network administrators to support or with which to contend. Everyone can set up his or her own shared folders, printers, and CD-ROMs. This situation can become an enormous nightmare in terms of securing and protecting the data. With this type of setup, the server is also more prone to accidental midday reboots and lockups, as the user of that PC puts the system through its daily trials and tribulations. If the small business owner thinks the current peer-to-peer solution is adequate, take time to ask the following:

❑ How is data backed up, verified, and restored? What kind of tape rotation and off-site storage plan are in place for each server?

❑ How is security applied for each server? Does the entire company share one password? What happens when the password is leaked out or when someone is terminated? How do you differentiate between what everyone needs access to and what only specific people should have access to (public vs. private files)? Are you aware Windows 95/98 isn't designed to be a secure operating system, and the passwords are basically meaningless?

❑ How much is the data on the server worth to the business? If the server were down for four hours during the workday, what would be the impact on the business? What about one full day? What about one week? What if the data were unrecoverable?

❏ How is Internet access set up today? What happens when people need to go to a vendor or customer Web site? What happens when people need to send or receive e-mail? Does the entire company share just one e-mail address? How are productivity and security concerns addressed? Have you started installing a separate modem, ISP dial-up account, and analog line for each person who needs Internet access? Isn't this going to get expensive after a while? Aren't you concerned about security ramifications with the many potential points of entry into your firm?

With an SBS network, data storage, tape backup, security, folder and file sharing, and auditing are all centralized. This generally makes the network much easier to administer and the data much easier to protect. In addition, having the entire office share resources such as network faxing, company and Internet e-mail, and high-speed Web browsing becomes cost-effective.

NetWare Environment

When selling SBS into a small business that already has a NetWare network, begin by determining which version of NetWare is being run. If the company had NetWare installed more than two or three years ago, the firm is more than likely running NetWare 3.1x for basic file and printer sharing. To add more services such as a secure, shared gateway to the Internet for Web browsing, e-mail, groupware, or Web sites, you're almost always looking at investing in additional software and hardware. For a small business with NetWare, focus on explaining what comes in the box with SBS 4.5 without having to purchase additional software.

Tip

For competitive information that compares Windows NT Server and SBS to various versions of Novell NetWare, see the Microsoft Direct Access Web site at *www.microsoft.com/directaccess*.

SBS also includes a rich set of tools for migrating from NetWare. If need be, SBS can also coexist with NetWare. Running SBS alongside of NetWare might be required if your client has an application that requires NetWare and that has no Windows NT or BackOffice Server compatible equivalent. For most modern industry-specific applications, ISVs make the effort to insure their applications run on both platforms. Nevertheless, you can add the NWLink or IPX protocol to interoperate with NetWare servers in addition to TCP/IP, which SBS installs by default.

Gateway Services for NetWare (GSNW), when used in conjunction with the NWLink protocol, allows the SBS system to communicate with NetWare servers as a NetWare client. Once the Windows NT Server 4.0 portion of SBS is configured for GSNW, SBS clients communicate with the NetWare server through a single connection on the SBS system. The SBS clients can reach the NetWare server without the need to run two protocol stacks and client software redirectors.

If your client's desktop PCs are already configured for IPX/SPX, File and Print Services for NetWare (FPNW) can be installed on the SBS system to make SBS look like a NetWare server to NetWare clients.

So how do you decide when to migrate from NetWare vs. when to run the two servers side by side? As mentioned above, if your client needs a niche application that's only compatible with NetWare *and* there are no industry-specific or off-the-shelf alternatives, running side-by-side might be the best and only course of action. If you can help your small business client migrate to SBS, however, they'll get many benefits including centralized security, administration, tape backups, and user account maintenance.

The Migration Tool for NetWare is installed automatically when GSNW is installed. This utility can help you migrate users, groups, files, and directories. In order to use the Migration Tool for NetWare, the NetWare server must either be version 2.x, 3.x, or running in bindery emulation mode. For more details on usage of GSNW, FPNW, or the Migration Tool for Netware, see the Microsoft TechNet Web site at *www.microsoft.com/technet*.

NetWare vs. Windows NT in the Small Business Market

An August 1998 report in *Aaron Goldberg's InfoBead Insider*, "LANs in Small Business: Not a Rare Occurrence," points out how roughly 65 percent of small businesses in the United States have LANs of some sort, where "NT and NetWare are ruling the roost."

The report also identifies that during the past year the market share for Windows NT in small business is up while NetWare's market share is dropping.

In addition, the report points to lesser players in the small business networking arena: UnixWare, OS/2, LANtastic, and Macintosh.

Macintosh Environment

How do you pitch SBS to a small business that already has a sizable investment in Apple Macintosh technology? For starters, unless small business owners tell you specifically that they're open to talking about replacing Macs with PCs, don't go there. By 2000, if the small businesses are still running their organizations on Macs, chances are the firm is *extremely* committed to the platform. Although it often defies logic, Mac users' loyalty has been compared to the type of devotion of cult members or religious zealots. Given the monumental effort required to convince the small business owners to send the Macs to the Dumpster and order across-the-board PC replacements, you need to focus on how SBS can fit into their existing network infrastructure.

Many small businesses with Macs also have PCs. In an advertising agency for example, the creative staff might be wedded to Macs while the back office accounting and operations staff runs their day-to-day applications on PCs. In this type of environment, you can position SBS to bridge the two platforms. Focus on how Mac clients can make use of many of the core SBS 4.5 services such as the following:

- **Windows NT Server 4.0 Services for Macintosh (SFM)** is included with SBS 4.5 and lets you share files and printers. With SFM, the SBS system functions as an AppleTalk router. Perhaps the best part of SFM is Mac clients don't need any special software.

- **Outlook for Macintosh** messaging client can be ordered for a nominal fee through Microsoft Inside Sales (for details see the SBS Web site at *www.microsoft.com/smallbusinessserver*). Using this Mac-compatible client, you can send and receive e-mail through the SBS 4.5 Exchange Server 5.5.

- **Internet Explorer Macintosh Edition** can be used by end users with Mac clients to browse the Web through Proxy Server 2.0.

Note

Only three major SBS services aren't available to Mac clients: Modem Sharing Service, Fax Service, and Remote Access Service (RAS).

The Bottom Line

Whether or not you're a great schmoozer, you need to adopt some type of sales style with which you feel comfortable. My goal in this chapter was to give you the tools to succeed in selling to small business decision-makers, speaking to their hot buttons, overcoming common objections, and relating your message to bottom-line savings. At the most basic level, this involves analyzing your client's requirements and crafting a cost-effective solution. It also includes positioning SBS 4.5 in various small business environments where entrenched, competitive solutions exist.

Transforming the Technology Roadmap into the Project Plan

After uncovering the needs of a small business with the technology roadmap and successfully pitching Microsoft BackOffice Small Business Server 4.5 as the centerpiece of the solution, SBS VAPs need to transform these goals into concrete, manageable tasks. This chapter will help you assemble the project to do list and create the documents that will ultimately comprise the project plan packet.

Chapter 9 begins with an overview of what some typical SBS VAPs include in their network design and specification documents. Next, the chapter covers how to use the IT audit and site surveys from Chapter 7 to develop a desktop standardization plan, project timetable, and cost estimates. During these early stages of the SBS rollout, discussing any potential problems and establishing what areas are your firm's responsibility vs. what areas are the client's responsibility is crucial.

The next section of the chapter deals with product issues. In particular, it looks at how to select the hardware, software, and peripherals for the project plan packet. The topics include hardware standardization, network cabling, data protection, licensing, and securing price quotes. The final section of this chapter deals with selecting an Internet service provider (ISP) and telecommunications lines.

Tip

For more detailed information on selecting an ISP, and making use of the "ISP Selection Matrix" template on the CD-ROM, see Chapter 18.

Drafting the Documents

I've introduced several documents in this book that are part of the technology roadmap phase of the project. (All of the documents are included on the CD-ROM for this book.) The following list summarizes these documents in the order they are most commonly implemented:

1. **"Letter of Engagement for Initial Consultation"** (Word template) clarifies the scope, deliverables, and fees for the initial consultation. Even more importantly, the document spells out which items are beyond the scope of this relatively low-cost initial analysis.

Tip

The "Letter of Engagement for Initial Consultation" should be *the* first document delivered to the prospect or client. It helps to instill the idea that your firm gets paid for objective, professional advice and *isn't* in the business of providing free advice that only benefits competitors.

---

2. **"Roadmap Template for SBS Network"** (Excel workbook) helps you plan, at a high level, the project areas that will need closer examination, including the number of existing and required desktop PCs, laptops, servers, and network end users. The roadmap workbook also functions as a checklist of 20 distinct project phase areas and organizes the areas into three categories: current (what the client has today), planned (what needs to be implemented in the initial SBS rollout), and future (what the client is considering adding at some point in the near future).

3. **"IT Audit Opportunity"** (HTML document) is one of my "VAPVoice: Notes from the Field" columns from the Microsoft Direct Access Web site (*www.microsoft.com/directaccess*). This docu-

ment takes you through 10 key areas to cover in a basic IT audit of a small business. You should use the topic list in this column in conjunction with the roadmap template as the basis for organizing your questions and agenda items for the initial consultation.

Tip

Covering the topics broached in the roadmap template and IT audit column is often the difference between a sales call and a true billable, in-depth initial consultation.

4. **"Summary of Findings from Initial Consultation Meeting"** (Word template) spells out high-level goals and objectives for the project, defines the problem, lays out high-level preliminary technical requirements, red flags any contingencies, identifies key contacts, and summarizes your professional credentials.

5. **"Letter of Engagement for Network Design"** (Word template) itemizes the next steps beyond the initial consultation, establishes hourly estimates for each task, and moves the project from a fixed-price overview analysis to a more in-depth, billed-by-the-hour examination of what it'll take to implement all of the client's needs.

6. **"Site Survey Inventory (Word)"** (Word template) should be customized for your firm's specific needs and printed out before you go to the client site to perform site surveys of the hardware, software applications, and system configurations.

7. **"Site Survey Inventory (Excel)"** (Excel workbook) can be used either in conjunction with the "Site Survey Inventory (Word)" or as an electronic replacement. With this workbook loaded on your laptop and customized for your firm's specific needs, you can capture all the information in a format that can be reused and revised for additional future needs.

Tip

You might even want to use the "Site Survey Inventory (Excel)" workbook as the basis for building a Microsoft Access database for storing all of your clients' site survey and inventory data.

8. **"30-Point PC Security Check-Up"** (Word template) should be customized for your specific needs and printed out before going on-site to the client. The "Check-Up" helps you uncover the adequacy of the client's data backup, disaster recovery planning, security, power protection, and virus protection.

9. **"Quarterly Update Report"** (Word template) summarizes your existing client's current high-level standards, projects in progress and projects completed in the quarter, and projects planned to start.

For detailed explanations of how each document fits into the technology roadmap, see Chapter 7.

Designing the Network and Detailing the Specifications

As you review the information you recorded in the "Summary of Findings from the Initial Consultation Meeting" and your notes from the "Site Survey Inventory" and "30-Point PC Security Check-Up," you'll be able to begin visualizing and synthesizing some of the key elements that need to be included in your network design report. In preparing this report, you'll definitely want to use the above documents and any additional notes as the basis for making sure you've covered all bases.

Tip

Because the details are so crucial when writing a thorough network design report, I usually photocopy the existing documents (as prepared in Chapter 7) and either check off or highlight each line item as I incorporate data into the report.

For example, if the IT audit reveals three employees need to work daily on a top secret, mission critical Access database application, the network will need the security of both Microsoft Windows NT Workstation and Server, a very reliable tape backup solution, and a server-grade UPS (uninterruptible power supply). If the technology roadmap reveals that Internet e-mail for each employee is a high priority, then planning how to implement Microsoft Proxy Server and some type of dial-up or permanent connection to an ISP becomes an integral part of the network design.

Before you begin writing your network design report, review all of the documents prepared thus far, as well as any additional notes, and seek out any potential holes or areas of ambiguity that need clarification. Once you've amassed this shortened list of discussion points, review the following topics one more time with the client:

- ❑ What's the single biggest need driving the project?

- ❑ What are the client's top three expectations of what the network needs to be able to provide once the rollout is completed?

- ❑ What are the client's top three industry-specific concerns that need to be addressed?

- ❑ What are three most important software applications already in use that need to continue being used?

- ❑ What's the approximate budget for the initial rollout? For what timeframe is the budget available? Will budgetary reasons dictate a more phased rollout? Who has the final authority to approve the project kickoff?

- ❑ Do any underlying business or scheduling reasons exist that would drive a certain start or completion date?

To help you organize your network design report, the CD-ROM includes an Excel workbook, "Network Design Report," with four worksheets:

- "Summary of Users List"
- "Supported Application Matrix"
- "Time Budget"
- "Materials Budget"

Nailing Down the User List

Until now, you've asked the small business owner or main decision-maker for a ballpark idea of how many end users need access to the planned SBS network. Once you begin amassing an actual user list for your network design report, however, your initial estimate likely will be revised upward.

The "Summary of Users List," which is shown in Figure 9-1 on the next page, should spell out, quite literally, the following information about users:

- The first and last name of all potential SBS network users (This includes users with and without their own PC.)

- A summary of their current hardware specifications (brand of computer, CPU speed, hard drive size, and RAM)

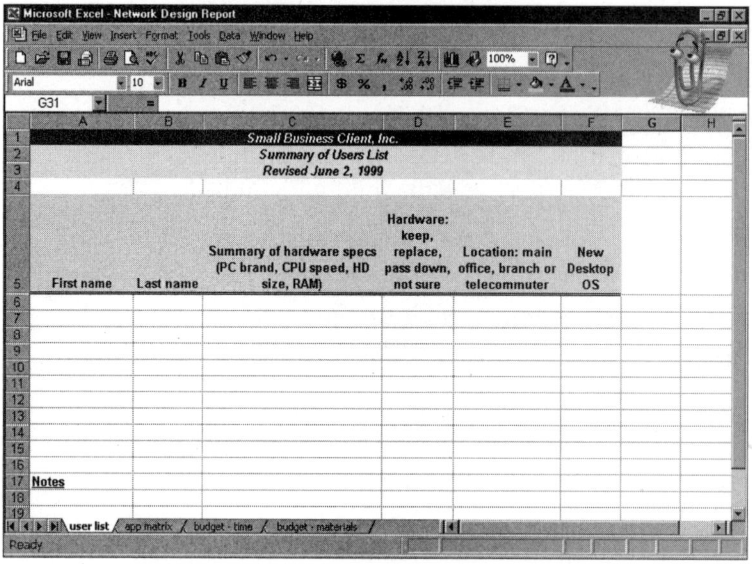

Figure 9-1

The "Summary of Users List" will help you and your client to start finalizing decisions for each individual SBS end user.

- Whether their hardware will be kept, replaced with new hardware, or passed down to someone else *and* replaced with new hardware, or whether no one is sure what to do with the hardware at this point

- Location of the users, such as the main office on the LAN or a branch or home office through dial-up networking

- Designation of which desktop OS each user will have in place on the new network (If at all possible considering application and budgetary constraints, you should try to use Windows NT Workstation 4.0 across the board for increased security, performance, and reliability.)

Fleshing Out the List of Supported Applications

Nothing is more frustrating than starting an SBS rollout and having the client inject, "Oh, by the way, we need the network to run this _____ application."

Just as the "Summary of Users List" helps you bring to the surface any end users overlooked during the early planning stages (the stragglers), the "Supported Application Matrix," an Excel worksheet shown in Figure 9-2, helps you find stray software programs required by any end user on the SBS network. Knowing that these programs exist is particularly important for both licensing and compatibility concerns. In addition, being aware of these pro-

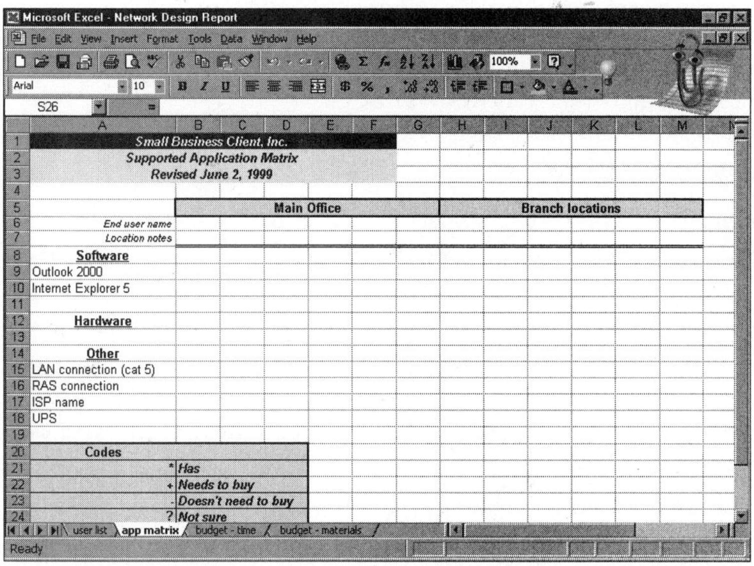

Figure 9-2

The "Supported Application Matrix" will help you identify and hopefully prevent expensive change orders during the project rollout.

grams from the start helps you to avoid making last minute changes to your plans just to accommodate these stray software programs, changes that can be quite time consuming for your firm. As a result, many SBS VAPs charge some kind of fee for change orders. (This topic is addressed in Chapter 10.)

The "Supported Application Matrix" organizes the end user by location (main office vs. branch offices). For each end user on the network, you'll need to list his or her relationship with various software programs, hardware devices, and other pertinent resources. At the bottom of the worksheet, a legend helps you assign each person one of the following statuses using a symbol:

*   for Has (the user already has a certain program, device, or other resource)

+   for Needs to buy (the user needs a certain program, device, or other resource)

−   for Doesn't need to buy (the user doesn't have or need a certain program, device, or other resource)

?   for Not sure (no one is sure whether the user needs a certain program, device, or other resource)

Like the "Summary of Users List," this matrix isn't meant to be the be-all, end-all worksheet. The "Supported Application Matrix," however, should help you and the client flesh out who needs what.

Estimating the Labor Cost

With a firm handle on how many end users will be on the network and what applications need to be supported, you can now estimate how many hours of labor will be required for each phase of the rollout. The "Time Budget" Excel worksheet, shown in Figure 9-3, has two main groups of columns: "Budgeted Hours" and "Timeline Planning." The first column in the first group, which is also called "Budgeted Hours," lists the total hours estimated for each phase and distinct task. A running total of billable hours incurred is listed in the "Billed Through" column. "Estimated Balance" is simply the difference between "Budgeted Hours" and "Billed Through."

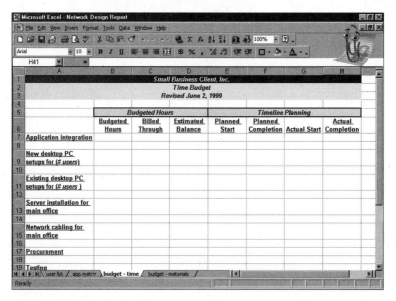

Figure 9-3

The "Time Budget" worksheet can be used to estimate hours of labor required for each phase, to track how each phase is progressing against the budget, and to organize each phase into a calendar or schedule.

Because of these columns, the "Time Budget" worksheet is useful well beyond the "Network Design Report." This worksheet is a great planning tool to use throughout the rollout to help you give status updates to the client on how your firm is progressing against the budget. The "Time Budget" can also be a great way to red flag potential problems before they snowball into major dilemmas.

For example, let's say you've budgeted 12 hours for working with the client's applications. Because of one particularly troublesome industry-specific application, you've incurred 8 hours already and you've barely scratched the surface. Tracking time this way is great for keeping your client in the loop. "Look Pat, I know we budgeted 12 hours for application integration; however, that one bar-code application is a lot more challenging to configure than we could've ever anticipated. Do you have a contact at the software vendor we can speak with? Do you know of any other companies like yours running this application that we could speak with? Do you want to consider an alternative?" Regardless of which direction you and the client mutually agree to pursue to resolve the problem, tracking budgeted hours against incurred hours helps to clarify how the project is proceeding against budget. (Project management techniques will be explored in detail in Chapter 11.)

The other group of columns in the "Time Budget" worksheet, "Timeline Planning," helps track when each phase is planned to start and to complete and compares these dates to the actual start and actual completion dates. While not meant for budgeting per se, these columns will be the basis for preparing a project timetable, or calendar of events if you will, for the rollout.

The "Time Budget" is also organized horizontally into rows for each distinct project phase. These phases include:

- Application integration
- New desktop PC setups for (# *users*)
- Existing desktop PC setups for (# *users*)
- Server installation for main office
- Network cabling for main office
- Procurement
- Testing
- Training
- Documentation

As appropriate, you should add itemized tasks below each major project phase heading that are specific to your client engagement. In addition, you might end up shuffling the order of the phases depending on individual clients' needs.

Estimating the Materials Cost

Once you've prepared the "Time Budget" and factored in some kind of cushion reserve factor, you'll be able to give your client a labor estimate by simply multiplying your hourly billing rate by the total budgeted hours. Your labor should have a relatively high profit margin. The profit margin on the labor or consulting services is the difference between what the client pays your firm and what you pay your employees.

In sharp contrast to the profitable nature of providing consulting services, reselling hardware, software, and peripherals is many times a business proposition that barely breaks even. Chapter 5 delved into this topic.

Because many SBS VAPs are avoiding the business of reselling products and because the profit margins are so different than service margins, the "Network Design Report" workbook includes a separate worksheet, "Materials Budget," for estimating product costs and other related items.

The "Materials Budget" worksheet, shown in Figure 9-4, helps you forecast expenses for desktop PCs, server, software, peripherals, telco and ISP accounts, and network cabling. In addition to a column for indicating the vendor who's supplying the materials (whether it's your firm or another), the worksheet has a group of "Timeline Planning" columns as well. The "Materials Budget" worksheet has a timeline that's separate from the "Time Budget" worksheet because different materials have varying lead times. For example, you might need only one week's lead time for acquiring software and peripherals; however, certain types of telco accounts might take six to eight weeks to set up.

Assembling the Worksheets into a Report

No matter how concisely you present your network design report, your client will have a lot to review. You can use the "Network Design Cover Sheet," a Word document included on the CD-ROM, to provide a one-page summary of what's included in your network design report. The "Network Design Cover Sheet," which is shown in Figure 9-5, also helps to finalize your deliverables and synthesizes the worksheets into a format that'll be easily accessible for review purposes throughout the SBS rollout.

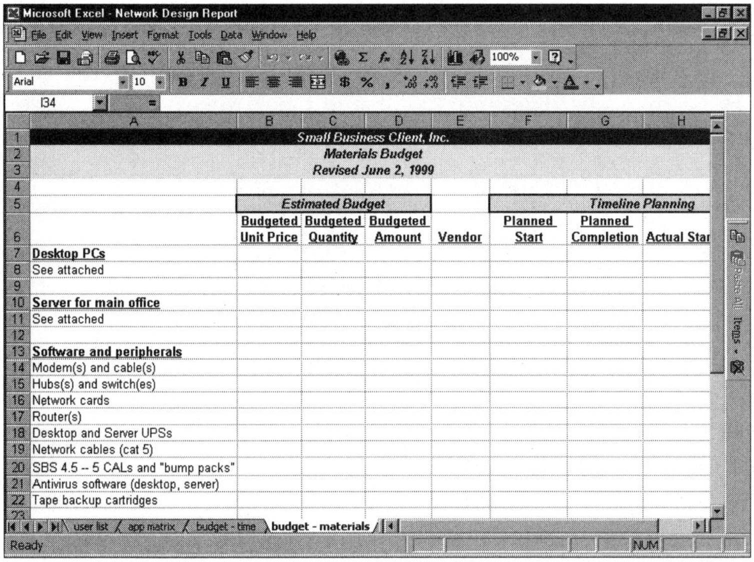

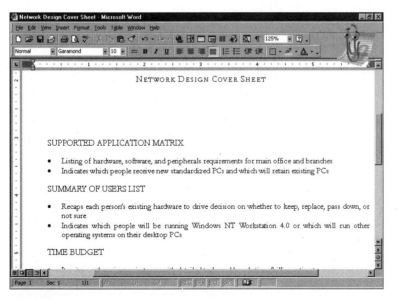

Figure 9-4

The "Materials Budget" should be used to estimate costs, indicate selected vendors, and plan timelines for ordering materials.

Figure 9-5

The "Network Design Cover Sheet" should be used to encapsulate your network design report and other hard-copy deliverables.

Using the Results of the IT Audit

Now that you have assembled the deliverables that comprise the network design report, you're ready to develop the plan to standardize desktops. Much like the way you needed to educate the small business owner on the benefits of proactive technology planning, desktop standardization will require you to educate the client up front.

In reality, desktop standardization is nothing more than an extension of proactive planning. Let's take a fairly typical small business. It has eleven desktop PCs from eight different PC OEMs, with four different desktop operating systems, six different word processing applications, and five different network cards. Now think about what this firm's cost would be for an annual support contract with your firm.

New SBS VAPs and small business owners might think desktop standardization is only useful for large Fortune 1000 IT departments. Once your small business client has grown beyond four or five desktop PCs, however, desktop standardization has huge benefits, including:

- Training and help desk support is much easier.

- You can roll out a dozen or more fully configured desktops in a day or two, as opposed to several days.

- You can restore corrupted desktops to their original, standardized state in a matter of minutes.

Then consider a small business down the street, which was just set up by your firm with a new SBS network. This other firm has eleven PCs as well, but its newly installed base is virtually identical, with each desktop PC having 64 MB RAM, 8-GB hard drives, Pentium II 400-MHz CPUs, Windows NT Workstation 4.0, and Microsoft Office 2000 Professional. As you can imagine, the firm with identical PCs has *much* lower support costs.

So why would you want to shoot yourself in the foot and recommend a solution that takes service dollars away from your firm? Because lack of desktop standardization causes downtime. You'll spend all of your time and your client's annual technology budget chasing down device drivers and patches when that time could be much better spent providing more value-added, higher-level services.

Think about services that provide a bigger bang for the buck (or ROI) for your client and services for which you can easily justify charging a higher rate. Would your client rather pay your billing rates for tracking down video drivers or for building a database-driven Web site?

Once you've sold your clients on the benefits of desktop standardization, you'll need to develop a basic plan. Automating the desktop rollout is the focus in Chapter 12. If you've been using the CD-ROM templates and worksheets for Chapters 7 and 9, the desktop standardization discussion and decision should be very straightforward. The "Supported Application Matrix," a worksheet in the "Network Design Report" on the CD-ROM, can serve as the basis for the plan to standardize desktop PCs.

Tip

Many SBS VAPs also add value to the desktop standardization efforts by implementing system policies that restrict user access to various operating system functions. System policies prevent end users from tampering with their configuration settings and installing unauthorized software that might introduce system instability, lockups, viruses, and licensing violations (all of which are potentially very expensive propositions).

Preparing the Initial Project Timetable

Before you can prepare the initial project timetable, you need to recognize the stigma associated with deadlines within our profession. IT projects are notoriously late and over budget. That's no excuse, however, to adopt a *laissez-faire* attitude about the situation. By preparing a time and materials budget with well thought-out, detailed phases and specific tasks, you'll be able to forecast the projected starting and ending dates with much greater accuracy.

Revising the "Time Budget" and "Materials Budget" worksheets every few days during the course of the rollout project is crucial. In particular, you'll need to document in the "Notes" section of each worksheet any dates and phases that are pushed back and the reasons for the delay.

Establishing realistic dates for implementation of deliverables at the outset might seem obvious, but it bears repeating. Although you might be tempted to give in to your client's wishes that you complete the rollout sooner, you'll need to set up a schedule for staff members or at least have a rough idea of their availability before you can commit to deadlines.

Also, make sure your client is aware the clock begins ticking when the contract is signed. If the planned completion date for the final phase is September 1, based on a May 1 start date, you have a four-month schedule with which to contend. So if your client sits on the letter of engagement and doesn't give you the retainer until July 1, the planned completion target date should be moved to November 1.

You also need to warn your clients that the four-month timeline estimate you're providing is based on staff availability at the time the document is prepared. If the client doesn't execute the project for two months, your four-month timeline might need to be adjusted to five months or six months if you've taken on large projects during the interim.

Tip

Small business owners are notorious for wanting to believe that they are your *only* client. Make sure to take whatever subtle, or not so subtle, steps are necessary to show the client that, although you value the business, you're not going to ask how high when they demand that you jump.

Estimating Costs

Regardless of how much buy-in you receive from the client on the value of proactive technology planning; the small business owner is always going to be intently interested in the bottom-line cost. Be prepared, though. Once the client has an idea of the project cost, the client will either love or hate the estimate.

The cost estimate numbers, however, shouldn't be sticker shock at this late stage of the game. During the initial consultation, you'll have a very rough idea of preliminary hardware and software requirements. You'll refine and detail those preliminary estimates during the network design phase. Because the network design phase is fee based at your prevailing hourly billing rates, this pricing model will have already been dismissed by many small businesses who don't have the foresight to invest in a professionally installed network.

Record estimated labor costs in the "Time Budget." This worksheet lists the number of hours of labor for each phase and task of the project. Some SBS VAPs list their hourly billing rates for the rollout project and the resulting project consulting fees right on the "Time Budget." Other SBS VAPs assume this worksheet might be shared with people on staff or other parties who shouldn't be privy to the hourly billing rate that you've negotiated with the client. For this reason, you might want to formalize the hourly billing rate on the letter of engagement for the rollout, which is discussed in Chapter 10.

Note

Some SBS VAPs don't bill out their labor by the hour, but rather base their fees on a fixed-price bid. Adopting either method has many pros and cons. Because I've found more success with billing by the hour as have most of the VAPs in the focus group for this book, the templates on the CD-ROM assume you're billing your small business clients by the hour.

Most SBS VAPs will add some kind of cushion factor to their estimate through either a separate line item or within the estimate itself. This is to help plan a little for the unexpected. In most cases, you'll want to hit the time budget estimates in your network design report or come in a little below. If you're going to exceed the estimates, you must discuss this with your client as early as possible. By establishing the framework of a time budget with weekly or bi-weekly updates, you should be able to get a strong pulse on how your firm is progressing against the time budget.

Many clients truly appreciate receiving schedule updates with their invoices or during regularly scheduled progress meetings. Unpleasant news is never easy to convey. By advising your client about the problem as early as possible, you'll go a long way toward preventing rifts. Because estimated costs are truly *estimated* costs, the name of the game is keeping your client in the loop about any anticipated budget overruns or scheduling delays.

By now you should've decided whether your firm is reselling products for this project or whether you'll simply advise clients on where to purchase their hardware, software, and peripherals. The "Materials Budget" worksheet should reflect this information. The "Notes" section at the bottom of the "Materials Budget" worksheet states that prices, specifications, and availability on products fluctuate daily. Make sure that your client is aware of this fact. The longer the client waits to give you the go-ahead, the greater the chance you'll need to spend some additional (*billable*) time reconfirming prices and availability.

The "Materials Budget" is directly impacted by how much existing hardware, software, and peripherals the client is able to continue using. On the hardware front, site surveys and the "Summary of Users List" will help to force the decisions about which PCs should be kept, replaced, and passed down to other users. You also need to find out whether the applications the small business is using are 32-bit, SBS-compatible, and require version upgrades and whether the client is legally licensed for their usage. If any of these software questions send up any red flags, stop. Do not pass Go. Do not collect $200. These issues *must* be ironed out. Ignoring them could derail the project midstream.

Red Flagging Potential Obstacles

Getting a handle on all potential obstacles and contingencies before you and the client sign on the dotted line is important. To help stem potential problems, try to gather as much information as possible up front. The goal is to prevent unpleasant surprises.

To help cover your bases, read and reread all of the memos, notes, and deliverables that have been prepared for this project so far. In fact, if other staff members from your firm will be involved, have one of them take a second glance at the recommendations. Make sure no loose ends need to be tied up. The worksheets and documents you've prepared might contain various notes and assumptions. If a specific note or notes are mission critical to the project, you might want to have the client specifically initial a sentence or two to indicate that he or she has read the clause *and* just as important, understood its meaning and the impact on the project. Other more project specific areas that are worth double-checking include:

❑ Can ISDN or other high-speed Internet access options be installed at the client's location? You might need to check with multiple telco providers and ISPs to get the answer. Don't forget to budget some additional research time if you feel this could be an issue.

❑ Is the client allowed to install category 5 cables for the Ethernet connections in the walls and ceilings? Some landlords and building regulations prohibit this.

Tip

Some local building ordinances also require that the category 5 cable have a plenum coating. In the event of a fire, the cable won't spread fire in the dropped ceiling.

❑ Have all of the software applications that your client has requested or recommended for inclusion in the network design been checked out yet or tested by your firm? Depending on how critical the application is, you might want to insist on getting an evaluation copy from the ISV for testing both in your lab for technical issues and at the client location for business issues.

❑ Does your network design report contain software, hardware, and peripherals that are bleeding edge? If so, make sure your client is aware of this issue. With very few exceptions, small businesses are definitely not the place to try out bleeding edge technologies.

Tip

A leading edge application is one that's generally considered very current or the latest and greatest. An extreme case of the leading edge application is bleeding edge, where you're so close to the edge that you may get a little nicked or cut in the process of deployment.

❑ Are the client's existing industry and custom applications SBS-compatible? In nearly all cases, if the application carries the Microsoft BackOffice compatible logo, the application will be fully compatible with SBS.

❑ Are other consulting firms involved in the project? If so, communication should be a top priority. Also, you'll need to figure out some checkpoints to make sure you can assess their quality of workmanship. The last thing your client needs is finger-pointing.

Tip

As mentioned in Chapter 6, you need to ascertain who are the proper contact people at the other technology vendors involved with the project.

❑ Is custom programming being done during this same timeframe? If your firm is doing the development, be careful with incurring more billable hours than are budgeted. If someone else is developing custom applications, be suspicious of compatibility issues until you have verified compatibility.

❑ Are products in use that might cause a problem? The typical culprits include devices such $29 flatbed scanners and $19 modems. Nonbranded hardware is often liquidated at bargain basement prices for good reason. While your fears could be totally unfounded, a healthy dose of skepticism can't hurt. If you sense trouble, add some clauses to the letter of engagement to protect yourself.

Identifying Client vs. VAP Responsibilities

Some small business clients will want to take a very active role in the SBS networking project. The small business owner and staff will listen intently to your every word, will read and reread your written documents about deliverables multiple times, and have some well thought-out questions waiting for you at each and every meeting. Other small business clients will take a totally hands-off approach. If you get the "just send me the bill" attitude, tread carefully, very carefully.

Most small business clients take a stance without realizing it that's somewhere between an active role and a hands off approach. They want to know what's going on and they want to learn about networking issues to a certain degree, but they recognize that certain tasks are best left to experts. Because of this inherent neither here nor there attitude, make sure your clients are aware of what you're expecting from them beside prompt payment. Some typical client responsibilities include:

- Helping you prepare the user lists and lists of supported applications

- Providing installation media and license agreements for any applications that need to be migrated to the SBS 4.5 network

- Devising user groups and file folder structure for the server shares (They'll need to specify the user groups and folder structure on paper before your firm can implement them.)

- Figuring out who belongs in various e-mail distribution lists

- Being receptive to end-user and administrator training when appropriate (detailed in Chapter 20)

Product Issues

As you move from the technology roadmap to a more definitive project plan, you'll need to start finalizing which hardware, software, and peripherals need to be purchased. The "Materials Budget" worksheet will help you consolidate this information and present it for simplified review and discussion with your small business client. As you begin to gather information to complete the "Materials Budget," you'll want to be aware of some areas of concern:

- The type of hardware on which to standardize

- How to handle data cabling needs

- What type of data protection solutions to implement

- How best to license SBS

Standardizing Hardware: Clones vs. Branded PCs

Regardless of whether your firm assumes the traditional reseller role or not, you'll be called upon for a PC brand recommendation. Some SBS VAPs feel the best choice for small business desktops and servers is a clone or white box system. Clones are PCs that are assembled from brand-name components, but lack a brand-name vendor for the overall system. On the other hand, many SBS VAPs think that the best course of action for small businesses is to purchase desktop and server hardware from top tier brand-name vendors, such as Compaq, Dell, Gateway, Hewlett-Packard, or IBM.

Regardless of whether you're a believer in branded PCs or in clones, client hardware selection criteria shouldn't be taken lightly. Cutting corners on hardware can create major support problems later. More often than not, small businesses decide upon which PCs to buy by the price tag alone. In most cases, however, consumer PCs bundled with TV tuner cards, speakerphones, and other multimedia gizmos don't necessarily make the best desktop productivity clients on an SBS network.

Some SBS VAPs even insert clauses in their proposals, letters of engagement, or project plans to protect their firm from the fallout associated with substandard hardware. The basic idea is that if the client insists on substandard hardware, the client should be prepared to pay for additional support costs. Such a clause should also give your firm the option to walk off the job. Most small business clients will see these statements and acquiesce to your professionally grounded product recommendations. At the very least this type of protection demonstrates that sometimes you need to put your foot down to avoid being backed into a corner.

Regardless of whether you recommend white box or branded PCs and servers, you'll be able to provide support to your small business clients much easier if you have a consistent set of hardware standards installed at all of your SBS client sites. As mentioned earlier in this chapter, standardization lowers supports costs, makes deployment go much quicker and smoother, and allows for rapid recovery of corrupted builds and damaged hardware.

Identifying the Cabling to Be Installed

Network cabling is another major area of any SBS rollout and accordingly has a separate section in the "Materials Budget." Most SBS VAPs don't do the cabling themselves, but rather partner with, subcontract to, or just recommend a local firm that specializes in installing *and* certifying category 5 unshielded twisted pair (UTP) cabling.

As indicated in "Red Flagging Potential Obstacles" earlier in this chapter, make sure the client can put cabling through walls and ceilings. Even if the building owner has no restrictions regarding cabling, the construction of the building might make cabling difficult. Many small businesses are located in buildings originally designed for residential use. As a result, the cabling might be very difficult and expensive. This is the more reason SBS VAPs tend to rely on outside experts for cabling between the patch panel and desktop jacks.

If the cabling subcontractor hasn't done a site survey yet, most SBS VAPs insert a note in the "Materials Budget" that stipulates cabling costs are estimates that won't be finalized until after the cabling contractor's walk-through. Most

SBS VAPs will want to be present during the walk-through and, if possible, during the actual cabling work. While your small business clients certainly aren't going to pay your firm to baby-sit the cable contractor, questions often come up during the course of the cabling installation that only your firm can answer. Your best bet is to schedule yourself to be on-site doing a task such as preparing desktop PCs or the server during the cable installation.

Selecting a Tape Backup Solution, UPS, and Antivirus Software

Another major area of concern for your network design report and the "Materials Budget" worksheet is selecting the proper solutions to protect data. The site surveys and "30-Point PC Security Check-Up" will be very helpful as you begin to finalize your recommendations for data protection hardware, software, and peripherals, such as tape backup drives and associated software, uninterruptible power supplies (UPSs) and monitoring software, and antivirus software. SBS VAPs tend to be brand loyal in the data protection category. Once they've found a vendor solution they're comfortable with, they stay put.

Most SBS VAPs recommend 4-mm DAT tape backup drives. While it's possible to go with a lower-cost Travan-based drive, this often proves too slow for backing up 4 to 9 GB of data each night.

I've seen some SBS VAPs choose to install the tape backup drive for the network on a workstation, so an over-the-network backup is run overnight when the office is empty and the network isn't being used. This is generally implemented through a workstation-class, Travan tape backup drive, primarily to save money. In this type of configuration, the tape drive controller usually uses either the floppy drive or IDE controller as opposed to a higher-performance SCSI adapter. I've also seen some SBS VAPs implement a workstation-based backup solution to make troubleshooting and replacing the tape drive easier, without having to shut down the server.

Regardless of the reasons for using them, workstation-based backup solutions often miss the mark when backing up the server registry, Exchange Information Store and Directory Store, and SQL Server databases and transaction logs. (Workstation-based backup solutions generally only back up files that are not in use.) Make sure that your client isn't being penny-wise, pound-foolish.

Tip

Check to insure that scheduled tape backup jobs are set up properly, verified, and tested. Chapter 23 covers how to test the tape backup solution.

A server-class UPS typically is connected to a server for monitoring and automated shutdown. Make sure your client orders the proper serial cable for this function. A UPS without a serial interface and appropriate software can protect the server. If the power is out for an extended period of time overnight, however, you're risking major data corruption and data loss while the server is on and no one is around to shut it down properly. Most UPS monitoring software packages feature unattended shutdown routines that take over when the server has been running on battery power for a specified amount of time.

As your small business clients get Internet-enabled e-mail accounts and Web browsing privileges, antivirus software moves to a mission critical status. Most third-party antivirus software packages have individual modules that protect the server, workstations, Exchange Server, and the Proxy Server firewall. You also need to make sure the scanning engine and signature or pattern files are kept up to date.

While a robust tape backup, power protection, and antivirus solution are required for the server, don't overlook the desktop PCs on the SBS network. Make sure each PC has antivirus software with the most current scanning engine and signature files. At the bare minimum, each workstation should also have a network grade surge suppressor. As the prices of entry-level UPSs have dropped below $100, most SBS VAPs are also advocating every PC have its own UPS.

Tip

Chapter 23 details procedures for checking for proper installation of the tape backup solution and UPS.

Deciding on SBS Licensing

In addition to making decisions on what type of hardware on which to standardize, how to handle data cabling needs, and what type of data protection solutions to implement, you'll need to advise your client on how best to license SBS.

SBS is available through three distinct licensing/packaging mechanisms:

- **Full packaged product (FPP)** includes documentation and media and is available through authorized Microsoft distributors such as Ingram Micro, Merisel, and Tech Data. For a full list of authorized Microsoft distributors, see the Microsoft Direct Access Web site (*www.microsoft.com/directaccess*). For the list of FPP part numbers, see the SBS Web site at *www.microsoft.com/smallbusinessserver*.

- **Microsoft Open License** unbundles the documentation and media to give the small business the lowest possible acquisition costs, as well as lower asset tracking costs. Open License is available from conventional authorized Microsoft distributors, as well as specialty Open License distributors such as License Online (*www.licenseonline.com*). For more details on Open License, see *www.microsoft.com/mlo*.

- **Authorized PC hardware vendors (OEM/System Builder program)** offer special servers bundled with SBS. For a complete list of top-tier PC OEMs that bundle SBS, see the SBS Web site at *www.microsoft.com/smallbusinessserver*. Smaller OEMs can also become authorized to bundle SBS with their white box servers by enrolling in the Microsoft System Builder program. For details see *www.microsoft.com/oem*.

Securing Price Quotes

Throughout the first eight chapters of this book, you've seen how some SBS VAPs are both resellers *and* consultants while other SBS VAPs are just consultants or pure service providers. Chapter 5 looked at some of the quandaries SBS VAPs face when they grapple with whether to resell products or not.

First and foremost as an SBS VAP, you'll need to be some type of technology provider or consultant. Then, if you want to *and* the customer wants you to *and* the margin is sufficient, you might choose to resell some or all of the many products required for an SBS rollout. These include the hardware, software, and peripherals you've itemized in the "Materials Budget" worksheet. By reselling products to your small business clients, you can provide a complete, end-to-end solution.

Note

Some SBS VAPs view reselling products as an all or nothing proposition. You can deal with the margin erosion issues, however, in many ways. Some SBS VAPs, myself included, will resell software and peripherals *when* profitable. We won't resell brand-name desktop PCs, laptops, or servers, as they are rarely profitable. In the white box market, however, SBS VAPs should almost always be able to clear over 10 percent net profit margins.

You should be aware that more and more SBS VAPs are writing the product specifications and then having small business clients purchase the products somewhere else. In this scenario, the SBS VAP takes on more of a strategic advisor role and becomes a pure service provider because the VAP isn't reselling products.

I've seen one other variation on the product reselling decision handled quite successfully by some SBS VAPs. In this situation, the SBS VAP will sometimes be a traditional reseller (that is, selling products) and other times will just be the consultant (that is, pure service provider). The linchpin of this margin preservation strategy: the decision is based on customer preferences and the potential profitability of the products required for the project. Effectively, the SBS VAP customizes the role for each unique client situation.

Connectivity Issues

As part of finalizing the definitive project plan, you'll need to talk with your client about connecting the SBS network to the Internet. This includes selecting an Internet service provider (ISP) and telecommunications lines. Chapters 13 and 18 deal with configuring Internet connectivity on an SBS network.

Identifying an ISP

If your small business client has no desire for Internet-enabled e-mail and Web browsing from the desktop, your job will be quite easy. Just skip this section and roll your eyes. How could any firm, no matter how small, forgo the basic communications tools for the next century? Can you even envision a business card without an e-mail address and Web site URL? Because of the vast array of choices available from ISPs and the huge variations in cost for different types of services, the small business client's choices will usually be somewhat constrained by cost.

Some SBS VAPs perform network-consulting services for small businesses *and* are traditional ISPs. They can provide a wide array of offerings for small business clients. However, most SBS VAPs *aren't* in the business of being ISPs. To keep their finger in the ISP pie, some SBS VAPs have a co-located Web/mail server within an ISP's network-operation-center (NOC) facilities so they can host client's Web sites and e-mail. Almost no SBS VAPs get involved in reselling dial-up or permanent Internet access services unless the firm is a hybrid SBS VAP and ISP.

Tip

For more information on co-location, see "ISP Web Site Co-Location Service" in Chapter 6.

Most often, SBS VAPs either partner with ISPs, subcontract with ISPs, or just have a preferred ISP or a list of ISPs to which they refer clients. SBS VAPs in the United States are also eagerly awaiting widespread availability of low-cost, high-performance broadband offerings such as xDSL.

Identifying the Telecommunications Lines to Be Ordered

Just as most SBS VAPs aren't involved in being ISPs, VAPs are rarely involved in ordering telecommunications lines. As with ISP access accounts, e-mail, and Web hosting, however, SBS VAPs are routinely called upon and expected to spec the requirements for various dial-up and leased lines. Just as for ISP accounts, cost becomes *the* limiting factor for small businesses when specifying telecommunications lines for Internet access and other wide area network connections. In most areas, typical options include analog lines (standard dial-up lines), ISDN (dial-up or full-time Centrex), xDSL (broadband over copper), cable modem, frame relay, and fractional T1.

SBS VAPs rarely get involved in the inside wiring for telecommunications lines. If inside wiring is required and the telephone company doesn't provide that service, SBS VAPs will often call upon the same cabling company that provided the category 5 UTP cabling for the LAN.

Tip

Inside wiring is the portion of the wiring that runs from the phone jack in your small business client's office to the network interface box (NIB) or point-of-demarcation outside the building. Some landlords and property managers of certain types of commercial buildings require all inside wiring be done by an authorized contractor.

The Bottom Line

You should now have a good idea of how to assemble the project to do list and create the documents that will ultimately comprise the project plan packet. The first section of this chapter looked at how to assemble data for your network design report. Next, the chapter drilled down on a few potentially troublesome areas of the network design to help highlight areas for additional review, as the project plan is finalized and executed through a letter of engagement. The final section of this chapter introduced background information on how to talk with your small business clients about connecting the SBS network to the Internet.

Chapter 10

Building Client Consensus and Moving Forward

No matter how many times you meet with your small business clients before starting a rollout for Microsoft BackOffice Small Business Server 4.5, a few "oh, by the ways" are bound to come up during the project. Your project planning goals and the emphasis in Part 3 are twofold.

First, get your clients to think about the big picture and being proactive about their technology planning. This largely involves helping your clients move beyond just seeing the installation of a network as a shopping list of hardware and software.

Then, once you've introduced your small business clients to your firm's role as the virtual IT department and your unique role as their virtual CIO and technology visionary, establish a concrete plan of attack. Your network design report is the primary deliverable for this purpose and includes priorities, target dates, responsibilities, time and materials estimates, timelines, and project dependencies.

Even if your small business clients are willing to sign off on the project without additional discussion, this usually isn't the best course of action. While you certainly wouldn't want to talk yourself out of the sale, open communication is the linchpin of SBS deployment success. Even if your clients don't initiate a request for another meeting, establishing an open dialogue with small business owners, internal gurus, power users, and any other influential constituencies at the client sites is crucial.

Chapter 7 introduced a number of documents that can help you build the SBS technology roadmap and lay the groundwork for open communication:

- ❏ "Quarterly Update Report"
- ❏ "Roadmap Template for SBS Network"
- ❏ "Letter of Engagement for Initial Consultation"
- ❏ "Summary of Findings from Initial Consultation"
- ❏ "Letter of Engagement for Network Design"
- ❏ "IT Audit Opportunity"
- ❏ "30-Point PC Security Check-Up"
- ❏ "Site Survey Inventory (Word)"
- ❏ "Site Survey Inventory (Excel)"

All of these documents are on the CD-ROM at the back of the book.

Chapter 8 focused on how to sell the concrete benefits of SBS to small business decision-makers, even when you're confronted with obstacles concerning existing network solutions.

Chapter 9 emphasized how to take the data you captured with the "Summary of Findings from Initial Consultation" and "IT Audit Opportunity Column" and add it to the "Network Design Report," an Excel workbook that contains these worksheets: "Supported Application Matrix," "Summary of Users List," "Time Budget," and "Materials Budget." (All of these documents can be found on the CD-ROM at the back of the book.)

Why make so much effort to gather information up front and analyze requirements? By using the methodologies presented throughout this book you'll take a thorough, well thought-out professional approach to planning the SBS implementation project. This is in sharp contrast to many local VAPs, perhaps your less enlightened local competitors, who often rely on back of the napkin calculations and take imprudent risks with both their own and their clients' resources. Also, when you look at the magnitude of your small business client's potential technology investments, making sure the project will be successful—or at least will proceed with minimal aggravation—is crucial.

On the flip side, if your small business clients wanted to take an amateurish or hobbyist approach to implementing a network, they probably would've asked their internal gurus to take on the project. By calling in your firm, however, they've indicated they want small business-networking experts managing the implementation and ongoing support responsibilities. These final meetings with your clients before the official start of a project also afford your firm one final opportunity to assess the urgency of the situation.

This chapter will help you build consensus among the various affected parties associated with the client and get your client up to speed on the meaning of your planning deliverables and accompanying conclusions. You'll also learn how to help your client solidify an Internet usage policy and how to establish procedures for payment terms and change orders. Chapter 10 will conclude Part 3 of the book by helping you identify potential showstoppers before they develop into major problems.

Reviewing the IT Audit

Now that you've taken the client through your initial consultation (Chapter 7) and have authored at least a first draft of your network design report (Chapter 9), you need to plan a meeting agenda to review your analysis and the various worksheets and documents you've prepared with your client.

Roadmap Template

The "Roadmap Template for SBS Network" is used early in the initial consultation meeting to make sure you gather all the required information on the first pass. Think of the "Roadmap Template" as a set of guidelines for your 30,000-foot aerial view of the technology needs of your small business client.

Because it might now be several weeks since this information was first recorded, review and reconfirm each detail with the client. Also explain the meaning of each line item and how the information discussed will ultimately impact the project deployment. Highlights to bring out include:

❑　Reconfirm the number of current, planned, and needed desktop PCs, laptops, servers, and network users. (This information will be reinforced by the "Supported Application Matrix" and "Summary of Users List" worksheets in the "Network Design Report.")

❑　Review the client's current, planned, and future (at least one full quarter following deployment) needs for the major categories of virtual IT services. These services include file, printer, and CD-ROM sharing; network faxing; internal and external e-mail; groupware; Web browsing; remote access, control, and management; database development and custom programming; security and disaster recovery planning; cabling; procurement; documentation; and training.

❑ Discuss the estimated start date, estimated completion date, and how much time the SBS VAP will need to allocate to the project each week during deployment.

Quarterly Update Report

The "Quarterly Update Report" is a tool that should be used to keep the client in the loop about the progress of major projects. Once buy-in is received to move ahead with each distinct project, the project should be micromanaged and compartmentalized into distinct phases and tasks, in a fashion that's similar to the "Time Budget" worksheet presented in Chapter 9.

In addition, the "Quarterly Update Report" documents the company standards and supported applications. Because these standards and applications will evolve over time as different projects are implemented and completed, the "Quarterly Update Report" should be viewed as a snapshot that's taken four times a year.

With new small business clients, consider completing a preliminary version of the "Quarterly Update Report" and discuss how this template can be used as a high-level planning tool. In addition, you'll want to discuss the importance of company standards for operating systems, PC hardware, applications, e-mail, and database applications. Some of the many benefits of standardization to emphasize include lower support costs, ease of support from fewer vendors, fewer integration headaches, easier cross-training among employees, ease of recovery from disasters, and a flatter learning curve for new staff.

Summary of Findings from Initial Consultation

The most challenging part of planning an SBS rollout often is knowing where to start and how to tackle the dozens of interrelated tasks. The "Summary of Findings from Initial Consultation" solidifies your preliminary analysis and sets up the next steps required for network design. To make sure that your firm has gotten a handle on the true problem and objective, especially given the more in-depth network design report that you've drafted since the initial consultation, make sure to recap the most important details, which include:

❑ High-level objectives and goals, findings, and definition of the problem

❑ Preliminary requirements for desktop and server operating systems and applications, hardware, data security, and telecommunications lines

❑   Correct contacts for financial and business impact decisions and technology and operational decisions (If each decision is made by a different person, make sure you discuss who has veto power in the event of internal disagreements.)

30-Point PC Security Check-Up

The "30-Point PC Security Check-Up" drills down on how well the client's data is protected from various risk factors such as data corruption, data loss, power interruptions, viruses, hackers, tampering, and accidental deletion. Take time to bring out a few select highlights from your assessment of the client's existing solutions (or lack thereof) for data backup, disaster recovery, overall security, power protection, and virus protection.

Then, follow that up with a *very* brief overview of how these findings translate into various project phases and hardware, software, and peripherals requirements. (These observations should correlate with line items on the "Time Budget" and "Materials Budget" worksheets introduced in Chapter 9.)

Site Survey Inventory

Once again, the goal of this meeting is to review your findings from the IT audit. You shouldn't be reading every last detail of the results to the client. (By all means, you should provide full copies of the inventory if the client wants it, however.) As with the "30-Point PC Security Check-Up," select a few highlights from the "Site Survey Inventory (Excel)" worksheet or the "Site Survey Inventory (Word)" document that represents the installed base of PCs, operating systems, and applications. Topics to cover include:

❑   Relative age of the hardware, desktop operating systems, and software applications

❑   The client's standardization, or lack thereof, with respect to hardware, software, and operating systems

❑   Adequacy of hardware (processor speeds, RAM, hard drive sizes) for 32-bit applications on an SBS network

❑   Adequacy of hardware, or lack thereof, will be reiterated throughout the "Supported Application Matrix," "Summary of Users List," "Time Budget," and "Materials Budget" worksheets in the "Network Design Report"

Educating the Client About the Technology Roadmap

Before proceeding with the SBS rollout, make sure that everyone concerned is on the same page. The previous section of this chapter covered how to review the findings from the IT audit with your client. Next, the chapter shows how to educate the client about the elements of the technology roadmap, which is principally composed of the previously discussed deliverables and your network design report.

These discussions can either take place at the same meeting as the review of the IT audit findings or in a subsequent session. The scheduling of additional agenda items when discussing the roadmap usually depends on how smoothly the first meeting goes. Some SBS VAPs will have just one meeting to review all findings and the network design. Other SBS VAPs spread out these discussions over two or three shorter sessions. The decision on whether you need one meeting or two (or more) meetings depends on several factors, including:

- Length of your relationship with the client (and the client's level of trust in you)

- Complexity of the client's needs

- Client's comfort level with technology

- Involvement of any other technology providers

Network Design Cover Sheet

Your small business client might be somewhat intimidated, or at least confused, when receiving a thick report. The "Network Design Report Cover Sheet" introduces the client to each item in the "Network Design Report" packet. The elements include the "Supported Application Matrix," "Summary of Users List," "Time Budget," and "Materials Budget."

Supported Application Matrix

During individual site surveys, you probably identified a hodgepodge of hardware, software, operating systems, and peripherals. Now based on your evaluation of the client's needs and the goal to implement an SBS network, you can use the "Supported Application Matrix" to match the various recommended products and solutions with individual end users.

The left-hand column shows your recommendations for hardware, software, and other supported requirements (peripherals, cabling, e-mail accounts, and so forth). Across the top of the matrix, each end user in the main office and branch offices is listed. At the intersection of each end user and product line item, entries are classified as "has," "needs to buy," "doesn't need to buy," or "not sure."

While these four classifications aren't always mutually exclusive, the "Supported Application Matrix" provides a great starting point for specifying the actual standards for the company and how each end user complies with these newly recommended standards. The matrix can also be used as a starting point for developing timetables and scheduling, as well as the springboard for the time and materials cost estimates.

You might find it helpful to point out to your client some of the more obvious examples of why the matrix is so valuable. For example, sharing documents might be a high priority among the small business end users. The company, however, currently has 11 different word processor versions across 21 end users. This includes 4 different versions of Corel WordPerfect, 2 different versions of Lotus WordPro, and 5 different versions of Microsoft Word, spanning from 2.0c to 2000. By standardizing on a 32-bit Windows operating system and desktop productivity suite, such as Windows NT Workstation 4.0 and Office 2000, document sharing will become a reality.

Summary of Users List

In a small business, sharing PCs is common because of big discrepancies between the number of employees and number of PCs. You should have already uncovered this in many earlier parts of the client engagement such as the site surveys. Because of hardware acquisition issues and licensing costs of the desktop operating system and applications, you need to get a firm grasp on the list of users who will be accessing the SBS network. Once the list is compiled, you can figure out which end users will share which PCs.

The "Summary of Users List" shows a summary of PC hardware specs for each person who will use the network, each user's location, and whether the PC used by each user will be kept, replaced, passed down (to someone else), or not sure (to be determined). The "Summary of Users List" is another tool that helps force the client to make tough decisions on PC hardware and operating system standardization.

Note

Small business owners are generally reluctant to retire hardware. Finding small business owners and end users clinging to 486 PCs with 12 MB RAM and 340-MB hard drives isn't unusual. Once the small business owner is sold on the dozens of benefits SBS provides and company-wide standardization, however, supporting one or two stragglers from the old MS-DOS/Microsoft Windows 3.x days becomes quite expensive.

Generally prepared concurrently with the "Supported Application Matrix," the "Summary of Users List" is focused on solidifying the list of network users, as well as the desktop PC hardware and desktop operating system that each user will have when the network deployment is complete.

Time Budget

The "Time Budget" should be used as a working document throughout the SBS rollout. It shows estimated hours required for each phase and itemized task. Depending on how you want to present your billing rate, you might want to incorporate your hourly consulting fee into the "Time Budget" or save that information for a separate letter of engagement.

In addition to being used to plan the timeline and project calendar, the "Time Budget" can be used to compare estimated hours against how they're actually being spent and to determine whether the project is on track.

Materials Budget

Years ago, the time and materials budgets would've almost certainly been presented within the same document. Many SBS VAPs, however, now choose to be pure service providers and don't engage in product reselling.

To allow for separation of consulting services from product sales, the "Materials Budget" is broken out *a la carte* and includes categories for grouping various estimated expenditures. The "Materials Budget" includes quantities, cost estimates, and selected vendors for desktop PCs, servers, software, peripherals, telecommunications and ISP accounts, and network cabling. This worksheet also has same timeline planning columns as the "Time Budget."

Tip

When the estimated starting and completion dates are combined from the "Time Budget" and "Material Budget," you'll have the foundation of the project timetable.

Spec Sheet Details

With so many of the large PC OEMs and distributors providing custom assembly for desktop PCs and servers, you might want to keep the "Materials Budget" less cluttered and just point to more detailed spec sheets. These custom documents are easy to create on PC OEM Web sites, such as those owned by Compaq (*www.compaq.com*), Dell (*www.dell.com*), and Gateway (*www.gateway.com*). Figure 10-1 shows a detailed spec sheet for a fully configured SBS 4.5 server, which I created on *www.dell.com*. Included as separate attachments within your network design report, these spec sheets or "shopping cart" details prevent you from repeating or retyping the same information. In addition to saving the effort of entering redundant information, you lessen the possibility of typos by pointing to an attachment because the information isn't copied manually from one format to another.

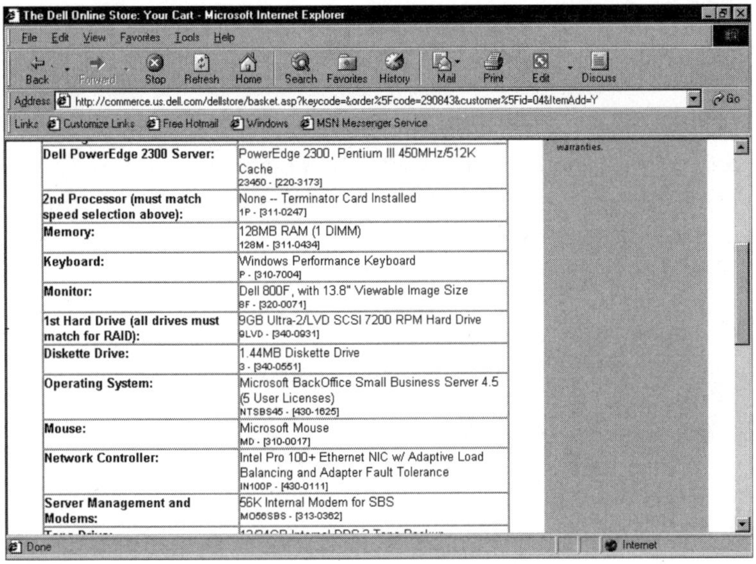

Figure 10-1

By attaching a spec sheet to the "Materials Budget" in the "Network Design Report,"
you eliminate the need to retype very detailed information.

To make your job even easier, many PC OEMs and distributors also allow you to save your shopping cart online for later retrieval or for establishing standard configurations. See Figure 10-2.

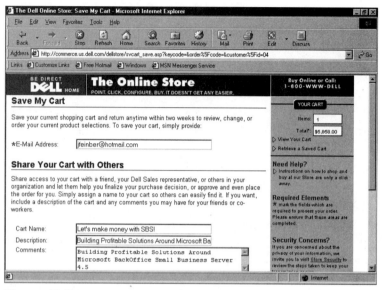

Figure 10-2

Save your shopping cart for future retrieval.

Tip

If the shopping cart quote is based on wholesale prices and your firm wants to add markup, make sure the spec sheets either omits the wholesale price or shows your customized retail price.

Establishing E-Mail and Internet Usage Policies

Why should your small business clients adopt a written policy concerning e-mail and Internet usage? Isn't this type of paranoia just for Fortune 1000 IT departments?

While you and your small business clients shouldn't lose sight of the tremendous benefits of company-wide access to Internet e-mail and Web browsing, protecting against potential dangers is important as well. The "Company E-Mail and Internet Usage Policy Planning Worksheet," a Word template included on the CD-ROM for this book and shown in Figure 10-3, is designed to help you plan what topics to tackle in your clients' policy statements. That way, your clients will have a thorough, concrete grasp of which issues are most relevant *before* they consult with their attorneys. The policy statement should detail both appropriate and inappropriate uses of these company resources, as well as the sanctions for violating company policies.

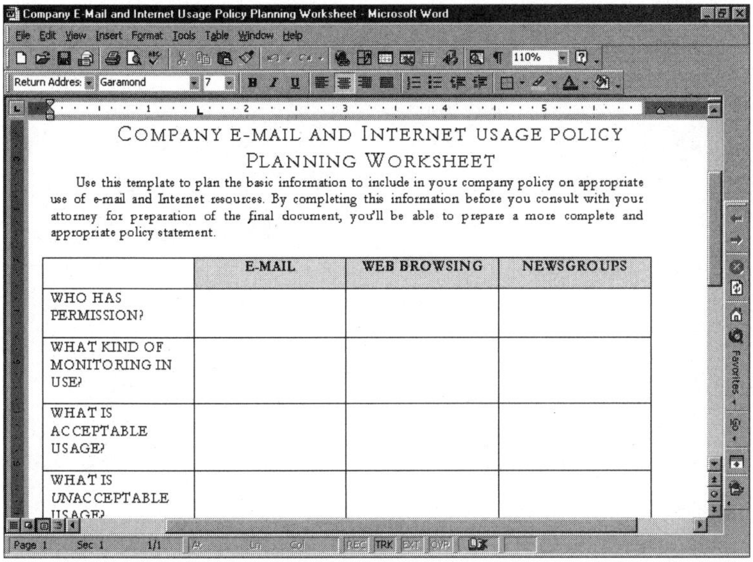

Figure 10-3

The "Company E-Mail and Internet Usage Policy Planning Worksheet" should be used to decide what belongs in your client's policy statement.

Tip

The attorney who prepares the final policy statement should have a firm grasp on local labor laws.

Once implemented, the written policy should be updated and disseminated at least twice a year and given to all new hires. All employees should review the document and sign off to acknowledge their understanding of the policies and sanctions. Copies should also be retained by employees and posted prominently on company bulletin boards and intranets.

Because this area of the SBS client engagement crosses into legal and ethical issues, you might not feel entirely comfortable broaching the topic with your client. Ignoring this problem, however, is a substantial risk. If you want to assume the virtual CIO role, be prepared to at least read up on the topic so that you can advise your client on how to proceed.

As an SBS VAP, your goal should be twofold. First, get your client to think about what needs to be in the written policy. Second, encourage your client to consult with an attorney before issuing the policy statement.

Benefits of a Written Policy

Given the general desire of small businesses to be more nimble, better implementers, and lower-cost producers than their larger competitors, why bother with the formality of a written policy on appropriate usage of company e-mail and Internet resources? Some of the benefits include:

- Protection against litigation and liability (Some attorneys won't even consider taking on a case against your client if they know your client had a tight, written policy.)

- Avoiding invasion of privacy claims by putting employees on notice that monitoring of Internet usage might take place

- Reducing employee confusion

- Preventing problems with undesirable behaviors

- Insuring that employees know that they have no privacy and conveying that almost all activities can be traced (In fact, administrators have the ability *and* obligation to monitor usage.)

- Specifying that your client owns the system and controls content of messages and all documents (This is especially important because individual accounts and passwords might create the illusion that personal computer usage is private.)

- Helping to protect company trade secrets

- Deterring employees from wasting company time on personal matters

Deciding what individual penalties, sanctions, and consequences for misconduct and unauthorized use is an individual decision. In order to hold up in court in many jurisdictions, these penalties and monitoring must be applied consistently across the board to all employees. Because the consequences in the policy statement often can include everything up to and including prosecution and termination, getting an attorney involved in drafting the document is critical.

What's Usually Prohibited

Once again, the individual small business owner needs to decide what specific activities should be banned at the workplace. The following behaviors, however, are commonly prohibited when a written Internet usage policy is adopted:

- Circulation or possession of obscene, sexual, or other vulgar material
- Any form of harassment, including making or having libelous, defamatory, offensive, discriminatory, racist, or hate statements or material
- Illegal activities at the local, state, or federal level
- Commerce for personal gain (side businesses) or any other excessive or inappropriate personal use of company equipment or resources
- Entertainment activities and games
- Sending spam or other unauthorized mass mailing
- Copyright infringement (when downloading and forwarding information)
- Dissemination of viruses
- Attempts to hack into unauthorized systems or to obscure or to alter the origin of messages or any downloaded material
- Leakage of sensitive information of a personal, confidential, or protected nature
- Software piracy
- Any other grossly inappropriate conduct not expressly prohibited

E-Mail Guidelines

Now that you have an idea of what types of behavior are often expressly prohibited, you need to understand what issues specifically relate to e-mail. These issues include the following:

❏ Does your client plan on monitoring individual e-mail accounts and messages at random? Who has authority and responsibility to monitor? What are the monitoring procedures?

❏ Do employees know their e-mail is not private?

❑ Do employees understand that people other than intended recipients might intercept e-mail?

❑ Do employees realize that deleted e-mail is not deleted?

❑ Are employees aware that the same care should be taken in composing e-mail as in other forms of office communication (phone, fax, letterhead, memo, and so forth)?

❑ Do employees think of e-mail from @yourcompanyname as being on electronic letterhead?

Web Browsing Guidelines

Now with an understanding of policy issues specific to e-mail usage, defining how the policy translates to Web browsing and other Internet resources is important. Some questions you might ask include the following:

❑ Does each staff member have his or her own unique logon and password? Are staff members aware that passwords aren't to be shared?

❑ Is Proxy Server being used to control which staff members have access to the Internet or which sites might be accessed or blocked?

❑ Does each staff member know that his or her usage is being logged and monitored?

❑ Do staff members who participate in chats and newsgroups specifically need that access to perform their job? Further, do they understand the appropriate usage guidelines and how their participation reflects on the company?

Determining Payment Terms

As you get closer to beginning the actual SBS rollout work, you need a grasp on how your firm will be paid by the small business client. SBS VAPs are literally all over the map when it comes to payment terms, credit policies, and billing procedures. Some SBS VAPs insist on cash-on-delivery (COD). Others place huge stakes in the value of a gut feel and handshake and assume literally *all* of the risk. Most SBS VAPs are somewhere in the middle, offering some type of payment terms but requiring up-front deposits and holding tight reins on due dates.

Regardless of how you decide to handle payment terms, remember you've already established some type of precedent with your small business client. The

"Letter of Engagement for Initial Consultation" and "Letter of Engagement for Network Design" both spell out payment terms and requirements for up-front deposits. By providing some limited payment terms early on for relatively small dollar amounts, you can begin to assess your client's payment habits. If you intend to deviate substantially from how the client was billed for the planning work, be prepared to provide an explanation on why you have different billing and credit policies for different parts of the project.

If you decide to extend payment terms to your small business clients, you'd be wise to consult with your attorney and accountant to develop specific guidelines as to what constitutes acceptable and unacceptable credit risk. In addition, you'll certainly want to insist on the small business client's completion of a thorough credit application. The CD-ROM at the back of this book includes "Credit Application," a Word template on which you can base your own credit application. See Figure 10-4.

Tip

This credit application is primarily intended for use in the United States. Be sure to consult your attorney and accountant to adapt this type of template for local use.

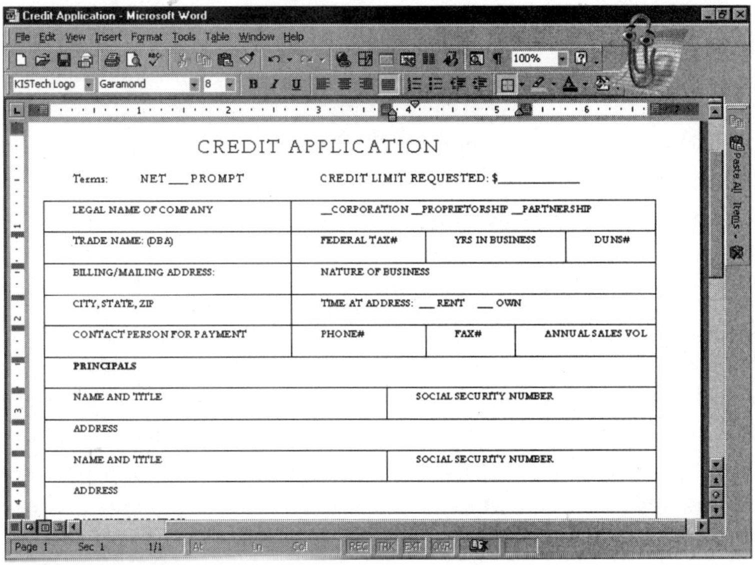

Figure 10-4

Don't even think about granting any substantial amount of credit to a small business client without securing and processing a completed credit application.

Creating Procedures to Handle Change Orders

Even with the most thorough up-front needs analysis and network design, your small business client is bound to come up with some additional work items once the project is already underway. These "oh, by the way" types of items are commonly referred to as change orders.

Change orders can make or break the project depending on how you handle them. At the bare minimum, change orders typically require anywhere from minor to major revisions of the "Time Budget" and "Materials Budget." In particular, change orders often directly impact time estimates, materials estimates, start dates, and completion dates. So clearly you need to establish at the outset how you and your small business client will deal with change order requests during the SBS rollout.

Tip

Occasionally the SBS VAP will initiate a change order. More times than not, however, the change originates with the small business owner, internal guru, or affected end user.

A change order should always be written up and subject to appropriate authorizations from both parties. The change order must be mutually acceptable or revised to be mutually acceptable or additional complications will ensue.

You should also discuss whether any type of service charges will be necessary for processing change orders. Given the often time-consuming adjustments that must be made to scheduling and purchasing timelines, nominal service charges are often par for the course.

To make sure that change orders aren't mired in weeks of bureaucratic Ping-Pong, you should also establish a tiered-approval process. Assuming your small business decision-maker is in agreement, you might want to set up a ceiling of anywhere from $200 to $500 or perhaps one to six hours of estimated labor as a nonmaterial change order so you can accept a verbal authorization.

Once that threshold has been reached, someone with authority needs to sign off on the change order documents. Sometimes the affected end user can do that. Sometimes the internal guru can. More times than not, the small business owner wants to have a say in any substantial cost escalations or schedule slippages. Regardless of who's the commander in chief of the change order process, you'll need a clear chain of command. That way if an urgent decision needs to be made *and* the primary business and technical decision-makers aren't available, you'll know whether the project should be put on hold or whether an alternate staff member can be consulted.

Making Sure All the Client's Main Decision Makers Buy into the Project

Although small business clients are much less prone to protracted political squabbles than their Fortune 1000 equivalents, making sure all key parties are in favor of what you're proposing is critical. If the small business owner is totally gung ho about the SBS deployment project, but every one of the owner's staff members is bitterly resistant, your life will be a living nightmare. You also have an excellent chance that the small business owner will be forced to pull the plug midproject and that your firm will be forced to eat some nonbillable hours (or risk alienating the client with vigorous collection efforts).

You can avoid a lot of this potential aggravation by taking precautions up front to make sure you've heard from all the major client constituencies. These include:

- Small business owners

- Internal gurus

- Power users

- Novice or beginner users

Talking to these people is really your final opportunity to probe newly discovered topics that you need to address and to ask for additional clarification. Make sure you thoroughly understand their expectations and that they understand yours.

Having the small business owner stay actively involved in the project is important. If the problem you're going to tackle isn't urgent enough to demand the small business owner's attention or if the small business owner becomes disengaged, you've encountered a major red flag of potential problems.

Regardless of how competent, experienced, and resourceful your firm is, the small business owner can't completely outsource the decision-making and oversight. You'll still need periodic feedback and guidance from the owner at certain key decision intervals, such as at the conclusion of each distinct phase in the "Time Budget."

You should take great pains to insist that the small business owner stays actively involved during the rollout. Project failures usually come about when the owner wants the project done yesterday, but doesn't have time to explain what's needed.

Although the primary financial and technical decision-makers need to stay actively involved, understanding who has veto authority is critical. If the small business owner doesn't have time to stay personally involved with the project, then he or she needs to delegate to someone who does have the time. Otherwise, your project will stand a large chance of failure midstream.

The Bottom Line

Successful SBS rollouts require full client agreement and cooperation. Spend time early on explaining your findings and recommendations to the key client decision makers. Once your small business understands your network design report and is comfortable moving forward, take time to discuss Internet usage policy, as well as credit and change order procedures. Finally, before your client signs on the dotted line and writes the down-payment check, make sure all affected constituencies at the client are in favor of the SBS deployment.

Chapter 11

Project Management Techniques

Parts 1 through 3 in this book have helped you establish the technology plan, build a solid relationship with the small business owner or other key decision-maker, and obtain formal approval to schedule the consulting work and order the required hardware, software, and peripherals. The CD-ROM for this book includes a "Letter of Engagement for SBS Rollout," a Word template, to make sure you've covered as many bases as possible in your project management. See Figure 11-1 on the next page.

Part 4 drills down into the nitty-gritty of doing the actual installation. When I refer to installation, I'm talking about work substantially more involved than just running setup.exe on Microsoft Small Business Server 4.5 CD-ROM 1. Any novice—or internal guru—can insert a CD-ROM and accept the defaults. Experienced SBS VAPs know that amateurs often fall flat on their face when installing SBS. A successful implementation requires a plan of attack. This is what Part 4 is all about.

This chapter kicks off Part 4 with a discussion of project management techniques. Contrary to the often esoteric, ivory-tower project management

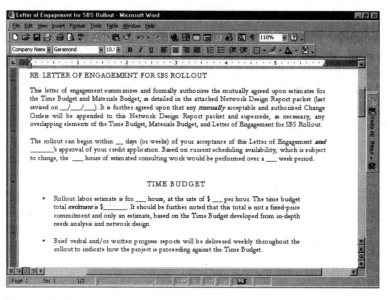

Figure 11-1

Cover your bases with the "Letter of Engagement for SBS Rollout" template.

material applicable only to big five consulting firms or Fortune 1000 IT departments, Chapter 11 is loaded with hard-hitting, concrete advice about keeping the SBS rollout on track.

Chapter 12 shows how you can save valuable time and leave more money in the budget for higher-margin value-added services by deploying the desktop OS with as little manual configuration as possible.

Although a novice SBS VAP might think the SBS installation is complete when the highly automated setup program finishes running two to four hours later, literally dozens of individual, interrelated, crucial steps need to be performed *after* the setup program is done. Chapter 13 gives you a structured methodology for tackling the various configuration, data protection, and connectivity tasks that are part of the installation process.

SBS 4.5, like its predecessor, features a customizable server console, based on HTML and Active Server Pages (ASPs). The SBS Console centralizes the most commonly used administration tasks and provides easy-to-use wizards. Chapter 14 shows you how to add tremendous value to your client's installation by customizing the SBS Console.

Chapter 15 focuses on how you can help prevent expensive downtime from occurring at your small business clients' offices. The Server Status Tool, new to SBS 4.5, should be the basis for your proactive maintenance program. With the Server Status Tool, you can preconfigure certain log files and reports to be e-mailed or faxed to your firm at specified intervals. In addition, Chapter 15 shows you how to add additional value to your proactive maintenance efforts by customizing the Server Status Tool.

Chapter 16 discusses how you can save time and prevent configuration errors by adding additional software applications to the unattended setup routine already in place for the SBS client applications. In Chapter 17 you'll get a behind-the-scenes look at the Set Up Computer Wizard and client setup disk. In addition, you'll learn about the few remaining, manual steps that need to be performed at each desktop PC.

Many SBS VAPs had difficulty getting all of the Internet services to function properly and reliably in SBS 4.0. Microsoft completely redesigned the Internet Connection Wizard (ICW) in SBS 4.5 to make it easier for you to set up secure Web browsing, Internet e-mail, and Web publishing. Chapter 18 begins with an overview of Internet Service Providers (ISPs) and various acronyms you'll need to get a basic grasp on the solution. The remainder of the chapter focuses on Microsoft Proxy Server, Internet access, bandwidth, publishing, and e-mail options.

Establishing the Single Point of Contact

During the planning stages of the SBS rollout when you utilized the templates in Chapters 7, 9, and 10, you should have tried to speak with as many different people as possible at the client site. Talking to these people can help you reach unbiased conclusions about the true needs of the client. Once the project specifications and timetables are finalized, however, you'll no longer have the luxury of being able to solicit everyone's opinion. One person at the client needs to be designated as the go-between. Too many cooks will definitely spoil the SBS rollout. Once a person who is *the* main contact is appointed, you must stick to taking all your orders from this one person *at all costs*. Many SBS VAPs even go so far as contractually obligating the small business owner to designate a single point of contact.

Successful SBS VAPs learn early that having a single point of contact is crucial to success. During the early stages of needs analysis and network design, the templates and discussions require that you identify the main business and technical decision-makers. If you're fortunate, this will be the same person. If the person authorizing the purchase orders and letters of engagement is *not* the same person as the technical implementation decision-maker, however, you need to establish which of the two people has the final say.

Without a designated single point of contact, you run a major risk of getting conflicting and often contradictory instructions from different people at the client site. Someone, not "some ones" (plural), needs to be in charge. Most SBS VAPs caution that if you detect such a problem, it must be caught and dealt with very early before the confusion gets out of control.

Another way to know whether you have a potential problem on your hands is when simple questions receive different answers from different parties. Many SBS VAPs experience this when they involve multiple people in decisions on naming conventions for users, computers, and directory structures. Typically when this happens, no one steps up to the plate to accept responsibility. In essence, if everyone is in charge, no one is in charge; hence the need for a *single* point of contact.

If key power or end users at the client have requests and want input, they should be instructed both by the small business owner and by you to have all their requests funnel through the single point of contact. Because even a minor change order can dramatically alter a project timetable, you need to have the single point of contact assess each request and prioritize it before discussing the item with you.

End users often see only a very small piece of the puzzle, and their requests are usually quite small in the whole scheme of things. For example, while I was with an SBS client recently to help finalize the company's Year 2000 compliance, one end user questioned why her wallpaper bitmap file wasn't transferred from her old PC to her new one. While I could've easily transferred the file, the main contact at the client felt strongly that the task was quite trivial and I shouldn't do it at the risk of jeopardizing the project timetable.

Arbitrating end users' requests can be quite hazardous to your firm's longevity and relationship with the client. Taking sides can make servicing the small business client incredibly and unnecessarily complex because your firm will undoubtedly end up in the middle of political turf wars.

Sticking to the Deliverable Schedule

Often the key to managing a complex SBS rollout is compartmentalizing the project or breaking the seemingly humongous project or phases into more manageable tasks. That's what your network design report is all about. Chapter 9 introduced the "Time Budget" and "Materials Budget" worksheets, each of which has a set of columns for scheduling tasks, identifying milestones, and benchmarking progress against the goals. The "Timeline Planning" columns in these worksheets include the following dates:

- Planned Start

- Planned Completion

- Actual Start

- Actual Completion

Some SBS VAPs don't provide the type of microschedules in the "Time Budget" and "Material Budget" or at least don't turn them over to the client. Rather, these SBS VAPs itemize the work to be done and provide an estimated timeframe for completion. For example, if your time budget forecasts 60 hours of project work, you might choose to tell the client that the project will be completed in six to eight weeks. For most clients and SBS rollouts, however, the detailed project timetable becomes an invaluable tool for keeping the project on track and revising targets when inevitable delays arise.

Tip

Some clients value face time tremendously; many SBS VAPs, however, prefer to do a portion of the work back at their offices. This can be especially helpful when you're preparing multiple desktops and servers for several clients simultaneously. One SBS VAP that I know upgrades servers by picking up the server on a Friday evening, upgrading the hardware and software over the weekend, and returning the server to the client early Monday morning.

Potential Showstoppers

Many potential showstoppers can prevent your firm from sticking to the deliverable schedule and milestones. Armed with a list of some of the more common issues, you'll be most effective at spotting *and* addressing the following potential problems before they evolve into major catastrophes:

- **Too many cooks in the kitchen.** As indicated in the previous section of this chapter, you need *one* person driving the project for the client. If two or three people give you orders, who's really in charge? When you get contradictory orders, you waste valuable time. Disputes often ensue about who should pay for this time, you or the client. Insist upon one main contact.

- **Static project timetable.** While you may be tempted to print out the project timetable and deliver just one version to the client, making the timetable a live document is important. More than likely you'll update the timetable almost on a daily basis to reflect progress and any problems or delays. Nearly every item within this bulleted list of potential showstoppers could easily trigger a timetable update.

- **Product or service provider delays.** When you're coordinating telco or ISP account activation or product shipments from multiple distributors, you'll often run into unanticipated delays. Most small business clients will be content with just being kept in the loop as long as the delay is reasonable. Make sure to get scheduling commitments from all subcontractors and write appropriate contingencies into the master letter of engagement or contract to protect your firm.

- **The dreaded "oh, by the way…"** Nothing is more frustrating to SBS VAPs than requirements that weren't mentioned by the client during the needs analysis and network design phases. Watch out when the client says "just" and "only," such as, "It will *only* take a few minutes" or "It's no big deal, but I *just* need _____ (fill in the blank)."

- **Skipping the planning phase to save money.** If your firm skipped some of the preliminary needs analysis and didn't use the type of templates and worksheets described in Chapters 7 and 9, you may have overlooked some key areas that require additional time or purchases.

- **Ambiguous software ownership.** If the client is getting new PCs, make sure the client has the media *and* correct number of licenses available. If the software installation requires nonstandard or nonintuitive configuration, make sure you also have all the configuration settings and procedures well-documented.

- **Software incompatibility.** Experienced SBS VAPs don't take software compatibility for granted…*ever*. A small business end user could be wedded to an MS-DOS-based application, circa 1989, that simply wreaks havoc on a 32-bit desktop OS and SBS.

- **Hardware incompatibility.** Make sure to check that *all* the server hardware that you're ordering and depending on is on the SBS hardware compatibility list (HCL). As a corollary, watch out for any nonstandard hardware not provided or recommended by your firm.

Tip

The SBS hardware compatibility list is located on the SBS Web site at *www.microsoft.com/smallbusinessserver*.

- **All data not transferred from old PCs.** Small business end users often think their years of stored data files will somehow magically get copied or moved from their existing PC to their new PC or server folder. As a result, they rarely mention all, if any, of their data files. In your individual site surveys, make sure you scour their local drives for stray data files, especially those with recent time and date stamps.

Tip

You can use the Find feature in Microsoft Windows 95/98 and Microsoft Windows NT Workstation 4.0 to help locate recently modified data files. Click the Start button, select Find, and click Files Or Folders.

- **No server data backup.** If you're installing SBS on an existing server, make sure you have a complete *and* verified backup of all the volumes, services, and the registry on the existing server just in case you need to roll back to the original configuration.

- **Unfamiliar ISPs.** Delays often occur when you're working with an unfamiliar ISP that the client either is presently using or insists upon using.

- **Too many client commitments**. Because most SBS VAPs tend to be small businesses themselves, take extra caution not to spread your firm's resources too thin.

- **End of project dragging on.** Often the follow-up work or tweaking can drag on for weeks. Know at the outset what types of tasks are in scope and which are out of scope. When in doubt, refer to the latest revision of your time budget. If necessary, don't hesitate to invoke the agreed upon change order procedures.

- **Client control of scheduling**. Unless your small business clients are prepared to pay for your staff's training, downtime, overhead, taxes, insurance, and fringe benefits, small business clients need to remember that your firm's staff aren't their employees.

Regardless of which gotchas you red flag and stop from compromising your deliverable schedule, open communication is the cornerstone of effective project management. Most SBS VAPs recommend that you keep in touch with the main contact person at the client at least once or twice a week. This type of dialog keeps your single point of contact informed of the latest developments and provides an opportunity for you to solicit interim feedback while you still have an opportunity to address the comments and concerns in a nonthreatening atmosphere.

Providing Detailed Status Reports and Invoices

Throughout this chapter, I've avoided the jargon typically associated with project management and have focused solely on how to be an effective SBS VAP project manager. To that end, keeping your main contact person at the client in the loop is key. Adopt whatever style works best for you and each individual client, but be sure to keep the communications channel open. If you anticipate delays, most small business clients would prefer to get the bad news as early as possible. Waiting until the last minute to inform the client of unpleasant surprises tends to create feelings of distrust and resentment, which may ultimately create a rift between your firm and the client.

Status Reports

Most SBS VAPs either give brief verbal or written status reports once a week during the course of the rollout. This is intended to keep the client abreast on:

- Work performed this past week

- Problems encountered

- Schedule for next week

- Progression of the project against the timetable

Invoices

Some SBS VAPs choose to invoice all the time and materials at the end of the project when the project is relatively small. At the other extreme, some SBS VAPs will invoice all the time and materials up front and provide a payment schedule that is spread throughout the rollout. Most SBS VAPs, however, customize their billing frequency on a per-client or per-project basis and tend to prefer sending the client a series of smaller invoices, as opposed to one large invoice.

The summary invoice is usually accompanied by detailed time sheets from the consultants assigned to the job. These logs typically list the hours, the tasks performed, summary of results, and the consultant who did the work. Regardless of whether the small business owner or other key decision-maker actually reviews every detail, most SBS VAPs include the work detail to protect themselves.

On the flip side, if an invoice or progress report has too much detail, the client simply won't read the document. If a dispute arises between you and the client, you'll be back to square one—you'll end up explaining what's been written. So make sure you know your client's preferences for detail. This will go a long way toward preventing you from wasting an hour or two writing up a report, when a half-dozen one-line bullet points on a half-page would've been more than adequate.

Progress payments are another invoicing method that SBS VAPs frequently utilize. This way a steady flow of payments comes into your firm, and your client can write relatively small checks on a regular basis. Progress payments also give your firm more leverage and a cushion against disagreements of materiality or relative importance of problems.

For example, let's say your firm sells the small business client a white box server for SBS 4.5 that costs approximately $4,500 fully configured. For whatever reason, the Microsoft Mouse that was supposed to be included with the server is on back order with your distributor for about six weeks. During the interim, you loan your client a slightly used Logitech mouse from your lab. The client, actively seeking any excuse not to pay on time, decides to withhold your entire payment for the server. If you had red flagged the component shortage early on, moved the back-ordered mouse into a change order, and reduced the main server invoice by the retail price of the mouse, you would have been able to insist on being paid for what's been delivered thus far. At the same time, the client would've felt more confident paying the invoice, because you're not expecting the client to pay for something not yet received.

One of the SBS VAPs in the focus group for this book recounted how his firm *used to* put all the project time and materials on a single invoice at the end of the project. A few months ago, however, a client wasn't satisfied with one relatively small part of the project. (Of course, all of us have our own definition of small, and that's when your negotiation skills will truly be put to the test.) One user's PC couldn't send outbound faxes through the server. The client decided to withhold payment on the entire job until the problem was rectified. Ultimately, this SBS VAP discovered the problem had nothing to do with the SBS install. Rather, the desktop PC in question had some other applications, not installed by the VAP, that conflicted with the SBS fax client application. If the SBS VAP's client had been remitting progress payments all along, perhaps the project would be 85 to 90 percent paid for and the SBS VAP wouldn't have been forced into such a weak position.

Change Orders

When change orders are prepared and authorized, most SBS VAPs tend to bill for that work separately. For example, if any additional hardware or software is required, you need to keep this from making the client think that you've exceeded the materials budget. A change order invoice will greatly clarify any potential misunderstandings.

Many SBS VAPs prefer billing change orders separately. That way, in the event that any particular part of the project billing is disputed, you can at least collect on the project additions and change orders while the dispute is being settled. This ultimately will go a long way toward facilitating payment of the main invoice(s), even if there are relatively minor disputes or issues to be resolved.

Because the wish-list and "oh, by the way" requests inevitably appear toward the end of the rollout, you need to make sure the payments are kept fairly current, or up to date. This way, your small business clients will be less inclined to feel they have leverage on your firm or can twist your arm into providing free or nonbillable services. The question, "Can't you just throw it in?" is nothing more than the client trying to negotiate after the fact.

Deposits

Because the profit margins tend to be so thin on product sales (see Chapter 5), SBS VAPs usually insist upon a substantial deposit up front. I've seen SBS VAPs require deposits that are 10 to 100 percent of the cost of orders placed for hardware, software, or peripherals. If the entire amount isn't prepaid, you'll have to decide or negotiate with your client whether the balance of the cost of the order is due upon receipt or whether some limited net terms will be provided.

I've seen some SBS VAPs work without any deposit for their services. If the work is invoiced frequently *and* paid on time, this method of payment generally doesn't pose any major problems to the project. To lessen the risk, many SBS VAPs require that they get paid a percentage of the budgeted consulting bill up front. These percentages typically range anywhere from 10 to 25 percent. After that, the SBS VAP bills the client at various project milestones or on predefined percentages at designated dates.

Handling Change Order Requests

Can you predict the need for change orders? Generally not, so don't bother beating yourself up over change orders you might get. The best protection against unanticipated requests and delays is doing a thorough job with the need analysis and network design report. (See Chapters 7, 9, and 10.) Try to uncover the client's true needs and anticipate future needs as much as possible to prevent problems.

The impossible task of trying to predict the unknown is shown in *Dilbert* when the pointy-haired boss asks Dilbert for a schedule of all the *unplanned* network outages. To this seemingly absurd request, Dilbert supplies a document that lists not only the unplanned network outages, but also all the hurricanes and tornadoes for the next several months.

Given that it can be extraordinarily difficult to predict when the "oh, by the way" requests might occur, what's the best way to proceed? If change order requests pop up during the rollout, most SBS VAPs recommend that you stop and explain to clients that their requests weren't part of the original project plan estimates. They need to be aware that fulfilling their requests will add to the cost of the project and will indeed impact the project timetable. The "Change Order" Word template included on the CD-ROM for this book should be used to evaluate and manage all potential change order requests. See Figure 11-2 on the next page.

Delays Caused by Change Orders

How can you deal with unanticipated delays caused by change orders? Most SBS VAPs recommend that you stay as flexible as possible. Let's say your project has eight distinct phases. If phase three involved connecting the SBS 4.5 server to an xDSL line on the Internet and the ISP or telco is delayed in installing the service, you should look at the project timetable and determine what tasks or phases you can accomplish next while you wait. For example, you may be able to move to phase four or five, which perhaps involves installing a tape backup solution, UPS, antivirus software, or installing workstations on the LAN. Whenever possible, try to maintain project continuity and prevent the rollout from grinding to a halt.

Anytime change orders affect project scheduling—and they almost always do—you should revise the schedule, even if you anticipate that the delay will only be minor. Remember, several minor delays can easily lead to a major project snafu. Failure to revise the schedule regularly may result in the client

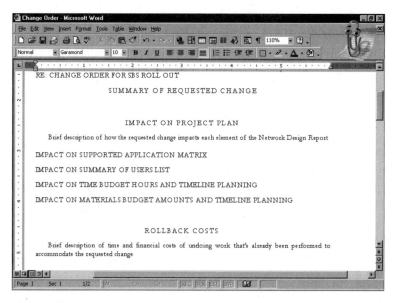

Figure 11-2

The "Change Order" template can help you manage change order requests.

exerting incredible pressure on your firm to deliver on the original estimated project completion date.

In Chapter 10 I suggested that you talk with your client about establishing financially tiered procedures and guidelines for making decisions about change-orders. For example, if the request is estimated to take less than two to four hours to accomplish or involves less than $200 to $500, perhaps a verbal authorization from the main contact person is adequate. If the estimate is for any greater amounts, a written change order, appended to the project plan, should require written client authorization and be invoiced separately.

Evaluation of Change Orders

As tempted as you might be to think of handling change orders as cut and dry or having them down to a science, all change order requests should be evaluated individually. Ask the following questions for each change order request:

- Is the client's change order request something that your firm would recommend implementing? If it isn't, most SBS VAPs say that you try to dissuade the client from proceeding.

- Can the project timing afford the schedule slippage that will be caused by the change order?

- Is the client aware of the different ways that your firm can help the client achieve the desired outcome of the requested change orders? Have you presented alternatives?

Note

Sometimes small business clients will initially opt for the scaled-down, low-budget versions of hardware, Internet access, or the like, only to later change their minds. Be flexible, but don't allow change orders to trash the schedule unless absolutely necessary. Remember how you emphasized that change orders must be mutually acceptable in your client consensus-building meeting? If necessary, recap your understanding of the decisions that you and the client *jointly* reached during that meeting.

Coordinating Vendors and Subcontractors

As discussed in Chapter 6, SBS VAPs can rarely provide all the pieces of the rollout puzzle. Frequently you'll partner with other firms or subcontract with various vendors. As these vendors' work become an integral part of the project timeline, understanding the impact of their schedule on other parts of the project is crucial.

Even a minor schedule slippage by another vendor or subcontractor can easily wreak havoc on your schedule. The best protection against this is an open line of communication between your firm and the other technology provider. As the project manager, also make sure to keep your main contact at the client apprised of any potential project timetable revisions that might need to take place as a result of vendors missing deadlines.

What can you do proactively when coordinating vendors and subcontractors for an SBS rollout? For starters, build some cushion into your schedule. If you know it typically takes 10 days to order a server and have it delivered, allow yourself at least 14 days in your schedule for the server to arrive. Adding extra time to the schedule is important when working with ISPs and telco companies because they're well known for being chronically late in many parts of the world.

Delays Caused by Subcontractors

When you subcontract for work and *your* subcontractor fouls up, you'll want to step in and make good on the work. Because this can eat into your service margin on the project, allow yourself some hedge against subcontractor problems in your time budget. In general, finger-pointing between you and the subcontractor greatly irritates your small business client. As a result, passing the buck should be avoided at all costs.

Most SBS VAPs just point out to clients what the delays are and the source of the delays. They let their clients come to their own conclusions. To be judgmental or adopt an "I told you so" kind of attitude is generally counterproductive. Do this among your staff if you must, but you should refrain from these types of discussions in front of clients, especially when the vendors are ones that your firm has *not* specifically recommended.

To help prevent misunderstandings during the project, make sure the vendor or subcontractor knows when the project is expected to be approved and when the work needs to be completed. When selecting vendors, also make sure you compare the vendor's availability to the project schedule. If you're depending upon a cable contractor for work in the next two to four weeks, but that firm's technicians are booked solid for the next three months, the project schedule will be thrown off.

Other Vendors Hired by the Client

Most SBS VAPs recommend that you avoid giving the client a choice in scheduling the work of other vendors and subcontractors unless absolutely necessary. Subcontractors work for your firm, not your client. Thus all of their instructions should come directly from your firm's project manager, *not* your small business client's single point of contact.

If your client doesn't want your firm subcontracting work and they in turn decide to hire the other needed vendors, you have a few creative ways to work within these confines. For starters, you can write the specs of what's needed from the other vendors and help your client qualify and interview the other technology providers. In addition, many SBS VAPs offer their clients the option to have your firm supervise the other technology providers for a fee.

The Bottom Line

Dealing successfully with technical issues, which Chapters 12 through 18 cover, is extremely important to being an SBS VAP. But projects live and die based on the execution of simple administrative details, such as schedule tracking. In this chapter you learned how to plan a successful SBS rollout and keep it on track with concrete project management techniques.

Chapter 12

Automating the Desktop Rollout

Tight timetables and thin budgets often necessitate automating the installation of the desktop OS and applications. At the same time, automating software installation helps maintain the quality control. Microsoft Small Business Server VAPs and their small business clients often miss out on this highly underrated way to save your client's budget *and* leave more money in the budget for higher-margin value-added solutions that are discussed throughout this book.

This chapter introduces you to techniques for automating the deployment of desktop operating systems with as little manual configuration as possible. Chapter 16 will present ways to automate the installation of the remainder of the SBS desktop, including SBS client applications and third-party software applications.

Paradigm Shift Toward Windows NT Workstation 4.0

During the past two years, Microsoft Windows NT Workstation 4.0 has gained tremendous momentum in the small and medium-sized business market. As recently as late 1997—around the same time as the SBS 4.0 release—Windows NT Workstation 4.0 was still being deployed *en masse* only by well-funded Fortune 1000 IT organizations. Windows NT Workstation 4.0 was installed primarily for power users with financial modeling, statistical, highly quantitative, or scientific applications. The PC hardware required to run Windows NT Workstation 4.0 was, at the time, still quite costly: around $3,500 to $5,000 for a desktop PC that could run the OS with acceptable performance. Application compatibility also still wasn't assured. And it was only after the release of Microsoft Windows NT 4.0 Service Pack 3 (SP3) that most IT professionals began to perceive Windows NT 4.0 as a truly stable OS.

By early 1998, two major shifts had occurred in the Windows NT Workstation 4.0 landscape. First, component prices on CPUs, RAM, and hard drives plummeted. As a result, leading PC manufacturers (OEMs) aggressively drove down price points for Windows NT Workstation 4.0 capable desktop PCs. In the United States, most major OEMs offered fully configured mainstream PCs that were ready for Windows NT Workstation 4.0, for in the neighborhood of $1,500. This configuration was similar to the following specifications: 233-MHz Pentium II CPU, 32 MB RAM, and a 4-GB hard drive.

Second, these same OEMs also began to offer Windows NT Workstation 4.0 as a time-of-purchase upgrade option with most of their mainstream desktop PCs. For about $100 (less than 10 percent of the purchase price), most major PC manufacturers would let you upgrade from the bundled desktop OS—Microsoft Windows 95 or Microsoft Windows 98—to Windows NT Workstation 4.0.

This sea change didn't exactly go unnoticed. In March 1998, I launched the "Small Business Smarts" column in *Selling Windows NT Solutions* magazine. The column discussed why small businesses weren't being well served by Windows 95 and why they needed Windows NT Workstation 4.0. ("NT Makes Small-Business Sense: Pack your small-business sales kit with these compelling reasons to go NT")

By June 1998—around the same time as the Windows 98 product launch—Microsoft released a white paper titled "Choosing the Best Windows

Desktop Platform—Small Business Guide," which detailed the numerous benefits of Windows NT Workstation 4.0 over Windows 95 and Windows 98 for small business users. In less than 12 months, the Windows 95/98 platform was moved from the mainstream business desktop OS to more of the consumer-oriented OS. Windows NT Workstation 4.0 was rapidly becoming the mainstream desktop OS for businesses of all sizes.

By early 2000, many of your small business clients still won't have heard of Windows NT Workstation 4.0. Compared to just 12 to 18 months ago, though, basic awareness of the OS has increased dramatically. As an SBS VAP, the key decision-maker at the small business client will likely need some basic education on the main differences between the Windows 95/98 platform and Windows NT Workstation 4.0. In addition to articles on the CD-ROM for this book, you'll find a wealth of information on the Microsoft Direct Access Web site (*www.microsoft.com/directaccess*) on why Windows NT Workstation 4.0 makes sense for small businesses.

Handling the In-Place Windows NT Workstation 4.0 Installation

An in-place installation is when you install an OS on a PC that already has an existing *and* functional OS. For example, your small business clients might have existing PCs with Windows 95. Your needs analysis and network design report concludes that their data security needs will be better served by adopting Windows NT Workstation 4.0 as the desktop OS standard. You're now confronted with an often confusing choice.

You can wipe the PC hard drives clean by reformatting or repartitioning the drives. Thus your Windows NT Workstation 4.0 installation would proceed just as if the OS was being installed on a new PC with an empty hard drive.

Alternatively, you could install Windows NT Workstation 4.0 on top of Windows 95. While this latter choice would more than likely save time, it's not usually the best approach.

A clean installation of Windows NT Workstation 4.0 has several major benefits: removing years of .dll and other system file clutter, increasing the system performance with the ultimate system defrag, and greater system stability as underlying system file conflicts are eradicated.

Benefits of Windows NT Workstation 4.0 over Windows 95/98

- **More crash proof.** With Windows NT Workstation 4.0, a single application is unlikely to compromise the stability of the entire desktop OS.

- **More scalable.** With Windows NT Workstation 4.0, performance increases substantially as you add RAM, faster processors, and a second processor.

- **More secure.** Windows NT Workstation 4.0 can use the NTFS local file system security and enforce a mandatory logon.

- **Familiar user interface (UI).** Windows NT Workstation 4.0 has the same basic UI as Windows 95 and Windows 98.

- **More tamper proof.** With Windows NT Workstation 4.0 and the modularity of various user rights, you can lock down the OS to prevent configuration tampering.

While SBS 4.5 still completely supports Windows 95 and Windows 98, I strongly recommend and implement Windows NT Workstation 4.0 as the standard desktop OS at small business clients. Most SBS VAPs worldwide are seeing increased demand for Windows NT Workstation 4.0 as the preferred desktop OS. To that end, this chapter will focus on automating the desktop rollout of Windows NT Workstation 4.0. For information on automating the setup of Windows 95, see the *Microsoft Windows 95 Resource Kit,* Chapters 4 through 6. To get assistance with automating the deployment of Windows 98, check out the *Microsoft Windows 98 Resource Kit*, Chapter 4.

This chapter is devoted to applying the base OS to desktop PCs. If your small business client is purchasing PCs from an OEM who already bundles and preloads Windows NT Workstation 4.0, many parts of this chapter won't be relevant.

For many SBS VAPs who are white box resellers, however, this chapter's content is *extremely* relevant. White box resellers purchase brand name components and assemble desktop PCs and servers with no brand name label on the front of the case. (Although some white box resellers do get stickers made up for the front of the case that display their firm's logo as the PC manufacturer.) For details on the decisions that go into reselling white box PCs or clones as opposed to brand name PCs, see Chapter 5.

Reviewing the Supported Application Matrix

Standardizing hardware and software saves a tremendous amount on acquisition and support costs. That's why this book emphasizes standardization throughout the needs analysis and IT audit and in your network design report.

Chapter 9 introduced the "Network Design Report," an Excel workbook on the CD-ROM. The worksheets in that workbook can only be completed properly after you've taken your small business client through a thorough needs analysis, IT audit, and individual site surveys. Besides forming the basis for the SBS roll out project plan, the "Network Design Report" workbook includes a "Supported Application Matrix," shown in Figure 12-1.

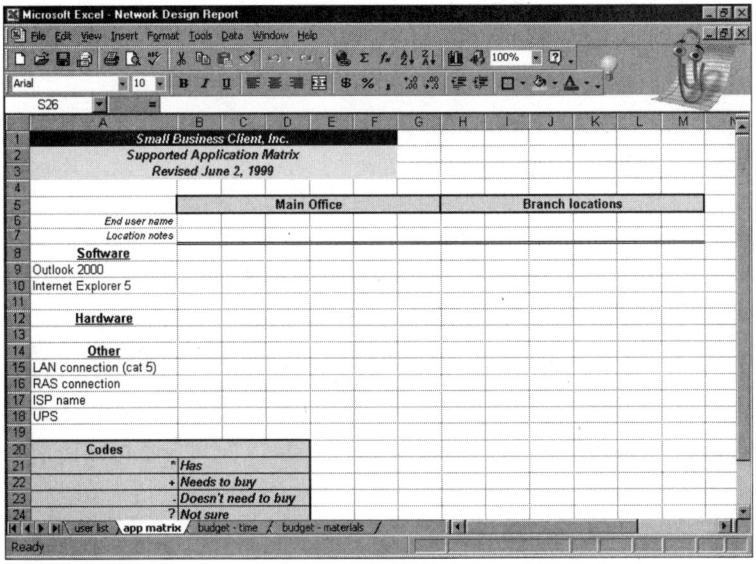

Figure 12-1

The "Supported Application Matrix" worksheet as originally introduced in Chapter 9.

The "Supported Application Matrix" helps to weed out the many problems associated with a lack of hardware and software standardization. A typical small business, which has *never* used a document like the "Supported Application Matrix," might have six different spreadsheet programs, five different word processors, and four different operating systems. On the hardware front, the small business might have five different brands of PCs with eight different network cards and four different video cards. A lack of standardization could easily deplete this small business' IT budget on seemingly trivial tasks, like chasing down the latest software patch or device driver. By standardizing the small business' PC platform, you'll be able to shift your firm's focus to higher-level activities, such as implementing groupware forms, intranets, relational database applications, and remote access.

Prior to rolling out the baseline desktop OS through methods described in this chapter, make sure you know about *and* have tested all the applications this particular client needs. Note that SBS 4.5 includes the following client applications that should also be tested with any additional required applications before proceeding:

- Microsoft Internet Explorer 5.0

- Microsoft Fax client

- Microsoft Modem Sharing client 4.5

- Microsoft Proxy client 2.0

- Microsoft Outlook 2000

- Microsoft Office 2000 Professional (included only with SBS 4.5 part numbers B58-00002 and B58-00009)

Tip

For more details on various SBS 4.5 SKUs and part numbers, see Chapter 2 and the SBS Web site at *www.microsoft.com/smallbusinessserver*.

Automating Deployment of the Desktop OS

You can automate the deployment of Windows NT Workstation 4.0 for your small business clients in two basic ways:

- **The Microsoft way**—primarily using answer files, unattended setups, uniqueness database files (UDFs), and system difference files

- **The third-party way**—primarily using cloning techniques and disk image replication

The balance of this chapter will help differentiate between these two methods and will help you select the one that will work best for your small business clients.

Regardless of whether you choose to roll out Windows NT Workstation 4.0 through unattended setup or cloning, you'll need access to either a CD-

ROM drive or a network share point. Most SBS VAPs choose the latter route, and then create a boot disk that can automatically connect to the network share point containing either the unattended setup files or disk image.

Preparing the Network Installation Startup Disk

One way to simplify creation of this magic boot disk is by using the Network Client Administrator program, which is part of Windows NT Server 4.0. The Network Client Administrator program can be found under Administrative Tools in the Start menu on any server running SBS 4.0, SBS 4.5, BackOffice Server 2.5 through 4.5, and Windows NT Server 4.0. The Network Client Administrator program has several functions, as shown in Figure 12-2. This chapter, however, discusses the program's ability to create a Network Installation Startup Disk easily.

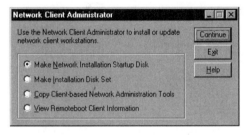

Figure 12-2
You can use the Network Client Administrator program to create boot disks, in addition to other functions.

Before you create this boot disk, or Network Installation Startup Disk if you will, you'll need to create a system disk on a system running MS-DOS 6.x or Windows 95/98. The Network Client Administrator copies files to this disk, so that when complete, you can boot the target PC and the PC will connect to a share point on the distribution server, from where the unattended setup or disk image replication programs are launched.

To support network installation, the Network Client Administrator program has device drivers available that support roughly 100 different network adapter cards. You will need to select one of these drivers to be installed on the Network Installation Startup Disk. In addition, the Network Client Administrator supports all three primary protocol stacks for a Windows NT network: NWLink or IPX, NetBEUI, and TCP/IP. Because TCP/IP is the default protocol installed with SBS 4.5 and its client workstations, most of the time you'll want to select TCP/IP and enable DHCP.

Tip

For more information on TCP/IP and DHCP, see Chapter 17.

When you create a Network Installation Startup Disk, make sure that you have accounted for the following:

- **Network adapter card settings**. The Network Client Administrator creates the Network Installation Startup Disk with the default settings for the network adapter card. Make sure you check your network adapter card's hardware configuration on the target workstation (primarily IRQ and base I/O address) and edit the relevant section of the protocol.ini file, which is in the net directory on the Network Installation Startup Disk, to match the actual hardware configuration.

- **User ID permissions**. Make sure the User ID used for network installation has access permissions to the distribution share point. Because that user's password is stored in plain text with unattended setups, your best bet is to create a special account (such as OSDeployer) that has read-only access to the distribution point. You will supply this User ID during the creation of the Network Installation Startup Disk.

- **System disk**. As indicated above, the Network Installation Startup Disk must be formatted as a system disk on an MS-DOS or Windows 95/98 system prior to running the Network Client Administrator program.

- **Net use path**. You'll need to edit the autoexec.bat file on the Network Installation Startup Disk to reflect any changes to the distribution point on the server.

Tip

For more information on Network Installation Startup Disks, see the *Microsoft Windows NT Workstation 4.0 Resource Kit,* Chapter 2.

Working with Answer Files, Unattended Setups, and UDFs

During a conventional Windows NT Workstation 4.0 installation launched by running the winnt or winnt32 setup program, you'll typically need to reply to at least a dozen different dialog boxes and configuration options. While not a real nuisance or barrier to installation for one or two PCs running Windows NT Workstation 4.0, multiply this effort over as few as 10 to 15 PCs and it becomes quite tedious. In addition, manual setup introduces many opportunities for configuration errors and inconsistent settings.

With an unattended setup, also known as a silent installation, you enter the setup information once. This not only saves time, but also reduces errors and assures consistency. Configuring an unattended setup for Windows NT Workstation 4.0 is also extremely helpful if you have a more senior-level consultant on staff who prepares the standards for more junior-level technicians to deploy at your small business client sites. You need to be careful, however, in designing and testing the unattended installation because one small mistake will be cascaded across dozens of workstations.

At the most basic level, an unattended setup requires three elements:

1. The winnt or winnt32 setup program

2. A customized unattend.txt file

3. Your answers to the questions posed in the unattend.txt file

Note

The winnt setup program is used the majority of the time by SBS VAPs because winnt can be run from MS-DOS, Windows 3.x, or Windows 95/98. The winnt32 setup program, on the other hand, can be run only from Windows NT Workstation 3.5x or 4.0.

Answer Files

An answer file, also known as an installation script or an unattend.txt file, answers the configuration questions posed by the winnt or winnt32 setup programs. When combined with the winnt or winn32 setup program, an unattend.txt file specifies the required configuration information.

An unattend.txt template, or sample if you will, is in the i386 directory of the Windows NT Workstation 4.0 CD-ROM. As the file extension implies, the unattend.txt file is simply a text file that can be modified in any standard text editor, such as Notepad. Although you can certainly edit the unattend.txt or answer file by hand, the Windows NT Setup Manager (setupmgr.exe), a GUI-based tool, can perform all of the most of the popular customizations for the unattend.txt file. The Windows NT Setup Manager is included on both the Windows NT Workstation 4.0 CD-ROM and the *Microsoft Windows NT Workstation 4.0 Resource Kit* CD-ROM.

Note

This chapter, and this book for that matter, assumes that your small business clients will be running Windows NT Workstation 4.0 on Intel CPUs or comparable CPUs from AMD or Cyrix. In the highly unlikely event that your small business clients are running Windows NT Workstation 4.0 on PCs with Alpha processors, you'll want to review the Deployment section of the Windows NT Workstation 4.0 Web site at *www.microsoft.com/NTWorkstation*.

The Network Installation Startup Disk needs a designated user account name and password to connect to the clients share on the server. This particular share, set up by the Network Client Administrator program, should hold the distribution files required for the unattended setup (in the i386 directory of the Windows NT Workstation 4.0 CD-ROM). In order to make the initial net use logon seamless, the unattend.txt stores the account name and password as straight text. Because this user name and password can be lifted or compromised so easily, you'll want to create a special user account with *extremely* restrictive read-only permissions to the clients share on the server.

Note

For security reasons, you definitely don't want to use your standard administrator account and password for the unattended setup.

The Windows NT Setup Manager walks you through creating the unattend.txt file, with predefined answers to prompts you'd normally have to respond to during Windows NT Workstation 4.0 setup. In sharp contrast to image files, which are discussed later in this chapter, an unattended setup can be used across a broad base of hardware. This means that PCs don't need to be identical. So an unattended setup can be used if your small business client doesn't have standardized client workstations. The only caveat is that the hardware must be on the Windows NT Hardware Compatibility List (HCL) *and* setup needs to be able to detect the hardware properly. This primarily affects network adapter cards, disk adapters, and video cards.

Tip

The Microsoft Hardware Compatibility List is located at *www.microsoft.com/HCL*.

The Windows NT Setup Manager divides the configuration choices into three broad categories: General Setup, Networking Setup, and Advanced Setup. See Figure 12-3. The configuration choices that can be found in each of these three categories are shown in Table 12-1 on the next page.

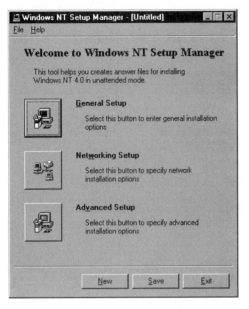

Figure 12-3

Windows NT Setup Manager configuration categories.

Note

When you have made all your selections in Windows NT Setup Manager, be sure to save your file by choosing the Save command from the File menu.

When you've completed preparing the unattend.txt file, you'll need to move the file to the distribution point on the server that contains a copy of the i386 directory from the Windows NT Workstation 4.0 CD-ROM, such as the clients share. As you begin to customize the autoexec.bat file on the Network Installation Startup Disk, you'll need to know about command syntax and switches for winnt and winnt32. The /s switch specifies the source file location where the i386 directory resides relative to the drive letter that you've mapped through a net use command. The /u switch specifies where the unattend.txt file resides also relative to the drive letter that you've mapped through a net use command.

General Setup	Networking Setup	Advanced Setup
User name	Manual or unattended network installation	Install new hardware abstraction layer (HAL)
Organization		Specify reboots
Computer name	Detect network adapter card	Specify file system
Product ID		Mass storage device drivers
Confirm hardware settings	List of network adapters cards to be detected	Display device drivers
Computer role		Keyboard device drivers
Domain name	Protocols	Device drivers for pointing devices
Target installation directory	Services	Boot files
Display settings	Modem (if RAS installed)	Advertisement
Time zone		

Table 12-1

Configuration options by category in Windows NT Setup Manager

Tip

For more information on answer files and unattended setup, see the *Microsoft Windows NT Workstation 4.0 Resource Kit*, Chapter 2.

UDFs

As you begin creating Network Installation Startup Disks for each target workstation, you'll notice the vast majority of the configuration choices remain the same, while a few key variables change, such as computer name and user name. To make the unattended setup more flexible, Microsoft gives you the ability to extend the capabilities of the unattend.txt files though UDFs. A UDF is like an answer file, although a UDF identifies the key differences between installation options for various workstations and users. A UDF also overrides any values in unattend.txt answer file that have same names.

When you run either the winnt or winnt32 setup program as unattended setups, the setup program merges the contents of the UDF file with the unattend.txt file. Within the UDF file, the [UniqueIds] header or section contains the unique identifiers for specific workstations.

**Tip**

For more information on UDFs, see the _Microsoft Windows NT Workstation 4.0 Resource Kit_, Chapter 2.

Difference Files

You can extend the unattended setup to include installation for additional
Microsoft and other third-party applications. SBS 4.5, however, already provides a facility for this: the Set Up Computer Wizard (SCW). Chapter 16 shows
how to take the base OS install that you've already deployed and set up the SBS
4.5 client applications _and_ other non-SBS applications.

Both the unattended setup options and customizing the SCW require that
the desired application have a scripted or silent installation option. For a variety of reasons, not all third-party applications support this kind of installation. For this purpose, Microsoft provides the sysdiff utility both on the
Windows NT Workstation 4.0 CD-ROM and with the _Microsoft Windows NT
Workstation 4.0 Resource Kit_.

Sysdiff is application independent, meaning that you can use sysdiff to
automate the application of virtually any software application. When configured properly, sysdiff can make the OS believe that the setup program for that
particular software application has been run. Sysdiff not only takes into account
file and folder installations, but registry modifications as well. In order to use
sysdiff to add applications to a PC, Windows NT Workstation 4.0 must already
be installed.

**Note**

Sysdiff can't automate an OS installation. To automate deployment of the
OS, use the unattended setup options first.

To use sysdiff, follow these steps:

1. Create a snapshot of the Windows NT Workstation 4.0 PC (the before
   state of the files and registry). Do this with the sysdiff /snap command.

2. Install the desired applications and make the relevant configuration settings.

3. Create a difference file to determine what's changed (the after state
   of the files and registry). Do this with the sysdiff /diff command.

4. Apply the difference file to the target workstation with the sysdiff/ apply command.

Tip

To examine the contents of a difference file, run the sysdiff /dump command.

Creating Image Files

Up to now, this chapter has covered the Microsoft methods of automating the deployment of Windows NT Workstation 4.0. Several third-party independent software vendors (ISVs) have an alternate method of getting the Windows NT Workstation 4.0 OS rapidly and consistently deployed on target PCs. The ISVs use image replication techniques, commonly known as cloning. Disk image replication can also be very useful when you need to rapidly recover a standard PC software configuration after an OS becomes corrupted or hardware fails.

Using Microsoft Systems Management Server 2.0 to Automate Deployment of Windows NT Workstation 4.0

An often overlooked option is to use Microsoft Systems Management Server (SMS) 2.0 to automate deployment of Windows NT Workstation 4.0. SBS VAPs often don't think of SMS because SBS does *not* include SMS.

If your firm has a Windows NT Server 4.0 system running SMS 2.0 or a system running Microsoft BackOffice Server 4.5, however, you could bring that server on-site to the client temporarily for a day or two to automate the desktop OS rollout. You could even have SMS 2.0 running on a well configured laptop to make the deployment solution truly portable.

Nevertheless, I'd recommend that you pursue this route only if your firm already licenses SMS 2.0 and has appropriate SMS expertise in-house. You shouldn't go out of your way to purchase a laptop and install BackOffice Server 4.5 just for automating Windows NT Workstation 4.0 rollouts. SMS 2.0 is primarily for system management in much larger environments than 2 to 50 seats. This chapter describes some much simpler and more cost-effective ways to automate desktop OS deployment.

For more information on implementation details and licensing for SMS 2.0 see the *Systems Management Server Resource Guide* in the *Microsoft BackOffice Resource Kit: Part Two* or the SMS Web site at *www.microsoft.com/smsmgmt*.

How does cloning work? You need to follow these steps:

1. Create a standard workstation image. Develop a prototype PC that has an identical hardware configuration to the target PCs, and get the software configuration perfect.

2. Use the disk image utility to create an image based on your perfect master PC.

3. Use disk image replication to deploy all of the standardized desktops.

While an in-depth hands-on discussion of cloning software is well beyond the scope of this book, I'd like to give you at least an overview of the pros and cons of cloning, as opposed to the unattended setups described earlier in the chapter. For more in-depth information on disk image replication tools, start by checking out the Web sites for these popular third-party disk image replication software utilities:

- Altiris RapiDeploy (*www.altiris.com*)

- ImageCast IC3 (*www.imagecast.com*)

- PowerQuest DriveImage Pro (*www.powerquest.com*)

- Symantec Norton Ghost (*www.symantec.com*)

Tip

As with unattended setups, you'll need to be *very* careful in testing the deployment of your disk images because one mistake will be cascaded across dozens of workstations.

Pros of Cloning

The positive aspects of using cloning to deploy standardized desktops include:

- **Speed of deployment.** Cloning is generally a faster process because compression is used, as well as multicast IP.

- **Ease and speed of preparation.** With cloning, you don't need to customize unattended setup scripts, UDFs, or sysdiff files. Although this customization is quite flexible, perfecting the scripts, UDFs, and sysdiff files can be very time consuming. Cloning eliminates the need for extensive trial and error with unattended setup scripts. You do much less work up front to get a disk image ready for deployment.

- **Faster learning curve.** With cloning, you don't need to learn about scripting languages and specialized requirements for third-party applications.

- **Works with data at a much more intimate level.** By taking an image of the disk sector by sector, cloning picks up data not visible to a file-by-file copy. Cloning takes a snapshot of *all* files, including hidden files and files that are in use.

- **More encompassing.** Generally speaking, cloning supports virtually any software application, while other unattended installation methods can be more limited. With cloning, you can even automate the deployment of applications that are difficult to automate. Cloning can also include shortcuts, desktops, persistent network connections, and service packs.

Cons of Cloning

The arguments against cloning include:

- **Licensing complexity and costs.** When using cloning solutions to automate deployment, you'll need to buy additional software. And to complicate matters, each vendor has its own unique licensing programs and requirements.

- **Identical desktop hardware requirement.** Unlike an unattended setup, which can detect a variety of HCL-approved hardware devices, disk images are specific to the hardware on which they were created. As a result, the target PC hardware must be identical to source image hardware.

- **Need for limited manual configuration.** Unlike unattended setups, machine and user specific settings must still be configured manually after the disk image is deployed to the target PC.

- **Lack of modularity.** Cloning is largely an all or nothing deal. Disk image replication utilities can't merge images with lists of different users and different applications.

Microsoft Support of Disk Image Utilities

Up until early 1998, the leading third-party cloning programs couldn't generate a unique security identifier (SID) when an image was replicated from a source to a target workstation. As a result, all of the target workstations on a given network would have identical SIDs. Because a unique SID is needed for successful communication between Windows NT systems on a given network, Microsoft opposed the use of cloning software.

IT organizations and VAPs, however, were deploying PCs running Windows NT Workstation 4.0 with identical SIDs and not experiencing problems. Microsoft warned that its Product Support Services (PSS) division wouldn't support cloning and that the next version of Windows NT, dubbed Windows NT 5.0 at the time, would *insist* upon unique SIDs.

Note

A unique SID is generated when a PC running Windows NT Workstation 4.0 joins a given domain.

By early 1998, however, various third-party ISVs tweaked their disk image replication utilities so they could in fact generate a unique SID. Shortly after that in June 1998, Microsoft released the Microsoft System Preparation tool, which legitimized cloning and offers PSS support for cloning with certain caveats.

Microsoft System Preparation Tool

The System Preparation tool, as the name implies, prepares a Windows NT Workstation 4.0 master PC to be imaged and replicated to target PCs. The System Preparation tool does *not* replace third-party disk image replication solutions, but rather supplements their usage. When used *prior* to taking a disk image with a third-party solution, the System Preparation tool helps to make sure your Windows NT Workstation 4.0 SIDs are unique. This allows the automated deployment of Windows NT Workstation 4.0 to be supported by Microsoft PSS.

The System Preparation tool can be licensed free by any Microsoft customer with an active volume licensing agreement. For details, see the Deployment section of the Windows NT Workstation 4.0 Web site at *www.microsoft.com/NTWorkstation*. Just bear in mind that the System Preparation tool has the same confines as cloning. This means your hardware on the master PC must *still* be identical to the hardware on the target PCs.

For more information on Microsoft's position on cloning tools and how the System Preparation tool fits into these types of solutions see:

- "Disk-Image Copying of MS Windows Operating Systems" (last updated 6/98, part number 098-80634). This white paper can be found on the Microsoft TechNet site at *technet.microsoft.com*.

- "Easier Windows NT Workstation 4.0 Deployment with Disk Image Copying and the Microsoft System Preparation Tool" (last updated 12/98). This white paper can be found on the Windows NT Workstation 4.0 site at *www.microsoft.com/NTWorkstation.*

The Bottom Line

Automating the deployment of desktop systems has several advantages: it's cost-effective, saves time, and helps maintain quality control. This chapter introduced you to techniques for automating software installation with as little manual configuration as possible. These techniques include using Microsoft solutions, such as using answer files, unattended setups, uniqueness database files (UDFs), and system difference files, or using third-party utilities for disk image replication.

Chapter 13

Post-Installation Server Configuration Tasks

Loosen your tie, unbutton the top button of your shirt, roll up your sleeves, and don your favorite SBS pocket protector. You've reached the more "techie" section of the book.

This chapter shows how to make sure you have a complete Microsoft BackOffice Small Business Server 4.5 installation. The problem is everyone has his or her own definition of complete. VAPs new to SBS might be tempted to think they're done with the SBS installation when CD-ROM 3 of the unattended SBS 4.5 setup is complete. This, however, isn't the case.

While the unattended parts of the SBS 4.5 setup are quite comprehensive, you'll need to take at least a dozen more steps before you'll be ready to turn the newly installed SBS 4.5 network over to your small business client's end users. This chapter will provide a structured way to tackle some of the more commonly required steps efficiently.

The SBS 4.5 Unattended Setup Program

As you've seen, SBS 4.5 is a very full-featured and complex NOS suite. The redesigned setup for SBS 4.5, however, makes it possible to install SBS 4.5 with a minimum of configuration effort. For highlights on the SBS 4.5 setup, read Chapter 2 to learn how Microsoft overhauled the SBS 4.5 setup to be more VAP-friendly. With that in mind, your greatest opportunity to add value as an SBS VAP is during the planning stages and post-installation customization phases. You'll help your small business clients chart a cohesive technology roadmap and strategy. Once that's complete, you can begin executing that technology plan by implementing a myriad of solutions. These might include a customized SBS Console and Set Up Computer Wizard (Chapters 14 and 16), a proactive maintenance program (Chapters 15, 19, 22, 23, and 25), high-speed, secure Internet access, and collaborative and messaging applications (Chapters 18 and 26), and remote access and faxing applications (Chapter 27).

For more in-depth information on the unattended setup routine, see Part 3, "Deployment," in the *Microsoft BackOffice Small Business Server 4.5 Resource Kit*. In particular, you might want to review Chapter 17, "Installing on New Machines"; Chapter 18, "Installing Small Business Server in Existing Environments"; and Chapter 19, "Small Business Server Setup Issues," in the *Resource Kit*.

Before You Get Started: Top 5 Tips and Hints

Originally, I was going to start this chapter by covering how to configure users, computers, and folders. (These topics are covered later in this chapter.) You, however, need to be concerned with a number of points immediately following setup before you begin administering the server. Think of the following topics as your orientation to post-installation server configuration tasks.

Don't Change the Computer Name or Domain Name

Don't change the name of the computer or of the domain following setup. Figure 13-1 might lead you to believe that doing this is possible. That figure, however, shows a Windows NT Server 4.0 dialog box, not a dialog box from the portfolio of SBS 4.5 administration wizards. For a list of the SBS 4.5 wizards, see Table 2-1 in Chapter 2.

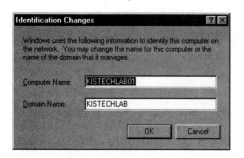

Figure 13-1

Avoid changing the SBS 4.5 server computer and domain names at all costs.

If you change either the computer or domain name, many of the SBS server applications won't recognize the new name. Too many dependencies exist between applications. Once the SBS 4.5 setup has recorded your computer and domain names, neither can be safely changed without ramifications.

Pay Close Attention to Service Control Manager Errors

Service control manager errors are indicated when you see a dialog box with the following message: "At least one service or driver failed during system startup." See Figure 13-2. If you receive this message on a fresh restart, don't casually dismiss the dialog box as insignificant. You should investigate further. This type of error usually means some relatively important service or device driver isn't functioning properly.

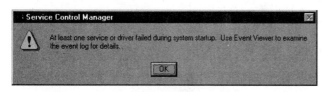

Figure 13-2

Always take Service Control Manager errors seriously.

An error like this will result in a new entry with a red stop sign in the System Log, which you can view in Event Viewer. See Figure 13-3 on the next page. For those of you who might be new to Microsoft Windows NT, you can reach Event Viewer by choosing Programs on the Start menu, then choosing Administrative Tools.

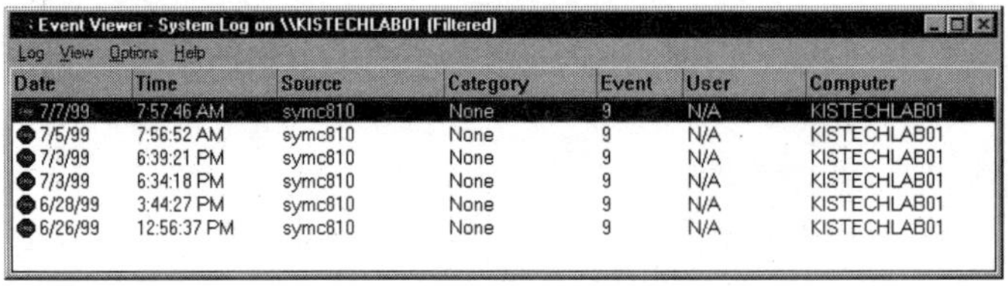

Figure 13-3

When you receive a Service Control Manager error, always examine the stop errors in the System Log through the Event Viewer.

Once you've double-clicked the most recent stop event and noted the source, event ID, and description, you can begin researching the error through the Microsoft Knowledge Base or through Microsoft Direct Access Technical Support resources for SBS VAPs (*www.microsoft.com/directaccess*).

Also note that several documented Event Viewer log errors in SBS 4.5 don't cause problems. For a list of these errors, see Table 53.1, Known Errors, in Chapter 53 of the *Microsoft BackOffice Small Business Server 4.5 Resource Kit.*

Avoid Changing the Parameters for Services

The SBS 4.5 setup configures the required Windows NT services for the appropriate startup type. Unless you have expert knowledge on SBS 4.5 and the related Microsoft BackOffice family of applications, avoid making random changes to services. See Figure 13-4. For a list of the default services installed with SBS 4.5, see KB article Q217999 in the Microsoft Knowledge Base (*support.microsoft.com*).

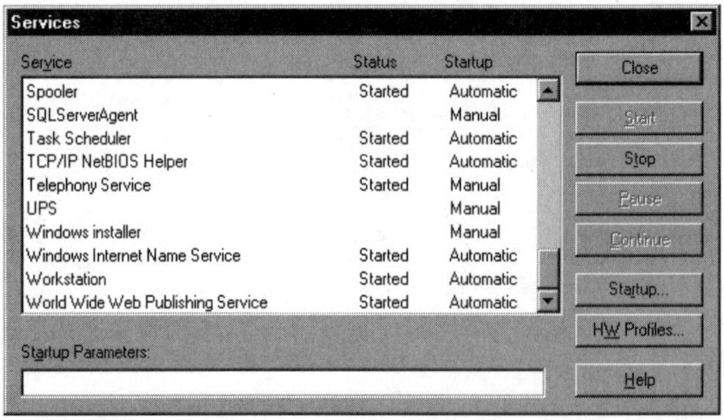

Figure 13-4

Be careful when making changes to services.

Check the Setup Log Files

If you encountered any difficulty during the unattended SBS 4.5 setup, you might be able to find clues in the setup log files. These text files are found in \Program Files\Microsoft BackOffice and in temp folders on the system drive. You can most easily locate these log files by sorting according to the most recent time and date stamp in Windows NT Explorer.

Change the Administrator Password the SBS Way

Although a number of ways exist to change a password associated with a user account name on a Windows NT Server, only one way is safe for changing the Administrator password on an SBS 4.5 system. Because of all the account credentials associated with dependent server services, you should only change the Administrator password by using the Change Password Wizard. See Figure 13-5. The Change Password Wizard is located on the Manage Users page, which you can access from the Tasks page of the SBS Console.

Figure 13-5

Always use the Change Password Wizard to change the Administrator password.

Configuring Users, Computers, and Folders

The To Do List on the SBS Console helps SBS VAPs a great deal with the tasks after unattended setup. See Figure 13-6. The remainder of this chapter will reference the To Do List as the basis for planning and organizing your post installation server configuration tasks.

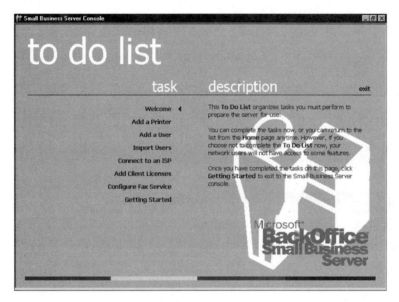

Figure 13-6
The To Do List page on the SBS Console helps you plan tasks after setup.

Understanding the To Do List and What It Means to Have a Complete Installation

As the name implies, the To Do List is one-stop shopping for accomplishing the most immediate tasks following installation. The To Do List appears the first time you log on to the server. Subsequently, you can launch the To Do List by clicking the first Favorites link on the SBS Console Home page, as shown in Figure 13-7.

Depending on which network applications your small business clients need, you might not need to complete *all* of the tasks on the To Do List immediately. You need, however, to have at least a superficial grasp on the purpose of all the tasks on the To Do List, which are explained in Table 13-1. That way when the need for a particular application arises, you'll know exactly where to turn for the most efficient configuration options.

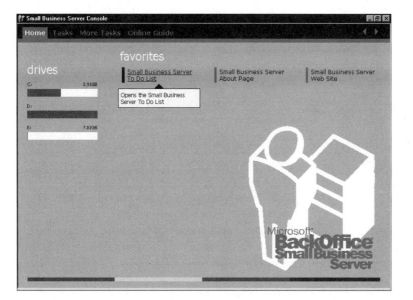

Figure 13-7

Open the To Do List from the SBS Console Home page.

Task	Description
Welcome	Introduces the To Do List
Add A Printer	Connects a printer directly to the server (such as parallel port LPT1) or to a network printer (such as a Hewlett-Packard JetDirect printer server connected to an Ethernet hub)
Add A User	Creates a user account, grants access to folders and other resources (e-mail distribution lists, Proxy Server Internet access, RAS, printers, and fax), and sets up a computer for an SBS end user
Import Users	Imports Windows NT Server 4.0 account information created by running the SBS 4.5 Migrate User Wizard on a Windows NT Server 4.0 domain controller or member server

Table 13-1

Tasks in the To Do List in the SBS Console   *(continued)*

Table 13-1 *(continued)*

Task	Description
Connect To An ISP	Launches the Internet Connection Wizard, the subject of Chapter 18, and connects the network to the Internet for e-mail and Web browsing and publishing (If your small business client has a full-time connection, you can even configure SBS 4.5 for use as a Web server and for virtual private networking.)
Add Client Licenses	Finds out how many client access licenses (CALs) have been purchased and adds additional CALs in increments of 5 and 20 users
Configure Fax Service	Configures one or more fax modems to receive faxes (SBS 4.5 setup configures fax devices to send faxes on each installed fax device but not to receive.)
Getting Started	Exits out of the To Do List and back to the SBS Console Home page

Configuring User and Computer Accounts

Two ways exist to add users to an SBS 4.5 network using the To Do List. After you click the Add A User task, the User Account Wizard walks you through adding a new user, granting the user appropriate permissions to network resources, and setting up a computer for the user. See Figure 13-8. Through the User Account Wizard, you can selectively grant permissions for the following:

- E-mail distribution list membership

- Read/write or read-only access to shared folders

- Network printers and fax printers

- Internet access

- Remote access to the server

- Administrative access to the server

Once you have decided which network resources the user of this newly created account should be able to access, the wizard will guide you through the Set Up Computer Wizard (SCW), creating a client setup disk to connect a computer to the SBS 4.5 network. The Add A User task is unique in that it combines establishing the user account and permissions with setting up the computer for the user. If you were to tackle these tasks outside of the To Do List framework, you'd need to visit both the Manage Users page from the Tasks page and the Manage Computers page from the More Tasks page in the SBS Console.

Figure 13-8

Use the User Account Wizard to create user accounts, grant permissions, and set up computers.

Batch User Add Tool

The User Account Wizard can be extremely helpful if you need to set up one user and computer at a time. If you're setting up 10 to 15 users simultaneously, however, you might welcome automation. The *Microsoft BackOffice Small Business Server 4.5 Resource Kit* includes the Batch User Add Tool, a Microsoft Excel spreadsheet with macros that automate the creation of individual user accounts and company-wide default values. See Figure 13-9 on the next page. Because the Batch User Add Tool is a standard Excel spreadsheet, you can simply copy and paste the user names you entered in the "Summary of Users List" worksheet in the "Network Design Report" workbook on the CD-ROM at the back of this book. (The "Network Design Report" was covered in Chapter 9.) Once you have filled out the spreadsheet and clicked the Create User File button, the Batch User Add Tool creates the users.txt file. This is a standard, editable text file, which should be copied to a diskette so that it can be used to import user account names into SBS 4.5 through the Import Users task on the To Do List.

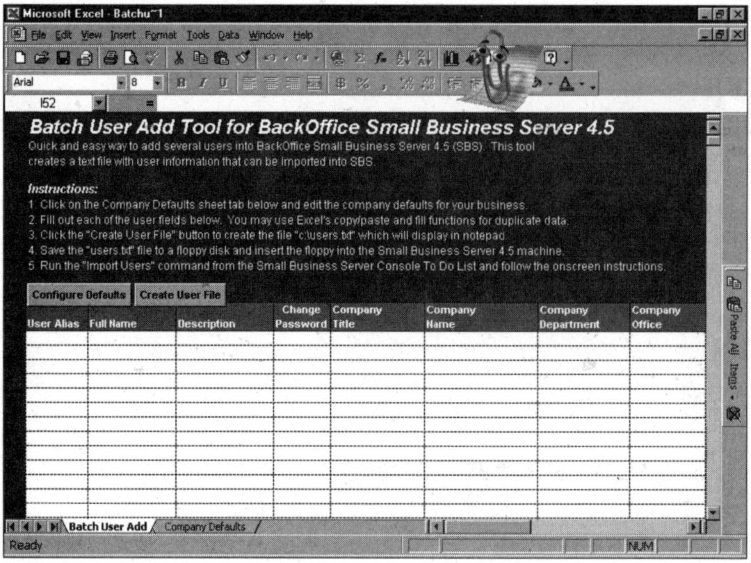

Figure 13-9

Batch User Add Tool can be found in the Microsoft BackOffice Small Business Server 4.5 Resource Kit.

Import Users

Although SBS 4.5 was designed and thoroughly tested for in-place upgrades of SBS 4.0, you can't do an in-place SBS 4.5 installation on top of Windows NT Server 4.0 and Exchange Server 5.x. Microsoft, however, found a lot of small businesses were migrating from this combination to SBS 4.0.

To help you migrate small business clients from Windows NT Server 4.0 and Exchange Server 5.x, Microsoft created the Migrate User Wizard. See Figure 13-10. The wizard extracts user account information from the Windows NT Server 4.0 registry and saves the data to a text file on a disk. Before you can import the user account information, you'll need to export users by running the Migrate User Wizard, which is launched from the autorun screen on SBS 4.5 CD-ROM 1. You can only export user accounts from a Windows NT Server 4.0 system because the Migrate User Wizard checks for specific registry entries. The Migrate User Wizard should be run on the Windows NT Server 4.0 system immediately prior to importing the user list into SBS 4.5.

Once you've created and edited the disk with the user account information through either the Batch User Add Tool or the Migrate User Wizard, you can import the data through the Import Users task on the To Do List.

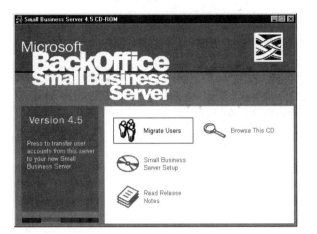

Figure 13-10
Use the Migrate User Wizard to import user account information from Windows NT 4.0 Server.

Creating Setup Disks with Set Up Computer Wizard

If you've used the Batch User Add Tool or the Migrate User Wizard to import a list of user account settings from an Excel spreadsheet or a Windows NT Server 4.0 domain controller, you'll still need to create client setup disks before the workstations can be properly installed on the SBS 4.5 network.

Note

Only the Add A User task on the To Do List can create user accounts and set up computers simultaneously. For more details on setting up desktop computers on an SBS 4.5 network, see Chapter 17.

You can use SCW to select an existing SBS 4.5 user account and create a client setup disk that will install the required client applications and add the computer to the SBS 4.5 domain. See Figure 13-11 on the next page. SCW is launched by clicking Manage Computers on the More Tasks page in the SBS Console.

Tip

For more details on how SCW configures SBS 4.5 workstations, see Chapter 17. You can also integrate third-party applications into the automated SCW (see Chapter 16).

Figure 13-11

When the required user account already exists, use the Set Up Computer Wizard to add a workstation to the SBS 4.5 network for the specified user.

Creating and Moving Company and Private Shared Folders

At the most basic level, most small businesses need two different types of file-based storage on the server: public and private. A public folder is fully accessible to anyone who has a valid user name logon account for the SBS 4.5 network. The unattended setup routine for SBS 4.5 prompts you to create a public folder in the Company Shared Folders directory. A private folder on the server is generally only available to one specific user name account. The unattended setup routine for SBS 4.5 prompts you to create the private folders in the Users Shared Folders directory. The public folder is created during the unattended SBS 4.5 setup. Each user's private folder is created when you configure the user account through the User Account Wizard.

When you run the client setup disk at each target workstation, the wizard places shortcuts on the desktop for the user's private folder and the company's public folder. I usually also map persistent drive connections to these shared folder locations using the same naming convention. The N drive is each user's personal, private network folder. The P drive is the company-wide public shared folder. Mapping these drives is explored in detail toward the end of Chapter 17.

Immediately following the unattended SBS 4.5 setup, your small client's server will often run low on available hard drive space on the system partition. You need to be able to move existing personal and private shared folders easily. This can be accomplished through the Move Folder Wizard, accessible through Manage Shared Folders on the Tasks page in the SBS Console. See Figure 13-12.

Figure 13-12

Use the Move Folder Wizard to move folders when space is low.

Configuring Shared Printers

Once the SBS 4.5 system is up and running and user accounts and shared folders are created, your small business client will likely want to share various printer devices through the network. From the Add A Printer task on the To Do List, you can launch the Add Printer Wizard. Those of you familiar with Windows NT 4.0 administration will recognize this wizard as the one included with Windows NT Server 4.0 and Windows NT Workstation 4.0. See Figure 13-13 on the next page.

The Add Printer Wizard can be used to set up shared printers that are directly attached to the server through a local printer port, such as parallel port LPT1. This wizard can also be used to configure network-based printers that are connected directly to category 5 cable through Ethernet connections (such as a Hewlett-Packard JetDirect printer server).

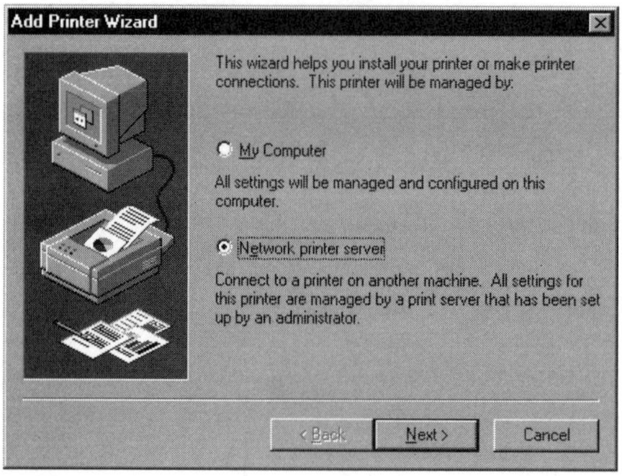

Figure 13-13

Use the Add Printer Wizard to set up shared printers on the SBS network.

Although not a common request with small business clients, printer pooling can also be enabled through the Add Printer Wizard. Printer pooling aggregates several identically configured printer devices into one logical printer. Once configured properly, end users can print to a single printer through a printer queue while the NOS decides to which available physical device to route the printing job.

Once shared printers are configured, you can selectively grant or deny access to the shared printer as you create new user accounts. In addition, you can review all the user permissions for a specific shared printer through the Printer Access Wizard. See Figure 13-14. To launch the wizard, click Manage Shared Printers on the Tasks page of the SBS Console.

In many cases, you'll grant everyone on the SBS 4.5 network access to all shared printers. In some cases, however, more restrictive permissions are in order. For example, take a printer that's stocked with blank checks or a printer that's extremely expensive to operate, such as color laser poster printer. Both devices can be controlled through permissions. In addition, auditing can also be enabled to track usage. For more details, see keyword "audit" in the Online Guide for the SBS Console.

Installing Client Bump Packs

Through the most common SBS 4.5 licensing scenario, your new small business clients will start with five CALs. To grow beyond that, your client will need

Figure 13-14

Use the Printer Access Wizard to review user permissions.

to purchase additional CALs in increments of five or twenty licenses. Also known as add-on packs or the bump packs, these CALs allow you to increase the number of workstations that can be connected to an SBS 4.5 network from 5 to 50. For details on SBS 4.5 licensing and product stock-keeping units (SKUs), see Chapter 2 or the SBS Web site at *www.microsoft.com/ smallbusinessserver*.

Tip

Don't confuse the workstation connection limit with the user account limit. Even with only five CALs, SBS 4.5 supports virtually an unlimited number of user accounts. Unless you bump up beyond five CALs, however, this unlimited number of users must share five workstations on the SBS 4.5 network.

In order to add more CALs to SBS 4.5, choose Add Client Licenses on the To Do List. This wizard begins by reviewing the number of currently owned and installed licenses. Because setup for adding bump packs needs to reboot the server twice, you'll likely want to schedule the bump pack installation for after hours.

Tip

Prior to rebooting the server, you should always make sure all affected end users are disconnected from the server.

In the event you need to apply multiple bump packs, be sure to number the order in which the bump packs were applied. This becomes crucial in case you need to reapply the bump packs for a reinstallation.

Using the i386 Distribution Point

The i386 directory on the SBS 4.0 CD-ROM 1 contains the setup code and device drivers to get a plain vanilla installation of Windows NT Server 4.0 functioning. In addition to its usefulness during installation, the contents of the i386 directory are frequently needed when configuring printers, modems, and various network components.

You can help control the physical installation media, speed up reconfiguration of new devices and services, and wow your small business clients simply by copying the i386 folder and its subdirectories to a volume on the server with at least 80 MB of available space. For example, let's say that you need to install a Hewlett-Packard Color LaserJet 5 as a shared printer on LPT1. Start at the To Do List and click Add A Printer, which launches the Add Printer Wizard. From there choose to install a local printer. Finally, when you've answered all the questions, SBS 4.5 prompts you with the Files Needed dialog box. See Figure 13-15. To copy the driver files, you can either hunt down SBS 4.5 CD-ROM 1, place it in your CD-ROM drive, and browse through the dialog box until you find them, or simply browse the i386 folder.

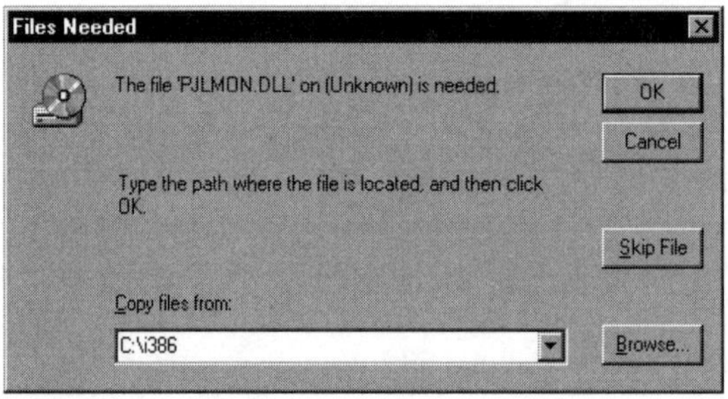

Figure 13-15

In the Files Needed dialog box, browse until you find the i386 folder to install a local printer.

Protecting the Data

Although data protection is an extremely important topic, the unattended setup for SBS 4.5 doesn't have a mechanism for dealing with each small business' unique data protection requirements. The early stages of the SBS 4.5 setup will detect and allow you to tweak device drivers for various disk and RAID controllers that are either part of the SBS or more general Windows NT hardware compatibility lists. The SBS unattended setup, however, has no cohesive framework for nailing down an airtight strategy for protecting your small business client's server-based data.

Once the SBS 4.5 setup is complete, you'll want to work through the data protection section of this chapter to jump start your data protection efforts. Later the book delves more deeply into ongoing data protection strategies. Chapter 19 takes you through the creation of a disaster recovery preparation and business resumption plan. Chapter 23 details steps to take to make sure your data protection strategies are in fact working.

Tip

Data protection isn't a one-shot deal; it's an ongoing commitment to guarding your client's most critical IT assets. Keeping tabs on your client's data protection plan on a regular basis is necessary to make sure the strategies are still working.

Building the NTFS Boot and Emergency Repair Disks

A typical SBS 4.5 server is configured with one or more SCSI-based hard drives connected to an on-board or third-party SCSI host adapter. Typically, the SCSI host adapter or comparable RAID adapter will have its own BIOS that allows the SCSI hard drive or drives to be bootable without additional hard drives or disks. Under the best scenarios, this works. Seasoned SBS VAPs, however, know a hard drive will fail sooner or later, and you can never start planning for it too early.

Immediately following the SBS 4.5 setup, you'll want to create an NTFS boot disk that can jump start an SBS 4.5 server hard drive in the event of unforeseen trouble. An NTFS boot disk can be invaluable when it comes to troubleshooting and recovering from a corrupt or missing boot loader (NTLDR) or ntdetect.com file, a damaged boot sector or master boot record (MBR), a virus infection, or a broken mirror set.

Tip

For more information on NTFS boot disks, see KB article Q119467 in the Microsoft Knowledge Base and in the *Microsoft Windows NT Server 4.0 Resource Kit*, Chapter 20.

Create an NTFS boot disk while your SBS 4.5 system is fully functioning and healthy. Insert a blank 3.5-inch disk in your disk drive, then follow these steps:

1. Format the disk under Windows NT. This copies the required boot sector that's required to jump start the NTLDR. Then use Windows NT Explorer to complete steps two through four.

2. Copy the NTLDR to disk.

3. Copy the boot.ini file to disk. (This file will generally vary based on the server configuration on your hard drives. Because of this, copy it directly from the root directory of the SBS 4.5 boot drive.)

4. Copy ntdetect.com to disk.

Tip

NTLDR, boot.ini, and ntdetect.com might have attributes set to system, hidden, and read-only. You don't need to change these attributes to copy the files to disk; you will, however, need to locate the files on the boot drive on the SBS 4.5 system.

Emergency Repair Disks

The NTFS boot disk would be used in the event the SBS 4.5 boot drive couldn't begin the boot process. Often the boot process will start; registry corruption, however, can prevent SBS 4.5 from successfully loading. To work around configuration problems in the registry, you'll want to have an up-to-date emergency repair disk (ERD) on hand.

Tip

Always label the ERD with the date it was created and the computer name to which it belongs. Then promptly store the ERD in a secure place. Because the ERD has registry information, a reasonably clever hacker could use an ERD to break into your client's SBS 4.5 system relatively easily.

Creating an ERD for SBS 4.5 is very straightforward. Follow these steps:

1. Insert a blank formatted disk in the server's disk drive.

2. In the SBS Console, open the More Tasks page and click Manage Disks.

3. Click the Create An Emergency Repair Disk button on the Manage Disks page.

4. Select Repair Disk Utility. This will start the Repair Disk Utility (the same utility as in Windows NT 4.0).

5. In the Repair Disk Utility dialog box, click the Create Repair Disk button. See Figure 13-16.

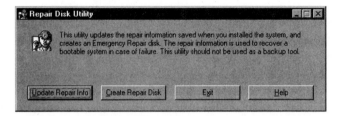

Figure 13-16

Create an Emergency Repair Disk in the event the server won't boot.

Retaining Several Generations of ERDs

I always advise my small business clients that one can't have too many ERDs. This shouldn't just apply to the server. All Windows NT Workstations should also be protected with current ERDs.

When an SBS 4.5 system is freshly built, I usually create two ERDs. Then before and after any configuration changes, I'll create updated ERDs. You might want to set aside a box of ten disks to use just for server ERDs. That way you can always be sure you'll have the state of the SBS 4.5 system on disk in the event you need to roll back to an earlier configuration.

Tip

For more information on planning a fault-tolerant drive configuration, see Chapter 10 in the *Microsoft BackOffice Small Business Server 4.5 Resource Kit*.

Installing UPS Monitoring, Tape Backup, and Antivirus Software

In addition to creating an NTFS boot disk and ERD, you need to look at several additional data protection concerns immediately following the SBS 4.5 setup. Use your needs analysis, IT audit, and network design report as the framework for implementing a comprehensive data protection solution. Small business owners often don't know they need to be concerned about data protection until too late. And even when they're made aware, small business owners often try to cut corners to save money on data protection until they experience the fallout first hand.

UPS

For many small business owners, power protection is a power strip picked up a local hardware store. The power strip is not even a surge protector, let alone battery backup or standby power supply. So their PCs and data are exposed to huge risks in terms of both physical hardware damage and data corruption and loss. You might need to educate the small business decision-maker about power protection solutions.

Chances are they've probably never heard of being able to log power fluctuations, such as an 8V blackout at 4:01 A.M. last Sunday morning. They probably are also unaware that server-grade uninterruptible power supply (UPS) solutions can provide unattended safe shutdown of all services and the server when on battery for more than the preconfigured number of minutes. As is typical with most SBS-centric solutions, an intelligent server-based UPS solution is something that all businesses need but only became affordable to small businesses within the past few years.

Tip

Bearing in mind the risk and reward equation and relatively low cost of these devices, all workstations on an SBS 4.5 network should also be protected through stand-alone battery backup units. UPS units for stand-alone workstations start at well under $100.

The serial interface on the UPS allows for real-time monitoring, event logging, and automated shutdown. When selecting a UPS solution for your small business clients, look for a product that includes the required serial interface cable as well as software that is BackOffice-family compatible.

Without the serial interface and monitoring software, your small business client's SBS 4.5 system will still be protected to a certain degree. The cable and the appropriately configured software, however, is what allows you to keep tabs on:

- Run time

- Battery capacity

- Utility voltage

- UPS temperature

- And dozens of other crucial statistics

In addition, the serial cable and software are responsible for alerting users on the network the server is shutting down, paging the SBS VAP to red flag the trouble, and safely shutting down all SBS 4.5 services.

Note

In the middle of writing this chapter, the New Jersey shore (from where I hail) experienced one of the worst heat waves and power outages in recent memory. As a result of rolling brownouts and blackouts, I saw a UPS in my office kick into gear 11 times within a 48 hour period. Similarly, SBS VAPs in regions particularly prone to hurricanes and earthquakes grow incredibly dependent on high-end intelligent UPS solutions.

Tape Backup

You need to be concerned for the tape backup solution as well. Once again, most small business owners are accustomed to pretty low-end solutions. Whether to save money or just out of lack of understanding, small business owners see IDE-based and parallel port-based tape backup drives and wonder why a $200 solution is not adequate.

Seasoned SBS VAPs know that tape backup drives are definitely one place where you don't want to go cheap. The tape drive for the SBS 4.5 system should be on the Windows NT hardware compatibility list (HCL). In selecting an appropriate tape backup solution, you'll also need to consider speed, performance, and reliability.

Tip

First and foremost, consider Windows NT compatibility when selecting tape backup solutions. Some tape drives, especially at the low-end of the market, want to bypass the OS for some functions and communicate directly with hardware. Although bypassing the OS doesn't pose a problem with Microsoft Windows 95/98, this can be especially problematic with Windows NT Server 4.0 and SBS 4.5.

If your small business client has purchased a third-party tape backup solution, now would be a great time to install the software. Otherwise, you should configure the tape backup drive at this point and perform an initial backup of one of the server volumes and Microsoft Exchange Server mailboxes through Windows NT Backup. To configure the hardware side of the tape backup solution:

1. Click Back Up And Restore Data on the Tasks page of the SBS Console.

2. Click Set Up Your Tape Drive, as shown in Figure 13-17. This action opens a help topic.

3. Click Tape Devices Utility. This action opens a window in Control Panel, which lists any detected devices.

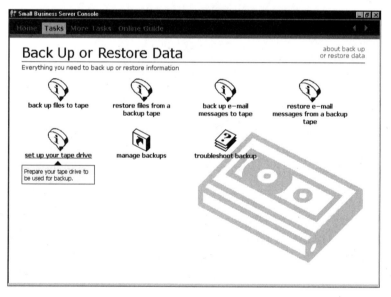

Figure 13-17

Set up your tape drive on the Tasks page in the SBS Console.

After you've configured the tape drive and rebooted, you can return to the Backup Or Restore Data page and click Back Up Files To Tape. This opens Windows NT Backup, which you can use to back up files, volumes, and Exchange Server mailboxes manually. Later in this chapter, you'll see how to automate this task to take place after hours.

Antivirus Software

Antivirus software is also usually an afterthought for most small business owners. Just like a power problem or data loss, small business owners only begin to get serious about virus protection after their firm's been devastated by a virus outbreak. SBS VAPs need to be proactive about recommending and installing antivirus software on the server and individual workstations.

In selecting the third-party antivirus solution, look for products that display the BackOffice logo for assured compatibility. In addition, make sure the virus-scanning engine and virus definitions are both kept current. Most virus experts routinely discuss how dozens of new viruses are discovered each month. As a result, antivirus software that hasn't been updated in months becomes virtually worthless. In addition to traditional antivirus products that protect files on workstations and servers, a host of third-party solutions now exist that can also specifically protect the Exchange Server Information Store, Microsoft Proxy Server, and Microsoft Internet Explorer against malicious applets.

Automating Tape Backups

Although having a reliable, speedy tape backup drive and tape backup software that works is important, automating the whole process is even more important. A surefire way to ensure tape backups aren't done on a regular basis is to rely on one person at your small business client's site to kick off the tape backup job each night. You can remove this barrier by setting up an automated schedule. Doing this has the following advantages:

- The steps for changing the tape take so little time no one can ever have the excuse of being too busy to do them.

- Cross-training others to handle backups is easier for those times when the internal guru is out of the office.

- Consistency is established so that the same options are selected every day.

In SBS 4.0, most SBS VAPs configured Windows NT Backup for unattended scheduling through either the AT command line syntax or the WinAt utility from the *Microsoft Windows NT Server 4.0 Resource Kit* (using the Windows NT Schedule service). With SBS 4.5 and the inclusion of Internet Explorer 5, you now have the Scheduled Task Wizard at your disposal as well. Many SBS VAPs also recommend that their clients purchase third-party tape backup software, which almost always includes built-in scheduling capabilities.

Tip

If you're planning to use the AT command line or the WinAt utility to automate the tape backup process, make sure the Windows NT Schedule service is set for Automatic startup and is in fact started. (Do this by clicking the Start button, selecting Settings, clicking Control Panel, and clicking Services.)

Regardless of whether you opt for the older or newer method, you'll need to know the command line parameters required to launch the Windows NT Backup job. Most SBS VAPs also choose to fold these command line parameters into a batch file and then subsequently call the batch file from the AT command line, the WinAt utility, or the Scheduled Task Wizard.

Tip

To get a list of command line parameters available to run with Windows NT Backup, type "ntbackup /?" at a prompt.

To configure the tape backup job with the Scheduled Task Wizard, open My Computer and double-click Add Scheduled Task. This displays the Scheduled Tasks window, listing any previously existing scheduled tasks along with summary details.

To configure the tape backup job with the Scheduled Task Wizard, follow these steps:

1. Open My Computer and double-click Scheduled Tasks.

2. Double-click the Add Schedule Task icon in the Scheduled Tasks window. See Figure 13-18.

3. Read the introduction and then click Next.

4. Browse to find ntbackup.exe. (The path is c:\winnt.sbs\system32\ntbackup.exe.)

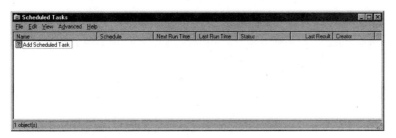

Figure 13-18

Use Scheduled Tasks to see what tasks are scheduled.

5. Name the task NTBackup, click Daily, and then click Next.

6. Choose 11:00 P.M. weekdays as the time to perform the task and click Next.

7. Enter a user name and the password for an account that has permission to back up files. Click Next.

8. Click Finish.

Voilà. Your tape backup job is now complete. Chapters 19 and 23 put this routine through more rigorous scrutiny.

Tip

If you enable logging tape backup statistics to a text file—and no reason exists why you shouldn't—you can incorporate that text file into the scheduled delivery of log files with the Server Status Tool. Chapter 15 shows you how to customize and extend the Server Status Tool.

All tape backup solutions should also use some kind of tape rotation plan. A small business will often use the same tape over and over again only to discover at some point this one tape is no longer reliable. Because the tape is overwritten each night, the small business can't roll back to a version of a file that existed a few days ago. Here's a typical scenario in which the company wants to roll back files a few days: the owner of the company updates a huge Excel file every Monday morning. One Monday morning, she opens the file and finds that it's corrupted beyond recognition. If the owner maintains several weeks of tape backup sets, you can walk the internal guru through retrieving the last known good copy of the Excel file.

Tip

I recommend that most of my small business clients purchase four complete sets of tapes. If the firm works Monday through Friday, these means they'll have 20 tapes. At the minimum, one week's worth of these tapes should always be off-site to protect against fires, floods, earthquakes, and other unpredictable events. This topic is covered in more depth in Chapter 19.

Special Exchange and SQL Server Backup Concerns

As your small business clients become more dependent on utilizing Microsoft Outlook 2000 to manage contacts, meetings, tasks, forms, and e-mail on Exchange Server 5.5, you need to make sure your daily backup encompasses both the Exchange Server directory and information store, as well as SQL Server. Windows NT Backup and numerous third-party solutions can back up Exchange Server mailboxes online while Exchange Server services are running.

You can also perform an offline backup of Exchange Server by disconnecting all users and stopping all of the following Exchange Server services:

- Microsoft Exchange Directory
- Microsoft Exchange Event Service
- Microsoft Exchange Information Store
- Microsoft Exchange Internet Mail Service
- Microsoft Exchange Message Transfer Agent
- Microsoft Exchange System Attendant

You need to be aware, however, that Windows NT Backup can't back up a SQL Server 7.0 database online. Windows NT Backup is not SQL Server aware. SQL Server 7.0 has its own unique way of backing up a database through the SQL Server Enterprise Manager. From the Tools menu, choose Backup Database. If you choose to back up a SQL Server database to a hard drive volume, you can then use Windows NT Backup to copy the database to tape. Numerous third-party solutions also support backing up SQL Server 7.0.

Tip

For a list of third-party solutions available for SQL Server 7.0, see the SQL Server Web site at *www.microsoft.com/sql*.

Running the Initial Tape Backup

Just as you should create two ERDs from the freshly built SBS 4.5 install, you should run two full backup jobs of how the server looks on its first day in service. Once these two backup tapes are created, write-protect the tapes, label them "DO NOT ERASE," and store one off-site.

In addition to your regularly scheduled automated tape backup routine, you want to ensure that both of these tape jobs were run with the verify option selected and logging. See Figure 13-19. Examine the text file log once the backup and verify is complete to inspect for any irregularities or other errors. In addition, you should try to restore a few files or folders just to make sure the tape backup drive and software are working properly.

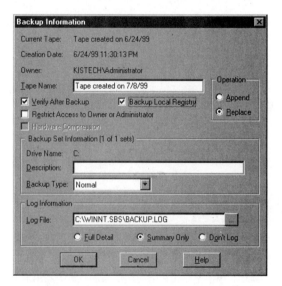

Figure 13-19

Select verify and log file options in Windows NT Backup.

Applying Antivirus Definitions and Application Service Packs

From the time you began reading Chapter 13 to now, new viruses probably have been created. One way to keep abreast of new viruses is by visiting the Microsoft Security Advisor Web site and subscribing to their e-mail newsletter (*www.microsoft.com/security*). Most of the leading third-party vendors with antivirus software solutions also maintain extensive Web sites with late-breaking information on viruses. For example, see Network Associates at *www.nai.com* and Symantec at *www.symantec.com*.

Regardless of how you choose to keep up with the endless flow of virus protection bulletins, make sure to install the most recent antivirus software scanning engine and virus definitions after you install an SBS 4.5 system. If you're not sure how current the antivirus updates are and need assistance on how to determine the date of the last update, check with the vendor's tech support department or read the frequently asked questions list (FAQ) on the vendor's Web site.

Like antivirus software, many of the SBS 4.5 server and client applications are also subject to constant changes. While client application upgrades are sometimes less critical, server application upgrades might improve on or fix something your small business client really needs. Because your client's SBS 4.5 might be running other third-party software, however, be sure to research and test each service pack (SP) that you intend to install. Also note that SBS service packs are different than Windows NT 4.0 service packs.

One way to keep up with server application service packs is by visiting the SBS Web site regularly and by subscribing to the BackOffice newsletter (*www.microsoft.com/smallbusinessserver*). SP information is also made available to VAPs through the Microsoft Direct Access Web site at *www.microsoft.com/directaccess*.

Assigning Server Administrative Privileges to the Internal Guru

Finally, you'll need to talk with the small business owner and internal guru about who should have administrative access to the server in assessing the post-configuration data protection. This is a highly individual decision and should be left to the small business owner.

Some SBS VAPs believe strongly that handing over administrative privileges to anyone at the client site is risky. VAPs in this camp believe someone not accustomed to administering SBS can do a lot of damage.

Most SBS VAPs do, in fact, build a close working relationship with the internal guru and feel 100 percent confident in setting up the guru with full administrative privileges to the server. For tips on what to teach the internal guru about SBS 4.5, see Chapter 20.

Even if you decide not to grant administrative permission to anyone at the client site, you need to know where to set the option so you don't inadvertently grant it. The right to log on interactively to the SBS Console is granted during the second-to-last dialog box of the User Access Wizard, as shown in Figure 13-20.

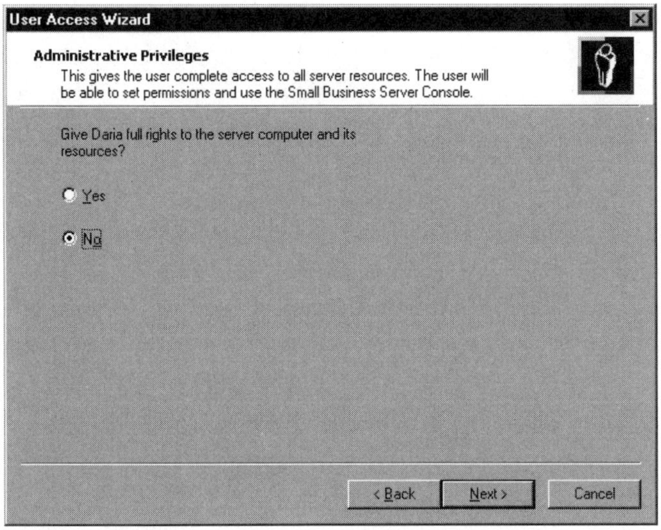

Figure 13-20

You can grant or deny administrator rights in the User Access Wizard.

Setting Up Connectivity

Just as you need to perform several steps after SBS 4.5 installation to configure user accounts and computers and to protect data, you'll need to perform several tasks to connect the SBS 4.5 network to various resources. These tasks are introduced during the remainder of this chapter and are then further detailed in subsequent chapters. Connectivity related applications include faxing (Chapter 27), e-mail (Chapters 18 and 26), Web browsing (Chapter 18), Web publishing (Chapter 18), and remote access (Chapter 27).

Configuring Fax Service

The Microsoft Fax Service is the subject of Chapter 27. So I won't go into much detail here, but rather I'll offer a few preliminary caveats and prudent preparation advice.

During the unattended SBS 4.5 setup, you were asked to confirm the modem selection choices. The success, or lack thereof, in properly configuring modems during the SBS 4.5 setup will impact your ease in installing and supporting Fax Service.

In general, the fax modem must be business class and class 1 compatible. The SBS Web site (*www.microsoft.com/smallbusinessserver*) has a pointer to the Windows NT Server 4.0 HCL, which lists fax modems that have been tested with Windows NT Server 4.0. If you want a truly painless experience with Fax Service, make sure the fax modem is on the HCL. As a safeguard, the SBS 4.5 unattended setup program pauses to give you the opportunity to confirm and modify your device driver selection during the early stages of setup.

In order for SBS 4.5 to install modem-dependent services, such as RAS, Modem Sharing Service, and Fax Service, the modems need to be detected first and installed. During the SBS 4.5 unattended setup, the modem firmware is queried for the unimodem ID. SBS setup needs to match the unimodem ID on the modem firmware with the unimodem ID in the modem device driver file (.inf) for Windows NT. In the event the setup program can't find a match, the modem will be temporarily labeled as an unsupported modem. This is meant to emphasize the potential problems of a mismatch between the unimodem ID in the device driver and the unimodem ID present in the firmware. Without a definitive match, faxing won't work properly.

Basic Network Connectivity Characteristics of an SBS 4.5 Network

The following are characteristics of an SBS 4.5 network:

- SBS 4.5 isn't routed or bridged to any other LANs or WANs except for remote access users and Internet access.

- TCP/IP, the standard, routable protocol of the Internet, is the primary protocol suite in SBS 4.5. Other protocols, such as NetBEUI (typically associated with small office environments) or IPX/SPX (NWLink), aren't needed unless the SBS 4.5 system needs to stay connected to one or more NetWare servers.

- SBS 4.5 can be licensed for up to 50 PCs, which is more than the 25 PC limit in SBS 4.0. The client PCs are generally running Windows 95, Windows 98, or Windows NT Workstation 4.0. You can, however, manually configure SBS 4.5 to have limited functionality with other operating systems, such as MS-DOS, Windows 3.x, Macintosh, and various UNIX flavors, such as Linux.

Note

The unsupported modem in SBS 4.5 is comparable to the standard modem in Windows NT 4.0. SBS developers, however, decided to change the name to unsupported modem to drive home the point that modems with firmware that don't match the .inf file are unsupported.

As you've probably already seen, the To Do List page contains a task called Configure Fax Service. This is required because Fax Service in SBS 4.5 is configured only to send outbound faxes by default. In order for the SBS 4.5 system to receive inbound faxes, Fax Service must be configured manually. You can enable which fax modem devices receive incoming faxes by opening Fax Server Properties, clicking the Receive tab if necessary, and selecting the devices in the Fax Reception Settings area. See Figure 13-21.

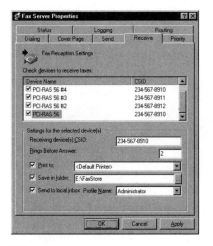

Figure 13-21

You need to configure Fax Service to receive incoming faxes.

Migrating from a Single Dial-Up ISP Account to Company-Wide Internet Access

The Internet is rapidly transforming the way that companies worldwide conduct business. Regardless of the industry, organizations of all sizes are anxious to have e-mail and Internet access for nearly every employee in the company. For most Fortune 1000 companies, this has already taken place. Small businesses, however, have often been forced to settle for one PC in the office configured with a dial-up ISP account. That meant whenever anyone needed to get to a vendor's or customer's Web site or to send or receive e-mail, that person would have to trek across the office to wait in line to use this one Internet-enabled PC.

Most small businesses wished they could afford to give everyone access at their own desktop. Many barriers prevented this kind of access, however, such as the need for a modem, analog phone line, and an ISP account for each person. In addition, no way existed to monitor activities centrally, back up crucial e-mail messages, or keep usage secure.

SBS 4.5 provides a turnkey solution for delivering secure, shared, high-speed Internet access and e-mail to each client workstation on the network. This is achieved through using Outlook 2000 and Internet Explorer 5 at each SBS client PC and Exchange Server 5.5 and Proxy Server 2.0 on the SBS 4.5 system.

In order to make company-wide Internet access and e-mail a reality, you'll need to assist your small business clients in migrating from a single-user account to a network-based account. This subject is the focus of Chapter 18.

For the time being at least, knowing how SBS 4.5 makes it easier for you to approach this often-daunting set of tasks is important. Understanding how you can begin to plan your efforts is also helpful.

Benefits of External Modems

Small businesses are often attracted to internal modems largely due to up-front purchase price cost savings. The small business decision-maker or internal guru usually doesn't understand the many benefits of external modems and why the small cost difference is money well spent.

Seasoned SBS VAPs tend to stick with external modems for many reasons. The status lights on the front of the modem can be invaluable when it comes to troubleshooting problems. In addition, you can reset each modem when problems arise without having to reboot the server. Because the internal modem would reside within the SBS 4.5 system, you'd literally have to take down the network just to clear phone line congestion and perform a hard reset on a modem. Many SBS VAPs also choose external modems because they're almost always easier to configure. In short, external modems should be a no-brainer requirement for any SBS 4.5 network needing Fax Service.

Tip

If you need to use an external network adapter card to connect to the ISP, wait to configure the secondary network interface card (NIC) until the unattended SBS 4.5 setup is complete.

On the To Do List page, click Connect To An ISP to launch the Internet Connection Wizard (ICW). A significant improvement from the wizard in SBS 4.0, ICW now walks you through the process of signing up new accounts with an SBS-compatible ISP or simply configuring your existing ISP accounts to work with SBS 4.5. See Figure 13-22. Microsoft has also dramatically simplified the process of gathering information from your ISP by creating templates for the three types of Internet access supported by SBS 4.5—analog modem or terminal adapter; router; or full-time, broadband modem. See Table 13-2 on the next page.

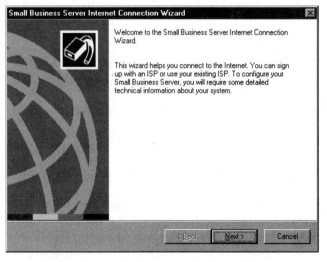

Figure 13-22
Internet Connection Wizard (ICW) lets you select a new ISP or configure existing ISP accounts.

Note

Unlike SBS 4.0, the FTP service is no longer installed with SBS 4.5 by default. This doesn't affect outbound FTP support through Proxy Server 2.0, but rather it prevents inbound FTP access to the SBS 4.5 system unless you explicitly add this service. Left out only for security reasons, the FTP service can be easily added back through IIS 4.0.

Internet access method	Distinguishing characteristics
Modem or terminal adapter	Supports dial-up connections
	Generally adequate for low-volume usage
	Available as analog/PSTN (speeds from 28.8 to 56.6 Kbps) or ISDN (speeds from 64 to 128 Kbps and quicker call setup time)
Router	Supports Centrex ISDN, frame relay, and fractional T1/T3
	Generally meant for higher-speed, dedicated Internet connectivity
	Uses external network adapter card
Full-time/broadband modem	Supports cable modem and xDSL
	Uses external network adapter card

Table 13-2

Characteristics of three types of Internet access supported by SBS 4.5

Installing the Exchange POP3 Gateway Add-On Pack

Not all small businesses with SBS 4.5 can afford or justify the expense of a full-time Internet connection. To keep costs down, these small businesses often rely on dial-up analog lines (ideally running at their full v.90 potential) or dial-up ISDN lines running at either 64 or 128 Kbps. Widespread rollouts of affordable broadband technologies, such as cable modems and xDSL, are likely to change the dynamics of this equation within the next 12 to 18 months. For the time being, however, SBS VAPs need to deliver company-wide e-mail solutions through SBS 4.5 even when no full-time Internet connection exists.

One way to provide e-mail to each SBS 4.5 user on the network is by configuring a POP3 gateway to interface with Exchange Server 5.5. Shortly following the release of SBS 4.5, Microsoft made a free connector, Microsoft Exchange Connector, available for POP3 mailboxes. The connector allows your small business clients to make their Exchange Server Internet-enabled quite cost effectively, by using a single POP3 e-mail account for multiple internal mailboxes on Exchange Server 5.5.

You can find more information about Exchange Connector for POP3 mailboxes on SBS 4.5 systems on the SBS Web site at *www.microsoft.com/ smallbusinessserver*. Chapter 26 looks at Exchange Connector for POP3 mailboxes in more detail.

Granting Remote Dial-In and Internet Access Privileges to Select Users

In a traditional Windows NT Server 4.0 environment, you'd need to use several tools to administer remote access and Proxy Server–based Internet access. SBS 4.5 makes administration of remote access and Internet access simple through the User Account Wizard, the same wizard used to create user accounts. The User Account Wizard takes the place of User Manager for Domains, Proxy Server Manager, and Remote Access Administrator. See Figure 13-23.

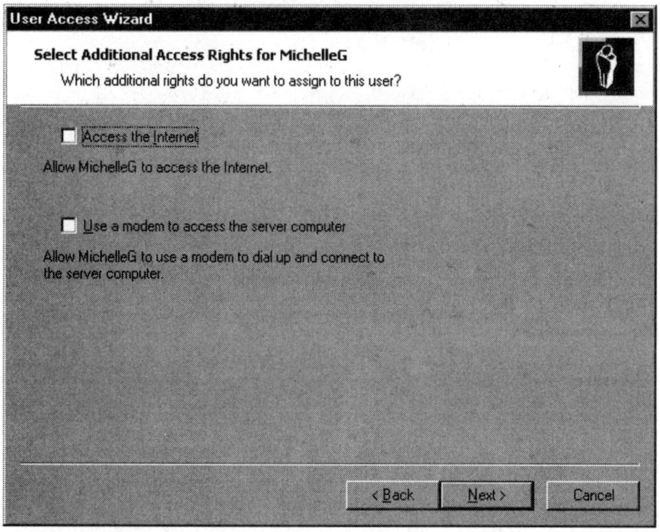

Figure 13-23

You can grant remote dial-in and Internet access through the User Account Wizard.

Remote dial-in access is generally important for telecommuters, road warriors, and individual end users working in very small branch offices. Once configured properly, remote access users can share files and printers, surf the Web, send e-mail, send faxes, and schedule meetings just as if they were working as a node on the SBS 4.5 LAN in the office. The only problem is that system performance is generally much slower for remote access users. Remote access is the subject of Chapter 27.

A big trend now involves using virtual private networks (VPN) or Point-to-Point Tunneling Protocol (PPTP) in lieu of traditional dial-in modem bank solutions. PPTP connections are established by dialing in through a local ISP over the Internet as opposed to dialing directly to SBS 4.5 modems. VPNs are also explored in Chapter 27.

Tip

PPTP must be enabled when ICW runs (detailed in Chapter 18) to open the appropriate ports on the firewall in Proxy Server 2.0.

Proxy Server 2.0 controls Internet access privileges on an SBS 4.5 network. SBS VAPs can determine on a user-by-user basis who can surf the Web and run Winsock applications such as RealPlayer, PointCast, and AOL. In addition, you can enable detailed logging and explicitly grant or revoke the right to visit selected Web sites. Proxy Server 2.0 administration is explored in Chapter 18 and picked up again in Chapter 23.

Tip

A PPTP RAS solution is more ideally suited for small business clients with dedicated, full-time ISP connections vs. dial-up or on-demand connections.

The Bottom Line

Those who are new to SBS might think they're done with the installation when the unattended setup is complete. While the unattended parts of the SBS 4.5 setup are quite comprehensive, you'll need to take at least a dozen more steps before you'll be ready to turn the network over to your small business client's end users. This chapter showed you how to make sure you have a complete Microsoft BackOffice Small Business Server 4.5 installation by tackling some of the more commonly required tasks, such as configuring computers, peripherals, and user accounts; setting up hardware and software to protect the client's data; and handling connectivity issues.

Chapter 14

Customizing the SBS Console

Most administrative functions in Microsoft BackOffice Small Business Server 4.5 can be performed directly from the SBS Console, the central management console. Microsoft has redesigned the SBS Console for SBS 4.5 to make network administration even easier for you and your clients. The SBS Console pulls together all the commonly needed SBS 4.5 administration tasks into a consolidated user interface.

Comprised of linked Active Server Pages (ASP), the SBS Console is organized into five basic sections:

- **To Do List**—Contains the tasks that you'll need to do immediately following the unattended SBS 4.5 setup. Mainly used for the initial setup, the To Do List is designed to make sure you have a complete SBS installation. It's the first page you see upon your initial logon to SBS 4.5 (Ctrl+Alt+Del).

Tip

Chapter 13 drills down in the To Do List.

Changes in Technology Underlying the Console

In SBS 4.0, the Manage Server Console was actually a full-size Internet Explorer 3.x or Internet Explorer 4.x window.

With SBS 4.5, the SBS Console has been retooled as an Internet Explorer 5.x window hosted within the Microsoft Management Console (MMC). In order to prevent confusion, however, the MMC splash screen is suppressed with the /s switch. See Figure 14-1.

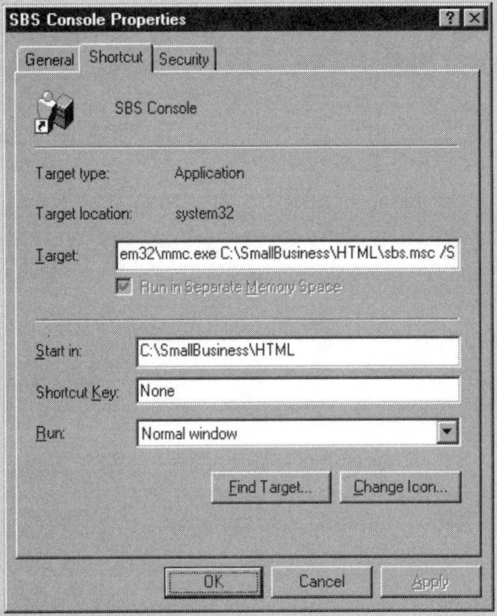

Figure 14-1
The SBS Console is actually hosted within Microsoft Management Console; however, the splash screen is suppressed.

The Manage Server Console in SBS 4.0 was difficult to administer remotely because of the large size of the files, which often had to be transmitted over an analog modem connection. The SBS Console has fewer ornate icons and buttons than the Manage Server Console so the SBS Console loads more quickly for remote administration. Microsoft NetMeeting is the preferred route for remote management of the SBS Console. This topic is explored further in Chapter 25.

The SBS Console is also fully scalable. In SBS 4.0, the Manage Server Console couldn't be resized. In SBS 4.5, the SBS Console can be resized from a full screen down to the size of a postage stamp. (At some point, it definitely becomes illegible, though.)

- **Home page**—Shows total drive space and a graphical representation of free space available on each drive volume. The Home page is the first page your clients will see when they launch the SBS Console. It also alerts them to critical stopped services through an ActiveX applet. You can attempt to restart the stalled services by a click of the mouse. Since the Home page is like a main table of contents or front door, this is a great place to create a link to a custom Web page your firm has designed, as well as to your firm's Web site home page.

- **Tasks**—Displays the SBS 4.5 tasks you need to perform most often. This includes managing users, printers, and shared folders. The Tasks page answers the question, "What do I need to do frequently?"

- **More Tasks**—Lists the SBS 4.5 tasks you perform less often. This includes managing computers, modems, faxes, and e-mail distribution lists. More Tasks answers the question, "What do I need to do with SBS 4.5 once in a while?"

- **Online Guide**—Is loaded with background information, step-by-step procedures, and troubleshooting guidelines. The Online Guide is mission control for SBS 4.5 online help.

SBS VAPs have a unique opportunity to add value to their installations by customizing the console. This chapter will introduce you to designing a customized SBS Console.

Understanding the Small Business Server Customization Tool

By adding and manipulating various registry keys, you can extend the SBS Console. Table 14-1 on the next page shows the registry keys for pages in the SBS Console. Unless you enjoy the tedium and associated risks of modifying the registry, however, you should have no reason to make registry changes for console customization. The only exceptions to this would be if your firm is an independent software vendor (ISV) customizing the SBS Console *en masse* or you have some very unique needs.

If you're not going to modify the registry to customize the SBS Console, how do you make the changes? Although the SBS Console pages are built as ASPs, you shouldn't modify the console pages directly. Even though your modifications to the ASP code will more than likely work, any customizations you make will be overwritten if the SBS Console needs to be upgraded or reinstalled.

SBS Console	Registry key
Home page	\HKEY_LOCAL_MACHINE\SOFTWARE\ Microsoft\SmallBusiness\Console\Favorites\Custom
Tasks page	\HKEY_LOCAL_MACHINE\SOFTWARE\ Microsoft\SmallBusiness\Console\CustomSmTasks
More Tasks page	\HKEY_LOCAL_MACHINE\SOFTWARE\ Microsoft\SmallBusiness\Console\CustomBgTasks

Table 14-1

Registry keys for SBS Console pages

Microsoft created the Small Business Server Customization Tool to make it easy for SBS VAPs to customize the SBS Console without having to edit the registry directly. See Figure 14-2. Customizing SBS no longer needs to be a highly esoteric process, only accessible to those with an intimate knowledge of registry entries, HTML, ASP, and VBScript. Because the immediate benefits are so compelling, the majority of this chapter is devoted to what you can do with the Small Business Server Customization Tool.

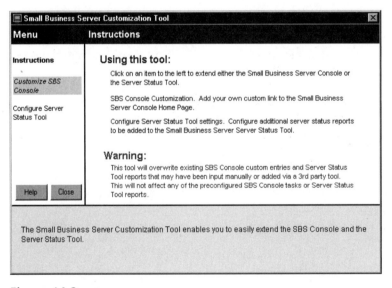

Figure 14-2

Use the Small Business Server Customization Tool to customize the SBS Console.

Note

The Small Business Server Customization Tool is part of the *Microsoft BackOffice Small Business Server 4.5 Resource Kit*. The file name for the Customization Tool is sbscustom.exe, and it was written in Visual Basic.

Tip

The Small Business Server Customization Tool can be used to add links to the Home page, Tasks page, or More Tasks page. It can't be used to modify the Online Guide, which you can only extend programmatically. For more information, see "Extending the Online Guide" later in this chapter.

New to SBS 4.5, the Small Business Server Customization Tool is a huge boon to SBS VAPs looking to customize the console. And the best part...you don't need to edit the registry or get involved in the nitty-gritty of coding HTML, ASP, or VBScript.

Note

The Small Business Server Customization Tool can also be used for customizing the Server Status Tool (SST) reports. See Chapter 15.

Adding Links

The Small Business Server Customization Tool adds custom links to SBS Console pages, so you can easily update the appropriate keys and hives in the registry for console customization. If you really want to, you can still edit the registry directly. My gut feeling, however, is that most SBS VAPs will be well served by this GUI-based tool, in much the same way that many SBS VAPs prefer using the WinAt utility for unattended scheduling over the AT command line.

You should pay particularly close attention to the warning in the Small Business Server Customization Tool instructions, as shown in Figure 14-2. The Small Business Server Customization Tool will overwrite any console customizations you've already created through the registry or that have been performed by ISVs. The default links placed on the console pages by the SBS 4.5 setup, however, won't be affected.

> ### Benefits of Using the
> ### Small Business Server Customization Tool
>
> For console customization, the SBS Customization Tool has these benefits:
>
> - It doesn't have a steep learning curve.
>
> - The need for extensive research and development (R&D), trial and error, and testing is eliminated.
>
> - You're shielded from the huge potential to corrupt the registry and trash the NOS installation.
>
> - Configuration of requisite registry entries is automated.

Note

Never edit the console ASP files directly. If you do, your changes will be overwritten during upgrades or reinstalls. Always make all your customizations through the registry or better yet, with the Small Business Server Customization Tool.

To begin customizing the console, click Customize SBS Console on the left side of the page. This action will bring up the Extending the Small Business Server Console page, where you enter customization instructions. See Figure 14-3.

Configuring Links

When using the Small Business Server Customization Tool, you can configure two different types of links. The links can either launch custom HTML pages (or locally stored ASP) or external, fully qualified URLs. If you're creating custom HTML pages or ASP files, you can use Web page editors such as Microsoft FrontPage 2000 or Notepad. You might also want to use existing pages in the HTML folder in the SmallBusiness directory as templates for creating custom pages. Remember that nothing is proprietary about customizing the console. The files for extending the console are all standard HTML or ASP-based pages.

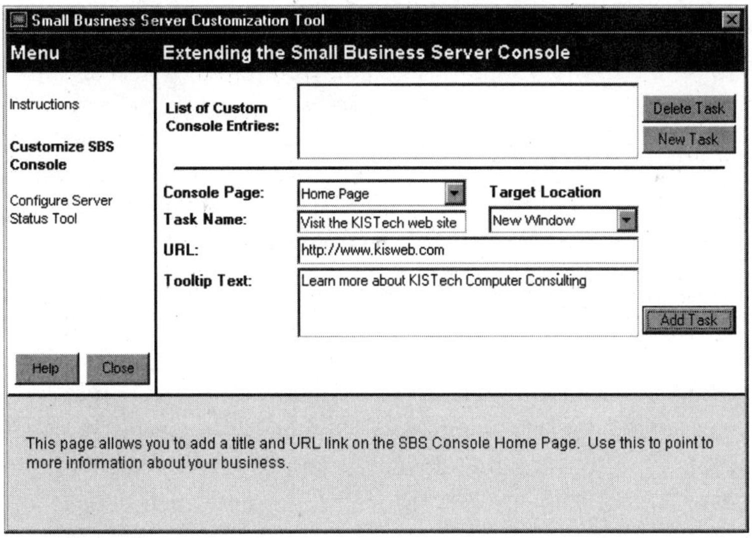

Figure 14-3
Make customization changes on the Extending the Small Business Server Console page.

Note

You can't use the Small Business Server Customization Tool to link to an executable file.

Tip

To learn more about creating custom Web pages to link to the console, start with *Running Microsoft FrontPage 2000* from Microsoft Press.

In addition to supporting both internal and external hyperlinks, the Small Business Server Customization Tool can place links on the Home page, Tasks page, or More Tasks page. Use the drop-down list next to the Console Page box to place the links. If the link is on the Home page, you'll have a choice of making the link either within the frame or outside the frame.

Now, let's take a typical example, where you place a link to your firm's Web site on the SBS Console Home page.

1. Click the New Task button on the Small Business Server Customizaton Tool.

2. On the Console Page drop-down menu, make sure Home Page is selected (as opposed to the Tasks or More Tasks page).

Tip

As you move from field to field, pay close attention to the context sensitive help displayed at the bottom of the dialog box in the yellow area.

---

3. Give your task a descriptive name or title that will appear on the SBS Console page (such as "Visit the KISTech Web site").

4. On the Target Location drop-down menu, select New Window. By selecting this option, you cause a new browser window to be opened containing the target destination when the user clicks the link. Microsoft recommends you select New Window for links to pages that are external to the server and select In Frame for any pages that are stored locally. Note this drop-down menu is relevant for only the Home page. Even though this drop-down menu is always active, this selection would have no bearing if you were placing the link on the Tasks or More Tasks page.

5. Enter your Web site address in the URL box (for instance, *http://www.kisweb.com*). Alternatively, you could enter the file name of any HTML file stored locally in the default HTML folder in the SmallBusiness directory. Because the Small Business Server Customization Tool doesn't perform validation of your entries here, make sure to check the entry in Internet Explorer before entering it in the URL box.

6. In the Tooltip Text box enter the text you want to appear when a user hovers over the link (such as "Learn more about KISTech Computer Consulting").

7. Click the Add Task button.

The Registry Editor confirms your changes have been entered, as shown in Figure 14-4.

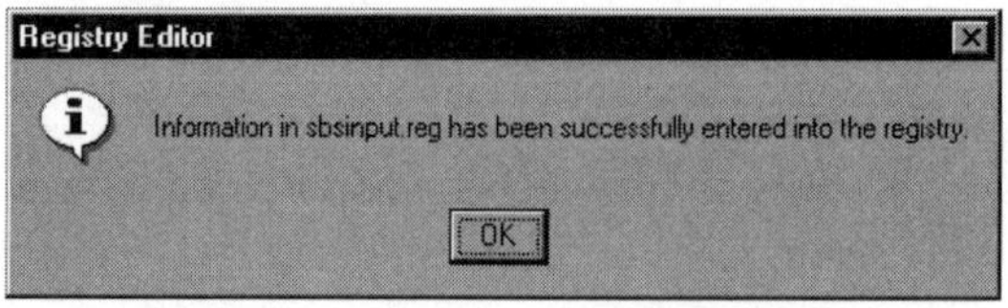

Figure 14-4

The Registry Editor confirms changes made to the Home page.

When I click the Home page and hit the F5 button to refresh (or right-click and choose the Refresh command), I'll see the new link on my small business client's console to my firm's Web site. *Voilà!* See Figure 14-5.

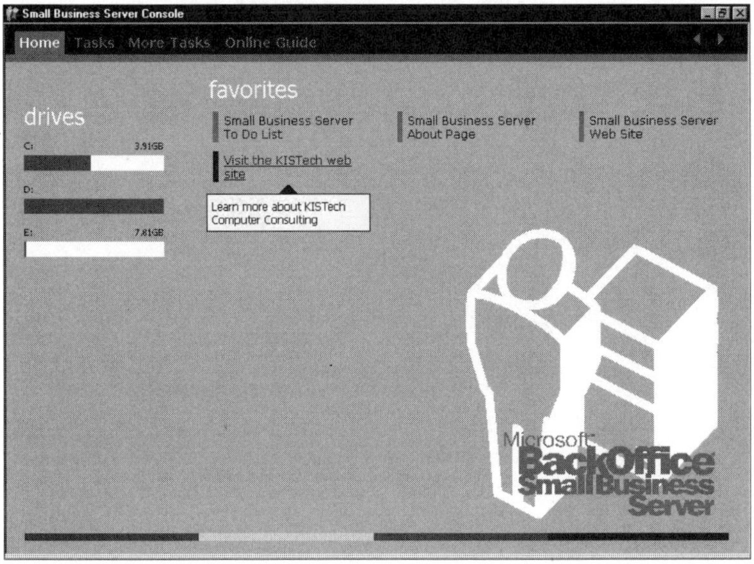

Figure 14-5

Updated SBS Console Home page has a link to my firm's Web site.

What happens if I need to edit the link on the Home page? Suppose my firm is acquired by another company and we decide to change the name of the company to Josh's House of SBS Pros. Simply go back to the Small Business Server Customization Tool and follow these steps:

1. Choose Customize SBS Console.

2. Select the desired task from the List of Custom Console Entries. Once selected, the form entries will populate the appropriate fields.

3. Make your changes in the Task Name and Tooltip Text boxes.

4. Click the Update Task button.

To confirm your changes have taken effect, switch back to the SBS Console Home page, refresh the page, and you should see the new title and Tooltip. See Figure 14-6 on the next page.

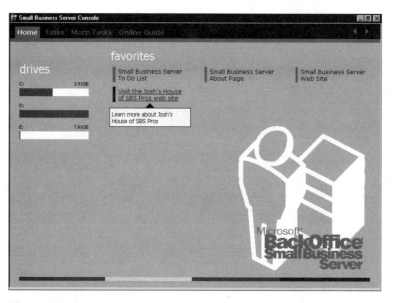

Figure 14-6

The updated SBS Console Home page with new title and Tooltip.

Note

The Small Business Server Customization Tool can only modify the Home page, the Tasks page, and the More Tasks page. If you need to create a second-level page (that is, a page one level below one of these three pages), you'll need a detailed understanding of HTML, ASP, and a scripting language, such as Microsoft Jscript. To learn more about adding second-level pages to the console, see Chapter 43 in the *Microsoft BackOffice Small Business Server 4.5 Resource Kit*.

In planning your console customization efforts, ask yourself these questions:

- Will any console customizations made through the registry or by an ISV be affected?

- On which Console Page should the link be placed: Home page, Tasks page, or More Tasks page?

- What's the task name (the title displayed on the console page)?

- If placed on the Home page, is the link to an internal or external page or file?

- What's the URL?

- What should the Tooltip text contain?

Tip

In order to make console changes, you need to be logged on as Administrator (or equivalent user account).

Leveraging SBS Console Customization

Now that you know the mechanics of placing links on SBS Console pages, what can you do with this tool to add greater value to your clients' SBS installations? The basic goal should be to transform the ordinary default SBS Console pages, especially the Home page, into a Web portal that directs your small business clients to additional services your firm can provide.

Tips on Console Customization and Style

Establishing a consistent, easy-to-read style on SBS Console pages helps users find what they need quickly. Here are tips for customizing the console:

- Be consistent in regard to the existing links on the page.

- Keep your sentences succinct and to the point.

- Build the links for the average SBS administrator, which will likely be the internal guru, who has some Windows experience but limited knowledge of networking and SBS applications.

- Make sure the links are completely intuitive and visually obvious. The user shouldn't need to hunt for information.

- Organize the links hierarchically so that the most general and most important links jump out at users.

    You can't control layout on the page. A new link to a local HTML page or ASP or to an external link occupies the next available position on the console page. If too many links on a page are visible, scroll bars will appear.

Adding Value Through Customization

In April 1999, my monthly Microsoft Direct Access SBS Sales Center column was titled, "The Portal to More Value-Added Services: Customizing the Small Business Server Console." In this article, which is included on the CD-ROM in the back of this book, I discuss 10 simple ideas for console customization.

By adding links to the SBS Console Home page, your small business clients can easily do the following:

- **Place technical support requests.** This link points to a password-protected form on your firm's Web site where clients can enter help desk requests and track the status of open help desk tickets.

- **Order hardware and software.** This link takes clients to an e-commerce area of your firm's Web site where they can order anything from additional SBS 4.5 CALs to a cable drop or an extra laptop battery.

- **Learn about training classes.** This link brings clients to descriptions of current training classes offered by your firm and a class schedule.

- **Update virus definitions.** This link leads your clients to either your site or the site of your preferred antivirus ISV. There the clients can learn about the latest viruses and upgrade to the latest virus signature files (if no automated facility is available for updates).

- **Get the latest device drivers.** This link delivers your clients to a page on your site where you have downloadable drivers and vendor links for your most commonly sold and configured hardware devices.

- **Retrieve Web site stats.** This link points to the ISP's Web site stats area so your clients can find out about their Web site traffic.

- **Retrieve event log summary and check server health.** This leads your client to a dynamically generated, password protected page on your firm's Web site that has a summary of the event logs most recently retrieved by your weekly Server Status Tool report.

- **Find industry specific links.** These links vary, depending on the industry for which your firm installs SBS. If you plan on installing SBS for local realtors, make sure your industry links are loaded with Web sites for townships, school districts, other realtors, and multiple listing services. If your SBS installations are primarily for accounting firms, make sure your industry links include taxation and regulatory sites, trade groups, and accounting magazines.

Tip

Many SBS VAPs are also placing links on their small business clients' home page that allows the client to page or beep the VAP. This is typically done by linking to the URL of the paging company that offers their customers the ability to send Web-based alphanumeric paging messages.

Figure 14-7 shows how the SBS Console Home page looks when all of these links are added. Note that in addition to the three links included by Microsoft on the Home page, six additional links have been added. By design, the Home page of the SBS Console can only accommodate a total of nine links. Additional custom links can be easily accommodated on the Tasks or More Tasks console pages.

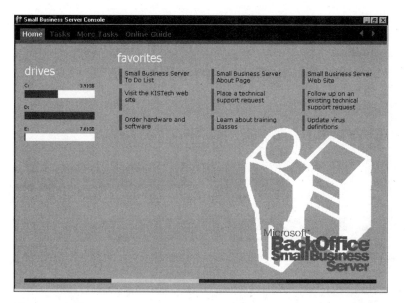

Figure 14-7

A customized SBS Console Home page, with six links to external Web sites.

Tip

If you back yourself into a corner while trying to customize the console, see KB article Q222531 in the Microsoft Knowledge Base.

Extending the Online Guide

The Online Guide is your single point of contact for immediate SBS assistance. You can access elements of the Online Guide from the SBS Console in three ways:

- Many second-level pages have links to online help, which is part of the Online Guide. For example, clicking Troubleshoot A User's

Problem on the Manage Users page opens the Online Guide. See Figure 14-8.

- From the Online Guide Contents view, you can click and scroll through help screens organized like a table of contents. For example, if you expand the Backups section by clicking the plus sign, you can find help on restoring e-mail messages from a backup tape. See Figure 14-9.

- If you know a keyword, you can search for help in the Find view of the Online Guide console page. For example, if you need help on routers, just type your request and review the list of results. See Figure 14-10.

Note

The Find view of the Online Guide uses Microsoft Index Server 2.0, part of the Windows NT Option Pack included with SBS 4.5.

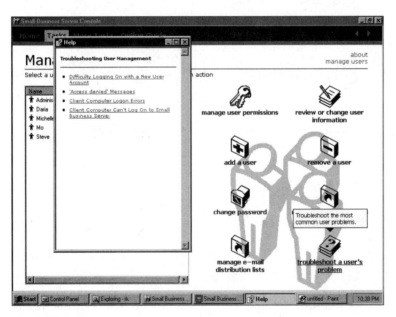

Figure 14-8

Find help about managing users from a console page.

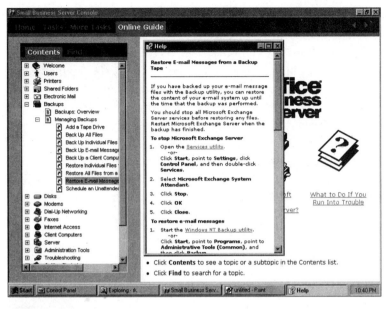

Figure 14-9

Find help in the Contents view of the Online Guide.

Figure 14-10

Find help in the Find view of the Online Guide.

What happens when you need to add your own help files to the Online Guide? Unfortunately, this process isn't nearly as straightforward as adding links to the Home, Tasks, or More Tasks console pages. As mentioned earlier, the Small Business Server Customization Tool can't be used to modify the Online Guide. Rather, the Online Guide can only be extended programmatically.

Files for the Online Guide are stored in c:\winnt.sbs\help\sbs.srv\htm. Even though no GUI-based tool exists for easily extending Online Help, the required files are still really just HTML or ASP code. The primary way the Online Guide is extended is through the oem.hhc file, which is an HTML file. The oem.hhc file must be created the first time the Online Guide is customized. In addition, you'll need to create another .hhc file for your custom help files and have that file referenced in the oem.hhc file.

Tip

You can find sample backgrounds and styles to use for custom Online Guide pages in c:\winnt.sbs\help\sbs.srv\htm.

When the Online Guide generates its views, SBS 4.5 appends the oem.hhc file to the main table of contents file (contents.hhc). Once the .hhc files are saved to c:\winnt.sbs\help\sbs.srv\htm, they are automatically picked up for processing by Index Server 2.0.

Tip

For information on extending the Online Guide, as well as sample code, see Chapter 43 in the *Microsoft BackOffice Small Business Server 4.5 Resource Kit*.

The Bottom Line

The SBS Console, which pulls together all the commonly needed SBS 4.5 administration tasks into one single consolidated user interface, is a powerful tool. This chapter taught you to use the SBS Console, including how to customize and extend it to benefit both you and your clients.

Chapter 15

Adding Value with the Server Status Tool

Downtime costs small businesses money. Anything you can do as a Microsoft BackOffice Small Business Server VAP to prevent downtime is a real bonus for your clients. The new Server Status Tool (SST) in SBS 4.5 should be the foundation of your proactive maintenance program. In this chapter, you'll learn about the SST and how to use the application to monitor your clients' available disk space, the status of Microsoft Windows NT services, and Microsoft Proxy Server logs. You'll also learn how to add log files for third-party applications to the SST e-mails or faxes that your firm receives.

Tip

Chapter 25 looks at how you can fine-tune the SST reports and analysis to maintain SBS operation and client satisfaction.

The Real Cost of Downtime

My Microsoft Direct Access SBS Sales Center column for April 1999, "The Portal to More Value-Added Services," showed how you could use SST as the basis for selling a proactive maintenance program to your SBS clients. The column is included on the CD-ROM for the book.

Before you can implement such a program, you'll need to help your small business clients understand the real cost of their downtime. This way they'll know what the proactive maintenance program is protecting against or what's at stake, essentially. Gather the following information about your client:

A.   Client's annual net income

B.   Number of business days each year (usually about 250)

C.   Number of hours in each business day (usually about 8)

Calculate the cost of downtime with the following equations:

- Daily cost of downtime = A/B

- Hourly cost of downtime = $A/(B{\times}C)$

For example, if your small business client's annual net income was $2,000,000 last year (variable A), the daily cost of downtime is $8,000 ($A/250$) and the hourly cost of downtime is $1,000 ($A/2000$). Once you and the small business owner have a handle on these costs, you'll see how a proactive maintenance program can be a huge win-win for you and your small business client even if you just prevent one or two days of downtime a year.

Note

"The Portal to More Value-Added Services," my April 1999 Microsoft Direct Access SBS Sales Center column (which is on the CD-ROM), covers how I saved the day by using the Spooler service, which alerted me to a stalled network printer before my client called me. The Spooler service isn't included in the list of default Windows NT Server services that are monitored by SST. In order to keep tabs on network printers, you'll need to add the Spooler service to the list. To do this, locate \HKEY_LOCAL_MACHINE\SOFTWARE\ Microsoft\Small Business\VAPReporting\Services in the registry and add a new DWORD named Spooler with a value of 1 (for enabled). Use the other services listed in this registry key as your example. Just make sure you've backed up the registry before you make this change. Note this is one of the *very* rare times where I advocate even going near the registry. In most cases, you should completely exhaust every GUI-based way to modify the registry before trying to edit it directly.

The Basis for a Proactive Maintenance Program

The goal of using SST is to catch minor problems through proactive monitoring and maintenance before the problems develop into major emergencies. SST is integrated in the SBS Console and can be accessed from the Administration Tools section of the Tasks page. SST works in conjunction with the Scheduled Task Wizard, Microsoft Fax Service, and Microsoft Exchange Internet Mail Service (IMS).

Note

The Scheduled Task Wizard comes to SBS 4.5 as a component of Internet Explorer 5.x.

Comparing the Scheduled Task Wizard to AT/WinAt Tools

Using the Scheduled Task Wizard has some advantages over using more conventional AT/WinAt Tools. These advantages include:

- Events can be triggered on server reboot, logon to server, or when the server is idle (not just on specific dates and at specific times).

- You can set permissions on events using NTFS and standard access control lists.

- You can configure auditing on the event in a .job file.

- Events are portable. Tasks are saved with a .job file extension (under \winnt.sbs\Tasks), which makes moving tasks between computers easier (such as between the lab and client site). You can even transfer .job files as e-mail attachments or use RAS to transfer them. You'll need to reestablish security credentials after you've moved a .job file from one SBS system to another.

Tip

For more information on AT/WinAt and the Schedule service, see the *Microsoft Windows NT Server 4.0 Resource Kit*.

Setting the SST Password

SST reporting runs under a specific user account and password context. The SBS 4.5 Password Change Wizard, however, won't change the password for an account used for SST. To change the password, follow these steps:

1. Open My Computer and double-click the Scheduled Tasks icon.

2. In the list of Scheduled Tasks, right-click the desired task and choose Properties.

3. Click the Set Password button and enter the desired password. See Figure 15-1.

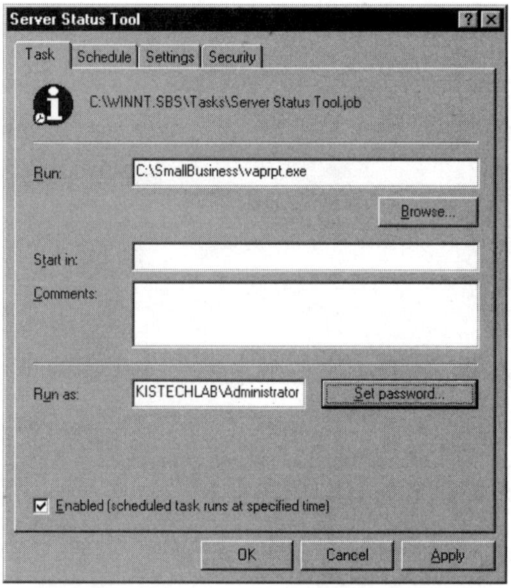

Figure 15-1

Click the Set Password button on the Task properties page to change the password.

You can find step-by-step instructions on how to change the passwords used by SST by searching for help on "server reporting password" in the SBS Console Online Guide.

Using Log Files

By default, SST can send up to five preconfigured log files to a specified SMTP e-mail address or fax number daily at 2 A.M.

Tip

In order to send SST reports through SMTP e-mail, first you need to run the Internet Connection Wizard (ICW), which Chapter 13 introduced. Chapter 18 drills down further on ICW.

For example, SST can monitor key Windows NT Server services and alert the VAP or other SST report recipients to the status of these services. This way, the off-site VAP can monitor the status of services without having to visit the client or connect to the server remotely to use the Control Panel Services applet or to run a Net Start command at the command prompt.

Tip

Although you can use SST to send log files by fax, make sure to get a handle on the log file size before choosing fax or e-mail. While fax reception is probably acceptable for relatively short one or two page logs, the Microsoft Internet Information Server (IIS) and Proxy Server logs can get quite large very quickly. If you're in doubt, just ask yourself whether you'd prefer to receive a 20-KB e-mail attachment or a 20-page fax.

With SST, you can specify how often log files should be sent. The frequency metrics can either be set based on time and date—such as a one-time or recurring event—or based on certain events—such as when the SBS 4.5 system starts up or when someone logs on interactively on the SBS 4.5 system. You can also use multiples of these criteria. See Figure 15-2 on the next page.

You can also force SST to send reports on demand. This can be especially useful if you need to walk a less experienced end user at the small business client through sending you the latest batch of SST logs immediately. To send an SST report manually, simply go into the Tasks page on the SBS Console, open the Administration Tools page, and choose Send Server Status. See Figure 15-3 on the next page.

Tip

If you have a lot of SBS clients set up for SST, you can generate e-mail messages and faxes containing custom subject lines. This way you know which client the reports represent and why the reports were sent. This is especially helpful for reports that aren't tied to recurring time and date events, but rather are sent following system startup or interactive logon.

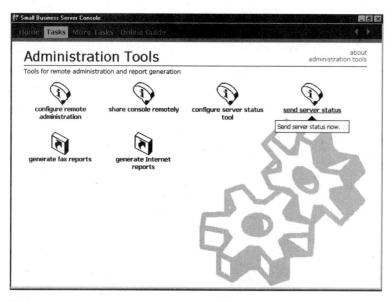

Figure 15-2
You can choose to have SST send you certain log files each time the SBS 4.5 system is booted.

Figure 15-3
You can send an SST report on demand by clicking Send Server Status.

Note

You can't send SST logs by fax until you've added the Fax Mail Transport service to the Administrator's mailbox profile in Microsoft Outlook 2000. This is done on the server through the Mail applet in Control Panel. Once complete, disconnect all connected end users, then shut down and restart the server.

Why Some SST Reports Don't Contain Five Log Files

SST always searches for the most current log file that matches the specified file pattern. This means that some log files might not be on every SST report if the log files haven't changed since the last time SST folded them into a report.

Later in this chapter, you'll learn how to extend SST's capabilities by adding a custom log file to the SST report batch.

Note

SST doesn't have an associated .hlp file because SST doesn't support Windows Help. If you press F1 within SST, you'll get a dialog box with an error message, "Cannot find the c:\smallbusiness\vaprpt.hlp file." Notice also that the upper right corner of the dialog box doesn't have a question mark icon. For more details, see KB article Q225297 in the Microsoft Knowledge Base.

Default Logs Included with SST

The five default log files, which can be included with any SST reports and sent by SMTP e-mail or fax service, are listed on the Reports tab of the Server Status Configuration dialog box. These default logs are Hard Disk Space, Server Status, IIS Logs, Web Proxy Logs, and Winsock Proxy Logs. See Figure 15-4 on the next page. An SST e-mail report can include any of these logs, as well as others, as attached files, as shown in Figure 15-5 on the next page.

Hard Disk Space   The Hard Disk Space log lists the percentage (%) of hard disk space available on all local hard disk volumes. While this log also lists any other drive letters on the server, such as floppy disk, CD-ROM, and mapped network drives, the Hard Disk Space log only reports on local hard disk volumes.

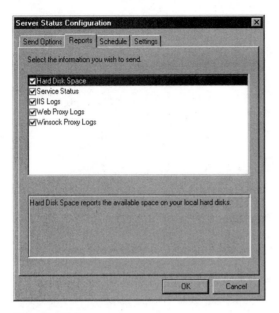

Figure 15-4
The five default reports for SST.

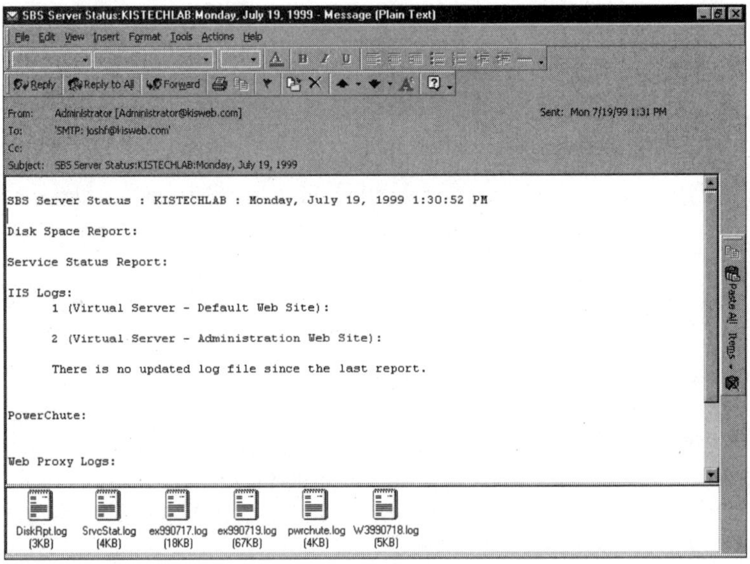

Figure 15-5
An SST e-mail report with several attached log files.

The Hard Disk Space log is attached to e-mail SST reports as DiskRpt.log. See Figure 15-6.

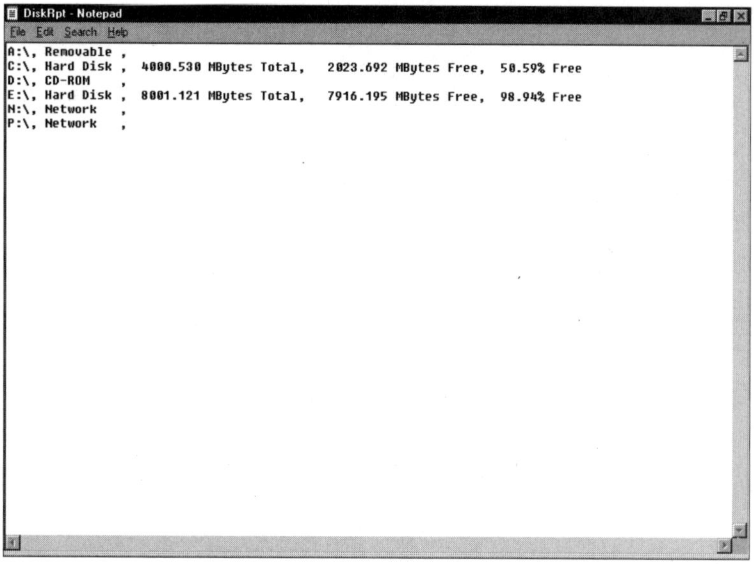
DiskRpt - Notepad
File Edit Search Help
A:\, Removable ,
C:\, Hard Disk , 4000.530 MBytes Total, 2023.692 MBytes Free, 50.59% Free
D:\, CD-ROM ,
E:\, Hard Disk , 8001.121 MBytes Total, 7916.195 MBytes Free, 98.94% Free
N:\, Network ,
P:\, Network ,

Figure 15-6

The Hard Disk Space log.

Service Status The Service Status log shows the status of each Windows NT service supported by SST. The list of services supported by SST can be extended by editing the registry if absolutely necessary, as I described earlier with the Spooler service example. See Figure 15-7 on the next page. The log file included with SST shows the following information:

- Name of the service
- Status of the service—Stopped, Running, or Paused
- Startup type of the service—Manual, Automatic, Disabled, or Not Installed

The Service Status log report is attached to the SST report e-mail as SrvcStat*x*.log, where *x* is a sequential number appended to the file name each time SST generates a new Service Status log. See Figure 15-8 on the next page.

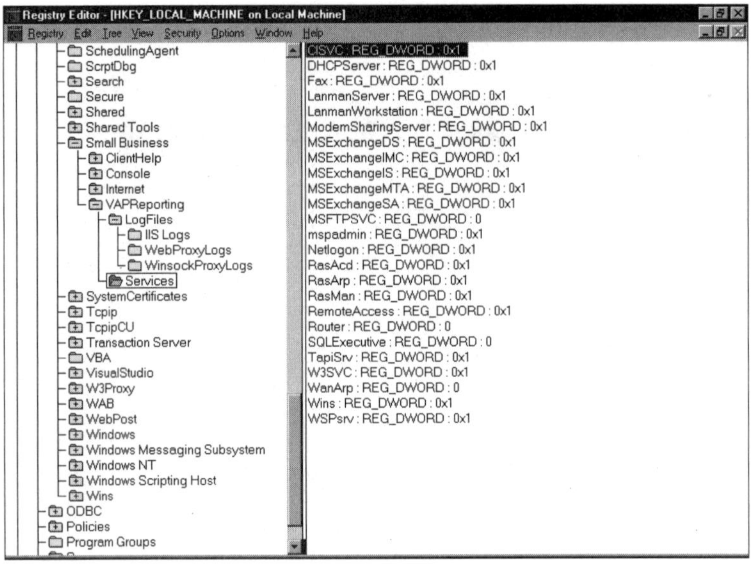

Figure 15-7

The default services monitored by SST as they appear in the registry.

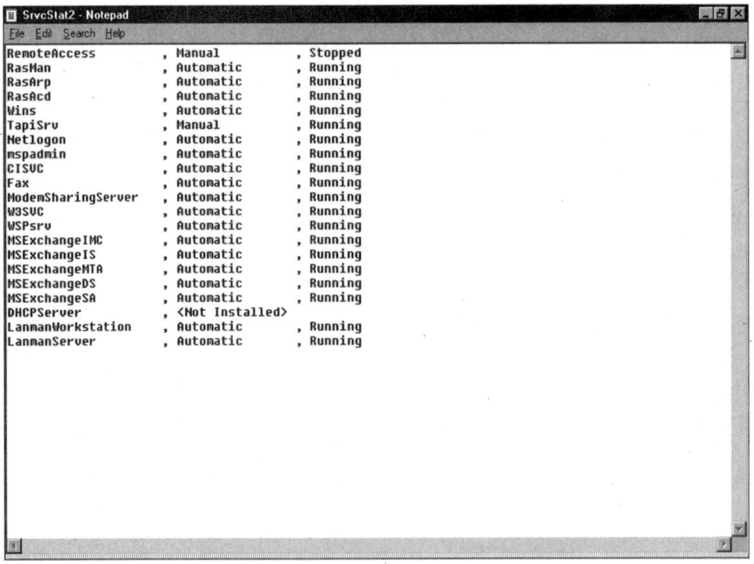

Figure 15-8

SBS Server Status log.

Note

Figure 15-8 shows the DHCPServer as <Not Installed>. Under normal circumstances the DHCPServer service would be shown as having an Automatic startup type and a Running status. In order to write this book and have several SBS servers coexisting on the same subnet, however, I had to disable the DHCPServer service on all but one SBS 4.5 system. Under normal usage, you should never disable the DHCPServer service. In fact, if SST logs for your small business clients shows DHCPServer as <Not Installed>, end users will be unable to log on to the SBS 4.5 system once their DHCP lease has expired. For more information on DHCP and leases, see Chapter 17.

Tip

For more information on Windows NT Server services, see the *Microsoft Windows NT 4.0 Server Resource Kit*.

IIS Logs   The IIS logs display Web site usage, which includes activity type and source IP address, and answer the questions of who's visiting your client's Web site and what they're viewing on that Web site. These logs are also often useful for red flagging security holes and provide at least a starting point for an audit trail back to a hacker.

The external IIS Web logs will be relevant only if your small business clients have full-time, dedicated Internet connections *and* choose to host their own Web sites. Many small businesses still choose to have their Web sites hosted on ISP-owned servers.

Web Proxy Logs   Web Proxy logs show which Web sites are being visited by which end users at the client site. Through further analysis, the logs can also reveal what times of day and week Web viewing activities take place, which are the top Web sites visited, and which end users are browsing the Web the most.

Winsock Proxy Logs   The Winsock Proxy logs perform the same basic functions as Web Proxy logs, but for Winsock-based applications. Popular Winsock applications include PointCast, AOL, POP3 e-mail (such as Microsoft Outlook Express), RealPlayer, and Microsoft NetMeeting.

Note

Unlike the Hard Disk Space and Service Status logs, the IIS, Web Proxy, and Winsock Proxy logs can grow very large very quickly. Be sure to evaluate estimated log files size and available bandwidth as you configure SST reports for these three log files.

Tip

Discussing the availability of these logs with the small business owner is important. If you haven't already broached the big brother types of issues when you helped craft a company e-mail and Internet usage policy (covered in Chapter 10), now would be a great time to have a heart-to-heart with the primary decision-maker at the client. The Web Proxy and Winsock Proxy logs can be great tools for helping the small business owner keep abreast of Internet usage; make sure, however, that all parties are on the same page with respect to how sensitive information will be used.

Adding Your Own Log Files to the SST Reports

In addition to the five preconfigured log files that SST can automatically fax or e-mail, you can extend SST to include log files from any number of third-party or custom applications. The best part: this customization can be performed without touching the registry or writing so much as a single line of code. You'll simply need the Small Business Server Customization Tool, the same application used in Chapter 14 to customize the SBS Console. An in-depth example of customizing SST will be provided toward the end of this chapter.

Tip

The Small Business Server Customization Tool is part of the *Microsoft BackOffice Small Business Server 4.5 Resource Kit*.

Configuring SST Reports and Log Files

The steps you take to configure SST reports and attached log files depend on whether you're choosing only from the included five default logs or whether you're adding your own custom logs.

Default Reporting

Follow these steps to configure SST reports with only the five default logs:

1. Choose Administration Tools on the SBS Console Tasks page.

2. Click Configure Server Status Tool. See Figure 15-9.

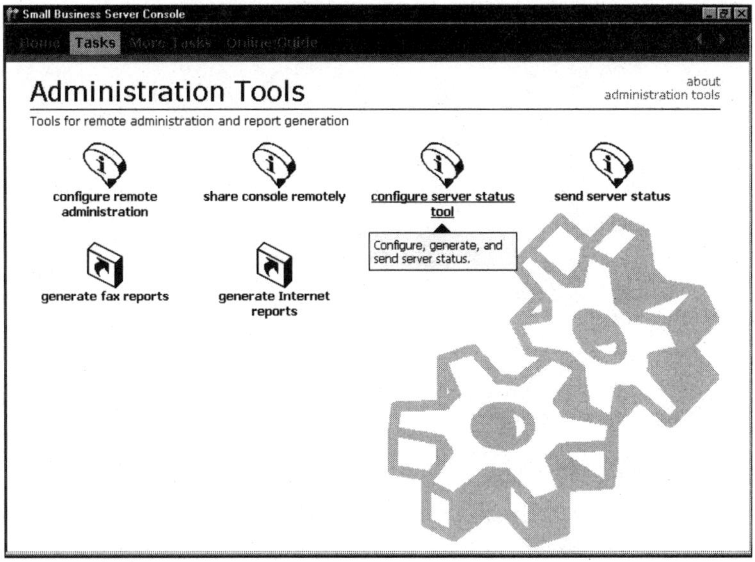

Figure 15-9

Click Configure Server Status Tool.

3. Select Server Status Configuration in the Help window that appears. See Figure 15-10 on the next page.

4. Click the Send Options, Reports, Schedule, or Settings tab of the Server Status Configuration dialog box and make your configuration choices. Doing this enters information in both the registry and the Scheduled Task Wizard. When an SST event is triggered by the Scheduled Task Wizard, SST sends logs by SMTP e-mail or fax to the desired recipient.

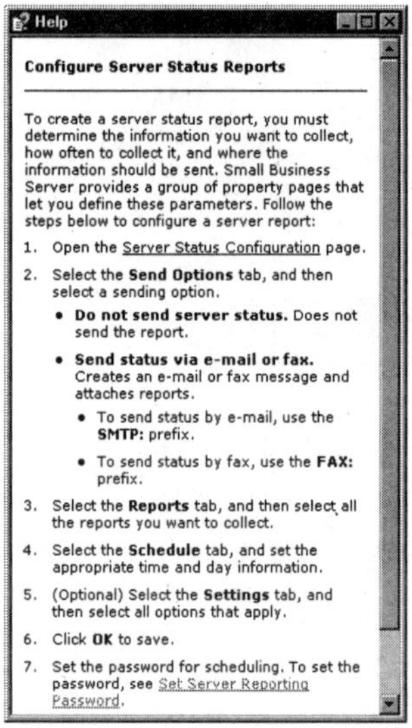

Figure 15-10

Click Server Status Configuration within the Help window.

Custom Reporting

Setting up your own logs to be included in SST reports isn't that different from selecting among the five default reports. Before you follow the steps in the preceding list, you'll need to use the Small Business Server Customization Tool to define the log parameters. See Figure 15-11.

Once you've entered the Report Name, File Pattern, File Path, and Description, your log definition is updated in the registry and the log becomes available on the Reports tab of the Server Status Configuration dialog box. A detailed example will be provided later in the chapter.

Configuration Choices

Although SST is quite powerful and extensible, the configuration choices really boil down to four tabs on a single Server Status Configuration dialog box: Send Options, Reports, Schedule, and Settings.

Send Options   The Send Options tab tells SST where logs should be sent. As indicated earlier, the reports can either be sent to an SMTP e-mail address or to a valid fax number.

If you configure SST to use an e-mail address, the SMTP: prefix is required, as shown in Figure 15-12. This uses IMS. So if IMS isn't configured through ICW, SST won't work through SMTP e-mail.

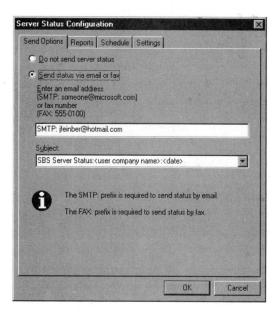

Figure 15-11

You can add more log choices to SST by using the Small Business Server Customization Tool.

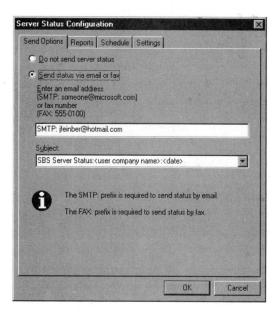

Figure 15-12

Configuring SST to use an SMTP e-mail address.

Alternatively, you can configure SST to send its logs to a fax number. If you choose this option, the "FAX:" prefix is required, as shown in Figure 15-13. This uses Fax Service. If Fax Service wasn't previously configured, SST won't work through fax.

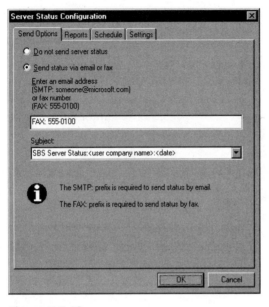

Figure 15-13

Configuring SST to send logs to a fax number.

You can also customize the subject line through the Send Options tab by simply editing the Subject line. This can be particularly useful if you have several different reports for a given small business client, such as daily, weekly, and monthly. By default, SST customizes the:

- <user company name> (SST picks the company name up from the domain name.)

- <date> (SST picks up the date from the system clock date in Windows NT Server 4.0)

Tip

If you choose to customize subject lines, you could use the Rules Wizard in Outlook 2000 to place logs for each client in a shared Public Folder on your firm's Exchange Server until monthly reports are compiled. You can find out how to use this feature by searching for help on Rules Wizard in Outlook 2000 online help.

You can also select Do Not Send Server Status on the Send Options tab to disable SST.

Reports   On the Reports tab of the Server Status Configuration dialog box you can select which reports should be sent. These reports were covered earlier in this chapter in "Default Logs Included with SST."

Any custom logs that you add, either through direct registry manipulation or, preferably, through the Small Business Server Customization Tool, will be displayed on the Reports tab. The description that you add will be displayed at the bottom of the Reports tab when the desired report is selected.Figure 15-4 shows how the Reports tab looks before you add custom log files.

Schedule   The Schedule tab ties SST reporting to the Scheduled Task Wizard. By default, SST sends its full report batch every Sunday at 2:00 A.M. See Figure 15-14 on the next page. As the Show Multiple Schedules check box at the bottom of the Schedule tab indicates, SST supports multiple scheduling events. You can set different reports to come at different intervals. These include:

- Daily
- Monthly
- Weekly
- Once (one time only)
- At system startup (when the computer starts)
- At logon (when someone logs on interactively to the server)
- When idle

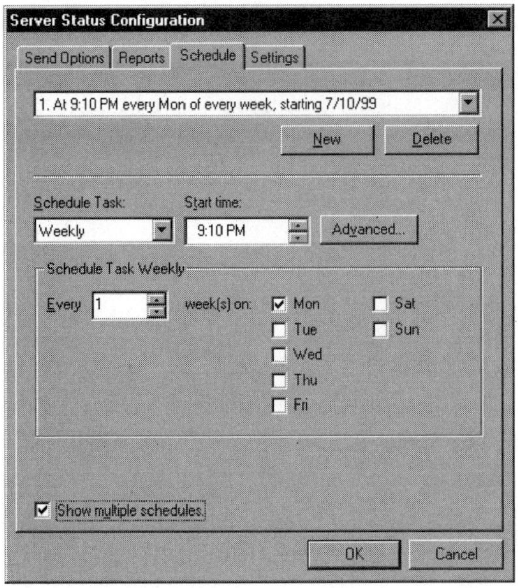

Figure 15-14
The Schedule tab of the Server Status Configuration dialog box.

For example, you might want to see some custom reports daily, while others you'll only want to see weekly. Perhaps you'll want to keep tabs on the progress daily for tape backup. Maybe for the UPS monitoring software, you'll care to see the logs only weekly.

Settings   The Settings tab controls whether tasks are deleted on completion and are stopped if they run longer than a predetermined amount of time (that is, if an application hangs). See Figure 15-15.

The Settings tab also configures how idle time and power management are dealt with in relation to SST reports. For example, if generating and sending a log file proves to be CPU intensive, you might want to set the report compilation to occur only when the server has been idle for a while. Power management settings allow the SST task to be bypassed or aborted if the server begins running on batteries.

Tip

To determine whether or not SST report logs have been sent, open up Administrator's mailbox in Outlook 2000 and look under Outbox and Sent Items.

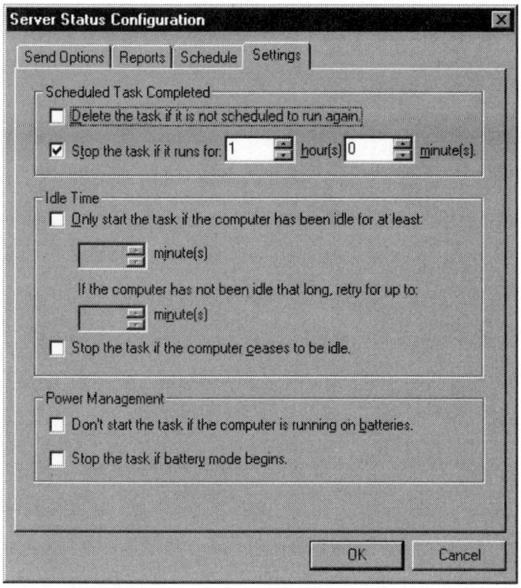

Figure 15-15
The Schedule tab of the Server Status Configuration dialog box.

Customizing and Extending SST

As explained earlier in the chapter, you can add more log files to SST's repertoire in two ways. The first way is through direct manipulation of registry keys and values. Since this way is fraught with risk and has the overhead of extensive testing, forget you ever heard that here and just focus on how easy it can be to extend SST through the GUI-based Small Business Server Customization Tool.

Ideas for Extending SST

Dozens or perhaps even hundreds of applications exist for extending SST's abilities by delivering additional log files to you through e-mail attachments. A few of the more common log files you'll likely encounter are:

- Tape backup logs
- Antivirus logs
- Accounting application logs
- Custom database application logs
- Vertical application logs
- UPS monitoring logs

The final section of Chapter 15 looks at how you can add logs from American Power Conversion (APC) PowerChute *plus* version 5.1, a UPS monitoring software application. I find this section to be particularly apropos because the area of New Jersey where I work and live was hit particularly hard by rolling blackouts and brownouts the week before I wrote this chapter.

The Mechanics of the Small Business Server Customization Tool

The Small Business Server Customization Tool, sbscustom.exe, was developed in Microsoft Visual Basic to make it easy for VAPs to add custom reports to SST. See Figure 15-11.

To begin customizing SST, open the Small Business Server Customization Tool and click Configure Server Status Tool. The List of Custom Reports shows all the reports added to SST. (These reports are in addition to the five default reports, which aren't visible in the Small Business Server Customization Tool.) By selecting a report, you can edit its configuration parameters. Alternatively, you can select a report and click the Delete Report button to remove the log from SST. By clicking the New Report button, you'll be on your way to adding a custom log to SST.

The bottom half of the dialog box outlines the four required parameters for extending SST: Report Name, File Pattern, File Path, and Description.

Report Name   The Report Name is displayed on the SST list of reports, which is on Reports tab of the Server Status Configuration dialog box. See Figure 15-4. The Report Name is also displayed within the body of the e-mail on an SST report.

Small Business Server Customization Tool enters the Report Name in the registry in the DisplayName value in \HKEY_LOCAL_MACHINE\SOFTWARE\ Microsoft\Small Business\VAPReporting\LogFiles*ReportName* where *ReportName*= DisplayName.

File Pattern   File Pattern is used behind the scenes to find the desired log report that matches the requested file pattern. If the log's name is always the same, File Pattern will be a file name. If log's name varies by one or more prefixed or appended characters, a wildcard character (*) is used to locate the file. When SST finds multiple files with the same File Pattern, SST always selects the most recent log file for the report.

Small Business Server Customization Tool enters the File Pattern in the registry in the LogFileNamePattern value in \HKEY_LOCAL_MACHINE\ SOFTWARE\Microsoft\Small Business\VAPReporting\LogFiles*ReportName*.

File Path File Path is also used behind the scenes to find the desired log report. As with File Pattern, File Path has no Browse button and doesn't perform validation on your selection. So you want to be especially careful here. You'll need to include the local drive letter and full path (for example, c:\winnt.sbs\temp\logs).

Small Business Server Customization Tool enters this in the registry in the LogFilePath value in \HKEY_LOCAL_MACHINE\SOFTWARE\Microsoft\ Small Business\VAPReporting\LogFiles*ReportName*.

Description Description is displayed at the bottom of the Reports tab in the Server Status Configuration dialog box. This allows the person configuring SST to get more information about the custom Report selection. See Figure 15-4.

Small Business Server Customization Tool enters the description in the registry in the Description value in \HKEY_LOCAL_MACHINE\SOFTWARE\ Microsoft\Small Business\VAPReporting\LogFiles*ReportName*.

Other Behind the Scenes Information Tracked by SST

In addition to the four fields captured by the Small Business Server Customization Tool that are stored in the registry, two additional values in \HKEY_LOCAL_MACHINE\SOFTWARE\Microsoft\Small Business\ VAPReporting\LogFiles*ReportName* are tracked for each default or custom log:

- LastSentFileTime is a hex value that keeps track of when the log file was last sent using SST.

- SendLog defaults to a value of 1 to indicate that the log file is enabled for sending with SST. A value of 0 prevents the log from being sent with SST.

Try to use the GUI-based Small Business Server Customization Tool whenever possible. Direct registry editing should only be attempted as an absolute last resort. Because of the risks associated with direct registry manipulation, make sure all end users are disconnected from the server and you have a full backup of the registry in the event you need to roll back.

Note

The Small Business Server Customization Tool will overwrite any logs with the same name that have been added to SST by an ISV. The tool also will overwrite any logs for SST with same name that were added manually through registry manipulation. As a general rule of thumb, if an ISV purports an application to be SBS-compliant, check the SST list of reports (Reports tab) for any ISV-added SST reports before customizing SST.

Adding a UPS Monitoring Log to the SST Reporting Logs

The final part of this chapter explains how to add the APC PowerChute *plus* log file to the list of available SST report selections. Then the chapter shows how to do an immediate SST report transmission to verify that the PowerChute *plus* log file was in fact added successfully to the SST report batch.

PowerChute *plus* is used to monitor the UPS through a serial cable. It provides real-time and logged information such as Battery Capacity, Run Time, Utility Voltage, UPS Temperature, and UPS Load. See Figure 15-16. I'm particularly interested in the Event Log that PowerChute *plus* stores so that I can tell when my small business client has experienced power fluctuations such as spikes, blackouts, sags, brownouts, and high input line voltages. See Figure 15-17. The Event Log shows the precise time of the power fluctuation as well as the magnitude of the problem in volts. So the report is of high value to SBS VAPs.

To add the Event Log to SST's available list of log reports, you first need to find out its file name and where the log file is stored. In the case of PowerChute *plus*, the log file is stored under c:\Program Files\Pwrchute\Pwrchute.log. Often you can locate this file through visual inspection of the hard disk directories or in the application's online help. Alternatively, you could always call the vendor's technical support group or check the vendor's Web site to find the log file location and file pattern.

With this information in hand, I can now launch the Small Business Server Customization Tool. To add the PowerChute *plus* log file as the Event Log, follow these steps:

1. Choose Configure Server Status Tool, and click the New Report button.

2. Enter "APC PowerChute log" in the Report Name box.

3. Enter "pwrchute.log" in the File Pattern box. (You don't need to use wildcard characters for this log file because APC always appends

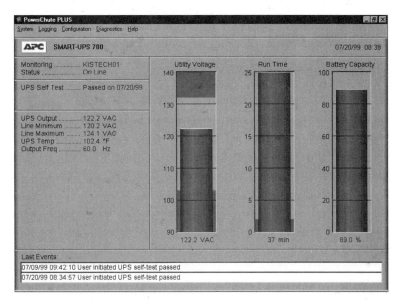

Figure 15-16

Main console screen of APC PowerChute plus *version 5.1.*

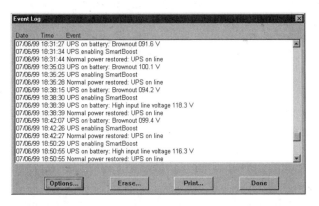

Figure 15-17

Manually displaying the Event Log from PowerChute plus.

new data to the same log file. The use of wildcards vs. fixed file names, however, will vary on an application-by-application basis.)

4.   Enter "c:\Program Files\Pwrchute" in the File Path box. (Remember to be careful what you type in the boxes for File Pattern and File Path because SST doesn't validate this information.)

5. Enter "Shows power fluctuations such as sags, spikes, brownouts, and blackouts" in the Description box. See Figure 15-18.

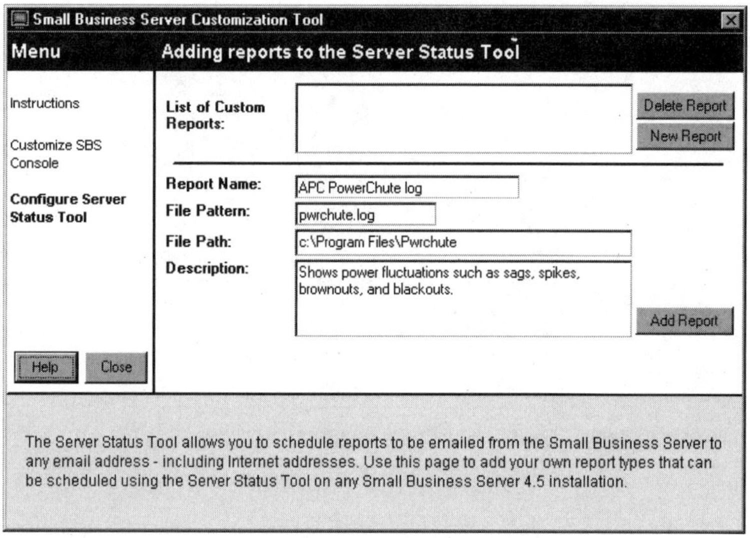

Figure 15-18

Completed dialog box to add Event Log.

6. Click the Add Report button to commit the changes to the registry. A dialog box will appear, confirming that your information has been successfully added to the registry.

Now when I return to the Reports tab in the Server Status Configuration dialog box, I'll see that APC PowerChute log has been added to the list of selectable log reports, between Service Status and IIS Logs. See Figure 15-19.

To test the ability to include PowerChute logs in my SST reports, I'll return to the Administration Tools page and click Send Server Status. See Figure 15-3. This will queue up the SST report to be sent out using the configured options.

Assuming SST is configured to send reports to your SMTP e-mail address, you'll shortly see an SST report containing the Pwrchute.log file in your Microsoft Outlook Inbox. The report will look similar to Figure 15-20.

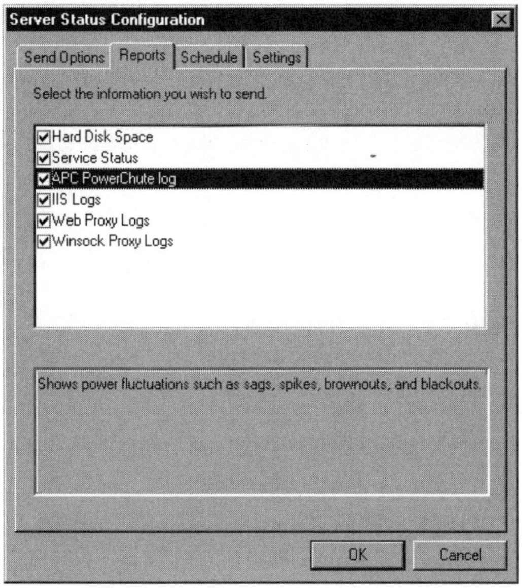

Figure 15-19

The APC log has been added to list of available SST logs.

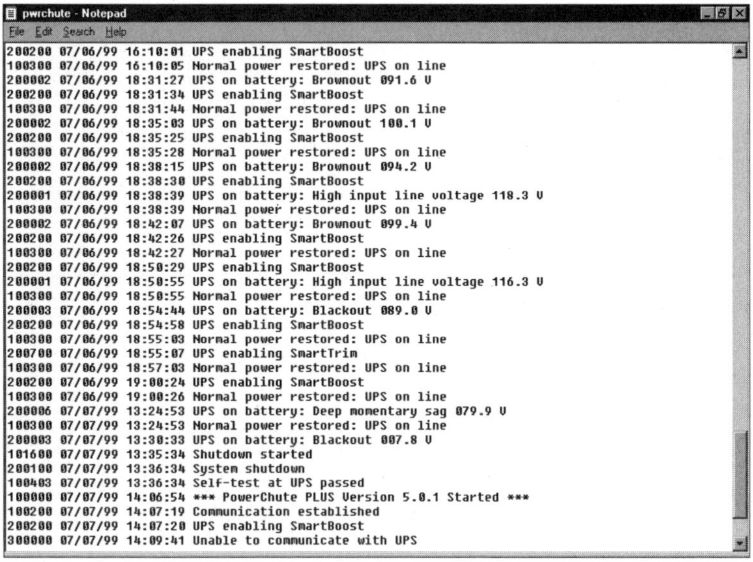

Figure 15-20

The SST report containing the Pwrchute.log file.

Tip

Power protection is an extremely important part of any SBS solution. As a result, this book will cover various aspects of power protection solutions as they relate to different parts of an SBS client engagement in Chapters 19, 22, 23, and 25.

Tip

For more information on power protection, APC UPS, and PowerChute _plus_ software, see the APC Web site at _www.apcc.com_.

The Bottom Line

Downtime is expensive for small business owners. Without a full-time IT staff on-site, small businesses are particularly vulnerable to server problems. The Server Status Tool gives SBS VAPs a mechanism to stay easily and proactively on top of various facets of the SBS 4.5 system's performance and overall network well-being.

Chapter 16

Extending the Set Up Computer Wizard

Manually installing application software can be tedious and subject to operator errors. In this chapter, you'll be introduced to a way you can add value to your small business client's Microsoft BackOffice Small Business Server installation by customizing the Set Up Computer Wizard (SCW). The SCW allows you to trigger unattended installations of applications included with SBS 4.5 and popular third-party software by running the main SBS client setup disk. By building upon the SCW infrastructure, you can make it easy for your small business client's internal guru to install and update a variety of client applications without expensive service calls.

In Chapter 16, you learn about how to prepare the SBS 4.5 system for adding new client computers and applications. Then, in Chapter 17 you'll look at the flip side of the equation by drilling down on the steps required at each client workstation.

High-Margin vs. Low-Margin Services

You might wonder why you'd want to extend the SCW to make it easier for your small business client's internal guru to install client applications. Wouldn't that be taking service income away from your firm? Yes and no.

As their client's virtual IT department, most SBS VAPs recognize that they need to be prepared to provide everything and anything under the sun in terms of hand-holding. On the other hand, installing a Web browser, e-mail client, or utility program on a desktop PC is a repetitive, relatively low-level task. In other words, you needn't have skills that rival a Microsoft Certified Systems Engineer (MCSE) to be able to install Microsoft Internet Explorer, WinZip, or Acrobat Reader.

By training the internal guru to handle some of the more mundane tasks, you'll be freeing up your resources to concentrate on perceived value-add services. These might include preparing a disaster recovery plan and data protection evaluation (Chapters 19 and 23), building collaborative applications with Microsoft Exchange Server (Chapter 26), or implementing a RAS server or Microsoft Fax Service (Chapter 27).

Keep your eye on the ball. Your skills need to stay sharp and on the cutting edge to a certain degree. Value-add is definitely a moving target. If your firm isn't at least thinking about offering some of these higher value-added services, perhaps you'll want to reread Chapters 2 and 3 to learn about the short shelf life of training.

Role of Set Up Computer Wizard

The goal of this chapter is to show you the two main ways to extend SCW and provide a few examples and techniques you can use for other application needs.

Extending SCW is only pertinent to applications with standard setup programs (such as InstallShield) that are capable of silent installations. As a general rule of thumb, if the application in question can't be pushed out (sent from the server to clients) from Microsoft Systems Management Server (SMS), it probably can't be integrated with SCW.

Note

SMS isn't part of SBS 4.5 and generally isn't a good fit for small businesses with 5 to 50 client PCs. For more information on SMS solutions and licensing, see *www.microsoft.com/smsmgmt*.

Although most independent software vendors (ISVs) aren't up to speed yet on the requirements for integrating an application with SBS 4.5 SCW, most ISVs will be familiar with integrating their application with SMS. If the ISV has no information on how an application fits in with SCW, use the ISV's SMS technical support bulletins and knowledge base articles as starting points.

Tip

If you happen to be a product or development manager, you have a tremendous market opportunity by making your application more SBS-friendly. This often can be accomplished with relatively few development resources by leveraging SBS's built-in customization mechanisms.

SCW can be started by clicking the More Tasks tab on the SBS Console, opening the Manage Computers page, and clicking Set Up A Computer. See Figure 16-1 on the next page. SCW, which is also launched at the end of the Add User Wizard, automates the configuration of client computers for an SBS 4.5 network.

Tip

Although the steps in SCW can be accomplished manually, the SBS Console and wizards are designed with the idea that you'll use the SBS wizards whenever possible. Experienced SBS VAPs know setup and administration goes much more smoothly when you don't stray from the SBS wizards.

Tip

SCW works with SBS clients running Microsoft Windows 95, Microsoft Windows 98, and Microsoft Windows NT 4.0.

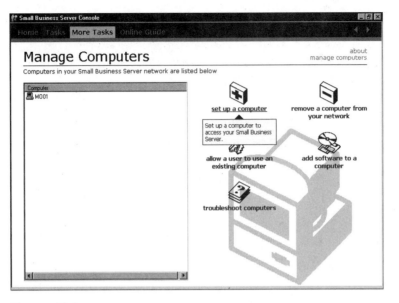

Figure 16-1

Clicking Set Up A Computer launches SCW.

When you install Microsoft and third-party applications on a desktop or laptop client, you typically take a set of disks or CD-ROMs with you to each client, run a setup program, and respond to a bunch of dialog boxes. While this method works well when you're installing one or two applications on a very small number of PCs, it grows old when you're installing a larger volume onto nearly identical PCs at your small business client.

Tip

If your small business clients are running Windows NT Workstation 4.0, SCW also installs Windows NT Service Pack 4 (SP4). For details on how to integrate subsequent Windows NT Service Packs with SBS 4.5, check the SBS Web site at *www.microsoft.com/smallbusinessserver*.

To get around this tedium, speed up the deployment, and ensure compliance to standards, IT professionals and SBS VAPs often recommend unattended setups, otherwise known as silent installations. Chapter 12 covered how to automate the deployment of Windows NT Workstation 4.0 as the desktop OS for an SBS rollout. With SCW, the SBS client applications and third-party applications are layered on top of the baseline OS.

In order for SCW to add the SBS 4.5 client applications and ISV applications to the SBS 4.5 clients, the application setup files need to be stored on a share on the server. Because the installation files are stored on the server, you don't need to carry CD-ROMs and disks from one client PC to the next.

Tip

SCW can only push out an installation; it can't remove applications. To remove individual applications installed by SCW, use Add/Remove Programs in each client's Control Panel.

In addition to building a customized client setup disk each time it runs, SCW creates and overwrites several configuration files for an existing client. The files affected by SCW include the logon script, application .inf files, the client optional component information file (clioc.inf), and the installed file.

Logon Script

A logon script is run each time a user logs on to the SBS 4.5 network. SCW uses a logon script template to create individual logon scripts for each user account. The template, template.bat, is stored in \SmallBusiness\Template and includes environmental variables for SBSUser and SBSServer. SCW uses the template.bat file as the basis for creating each user's logon script, which is then stored in the \winnt.sbs\system32\repl\import\scripts\SmallBusiness folder (sometimes referred to as the NETLOGON share).

You should note that SCW doesn't customize logon scripts. SCW just copies the template.bat file to the NETLOGON share and renames it for the target user account. Because of this, SBS VAPs might be tempted to modify each user's logon script for any desired changes. This, however, would be a huge mistake. Logon scripts are overwritten by SCW, so you should never modify an individual's logon script. You can, however, modify the logon script template using a standard text editor. This might be useful, for example, if you wanted to synchronize time between the SBS 4.5 server and the clients. You could just add a net time command to the template, such as net time \\servername /set /yes, as shown in Figure 16-2 on the next page. The moral of the story: don't waste time modifying individual logon scripts for SBS 4.5 users. Always modify the template.bat file directly.

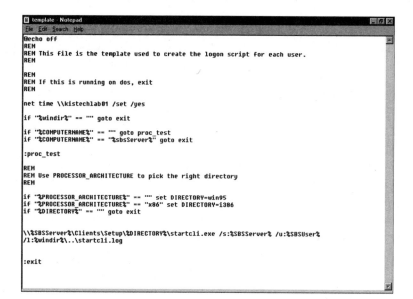

Figure 16-2

Customize SBS 4.5 user logon scripts by modifying the template.bat file.

Tip

Before editing any file, you should always make a backup copy in case you need to roll back to your original. In this case, you could create a copy of template.bat named template.old before continuing.

Once SCW has configured a user's logon script and application response files, each time the users logs onto SBS and the logon script runs, the startcli.exe program checks to see if the installed file exists before any applications are installed. This results in a command prompt window opening immediately following logon to the SBS 4.5 network. The Client Installation Wizard creates the installed file for each user when all of the SCW application installation programs have completed.

If the Client Installation Wizard does in fact install SCW-selected applications, upon completion the Client Installation Wizard creates the installed file in the Response folder for the appropriate client. The existence of the installed file blocks all subsequent attempts to install applications by the Client Installation Wizard.

The installed file is stored in the \SmallBusiness\Clients\Response folder (on the Clients share) for each client on the network. If an installed file exists, SCW stops and no applications are installed. If startcli.exe is unable to find an installed file in that client's Response folder, the Client Installation Wizard takes over and begins installing the applications selected during SCW for that client (the client in this instance is a combination of the user and computer).

Startcli.exe Syntax

In case you need to troubleshoot SCW or a logon script, the following switches are used with startcli.exe:

/s   name of SBS sever

/u   name of user

/l   name and location of log file

Tip

If you want to force the Client Installation Wizard to reinstall SCW-selected applications for a client, simply delete or rename the installed file from the Response folder. On the flip side, SCW will delete the installed file for the appropriate client if it finds one. This will in turn trigger unattended application installation on the client computer the next time that user logs onto the SBS 4.5 network from that client workstation.

Client Optional Component Information File

In addition to the installed file, the Response folder for each client on the server also contains a client optional component information file (clioc.inf) as well as application-specific .inf files. The clioc.inf is the top level .inf file and provides Client Installation Wizard with a list of applications to be installed on the SBS client computer. See Figure 16-3 on the next page.

The clioc.inf for individual clients is created from the clioc.inf template in \SmallBusiness\Template. Each client's clioc.inf changes are overwritten every time SCW is run for that client, just as when SCW copies the logon script template to the NETLOGON share. So once again, if you must modify the clioc.inf file, only make changes directly to the clioc.inf template, not clioc.inf files stored in individual client directories.

```
clioc - Notepad                                                    _ 6 X
File  Edit  Search  Help
;
; clioc.inf
;
; top-level inf file for use with the Sam client installation

[Version]
Signature = "$Windows NT$"

[Components.w95]
fax = "","",clifax.inf
ie = "","",cliie.inf
proxy = "","",cliproxy.inf
mshare = "","",climshr.inf
office_cd1 = "","",clioff.inf
office_cd2 = "","",clioff2.inf
client = ..\..\setup\win95\ocsam.dll,OcEntry,client.inf

[Components.x86]
ntfax = "","",ntfax.inf
ie = "","",cliie.inf
proxy = "","",cliproxy.inf
mshare = "","",ntmshr.inf
office_cd1 = "","",clioff.inf
office_cd2 = "","",clioff2.inf
client = ..\..\setup\i386\ocsam.dll,OcEntry,ntclient.inf

;the HKLM keyword lists a regval to be found in HKEY_LOCAL_MACHINE that indicates
;whether the specified component is truely installed.  If it is installed, the value
;exists, if uninstalled, it should have been removed.  There must be one entry for
;each component, if the installer is to successfully determine the installation state
;of the component.

[proxy]
HKLM="SOFTWARE\Microsoft\Windows\CurrentVersion\Uninstall\Microsoft Proxy Client","DisplayName"
```

Figure 16-3

A Client optional component information file, clioc.inf.

Tip

When a system is upgraded from SBS 4.0 to 4.5, the clioc.inf is overwritten. A copy of the file, however, is preserved as clioc.old so that you can copy and paste settings as needed.

Once startcli.exe fails to find an installed file, the Client Installation Wizard launches and uses the clioc.inf to determine which applications are already installed and which need to be installed. The Wizard looks for a specific HKEY_LOCAL_MACHINE registry value, which appears toward the bottom of the clioc.inf file for a particular application.

Tip

The Small Business Server Client Setup Integration Wizard, introduced later in this chapter, is a GUI-based tool that largely eliminates the need to modify the clioc.inf template directly.

Note

Take a look at the fourth line in the clioc.inf file, which has the semicolon in front of it (a comment line): "; top-level .inf file for use with the Sam client installation." Also note the ocsam.dll file, which is referenced for the Client Installation Wizard in two separate lines, one for Windows 95 and the other for Windows NT Workstation 4.0. Apparently, the SBS developers were referring to SBS by its original circa-1996 code name Sam (for SAM'S Club warehouse stores). For more details on the history of SBS and why it was originally code-named Sam, see the white paper entitled "Roots of SBS" on the CD-ROM in the back of the book.

Application .inf Files

Each application tagged by SCW to be pushed out by the Client Installation Wizard must also have its own .inf file that details how to install the application. Each application's .inf file should be placed in the Template folder so SCW can copy the .inf file into each client's Response folder on the server.

The application's .inf file will need various items defined such as InstallCmd, DiskSpaceEstimate, and UnInstallCmd. If the ISV doesn't have an .inf file that works with SCW, you can use an existing .inf file as your model, such as the one shown in Figure 16-4 on the next page. The application setup files, which would normally be on a CD-ROM or disk, need to be copied to the ClientApps share and folder on the server. Also, each application's set of installation files should be placed in its own folder. The unattended installation information file (.inf) should be placed in the Template folder.

Table 16-1 on the next page shows the.inf files for SBS 4.5 client applications.

Tip

You don't actually need an application .inf file as a prerequisite for integration into SCW. If the target application can be installed without an .inf file, the Client Installation Wizard should be able to perform an unattended installation without the .inf file.

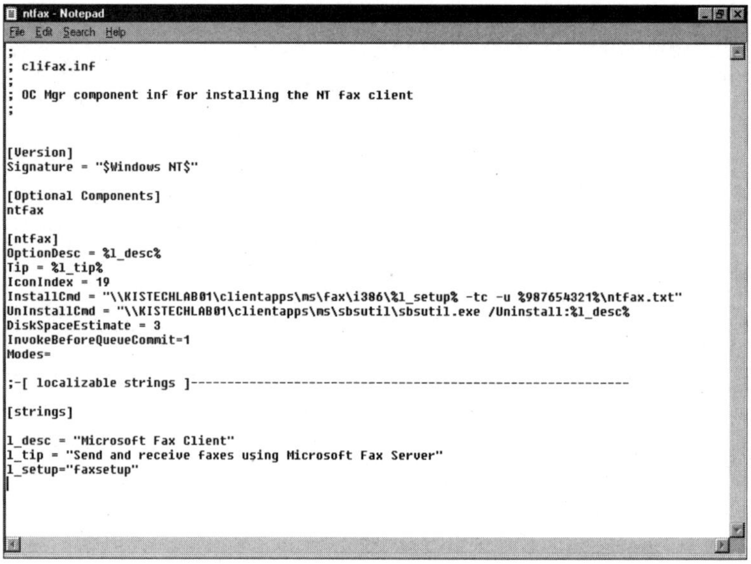

```
ntfax - Notepad
File  Edit  Search  Help
;
; clifax.inf
;
; OC Mgr component inf for installing the NT fax client
;


[Version]
Signature = "$Windows NT$"

[Optional Components]
ntfax

[ntfax]
OptionDesc = %1_desc%
Tip = %1_tip%
IconIndex = 19
InstallCmd = "\\KISTECHLAB01\clientapps\ms\fax\i386\%1_setup% -tc -u %987654321%\ntfax.txt"
UnInstallCmd = "\\KISTECHLAB01\clientapps\ms\sbsutil\sbsutil.exe /Uninstall:%1_desc%
DiskSpaceEstimate = 3
InvokeBeforeQueueCommit=1
Modes=

;-[ localizable strings ]----------------------------------------------------

[strings]

1_desc = "Microsoft Fax Client"
1_tip = "Send and receive faxes using Microsoft Fax Server"
1_setup="faxsetup"
```

Figure 16-4

An .inf file for Fax Service client software for Windows NT Workstation 4.0.

Client application	.inf file
Fax Service Client 4.5	clifax.inf for Windows 95/98
	NTFax.inf for Windows NT Workstation 4.0
Internet Explorer 5	cliie.inf
Microsoft Proxy Server Client	cliproxy.inf
Modem Sharing Service Client 4.5	climshr.inf for Windows 95/98
	ntmshr.inf for Windows NT Workstation 4.0
Microsoft Outlook 2000 or Microsoft Office 2000 Professional	clioff.inf (Office CD 1) clioff2.inf (Office CD 2)

Table 16-1

.inf files for included SBS 4.5 client applications

Criteria for Integration with SCW

Not all applications are prime candidates for integrating with SCW. For starters, MS-DOS-based applications and 16-bit applications are off limits for SCW because the SCW process relies on checking registry entries. What are the basic criteria for whether or not an application can be integrated with SCW?

In a perfect world, you'd be able to go to an ISV's Web site or contact its technical support department and get simple answers to these simple questions: "Will your app work with SCW? What do I need to do to make it work?" Because many ISVs are still SBS newbies, you might need to explain what SCW and SBS are.

Tip

When faced with SBS-clueless ISV tech support, I generally liken SCW to a small subset of the software management functions found in SMS within Microsoft BackOffice.

Barring the ISV's ability to tell you whether the application works with SCW, the application needs to install silently, with no user interaction required, to be an SCW candidate. The application should also have no order dependencies on other applications in the unattended setup batch because you can't dictate the order in which unattended installations are launched.

Tip

If the application setup program is based on InstallShield, find out if you can you use the –sms option to prevent unattended setup from starting another process for the install. This one command line switch is often the difference between success and failure with SCW integration.

Finally, in order to integrate an application with SCW, you need a way to suppress the reboot prompt. Applications usually prompt you to reboot following installation. SCW generally can't function properly with these types of reboot requests. If the ISV has SMS integration instructions, chances are this concern is addressed.

GUI vs. Text-File Extension Methods

Chapters 14 and 15 covered how you could use the Small Business Server Customization Tool in the *Microsoft BackOffice Small Business Server 4.5 Resource Kit* to avoid having to script, program, or modify the registry. While the GUI-based Customization Tool is not quite as powerful as manual extensions would be, it eliminates tremendous risk and lessens the learning curve for SBS VAPs. By using GUI-based tools to customize and extend various facets of SBS, you are free to concentrate on providing the additional solutions covered throughout this book.

Small Business Server Client Setup Integration Wizard

When extending SCW, you have two choices. You can use the Small Business Server Client Setup Integration Wizard (SCWCustom.exe) in the *Microsoft BackOffice Small Business Server 4.5 Resource Kit* or you can edit lots of text files and registry keys. The GUI-based tool, shown in Figure 16-5, takes care of the basics by lessening the dangers associated with direct registry manipulation, flattening out an often steep learning curve, and getting rid of the need for hours of tedious trial and error.

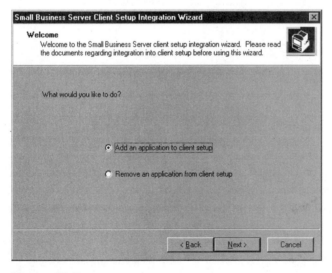

Figure 16-5

The Small Business Server Client Setup Integration Wizard.

With the Small Business Server Client Setup Integration Wizard, you can add or remove an application from SCW and capture the following information:

- Name of the application (how it's to appear in client setup)

- Short name of the application (used internally; up to eight characters long)

- With which OS the application works (Windows 95/98, Windows NT, or both)

- Application selected by default in SCW (Yes/No)

- Description of application (used by Client Installation Wizard—shows up on the client side of setup)

- Disk space estimate (MB)

- Installation command (defaults to \\servername\ClientApps; you'll need to append the folder created for the application installation files and the install command—for example, setup.exe—to this default)

- Installation key (the registry key and value used to figure out whether an application has been installed)

- Unattended file required for setup (Yes/No)

- Location of unattended (.inf) file relative to SmallBusiness directory (preferred location is the Template folder)

- Source name of unattended .inf file (in the Template folder)

- Destination name of unattended .inf file (in the user's Response folder)

We'll use the Small Business Server Client Setup Integration Wizard later in this chapter to add a third-party application to SCW.

The Gray Hair Way

In order to master the gray hair way of extending SCW, you should thoroughly read and understand the role of the logon script, clioc.inf, and application .inf files as discussed earlier in this chapter. In addition, you'll need to modify the SCW initialization file (scw.ini) in the SmallBusiness folder on the server so the new application can show up in the list of SCW applications.

Tip

As with all text files discussed in this chapter, always back up the primary text file before making changes to it so you can roll back to the original if necessary.

Scw.ini contains a [SCW_OptionalApplications] section with the setting SCW_NumberOfApps. In order to add another application to SCW, the SCW_NumberOfApps needs be incremented by one. The SCW_NumberOfApps value should be incremented in numerical order, starting at zero.

Tip

When upgrading from SBS 4.0 to 4.5, the scw.ini is overwritten. A copy, however, is preserved as scw.old.

To learn more about extending SCW manually, see the *Microsoft BackOffice Small Business Server 4.5 Resource Kit* Chapter 44, "Extension Mechanism for the Set Up Computer Wizard," and the "Microsoft BackOffice Small Business Server 4.5 Client Setup White Paper" located on the SBS Web site at *www.microsoft.com/smallbusinessserver.*

Adding Antivirus Software

A number of third-party ISVs make antivirus solutions that are SBS-compatible. For the purpose of this example, I'll look at how you can integrate Network Associates VirusScan 4 for Windows NT with SCW, primarily through the Small Business Server Client Setup Integration Wizard.

Tip

You can learn more about VirusScan and Network Associates (the ISV for VirusScan) at *www.nai.com.*

Before you can even think about adding an application to SCW, you need to need learn about what it takes to make the application install in an unattended fashion. To meet the other two criteria for integrating with SCW, you should find out from the ISV whether the application has any installation order dependencies and whether the reboot prompt can be suppressed. Because Network Associates provides documentation on how VirusScan can be rolled out using SMS, I was able to read between the lines to find what was required to integrate VirusScan with SCW.

Tip

In addition to the 1.5-MB Vnt31doc.pdf file, the installation files include an extremely valuable what's new file (whatsnew.txt). Both contain detailed information on silent installations to use in crafting your SCW customization plan. Whenever you're confronted with a new application, you should always first try to seek out this type of documentation.

Just as with WinZip and the Acrobat Reader, which will be discussed in the next section, you can't prepare the installation files for a silent installation by using only the single-file self-extracting executable most often found on an ISV's Web site. Many ISVs compile these self-extracting executable files using WinZip, so you can easily extract the single-file contents to a folder using a client that already has WinZip installed.

Preparing a silent installation with VirusScan is typical of many third-party applications. You run through setup.exe the first time in record mode, so your configuration choices are logged to a file. Then at the target client, you play back the configuration choices in an unattended setup.

Note

Because VirusScan 4 for Windows NT is designed to run only on Windows NT Workstation 4.0 systems, it's important to prepare the silent installation from a Windows NT Workstation 4.0 client. The recording part of the silent installation process also, as a byproduct, installs VirusScan 4 for Windows NT. Network Associates has another product called NetShield that runs on the Windows NT Server 4.0 portion of SBS 4.5. If your clients run Windows 95/98, you'll need a different version of VirusScan 4 that's written specifically for the Windows 95/98 operating system.

In order to customize the silent installation, you'll first run setup.exe with the –r switch (for record). This creates setup.iss, which is generally placed in the winnt or windows folder. Setup.iss will need to be copied to the same place where you copy the extracted installation files on the SBS share point. For the purpose of this example, copy the extracted installation files and setup.iss to the Vscan4NT folder in the ClientApps directory on the SBS 4.5 system. To play back the setup.iss file for the silent installation, simply run setup.exe –s.

Note

Although many third-party applications use very similar record and play-back switches and setup.iss files, the setup.iss file is product and platform specific. This is the case within the Network Associates product line. You can't reliably use a setup.iss for VirusScan 3.x for Windows95/98 with VirusScan 4.x for Windows NT.

Now that you know how to manage a silent installation of VirusScan, how do you integrate VirusScan with SCW? Follow these steps:

1. Launch the Small Business Server Client Integration Wizard.

2. In the Welcome dialog box, choose to Add An Application To Client Setup. See Figure 16-5.

3. Click the Next button.

4. In the Application Information dialog box, enter VirusScan 4 for NT as the name of the application and Vscan4NT as the short name for the application, which can be up to 8 characters. See Figure 16-6.

    The application name flows through to the scw.ini as DisplayString and the Vscan4NT.inf file as desc string. The short name is used to name the application .inf file, as well as the AppName in scw.ini, and is referenced in the clioc.inf. The application name is also listed in both SCW and Client Installation Wizard.

5. For the OS, select NT 4.0 from the drop-down menu because this version of VirusScan works only with Windows NT 4.0.

    The OS selection flows through to ArchitectureList=i386 in scw.ini, Signature=$Windows NT% in vscan4nt.inf, and the [Components.x86] section of clioc.inf.

6. Click the Next button.

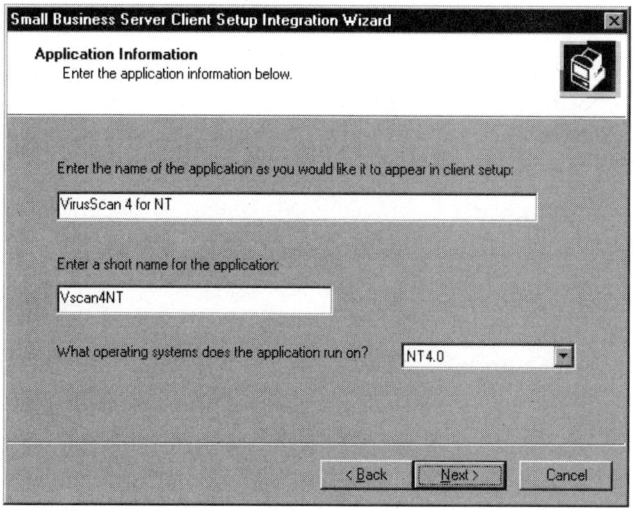

Figure 16-6

Application Information dialog box.

7. In the Additional Application Information dialog box, choose Yes
   for Should The Client Be Selected By Default In Client Setup. See
   Figure 16-7.

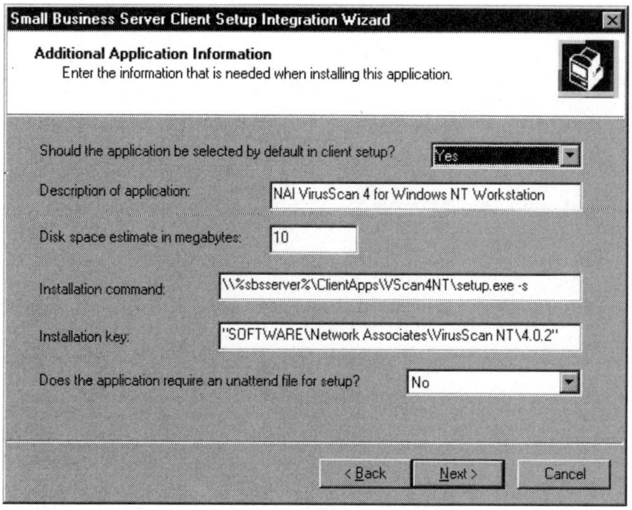

Figure 16-7

Additional Application Information dialog box.

This setting flows through directly to the Application Information dialog boxes in SCW and Client Installation Wizard, as well as the SelectedByDefault variable in scw.ini.

8. Type NAI VirusScan 4 for Windows NT Workstation for Description Of Application.

This setting flows through to the Client Installation Wizard at the client and is stored in the tip string in VScan4NT.inf.

9. Type 10 for Disk Space Estimate In Megabytes.

The disk space estimate is visible both to the SCW and Client Installation Wizard and is stored in the DiskSpaceEstimate variable in the VScan4NT.inf file.

10. Append \VScan4NT\setup.exe -s to the existing Installation Command text.

The wizard includes \\%sbsserver%\ClientApps at the beginning of the path and stores the path in the InstallCmd variable in VScan4NT.inf.

11. Type "SOFTWARE\Network Associates\VirusScan NT\4.0.2" for Installation Key.

The Installation key in the registry is used to determine whether or not an application has been installed on the client and is referenced in the clioc.inf.

Tip

In order to get SCW working properly with VirusScan, I had to edit the Installation key reference in clioc.inf directly, using other included applications as my model.

Although the GUI-based tool is definitely a huge time saver, I had to edit scw.ini directly in order to complete the integration of VirusScan with SCW. I began at the top of the file by incrementing the SCW_NumberOfApps from 15 to 16. See Figure 16-8.

After the last of the fully described SCW applications, MS_OFFICE_PUBLISHER, I appended a set of variables for VirusScan. Using another application as my model, I incremented all of the variable numbers by one and filled in the blanks as appropriate. See Figure 16-9.

```
scw - Notepad
File  Edit  Search  Help

;
; This file contains information that the Setup Computer Wizard needs
; to do its' job.
;
;
; This section lists the paths to the individual setup programs for the
; optional applications and the name of each application.

[SCW_OptionalApplications]

SCW_NumberOfApps=16

; Entries are as follows:

    Note: White space is NOT allowed in the SCW_AppName entry.

    SCW_AppName<n>=<the name of the n'th application>

    SCW_AppDisplayString<n>=<the string to be displayed in the application listbox
                            for the n'th application>

    Note: The SCW_AppSelectedByDefault entry specifies whether the n'th application
          is selected for installation by default.

    SCW_AppSelectedByDefault<n>=<YES | NO>

    Note: The SCW_AppRequiresUnattendedTextFile entry specifies whether the n'th
          application requires a special file for unattended mode installation.

    SCW_AppRequiresUnattendedTextFile=<YES | NO>

    Note: The SCW_AppTemplatePath entry specifies the path, relative to the "SmallBusiness"
          directory, to the template for the special file that the n'th application
          requires for unattended mode installation.
```

Figure 16-8

Incrementing the SCW_NumberOfApps.

```
scw - Notepad
File  Edit  Search  Help

SCW_AppName15=UScan4NT
SCW_AppDisplayString15=VirusScan 4 for NT
SCW_AppSelectedByDefault15=YES
SCW_AppRequiresUnattendedTextFile15=NO
SCW_AppTemplatePath15=
SCW_AppTemplateSourceName15=
SCW_AppTemplateDestName15=
SCW_AppSetupInfPath15=Template
SCW_AppSetupInfSourceName15=UScan4NT.inf
SCW_AppSetupInfDestName15=UScan4NT.inf
SCW_AppArchitectureList15=i386
SCW_AppParent15=


;
; This section specifies information related to the Operating System(s)
; that may beinstalled to the client computer.
;
; Note that the paths specified here are relative to the SAM Clients share.

[SCW_ClientOS]
SCW_ClientOSPathWin95=MS\Win95

; Note: %RespFile% will be expanded by the ICS process
SCW_ClientOSSetupCommandWin95=Setup.exe /IS %RespFile%
SCW_ClientOSPathWinNT=i386
SCW_ClientOSSetupCommandWinNT=Winnt /b /u:

;
; This section specifies the path to the base directory under which all of the
; Operating System Response files are to be stored and the path to the directory
; in which the source templates are stored.
;
```

Figure 16-9

Creating a new set of app variables in scw.ini.

Now the big test...drum roll please. Can you use SCW and the Client Installation Wizard to push out an unattended setup of VirusScan 4 for Windows NT, along with the other included SBS client applications? To that, you can now answer a resounding yes. If you've followed the steps above, SCW shows VirusScan 4 for NT at the bottom of the list of available applications, selected by default, with a requirement of 10 MB of available hard disk space. See Figure 16-10.

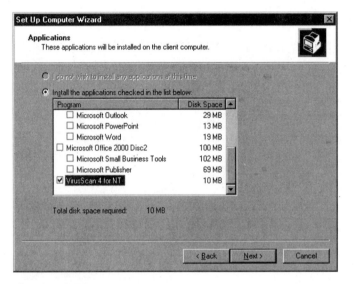

Figure 16-10

SCW extended with VirusScan 4 for NT.

To test the silent installation of VirusScan through SCW, log on to the target client PC. As expected, startcli.exe is launched by the logon script *and* fails to find the installed file, so the Client Installation Wizard is launched. At the bottom of the list of available applications in the wizard, VirusScan 4 for NT is already preselected, showing estimated disk space of 10 MB. See Figure 16-11. Click the Next button, and the Client Installation Wizard performs the silent installation of VirusScan.

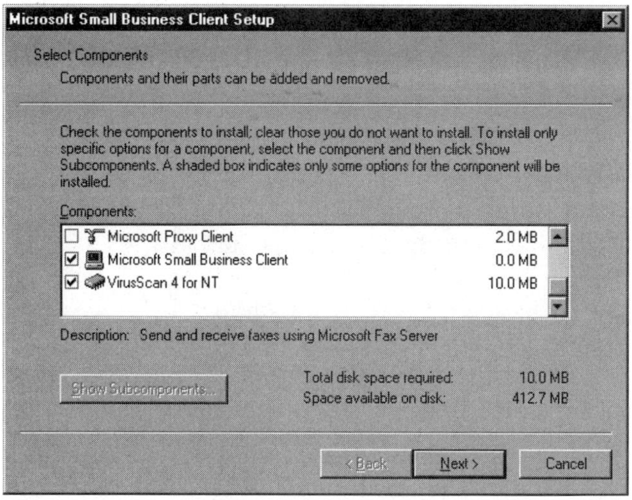

Figure 16-11

Client Installation Wizard with VirusScan 4 for NT.

Adding Utility Software

Using what you've learned about SCW and Client Installation Wizard and the techniques used with VirusScan and the Small Business Server Client Setup Integration Wizard, you can add a myriad of third-party applications to SCW. While I won't be taking you through step-by-step examples for other third-party applications, I do have tips and pointers for integrating two popular utility programs, WinZip and Acrobat Reader, with SCW.

WinZip

Like VirusScan, WinZip is typically downloaded from the Web as a single, self-extracting executable file. This means it doesn't have a setup program that you can use to plan and execute an unattended setup for SCW. Before proceeding with integrating WinZip with SCW, you'll want to use a client PC that already has WinZip installed to extract the files to the ClientApps share on the SBS 4.5 system.

Tip

You can learn more about WinZip and Nico Mak Computing, Inc. (the ISV for WinZip) at *www.winzip.com*.

Because WinZip has a fairly limited set of configuration options, you needn't use the record/playback scenario for a silent installation. Rather, you can use the /Autoinstall switch to perform an unattended setup of WinZip with default options and the Classic interface. The results of the installation will look just as if you had installed WinZip with the Express Install option.

The unattended setup command line for WinZip will be something similar to \\%sbsserver%\ClientApps\winzip\winzip32.exe /autoinstall.

Acrobat Reader

The key to successfully integrating Acrobat Reader with SCW is the setup.iss file. Notice that this file has the same name as the file used for the silent installation of VirusScan.

Tip

You can learn more about Acrobat Reader and Adobe (the ISV for Acrobat) at *www.adobe.com*.

First, record your Acrobat Reader configuration preferences for the setup.iss script by running through the setup in record mode: \acroread\setup.exe –r. This creates the setup.iss file, which is typically written to the windows, winnt, or winnt.sbs folder.

Tip

If you're having trouble locating the appropriate setup.iss file or distinguishing among several setup.iss files, use the Find File feature to locate files named setup.iss on all local drives. Then sort by the time/date stamp so that you see the most recently created setup.iss file.

Once you've located the appropriate setup.iss, copy it and the related extracted installation files to the ClientApps share point on the SBS 4.5 system. You might want to place the files in \\%sbsserver%\ClientApps\Acrobat.

Tip

If you're having difficulty initiating a record and playback session, make sure you've extracted all of the files from the self-extracting file you downloaded from the Web.

Then play back the setup.exe and setup.iss for a silent installation. This is done by running a command that's similar to \acroread\setup.exe –s.

If you want to extend the silent installation of the Acrobat Reader further, you'll find additional documentation on the setup.iss file in the Acrobat SDK (which is also downloadable from the Adobe Web site).

Tip

To pick up valuable troubleshooting techniques for SCW, see KB article Q214688 in the Microsoft Knowledge Base.

Adding Microsoft Office 2000 Professional

Although two stock-keeping units (SKUs) bundle SBS 4.5 with Office 2000 Professional, your small business clients might have purchased Office 2000 Professional and SBS 4.5 separately. Or perhaps your small business clients might have received a free version upgrade from SBS 4.0 to SBS 4.5, and then purchased Office 2000 Professional.

Tip

For information on SBS licensing and SKUs, see Chapter 2 or the SBS Web site at _www.microsoft.com/smallbusinessserver_.

But who wants to install a dozen or more licenses of Office 2000 Professional manually? With a few simple steps, you can easily add Office 2000 Professional to the SCW and Client Installation Wizard, just as if you'd already purchased the SBS 4.5 with Office 2000 Professional SKU. Follow these steps to add Office 2000 Professional to the SBS 4.5 SCW:

1. Delete the existing Outlook 2000 files (Office_CD1) from \\%sbsserver%\ClientApps\ms\office.

2. Run an administrative setup of Office 2000 CD 1 (setup /a), pointing to the installation of \\%sbsserver%\ClientApps\ms\office\CD1.

3. Launch an administrative setup of Office 2000 CD 2 (setup /a), pointing to the installation of \\%sbsserver%\ClientApps\ms\office\CD2.

4. Rename scw.ini to scw.no and scw.o to scw.ini in the SmallBusiness folder.

5. Rename clioc.inf in the Template folder to clioc.no and clioc.o in the SmallBusiness folder to clioc.inf.

Tip

If clients already have Outlook 2000 installed, you must manually remove Outlook 2000 before adding Office 2000 Professional with SCW and Client Installation Wizard.

The Bottom Line

Right out of the box, SCW saves you and your small business clients a tremendous amount of time and cuts the potential for errors by pushing out unattended installations of client applications included with SBS 4.5. As an SBS VAP, however, you have an opportunity to add even more value to the installation by integrating additional third-party applications with SCW and Client Installation Wizard. In this chapter, you learned about the underlying files that drive SCW and Client Installation Wizard, as well as an easy-to-use GUI-based tool for making the process even more VAP friendly.

Chapter 17

At the Desktop: Client Setup

With the up-front planning and preparation in the earlier chapters behind you, the visit to each client desktop PC should be remarkably quick. This chapter will help you understand the creation of the client setup disk, what preparatory steps to take before running the client setup disk, what happens when you run the client setup disk, how to create naming conventions, and how to get a better grasp on the network TCP/IP properties that are affected by the Set Up Computer Wizard. By the end of the chapter, you'll also know how to configure each SBS user's desktop work environment, including shared folders, printers, and default paths.

Behind the Scenes with Set Up Computer Wizard

As explained in Chapter 16, the Set Up Computer Wizard (SCW) helps auto-mate two main functions:

- Adding Windows 95/98 and Windows NT 4.0 desktop clients to the SBS network

- Installing SBS client applications on desktop computers

Running SCW on the server creates a setup disk for each desktop client. Follow these steps:

1. Click Manage Computers on the More Tasks tab in the SBS Console.

2. On the Manage Computers page, click Set Up A Computer. This launches SCW. See Figure 17-1. Click the Next button.

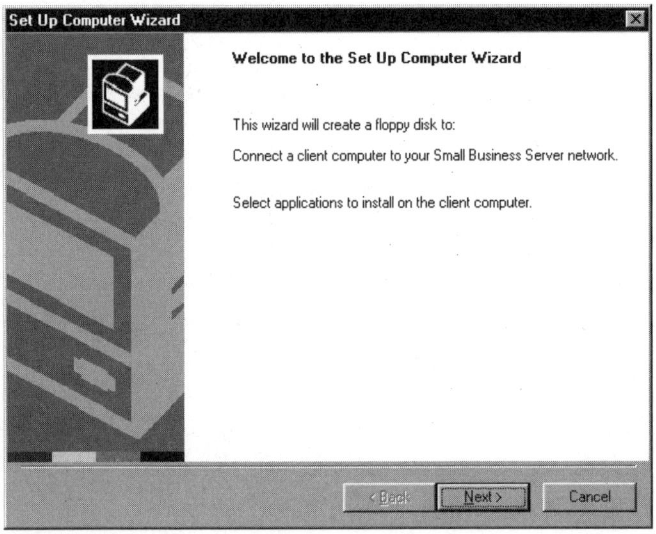

Figure 17-1

The SBS Console pages are based on HTML and hyperlinks. The Set Up Computer hyperlink launches the sbs.exe file that resides in the SmallBusiness folder on the server.

The Semantics of the Term "Client"

The term "client" takes on two completely different meanings for SBS VAPs. When used in the context of your customer, client refers to the small business owner that hires your firm. When used in the context of an SBS client/server network, client refers to the desktop and laptop computers on the SBS network that log on to the server. Since this double entendre can really throw most people for a loop, consider pointing out the double meaning to the small business owners at the outset of the project.

If this wasn't enough to get your head spinning, Chapter 18 explains two different meanings for the word domain.

3. Select a previously created user account in the Select A User dialog box. This user account will be associated with the client desktop computer that you're setting up now. Click the Next button.

Tip

For details on setting up user accounts, see Chapter 13.

4. In the Computer Name dialog box, accept the name that SCW recommends by clicking the Next button. Alternatively, you can type a different name, then click the Next button. The recommended computer name appends 01 to the user account name that you selected in the previous step. For example, user account joshuaf results in the recommended computer name JOSHUAF01.

5. Select which desktop operating system will be used by the computer that you're setting up. You have two choices: Windows 95/98 and Windows NT Workstation 4.0. Note that I selected Windows NT Workstation 4.0, which is my standard recommendation when a small business has no compelling business or technical reason to stay with Windows 95/98. Click the Next button.

Tip

You can configure other operating systems to use some SBS 4.5 services, such as file and printer sharing, Web browsing, and e-mail. The core SBS client applications, however, can be run only on 32-bit Windows operating systems. As a result, SCW supports only Windows 95, Windows 98, and Windows NT 4.0.

Tip

Although it's a bit far-fetched to think of a small business end user running Windows NT Server 4.0 as the primary desktop operating system, the client setup disk can also be run on a Windows NT Server 4.0 system.

---

6. In the Applications dialog box, pick which applications you want to install on the SBS client desktop when you run the client setup disk. See Figure 17-2. This is one of the big benefits of SCW because it largely eliminates the need to carry around a stack of CD-ROMs or to connect to a bunch of network shares to install the client applications. By default, the Applications dialog box will have all SBS client applications selected. As you modify choices, you'll notice the total

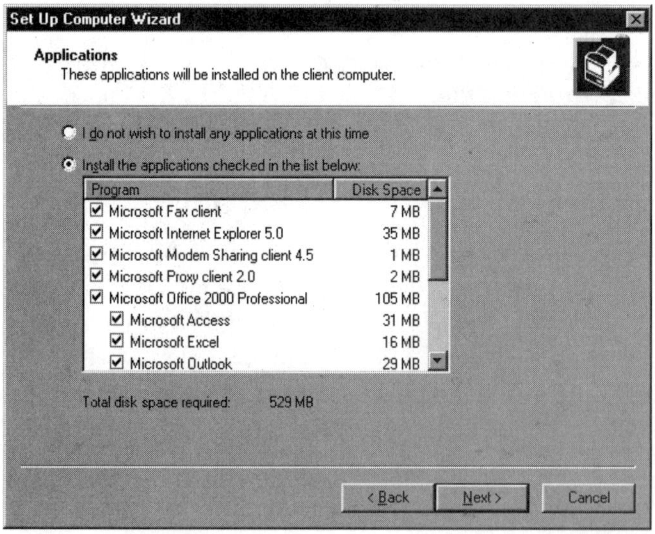

Figure 17-2

In the Applications dialog box, you select which SBS client applications will be installed on the client when you run the client setup disk.

disk space required (on the target desktop computer) changes to reflect the disk space requirements. Click the Next button.

7. The subsequent dialog box is strictly informational in nature, so all you do is click the Next button. (This dialog box tells you to label the client setup disk for the intended computer and insert the blank high-density 3.5-inch disk in your disk drive.)

Tip

If you're going to be doing lots of SBS 4.5 installations and you want to add a nice professional touch to your work, consider preprinting peel-and-stick labels. You can purchase Avery Laser Diskette Labels (#6490) and use Microsoft Word to prepare client setup disk labels. Also, be sure to keep a few boxes of blank 3.5-inch disks in your tool bag.

SCW will then format your disk, copy the needed files to the disk, and create the required files on the server share for unattended installation of SBS client applications.

Now that the customized settings files are on the client setup disk and server installation share, a dialog box confirms that SCW is complete and outlines what steps you need to take next:

1. Boot the computer that you're adding to the SBS network and log on with an account equivalent to administrator.

2. Launch the setup program on the client setup disk by selecting Run from the Start menu and typing a:\setup. (You can also launch the setup program from Windows Explorer or from the command prompt.)

3. Follow the wizard's instructions on the screen.

Preparing to Run the Client Setup Disk

Before running the client setup disk on a Windows NT Workstation 4.0 computer, I typically perform several preparatory steps while logged on as an administrator (or equivalent):

1. Close all open programs.

2. Disable any antivirus software.

3. Disconnect any local area network or dial-up network connections.

4. Create an updated emergency repair disk (ERD) for the client desktop computer. By running rdisk /s, you're also updating the local registry repair information on the system drive.

5. Once the ERD is prepared, label it with the date and computer name. Then store the ERD securely because security information is on that disk.

If the target Windows NT Workstation 4.0 drive isn't yet running NT File System (NTFS), convert the drive from the FAT file system to NTFS by typing convert c: /fs:ntfs at the command prompt. Or substitute the target drive letter for c: as appropriate. You can check which file system a specific drive partition is running on by right-clicking the drive letter in My Computer and selecting Properties. See Figure 17-3. Although this step isn't required by the SBS client applications, it makes the client much more secure.

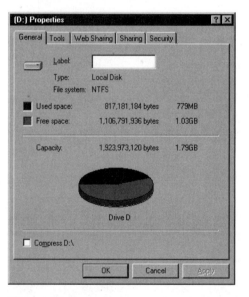

Figure 17-3

Check which file system is in use on the Windows NT 4.0 system, by opening My Computer, right-clicking the drive letter in question, and examining the drive volume's properties.

Can You Avoid the Client Setup Disk?

You can avoid using the client setup disk to configure each desktop PC. The SBS client applications, however, won't install automatically on each user's computer unless you run SCW for each user account and computer. Unless you're at a fairly advanced technical level with SBS, my recommendation is that you create a client setup disk for each computer to save yourself time and potential aggravation.

Using the client setup disk at each desktop computer isn't mandatory. While manual configuration certainly gives you more control over the client setup process, you lose many of the time-saving benefits of the Set Up Computer Wizard. If you insist on trying to work around the disk or are just curious about its internals, see KB article Q216106 in the Microsoft Knowledge Base at *support.microsoft.com*.

I know VAPs who put much effort into trying to outsmart the SBS wizards. In most cases, they could've completed the task at hand and moved to their next scheduled appointment in the time it took to bypass the wizard. When bypassing the SBS wizards, you also run the risk of causing more complications than intended. If you are truly an anti-wizard VAP and these types of debates keep you up at night, SBS might not be the best platform for your firm to support.

I also usually decrease the default Windows NT Workstation 4.0 boot delay from 30 seconds to 3 seconds. This not only saves time, but also deters curious end users from experimenting with nondefault boot choices. The boot delay can be changed most easily by following these steps:

1. From the Start menu, choose Settings, and then Control Panel.

2. Open System and select the Startup/Shutdown tab.

3. Change the Show List For value from 30 seconds to 3 seconds. Then click the Apply button. See Figure 17-4 on the next page.

Warning

If you decrease the boot delay to 0 seconds, you might inadvertently make your own troubleshooting efforts more complicated than necessary down the road.

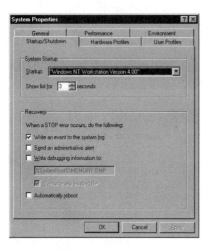

Figure 17-4

By decreasing the Windows NT Workstation 4.0 boot delay, you save time and deter curious end users from exploring nondefault boot choices.

When you install and remove various device drivers and services from a Windows NT Workstation 4.0 desktop client, you're often prompted to insert the OS installation media so that the appropriate files can be copied to the local drive. You can save a great deal of time and effort by copying the contents of the i386 folder from the installation media to the local drive. This solves two potential problems. First, you won't need to hunt around for the installation CD-ROM when adding or troubleshooting various device drivers and services. You'll simply point the dialog box to the local drive, as shown in Figure 17-5. Second, because they don't need to have installation media in their possession, the end users you support will be less likely to attempt to reinstall their operating system when something goes wrong with their computer.

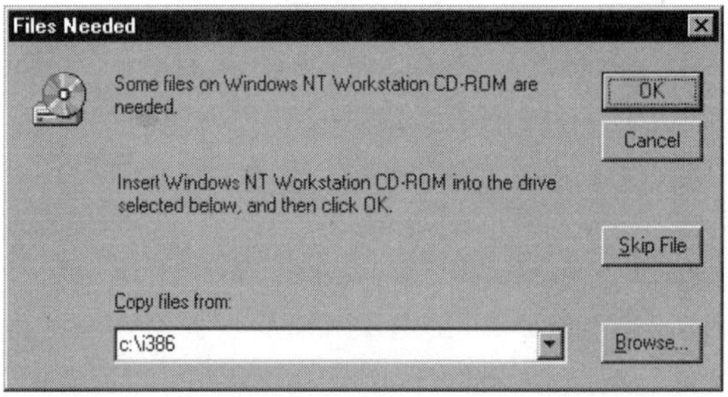

Figure 17-5

You can save lots of time, effort, and potential help desk call by copying the i386 folder from the installation media to the local drives.

Next, remove network services or protocols that won't be needed from the desktop computer. Do this by opening the Network applet in the Control Panel and by editing the Services tab, shown in Figure 17-6, and the Protocols tab, shown in Figure 17-7. If the small business doesn't have past or future connectivity needs beside the SBS 4.5 network, your configuration choices should be almost identical to Figures 17-6 and 17-7.

Figure 17-6

Typical services for a Windows NT Workstation 4.0 desktop computer.

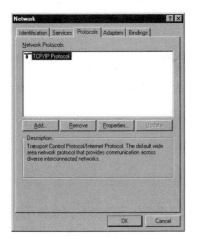

Figure 17-7

Typical protocols for a Windows NT Workstation 4.0 desktop computer.

While you have the Network applet open, check out the Identification tab, shown in Figure 17-8. If the client setup disk finds that the Windows NT Workstation 4.0 desktop computer already belongs to another domain, the install probably won't be successful. (A Windows NT 4.0 domain is a collection of desktops and servers that share a common security database.) By clicking the Identification tab, you'll be able to see whether the computer is part of another domain.

Caution

If the Windows NT Workstation 4.0 desktop computer is already part of another domain, this should be a red flag. Think through the implications before removing the computer from the domain.

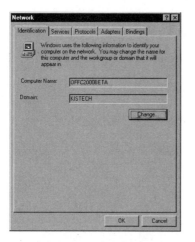

Figure 17-8

The Identification tab displays the computer and domain name information.

If you've determined that the Windows NT Workstation 4.0 desktop computer needs to be removed from its present domain, follow these steps:

1. Click the Change button on the Identification tab. The Identification Changes dialog box opens.

2. Select the Workgroup option and type in a temporary workgroup name such as WORKGROUP. (The client setup disk, working with SCW, will later change the domain to that of the SBS 4.5 system.)

3. Click the OK button twice.

4. When prompted, reboot the system. Upon restart, this system will no longer be a member of its old domain.

Preparing to Run Client Setup

Here is a summary of preparatory steps to take before running the client setup disk on a Windows NT Workstation 4.0 desktop computer:

❑ Close all programs, disable antivirus software, and disconnect any local area network or dial-up networking connections.

❑ Create an updated ERD.

❑ Make sure the target drive is converted to NTFS. (This step is optional, although highly recommended.)

❑ Decrease the boot delay from 30 seconds to 3 seconds.

❑ Copy the i386 folder from the installation media to the local drive. (This step is optional, although highly recommended.)

❑ Remove any extraneous networking services and protocols from the client computer.

❑ If the client computer belongs to a Windows NT domain, remove it from the domain before proceeding.

Behind the Scenes with Client Setup Disk

Now you're finally ready to run the client setup disk on a Windows NT Workstation 4.0 desktop computer. If you're starting to get the feeling that the rollout is 90 percent planning and 10 percent execution, you're on the right track. In fact, you'll start seeing some handsome payback on your meticulous attention to details within five minutes. The client computer will be fully configured for TCP/IP and added to the SBS 4.5 domain. Several client applications will also be installed on the computer.

To begin, insert the client setup disk into the disk drive on the client computer. From the Start menu, choose the Run command and type a:\setup. Once the setup program initializes, a dialog box opens that explains the steps that SCW is about to perform. See Figure 17-9 on the next page. The computer will be configured for a specific person, user account, and computer name, which you previously selected while running SCW on the server.

Once you click the Next button in the dialog box shown in Figure 17-9, SCW takes over and performs the following tasks:

1. Prepares the client for network setup

2. Attempts to detect and install the network adapter if it's not already installed

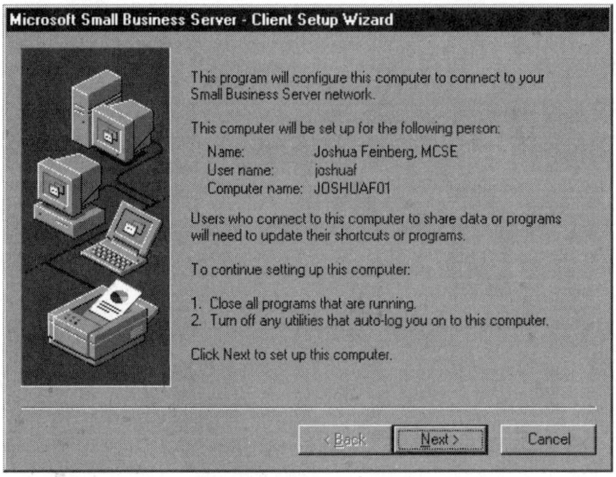

Figure 17-9

Once the client setup disk program has loaded, you'll see a dialog box that explains what SCW is about to do on the client computer.

3. Configures default services: RPC Configuration, Net BIOS Interface, Workstation, Server, Computer Browser, and Remote Access Service

4. Changes Name, User Name, and Computer Name and adds the client to the new domain

5. Notifies you of success and prompts you to reboot

Upon reboot and removal of the client setup disk, the Small Business Workstation Setup program starts. Following successful logon with the intended user account, the Small Business Workstation Setup program applies Service Pack 4 (SP4) to the Windows NT Workstation 4.0 client computer and then reboots the system.

Following the reboot and next successful log on under the end user's account name, the Small Business Workstation Setup program installs Microsoft Internet Explorer 5.0 and then reboots the system again.

After the reboot and logon, Small Business Workstation Setup passes control over to the Client Setup Wizard, which completes the installation of all previously selected SBS 4.5 client applications.

The Select Components dialog box appears with the previously selected SBS 4.5 client applications enabled by default for installation. See Figure 17-10. This dialog box allows you to make any final changes to the components that are to be installed. By selecting each component, you can get a brief description of its function. The dialog box indicates how much disk space is required and how much space is available. As you can see in Figure 17-10, the client computer had a shortage of available disk space.

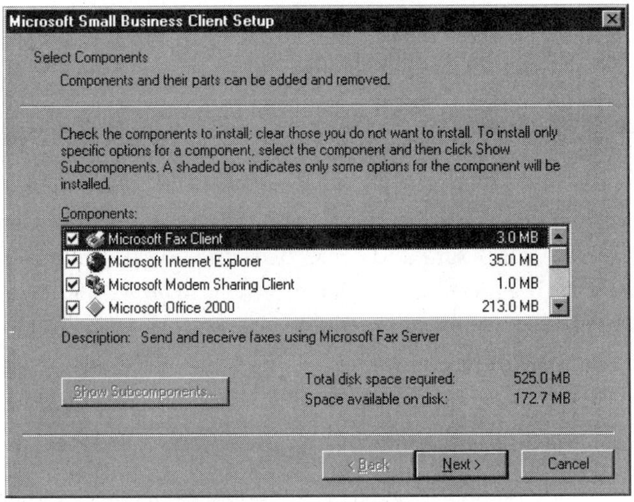

Figure 17-10
The Select Components dialog box gives you the ability to make last minute changes to the list of SBS 4.5 client applications for installation.

Because this was brought to my attention before the unattended installations began, I was able to switch over to Windows Explorer and remove unnecessary folders and files. Then I switched back to the Client Setup Wizard and clicked the Next button so that setup could proceed.

As each SBS 4.5 client application is installed silently, the Current Status indicator in the dialog box keeps you up to date on what's happening.

User and Computer Naming Conventions

Each user account and computer needs unique names. A consistent, understandable naming convention is crucial to any SBS 4.5 implementation. You'll need to make sure that the naming scheme isn't too confining or controversial. For example, if you named computers after planets, what would happen when you wanted to add the tenth client desktop? If you named computers after heavy-metal rock groups, wouldn't you risk offending some of the staff for your small business client?

Tip

Don't make a political *faux pas* on something as basic as naming conventions. Remember: learn about your client's culture as the engagement begins. For example, if your client is an entertainment agency or recording studio, naming the computers after bands or musical artists might be appropriate.

The naming convention has to be easy to remember, too. And that's where naming computers after recording artists, cities, Greek gods, or baseball teams begins to lose its luster. After all is said and done, a simple, elegant naming convention is best. That's why the SBS 4.5 SCW defaults to taking the user name and appending a number when creating the suggested computer name. See Table 17-1 for examples of computer names.

Full name of small business end user	User account name (a.k.a. logon name)	Computer name
Firstname Lastname	*Firstname*	*FIRSTNAME01*
Biff Duncan	Biff	BIFF01
Susie Que	Susie	SUSIE01
Wally Jones	Wally	WALLY01
Mildred Smith	Mildred	MILDRED01

Table 17-1

Sample company naming conventions

While it might seem more democratic to ask your small business clients what naming convention they'd prefer to use, you'll accumulate less gray hair by adopting a simple naming convention that you can apply across all your small business clients. Your clients will benefit as well. When you get beeped at 11 P.M. by the owner of your largest client when he can't log on, you'll know exactly what his user and computer names should be.

The *Microsoft BackOffice Small Business Server 4.5 Resource Kit* has the Batch User Add Tool, a don't-miss utility for structuring account names and gathering the complete information up front from your small business clients. The Batch User Add Tool turns Microsoft Excel data into a text file that can be imported directly into the SBS Console To Do List. Instead of sitting in front of the SBS Console doing much data entry in dialog boxes, you can prepare all the required user account information before going on site for installation. Plus, using the Batch User Add Tool provides you with a copy of how all the client's account information looked prior to the initial installation.

Standardizing on TCP/IP

When I meet prospective clients for an initial consultation or IT audit, I often hear complaints about the performance and reliability of their existing networks. Usually these clients have peer-to-peer networks based on Windows 95/98.

When using the Network applet in Control Panel, I often discover that these clients also have protocol mismatches between computers. Windows 95/98 and Windows NT Workstation 4.0 computers have three main protocol suites:

- NetBEUI

- IPX/SPX (called NWLink in the Windows NT world)

- TCP/IP

If you have eight Windows 95 computers and two are running NetBEUI, four are running both IPX/SPX and NetBEUI, and the remainder are running only TCP/IP, you have big potential for protocol mismatch problems. Small business networks that use SBS 4.5 and have no other servers with alternative network operating systems need only the TCP/IP protocol. Because SBS 4.5 has so many applications that depend on Internet connectivity, Microsoft has adopted TCP/IP as the default protocol for SBS 4.5. TCP/IP is the only protocol SBS 4.5 requires under most circumstances.

NetBEUI tends to be used in small workgroups of computers and was popular in small businesses before the rise of the Internet. In most small businesses with SBS 4.5, NetBEUI isn't necessary.

IPX/SPX is used by Novell NetWare servers. So if you add an SBS 4.5 system to a small business that already has a NetWare server and the two servers need to communicate, you can include both TCP/IP and IPX/SPX (or NWLink) on the client computers. Through Gateway Services for NetWare (GSNW) running on the SBS 4.5 system, however, you can virtually eliminate IPX/SPX (or NWLink) on your SBS 4.5 desktop clients. GSNW can be added to an SBS 4.5 system through the Services tab in the Network Control Panel applet.

Tip

For more information on integrating SBS 4.5 into an existing Novell NetWare network, check out the *Microsoft BackOffice Small Business Server 4.5 Resource Kit*, the SBS Web site (*www.microsoft.com/smallbusinessserver*), the Direct Access Web site (*www.microsoft.com/directaccess*), and the TechNet Web site (*www.microsoft.com/technet*).

Tip

To learn more about TCP/IP see *Microsoft TCP/IP Training*.

Understanding DHCP, DNS, and WINS

Although SBS 4.5 hides the complexity of configuring individual computers, you need to understand some of the basic settings that are configured behind the scenes on Windows 95/98 and Windows NT Workstation 4.0 systems running on an SBS 4.5 network.

Each computer on the Internet and on an SBS 4.5 network has a unique identifier called an IP address, which is made up of four numbers separated by periods. For example, the server on an SBS 4.5 network has a default IP address of 10.0.0.2 (read by those in the know as ten dot zero dot zero dot two).

Each computer on an SBS network needs its own internally unique and valid IP address. If two computers end up with a duplicate IP address, major and immediate communications problems ensue. The Windows NT Server 4.0 portion of SBS 4.5, however, has DHCP (short for dynamic host configuration protocol), which manages the pool of available IP addresses and ensures that two DHCP-enabled computers don't try to lease the same IP address as their own.

The client setup disk configures each SBS 4.5 client computer for using the TCP/IP protocol, with DHCP enabled. Once the client computer is rebooted, it gets its own personal IP address. For example, the SBS 4.5 server is statically configured for 10.0.0.2, while JOSHUAF01 is configured for 10.0.0.11, and WALLY01 is configured for 10.0.0.17.

Now Wally, being an absent-minded director of sales, keeps forgetting to save all his direct marketing letters on the server. As his VAP, I like to log on to a client computer in Wally's office once a month, connect to his PC, and copy his newly created Word documents to a folder on the server. The trouble is that I have a hard time remembering Wally's IP address. I find it easy to remember his computer name, however, since it's just his first name plus 01 at the end.

In order for computers to communicate on a TCP/IP-based network by using friendly names like WALLY01 as opposed to difficult to remember IP addresses like 10.0.0.17, the computers need to have some way to keep track of the relationships between computer names and IP addresses. A Microsoft-based network has three ways to do this: HOSTS or LMHOSTS files, name servers, or the broadcast mechanism.

The first way of associating computer names and IP addresses involves each computer having its own copy of a text file, called a HOSTS or LMHOSTS file. Although relatively easy to set up, these text files are a real bear to maintain on networks with lots of computers and lots of changes. Each time a computer's name or IP address changes or an employee joins or leaves the company or network, someone will need to update the HOSTS or LMHOSTS file on every computer. Because small businesses typically don't have in-house IT staff, such a process is basically impossible for the small business to maintain.

Even in larger organizations where dozens, if not hundreds, of qualified IT staffers could run around all day and update these files, the maintenance workload would be next to impossible.

The preferred way to keep track of the relationships between IP addresses and computer names is through a centralized service called a name server. Changes to the relationships between IP addresses and names only have to be updated in one place, and in some cases it's even handled dynamically. You'll encounter two types of name servers in the Microsoft networking world: DNS and WINS.

DNS, short for Domain Name System, is the primary name resolution method on the Internet. For example, when I want to point my Internet Explorer 5.0 Web browser to the Microsoft Press Web site, I don't need to know that its IP address is 207.46.142.45. I just need to remember *mspress.microsoft.com*, and my ISP's DNS server handles the rest of the details.

Although SBS 4.5 can run DNS for resolving names internally and externally, the service isn't installed by default. Microsoft networks often use another name server called WINS, short for Windows Internet Naming Service. The primary advantage of using WINS over DNS is that WINS generally requires less administrative overhead and maintenance. WINS is installed during the earliest part of the unattended SBS 4.5 server installation. SBS 4.5 clients, however, don't need to use a centralized name server because name resolution requests are typically handled through the broadcast mechanism.

The broadcast mechanism is the third way to resolve the relationships between computer names and IP addresses on a TCP/IP-based network. Although used only on small, single-location networks, broadcast is an efficient way for name resolution to take place on an SBS 4.5 network. When client computers are configured for this option, they broadcast announcements to all computers on the network, announcing their computer names and IP addresses to all within "earshot" (that is, on the same subnet).

The ipconfig /all command line utility lets you view the assigned TCP/IP protocol settings on a Windows NT Workstation 4.0 client computer. See Figure 17-11. With a Windows 95/98 client PC, run winipcfg from the Run command on the Start menu to see the equivalent TCP/IP configuration data in a GUI utility. See Figure 17-12.

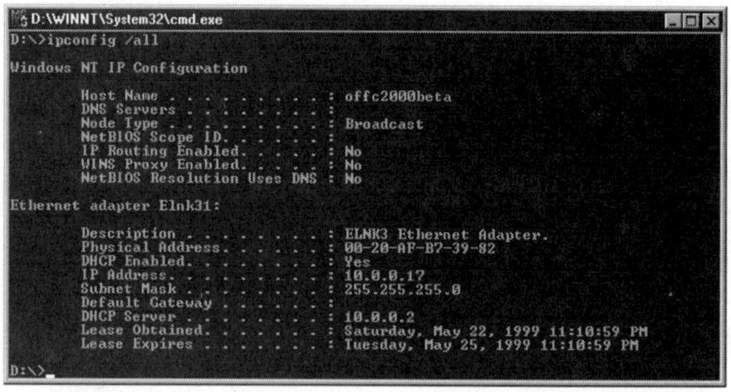

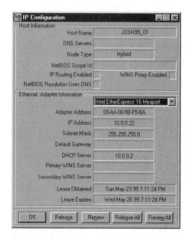

Figure 17-11

Use ipconfig /all to view what TCP/IP configuration choices have been made on a Windows NT Workstation 4.0 client computer.

Figure 17-12

Use winipcfg to view what TCP/IP configuration choices have been made on a Windows 95/98 client computer.

Setting up Persistent Network Drive and Printer Connections

The SBS 4.5 Client Setup Wizard places shortcuts on the desktop for each user's personal share location and the company share location on the server. While many find these desktop shortcuts quite handy, some small business end users who are accustomed to using stand-alone computers or older legacy software might be more comfortable referring to these server-based storage locations by a drive letter.

You could ask your small business clients for their personal preferences on network drive accessibility. If you're supporting a dozen different SBS 4.5 installations, though, how will you keep track of who's using desktop shortcuts, who's using drive letters, and which specific drive letters are being used?

As with the user account and computer naming convention, give serious thought to adopting one consistent way of referring to network drives across all of your small business clients. Table 17-2 shows a method for keeping track of network connections and drive letters on client computers.

Drive letter	What the drive letter represents	Who has access to the drive letter
A:	Local 3.5-inch disk drive	Anyone at that computer
C:	Local hard disk drive	With Windows 95/98, anyone at that computer; with Windows NT Workstation 4.0 and NTFS, one or more specific users
D:	Local CD-ROM drive	Anyone at that computer
N:	Private network share, in the form \\servername\username (for example, \\KISTECHLABS01\JOSHUAF)	One or more specific users
P:	A public network share, in the form \\servername\company (for example, \\KISTECHLABS01\COMPANY)	All users on the network

Table 17-2

A method for assigning drive letters

A persistent connection to a network drive is restored each time a user logs on to the SBS 4.5 network from his or her computer. You can configure a persistent network connection on a client workstation in a number of ways. One of the simplest methods follows:

1. Right-click My Computer and choose Map Network Drive.

2. Once the Map Network Drive dialog box appears, select N: from the Drive drop-down list box. See Figure 17-13.

3. In the Path box, type the server and share names in this format: \\servername\sharename (in this case, \\KISTECHLABS01\JOSHUAF).

4. Leave Connect As blank, and make sure that Reconnect At Logon is enabled to ensure that the drive mapping is persistent.

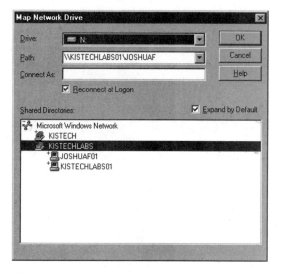

Figure 17-13

Use the Map Network Drive command to setup a persistent drive connection from each user's computer to his or her personal network share on the SBS 4.5 server.

You can use the same technique for mapping a persistent connection to the public shared folder on the server for each user.

Once you've completed mapping the persistent drive connections, you can verify that your configurations have taken effect by opening up My Computer and examining the available drive letters.

As with server-based folders, you can connect SBS 4.5 client computers to shared network printers. As with mapping persistent drive letter connections, you have a number of ways to set up a connection from an SBS 4.5 client to a network printer. One of the simplest ways is through My Computer. Follow these steps:

1. Double-click Printers in My Computer.

2. In the Printers folder, double-click Add Printer to launch the Add Printer Wizard.

3. Select Network Printer Server and then click the Next button. This opens the Connect To Printer dialog box, which shows you the list of available network printers. See Figure 17-14. Once you've found the desired printer, double-click the network printer share name. A dialog box opens, confirming success.

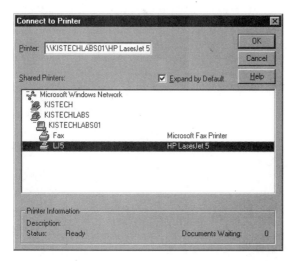

Figure 17-14

In the Connect To Printer dialog box, double-click the network printer to which you wish to print.

Caution

The above example was greatly simplified because I was configuring a Windows NT Workstation 4.0 client computer to connect to a Windows NT Server 4.0 network printer. If I'd been connecting from a Windows 95 client computer, I might have been prompted to select an appropriate printer driver and provide relevant device driver files. You can, however, configure a network printer on a Windows NT Server 4.0 computer to provide appropriate device drivers for Windows 95/98 client computers.

Configuring Default Paths in Office

When small business end users are first getting used to working with centralized file storage on a server, their inclination might be to save their data locally on their hard disk drives. Because this negates the many benefits of SBS 4.5, such as centralized data security, data backup, and antivirus and power protection, helping end users remember to store their files on the server is in your best interest. One way to encourage this behavior—without mandating it—is by configuring default file paths in Word and Excel.

With default file paths in Word, you can also point your small business end users to the company's central repository of templates. This one simple configuration will go a long way toward making sure everyone is using the same version of Word templates for documents such as memos, fax cover sheets, and direct mail letters.

To configure a default document path in Microsoft Word 2000, follow these steps:

1. Choose Options from the Tools menu.

2. In the Options dialog box, click the File Locations tab. See Figure 17-15.

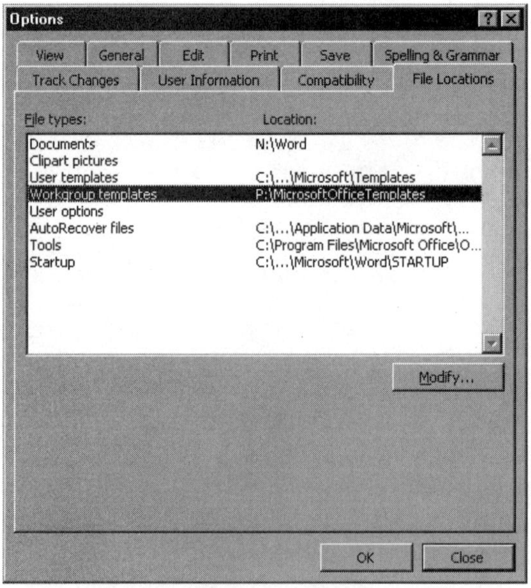

Figure 17-15

Configure a default document location in Word on the File Locations tab.

3. Select Documents from the list of File Types and then click the Modify button. This opens the Modify Location dialog box.

4. Browse through the Look In drop-down list box to find the drive letter you want as the default. In the Folder Name drop-down list box, find the folder where you want this end user to store Word documents. Click OK twice.

As an example, I created a Word folder on joshuaf's N: drive. So the default Word document path becomes N:\Word. Once this default is defined, Word will point to N:\Word when the end user opens or saves a file.

To configure the default Microsoft Office template location on the company shared drive, follow the same basic steps as above, but select Workgroup Templates from the list of File Types.

As an example, I created a MicrosoftOfficeTemplates folder on joshuaf's P: drive for company-wide templates and made this the default for the end-user's Word workgroup templates. Choosing New from the File menu will result in a display of the company-wide templates in the P:\MicrosoftOfficeTemplates folder.

Configuring the default file location in Microsoft Excel 2000 is a similar process. Follow these steps:

1. Choose Options from the Tools menu.

2. In the Options dialog box, click the General tab.

3. Enter the desired drive letter and folder name in the Default File Location box. See Figure 17-16 on the next page. (Unlike Word, Excel has no browse capability for selecting a drive letter and folder name.) Then click OK.

As an example, I created a Excel folder on joshuaf's N: drive. So the default Excel workbook path becomes N:\Excel. Once this default is defined, Excel will point to N:\Excel when a user opens or save a file.

Tip

If your small business end users are still using Microsoft Office 97, the instructions for configuring default paths are virtually identical.

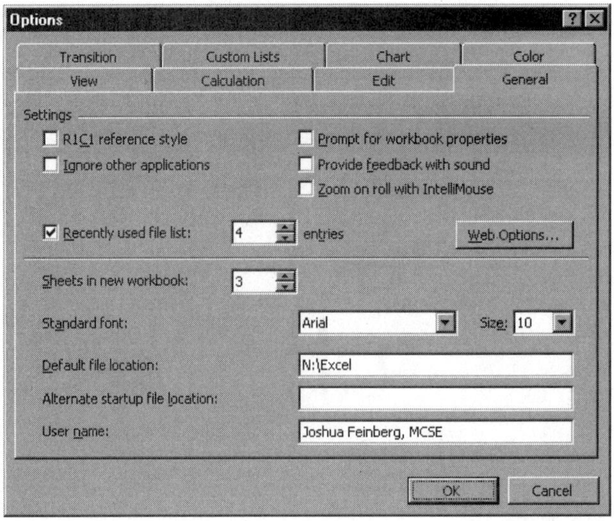

Figure 17-16

Configure a default document location for Excel on the General tab.

The Bottom Line

Much of the value-add that you bring to the table comes from how creatively and innovatively you customize the off-the-shelf SBS 4.5 setup. This chapter showed you how to use the client setup disk for maximum benefit. This includes:

- Understanding the creation of the client setup disk

- Taking preparatory steps before using the client setup disk

- Learning what happens when you run the client setup disk

- Creating naming conventions

- Seeing how the Set Up Computer Wizard affects TCP/IP properties

- Configuring each SBS user's desktop work environment, including shared folders, printers, and default paths

Chapter 18

Configuring Internet Access, Web Publishing, and E-Mail

When Microsoft BackOffice Small Business Server 4.0 was first released in October 1997, Microsoft anticipated the Internet would be an important competitive tool for small businesses. During the past two years, however, the Internet has become the killer app that has the power to level the playing field for small businesses competing with the big guys.

SBS 4.5 was redesigned with the idea that small businesses want to leverage the power of the Internet. This chapter will help you to understand the myriad of technical and business implications behind each Internet access, Web browsing, Web publishing, and e-mail configuration choice.

Navigating the ISP Maze

SBS 4.5 has Microsoft Exchange Server 5.5, which provides internal e-mail and collaborative applications, such as group scheduling, contacts, and task management. In order to extend the SBS 4.5 network to the Internet for Web browsing, e-mail, or other applications, however, your small business clients will need to contract with an Internet service provider (ISP). As your small business client's virtual CIO, you're in a unique position to advise your clients on selecting an ISP that will work best with the SBS 4.5 network you've just installed.

Evaluating ISPs

Before you begin looking at ISPs, you need to determine whether an ISP who's local, regional, or national in scope will best serve your client. National ISPs, also known as tier-one ISPs, tend to be most comfortable offering commercial grade services. As a result, national ISPs generally provide greater reliability, redundancy, and breadth of services, but in turn tend to have higher prices than local and regional ISPs. For some small businesses, such as those with a heavily trafficked e-commerce site, paying extra for more assurances of uptime might make sense.

The vast majority of small business owners aren't yet running mission critical applications on their Web sites. (Although it's worth noting that the incredibly successful Internet bookstore Amazon.com did start as a very small business in the founder's spare bedroom.) In addition, most small business owners tend to be pretty price sensitive. As a result, SBS VAPs typically help their small business clients select a local or regional ISP.

In order to get accurate and total assessments of ISPs, you'll want to compile comparative information on their Internet access, e-mail hosting, Web site hosting, customer service, and costs.

Tip

For a comprehensive list of criteria on which to evaluate an ISP, see the "ISP Selection Matrix," an Excel workbook on the CD-ROM with this book.

Internet Access

Internet access is one of the most fundamental issues for any small business that wants to get online. First and foremost is the concern of geographic availability. A given ISP needs to have local presence in your small business client's immediate area so your client is only responsible for basic local loop charges.

In some remote areas of the United States and the world, this might not always be possible. So you'll typically settle for an ISP that's within the same county, province, region, or area of the state. Begin your first conversation with an ISP by asking if the ISP has a point of presence (POP) within local calling distance of your small business client.

Tip

POP, which indicates where an ISP has local presence, shouldn't be confused with the post office e-mail delivery protocol (POP3) discussed later in this chapter and in Chapter 26.

If you're discussing analog or ISDN dial-up Internet access accounts, request the POP phone numbers. Then have your small business clients check the front of their local phone books or with their telephone companies to see if the POP is within local calling distance.

Once you've confirmed geographic availability, you'll want to find out how various Internet access offerings are priced. Some access methods are always sold as fixed price. No matter whether your small business clients are logged on 40 hours a week or 7 × 24, they pay the same monthly fee to the ISP.

Other access methods are sometimes metered. With this type of offering, your small business clients are typically given a pool of hours to use each month. Once your clients exceed the included number of hours, they're billed for each additional minute or hour at an additional rate. Some ISPs sell a given access method as metered, while competitors down the street provide a similar offering on a fixed-price basis.

Dial-Up Lines   Analog dial-up lines tend to the most pervasive access method that small businesses utilize before an SBS VAP begins serving as their technology advisor. Most ISPs now support a standard that allows analog dial-up modems to connect at a theoretical maximum of 56.6 Kbps. (Although in the United States, FCC regulations prevent that ideal from being reached.) Some ISPs sell plans that provide unlimited usage for a fixed monthly fee. Others allow usage of a predetermined number of hours and then bill for any usage above and beyond the monthly allowance.

ISPs tend to be more profitable when they have a very large number of subscribers dialing into a relatively small number of modems. As you can probably imagine, this results in frequent busy signals for your small business clients. So you need to ask the ISP at the outset about the ratio of user accounts to dial-up ports.

In many parts of the world, ISDN tends to be the second most popular Internet access method for small businesses. ISDN is usually available in one of two ways, Basic Rate Interface (BRI) or Primary Rate Interface (PRI). For cost reasons, your small business clients will be most likely interested in BRI, as opposed to PRI.

An ISDN BRI typically provides two B channels of 64 Kbps (in addition to a 16 Kbps D channel usually used for in-line signaling) that when bonded together provide a combined bandwidth of 128 Kbps.

Just as with analog lines, geographic availability is always an issue with ISPs offering ISDN service. Because ISDN has unique circuit provisioning requirements from the telephone company, your small business clients are likely to have additional geographic constraints beyond the ISPs. Before approaching an ISP to inquire about ISDN offerings in a local area, have your small business clients contact their telephone companies to find out if ISDN service is available for their locations.

Assuming the telephone company and ISP have ISDN available in the immediate geographic area of your small business client, you should proceed with interviewing the ISP. Find out whether its ISDN offerings include a single 64 Kbps channel or dual channels for a total of 128 Kbps. Obviously, 128 Kbps of bandwidth is preferable to 64K bps; some ISPs, however, aren't capable of providing dual channel ISDN service in all of their POPs. Other ISPs price dual channel accounts in such a way so that the price is prohibitive for many small businesses.

Also ask the ISP whether the ISDN access is fixed price or metered.

ISDN Internet access lines are subject to the same kind of usage constraints as analog lines. From a profit standpoint, ISPs have incentive to sell a very large number of ISDN access accounts that use a relatively small number of dial-up ports. Because dual channel ISDN access uses two channels, inquire about the ratio of users to dial-up ports.

Full-Time Analog and ISDN Connections

For a premium price, some ISPs will sell dedicated analog or ISDN solutions, giving your small business client 7 × 24 guaranteed access to a phone number that no other ISP users are given. Dedicated accounts are almost always sold on a fixed-price basis and ensure your client never receives a busy signal. Depending on the competition in the local market, however, you might discover a dedicated dial-up line approaches the price of an entry-level, permanent Internet access connection.

Using Microsoft Proxy Server to Save on Metered Charges

If the ISP or the telephone company meters usage, you can help your small business client control Internet access costs by restricting the hours of use through Microsoft Proxy Server Auto Dial. For example, if your small business client keeps conventional business hours, you could limit Proxy Server from autodialing any time outside of Monday through Friday, 8 A.M. to 6 P.M., as appropriate. You can accomplish this on the Configuration tab of the Proxy Server Auto Dial properties dialog box. (See Figure 18-1.)

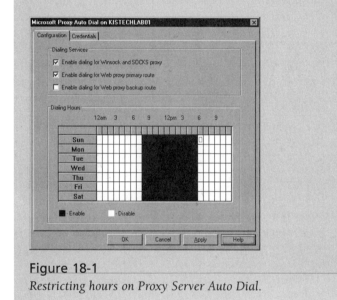

Figure 18-1

Restricting hours on Proxy Server Auto Dial.

Dedicated Lines   In contrast to dial-up lines, which can either be dialed or disconnected, a dedicated (that is, leased) line is always connected with the exception of unplanned outages. Because disconnection is extremely un-likely, dedicated Internet access lines are almost always sold on a flat fee or fixed-price basis.

Dedicated line offerings vary tremendously in different parts of the world. The only constant is change. So if you checked on dedicated lines for your small business client in early 1999, you'll likely have a host of different offerings and more aggressive prices by the time you refresh your ISP survey three, six, or twelve months later.

Traditionally, dedicated Internet access lines have been out of the financial reach of most small businesses. As prices keep coming down and small business' Internet needs grow more complex, you'll see more small businesses investing in full-time Internet access connections through offerings such as frame relay and point-to-point T1 and T3 lines, as well as the fractional equivalents.

Broadband Internet access is also making it much more affordable for small businesses to have full-time Internet access connections. Although their geographic availability tends to be sparser than frame relay and point-to-point T1 and T3 lines, broadband offerings such as cable modem and digital subscriber line (xDSL) are proving to be quite popular among small businesses worldwide.

Note

ADSL is a type of xDSL common broadband offering and is short for asymmetric digital subscriber line. It's referred to as asymmetric because download bandwidth is usually much greater than upload bandwidth.

Although static IP addresses are generally a given with conventional dedicated Internet access lines such as frame relay and point-to-point T1 and T3, you'll want to inquire about the availability of static IP addresses for dial-up and broadband connections. A static IP address (a fixed IP address) is required for certain Internet applications such as SMTP mail dequeuing under Microsoft Exchange Server 5.5 with ETRN and provides for a quicker call setup time for dial-up connections. (ETRN is short for extended-turn, an SMTP command, and is covered in more detail in Chapter 26.)

E-Mail Hosting

In selecting an ISP, you also need to consider the client's e-mail hosting capabilities. Before you begin discussing various e-mail offerings with ISPs, you need to understand how market forces have carved out two distinct ISP niches. Some ISPs offer Internet access, e-mail hosting, and Web site hosting. Other ISPs consider themselves Web hosting companies and strictly concentrate on offering e-mail and Web site hosting.

No hard and fast rules exist to help you decide whether to choose one ISP for Internet access and another for e-mail and Web site hosting, or consolidate all procured services under one roof. While you might have price incentives and the feeling of a single point of accountability to purchase all services from a single ISP, many small businesses and SBS VAPs are successfully ordering ISP services à la carte.

Regardless of whether the e-mail hosting is provided by the same ISP offering the Internet access, you'll need to discuss the ISP's e-mail capabilities. If your small business client is planning to use Exchange Server 5.5 Internet Mail Service (IMS) to handle Internet mail, you'll have to find out how the ISP handles SMTP mail queuing. With a static IP address, your best bet is usually being able to configure SBS 4.5 and Exchange Server 5.5 to signal mail dequeuing by the ETRN command.

Tip

ETRN and SMTP mail dequeuing is covered in Chapter 26.

If Exchange Server 5.5 isn't being used to send and receive Internet e-mail, POP3 is another, albeit a less robust, option. If you plan on utilizing POP3-based e-mail through the Proxy Server connection on SBS 4.5, you'll want to find out if the ISP offers a single, global POP3 mailbox or individual POP3 mailboxes. A global POP3 mailbox collects all of the e-mail from an entire domain in a single mailbox. For example, if I order a global POP3 mailbox from my ISP, any e-mail addressed to any alias in the kisweb.com domain is deposited into this one mailbox.

In contrast, many ISPs will set up individual POP3 mailboxes so users can retain their privacy and e-mail individuality. When the ISP offers individual POP3 mailboxes, find out how many mailboxes are included in the base offering, as well as the cost to add additional POP3 mailboxes.

The Importance of Domain Names

To keep entry-level costs down, most ISPs offer individual POP3 mailboxes that are associated with their own domain name. For small businesses, this is a dead-end offering and should be avoided at all costs.

If I set up an e-mail alias called josh@myinternetserviceprovider.com, for example, I lose two major benefits of having aliases created for a domain name such as josh@kisweb.com. For starters, I can't transfer my e-mail address to another ISP. Second, I lose valuable branding that goes along with having the domain for all company e-mail addresses in my organization (kisweb.com) match the domain in the Web site URL (*www.kisweb.com*). With prices as low as they currently are, all of your small business clients should have their own domain names for their Web sites and e-mail.

Tip

An increasing number of ISPs have added Web-based interfaces that al-low SBS VAPs, or small business internal gurus, to perform their own administration of POP3 mailboxes without having to submit requests to the ISP.

Web Site Hosting

In assessing the Web site hosting capabilities of an ISP, consider these factors:

- How much storage space (MB) is included before surcharges?

Note

Entry-level Web sites with static pages rarely occupy more than a small fraction of the available space on the ISP's Web server.

- How much monthly data transfer (GB) is included before surcharges?
- How many T1 and T3 lines are there? And is Web site hosting band-width shared with Internet access bandwidth?
- Is Microsoft FrontPage Server Extensions (FPSE) for FrontPage 2000 supported? Microsoft Office 2000 Server Extensions (OSE)?
- Is statistical reporting included?
- Is FTP access available?

Note

FTP access is required to use the Small Business Server Web Publishing Wizard.

- Can secure sockets layer (SSL) be configured?
- Can Active Server Pages (ASPs) be configured that make use of Microsoft Access and Microsoft SQL Server databases?

Tip

Depending on how specific your small business client's needs are, you might also want to inquire whether the server the ISP uses for Web host-ing runs Microsoft Windows NT Server 4.0 with Microsoft Internet Infor-mation Server 4.0 (IIS) or if it runs some type of UNIX-based Web server.

Customer Service

Now that I've covered some of the technical factors that influence ISP selection, I'll turn my attention to some of the more intangible customer service aspects. Here are questions you should ask ISPs:

- What are the standard hours for monitoring? Is it just Monday through Friday, 9 to 5? Is someone on call 7 × 24? Is staff on-site monitoring the Web servers?

- What are the hours for technical support? What types of issues are included in basic technical support?

- What's the ISP's level of experience in supporting SBS 4.5 and Exchange Server 5.5?

- What kinds of data protection measures are taken in terms of backup, redundancy, power protection, fault tolerance, and security?

- On whose backbone is the ISP?

Tip

"ISP Selection Matrix," an Excel workbook included on the CD-ROM in the back of this book, can also be used to help compare and contrast various ISP offerings.

Costs

Here are questions to ask ISPs about cost factors:

- What are the setup charges for the services being discussed?

- What are the monthly recurring charges?

- What are the payment terms?

- Which services are metered? Which are fixed price?

- What is the minimum contract length?

- What's the cost to register a new domain name or transfer an existing domain name (above and beyond InterNIC charges)?

Tip

For more information on criteria for selecting an ISP, see the *Microsoft BackOffice Small Business Server 4.5 Resource Kit*, Chapter 11, "Planning for an Internet Presence."

Explaining the Maze of Options in Lay Terms to the Client

Selecting an ISP using the criteria above isn't likely to be something small business owners or even their internal gurus will feel comfortable tackling. Interviewing and selecting an ISP is generally the sole domain of SBS VAPs.

Sooner or later though, you'll need to educate small business owners and their gurus on some of the key issues surrounding Internet access, Web browsing, e-mail, and Web hosting. By late 1999, many small business owners are already familiar with the stand-alone way of getting online. In this type of office, each PC has a modem, analog line, and ISP account. Or in some cases, one PC has a modem, analog line, and ISP account that everyone must share. Whenever anyone needs to send or receive e-mail using the main company e-mail account or visit a Web site, they just walk down the hall and stand around looking at their watch, waiting to use the PC.

> **Tip**
>
> Microsoft Direct Access created an SBS 4.5 marketing toolkit for SBS VAPs that includes a series of light-hearted ad slicks titled, "You know you need a network server when..." The Direct Access web site is located at *www.microsoft.com/directaccess.*

Why a Proxy Server

Often the best place to start when outlining the advantages of using SBS 4.5 with Proxy Server 2.0—as opposed to individual modems, analog lines, and dial-up ISP accounts for every person in the office—is to compare the two methods. Here are the advantages of using Proxy Server:

- Lower hardware, setup, and ongoing costs as you spread a fixed cost among many users. This way your small business client doesn't incur variable costs each time another user is granted Internet access.

- Lower administrative costs because the client has to keep tabs on only one connection, ISP account, and telco line.

- Better management control of Internet access through access control, granular permissions, monitoring, logging, and alerts.

- Security through the firewall that uses dynamic packet filtering. The required TCP/IP port is only opened when needed and then closed again right away. The connection doesn't stay open and expose the network to huge security risks. Stand-alone PCs generally have no protection from hackers compromising your client's network and server security. Because of this, most Fortune 1000 IT organizations won't even allow end users to have modems.

- Superior performance with caching of recently retrieved objects.

- No more bottlenecks as employees stand around waiting to use the one PC in the office with Internet access. Now the small business owner can afford to provide everyone in the office with high-speed, secure Internet access on his or her desktop PC.

- No more privacy issues with multiple people sharing a single PC with a single e-mail inbox, Web browser history list, and Web browser favorites list.

SBS 4.5 Server Applications for Getting Online

While small business owners and internal gurus might have a hard time conceptualizing topics like ETRN, SMTP, POP3, and SSL, they usually can relate to purchasing shrink-wrapped hardware and software. As a result, you'll find it useful to get them up to speed on the following server and client applications their office will be using for various Internet services:

- **Proxy Server 2.0**—Provides shared connectivity (a gateway) to the Internet, as well as security through a firewall that blocks unauthorized inbound traffic from the Internet. Proxy Server 2.0 also provides a performance boost through caching, which minimizes the need to dial-on-demand for small business clients without the luxury of a full-time Internet connection.

- **IIS 4.0**—Most useful for building an intranet for small businesses. In rare cases, small businesses might want to host their own Web site. IIS 4.0 is also used behind the scenes by the SBS Console and Online Guide.

- **Exchange Server 5.5**—Responsible for managing internal and external e-mail communication, group scheduling, contacts, task management, and shared folders. IMS and Exchange Connector for POP3 Mailboxes provide Internet connectivity for e-mail messages.

- **Remote Access Service (RAS)/Dial-Up Networking (DUN) from Windows NT Server 4.0**—Used when there is no permanent connection to the Internet.

SBS 4.5 Client Applications for Getting Online

The Setup Computer Wizard (SCW) and Client Installation Wizard can install the following applications:

- **Proxy Server client**—SBS 4.5 client that uses internal private IP addresses, with all Internet access requests going through Proxy Server. Installing the Proxy Server client also puts WSP Client applet in Control Panel.

- **Outlook 2000**—Messaging and collaboration client. SCW configures internal and Internet e-mail through Exchange Server. To connect directly to POP3 e-mail host, add Internet e-mail service to the mail profile.

- **Internet Explorer 5.0**—Web browser.

- **Outlook Express**—POP3 mail client that's not nearly as full-featured as Outlook 2000. I recommend that you use Outlook Express for newsgroup support only.

- **FrontPage 98**—Web authoring software. Although not installed by SCW, it's included with SBS 4.5. The installation files can be found in the FrontPg folder on SBS 4.5 CD 2.

Using Domain Name Registrars and DNS

Regardless of whether your small business clients host their own e-mail and Web sites, their domain names need to be registered in the domain name service (DNS) directory so host name requests resolve to the correct IP address. Assuming they go with Microsoft's suggested route and outsource e-mail and Web site hosting to an ISP, your small business client's DNS entries will point to the ISP's e-mail and Web servers.

All domain name registrations used to funnel through Network Solutions (*www.networksolutions.com*). While Network Solutions still processes and maintains a substantial amount of the DNS records, the domain name registrar process was opened up to several additional firms in April 1999. The Internet Corporation for Assigned Names and Numbers (ICANN) is a nonprofit organization that administers IP addresses and domain names. To get an up-to-date list of firms that can process domain name registrations, see the ICANN Web site at *www.icann.org*.

Mastering the Art of Double Entendres— Windows NT Domains vs. Internet Domains

New SBS VAPs or those new to Windows NT might be confused about domain names at first. A Windows NT domain isn't the same thing as an Internet domain.

A Windows NT domain is a group of computers that share a common user account security database. In the case of an SBS 4.5 network, the SBS 4.5 domain is made up of the SBS 4.5 primary domain controller (PDC), Microsoft Windows 95/98 clients, Windows NT Workstation 4.0 clients, and perhaps one or more additional Windows NT Server 4.0 member servers.

An Internet domain name is part of the DNS hierarchy and is the friendly name for an IP address of a host that uses DNS servers for name resolution.

Not to confuse the issue, but a Windows NT domain name and Internet domain name can have the same value. For example, I could name my SBS 4.5 domain KISWEB (the PDC system is named KISWEB01) and have kisweb.com as my Internet domain name (my Web site is *www.kisweb.com* and e-mail name space is @kisweb.com).

Because changing the SBS 4.5 domain name is next to impossible once SBS is installed without reinstalling from scratch, take great care in selecting the Windows NT domain name.

Tip

Most ISPs will be happy to process domain name registrations and transfers on your behalf. Since the process can often be quite confusing, I'd advise you to have the ISP take care of all issues related to DNS registration and transfer. Just be sure the whois records accurately list all the registration, billing, and contact information.

What does SBS 4.5 do with the domain name for your small business client? You'll enter the domain name in the Configure Internet Domain Name page in the Internet Connection Wizard (ICW). See Figure 18-2 on the next page. This entry updates the e-mail reply addresses as you configure recipients in the Exchange Server 5.5 Global Access List (GAL). In SBS 4.5, mailbox recipients are created when you run the User Account Wizard. In addition, Exchange Server 5.5 requires the domain name for the SMTP mail entries in IMS.

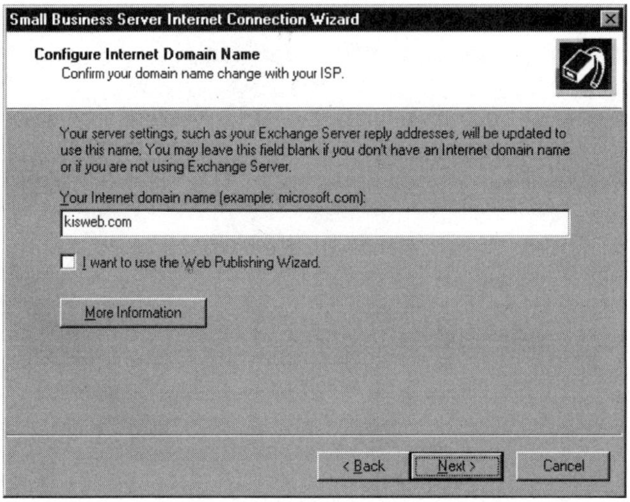

Figure 18-2

Enter the Internet domain name in the Internet Connection Wizard.

Tip

Before your small business clients print company Web site URLs and e-mail addresses on everything from business cards and letterhead to golf umbrellas, make sure they're comfortable with the second-level domain names they've selected.

Behind the Scenes with DNS Entries

In order for e-mail domain and Web site hosting to work properly, the ISP needs to register two different types of DNS entries:

- MX—The mail exchanger record in DNS used to connect Exchange Server IMS (SMTP protocol) to the Internet. If you decide to have your small business client host its own e-mail, the client will need a static IP address when the MX record is configured to point to the SBS system.

- A—The host record address and PTR record used for reverse lookup. The A record relates the host name to the static IP address.

To learn more about DNS entries, see *Microsoft TCP/IP Training*.

Second- and Third-Level Domain Names

Every Web site URL and e-mail domain name is configured for either a second- or third-level domain name. How do you know which one is better to have? Although small business clients might be tempted to gravitate toward third-level domain names, SBS VAPs should strongly recommend their small business clients make the nominal investment in establishing their own second-level domain name. The selection of a domain name to use as a Web site URL and e-mail domain name gets at the heart of naming conventions, so great care should be given to its selection.

An example of a third-level domain name Web site URL is:

- kisweb.myinternetserviceprovider.com

Examples of third-level domain e-mail name space include:

- josh@kisweb.myinternetserviceprovider.com
- inbox@kisweb.myinternetserviceprovider.com
- getinfo@kisweb.myinternetserviceprovider.com

An example of a second level domain name Web site URL is:

- www.kisweb.com

Examples of second-level e-mail name space include:

- josh@kisweb.com
- inbox@kisweb.com
- getinfo@kisweb.com

Second-level domain names are shorter (that is, less cumbersome), provide consistency between the Web site URL and e-mail address space, preserve brand name identity of the small business client, and allow for portability in case your small business client wants to change the ISP relationship.

Proxy Server and Internet Access Issues

Now that you have a better understanding of Internet access, e-mail hosting, Web site hosting, and DNS, you're ready to take a more in-depth look at configuring Proxy Server 2.0 through ICW. This section will drill down on configuring modem, router, and broadband Internet access connections, as well as a host of related Proxy Server–specific topics.

Using the Internet Connection Wizard

ICW makes it easy to configure all the settings related to basic SBS 4.5 Internet usage in one central place. SBS 4.5 supports three different types of hardware devices and provides worksheets to help you gather all the required configuration information on the Configure Hardware page in ICW. See Figure 18-3. Simply selecting the appropriate hardware selection and clicking the Form button retrieves the relevant worksheet. For example, Figure 18-4 shows the "Connection with a Router" worksheet, which you can print out and fax to your ISP to capture all the router configuration data before the installation.

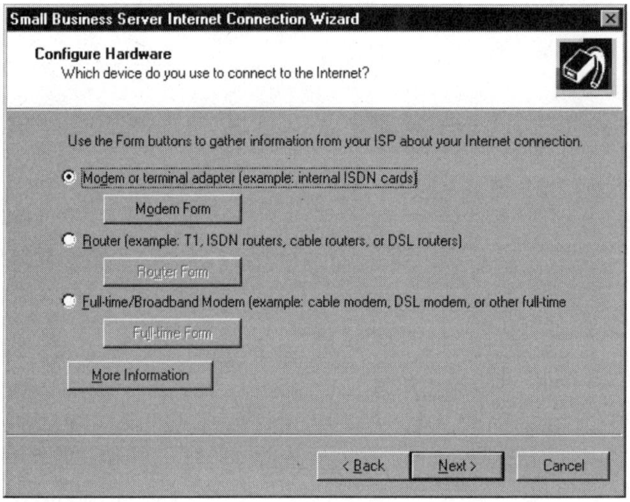

Figure 18-3

The Configure Hardware page within ICW.

ICW can be launched from multiple places on the Manage Internet Access page:

- Configure Internet Hardware (opens to specific page within the wizard)

- Connect To The Internet

- Change Internet Settings (opens to specific page within the wizard)

    You can also start ICW by clicking Connect To An ISP on the To Do List.

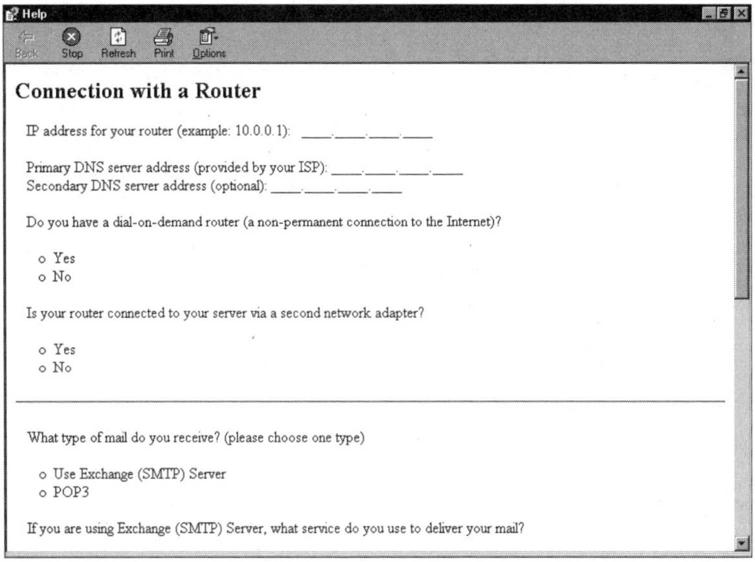

Figure 18-4

The "Connection with a Router" worksheet.

> **Tip**
>
> For more technical information on ICW, see the white paper on the SBS Web site (*www.microsoft.com/smallbusinessserver*), "Internet Connectivity and the Microsoft BackOffice Small Business Server Internet Connection Wizard."

Configuring Modems, Routers, and Broadband Hardware

Prior to running ICW, all hardware devices need to be physically installed and configured. If you need assistance with the installation of hardware, consult the documentation that came with the device, the vendor's Web site, or the vendor's technical support organization.

> **Tip**
>
> For lists of hardware devices that have already been tested with SBS 4.5 and Windows NT Server 4.0, check out the Recommended Hardware page on the SBS Web site at *www.microsoft.com/smallbusinessserver*.

Dial-Up Connection

A dial-up Internet access connection for Proxy Server works through the DUN and RAS capabilities of Windows NT Server 4.0. A conventional analog modem or an ISDN terminal adapter can make dial-up connections. Both types of devices should be configured through the Modems applet in Control Panel before launching ICW and then set up as ports through RAS with dial-out access. Dial-up devices establish temporary connections to the Internet and can be installed as internal cards (ISA or PCI) on a serial port or on a multiport serial board.

When configuring a dial-up modem connection to the Internet, ICW will prompt you to complete the Set Up Modem Connection To ISP page to indicate the appropriate RAS/DUN phone book entry and credentials (ISP account name and password), as shown in Figure 18-5. Proxy Server uses this information as the credentials for Microsoft Proxy Auto Dial and for Exchange Server IMS (on the Dial-Up Connections tab).

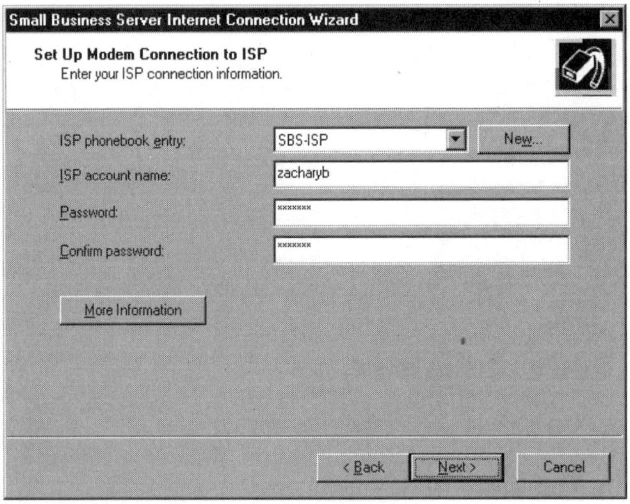

Figure 18-5
The Set Up Modem Connection To ISP page.

Once ICW configures the Auto Dial entry in Proxy Server, SBS 4.5 will connect to the ISP when a client or another service, such as Exchange Server IMS or the Exchange Connector for POP3 Mailboxes, makes a request. The Auto Dial connection disconnects only when the line is idle for the preconfigured amount of time or if the ISP or telco drops the call.

The High Costs of 7 × 24 Metered Dial-Up Connections

SBS VAPs need to be especially concerned with the disconnect on Auto Dial working properly if small business clients are paying for metered service (by the minute or by the hour) to the ISP and/or telco. Because a given month has over 700 hours, leaving a metered connection open 7 × 24 is expensive. If the small business truly needs 7 × 24 Internet connectivity, fixed-price full-time Internet connection alternatives are usually much more cost effective.

Note

If RAS/DUN connections seem to drop for no apparent reason, contact the ISP. Some of the more consumer-oriented ISPs actually will time the call and have a special feature that drops calls after the call has been connected beyond the configured call time limit threshold, regardless of whether or not the connection is in use. Other ISPs drop calls only when the connection has actually been inactive for a specified time period.

To set the number of seconds a connection can be idle before SBS disconnects, follow these steps:

1. Open Dial-Up Networking in My Computer on the SBS 4.5 system.

2. Click the More button and choose User Preferences. (If there is more than one connection, you'll need to perform these steps separately for each connection.)

3. On the Dialing tab, type the number of seconds in the Idle Seconds Before Hanging Up box. (See Figure 18-6 on the next page.) With an analog dial-up connection, you should probably set this to 300 seconds. For an ISDN dial-up connection with a much quicker call setup time, you should set the value to 60 seconds.

Figure 18-6

Configure the number of idle seconds before the call is disconnected on the Dialing tab in User Preferences for Dial-Up Networking.

In a perfect world, Idle Seconds Before Hanging Up would work as expected and your small business client would never have any chest pains when receiving the ISP or telco bill for metered service. Here a few of the more common reasons why RAS doesn't disconnect as expected:

- Active caching is updating the Proxy Server cache proactively. Unless your small business client has a full-time dedicated connection, active caching should be left disabled (the SBS 4.5 default) for small business clients. Check to make sure active caching is in fact disabled by opening the Web Proxy Service Properties. See Figure 18-7. This is located in the Microsoft Management Console, accessible from the Microsoft Proxy Server program group on the Start menu.

- The ISP or other Internet users are sending some type of TCP/IP traffic. This can often be difficult to troubleshoot unless you're skilled at using a protocol analyzer, such as the Windows NT Network Monitor or the more full-featured SMS Network Monitor.

- A Web browser (Proxy Server client) is pointing to a Web page with a refresh tag.

- A Winsock application on a client is open.

- PPP LCP extensions are enabled. This configuration choice is on the Server tab of the relevant Phonebook Entry. See Figure 18-8. If PPP LCP extensions are enabled, the RAS/DUN call timer is periodically reset.

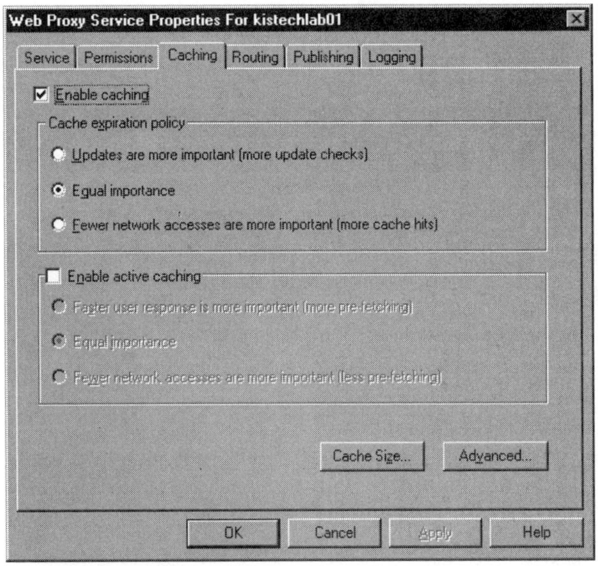

Figure 18-7

Make sure active caching is disabled.

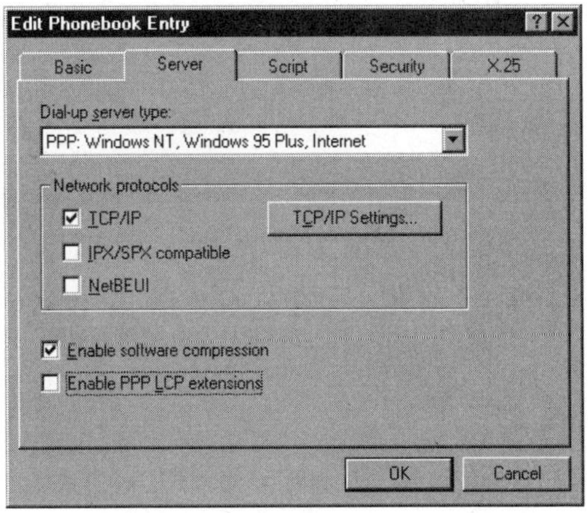

Figure 18-8

Make sure PPP LCP extensions are disabled.

- A WINS client (TCP/IP) is bound to an external NIC. In addition to making sure Auto Dial disconnects more predictably, unbinding the NetBIOS Interface from the external NIC makes the server all the more secure. This configuration is made on the Bindings tab in the Network applet in Control Panel. See Figure 18-9.

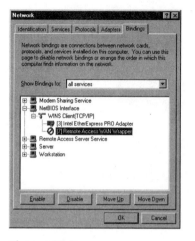

Figure 18-9

Unbind the NetBIOS Interface from the external NIC.

- The RAS Autodial Manager is enabled. Disable it through the Services applet in Control Panel. See Figure 18-10.

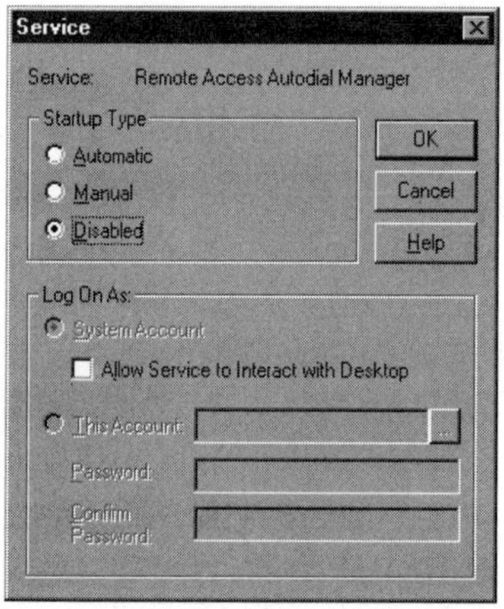

Figure 18-10

Disable the RAS Autodial Manager.

Tip

For more information on troubleshooting Proxy RAS Autodial and Auto disconnect, see KB article Q181407 in the Microsoft Knowledge Base.

Router Connection

Although dial-up connections are limited to analog and ISDN lines, routers can connect small businesses to the Internet for a much wider variety of connection types, including analog, ISDN BRI or PRI, point-to-point T1 and T3, and frame relay. Unlike a dial-up connection, routers don't use the RAS/DUN services of Windows NT Server 4.0 and aren't recognized as modems in Control Panel. Rather, when configured in the Microsoft preferred topology, routers are directly plugged into a second network interface card (NIC) in the SBS 4.5 system.

While dial-up connections are temporary by design, even when used 7 × 24, routers can either support full-time connections or be configured for dial-on-demand. Analog and ISDN BRI routers will typically support dial-on-demand, while ISDN PRI, point-to-point T1 and T3, and frame relay are designed for continuous Internet connectivity. Not to worry though—ICW supports both dial-on-demand and full-time routers.

If you select Router from the ICW Configure Hardware page, which is shown in Figure 18-3, the Set Up Router Connection To ISP page opens. See Figure 18-11 on the next page. Leave the default selection of My Router Is A Dial-On-Demand Router enabled and click the Next button. ICW will open the Configure SMTP Mail Delivery page so you can configure the Exchange Server IMS to forward outgoing mail to an SMTP relay host. See Figure 18-12 on the next page.

This process is in contrast to the advice you'd receive from ICW if you didn't indicate you had a dial-on-demand router. By deselecting My Router Is A Dial-On-Demand Router, you're indicating to ICW that you have a full-time Internet connection. As a result, ICW will recommend the selection of Use Domain Name System (DNS) For Name Resolution For Message Delivery. This means Exchange Server IMS will make its own DNS queries to deliver mail to MX hosts, as opposed to forwarding all mail to your ISP's SMTP relay host.

SCW supports two possible topologies for connecting a router. In the first method, the router is plugged into a second NIC on the SBS 4.5 system, so the router is effectively hidden behind the Proxy Server 2.0 firewall. Because of the security that Proxy Server brings to the table, this is the preferred router configuration method.

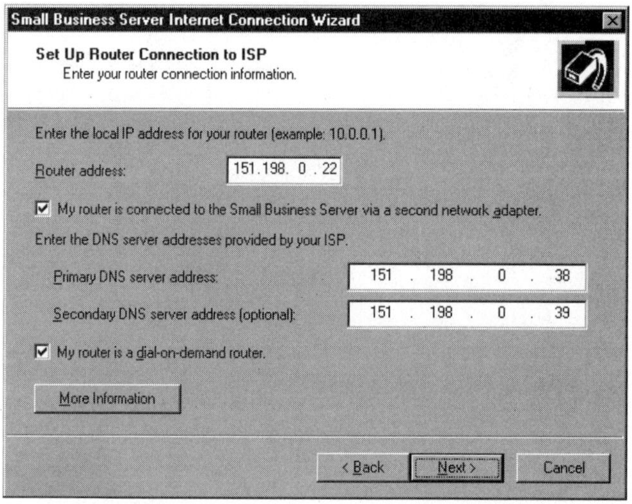

Figure 18-11

The Set Up Router Connection To ISP page in ICW.

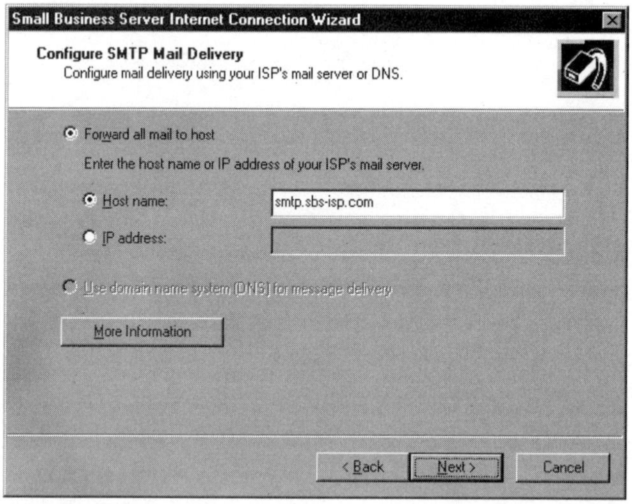

Figure 18-12

The Configure SMTP Mail Delivery page in ICW.

Alternatively you could connect a router directly to an Ethernet hub on an SBS 4.5 network. With this configuration, each SBS 4.5 client desktop has the IP address of the router as its default gateway, which is configured through the Network applet in the client Control Panel. Because this isn't supported by SCW and it leaves the network potentially more vulnerable to Internet security breaches (that is, hacking), this method isn't endorsed.

Preferred Router Topology   In the Microsoft recommended configuration, the router is connected to the SBS 4.5 system through a second NIC in the server. Just as with a dial-up connection to the Internet, the server will have no default gateway on the internal NIC. The server, however, will have a default gateway configured on the external NIC that's the same as the local IP address of the router. The router, in turn, will have a default gateway value that's on the same subnet as the IP address of the secondary NIC, the router, and a router back at the ISP POP location.

Just like clients on an SBS 4.5 system connected to the Internet through a dial-up connection, the Proxy Server clients won't have a default gateway. The clients connect to the Internet through the Proxy Server firewall. Because the Proxy Server firewall is between the LAN and Internet, the internal network is protected from outside hacker attacks.

Tip

Although the secondary NIC has to be installed and configured before running ICW, you shouldn't install the secondary NIC in the server until after the unattended SBS 4.5 setup has completed.

Understanding Call Setup Times

When comparing analog dial-on-demand routers with ISDN dial-on-demand routers, be aware of call setup times. With an analog connection—even with a static IP address—you're looking at 20 to 30 seconds of call setup time for each connection. With ISDN, on the other hand, call setup time should drop to 2 to 3 seconds. This means a Web-browsing user probably wouldn't even be able to tell the difference between the connected and disconnected state of an ISDN dial-on-demand router. In essence, an ISDN dial-on-demand router is the next best thing to having a full-time connection.

To configure a router connected to a secondary NIC with SBS 4.5, launch ICW, choose the Router option on the Configure Hardware page, and click Next. This opens the Setup Router Connection To ISP page. Enter the local IP address of the router. Remember, the IP address for the router needs to be on the same subnet as the secondary NIC.

Tip

The term secondary NIC is synonymous with external NIC—the NIC that connects the SBS 4.5 system to the Internet. The term primary NIC is the same as the internal NIC—the NIC that connects the SBS 4.5 system to the clients.

Once you indicate the existence of a secondary NIC, the Network Interface Card Configuration page will open. See Figure 18-13. This tells SBS which NIC is used for the LAN and which is used to connect to the Internet.

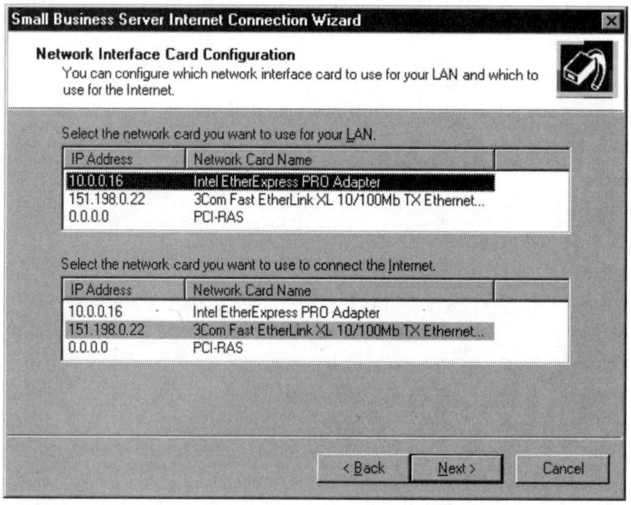

Figure 18-13

The ICW Network Interface Card Configuration page.

Proxy Server Local Address Table The IP addresses associated with the internal NIC should be in the Proxy Server Local Address Table (LAT). The LAT lists the IP address range(s) of the internal address space and helps Proxy Server decide whether a client request is serviced by the Internet or by the intranet. Essentially, the LAT differentiates between internal and external IP addresses.

Tip

To learn how to tell if two IP addresses are on the same subnet, see *Microsoft TCP/IP Training*. Alternatively, you can just rely on your ISP to give you these values and enter them by rote. You'll find it useful to know more about TCP/IP just to keep the ISP honest.

Although it isn't recommended that you do so, if you must change the IP address of the SBS 4.5 system internal NIC, you'll need to update the LAT as well. The IP addresses associated with the external NIC shouldn't be in the Proxy Server LAT. LAT Configuration can be reached from the Service tab of the Web Proxy Service Properties dialog box.

Note

The IP address associated with the external NIC needs to be static. You can't have the IP address for the secondary NIC or router using DHCP client services.

Alternative Router Topology   Connecting a router directly to the LAN through an Ethernet hub is supported by ICW but not recommended because you don't have the security of the Proxy Server 2.0 firewall. Someday you might need to defend your choice of the preferred method described above, so I'll give you a 90 second crash course on the alternative router topology.

When the router is connected directly to the LAN, you lose the benefits of having an SBS 4.5 system in the first place. All clients on the LAN that need Internet access need the router's IP address set as their default gateway. With the preferred configuration, clients normally have their default gateway left as blank because Proxy Server 2.0 is on the same subnet as the clients, and it handles all Internet access requests on behalf of the clients.

Unless the router is capable of performing network address translation (NAT), every client also needs to have a valid external IP address. This makes the clients more vulnerable to outside hacker attacks and costs substantially more in terms of ISP fees. Unless the router vendor includes its own firewall software, the clients have no packet level filtering and, accordingly, no security.

Tip

Regardless of whether a router is used for the preferred or alternative configuration, you need to check if the router has a built-in DHCP server. If it does, the DHCP server on router must be disabled to prevent conflicts with DHCP server on the SBS 4.5 system. For more details, see KB article Q177610 in the Microsoft Knowledge Base.

Broadband Connection

The third and final category of Internet access connections supported by the SCW is broadband. Labeled in SCW as Full-Time/Broadband Modem, the most commonly found devices in this category are either xDSL or cable modems. By their nature, broadband devices always have a full-time connection. Because no provision for protection has been made within the devices currently on the market, broadband devices should never be connected directly to an Ethernet hub. Broadband devices should always be plugged into the external NIC on the SBS 4.5 system, so that the network can be protected by the Proxy Server firewall.

Just like routers, broadband devices don't use the RAS/DUN services. Rather, their physical connection to the server is through the secondary NIC interface, which is configured in the Network applet in Control Panel.

With a broadband connection, the external NIC needs to have a static IP address. You can't have a DHCP server and DHCP client on the same system. Because a second NIC is required, a broadband connection will have a similar topology to that of the router connected to the SBS 4.5 server through a secondary NIC. As a result, all inbound and outbound traffic will be filtered by the Proxy Server firewall.

Distinguishing Between ISP and Telco Charges

In addition to Internet access charges from the ISP, your small business clients will also be paying fees for the circuit to some kind of telephone company. You and your small business client need to be aware of the circuit charges from the telco, as even seemingly small fees can add up quickly.

For a dial-up connection through an analog modem or ISDN terminal adapter, telco usage is typically metered. For an analog dial-up business line, even if the ISP is a local call, your small business client might be subject to message units of approximately $0.40 to $0.80 an hour. For ISDN, sometimes the telco circuit is metered. Other times usage is fixed price or unlimited. Local market conditions and FCC tariffs (or equivalent local government regulations) will generally dictate how dial-up rates are billed.

If the ISDN circuit is metered, usually packages are available that include a certain number of single or dual B channel hours. Once the monthly allowance of single or dual B channel hours has been exceeded, your small business client is billed at a certain per-minute or per-hour rate above and beyond the included time.

Installation charges for an analog or ISDN line, at least in most parts of the United States, tend to be relatively modest. To present a comprehensive cost estimate to your small business client, however, you still want to get ballpark figures on setup charges from the telco.

Full-time Internet connections, such as point-to-point T1 and T3 and frame relay, typically are billed by the telco at monthly rates considerably higher than dial-up analog and ISDN lines. With that substantially higher rate structure usually comes fixed-price billing. Your small business client will generally be billed a predictable, flat fee each month for the permanent, leased line.

For full-time telco circuits, however, the installation charges can be quite substantial. In the United States, telco setup charges are commonly in the neighborhood of $500 to $2,000 for installation of a frame relay or a point-to-point T1 or T3 circuit.

In one situation, however, your small business clients won't need to pay a separate telco circuit charge above and beyond ISP Internet access fees. Cable modems, delivered over the same kind of coaxial cable used for cable television hookups, usually bypasses the local telco. So the local cable companies that offer cable modem Internet access are assuming the dual role of ISP and circuit provider.

Evaluating Permanent vs. Dial-Up Connections

In sharp contrast to mid-sized and Fortune 1000 IT organizations, most small businesses don't need full-time, permanent, dedicated Internet connections. Small businesses can easily function with a dial-up connection (ISDN or, if need be, analog) as long as the ISP handles e-mail and Web site hosting needs.

Although the economics and dynamics of this will definitely change as full-time, lower-cost, small business–friendly alternatives to expensive frame relay and point-to-point T1 and T3 lines become available. For example, the price of broadband cable modems and xDSL offerings are making it possible for small businesses to secure a dedicated Internet connection for a fraction of the cost of an entry-level fractional T1 solution.

For a permanent connection, a small business typically needs a router, ISDN terminal adapter, CSU/DSU, xDSL modem, or cable modem. For a dial-on-demand connection, a small business will need a dial-on-demand analog or ISDN router, ISDN terminal adapter, or analog modem.

The firewall protection afforded by Proxy Server becomes mission critical when the small business client has a permanent connection to the Internet. A permanent connection actually increases the security risk, even when e-mail and Web site hosting are outsourced because the small business client's SBS 4.5 system is constantly connected to the Internet. Because the Internet access connection is always open and always has the same IP address, hackers can more easily find your client's SBS 4.5 system.

A dial-up or dial-on-demand connection makes it harder for hackers to find your small business client's SBS 4.5 system. Even with a static IP address, the SBS 4.5 system is only connected at certain time intervals. Some of these time intervals are scheduled and predictable, but are relatively short in duration. At other times, a dial-up or dial-on-demand connection is online for longer time periods but at more random, usage-driven intervals.

Note

Not all ISPs make static IP addresses available with dial-up accounts. If this is an issue for your small business client, make sure you discuss this problem early on with both the ISP and small business owner.

Static IP Addresses

I've made reference to static IP addresses throughout this chapter. You'll see the concept at least once more in Chapter 26 on how to add value to Exchange Server. Why pay the ISP's extra fees for a static IP address, as opposed to using an IP address that's dynamically assigned at each logon? The reasons include:

- Exchange Server full-time connections or dial-up connections with ETRN require a static IP address where Internet e-mail uses IMS and SMTP, as opposed to the Exchange Connector for POP3 Mailboxes

- It's a faster call connection type.

- Internet applications, such as hosting a Web site, FTP site, or newsgroup or remote access connections over Point-to-Point Tunneling Protocol (PPTP), need it.

Tip

You can use a dynamically assigned IP address with SBSTURN for mail dequeuing, if the ISP supports this dequeuing command. Alternatively, you can use a dial-up account with a dynamically assigned IP address to retrieve POP3 mail using the Exchange Connector for POP3 Mailboxes.

Reverse Proxy

Small businesses, and SBS VAPs for that matter, aren't usually geared for setting up SBS 4.5 for hosting Web sites and Internet e-mail. Although a seemingly simple configuration task, hosting e-mail and Web sites requires 7 × 24 monitoring and around-the-clock IT staff for monitoring server performance and events. Even as the cost dynamics change and small businesses are able to install full-time broadband Internet connections, in most cases small businesses are still better off outsourcing their e-mail and Web site hosting to an ISP.

In the event a small business decides to assume the hosting burden, however, it will need something called reverse Proxy, which enables Internet users to connect securely to their server to view a Web site hosted on the IIS 4.0 part of SBS 4.5. Because this would also mean the Web site would be running on the same server as line-of-business applications, this could cause all kinds of performance, security, and reliability issues as well.

Unless you or your small business client has particularly strong expertise in being a micro ISP and a particularly strong stomach for being beeped at 2 A.M., just say no to reverse Proxy.

Point-to-Point Tunneling Protocol

PPTP is part of the routing and remote access service (RRAS) add-on for Windows NT Server 4.0. PPTP and how it can be used to access an SBS 4.5 system remotely will be covered in detail in Chapter 27.

When PPTP is configured properly to work with Proxy Server, SBS 4.5 allows incoming PPTP sessions from the Internet. PPTP is inherently very secure because all data is encrypted within a tunnel. If your small business client will be using PPTP, you need to open up the port on the firewall by selecting the PPTP option on the Configure Firewall Settings page in ICW. See Figure 18-14 on the next page. This will give inbound Internet users access to virtual private networking through PPTP.

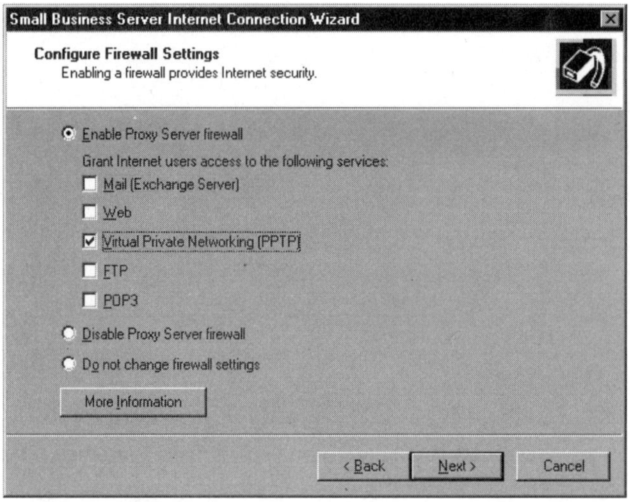

Figure 18-14
Enable inbound PPTP on the Configure Firewall Settings page.

Assessing the Proxy Server Defaults

While you're reviewing the ICW Configure Firewall Settings page, let's take a closer look at how this part of ICW can modify the Proxy Server default values. The page has three basic options:

- Enable Proxy Server Firewall

- Disable Proxy Server Firewall

- Do Not Change Firewall Settings

These settings affect only inbound access to the server. Selecting any options on this list won't affect clients' abilities to get out on the Internet for various services.

The second option, Disable Proxy Server Firewall, should be selected only if you consider yourself the be-all, end-all guru of firewall and Internet security. And even then, you should sleep on it before disabling the Proxy Server firewall. Selecting this option is akin to parking a brand new Porsche in a bad neighborhood with the keys in the ignition and a big sign on the windshield that screams out, "Steal me...Please!" Don't make breaking into your clients network easy for the hackers. At the bare minimum, make sure you select Enable Proxy Server Firewall.

The third option, Do Not Change Firewall Settings, assumes that you've already run ICW or made equivalent configuration changes directly to the Proxy Server Properties pages and don't want to mess with perfection.

The first option, Enable Proxy Server Firewall, merits the most attention. Selecting this option ensures that packet filtering is enabled. This blocks users from outside the SBS network from accessing the network.

The five check boxes underneath Enable Proxy Server Firewall allow inbound access. Be careful. By opening up ports on the firewall, you're allowing inbound traffic from the Internet. The types of inbound access include:

- **Mail (Exchange Server) (port 25)**—Select this if your small business client is using Exchange Server for Internet e-mail. Opening up port 25 allows the ISP to exchange e-mail with the Exchange Server IMS.

- **Web (ports 80 and 443)**—Open these ports only if you're doing your own Web hosting. This is relatively rare for a small business client and usually relevant only if there is a full-time Internet access connection.

- **Virtual Private Networking (PPTP) (port 1723)**—Use this for secure tunneling into the server for remote access. Usually it's relevant only if a full-time Internet access connection is used.

- **FTP (ports 20 and 21)**—Use this for *inbound* FTP access. It's usually relevant only if a full-time Internet access connection is used. This option has nothing to do with *outbound* FTP access from clients on the SBS 4.5 network.

- **POP3 (port 110)**—Use this for *inbound* POP3 access. This is a very rare configuration for a small business client and is usually relevant only if a full-time Internet access connection is used. This option has nothing to do with *outbound* POP3 access from clients on the SBS 4.5 network.

Fine-Tuning Proxy Server Settings

Once SBS 4.5 is installed and user accounts are created, you can use the Internet Access Wizard and User Access Wizard to set permissions for each user. These wizards in turn create the appropriate behind the scenes permissions on Proxy Server.

Tip

If your small business client is particularly concerned about appropriate use of company resources, the client can also buy Proxy Server plug-ins that keep restriction lists up to date. Restriction lists help to prevent users from accessing offensive and inappropriate Web sites. To learn more about third-party solutions for Proxy Server, see the Proxy Server Web site at *www.microsoft.com/proxy*. When contacting the ISV, also confirm that the plug-in has been tested with SBS 4.5.

You might also want to set up alerting to help you spot hacker attempts to break into SBS 4.5 network. Alerting is configured on the Alerting tab on the Security dialog box for the Web Proxy Service Properties. See Figure 18-15.

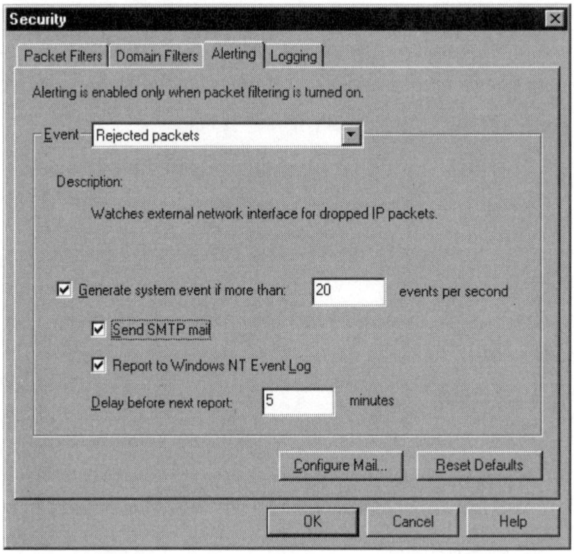

Figure 18-15

Set up alerting for Proxy Server intrusion attempts.

Tip

Chapter 23 drills down on testing the firewall.

You can also explicitly list the domains that users can access or are blocked from accessing. This is configured through the Domain Filters tab on the Security dialog box for the Web Proxy Server Properties.

Tip

For more technical details on Proxy Server, see the Microsoft Proxy Server documentation. This HTML-based help can be accessed from the Microsoft Proxy Server program group on the Start menu of the SBS 4.5 system.

Customizing Proxy Server Logging

Examining and customizing the Proxy Server logs is often useful. SBS 4.5 includes several standard reports that are accessible by clicking More Tasks on the SBS Console and then opening the Manage Internet Access page. Clicking Generate Internet Reports takes you to Online Guide with hyperlinks to ASP-driven reports, which are displayed in Internet Explorer 5.0. Figure 18-16 shows one such report, the Activity by Hour report.

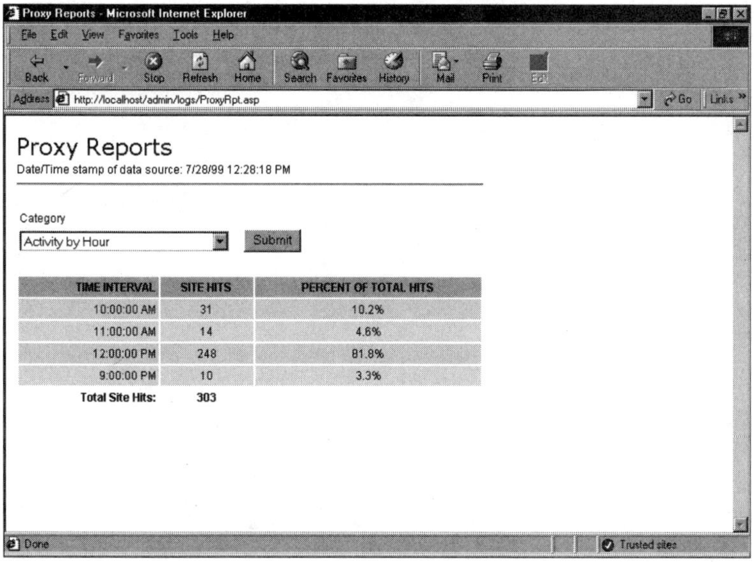

Figure 18-16
The Activity by Hour report is one of several reports you can generate.

Proxy Server logging is customized on the Logging tab on the Web Proxy Service Properties page. Take special care not to change the log file location because this is tied into the reports preconfigured for SBS 4.5. For details on customizing the logging, see Microsoft Proxy Server documentation.

Monitoring usage of Internet access tends to be a pretty sensitive issue for most small businesses. Chapter 10 covered how you can help your small business client craft a company e-mail and Internet usage policy. Your configuration choices should be made in consideration of the guidelines developed by your small business client.

In July 1999, I wrote a set of case studies for *Windows NT Magazine* on how three different small businesses were using SBS 4.0. One of the organizations discussed, the town of Spring Hill, Tennessee (home of the General Motors Saturn Corporation), needed to make sure the town's employees were appropriately using Internet access resources.

At the time I wrote the article, town employees on the SBS 4.0 network had Internet access through Proxy Server 1.0 and a dial-on-demand ISDN 128 Kbps connection. At the client's direction, SBS VAP Jeff Cate of PC Serv in Nashville, Tennessee, configured Proxy Server for user access security and detailed logging so that administrators could monitor Web browsing to ensure appropriate use of the town's resources. So in the end, Proxy Server logging gave the town administrator and citizens the confidence to know that the users on the SBS 4.5 network were complying with the town's policy on Internet usage.

Tip

That SBS 4.0 case study article can be found on the *Windows NT Magazine* Web site at *www.winntmag.com*.

Web Publishing Issues

Now that you've navigated through maze of ISP options, Proxy Server, and Internet access issues, I'll round out Chapter 18 by shifting attention to Web site publishing.

When you reach the ICW Configure Internet Domain Name page, you'll see this option: I Want To Use The Web Publishing Wizard. Selecting this option opens the ICW Configure Web Site Information page. You'll need the following information to proceed:

- Web page URL
- Web posting URL (usually an FTP site)
- Web posting account name (*usually* not the same as the Internet access or POP3 account)
- Password (and confirm password)

Configuring FrontPage 98

FrontPage 98 is included with SBS 4.5, but it's not installed by default. To install FrontPage 98 on a client, run the setup.exe program in the FrontPg folder on SBS 4.5 CD 2. Once a Web site is created, posting the site to an ISP with the Publish button will work transparently through Proxy Server 2.0. SBS 4.5 includes a wizard that copies the Web site content from the staging site to the live site at the ISP.

Tip

The SBS Console Online Guide also has instructions on how to install FrontPage.

Using the Web Publishing Wizard

The Small Business Server Web Publishing Wizard was created specifically for SBS and is different than using the Publish button in FrontPage 98. To access the Small Business Server Web Publishing Wizard, click More Tasks on the SBS Console, then open the Manage Internet Access page and click Publish On The Internet. See Figure 18-17.

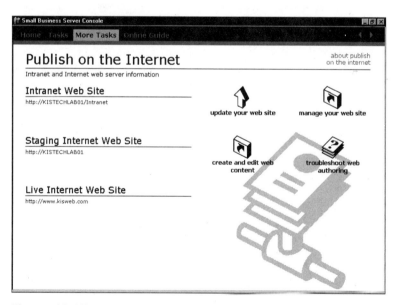

Figure 18-17

The Publish On The Internet page.

The Small Business Server Web Publishing Wizard uses outbound FTP through the Proxy Server to post Web site content from the staging site to the live site at the ISP. The staging site on an SBS 4.5 system is located in \InetPub\WWWroot. The idea behind having a staging site is that your small business client can review content before posting it live to the Web. When the content is ready to be posted, simply click Update Your Web Site and follow the Web Publishing Wizard's instructions.

The Bottom Line

A tremendous amount of detail goes into planning how your small business client will deal with Internet access, Web browsing, e-mail, and Web site publishing. In this chapter, you were introduced to ISP selection techniques and how ICW can help you configure modems, routers, and broadband devices for Internet access. In addition, the chapter looked at how to fine tune Proxy Server for customized Internet access and how to start publishing your client's Web site. Chapter 26 continues looking at Internet access and how it applies to connecting the SBS 4.5 network and Exchange Server 5.5 to Internet e-mail.

Chapter 19

Preparing for Disasters Before They Happen

Just because small businesses are small doesn't mean they're immune from big data disasters. Even small businesses have mission critical applications running on their PCs and networks. Often lacking full-time on-site IT staff, many small businesses are substantially more vulnerable to full-blown IT disasters than their Fortune 1000 counterparts. As smaller form factors on higher capacity hard disk drives continue to become more prevalent and data is more concentrated, disaster recovery planning becomes more important than ever.

This chapter begins Part 5, which is focused on testing the installation and training your clients. I'll pause between the immediate post-installation tasks (the subject of Part 4) and further growth opportunities (the subject of Part 6) to show you how to prepare a disaster recovery assessment (Chapter 19), provide training for the internal guru and end users (Chapter 20), jump start Office 2000 automation (Chapter 21), set the stage for regular software maintenance (Chapter 22), and test the backup, uninterruptible power supply (UPS), and firewall solution (Chapter 23).

Like the rest of this book, this chapter shows how to provide world-class reliability on a small business–friendly budget with ease of use for the internal guru. Bear in mind though, the greatest disaster recovery planning threat to small businesses often isn't the potential for a disaster to occur, but rather the massive denial by small business owners that a disaster could happen.

As you'll see throughout this chapter, you can't protect against every possible risk. Rather, your goal should be to work with the small business owner, internal guru, and other managers to develop a plan for disaster recovery that covers as many potential problems as possible.

Asking the Right Open-Ended Questions

As you work toward convincing small business owners that disaster recovery planning must be a priority now, you'll need to develop a short set of questions that gets them thinking seriously about the issue.

VAPs for Microsoft BackOffice Small Business Server often attend seminars that are sponsored by independent software vendors (ISVs) and hardware and peripheral vendors and that focus on topics such as disaster recovery, virus containment, power protection, and tape backup solutions. In this context, you're likely to hear the usual platitudes and marketing hype, such as:

- "You'll find only two types of small businesses—those who've experienced an IT disaster and those who will."

- "Small businesses without a sound backup and disaster recovery procedure never fully recover."

- "Small businesses without a sound recovery plan are likely to go out of business within months following a data disaster."

Regardless of whether you espouse the statistics, case studies, media dramatization, and traditional sales pitches, ignoring basic disaster recovery planning is very dangerous to your small business clients and to you. Think about it. If one of your small business clients were to experience extreme financial distress because of a lack of proper planning, where would this leave your firm? To get your small business clients to consider the ramifications, pose some of the following questions:

- If your employees were unable to get into your facility for several days, what are the most critical jobs and tasks that would need to be performed immediately?

- Do you have a disaster recovery coordinator, team, and plan?

- Does everyone on the disaster recovery team have a copy of the plan both at his or her desk and at home? Do employees have a list of home phone numbers and addresses for key personnel both at their desks and at home?

- Is a complete inventory of your hardware, software, and network configuration stored off site?

- Do you keep basic spare hardware parts on site to minimize downtime? Are hot or warm spares ready for critical hardware?

- Do you have an off-site location that could serve as the command center and temporary workplace in the event of an emergency?

- Who decides whether an event is a disaster? How should key staff and vendors be notified in the event of a disaster?

Procrastinating Can Be Deadly

As your small business client's virtual IT director, you need to impart a sense of urgency. While you can allow a client to put a Web site overhaul, an accounting software upgrade, or a server RAM upgrade on the back burner, disaster recovery planning shouldn't be postponed.

In fact, working with your small business clients to identify their specific vulnerabilities and to take concrete steps beforehand should be considered mission critical by your clients. While each small business has unique requirements, procrastination can be a serious threat to the longevity of your client. Disasters are sudden mishaps, certainly not events that show up on anyone's calendar. Lots of things can go wrong. Working with your small business client's designated disaster recovery coordinator, often the internal guru, you'll need to identify as many of these risks as possible and plan for them.

Types of Disasters with Natural Causes

Because of the enormous media attention, disasters resulting from natural causes are quite familiar to most small business owners. Natural disasters include:

- Earthquakes

- Fires

- Floods

- Hurricanes

- Lightning storms

- Tornadoes

- Typhoons

In reviewing these risks, note that certain areas of the United States and parts of world tend to be more prone to certain natural disasters than others. For example, most people are aware that California gets more than its fair share of earthquakes. Florida always seems to be preparing for or recovering from a big hurricane.

Experienced First Hand in the Field

Just like most novice SBS VAPs and small business clients, I used to think that most of my small business clients, both in central New Jersey and at the Jersey shore, weren't really in a high risk category for most potential natural disasters.

Although I advocated and practiced reasonably extensive disaster recovery planning precautions from a network standpoint, I never thought in a million years that one of my clients would be caught in a tornado. I always thought of tornadoes as something that happened more in the Midwest in the United States or in the movies like the 1996 movie *Twister*.

That was, of course, until the office roof for one of my small business clients was peeled off like the top from a sardine can during a very isolated tornado and rainstorm in the fall of 1998. Their entire office was flooded and the client's server, network printer, and several laptops and other office machines were drenched. Within hours of the accident, my client became very serious about replacing the Microsoft Windows 95 peer-to-peer network, which was at the time hanging on by a thread, with a more fault-tolerant SBS 4.0 server-class system, DDS-3 tape drive, mirrored hard disk drives, and an intelligent UPS.

Types of Disasters with People Causes

Besides disasters caused by weather or similar natural causes described above, many disasters are caused by people, various types of negligence, or building infrastructure failures. Examples of these types of disasters include:

- A flood in the computer room caused by a burst pipe or fire sprinkler over the server

Tip

If you find a water pipe in the computer room, have the pipe labeled for easy shutoff. You can also have your client invest in a water detector alarm, sold in many hardware stores for as little $5 to $10. Keep plastic tarps on hand to cover a server during an emergency.

- Huge temperature fluctuations in the computer room (or excessive humidity) caused by a malfunctioning or improperly programmed thermostat or other climate control system
- Cleaning supplies or other corrosive materials that leak or explode in the computer room
- Power outage (brownouts, blackouts) caused by downed power lines and utility grid failures
- Phone line outage caused by downed phone lines or central office switch failure

Tip

Many phone line outages and corresponding network outages are caused by utility companies and other contractors digging with a backhoe in the area. You'll often see accidental cuts in critical fiber optic or copper cables that feed phone service for an entire section of the city.

- Sabotage of network resources due to a lack of physical, internal, or Internet security (This can take the form of outside or inside hacking.)

Tip

Outside hacking can be easily thwarted many times by tracking failed dial-up attempts or failed inbound Internet attempts on the firewall. As an SBS VAP, you can monitor the logs produced by Event Viewer and Server Status Tool (SST) for potential red flags. To combat inside hacking, each person should have his or her own logon and password, which should have a minimum length and be composed of both numbers and letters of mixed case. Strong passwords are enforced through User Manager for Domains. In addition, all relevant user accounts should be disabled immediately after or, better yet, before someone is terminated or leaves the company.

- Theft and burglary due to a lack of physical security

- Collapse of the ceiling, physically damaging server hardware

- Riots

- Bombings

- Administrator or end user error, such as accidental deletion of critical files or data, typos during configuration of critical components, incorrect editing in the registry, or improper configuration of the system

- Inexperienced personnel in administrator roles

- Administrator account being used for something other than administrative purposes

- Someone tripping over the power cord due to a lack of physical security

- System powered down at the wrong time (that is, before all data is written to hard disk drives)

- Failure to back up system adequately before an upgrade that fails (no change management procedures)

- Server out of hard disk drive space

Tip

To keep tabs on server hard disk drive space, configure appropriate Performance Monitor alerts and SST reports. This topic is covered further in Chapter 25.

Types of Disasters with Technology Limitations as the Cause

In addition to disasters stemming from natural and human causes, small businesses are also highly susceptible to disasters due to technology limitations, such as the following:

- Failure of hardware components on the network, such as a server power supply, router, hard disk drive, or SCSI controller

- Lack of fault-tolerant RAID hard disk drives

- Failed hard disk drive in a RAID array not replaced promptly enough

Note

RAID, which is short for a redundant array of independent drives, is supported by Microsoft Windows NT Server 4.0 and SBS 4.5 through mirroring and duplexing (RAID 1) and stripe sets with parity (RAID 5).

- Data corruption
- Virus contamination because antivirus software isn't installed or isn't configured properly, or engine or signature files haven't been kept current

Tip

Antivirus software on an SBS 4.5 network needs to protect the server, e-mail files, firewall, and client PCs. This is discussed further in Chapters 22 and 23.

Sounding the Call to Action

Now that you've gotten your small business clients to ponder some of the above-mentioned causes of small business disasters, remind them that in most cases no one can predict or prevent a disaster. You can, however, plan for how you'll deal with different scenarios. That's what this chapter is all about.

Every disaster recovery plan needs to begin with a goal, which can be expressed in two or three succinct bullet points. The specific goals will inevitably vary by company but should focus on getting your small business client back to normal as quickly as possible. Once the brief goals are finalized, your client should consider these questions:

- What is the client's core business?
- What is your client trying to protect against?
- What are the recovery objectives?
- What kind of staff, supplies, equipment, hardware, software, and telecommunications lines would be needed to meet your client's most immediate commitments? (Tier 1)
- How would your client continue to do business during and after a disaster? (Tier 2)
- How does the company get back to normal? (Tier 3)

- How dependent is your small business client on its data and SBS 4.5 network? Do any other major IT resources (mainframe, UNIX, Novell, Macintosh, and so forth) need to be protected?

- How will your client deal with vendors and pay bills during the disaster? (Vendors deliver the goods and services the client needs to stay in business.)

- How will your client service customers? (Customers provide the income and profit to pay the bills.) How transparent will the disaster be to customers? How will your client invoice for products shipped or services rendered? How will your client track billing and receivables? What can your client do to make sure customers don't lose confidence?

- How will your client retain their employees? (Employees are crucial to producing the product or service your client provides.) How will your client pay employees? What steps need to be taken to protect the safety of employees? How will your client keep its most mission critical employees productive?

- What kind of data, IT resources, and records need to be protected? If nothing else, your small business client needs to protect data for regulatory, legal, and compliance reasons. How would your client prepare a corporate tax return, survive an audit, or defend against a lawsuit if all the company paper and electronic business records were unavailable or destroyed?

- How will your client generate financial statements to keep the banking relationship and lines of credit intact? (Immediately following the disaster, your client will likely experience unprecedented cash flow challenges.)

- How is disaster recovery planning integrated into all facets of the company? Is it discussed in the employee handbook, job descriptions, new hire orientation, annual reviews, and meetings? How often does the disaster recovery team meet to review and update the plan? Are disaster recovery instructions posted on company bulletin boards and in the computer room?

- Who will be in charge of communicating with the public, such as the media, customers, vendors, employees, employee families, regulators, or creditors? Have a checklist and phone script been developed for any conversations with the public? Is the person in charge of communicating with the public prepared to deal with potentially hysterical family members of employees if he or she happens to be the first one who tells the family members about the disaster?

To help you jump-start your small business client's disaster recovery planning, take a look at the "SBS 4.5 Disaster Recovery Planning Template," a Word template, included on the CD-ROM with this book. See Figure 19-1.

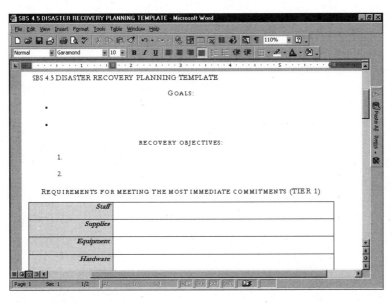

Figure 19-1
"SBS 4.5 Disaster Recovery Planning Template."

If you feel that you're technically inadequate to assist in disaster recovery planning or you're not prepared to do this for clients from a business operations standpoint, perhaps you'll need to involve a consultant who specializes in disaster recovery planning. These consultants' practices typically encompass technology, as well as all the people issues, financial and operational matters, and business processes. This chapter isn't designed to be a substitute for retaining a disaster recovery planning expert. As your small business client's virtual IT director, however, you need to stay in the loop as a member of each your client's disaster recovery planning teams. You might even want to partner with a disaster recovery consultant in your area.

Tip

For tips on partnering, see Chapter 6.

Understanding the Real Cost of Downtime

Many times small business owners will put disaster recovery planning on the back burner because they have yet to comprehend the cost of downtime. They haven't thought through the implications and ramifications of various disaster scenarios. How valuable is your client's data? Would they go out of business if they were without it either temporarily or permanently?

Tip

Chapter 15 covers a simple formula you can use to determine your small business client's hourly and daily cost of downtime. This coverage was adapted from a VAPVoice column I wrote for Microsoft Direct Access in April 1999. A copy of the article, "Be the Hero," an HTML document, is on the CD-ROM with this book for your convenience.

Small business owners who remember the pre-PC days will usually claim, "Well, if we had to, we could always go back to paper and pencil." To which you should add a healthy dose of skepticism with an "Oh, really?" In reality, even the smallest of small businesses have become enormously dependent on information technology. Business transactions move much faster than they ever did even five or ten years ago.

If employees really could temporarily revert to doing their jobs manually if they had to, this is a definite plus. Make sure, however, that your client has procedures and forms developed and field-tested for this contingency. This type of emergency paper processing should encompass the most critical software applications and be used as a stopgap measure until the mission critical applications are restored.

The budget for disaster recovery planning is usually directly proportional to how serious a problem downtime really is. So in the early stages of disaster recovery planning when assessing the real cost of downtime, make sure to find out:

- What are the restore and recovery expectations?
- What's the maximum tolerable downtime for various software applications, network services, and crucial business functions?
- What kind of financial loss is tolerable?

Building a Fortress Around SBS 4.5

Now that you're armed with an understanding of some of the big picture issues surrounding disaster recovery planning, I'll delve into some of the more technical aspects of protecting your SBS-dependent small business client.

Tape Backup Solution

People have a strong tendency with a tape backup solution to set it and forget it. While the tape backup solution must be highly automated in order to ensure jobs are launched both consistently and correctly, installing the drive and keeping your fingers crossed is risky. As the SBS VAP, you'll need to train the internal guru to operate the tape drive, supervise the guru's ongoing activities, spot-check the backup with regular restore tests, and constantly monitor the logs.

Unfortunately, like all disaster recovery planning, monitoring the tape backup solution generally isn't a priority until something goes wrong. If your customer is relying on the data stored on an SBS 4.5 system to run the business, you must keep tabs regularly on the tape backup solution.

Tip

Chapter 23 explains how to test the tape backup solution. Then Chapter 25 shows how to incorporate regular monitoring of the tape backup solution into the proactive maintenance plan.

Assessing Needs

To make sure the tape backup solution covers all bases for the small business client, you need first to take a few steps back and assess the client's tape backup needs and the current tape backup practices. Some relevant questions include:

- What types of data need to be backed up?
- Are all user data files backed up daily?

Tip

Users don't always keep all their data on the server. Make sure you examine whether locally stored data needs to be backed up.

- How much of this data is there today? How much will there be in 12 to 18 months?

- What's the backup window? (When are the server and network at their lowest utilization points?)

- How many different tapes are used? (What's the rotation plan?)

- Who performs the tape backup jobs? What about the restore jobs? How are the tape backup jobs supervised? What controls are in place to make sure the tape backup jobs are done according to the established plan?

- Who's the secondary tape backup operator, in the event the primary person is unavailable? Are these responsibilities part of the primary and secondary persons' formal job descriptions?

- What precautions are taken to guard the tapes against tampering or outright theft?

- How often are tapes permanently archived? How often are tapes removed from the rotation (to prevent the tape from wearing out and becoming unreliable)?

- Are tapes stored off site? Where? Is that location physically secure? How do the tapes get the off-site location? Who's responsible for sending the tapes off site, verifying that they've arrived, and retrieving the tapes? Can the off-site tapes be retrieved outside of business hours? How long does it take for the tapes to get between the main and off-site locations and vice versa?

- What's the turnaround time on a restore request if the tape is still on site? What if it's already off site?

- Are the backup jobs verified? Are results logged? Are the logs spot-checked to make sure they're accurate and complete? Who's responsible for investigating any irregularities in the log? How often are the logs examined? Who's supposed to be made aware of backup successes and failures (management, end users)?

- How often are individual file and folder test restores done? How often are individual mailbox test restores done? How often are full volume and full information store test restores done?

- Who configures and monitors the automated job backup schedule?

- If the tape backup solution fails due to a hardware error, how quickly can the hardware be replaced?

Windows NT Backup

Although you can choose one of several third-party alternatives for backing up data—two of which will be described in the next section—you can also use Windows NT Backup (NTBackup.exe), which is included in SBS 4.5. You can learn how to access this application by clicking Back Up And Restore Data on the Tasks page in the SBS Console. See Figure 19-2.

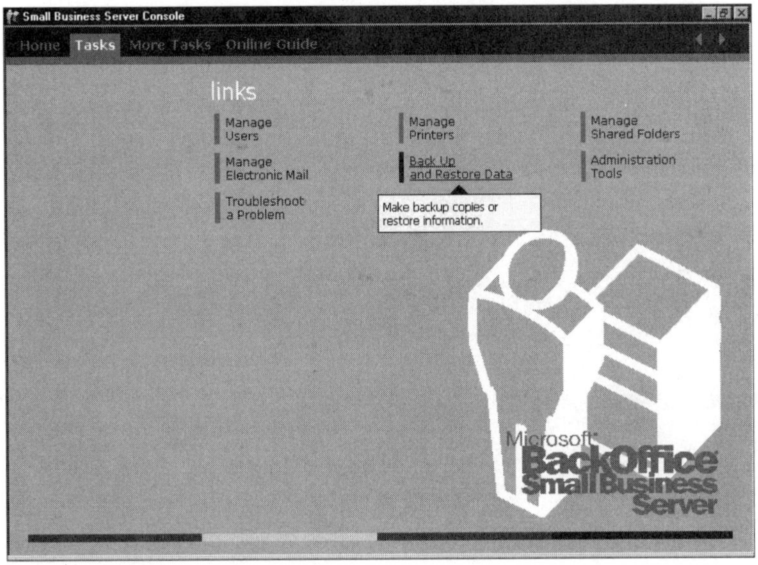

Figure 19-2

Launch Windows NT Backup from the Tasks page on the SBS Console.

Tip

Chapter 23 shows how to test various backup and restore scenarios using Windows NT Backup. Then Chapter 25 covers how to incorporate the tape backup logs into the proactive maintenance program.

Chapter 13 showed how you can configure the Scheduled Task Wizard to support unattended tape backup jobs with Windows NT Backup. In order to make optimal use of this capability, you'll want to create a batch file with command line switches for ntbackup.exe. To learn more about using these switches, you'll want to review two Microsoft Knowledge Base articles:

- **KB article Q162972**—"Troubleshooting Tape Backup Issues in Windows NT"

- **KB article Q152313**—"Using the AT Backup Command with Microsoft Exchange"

Tip

KB article Q152313 is a great reference for incorporating switches into the automated Windows NT Backup routine. But with SBS 4.5, the Scheduled Task Wizard has supplanted the AT/WinAt interface for job scheduling.

In addition to being able to back up OS files, application files, and user data files, you can run an online backup of the Exchange Information Store and Directory using an extension to Windows NT Backup that Microsoft Exchange Server 5.5 installs. See Figure 19-3.

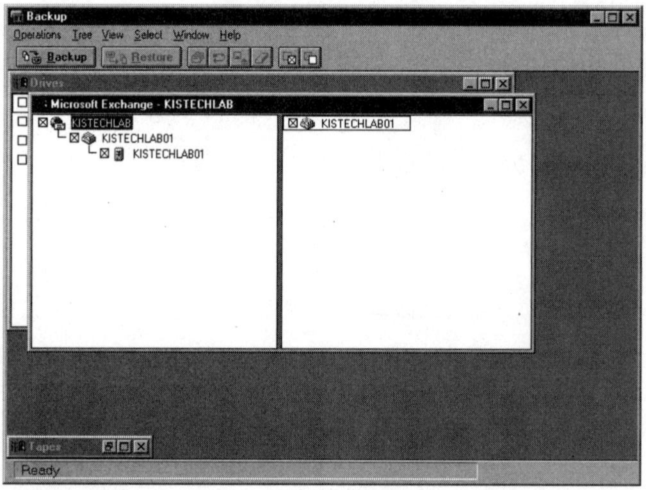

Figure 19-3
Use Windows NT Backup to launch an online backup of the Exchange Information Store and Directory.

Note

An online backup means that the backup can be run with all Exchange Server Windows NT services started (that is, with users connected and Exchange Server running). An offline backup or file-base backup requires all Exchange Server Windows NT services be stopped for the duration of the backup job.

Running an online backup of Exchange Server through Windows NT Backup provides an additional secondary benefit. The way the Exchange Server database is designed, requests to modify the Information Store and Directory are first recorded in transaction logs. This is designed to preserve transactional integrity in the event of system difficulty.

Note

If you don't use the Exchange window in Windows NT Backup or stop all Exchange Server Windows NT services, running an ordinary file-based Windows NT backup won't back up Exchange Server properly. On a recent trip out to Redmond, one of the SBS program managers recounted a sad tale of how one of his friends fell into this trap. From that moment on, we both vowed to make sure SBS VAPs everywhere learn how to back up Exchange Server 5.5 properly on SBS 4.5.

By default, Exchange Server is configured to let these log files accumulate indefinitely. When you run an online backup of Exchange Server using Windows NT Backup, however, the transaction logs that have been written to the Information Store and Directory are truncated. This prevents the transaction logs from consuming all available hard disk drive space. If transaction logs aren't pruned, they have the potential to crash the SBS 4.5 system by completely filling up the hard disk drive volume.

Tip

The third-party backup solutions described below are also fully capable of performing online backups and truncating the transaction logs.

If your small business clients are running Microsoft SQL Server 7.0 and using Windows NT Backup, you'll need a slightly different backup strategy. Although Windows NT Backup is Exchange Server aware, it isn't SQL Server aware. Windows NT Backup can't perform an online backup of SQL Server, although the third-party backup solutions discussed below can. In order to back up a SQL Server database using Windows NT Backup, you need first either to stop all SQL Server Windows NT services to perform an offline backup or use SQL Server 7.0 Enterprise Manager to do an online back up to disk. Then you can back up that file using Windows NT Backup.

Note

Windows NT Backup can back up the registry only on the SBS 4.5 server. It can't back up registries on remote Windows NT Workstation 4.0 or Windows NT Server 4.0 systems.

Third-Party Backup Solutions

While many tape backup software applications bear a Microsoft BackOffice logo, two products in particular have been designed specifically for SBS.

Tip

Always make sure each tape is clearly labeled with the date (or day in the rotation, such as Wednesday-B), computer name, and type of backup (full, incremental, and so forth).

Backup Exec Small Business Server Suite for Windows NT version 7.3

Backup Exec Small Business Server Suite for Windows NT version 7.3, which is from ISV VERITAS (*www.veritas.com*), includes these features:

- Online backup for Exchange Server, SQL Server, and Microsoft Internet Information Server (IIS)

- Brick-level backup and restore of Exchange Server (one mailbox at a time, as opposed to just backing up and restoring the entire Information Store with all mailboxes)

- Scans that detect and clean viruses before data is written to tape, preventing viruses from spreading during a restore

- Backup of client workstations

- Disaster recovery module that recovers an SBS system using three customized SBS boot disks, SBS CD 1, a special fourth disk for intelligent disaster recovery, and the latest full tape backup. (This module restores data quickly to the point of the last full backup without having to first reinstall the Windows NT Server 4.0 portion of SBS.)

Tip

Many small business owners will resist sending the tapes off site, insisting that the tapes are secure in the company's fireproof safe. While this sounds good in theory, an ordinary fireproof safe designed for protecting business papers usually won't protect the data on the tape. During a fire, the tape media will appear on the surface to be physically unharmed; the data on the tape, however, is often damaged beyond recognition. While a fireproof safe certainly protects against theft or misappropriation, don't depend on it to protect the data during a fire unless you have proof to the contrary. Some safe manufacturers offer "media safes," which are specifically designed for protecting magnetic media by keeping the internal temperature below 125 °F during a fire. Sentry (*www.sentrysafe.com*) is one such manufacturer.

ARCserve Storage Suite for Microsoft BackOffice Small Business Server

ARCserve Storage Suite for Microsoft BackOffice Small Business Server, which is from Computer Associates (*www.cai.com*), includes features that are, at the most basic level, nearly identical to Backup Exec Small Business Server Suite for Windows NT version 7.3.

Tip

Windows NT Backup can't perform a brick-level backup and restore of individual Exchange Server mailboxes. Without a third-party solution, restoring an individual mailbox requires that you first restore the Information Store to a spare Exchange Server system. This process can be somewhat cumbersome, even if you, as the VAP, bring a spare SBS 4.5 system on site during the emergency. For details, see the Exchange Server Web site at *www.microsoft.com/exchange*.

Power Protection Solution

Just as small business owners often vehemently resist installing a business-class tape backup solution, they often are in denial of power problems as well. If you stumble on a particularly stubborn small business owner who can't understand why the computers would need uninterruptible power supplies (UPSs), try saying something like this, "I see you have six applications open on your PC and twelve people connected to the server. What would happen if I yanked the power cord out of the wall right now without warning you to first save your files?" This usually drives the message home.

Why should small business owners and SBS VAPs be so paranoid about protecting against power disturbances? At the most basic level, utility companies can't provide electric power consistently and cleanly enough for PC-related hardware. Ultimately SBS VAPs and small business clients need a strategy to compensate for this lack of power reliability. They need to protect their hardware and, even more importantly, their irreplaceable data. As small business clients become increasingly dependent on their SBS network, making sure they can cope with utility companies that are stretched to the max with providing electricity is more important than ever.

Tip

Ironically, on the day I was editing this chapter last August, *The Wall Street Journal* ran an article titled, "U.S. Power Grid Is Put to Test by Rising Demand."

Power disturbances can take many forms, such as spikes, surges, sags, brownouts, and blackouts. While some power disturbances are beyond your client's control, some can be prevented. For example, in a small business I often see outlets overloaded with surge protectors piggybacked with more surge protectors. Not only is this practice a potential fire hazard, it diminishes the effectiveness of the surge protection.

Ascertaining which outlets are on which circuits is also important. For example, if a single outlet is on a dedicated 20-amp circuit, that outlet can provide a lot more power than if six outlets are on a 20-amp circuit. If you have any doubts about your small business client's electrical wiring, insist that they have a licensed electrician come on site to do an evaluation and perhaps set up a dedicated circuit for the server and related peripherals. A UPS can only go so far. If the client's electrical wiring is a mess, you'll have hours and hours of frustration later.

Tip

In evaluating whether a small business needs a UPS, look at how much run time is required. Depending on the need, a UPS might not be an adequate solution. Perhaps the small business needs a generator as well. To evaluate small business power protection needs properly, look at how much battery backup power is needed. Is it a matter of minutes, hours, or days?

To compensate for fluctuations in power, a UPS constantly monitors line voltage and trims any overages accordingly, while boosting power as needed. Because these changes in voltage are often incredibly fast, the UPS must be able to change over to battery extremely quickly to avoid data loss. In fact, often the difference between an entry-level UPS and a server-grade UPS is the transfer time between utility power and battery.

Tip

UPS batteries often wear out after three or four years. Be on the lookout for this so you and your small business clients aren't caught off guard. Red flags are raised whenever I do a site survey with a new client who has a NetWare 3.x server installed five or six years ago and who is still using a UPS model that hasn't been manufactured in years.

A server-grade UPS needs to have unattended shutdown capability. Through a hardware interface, generally implemented through a serial port, the UPS is in constant online communication with power monitoring software on the server. The unattended shutdown capability is designed to kick in when the server has been on battery for a preconfigured amount of time. Since servers are almost always running 7 × 24 and small businesses rarely have around-the-clock, on-site IT support, the UPS needs a way to shut down the server gracefully when no one is available to perform the task manually.

A graceful shutdown goes a long way toward preventing data corruption and possible data loss associated with hard shutdowns. Although Windows NT Server 4.0 has native capabilities for limited interfacing with the UPS, most UPS vendors have their own software application that leverages the native NOS UPS services and also provides significantly enhanced functionality. An example of this is American Power Conversion's PowerChute *plus*, which was covered in Chapter 15. Figure 19-4 on the next page shows that the server is configured to shut down after the UPS has been on battery for 7 minutes (420 seconds).

Tip

Chapter 23 shows you how to put the UPS solution through rigorous testing to make sure it's as reliable as you believe it to be.

Most server-grade UPS units with power management software also provide detailed logging capabilities. Chapter 15 showed how you could integrate the event log from PowerChute *plus* into the batch of SST reports.

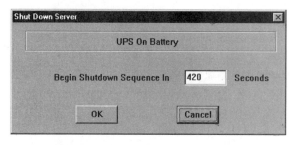

Figure 19-4

A UPS is configured for unattended shutdown.

What to Do When the UPS Shuts Down Immediately on Bootup of the SBS 4.5 System

During the SBS 4.5 bootup sequence, ntdetect.com sends a detection signal to each device attached to a port to find out what hardware is attached to that port. This normally doesn't cause a problem with printers, serial mouse devices, and external modems. Some UPSs that monitor serial ports, however, respond by turning off immediately.

To get around this problem, add the /NoSerialMice switch to the end of the relevant entry in the boot.ini file to disable COM port detection. For more information see KB article Q131976 in the Microsoft Knowledge Base.

Tip

Most UPS monitoring software applications will also periodically run a self-test on the UPS.

Figure 19-5 shows a sample from a PowerChute *plus* event log, listing the precise date, time, and magnitude of a spike and sag. This can be incredibly valuable for diagnosing a host of server problems. For example, I've noticed that servers with internal SCSI DDS-3 tape drives often have intermittent problems after unattended shutdowns from UPS units. The UPS event log allows me to pinpoint when the power disturbance occurred so I can narrow my troubleshooting efforts and determine whether the tape drive needs a firmware patch to fix a now easily identifiable problem.

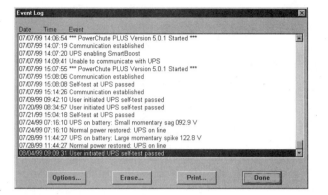

Figure 19-5

A UPS event log shows power disturbances and can help you track down problems.

Note

Most small businesses typically are in extremely poor shape when it comes to power protection. UPS vendors such as American Power Conversion (*www.apcc.com*) have detailed reseller materials on their Web sites to help you learn more about power protection. These materials include sizing matrices that help you identify the appropriate size of a UPS for specified equipment. Also, don't overlook the need for UPSs on workstations with valuable data, hubs, switches, and routers, and make sure to protect the data lines, including lines for analog modems, ISDN, PBX systems, and local area network (LAN) cabling.

Handling Logistics

Now that you know how to apply tape backup and power protection solutions to SBS 4.5 and understand why procrastination can be deadly, this chapter will look at what types of operational and logistics issues need to be considered in planning for disaster recovery.

Building a Warm Spare Server

Most small business owners will strongly resist the idea of investing in a second, fully configured SBS 4.5 server. After all, small business owners often need education on why a $499 consumer-oriented PC isn't meant to be used as a server. So how do you get your small business clients to conclude that they need a second server-class box? For some small businesses that aren't concerned at all about downtime, the point is moot. If the client doesn't mind the potential of being without the server, data, and applications for at least several days, a warm spare server definitely isn't required. For others, a warm spare server is mission critical.

Tip

If the warm spare server is constantly in an unstable state, such as having an open case and disconnected ribbon cables, it won't be much use in an emergency.

The cost of a warm spare server might seem high until weighed against the alternative of several days of lost orders that might cause irreparable damage to your client's reputation and bottom line. Some small business clients and SBS VAPs get around the need to have a truly redundant warm spare server by configuring a physically secure PC running Windows NT Workstation 4.0 with NTFS to replicate copies of the company and users shared folders on a spare hard disk drive or volume at least once daily. Although the core SBS 4.5 applications wouldn't be available until the server was replaced, at least employees could get to their personal data files.

Creative Ways to Provide a Low Budget Alternative to a Warm Spare Server

If a small business client doesn't want to spend or doesn't have the resources to spend on a warm spare server solution, consider alternatives. You could at least replicate Microsoft Office and other data files to a PC running Windows NT Workstation 4.0.

If your client wants to have SBS 4.5 actually running on the warm spare, you could take a recently retired desktop PC, add some RAM and perhaps a larger hard disk drive, and configure it for a less than optimal, but functional SBS 4.5 system to use in a pinch.

In addition, you might also want to use other recently retired PCs to set up clients on a small LAN at the hot site. Just make sure all the older hardware is Year 2000 compliant or else you could introduce unneeded problems at an inopportune time.

Tip

You can use the Scheduled Task Wizard to configure file copies between the SBS 4.5 system and a client workstation on the network.

If your small business client really wants a warm spare server, the data has to be replicated fairly regularly to be effective, generally at least once daily. In addition, the warm spare server can't be used as a test or production server if it's truly to be a warm spare, ready to be taken into action within a moment's notice with minimal IT intervention.

The warm spare server will have to meet minimum application requirements for SBS 4.5. To eliminate the potential for differences and last minute surprises from configuration or compatibility problems, the hardware should be nearly identical to the production server.

If your small business client is really serious about disaster recovery planning and feels that having to evacuate the office is a significant risk, the warm spare server should be kept at the designated off-site facility (that is, the hot site). In this case, incremental daily data replication would need to be done over a wide-area network (WAN), PPTP, or conventional RAS connection.

Preparing the Plan and Assigning Responsibilities

Each client's disaster recovery plan will be unique. It's developed as a result of thinking through the issues covered in this chapter and assessing the small business, as well as the owner's penchant for risk. Regardless of the measures taken, make sure the planning document is kept simple. (Remember the old keep it simple (KIS) principle.) The plan might be as simple as a detailed outline with bullet points, similar to "SBS 4.5 Disaster Recovery Planning Template," a Word template provided on the CD-ROM in the back of this book.

Ask yourself about what it would take for you to rebuild the organization for its most important business processes in 12 hours. Once you formulate the plan, you need to keep it current. When was the last time one of your client's LAN environments and business processes remained unchanged for more than a few months?

Tip

Encourage your small business clients to avoid analysis paralysis. Remind them that procrastination can be deadly. If it takes your client 18 months to finalize the plan, that's 18 months in which changes took place in the company that probably aren't reflected in the plan and 18 months in which the company went unprotected from potential disasters.

If your small business client is having a hard time getting the process started for a disaster recovery plan, questions you can pose to help your client include:

- Who decides that the business is in fact experiencing a disaster and activates the disaster recovery team and plan?

- Who needs to be notified of this decision and in what order should each person be notified? Who's on the phone chain in terms of employees, vendors, clients, and other parties? Does everyone on the disaster recovery team know what his or her roles are?

- What do the disaster recovery coordinator and team need to do as soon as they're on site? What's on the team's immediate task checklist? What happens if the primary person for an immediate task isn't available? Who is the backup? Are people cross-trained?

- Which software applications are mission critical to the company? Which data, fax, and voice lines need to be restored first? Who is responsible for calling the telephone company to activate remote call forwarding to the hot site during an emergency? How much of the plan relies on human intervention as opposed to automated processes?

- Have all departments within the company been consulted in developing the disaster recovery plan? (All too often, the plan has the danger of becoming IT-centric, without considering the impact on other parts of the company.)

- Which items required for mission critical functions have long lead times for ordering? Should any of these be ordered now and stored at the hot site?

- How current is the complete asset inventory of hardware, software, peripherals, telecommunications lines, and infrastructure? Which items in this inventory have a single point of failure?

Prearranging a Business Resumption Site

A business resumption site, also known as a hot site, is an alternate work site designed to be the location where your client's staff immediately relocates following a disaster and stays until their office or new permanent location is ready. The essential planning question becomes determining where your client and staff will meet if they can't get back into the office following the disaster.

The hot site should be a place that is easy to find and close enough to the area to be accessible, but far enough away from the office not to be subject to the same potential disaster. This is often a difficult decision because the convenience factor clearly has to be weighed against the risk. For some small businesses, the hot site can even be the owner's home. Others choose an easily reachable hotel or a branch office of the same company. Some additional issues to consider include:

- How will key personnel, that is, the disaster recovery team, get to the hot site? How will emergency travel reservations be made if necessary?

- How will transportation, meals, and accommodations be arranged? For many small businesses, this boils down to how to get cash quickly. (Remember, during a natural disaster where telecommunications infrastructure and power is lost, ATMs might not be available.)

- How will employees be notified if telecommunications infrastructure is affected? Is the employee contact list, as well as crucial vendor contact information, stored at the hot site? Contact information should include home, pager, and cell phone numbers, as well as home and e-mail addresses.

- Is ample telephone service available at the hot site to coordinate recovery efforts and serve as the command center? Can you get these phone numbers in advance to make sure that everyone who's internal to the client has them? In addition, make sure everyone who's internal to the client has easy-to-follow directions on how to get to the hot site. These documents should be prepared in advance. Employees should be instructed to keep a copy both in the office and at home.

Preparing Documentation for the Hot Site

First and foremost, the disaster recovery plan will never be carried out properly if the IT documentation is weak or nonexistent. In essence, standards and consistency need to be present; otherwise chaos will ensue. The documentation should include all relevant procedures and inventory. Documentation efforts also include making sure equipment and cables are labeled clearly ahead of time.

Tip

Many SBS VAPs use portable label makers such as the Brother P-Touch.

A typical SBS 4.5 disaster recovery documentation packet will include the following:

- Map of physical and logical layout of the server(s), clients, routers, hubs, and switches

- Naming convention instructions for users, computers, and shares

- Well-organized, well-understood folder and share structure

- Location of NOS, applications, and data folders on the server

- Internet Connection Wizard (ICW) settings, as configured in Chapter 18 (Often the best way to document these settings—which will generally include dial-up, router, or broadband connection configurations and e-mail settings—is by taking screen shots.)

- Server software and network configuration information, which should include a list of service packs and hot fixes applied for Windows NT Server 4.0 and BackOffice Server applications, the domain name and computer name, DHCP IP address scopes, protocol(s) in use, location of swap file, fault tolerance configuration, licensing, IP address, default gateway, and subnet mask for each NIC, and any dial-up or remote-access-service configuration details

- Server hardware configuration information, enumerating IRQ, DMA addresses, and I/O port settings (You can print a report listing this information from the Windows NT Diagnostics program under Administrative Tools. See Figure 19-6.)

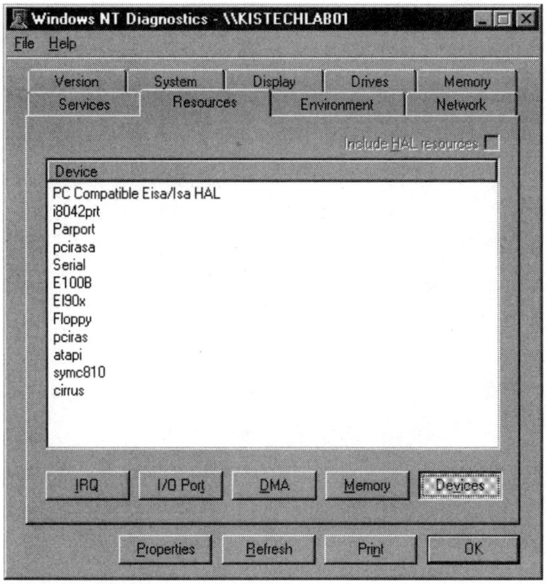

Figure 19-6

View and print the server hardware configuration with Windows NT Diagnostics.

- Server SCSI controller information, including brand, model, and BIOS firmware revision level, device driver version, configuration information, SCSI ID, and device description (You'll also want to note whether the server SCSI controller is internal or external and how devices are terminated. A diagram is often helpful as well.)

- Partition description listing what type of data is on each volume, whether the volume is FAT or NTFS (it should almost always be NTFS), the size of volume, and the assigned drive letter (An easy way to capture most of this information is by taking a screen shot of the Disk Administrator program under Administrative Tools. See Figure 19-7 on the next page.)

- Table listing daily tasks, periodic tasks with scheduled dates, and future tasks to be scheduled at a later date

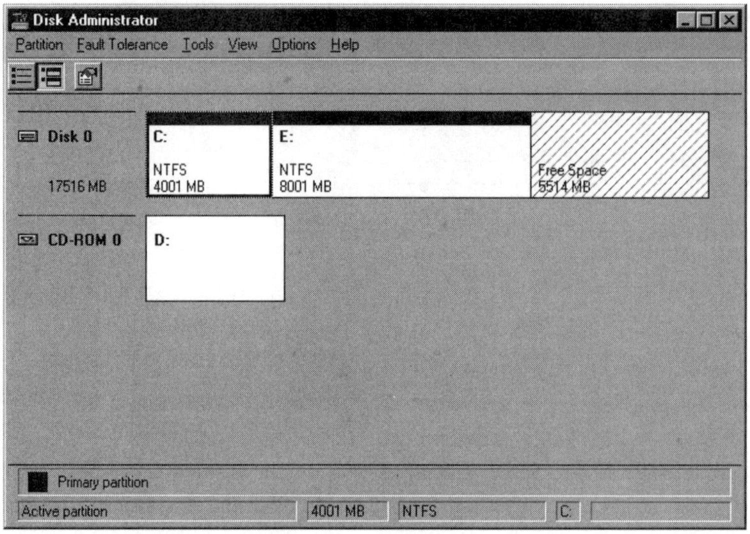

Figure 19-7

Document partitions on an SBS 4.5 system with Disk Administrator.

Other Content for the Hot Site Disaster Recovery Kit

In addition to the documentation requirements, the hot site also needs several other general items, including:

- The disaster recovery plan that you've designed with the client as a result of efforts stemming from this chapter

- The company employee manual

- Employee and vendor contact lists

- Bank statements

- Insurance policies

- Vendor agreements including preapproved emergency purchase orders with IT vendors and other suppliers

- Two-way radios and cellular phones

- Laptop with cellular fax modem

- At least one roll of quarters for pay phones

- Flashlight

- General office supplies such as paper, pens, stapler, and folders

- Temporary furniture, such as folding chairs and banquet tables

- Set of backup tapes from the most recent rotation

- NTFS boot disk and emergency repair disk (ERD), clearly labeled with the date of last update and computer name

- General office equipment such as a fax machine, phones, printers, UPS, and copier

Tip

When creating the ERD, make sure to run rdisk /s so that all of the registry keys are updated to the repair folder on the server and to the ERD. See Chapter 13 for instructions on how to prepare an NTFS boot disk and the ERD.

Note

The NTFS boot disk and ERD won't bring back data files. They're only used to jump start recovery efforts with the SBS 4.5 system when it won't boot. To recover, you still need a full verified tape backup. If the client has one of the third-party tape backup solutions (covered earlier in this chapter), you'll need the client's four startup disks and the SBS 4.5 CD 1 as well.

Testing and Maintaining the Disaster Recovery Plan

Once the plan has been developed and written up, you must test it. Testing is often the only way to uncover potential gaps in the plans. For example, many SBS VAPs and Fortune 1000 IT organizations spend a substantial amount of the recovery time gathering the required tools.

The testing is most effective when it's conducted without advanced notice, like a fire drill. In this scenario, some of the primary people for various tasks are likely to be out of the office, forcing the secondary people and cross-training issues to surface sooner rather later. By the end of the disaster rehearsal, you should be able to answer these questions:

- How long does it take to recover from a complete failure?

- Which tasks, responsibilities, and equipment were properly planned for? Which additional tasks, responsibilities, and equipment need to be added to the revised plan?

- Did any turf wars surface during the test? Does everyone know what his or her roles are?

As mentioned earlier, the disaster recovery plan likely will be outdated in a matter of weeks or months for a small business with an SBS 4.5 network. The disaster recovery coordinator needs to keep on top of revising the document and continually testing it. While the requirements for each small business will differ, the complete disaster recovery plan should reevaluated at least once a year, preferably two to four times a year. The chances of your client surviving the disaster increase tremendously when adequate preparation is taken.

The Bottom Line

While you can't anticipate every possible disaster, you need to encourage your small business client to take a thorough look at various circumstances that could arise. As an SBS VAP, you likely won't have the luxury of being able to specialize in disaster recovery planning. As your small business client's virtual IT department, your firm is probably staffed with well-rounded generalists, who perhaps have advanced expertise in a handful of areas. If your clients have more complex disaster recovery planning needs, don't be afraid to partner with a consultant who specializes in this area. At the end of the day, you want to make sure that your small business clients know what their recovery options are and how prepared they'd be to face various emergency scenarios.

Chapter 20

Providing Administrator and End User Training

Does your staff really want to get beeped every time a password needs to be reset at one of your small business client sites? As a Microsoft BackOffice Small Business Server VAP, you can provide tremendous value-add by bringing the in-house computer guru up to speed with highly targeted one-on-one training, customized documentation, and concise cheat sheets. By treating the internal guru as an on-site extension of your firm's total solution, you make it difficult for your client to contemplate seeking VAP alternatives. This tight relationship and the synergy that your staff has nurtured with the internal guru become the new standard on which any other future technology providers will be judged.

Once the internal guru has received the custom-tailored administration training, make sure the end users get up to speed. If this is your client's first network, the office staff also needs training. Your SBS implementation will be successful only if your client's staff takes full advantage of the network's features. While Fortune 1000 end users might be perfectly comfortable with the idea of local vs. network drives, e-mail, and Web browsing, your small business clients' end users might not be.

Some VAPs will train the internal guru on various end-user applications. Then the internal guru trains each user one-on-one. Other VAPs have their staff conduct end-user training. Many ultimately choose some middle ground, where VAP staff will train the first few end users, while the internal guru tags along to observe. The internal guru then trains the balance of the users on the newly installed client applications.

Encouraging Cross Training

Although intuitive for managers in larger organizations and often dictated by company policy, cross training is usually only an afterthought for small business owners and managers. Perhaps for certain mission critical functions, such as billing and payroll, small business owners have more than one person who's fluent in basic operations. But for small businesses that haven't had a proactive technology plan, you can bet that without a particular person on staff, the computers would slow to a crawl. In contrast to bigger companies, small businesses rarely have a lot of overlap or redundancy in skill sets, making cross training even more crucial.

Tip

You could adapt and extend the "Internal Skills Inventory," an Excel workbook introduced in Chapter 3 and included on the CD-ROM with this book, to help your small business clients figure out who knows what about various software applications.

Some of the barriers to cross training include:

- **Turf battles**—These are fought by people who have general concerns about job security.

- **Difficulty of training**—Knowing how to do a task and knowing how to train someone else to do that same task are two entirely different situations.

- **Not a priority**—With busy schedules and pressing deadlines, any kind of training is always the first thing pushed to the back burner until the lack of training causes or is very close to causing a business emergency.

- **Lack of patience**—People with the relevant skills don't always have patience to train others.

- **No motivation**—People with the relevant skills often have no financial or career incentives for sharing skills.

While this certainly isn't a problem that SBS VAPs can solve overnight on their own, you need to plant the idea that cross training is important with the small business owner. Even an inquiry as simple as, "So, how do you plan to address cross training among the staff?" is often enough to start the small business owner thinking about it.

Creating Targeted Cheat Sheets for the Internal Guru

IT isn't the primary job for the internal guru. The guru was hired for some other function, such as finance, accounting, operations, sales, or marketing, and he or she just happens to know more about computers than anyone else in the small business. Most of the guru's training has come from either playing with his or her computer(s) at home after hours, using trial and error on the computers in the office (hopefully the trial and error doesn't trash any PC configurations), or watching over the shoulder of the VAP's staff.

Because the guru isn't likely to take a five-day class on a BackOffice family application or read a 700-page book on a single topic, the SBS VAP somehow must bridge the gap for the guru's training needs. Often this training can be accomplished most efficiently by preparing some type of brief documentation pack or set of cheat sheets for the guru. For the documentation to be most useful, it must be kept short and simple. If it's too long or too detailed, the guru will likely bury it in a folder or binder at the bottom of his or her desk. The CD-ROM for this book includes an Excel workbook titled "Guru Documentation Pack," which you can use as the outline for training the internal guru on the unique aspects of the desktop client and SBS server configuration details.

Client Configuration Cheat Sheet

Besides being a great way to train the guru, a cheat sheet for client configuration is an invaluable tool for the internal guru when installing additional clients on the SBS 4.5 network and troubleshooting client setup problems after the rollout. "Client Configuration Cheat Sheet" is an Excel worksheet in the "Guru Documentation Pack," which is included on the CD-ROM with this book. See Figure 20-1 on the next page.

	A	B	C	D	E	F	G	H	I	J	K
				Client Configuration "Cheat" Sheet							
1											
2	Client name										
3	Domain										
4	Server (PDC)										
5											
6	local security	remove local accounts									
7		only SBS PDC accounts to be utilized									
8	screen saver	2 minutes									
9		blank screen									
10		password protected (uses SBS PDC account/password)									
11		can be overridden by Administrator									
12	network drives	N:	individual **NETWORK** drive		\\servername\user$						
13		P:	**PUBLIC** drive		\\servername\company						
14	Desktop pre SBS checklist										
15		1	rdisk /s	saves local registry repair info to c:\winnt\repair (or other equivalent on sys drive)							
16				create Emergency Repair Disk (ERD) - label with date - secure							
17		2	convert c: /fs:ntfs	if already done, confirm by right-click on c: in Windows Explorer							
18		3	convert d: /fs:ntfs	convert any other local drive partitions from FAT to NTFS							
19		4	local user account	create for temporary use until SBS PDC is completed							
20				remove local account once SBS rollout is completed							
21		5	local administrator pw	update- DO NOT WRITE DOWN!							
22		6	boot up delay	change from 30 seconds to 3 seconds							
23		7	i386 directory	make sure it's present							
24		8	BIOS check	record revision number on site-survey worksheet							
25		9	printer driver	make sure local or network printer is installed							

Figure 20-1

The "Client Configuration Cheat Sheet" can help you train the internal guru to configure SBS 4.5 clients.

SBS Configuration Notes

Another important area to document through a cheat sheet is the SBS 4.5 configuration details. The "Guru Documentation Pack" on the CD-ROM for this book contains "SBS Configuration Notes," an Excel worksheet that you use as a starting point for this part of the training for the system administrator (that is, the guru). See Figure 20-2. Items on this worksheet include the number of client access licenses (CALs), the auto-detected network card and modem(s), company contact information, applications installed, disk configuration, and access permissions.

LAN Cabling Notes

One final area to document is the network cabling. This is important so the guru understands which end users have been cabled to which network jacks at their desks. In addition, this document becomes invaluable when the guru has to troubleshoot or move network connections between the patch panel and Ethernet hub.

"LAN Cabling Notes," an Excel worksheet that is part of the "Guru Documentation Pack" on the CD-ROM with this book, will help you brief the guru on how the firm's network cabling has been configured. See Figure 20-3.

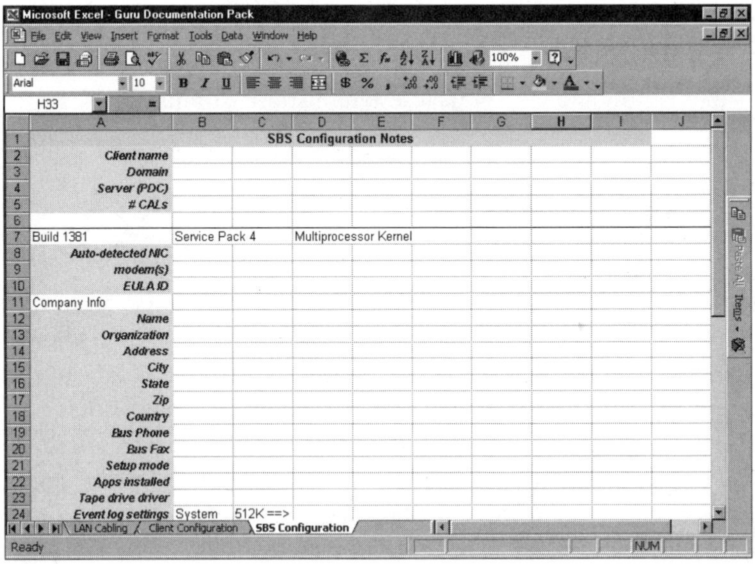

Figure 20-2

The "SBS Configuration Notes" should be used to document key settings and train the guru.

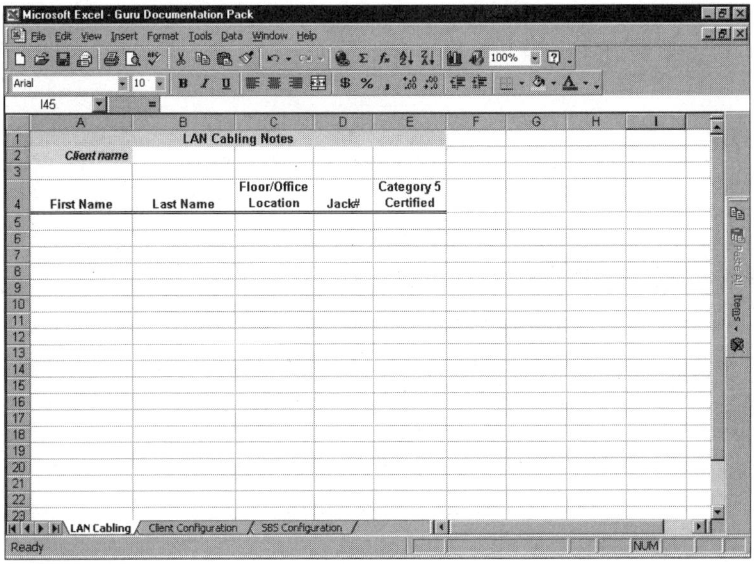

Figure 20-3

Use the "LAN Cabling Notes" worksheet to document network connections.

System Administrator Training

Every guru should know about several basic administrative training topics right off the bat.

Using the SBS Console

Those new to SBS might be tempted to use the Microsoft Windows NT Server 4.0 administrative tools (such as User Manager for Domains and Server Manager) to administer SBS. On the surface this might seem like a valid choice. Straying from the SBS Console and wizards, however, might end up causing all kinds of unforeseen configuration problems down the road. Whenever possible, all SBS administration needs to be done in the SBS Console. In those cases where you need to use applications outside of the SBS wizards to handle configuration tasks, the SBS Console will very clearly point you in that direction. In training the guru, make sure he or she is made aware of this crucial issue.

Creating User Accounts

As new employees join your client's company and computers are added to the network, the guru should be able to configure the proper user and computer accounts using the User Account Wizard. This wizard can be launched by clicking Add A User on the To Do List page in the SBS Console. Be sure to guide the guru through creating a complete setup for a new user and computer during your training session. For more details on the User Account Wizard, see Chapter 13.

Changing Passwords

Because end users are likely to forget their passwords from time to time or simply encounter difficulty changing their passwords from their client OS, the guru needs to know how to change a password from the SBS Console. The small business owner or another manager also might request that passwords be changed from time to time. This administrative task is accomplished by clicking Change Password on the Manage Users page, which is accessed from the Tasks page. For more information on passwords and the underlying security that Windows NT Server 4.0 provides to SBS 4.5, see my September 1999 VAPVoice column, "How to Sell the Security Features in Windows NT Server 4.0," on the Direct Access Web site. For your convenience, this article is included on the CD-ROM.

Deleting Print Jobs

Another important task for the guru to learn is how to delete jobs from network printers. This might be especially important when end users are using new applications and inadvertently send large documents to printers that clog up the printer, preventing other users from utilizing the shared resource. Make sure the guru knows how to delete print jobs by clicking Manage Printers on the Tasks page in the SBS Console and then choosing Manage Printer Jobs.

Restoring Files from a Backup Tape

The bulk of the guru's attention to tape backups will center on changing the tape daily and making sure the tapes go off-site, according to the plan you and the client developed for tape backup rotation and off-site storage.

Once in a while, the guru might need to restore a damaged or deleted file or group of files for an end user. If an entire volume or Exchange Server Information Store needs to be restored, the guru should call the SBS VAP because this is a complicated procedure. The guru, however, should feel comfortable restoring files selectively.

The big cautionary note to issue to the guru is that he or she shouldn't restore the file on top of the existing file. Always let the end user (owner) of the file replace the current version. To restore files, simply have the guru choose Restore Files From A Backup Tape on the Back Up Or Restore Data page, which is accessed from the Tasks page in the SBS Console. This will bring up a help page that has a link to Windows NT Backup and detailed instructions on how to perform a file restore. As with all steps above, you should make sure to do a few dry runs with the guru during your training session.

Best Practices for the Guru

In addition to covering hands-on, wizard-based administrative tasks, your administrator training session should cover a few additional topics to ensure the guru is ready for the huge responsibility associated with being the on-site junior-level administrator.

Physical Security

When considering how to protect the SBS 4.5 system from unauthorized usage, look at at least two major areas: network security and physical security. Network security is controlled by the permissions associated with shared folders, which the guru would typically see in the User Account Wizard. Whenever someone tries to map a drive to the SBS 4.5 system, properly configured network security keeps people away from files they're not authorized to access.

In addition to network security, physical security is required to ensure that the SBS 4.5 system can't be compromised while someone is physically at the server. Some popular and relatively easy ways to break into a server when someone has physical access include unauthorized use of the emergency repair disk (ERD) and removing the hard disk drive and installing it in another server. A host of substantially more sophisticated methods, which are primarily the domain of hackers, are quite easy when physical access is available.

When physical access is freely available, sooner or later the guru will forget to lock the keyboard when he or she walks away. (Press Ctrl+Alt+Delete, then choose Lock Workstation.) This leaves the front door open. Someone with physical access also has the ability to simply yank the power cord out of the UPS, causing the server to turn off immediately.

So now that you have told the guru about some of the many perils of failing to secure the server physically, you can provide some pointers to help the guru make the SBS 4.5 system more physically secure, such as the following:

- **Enable a password protected screen saver** that locks the server after a few minutes of keyboard or mouse inactivity. This ensures that even if the guru is forced to leave abruptly (for instance, the boss is screaming for help with Microsoft Outlook) and forgets to lock the server, the server will still lock itself after a few minutes. (I usually set this default to either 1 or 2 minutes on a server.)

- **Keep the server in a room** that is always kept locked. In evaluating the effectiveness of this tactic, make sure to find out who has access (with a key or keycard). Then ask if an alarm is set for the room after hours. Also find out if more than one person has access to the room. (No more than three people including the VAP should have access.)

- **Find a secure rack, table, or desk** for the server. Hard to believe, but some small business owners wouldn't think twice about putting a fully configured $5,000+ SBS 4.5 system on a flimsy $10 card table.

- **Install a dedicated electrical circuit** to make sure that the server and related peripherals aren't subject to high-voltage devices or motors that might interfere on the same circuit. The typical small business culprits that could wreak havoc include the office refrigerator, microwave, window-unit air conditioners, space heaters, cleaning equipment, and photocopy machines.

- Watch out for risks of water damage from pipes, fire sprinklers, and leaky windows above the server. Along the same lines, look for floors or ceilings that might buckle.

- Exercise common sense by adopting a zero-tolerance policy of no smoking, eating, or drinking in the computer room.

Sanctity of the Administrator Password

For many gurus, your SBS rollout will be their first opportunity to be responsible for a real production server, as opposed to a Windows 95/98 PC functioning in a peer-to-peer environment. Because of the guru's lack of experience in administering a server, you need to stress the importance of guarding the Administrator password.

Some tips and hints to cover in training the guru include:

- Never write down the Administrator password near the server or anywhere else that's visible. Better yet, don't write it down at all.

- Make sure the Administrator password isn't obvious, such as leaving it blank or making it the company name, the guru's name, the name of the guru's dog or spouse, or simply the word "password."

- Encourage dual account usage, where the guru uses the all-powerful Administrator account only when absolutely necessary and uses a standard domain user equivalent account for daily application usage on his or her own PC.

- Decide how often the Administrator password gets changed, and then put these dates in the Outlook calendar for the guru and the VAP. Another idea is to change the password four times a year, immediately following the meeting to review the quarterly update report.

- Change the Administrator password immediately if the password has leaked out to someone who shouldn't have it or if anyone who has the password leaves the company (resigns or is terminated).

- Always change the password using the SBS Console. Using any other method will definitely cause major problems with SBS 4.5.

- Use only a strong password for the Administrator account. No wimpy passwords allowed. This means the password must conform to a minimum character length, must be unique relative to recently used passwords, and must contain a mixture of numeric characters and uppercase and lowercase letters.

Developing the Production vs. Testing Mindset

Many small business owners and gurus mistakenly think, "Just install it and it'll work." They fail to consider these situations:

- The solution they're depending on to be the answer either doesn't work from a technology and/or a business standpoint.
- The new application conflicts with another important application.
- The new application trashes the OS or NOS.
- If complications ensue, expensive downtime is likely to occur.

To address these types of issues, experienced SBS VAPs typically have a test-bed PC and server. If the guru plans to introduce new software applications into a production environment, the guru should be encouraged to always have an extra PC on hand, even if it's one that's a little dated, to use strictly for testing new applications and service packs.

In addition to being used by key business managers to evaluate whether the application works as advertised, the guru's lab PC should be used to test for technical reliability and compatibility. Setting up a test system might seem expensive at first. Once the small business owner and guru have considered the potential risks and exposure, however, the cost of a dedicating one or two older PCs for this purpose become quite trivial in the whole scheme of things.

End User Training

Training end users is a critical task. Without proper training, end users might never scratch the surface on even 10 percent of the functionality of the included SBS 4.5 client applications. In order to devise a thorough and custom-tailored program for end users, you need to ask the internal guru and small business owner to work with your firm to develop training objectives and required skill sets.

If your firm is called upon to develop a custom training program for beginner level Microsoft Word 2000 users, perhaps you'd cover using bulleted and numbered lists, multicolumn text, styles, and templates. For the equivalent audience needing to learn Microsoft Excel 2000, you'd probably want to cover constructing basic formulas, using the Function Wizard, AutoFormat, sorting, filtering, and charting. Don't assume end users know the basics. Many times they don't. It's not that they don't have a desire to learn. They've just never been exposed to the concepts.

Logon and Password Procedures

Assuming the end users know how to turn on the PCs and have a basic level of understanding about OS concepts (using the mouse, the Start menu, folders, files, and so forth), the best place to begin is by showing each end user how to log on to the network and the potential pitfalls at this stage.

Tip

The small business owner and guru should make sure company policy dictates that accounts and passwords aren't to be shared under any circumstances.

End users whose PCs have Windows NT Workstation 4.0 installed need to know they'll have to press Ctrl+Alt+Delete to log on. Next they'll enter their User Name and Password and ensure that the proper choice is selected in the Domain drop-down list. Be sure to let each end user know that passwords are case sensitive, meaning they need to pay attention to the Caps Lock light on their keyboard.

End users whose PCs have Windows 95/98 installed will have a slightly different logon procedure. They don't need to press any key sequence to log on. They'll need to enter their User Name and Password. If the Network applet settings in Control Panel are correct (as they should be following successful completion of the Client Installation Wizard), the correct Domain name should be already displayed in the Domain field in the network logon dialog box. If it isn't or if it's incorrect, the end user will need to enter the correct Domain name in the field.

Local vs. Network Drives

Prior to explaining the difference between a local and network drive to end users, make sure they first have a grasp on the letters of the local drives on their systems (for instance, A: drive, C: drive, and so forth).

Most SBS VAPs and small business clients usually use the letters at the beginning of the alphabet for local drive letters. The letters in the middle and the end of the alphabet are typically used for network drive letters.

As was mentioned in Chapter 17, supporting hundreds of end users at different client sites is easier if you have some degree of consistency in naming the network drive mappings on an SBS 4.5 network.

Take time to explain how only they can see what's on their private space on the network but how anyone logged onto the network can see what's on the public space. You'll often need to create additional shares mapped to additional drive letters for various workgroup needs. These might include server-shared folders for staff in the accounting, marketing, or sales departments.

Also make sure each user is aware of the company's tape backup policy. For most this means any files stored on the private or public spaces on the network will be backed up nightly. Any files stored on local hard disk drives aren't backed up by default. Finally, take time to point out whether open files are backed up using the company's current tape backup solution.

Local vs. Network Printing

Just as local vs. network drives might be a totally new concept to end users whose companies never had a network, local vs. network printing usually needs to be explained (assuming their companies have shared network printers).

The concept should be fairly straightforward to explain to most end users. Either the document prints on the printer at their desk or prints somewhere else by virtue of the network. In terms of mechanics, make sure to show them how to change the print destination in Windows-based applications.

Also, point out how they can access the Printers folder through the Settings section of the Start menu. Then show end users how to find out which printer is selected as the default and how to change the default selection.

Sending and Receiving E-Mail

E-mail is one of the killer apps included with SBS 4.5. Whether used solely for internal purposes or, better yet, for internal and Internet usage, every small business end user, including the big boss, needs to know how to read and send basic e-mail.

End users on an SBS 4.5 network have their desktop OS profiles preconfigured to use Outlook 2000 as their messaging client. You'll want to make sure they know how to do the following:

- Open Outlook either from the Start menu or a shortcut on the desktop.

- Create a new e-mail message and select message recipients, including Internet recipients.

- Attach a file to an e-mail message.

- Spell check an e-mail message prior to sending.

- Set the importance of the e-mail message.

- Send the e-mail message to its final destination.

- Read a received e-mail message.

- Open an attachment.

Tip

For more advanced and more curious Outlook end users, you might want to show them how to organize their e-mail into folders within the Inbox.

Sending and Receiving Faxes Using Fax Service

The process of sending a fax through SBS 4.5 is very straightforward. If end users know how to change the printer selection, they already know how to send a fax from a Windows-based application. Just choose the fax printer listed on the Name drop-down list. The application prompts them to add the recipient name(s) and fax number(s), as well as cover page and scheduling information. Once end users click the Finish button, the outgoing fax is sent to Fax Service for transmission.

Also take time to explain to end users how incoming faxes are handled, assuming the small business client has inbound fax reception enabled. SBS 4.5 provides three different methods to handle inbound faxes, any of one of which can be used either separately or together:

- Inbound faxes are delivered to a single Outlook Inbox (such as the receptionist's) and then can be manually routed to appropriate end users.

- Inbound faxes are automatically printed to a network printer.

- Inbound faxes are automatically stored on a folder on the server.

Browsing the Web

One other immensely popular client application on an SBS 4.5 network is the Web browser. Although you might think that most end users in the year 2000 would have browsed the Web before, Web newbies exist and you're a lot more apt to find them working in small businesses than any other size business. You'll want to make sure they know how to do the following:

- Launch Microsoft Internet Explorer 5 (IE5) from both the desktop and Start menu.

- Use an URL to access different Web sites.

- Add their preferred Web sites to the Favorites list.

- Print Web pages. Despite promises of a paperless society, Web browsing end users love to print out their finds.
- Use a search engine.
- Download and save files.

Virus Prevention and Containment Training

End users can take a few basic precautions that go a long way toward preventing viruses from infiltrating their firm's LAN. Such precautions include:

- Resist the temptation to install unauthorized, downloaded, or non-commercial software on any PC under any circumstances. Always check first with the guru or VAP before installing software.
- Run a virus scan on any attachments received over e-mail. Always be suspicious no matter who sends the e-mail.
- If you receive any suspicious e-mail, don't open it or any attachments. Also never forward a suspicious looking e-mail. Call or beep the internal guru or VAP immediately.

The Bottom Line

Small business end users generally don't have anywhere near the level of computer literacy that their Fortune 1000 counterparts have. In order to make best use of their newly installed SBS 4.5 network, end users need to be brought up to speed quickly on basic skills. Use the topics outlined in this chapter to jump start your one-on-one training efforts with both the internal guru and end users at the client site.

Chapter 21

Adding More Value Through Microsoft Office Automation

This chapter shows how you can expose your clients to a rarely mined gem among smaller companies: Microsoft Office 2000 automation. In contrast to what some of the Fortune 1000 IT types turned Microsoft BackOffice Small Business Server VAPs might think, this chapter isn't about using Microsoft Visual Basic for Applications (VBA) and ActiveX controls to extend Office. Most small business clients need much more exposure to the fundamentals of using Office before you can even think about proposing custom programming. This chapter is all about helping your clients automate their daily business processes as they get familiar with some of the basic tools and capabilities of the Office suite. You also need to make sure your clients are aware of the differences between the versions of Office 2000, as shown in Table 21-1 on the next page, as well as the functions that each included application performs.

	Standard	Small Business	Profes-sional	Premium
Microsoft Word	✔	✔	✔	✔
Microsoft Excel	✔	✔	✔	✔
Microsoft PowerPoint	✔		✔	✔
Microsoft Access			✔	✔
Microsoft Outlook	✔	✔	✔	✔
Microsoft Small Business Tools		✔	✔	✔
Microsoft Publisher		✔	✔	✔
Microsoft FrontPage				✔
Microsoft PhotoDraw				✔

Table 21-1

Understanding the different versions of Office 2000

Office 2000 Small Business Tools

Office 97 Small Business Edition included Microsoft Small Business Tools—wizards and templates designed specifically to automate small business functions. To ensure the Office 2000 family of applications would be as helpful as possible for small businesses, Microsoft decided to include the improved and expanded Small Business Tools with all versions of Office 2000 except Office 2000 Standard.

The Office 2000 Small Business Tools include Microsoft Business Planner, Microsoft Direct Mail Manager, Microsoft Small Business Customer Manager, and Microsoft Small Business Financial Manager. Assuming you choose to install the tools from CD 2, which has a separate Setup program, Office 2000 Setup creates a Microsoft Office Small Business Tools program group on the Start menu.

The goals of the tools are four-fold:

- Simplify business processes and streamline workflow

- Reduce redundancy and duplication of efforts

- Move staff from clerical and administrative functions to more strategically important roles that go directly to the bottom line

- Transform individual productivity to company-wide productivity

Because new adds-ons, templates, and wizards are constantly being added to the Office 2000 Small Business Tools, visit the new Microsoft Office Update Web site (*officeupdate.microsoft.com*) on a regular basis. On this site, you can sign up for a free weekly e-mail newsletter and receive tips on using various parts of Office. Unless your clients happen to have an unusual zeal for exploring the features of Office 2000 on their own, you can add tremendous value to your SBS installations by helping end users, especially the small business owner and guru, become familiar with the four tools in Small Business Tools.

Microsoft Business Planner

One of the most daunting challenges facing any new small business or any small business looking to raise funds through bank financing, venture capitalists, or individual investors is writing a thorough, professional-looking business plan. Business Planner can help small businesses develop their business plans. Business Planner begins with a brief, browser-based interview of the small business owner. By the end of the three pages of questions, Business Planner will have gathered enough information—which it very clearly states is completely confidential—to point the user to specific how-to articles, templates, and worksheets in the included library that span planning, operations, legal, finance, and marketing. See Figure 21-1.

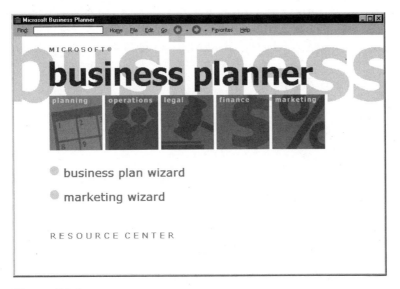

<u>Figure 21-1</u>

Use Microsoft Business Planner to develop a sophisticated business plan.

Once the basic plan is created, Business Planner can then tailor the plan for different purposes and different needs, such as those of bankers, investors, clients, or business partners. Once Business Planner is installed on an SBS client running Microsoft Windows 95/98 or Microsoft Windows NT Workstation 4.0, you can access Business Planner templates from each Office application by choosing New from the File menu and clicking the Business Planner tab. Even more templates and worksheets can be added to this collection by downloading updated files from the Office Update Web site (*officeupdate.microsoft.com*). The collection of Business Planner templates that ships with all Office versions except Standard includes:

- Bad Check Notice (Word)

- Break-Even Analysis (Excel)

- Business Contract Mediation Clause 1 (Word)

- Depreciation Worksheet (Excel)

- Press Release (Word)

- Trade Show Survival Kit (Word)

Microsoft Direct Mail Manager

Have you ever tried to assemble a small business direct mail campaign? Between entering the data, preparing the addresses, and designing the deliverables, a direct mail campaign can be a huge job. With Direct Mail Manager, shown in Figure 21-2, small business end users have an easy-to-follow way to import the address list, clean up the list so it follows U.S. Postal Service guidelines, and print envelopes, labels, and postcards.

Figure 21-2

Use Microsoft Direct Mail Manager to simplify creating a direct mail campaign.

Direct Mail Manager imports address information from popular formats, including Access, dBASE, Excel, Word, Paradox, and text, as well as Outlook Contacts lists, and ODBC compliant databases (such as Microsoft SQL Server 7.0). Once the information is imported, Direct Mail Manager can verify the addresses, clean up common spelling errors, identify duplicate records, sort records, go out through Microsoft Proxy Server to the U.S. Postal Service's national ZIP+4 database to get the correct nine-digit ZIP Codes, and even send the information directly to a mailing house for printing and adding proper postage.

Years ago, you'd have to buy expensive software to clean your mailing list or send out your mailing list to a service bureau. Direct Mail Manager makes it possible for you to accomplish these functions rapidly inhouse. In addition, the address verification and list cleaning process is important for getting the most favorable mailing rate discounts. In my test, I was able to verify 1,200 addresses, originally stored in an Access database, in about four minutes over a 256-Kbps connection to the Internet.

Once the mailing list is prepared, Direct Mail Manager can help users print in a variety of formats, including working with the mail merge wizards in Word and Publisher. Direct Mail Manager can then save the cleaned list results to an Excel, Access, or text file.

Microsoft Small Business Customer Manager

How many times have you wished for an easy way to take the customer data stored in an accounting program, such as Peachtree, QuickBooks, or Microsoft Money, and marry that data to the Contacts information stored in Outlook? Small Business Customer Manager, shown in Figure 21-3 on the next page, helps you do this.

Small Business Customer Manager can import data from several different sets of accounting files and local user Outlook.pst files and combine this information in an Access database with predefined queries, reports, and links to other Office applications. With this aggregated customer information, you can use Small Business Customer Manager to prepare letters, envelopes, labels, faxes, e-mails, appointments, tasks, and journal entries.

Because the database that Small Business Customer Manager creates is a standard Access 2000 database, you can use Access 2000 to provide security with passwords, permission levels, and individual logons. That way you can grant limited access to as many people in the company as you like with confidence that only one or two select users will have control over the overall database.

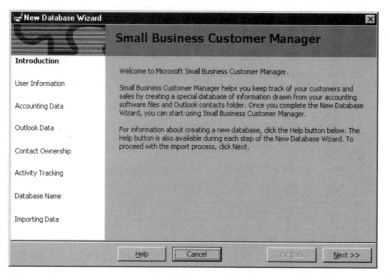

Figure 21-3

Use Microsoft Small Business Customer Manager to combine accounting information on customers with Outlook Contact information.

Tip

Download the Microsoft Office 2000 Small Business Customer Manager Toolkit from the Office 2000 page on the Microsoft Direct Access Web site (*www.microsoft.com/directaccess*). With the toolkit, you'll be able to customize the customer analysis queries, templates, views, and filters.

The real power in Small Business Customer Manager is the on the fly queries you can run across five custom drop-down menus. These queries are:

- **Hot Views**—Top Customers, Top Salespeople, Top Products, All Customers, All Products

- **Customers**—By Sales Volume, By Order Volume, By Time Since Last Order, By Product Ordered

- **Products**—By Sales Volume, By Quantity, By Time Since Last Order

- **Sales**—By Customer, By Product, By Region, By Salesperson, By Period

- **Profitability**—By Customer, By Product, By Salesperson

Microsoft Small Business Financial Manager

Unless small business owners were accountants, financial analysts, controllers, or CFOs in their prior career, they might need assistance to stay on top of their company's financial status. Small Business Financial Manager is designed to help small business owners make better decisions more rapidly by leveraging their existing accounting data files and using Excel. See Figure 20-4.

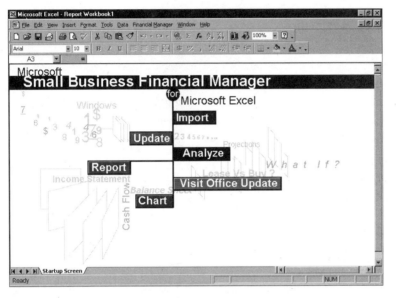

Figure 20-4
Use Microsoft Small Business Financial Manager to keep tabs on company finances.

Just like Small Business Customer Manager, Small Business Financial Manager can import accounting data from popular applications such as Peachtree, QuickBooks, or Money. From within Excel, Microsoft Small Business Financial Manager can produce standardized financial reports and charts, growth projection reports (needed for bankers and investors), and what-if scenarios that deal with profitability, receivables, payables, inventory, expenses, and taxes.

Tip

A number of upgrades to the wizards within Excel 2000 and Access 2000 have made integration of data from these applications with SQL Server 7.0 easier.

You can also use Small Business Financial Manager to compare financing options (that is, loans vs. leases vs. cash). Analyzing the buy vs. lease issue could be very useful to your small business clients who are contemplating whether they should buy or lease their hardware and software purchases. This is especially important because most direct PC vendors offer leasing options. The comparison feature even supports and customizes results for cars, computer hardware, computer software, equipment, and furniture. Small Business Financial Manager also can utilize any one of the four well-known depreciation methods (which harkens back to Accounting 101 from school).

Tip

To learn more, see "Extending Microsoft Office 2000," an October 1998 white paper that's on the SQL Server Web site (*www.microsoft.com/sql*).

In addition to generating standard accounting reports, such as a balance sheet, cash flow statement, income statement, ratios, and trial balance, Small Business Financial Manager can perform a business comparison to show how your client measures up to competitors in the same industry.

Making the Best Use of Toolbars

In addition to helping your clients understand how Office 2000 Small Business Tools can help drive more complete and rapid business decisions, many clients can benefit from a few minutes of instruction on some of the more basic toolbar buttons. For example, how many of your small business end users really know what the majority of the buttons do on the Standard and Formatting toolbars in Word and Excel? Further, how many of them know that if they hover over a button, they'll get a ToolTip explaining the button's function? This lack of knowledge is often a barrier in using Word and Excel more efficiently. As an SBS VAP, you have a unique opportunity to make end users aware of these time-savers and make a contribution to their daily productivity. Table 21-2 shows the buttons to emphasize in training.

Word	Excel
Undo and Redo	Spelling
Format Painter	Format Painter
Insert Table	Undo and Redo
Columns	AutoSum
Show/Hide	Paste Function
Zoom	Sort Ascending and Sort Descending
Numbering and Bullets	Chart Wizard
Increase Indent and Decrease Indent	Drawing
	Fill Color
Borders	Merge and Center
Style	

Table 21-2

Standard and Formatting toolbar functions

Once the small business end users understand how the above functions can be easily carried out, find out if they think they might still need to use drop-down menus for any tasks they perform in Word or Excel. Granted, only so much real estate is available to add custom buttons to these toolbars. If each user has one or two tasks that they need to perform a few times a week, however, consider customizing their Standard or Formatting toolbars to accommodate an additional menu-command button.

Tip

Make sure to point out how the new Office 2000 Clipboard and its accompanying toolbar can hold up to a dozen different chunks of data from any application.

Adding buttons to a toolbar in Word or Excel can be most easily accomplished through the following steps:

1. Click the down arrow on the right side of either toolbar in either application.

2. Choose Add Or Remove Buttons.

3. At the bottom of the menu, choose Customize. Then you can select virtually any pull-down menu command.

For example, by clicking Commands tab in the Customize dialog box in Excel, I can add a custom button to the toolbar for the Set Print Area command in the File menu. See Figure 21-5. Then from the Commands window, I can drag the Set Print Area command button to any location on any present toolbar.

Figure 21-5

Add the Set Print Area command button to an Excel toolbar.

Creating and Customizing Task-Specific Templates

Fortune 1000 companies have all kinds of templates prepared for various departments, job functions, and documents. Using a template with its accompanying formatting styles is often the difference between an amateurish and professional document appearance. Templates also give the document reader the message that consistently says, "We mean business."

SBS VAPs can leverage existing templates included with Office, as well as the templates that ship with the Office 2000 Small Business Tools, as the basis for helping their clients most efficiently prepare consistent and stunning sets of documents. And when people see this new professional image repeatedly, your client will be on the way toward building up brand name image and equity among vendors, customers, and business partners.

One goal might be to help your clients create a standard set of business form letters to reply to various information requests. Begin by making sure all document templates have your client's logo. (If your client doesn't have a logo, now would be a great time to have one created by a graphic designer.) Ideally, get the original logo file to insert into document templates. If that's not readily available, you could always scan the logo from a clean document.

Then ask your client's guru to gather up a set of the 10 or 20 most frequently used document types company-wide. From that collection, you can begin to identify trends and commonalities that will be useful in turning these documents into templates that can be used by everyone in the company. When you're done with this fact-finding mission, find out where each document's origination point is and where it ultimately ends up.

You'll probably discover that a small business owner or guru dramatically underestimates the number of document types in use. In your first meeting to explore template creation, your client might say, "Oh…we only have a few different types of documents. Maybe five or six tops." When the small business owner or guru begins to ask around, however, don't be surprised if they come back to the second meeting with a stack of two or three dozen different types of documents that their firm generates.

In terms of mechanics, creating a template is very straightforward. In Word, simply prepare the document (either from scratch or by creating it from another document or another template) and remove of any of the nonrepeatable information. Then add your client's contact information, such as company name, address, phone, fax, Web site URL, and so forth. Choose the Save As command on the File menu, change Save As Type to Document Template, then select the desired path and folder in which to save the file. Once each user's Word and Excel options are properly configured, users will see the new custom document templates when they choose New from the File menu.

If the document is a close match to a template that already exists in Office or the Small Business Tools, your job will simply be to customize the canned template for your client's unique needs. If the client has a large volume of templates to create or you anticipate that they'll need to create templates on a fairly regular basis, you might want to train their guru to assume this template creation function.

You could save the document templates to each SBS 4.5 client PC. You'll save a lot of time and effort in redistributing updates, however, by creating a Templates folder on the SBS 4.5 Company Shared Folders share and setting each person's Workgroup Templates file location to the appropriate path. Just make sure that each person in the company who needs access only has the Read permission. The guru will more than likely need full control to the templates and folder.

File Format Issues in Companies with Mixed Office 2000/Office 97 Installations

When discussing document templates for Word and Excel, you'll also likely get questions about file format compatibility between Office 2000 and Office 97. When Office 97 originally came out, many companies experienced some major compatibility problems when trying to share files between Office 97 and Office 95 users. Office 97 Service Release 1 (SR-1) ultimately remedied this.

Office 2000, on the other hand, should prove to be a much less stressful upgrade for companies that have mixed Office 2000 and Office 97 installations. With common file formats across Word, Excel, and PowerPoint, users can pass documents back and forth without having to resort to upward and downward conversion. While some advanced formatting features in Office 2000 applications simply won't be available in Office 97, these differences won't cause file compatibility problems. While Access 2000 doesn't share a similar file format with Access 97, Access 2000 does support saving a file in Access 97 format.

Applying Styles for Consistency

Style is one of more important buttons (in actuality, it's a drop-down list) on the Formatting toolbar in Word. Word templates include a set of styles designed to give documents a sense of consistency, corporate identity, and pizzazz. Small business end users usually don't even know what styles are, let alone how they can be used. Meticulous use of styles, however, is often the difference between mediocre or amateurish-looking documents and those prepared by professionals.

To help small business end users get started with styles and AutoFormat, ask them to show you a few typical documents and worksheets that they work with each week. Then gradually go through each document with them, their hands on the keyboard and mouse, and show them how to dramatically enhance the readability, professionalism, and appearance of their documents and spreadsheets.

Tip

The closest thing to styles in Excel is the AutoFormat tool in Excel, which is accessed from the Format menu. If your client is looking to prepare presentation-quality worksheets, this is a great feature to know about.

Understanding the Role of Wizards

In much the same way that a template and set of styles helps you to prepare professional-looking documents quickly and consistently, wizards can help end-users get complex tasks accomplished with ease.

Start Word beginners out with the Letter Wizard, shown in Figure 21-6. Launched from the Tools menu, the Letter Wizard is quite powerful. Just from the Letter Format tab—the first of four tabs—you can choose to incorporate several elements in your letter, such as today's date in any one of a number of formats, a header and footer, a page design from a template (including the dozens that came with Business Planner), letter block style, and letterhead size and location.

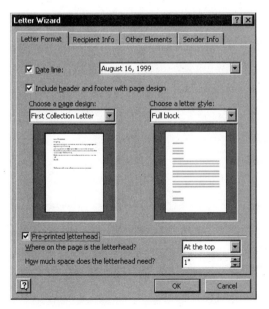

Figure 21-6

Use the Word Letter Wizard to create professional-looking letters quickly.

Another commonly used wizard in Word is Mail Merge Helper, which can create form letters, mailing labels, and envelopes. In addition to being able to query and sort on various criteria, Mail Merge Helper can pull in address data from Outlook address books as well as Word, text, dBASE, FoxPro, Access, and Excel files.

The Excel Paste Function wizard allows end users to avoid creating complex formulas by hand. Users can simply click the Paste Function button on the Standard toolbar and browse through a series of built-in functions organized by category such as Financial, Date & Time, and Text.

Tip

Because the Analysis ToolPak has additional functions, be sure to choose a complete installation of Excel 2000.

Looking through the functions, I discovered a useful one I didn't even know existed in Excel. The NETWORKDAYS function allows you to figure out how many working days are between two dates. See Figure 12-7. If I were teaching a reluctant group of end users, I'd present the function as one they can use to figure out how many days until a much anticipated event like their next vacation, next raise, or 401(K) plan vesting.

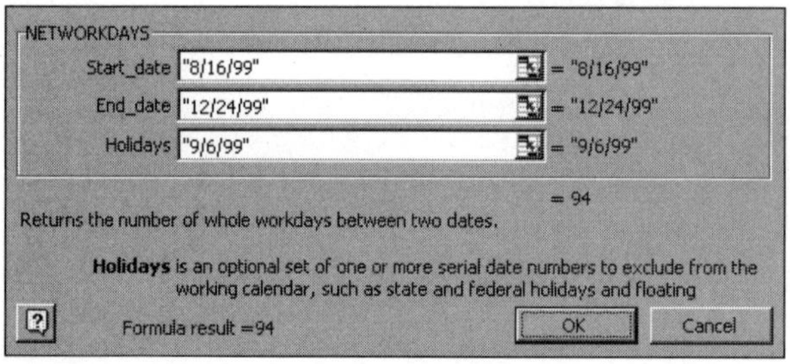

Figure 21-7

Set up the NETWORKDAYS function through the Excel Paste Function wizard.

Adapting Naming Conventions for Folders and Files

Most of your small business clients will desperately need your help in building a set of naming conventions for files and folders that works for them. The CD-ROM for this book includes an Excel workbook, "Company Shared Folders

Organizational Structure," which is designed to jump start your planning efforts with clients. See Figure 21-8. Although no hard and fast rules exist, ascertaining basic information as you plan the structure of the company's shared drive is important. This workbook will help you lay the framework for this type of crucial planning activity. If your clients are having difficulty getting started, you might want to begin by building a hierarchical outline (with roman numerals, letters, and numbers) or a tree (with branches) to establish the folder hierarchy.

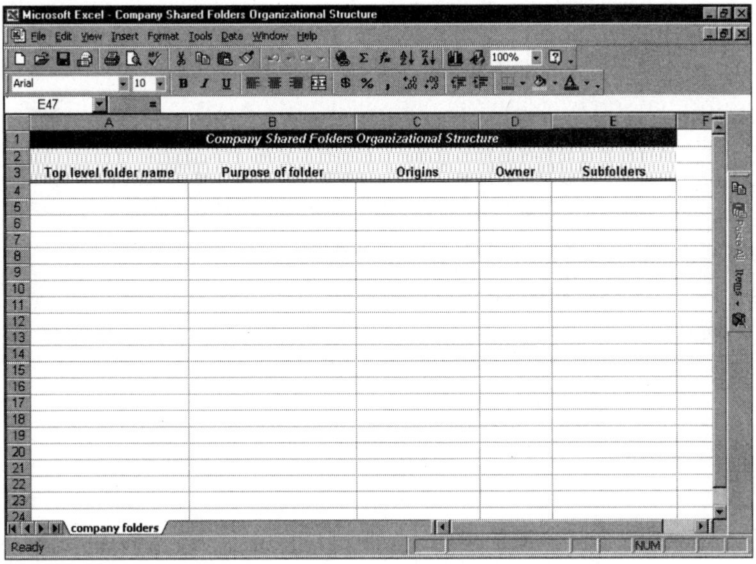

Figure 21-8

Use "Company Shared Folders Organizational Structure," an Excel workbook on the CD-ROM with this book, to help organize your client's shared drive.

The organizational structure for the company-shared folder on the server should meet three criteria:

- Files and folder names must be intuitive to end users.

- Files and folders must be able to reveal what's current and what's obsolete.

- Someone needs to be in charge (I'll call him or her the "shared folder Czar") and be responsible for enforcing the folder order and for assessing any requests for new top level folders.

Once you've decided on the structure, discuss some of the more common types of data files that will be generated and how end users should name them. For example, if you've created a series of document templates as outlined earlier in the chapter, now's a good time to talk about how file names will be determined for routine documents such as proposals, follow-up letters, fax cover sheets, and collection notices.

**Tip**

See Chapter 17 for more information on file and folder naming conventions.

The Bottom Line

Office skills are often sorely lacking among small business end users. This lack of training becomes a problem for you when it impedes your clients from taking full advantage of the SBS 4.5 network. When you see end users creating tables in Word with tabs and spaces or adding up numbers in Excel using an old-fashioned adding machine, you need to step in and propose instruction on how to automate tasks with Office 2000. Now more than ever, Office has tools to make your small business clients operate more efficiently. This chapter showed how you can rescue your small business clients from application atrophy and deliver them to turbocharged productivity.

Chapter 22

Software Maintenance

After the application of one or two service packs (SPs), software often is substantially different than the original release. Just take Microsoft Windows NT Server 4.0 for example. Once you apply the six SPs and the option pack, Windows NT Server 4.0 is more robust than the product Microsoft released in July 1996 and has more features. SBS VAPs will want to keep abreast of the performance enhancements, new features, and fixes introduced by interim software releases.

This chapter will introduce you to software that needs to be updated from time to time. First, the chapter covers how to keep up with hardware device driver and firmware revisions for crucial SBS network peripherals, such as modems, multiport serial adapters, network interface cards (NICs), routers, tape backup drives, and disk controllers. Then the focus shifts to antivirus, tape backup, and uninterruptible power supply (UPS) monitoring software. Finally, the chapter is rounded out with an overview of Microsoft SPs.

Keeping up with Device Drivers and Firmware Updates

Staying on top of the latest hardware device drivers and firmware has become dramatically easier during the past five years because network peripheral vendors have been putting up richly stocked technical support Web sites with frequently asked questions (FAQs), how-to articles, white papers, and downloads. Prior to this, the best you could hope for was a vendor-sponsored bulletin board service (BBS), which was often like a maze designed by someone who clearly was from another planet.

Tip

Many OEMs and software vendors have e-mail newsletters that provide push notification of software updates. As you visit each vendor's Web site, you may want to sign up for some or all of these listserv subscriptions, which are almost always free.

Download File Formats

Most of the downloads covered in this chapter are packaged as self-extracting executables, meaning you can double-click the downloaded file and either launch a setup program or extract the required files. Occasionally, you might need one of the more popular utility programs to extract or view files distributed by vendors.

WinZip, from Nico Mak Computing, compresses and decompresses files. This allows a hardware OEM to compress a complete set of files, such as a 4-MB download set, which might be an onerous download for some users. WinZip, however, can create a single-file archive that's a fraction of the size of the original 4-MB set of files. So you can download a relatively small file and then decompress the full set to a local or LAN-based hard disk drive (or any other appropriate storage media). You can download a fully functional evaluation version of WinZip from *www.winzip.com*. WinZip's standard file extension for its native files is .zip.

Acrobat Reader, from Adobe, is used to distribute documentation files and ensures that documents will look the same regardless of the OS, applications, or hardware on a given computer. In addition, users can't easily tamper with files created for Acrobat Reader. You can download Acrobat Reader free from *www.adobe.com*. The standard file extension for Acrobat Reader's native files is .pdf.

Why These Files Are So Important

A device driver, which is synonymous with driver, is a small piece of software written to control a hardware device, such as a NIC, disk controller, printer, mouse, video card, or modem. Often a seemingly minor patch can make a world of difference. For example, if your client purchased a 3Com Sportster 56K external modem in early 1998, the modem had firmware code and device drivers that were written before the V.90 standard was finalized. In order to make best use of the modem, you'd need to download updated code from 3Com. The modem will be more reliable, perform better, and have true V.90 compatibility once the updated firmware code and device drivers are installed.

Tip

Firmware that can be upgraded, or flashable firmware, is often a major differentiator between a $19 bargain basement modem and one that actually will work reliably on an SBS 4.5 network. To get a list of preferred peripheral devices for an SBS 4.5 system, often the best place to start is the Hardware Compatibility List (HCL) page on the Microsoft Web site (*www.microsoft.com/hcl*).

A great many device drivers are written by Microsoft and come with SBS 4.5 through the underlying Windows NT Server 4.0 NOS. Many types of hardware devices can be detected by Windows NT during SBS 4.5 setup, and the device driver for each is loaded automatically. Other times, the OEM will provide a driver in lieu of or as a supplement to a Microsoft-written device driver.

Note

One major benefit of dealing with brand-name systems that no one can deny is the ease of locating updated files for hardware components. For example, if your small business client has a Dell PowerEdge server, tracking down the latest device drivers and firmware revisions for various server components on the Dell Web site is a cakewalk.

OEM vs. Microsoft-Distributed Device Drivers

Industry professionals debate over which type of device drivers are preferable: those written by the OEM or those provided by Microsoft. Most SBS VAPs tend to agree that whichever driver is more current is preferable. Some think that the only way to get a stable driver is to rely on the one written by Microsoft and that you shouldn't buy a hardware device for which Microsoft has no device driver. Others feel that the OEM is in a much better position to know the hardware and to create a more reliable and efficient device driver.

To lessen the risk of introducing flaky device drivers, you can read product reviews in print and online publications, such as *Windows NT Magazine* (*www.winntmag.com*) and *Windows NT Systems* magazine (*www.ntsystems.com*)

and visit newsgroups on the Internet, such as those sponsored by Microsoft Product Support Services (PSS) and Microsoft Direct Access. Often the only way to know if the device driver will work well in your client's specific environment is to have a controlled test-bed environment either at your clients' sites or, more likely, in your own office where you can put new drivers through rigorous testing.

Tip

Some OEMs also have a much better reputation than others when it comes to writing stable device drivers. Don't be afraid to ask around for recommendations. One thing that SBS VAPs and other network administrators are never shy about is giving you their candid opinion on hardware vendors.

Although Microsoft considers only Windows NT Server 4.0 files with an .drv file extension to be device drivers, for all practical purposes, .sys (system) and .inf (setup information) files serve the same purpose. All three file types allow the Windows NT Server 4.0 portion of SBS 4.5 to communicate with various hardware devices. Once installed on a SBS 4.5 system, device drivers usually end up in one of three locations:

- \Winnt.sbs\system32
- \Winnt.sbs\system32\drivers
- \Winnt.sbs\inf

Device Drivers vs. Firmware

Device drivers for peripherals really can't be discussed in isolation. Peripherals almost always have some type of firmware software that's burned into a chip on the device. The device driver works in conjunction with the firmware to provide an interface between the NOS and the peripheral. Just like a device driver, firmware can often be updated by downloading a file from the OEM's Web site. Many times, certain device driver versions will work with or are optimized for only certain firmware versions. So you'll need to pay careful attention to file versions, as defined by size and time/date stamps.

Updating firmware can be quite risky, similar to updating the registry. If done incorrectly with devices such as modems and motherboards, the devices could be rendered worthless. Be meticulous in your pursuit of readme files and other supplied documentation.

Tip

Because SBS 4.5 is based on the Windows NT Server 4.0 NOS, you'll almost always want to look for the Windows NT 4.0 version of drivers. (In
some rare cases vendors might have specific download files for SBS.)

Windows NT 4.0 SPs can also inadvertently overwrite many device drivers or render them incompatible with the NOS. Often you can check with the
OEM through its technical support number or Web site about whether a specific device driver is bumped by a particular SP. Your best bet, however, is always to test an SP in a controlled lab environment before deploying the SP in
your client's production network. Many clues are often contained in the SP
readme. In addition, you may find active threads on specific device drivers in
the Microsoft Direct Access PSS-moderated newsgroups, such as:

- microsoft.private.directaccess.ntserver (for Windows NT Server 4.0)

- microsoft.private.directaccess.smallbizserver (for SBS 4.5)

Tip

SBS VAPs need to register for these newsgroups on the Support page of
the Microsoft Direct Access Web site.

Network Peripherals

When you consider the hardware that makes it possible for an SBS 4.5 system
to communicate with other clients on the LAN as well as other hosts on the
Internet and other wide area networks, focusing on how to keep network
peripherals functioning reliably and at optimal efficiency is important. Table
22-1 covers which hardware-related files often can be upgraded.

	Device driver	Firmware revisions
Modems	✔	✔
Multiport serial adapters	✔	✔
Routers		✔
Network interface cards or network adapters	✔	

Table 22-1

SBS 4.5 hardware-related files that are often revised

Tip

Routers and NICs differ in what it takes to keep them updated because they operate at different levels of the seven-layer ISO/OSI reference model. For details on this somewhat theoretical difference, see *Networking Essentials*, published by Microsoft Press.

Modems

Years ago, a distinction existed between modems and fax modems. Generally modems that could just send and receive data were less expensive than those that could also communicate with fax machines and other fax modems. As high-speed analog modems have evolved into a mature technology, however, nearly every major modem OEM includes both data and fax capabilities in even their lowest cost models.

Because SBS 4.5 has several services that depend on modems, such as Fax Service, Remote Access Service, Exchange Internet Mail Service, and Exchange Connector for POP3 Mailboxes, having a matched combination of modem device drivers and firmware becomes mission critical. This is especially important with Fax Service in SBS 4.5. Microsoft PSS found with SBS 4.0 that a substantial percentage of the support calls for Fax Service were caused by a mismatch between modem device drivers and firmware. On the Microsoft Direct Access PSS-moderated SBS support newsgroup the standard question that users with modem-related problems are asked is, "Do you have the latest driver and firmware from the manufacturer?"

Note

Fax Service is SBS-specific and doesn't exist in any other Microsoft products. It's not available with Windows NT Server 4.0 or BackOffice Server 4.5. From a hardware standpoint, Fax Service works best with modems that are business class and class 1 fax compliant. For assistance in selecting a fax modem, see the HCL page on the Microsoft Web site. For more information on configuring Fax Service, see Chapters 13 and 27.

The 3Com Courier V.Everything is one of the more popular modems among SBS VAPs. In fact, some SBS VAPs and PSS reps even swear by this modem. One reason for this is that 3Com has actually written a V.Everything device driver specifically for SBS. These same loyal fans of the V.Everything also warn, however, that you need to get the latest device driver and firmware revision. You can locate these files quite easily from the 3Com Web site (*www.3com.com*).

Tip

Many SBS VAPs also use various models and speeds of the 3Com Sportster product line. Regardless of which brand and model of modem you ultimately recommend for your clients, nearly all SBS VAPs and PSS reps agree that the modem should be external.

Multiport Serial Adapters

Most white box and brand-name servers usually include only two serial ports. This generally poses a problem for SBS VAPs and small business clients. The serial interface for a UPS occupies one of the two COM ports, leaving just one remaining serial port for other functions, such as a mouse, modem sharing, inbound and outbound faxing, remote access, and connection to an Internet service provider (ISP).

Not all small businesses need all services that depend on modems or even serial ports. For example, if a small business uses an xDSL connection to an ISP for Internet access, this will be connected to the SBS 4.5 system through a secondary (that is, an external) network adapter. If a small business uses this same broadband connection for mobile workers to connect to the SBS 4.5 system over the Internet (as opposed to directly to the server through modems) through Point-to-Point Tunneling Protocol (PPTP), this will eliminate the need for modem use for both remote access and ISP connectivity. Modem sharing would be required only if your small business clients needed to connect to systems that aren't set up to be accessed through a Web browser over the Internet, such as an IBM System/36 or AS/400 host. Finally, if the small business doesn't send many faxes, it might not need more than one modem connected to Fax Service. As a result, a small business client could easily get by with only two serial ports.

Tip

For more information on Internet access, see Chapter 18. For more information on remote access and PPTP, see Chapter 27.

On the flip side, if the small business does intend on sending and receiving a substantial amount of fax volume through SBS, has several mobile workers who need to dial in directly to the server to check e-mail and transfer files, and wants a backup Internet access connection in case their xDSL broadband line goes down, it'll need a lot more than two serial ports. This is where a multiport serial adapter or board comes into play.

A multiport serial board, as the name implies, provides additional COM ports to the system. With a typical SBS 4.5 system, a multiport serial board might be used to increase the number of serial ports from two to six or more. Many SBS VAPs choose Digi International as their OEM of choice for multiport serial adapters.

If you've never seen a multiport serial board up close, it's usually a PCI expansion card with a large proprietary connector taking up the bulk of the surface of the card. Into this proprietary connector, you plug a very thick proprietary cable that splits off into multiple COM ports. The Digi Web site (*www.digi.com*) has a number of pictures if you want to see what one of these devices looks like before ordering it for a small business client.

Tip

Digi, like many other vendors, also offers a number of products that have multiple V.90 modems built directly in the PCI expansion card, eliminating the need for bulky cables and proprietary connectors. For a more complete list of products, see the HCL page on the Microsoft Web site.

Routers

For those SBS VAPs who are totally new to wide area and Internet connectivity, a router takes packets of data from one network and routes it to another network. If you're looking for more background or a more elegant definition on routers and routing in general, see *Network Essentials* and *TCP/IP Training* from Microsoft Press.

SBS VAPs often use routers to connect the SBS 4.5 system to an ISP or in some cases to other company locations. Some of the more popular routers used by SBS VAPs include models from Lucent Technologies (from its merger with Ascend), 3Com, and Netopia.

Because a router communicates with SBS 4.5 on a very different level than a modem or multiport serial adapter (from an ISO/OSI reference model standpoint), routers don't need device drivers. They do, however, often require firmware upgrades.

To get updated firmware for a Pipeline router from Lucent Technologies, which is used primarily with ISDN and leased line connections, go to *www.ascend.com*.

Note

At some point in the future, Lucent Technologies will probably redesign the navigation on its Web site (*www.lucent.com*) to make it easier to reach technical support information for the former Ascend networking products. For the time being, it's much quicker to enter through *www.ascend.com*.

To download updated firmware for a 3Com router typically used for small business clients, such as the OfficeConnect ISDN LAN Modem, start at *www.3com.com*. If your small business client has a Netopia router, which like the Lucent Pipeline product line can be used for ISDN or leased line connections, go to *www.netopia.com* to update firmware.

Network Interface Cards

On an SBS 4.5 system, a NIC or network adapter is used to connect the server to the hub and from there, ultimately to client workstations. As you saw in Chapter 18, a NIC can also be used to connect an SBS 4.5 system to a router for an ISDN dial-on-demand or full-time Internet access connection. NICs are also used to connect SBS 4.5 systems to broadband access devices such as xDSL or cable modems. Although you can find a number of NICs listed on the HCL page on the Microsoft Web site, SBS VAPs tend to use NICs from either Intel or 3Com most often.

While NICs do have firmware burned into the card, you'll rarely see vendors making NIC firmware revisions available for download. A lot of this has to do with the low-cost, commodity-oriented nature of NICs in general. So the major concern with NICs would be ensuring that the latest device drivers are being used for optimal reliability and performance.

The Intel EtherExpress is a popular NIC product line with SBS VAPs. To get the latest device drivers, point your Web browser to *www.intel.com*. The 3Com EtherLink product line is also widely recommended by SBS VAPs. To locate updated device drivers for an EtherLink NIC, to the 3Com home page.

Tip

If you assemble white box systems or install NICs into existing systems on a fairly regular basis *and* your company is in the role of product reseller in addition to service provider, you might want to save money and bolster your profit margins by purchasing NICs in bulk. Both Intel and 3Com make their most popular NICs available in multipack boxes. Regardless of whether your company resells product or not, you'll want to have one or two spare NICs in your tool bag for troubleshooting.

Tape Backup Drives and SCSI and RAID Adapters

Beside the communication-oriented devices discussed above, SBS 4.5 storage related devices might also periodically need device driver and firmware upgrades.

Tape Backup Drives

Although a number of OEMs sell tape backup drives and many leading server OEMs have their own private label versions created, SBS VAPs tend to be most loyal to Hewlett-Packard (HP) and Seagate Technology tape drives.

To check for updated firmware and device drivers for a Seagate tape drive, start at the Seagate home page (*www.seagate.com*). If you see firmware on this Web page that's recommended or required, you'll need to send e-mail to or place a call to Seagate technical support.

For an HP tape drive, start at the HP home page (*www.hp.com*). Like many of the OEMs discussed in this chapter, HP also has a notify service where you can register to be e-mailed about any updates to the product's Software & Drivers page. This is a particularly great way to stay proactive.

SCSI Adapters

Some new SBS VAPs might be tempted to succumb to a small business owner's pressure to use desktop-class hardware with a server. Nowhere is this truer than with hard disk drives. SBS VAPs know the scene all too well. They meet with a small business owner to close a deal on an SBS 4.5 network rollout. Just as the small business owner's about to sign on the dotted line, he pulls out a circular from the Sunday newspaper showing the local office superstore's $199 sale on 13-GB hard disk drives. "Hey, Josh," he asks. "If these 13-GB drives are so inexpensive, why are you putting only 9-GB drives in our server?" I explain how the hard disk drives in a server should be based on a SCSI interface, as opposed to EIDE technology, because SCSI hard disk drives are better suited for the rigors of a server with multiple users.

Other things being equal, SCSI hard disk drives generally cost more. If the motherboard for the server doesn't include a SCSI host adapter, buying the adapter is an extra, albeit a crucial, expense as well. Many SBS VAPs choose a special type of SCSI host adapter for hard disk drives that provides built-in RAID capabilities and special cache memory dedicated to boosting the performance of the SCSI hard disk drives in a RAID array.

When hardware-based RAID isn't required or even when it's required and you need to have a SCSI-based tape drive and CD-ROM in the server, SBS VAPs still need a basic SCSI host adapter. Adaptec is one of the more popular SCSI adapter vendors among SBS VAPs.

To locate updated device drivers and firmware for one of Adaptec's best selling adapters, the AHA-2940, go to *www.adaptec.com.*

RAID Adapters

When setting up fault-tolerant RAID hard disk drive configurations, SBS VAPs have two basic choices:

- **Hardware RAID** (where a RAID adapter is utilized)—generally the higher performance option

- **Software RAID** (where any type of hard disk drive can be used and Windows NT Server 4.0 performs the fault-tolerance operations)— generally the lower performance option, but less expensive from an asset acquisition standpoint

Tip

When looking at RAID solutions with your small business clients, you'll also want to discuss the pros and cons of RAID 1 (mirroring and duplexing) as well as RAID 5 (stripe set with parity). For more information on planning a fault-tolerant drive configuration, see Chapter 10 of the *Microsoft BackOffice Small Business Server 4.5 Resource Kit.*

Assuming you select hardware-based RAID, you'll need to choose a RAID controller card. Many SBS VAPs prefer AMI RAID adapters, which are either sold under the American Megatrends (AMI) brand name or are part of servers sold by OEMs. To stay up to date on the latest device drivers and firmware revisions for an AMI RAID adapter, go to the AMI home page (*www.ami.com*).

Maintaining the Antivirus Software Engine and Definitions

Out of all the software maintenance covered in this chapter, one category stands out as the most important: antivirus software. Because of the alarming number of new viruses that are discovered each month, antivirus software has a very short shelf life. While hardware OEMs might update a device driver or firmware revision once, twice, maybe three times a year, antivirus software vendors have major updates available nearly every month of the year. Some vendors make updates available more frequently, on a biweekly or daily basis. All the leading antivirus software vendors also make patches available within hours of major outbreaks, such as the Melissa virus in March 1999.

Because antivirus software vendors recognize that updating their code is something that needs to happen on a regular schedule, their solutions are typically built to be updated modularly. Antivirus software usually has two pieces:

- **Scanning engine**—core code of the product, usually updated two to four times a year

- **Signature files**—also known as pattern files, typically updated every two to six weeks

Don't Let Your Small Business Clients Procrastinate on Antivirus Solutions

ICSA, a GartnerGroup affiliate, released "Fifth Annual ICSA Labs Computer Virus Prevalence Survey: 1999" in July 1999. Some notable highlights included:

- Despite major media attention and more companies than ever installing modern client/server antivirus solutions, the rate of infection continues to increase.

- The median monthly rates of infection doubled between the 1998 and January/February 1999 time periods and were up fourfold between 1997 and January/February 1999.

- Just between January 1999 and February 1999, virus infection rates increased by 20 percent.

  Full survey results can be downloaded from the ICSA Web site at *www.icsa.net*.

All of the leading antivirus software vendors now also offer e-mail newsletters that notify you when new updates are available. Most products are also configurable in such as way that the software can connect directly to the vendor's FTP site at prescheduled times and update itself. Given the rapid obsolescence of antivirus products, a new trend among the leading ISVs is to move to a subscription-based model, where your small business clients pay a specified amount per seat every year for unlimited upgrades to both the scanning engine and virus definitions.

Some of the more very popular antivirus software vendors among SBS VAPs include:

- **Trend Micro** (*www.antivirus.com*)—OfficeScan for Microsoft Small Business Server

- **Symantec** (*www.symantec.com*)—Norton AntiVirus

- **Network Associates** (*www.nai.com*)—McAfee Total Virus Defense

- **Computer Associates** (*www.cai.com*)—Inoculan AntiVirus Suite for Microsoft BackOffice Small Business Server

Maintaining the Tape Backup and UPS Monitoring Software

Tape backup drives and UPSs have associated software that's updated on a regular basis.

Tape Backup Software

The frequency with which you need to check for backup software version updates depends largely on whether or not your small business clients are using Windows NT Backup (ntbackup.exe), which comes with SBS 4.5 through Windows NT Server 4.0. Although Windows NT Backup has hardly changed since the July 1996 release of Windows NT Server 4.0, third-party tape backup solutions such as VERITAS Backup Exec Small Business Server Suite for Windows NT version 7.3 are updated quite frequently.

Any updates for Windows NT Backup would come from SBS 4.5 specific or Windows NT Server 4.0 SPs, which are discussed briefly in the final section of this chapter. Note, however, that installing Microsoft Exchange Server (which is installed by default during the unattended SBS 4.5 setup) adds features to Windows NT Backup that allow for an online backup of Exchange Server.

Tip

For more details on Exchange Server, see Chapter 26.

In SBS 4.5, scheduling tape backup jobs is usually accomplished through the Scheduled Task Wizard, provided in SBS 4.5 through Microsoft Internet Explorer 5 (IE5). So you need to be aware that any incremental updates to IE5 through an IE, SBS, or Windows NT Server 4.0 SP might affect the Scheduled Task Wizard.

Tip

For details on how to automate Windows NT Backup through the Scheduled Task Wizard, see Chapter 13.

Products generally have much more functionality when third-party backup solutions are used. Accordingly there's a lot more program code that potentially has to be updated.

VERITAS Backup Exec for Small Business Server, for example, regularly puts out associated build updates that upgrade the core program. To download these incremental upgrades, go to the VERITAS home page (*www.veritas.com*).

Tip

VERITAS has a reseller listserv where you can sign up to be notified by e-mail when various file updates are available.

Computer Associates also offers tape backup software designed specifically for SBS: ARCserve Storage Suite for Microsoft BackOffice Small Business Server. To find out more about the application and how to download file updates, visit *www.cai.com*.

UPS Monitoring Software

Although SBS 4.5 provides limited UPS monitoring and shutdown capabilities through Windows NT Server 4.0, most UPS OEMs, such as American Power Conversion (APC) and Tripp Lite, offer their own software. The applications are written to the Windows NT 4.0 API for UPS service and go way beyond the native UPS interface capabilities in Windows NT 4.0.

Many SBS VAPs rely on PowerChute *plus* from APC. Although PowerChute *plus* isn't updated nearly as frequently as other software discussed in this chapter, nevertheless it has regular upgrades that substantially enhance the application's feature set. To download an updated version of PowerChute *plus*, go to *www.apcc.com*.

Note

Although UPSs, such as those in the APC Smart-UPS product line, have firmware, the firmware rarely changes and generally isn't upgradeable.

Staying Abreast of Service Packs

Your clients don't need every Microsoft SP. Some SPs are released for applications your client might not even be using. For example, if an SP is released for Microsoft SQL Server 7.0, and your small business clients use Microsoft Access 2000, don't bother applying the SQL Server 7.0 SP.

SBS 4.5 ships with several SPs integrated into its unattended setup program:

- Windows NT Server 4.0 SP4
- Exchange Server 5.5 SP2
- Windows NT 4.0 Option Pack

Although not technically an SP, the Windows NT 4.0 Option Pack was released after the July 1996 release of Windows NT Server 4.0. The Windows NT 4.0 Option Pack gives SBS 4.5 such crucial components as Microsoft Internet Information Server 4.0 (IIS), Microsoft Management Console (MMC) 1.1, and Microsoft Index Server 2.0, all of which are required for various facets of the SBS Console.

Note

While Microsoft has no immediate plans to release an SP specifically for SBS 4.5, SBS 4.0 had an SP available that spanned two CD-ROMs.

As with all software that you download in this chapter, reviewing the readme file and any other included documentation is important. Testing the software in a controlled lab environment before deploying is just as important. With Microsoft SPs, these notes of caution become even more important because you're upgrading the core NOS suite. Before you upgrade, make sure you have at least one verified complete tape backup on hand. In addition, always be sure to have at least one updated emergency repair disk (ERD) on hand before applying the SP.

A few ways you can keep abreast of the latest SP information as it relates to SBS 4.5, Windows NT Server 4.0, and any other related BackOffice Server applications include:

- Visit the Microsoft Direct Access Web site (*www.microsoft.com/ directaccess*) Support page, which has a link to SP information on its list of resources.

- Order a Microsoft TechNet or TechNet Plus CD subscription or join the Microsoft Certified Solution Provider (MCSP) program. You'll get an updated set of SP CD-ROMs each month. This avoids the hassle of having to download large files. For more information on TechNet subscriptions, visit *www.microsoft.com/technet*. For more information on applying to the MCSP program, visit *www.microsoft.com/mcsp*.

- Subscribe to the weekly Microsoft Channel Flash, TechNet Flash, and BackOffice News e-mail newsletters, which all routinely announce new SPs. Visit *www.microsoft.com* to learn how to subscribe.

While the list of available SPs might seem a bit onerous at first, most SBS VAPs need to focus on only certain areas. Areas of primary concern are:

- Exchange Server 5.5
- Microsoft Office 2000
- IE5
- SBS 4.5
- SQL Server 7.0
- Microsoft Windows 95/98
- Windows NT Server 4.0 (Intel)

The Bottom Line

The days of being able to install a piece of software and let it sit unchanged for years are long gone. Hardware OEMs and ISVs are constantly releasing new software updates that warrant your attention. Sometimes these interim releases fix documented bugs. Other times they improve performance, fix security holes, or add new features. Regardless of where the software patch comes from, take time and do your homework. This includes reviewing any included documentation, performing testing in a controlled lab environment, and visiting relevant newsgroups. You can't be too careful when it comes to introducing new software into a production environment, even that of a small business client. Selecting hardware from the Windows NT HCL is also important. In this chapter, you saw how to keep on top of software for hardware devices, antivirus solutions, data protection tools, and Microsoft NOS-related applications.

Chapter 23

Testing the Tape Backup, Power Protection, and Firewall Solutions

Chapter 15 showed how downtime costs small businesses big money. Using a simple formula, you can help uncover your client's daily and hourly costs of downtime. Chapter 15 showed how a client who nets $2 million annually could lose $8,000 a day due to unplanned system downtime. Suddenly, $400 to $600 for a commercial grade UPS solution seems like pocket change.

Just as they rarely think about the devastating impact of server downtime, small business owners often have a hard time understanding why testing is necessary until it's too late. Too much, however, is riding on certain Microsoft BackOffice Small Business Server components to forgo thorough testing. This chapter will introduce you to key testing metrics for tape backup drives, UPSs, and firewalls.

Test Tape Backup and Restore Scenarios

Chapter 13 covered the many benefits of automating tape backup jobs. At the end of the day, though, the goal of a tape backup solution is to be a restore solution. The most crucial issue becomes how to get the data back into the server undamaged and as quickly as possible.

Note

Automation of tape backup jobs loses much of its appeal when jobs must span more than one tape. Since no one is likely to be around at your client's office to change tapes at 2 A.M., make sure to select a tape drive that is large enough, with ample room for growth, to back up all server volumes on a single tape. At the time this book went to press, the DDS-4 standard had just been announced for DAT tape backup drives. DDS-4 supports a native capacity of 20 GB, with compressed capacity of 40 GB. Although larger capacity solutions are and will continue to be available, DDS-4 will likely supplant DDS-3 as the server tape drive standard of choice for small business clients.

Saving Time on Windows NT Backup Jobs

Many third-party tape backup solutions will back up open files, but Windows NT Backup won't. If you're relying on Windows NT Backup, tape backup jobs might take longer because the program stops whenever it encounters any open files and pauses for 30 seconds to give the file time to close itself. I have yet to encounter files that cooperate with this 30-second waiting period.

Even if all the users on the network close all their files, a typical SBS 4.5 system will still have at least 30 to 40 system files left opened. To understand the magnitude of this issue, multiply this number of open files by a 30-second wait. So waiting for open files can easily add at least 15–20 minutes to a tape backup job. You can, however, get around these delays. See KB article Q104169 in the Microsoft Knowledge Base.

Because the tape backup solution runs on autopilot, many small business clients and new SBS VAPs might have a tendency to set it and forget it. While automation clearly has many benefits, this completely hands-off attitude can be very dangerous if no one is overseeing the process. The tape backup solution needs to be tested thoroughly following deployment and then subsequently at least four times a year.

Because you can never plan for data being destroyed by a fire, flood, hurricane, theft, or disgruntled employee, you can't be too diligent in keeping tabs on the tape backup, even if your client very seldom has the need for restores.

Protecting Basic Volumes, Files, and Folders

Before you launch a single wizard or pull up a dialog box, take a few steps back and make sure you've covered all bases with your small business client's tape backup solution. Key questions you need to answer before you test the tape backup solution include the following:

❑ Is all the data stored on the server or do certain workstations need to be backed up? To centralize data storage, can these clients' data files be migrated to the server?

❑ Do you have a list of everything that needs to be backed up on the server?

❑ Does the tape backup solution encompass all server volumes, as well as Microsoft Exchange Server and Microsoft SQL Server? Can the backup solution handle open files?

❑ How is security integrated into the backup and restore routines? Does the tape backup solution have its own security mechanism or does it leverage the Microsoft Windows NT Server 4.0 Security Accounts Manager database?

Note

If the tape backup solution doesn't back up open files, make the internal guru and end users aware of this limitation so that they can close files on their network drive(s) each day. You can even show some power users how to check Windows Explorer for the archive bit (A) to see whether their files have been backed up.

No matter how much planning you do, nothing can approximate the feeling of the rubber-meets-the-road impact of a test with live data. Regardless of which type of tape backup software is being used, you'll need to test individual file and folder restores. If adequate space is available on another physical drive, either on the same server or another system on the network, perform a full volume restore.

You'll also want to restore the backed up files to an alternate folder. Many times your client will be restoring data files, such as Word or Excel files, where data is corrupt. Since the end user probably doesn't recall the exact state the file was in at the time of the most recent backup, allow him or her to evaluate the damaged file side by side with the restored file and let them choose how they want to address mitigating their data loss.

Tip

If you don't have adequate space to restore files, folders, or a volume to the server, you can always point the restore to any mapped drive on the network.

In Windows NT Backup, for example, pointing a restore to an alternate file path is pretty straightforward:

1. In the Tapes window, choose Catalog from the Operations menu.

2. Once a catalog of the tape has been generated, select the tape backup set that you wish to restore.

3. Click the Restore button on the toolbar.

4. In the Restore Information dialog box, change Restore To Drive and Alternate Path fields as appropriate. You'll also probably want to select Restore File Permissions and Verify After Restore. See Figure 23-1.

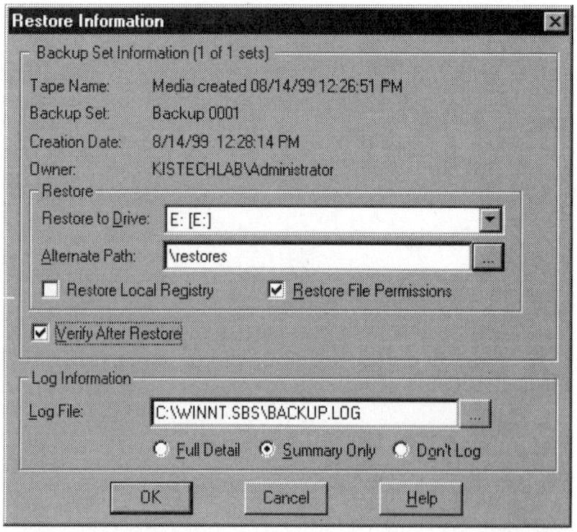

Figure 23-1

Restore a backup in an alternate folder location.

Each small business' data protection concerns will be unique. As you're developing the inventory of what files need to be protected, you should also be testing each scenario using the basic techniques described above to make sure that when the fateful moment arrives, the tape restore works. Be on the lookout for an "oh, by the way," such as when the head bookkeeper in accounting neglects to mention that he's been keeping the payroll records for the past five years on his hard disk drive, which of course isn't backed up or even password protected.

Also consider other e-mail besides Exchange Server in your small business clients' tape backup plans. For example, if clients are using POP3 mail through Proxy Server and maintaining local e-mail folders, contacts, and calendars, either migrate the .pst files to the SBS 4.5 system for integrated backup or back up workstations periodically over the network.

Creating the Low-Budget Warm Spare

With a larger client, many SBS VAPs will likely want to create an unattended job that copies company shared folders and user shared folders nightly to another system running Windows NT Server 4.0. This provides an extra measure of fault tolerance because the tape drive is often the least reliable component in any server. (It's also one of the few items in a server with moving parts.)

Since many of your small business clients will only have one server, you can use the Scheduled Task Wizard to copy company shared folders and user shared folders overnight to a highly secure client running Microsoft Windows NT Workstation 4.0 with NTFS and that has adequate hard disk drive space.

Not only does this method provide a backup for the tape backup solution, the Windows NT Workstation 4.0 client could provide file and print sharing services temporarily, with up to 10 simultaneous connections, in the event the server was down for whatever reason.

Unique Exchange Server and SQL Server Concerns

If your small business clients are utilizing Exchange Server 5.5, SQL Server 7.0, or both with SBS 4.5, unique backup and restore concerns exist that require attention. Windows NT Backup (NTBackup) can perform an online backup of Exchange Server while services are running, which was covered in Chapters 13 and 19. This, however, requires special configuration choices if the tape backup job is run manually. If the tape backup is automated, set up another

NTBackup job command line that encompasses backing up the Exchange Server 5.5 Information Store and Directory. For example:

```
ntbackup backup DS \\KISTECHLAB01 IS \\KISTECHLAB01 /d "Backup of
Exchange" /t normal /l "c:\temp\backlog.txt" /e
```

Tip

For more information on automating Exchange Server backup with Windows NT Backup, see KB article Q152313 in the Microsoft Knowledge Base.

Note that while you can do an online Exchange Server backup through Windows NT Backup, you can't perform a mailbox-by-mailbox backup or restore (that is, a brick-level backup) without a third-party solution. In order to recover an individual Exchange Server mailbox using Windows NT Backup, you'd need to restore the files to a spare server. You'll find several Exchange Server disaster recovery white papers that address this complex process on the Exchange Server Web site at *www.microsoft.com/exchange*.

For more information on disaster recovery preparation for Windows NT Server 4.0, see Chapter 5 in the *Microsoft Windows NT Server 4.0 Resource Kit*. For more information on disaster recovery preparation for Exchange Server 5.5, see Part 9 in the *Microsoft Exchange Server Resource Guide* in the *Microsoft Windows NT Server 4.0 Resource Kit*.

Caution

Windows NT Backup can't back up a remote registry. While you can map a drive to an additional Windows NT Server 4.0 system or to a client running Microsoft Windows 95/98 or Windows NT Workstation 4.0, if you perform an over-the-network backup, Windows NT Backup won't be able to back up that system's registry.

Although Windows NT Backup can perform an online backup of Exchange Server, it can't perform an online backup of SQL Server. Two ways to back up SQL Server if your small business client doesn't choose to purchase a third-party tape backup solution include:

- Use Enterprise Manager to back up a database to disk, then use Windows NT Backup to copy that disk-based backup to tape. (Or use Enterprise Manager to back up a database directly to tape.)
- Get all users to log off the database, stop the database in Enterprise Manager, and perform an offline backup using Windows NT Backup.

Since one of the major selling points of third-party tape backup software is their ability to truncate transaction logs in both Exchange Server and SQL Server, make sure any creatively assembled, homemade methods take this crucial concern into account.

Each small business client has unique needs. Some will rely on SQL Server and Exchange Server for mission critical functions. Others will be using less full-featured alternatives such as Microsoft Access 2000 relational databases or POP3-based mail through Microsoft Proxy Server. Regardless, the techniques described in these past two sections should be vigorously implemented and tested following implementation and then again at quarterly recurring intervals.

Factoring Antivirus Protection into the Tape Backup Solution

Chapter 22 covered how crucial it is to constantly update antivirus software. Because the incidences of virus contamination are increasing at alarming rates, virus protection needs to be considered in the context of a tape backup solution. The last thing you or your small business clients want to worry about is the possibility of restoring an infected file or set of files from tape.

While server and Exchange Server–based antivirus software should provide an adequate measure of protection against this frightening possibility, most of the leading independent software vendors (ISVs) for third-party tape backup software have recently shored up their product offerings by integrating virus protection into the backup and restore process.

In the event your client elects to stay with Windows NT Backup, you can use one low budget way to approximate this kind of virus protection without having true integration. Assuming your client has server and Exchange Server–based antivirus software that's being kept current, you could add a manual virus scan and clean job to the Scheduled Task Wizard. The job should be configured to run each night just before the backup job is launched.

Stay Proactive and Be Prepared

Tape backup is just one more part of an SBS network for which you'll need to stay proactive. Some tips on how to do that include:

- **Examine the logs**—Pay close attention to the tape backup logs whenever you're on-site (see Chapter 25) or, even better, integrate the tape backup logs into the Server Status Tool report (see Chapter 15).

- **Practice and be prepared**—Simulate a full-blown disaster recovery restore scenario with data from an entire volume or entire server. Also, prepare a one or two page document of the restore procedure that includes time estimates for various steps and checklists of what items are required. Then keep copies of the procedure both on-site at the client's office, as well as at your office. Everyone involved should know approximately how long it takes to restore a full server so expectations are in check with reality.

- **Rotate, archive, and retire**—While you have many ways to set up an effective tape rotation plan, one simple way is to use four weekly sets of tapes, with a total of 20 tapes. Every Monday morning, the previous week's set of tapes goes off-site while another set of tapes comes back on-site. In addition to these tapes, I always have clients order 12 more tapes to be used for permanent archive tapes, created on the last business day of each month. The permanent archive tapes should be write-protected, labeled, and stored off-site indefinitely. While different schools of thought on media replacement exist, tapes do wear out over time. A general guideline is to retire media once a year, so that once a tape has been recycled 13 times, it's put to rest for good.

Tip

If you sense your client is having problems keeping track of which set of tapes it should use for the weekly rotation, which tapes should be off-site, and other related issues, you might want to create a simple log book to keep by the server to control tape assets. If responsibility for changing tapes (daily) and bringing tapes back/forth off-site (weekly) is spread across multiple people, you can track exactly what's happening.

- **Keep the heads clean**—Some tape drives don't require head cleaning. Others do. Make sure to check the documentation for the tape drive and build head cleaning into the maintenance schedule if necessary.

Test the Alerting, Logging, and Shutdown Capabilities of the UPS

Just like the tape backup drive and the backup software, the UPS and its software need to be tested to ensure that no unpleasant surprises occur at inopportune times.

Tip

A good time to perform quarterly tests on the areas discussed in this chapter is on the same day as the quarterly update review meeting. To prepare a quarterly update report, see Chapter 7.

As you design and test power protection solutions for your small business clients, make sure to consider all impacted hardware, not just the obvious ones. Some often overlooked devices that need UPS protection include any related server peripherals, such as an external tape drive, modem, hub, router, or monitor as well as any phone and alarm systems. For many small business clients, also consider data-line protection in addition to electric utility protection. Data-line protection typically addresses surges that pass through telephone, cable TV, and network cable lines.

Prerequisite to Testing the UPS

Server-class UPS units almost always support a serial interface that allows the UPS to communicate directly with the SBS 4.5 system. If for some reason the UPS for the server doesn't have a serial interface, promptly get a UPS that does and move that less-featured UPS to another device on the network, such as a client workstation or Ethernet hub.

Through serial-port communication with the Windows NT Server 4.0 operating system part of SBS 4.5, the UPS and its accompanying monitoring software leverages four Windows NT services: Alerter, EventLog, Messenger, and UPS. Although none of these services are included by default in the Service Status report section of the Server Status Tool reports (see Chapter 15), these services all need to be running and set to an Automatic Startup Type. This provides you a value-added opportunity to integrate these services into the Server Status Tool reports.

Alerting

In order to test the UPS solution properly, you'll want to perform the tasks after hours. All the end users should be logged off the server or, at the minimum, all files should be closed. You can check to make sure all files are closed by opening the Tasks page in the SBS Console. In the Manage Shared Folders section select a shared folder and choose Manage Open Files.

You'll want to leave one or two client workstations logged on, preferably one with Windows 95/98 and one with Windows NT Workstation 4.0, to make sure alerting works properly.

Testing should be done immediately following deployment of an SBS system, then at least four times a year thereafter. Like testing the tape backup solution, UPS testing should be built into any service or maintenance contracts. Also make sure you watch for the Replace Battery indicator on the UPS unit because UPS batteries wear out over time. To be proactive, take time to learn how the UPS OEM that you recommend handles battery replacement and other warranty-related issues.

Tip

Before starting UPS tests, make sure the UPS is fully charged. The charge is usually indicated both on the front panel of any server-grade UPS and in the accompanying monitoring software.

Although most popular UPS monitoring applications have a variety of self-test mechanisms built-in, the test that best approximates real-life usage is simply pulling the UPS power cord out of the electric outlet. Everything plugged into the UPS should stay on. The UPS service, working in conjunction with the Messenger and Alerter services, will send messages to the SBS 4.5 system and to client workstations on the LAN, advising that the UPS is on battery and that the server will be shut down in a few minutes. In addition, the UPS will begin beeping audibly and the On Battery light will be displayed on the front of the unit.

Since you're just testing the alert features at this point, as opposed to shutdown features, you'll want to make sure that both the SBS 4.5 system and clients on the network have received the Messenger service notice.

Many times power outages are relatively short in duration, so that normal utility power is restored before the UPS initiates an automated server shutdown. When the UPS switches back to utility power before shutting down, clients on the LAN are notified that the server is back on utility power. To test this, plug the UPS back into the wall and watch for an updated Messenger service notice on both the SBS 4.5 system and network clients.

Most UPS software applications, such as American Power Conversion (APC) PowerChute *plus*, also work with the Windows NT Server 4.0 Server service to prevent client logons while the SBS 4.5 system is on battery power. If you anticipate that users will need this added checkpoint, by all means test the feature by attempting to log on to the SBS 4.5 system while the server UPS is on battery power.

Another type of UPS alerting sends messages to system administrators, such as the guru and VAP, by using e-mail, a pager, or both methods when an event defined as critical occurs. See Figure 23-2. If the system administrators are counting on these alert capabilities, make sure this facet of alerting is included in the testing process.

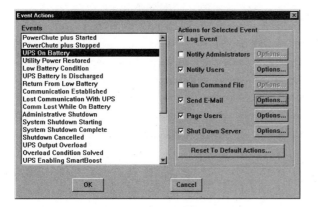

Figure 23-2

Alert administrators by pager or e-mail when the UPS is on battery power.

Logging

Chapter 15 showed how to integrate the PowerChute event log file with a batch of Server Status Tool reports. Logging is an extremely effective diagnostic tool. Because it keeps tabs on power statistics in the office, a PowerChute log is like a picture that speaks more than a million words.

Since UPS logs will be coming to you through Server Status Tool reports, you should incorporate some type of highlights of the logs into your monthly executive summary and quarterly update report and meeting. This could be as simple as stating, "ABC Company experienced 37 separate power disturbances this month, all of which were handled effectively by the UPS." You might also want to build a clause into your maintenance or service agreements that authorize your firm to follow up on any UPS log irregularities.

For example, if you walk into a client's office on a Wednesday morning and your client complains that half of the PCs were locked up on Monday morning, check the PowerChute event log. Chances are that a power disturbance occurred over the weekend, which the UPS compensated for and logged. This not only becomes a great tool for figuring out what went wrong, the statistics gathered by the PowerChute log become a great selling tool for placing desktop-grade UPSs on all client workstations. Without conveying an "I told you so" attitude, be sure to point out that UPSs on each workstation would have likely prevented the reported problem.

Because the logging capabilities of the UPS are valuable, test their functionality both initially and then each quarter. When you pulled the plug on the UPS in the alert testing section, this should've generated a blackout condition in the PowerChute event log. When you plugged the UPS back into utility power another event in the log should have noted the return to normal power. See Figure 23-3.

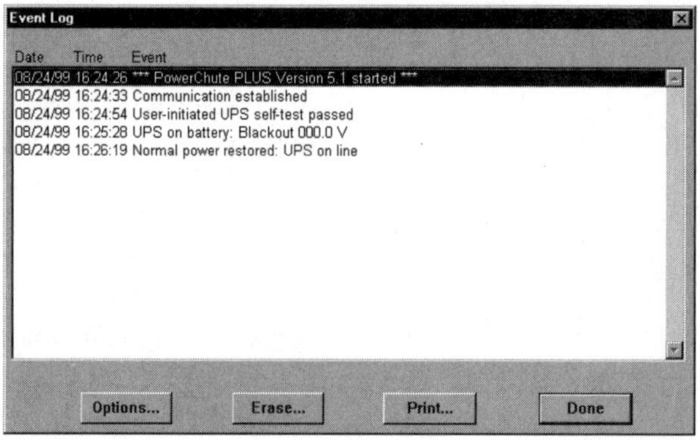

Figure 23-3

Assess the logging capabilities of the UPS.

Shutdown

The primary goal of a UPS is to minimize the huge risk of hardware damage and data loss that comes from sudden, uncontrolled shutdowns. Most small business owners might not intuitively understand the critical importance of the UPS being able to shut down the server gracefully during an extended power outage. If you encounter blank stares, try initiating a dialog similar to the following:

Josh the VAP: "The server data files could be severely damaged if the SBS 4.5 system loses power unexpectedly without an orderly shutdown."

Beth the guru: "That's nonsense. You're just trying to squeeze another $400 purchase out of us."

Josh the VAP: "Well, let's look at your PC, for example. I see you have Word running with four open files, Excel running with five open workbooks, and PowerPoint with one open file. Your PC has ten open data files, not including open files used by applications and the OS. Now what would happen if I yanked the power cord out of the outlet for your PC before you had a chance to save? Now imagine this happening to 15 end users connected to the SBS 4.5 system with a total of 150 open data files. That's going to be a tough crowd to deal with when everyone in the office just lost several hours of work that's corrupted and can't be salvaged, short of restoring from last night's tape backup."

Beth the guru: "Don't you dare unplug my PC! Okay, okay, you made your point. I can see the value of the server being able to shut off automatically."

By default, PowerChute *plus* will shut down the server after five minutes of being on battery. Depending on the size of the UPS and the load placed on the unit, you should be able to increase this time interval to 10 to 15 minutes (600 to 900 seconds) without any problem.

To test the unattended shutdown capabilities, allow the unplug test to run through the five-minute interval and observe the UPS and server behavior. When you plug the UPS back into the electric outlet, simulating the end of the blackout, the UPS and server should power back on and boot up on their own.

While a UPS has to be able to perform a graceful shutdown when the unit's been on battery for a prespecified amount of time, for many small business sites the UPS also needs to turn the SBS 4.5 server back on and boot back up after utility power is restored. This is an important feature to look for in UPS units for your small business clients.

You also need to consider UPS capacity. Make sure to find out the unit's run-time capacity at full load. If the devices plugged into the UPS are drawing current at the maximum capacity of the unit and power is lost at the same time, how long will the unit run? Because the run-time capacity varies based on each UPS model and the type of devices that are plugged into the UPS, most

UPS vendors have sizing guides on their Web sites. For example, see the sizing guide on the American Power Conversion Web site (*www.apcc.com*).

Assessing More Complex Power Protection Needs

If you've exhausted all the standard recommendations on power protection throughout this book and your small client still is experiencing unusual power disturbances or needs assurances of 7 × 24 mission critical 99.9 percent uptime, you have one additional option that's worth considering.

For more advanced testing of the electrical system, being be an SBS VAP or even an electrician isn't enough. APC has a consulting services group, made up of staff with dual backgrounds in system administration and electrical engineering. SBS VAPs can resell these services.

Although using the APC consulting group is often pricier than many small business owners would be able to justify, if your client is considering hosting a Web site and wants to become the next Amazon.com or eBay, the client might need a more advanced and reliable power protection design. While electricians in the United States will get the electrical system up to the National Electric Code (NEC), APC's consulting engineers will verify whether the electricity is operating at server-safe levels, as defined by IEEE.

Test Firewall Features on Proxy Server

With no full-time IT staff, small businesses tend to be particularly vulnerable to hackers compromising their network either through improperly secured modems or full-time Internet access connections. As more and more small businesses upgrade from dial-on-demand Internet connections, which generally have dynamically assigned IP addresses, to full-time broadband and routed connections, these small businesses need to make sure that at least minimal security is in place.

In contrast to Fortune 1000 IT staff or larger solution providers, SBS VAPs generally don't have in-depth expertise in firewalls or security. In many cases, this is because small businesses don't have the budget to spend $5,000 to $10,000 or more on a security audit. Unless security happens to be their specialty, SBS VAPs don't usually go out of their way to add complex firewall testing and troubleshooting skills to their training portfolio.

Fortunately for small business clients and SBS VAPs, Proxy Server 2.0 has a built-in firewall with appropriate defaults preconfigured. Proxy Server 2.0 uses dynamic packet filtering to secure the network from outside traffic. The only interface visible to the outside world is the external network card. With dynamic packet filtering, ports are only opened for a short duration during the requests. The appropriate port is then closed when the request has been fulfilled. Chapter 18 showed how the Internet Connection Wizard (ICW) helps to configure the firewall for popular applications.

As the virtual IT director for your clients, you need to assess why your small business client would or wouldn't be a target for hackers. For example, if your client is hosting an e-commerce Web site that accepts credit card numbers, your client is a target. If your client is a credit and collections agency with millions of dollars in billing information on the server hard disk drives, your client is a target.

The greater the value of the data to protect, the more concerned you'll want to be about assessing whether the default Proxy Server security configuration choices are adequate. For most small business clients, dynamic packet filtering will be more than adequate. If their needs demand it, however, you should call in a firm who specializes in security assessments.

Tip

To learn more about tightening up the Proxy Server firewall, see "Fight Fire with Firewalls" by Tom Moran (July 1998) on the MSDN online Web site (*msdn.microsoft.com*).

Although these security assessment firms generally bill at hourly rates that would make any SBS VAP's jaw drop in awe, the costs to your client might ultimately be quite trivial when you consider the value of the data to protect with Proxy Server 2.0. When I checked with PSS and SBS VAPs on the topic, I found the unilateral preference is to bring in a security expert to test firewalls. If your client truly has the need for these types of advanced services, don't skimp. An improperly configured firewall leads to a false sense of security. This complacency can be even more dangerous.

Tip

To learn more about the dos and don'ts of partnering with other technology providers, see Chapter 6.

In addition to fortifying the firewall portion of Proxy Server, clients with complex security needs also should have their Window NT Server 4.0 security permissions tightened up as well. While the default settings in SBS provide stronger security in areas such as RAS, IP forwarding, and private IP address scopes, a consultant who specializes in Windows NT security audits can help to craft a security policy and implementation specific to your client's unique needs.

To be effective in doing penetration testing, the security consultant must be intimately familiar with TCP/IP and security. This requires an understanding of various hacking techniques, such as IP address spoofing, denial of service attacks, intercepting packets with a protocol analyzer, and the ping of death. To be successful, the security consultant needs to able to think like the hacker. Because basic configuration mistakes regarding security can be like leaving the front door to a bank open overnight, even Fortune 1000 IT organizations will often outsource the testing and monitoring functions of the firewall to firms that specialize in this area.

The Bottom Line

Most small business owners typically won't ask you to test the tape backup, power protection, or firewall solution. Because many small business owners have never owned a network before nor heard accounts from other small business network owners, they have no idea that the out of the box defaults aren't always optimal or even functional without additional tweaking. Immediately following installation of the tape backup and power protection solution, you'll want to run vigorous tests on them. Depending on how complex your client's security needs, you might want to partner with a security consulting firm to have in-depth penetration testing performed on your client's firewall. Regardless of which methods and time frames you choose to work with, revisit these testing procedures at least once every three months.

Chapter 24

Developing the Service Contract

Part 5 looked at how to test the Microsoft Small Business Server 4.5 installation and train small business end users and gurus. Part 6 examines what it takes to keep both the client and the server happy. In particular, this section of the book outlines crucial steps to keep even your most demanding clients satisfied and the SBS 4.5 network humming along.

Chapter 24 will provide the framework for building long-term profitable and successful client relationships that will remain healthy for years after the server is installed. The service contract is a key link between the small business client and the SBS VAP. While no substitute for professional legal advice, this chapter will help you write mutually beneficial service contracts.

Planning Tips

While most SBS VAPs recommend that you consult with your attorney before finalizing your template for service contracts, you'll need to sort through the following issues before you can even get to that stage:

❑ What's included with the service contract and what's not?

❑ What are the service contract fees, terms, and rate premiums?

❑ What hardware and software is covered by the service contract?

To help jump start planning some of the main elements that go into a typical SBS VAP service contract, the CD-ROM for this book includes the "Service Contract Planning Worksheet," a Word template. See Figure 24-1.

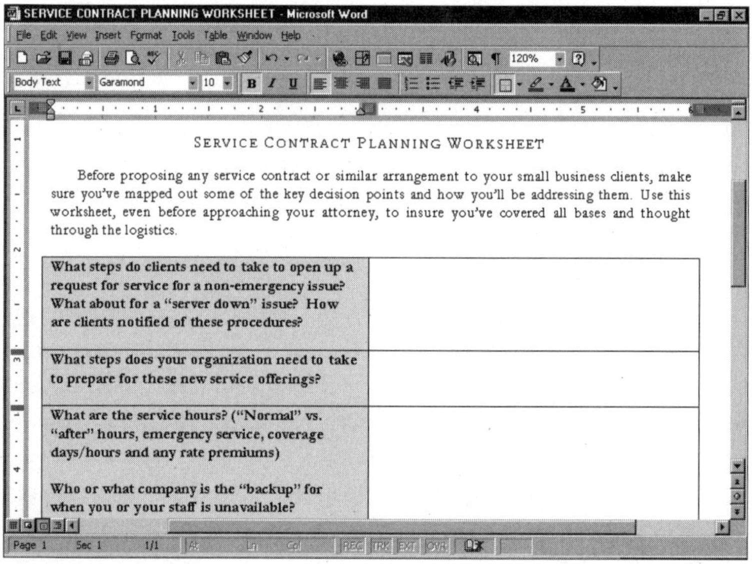

Figure 24-1
Use the Service Contract Planning Worksheet to write mutually beneficial contracts.

As you think about how small business clients will log their service requests with your firm, consider some of the tools in SBS 4.5. For example, you might want to create a custom Microsoft Outlook form that you'd distribute to clients to provide a more structured way of requesting service calls. To get started with Outlook forms, see Chapter 26 and my June 1999 Microsoft Direct Access

VAPVoice "How to Translate Sticky Notes into a Major Outlook Groupware Opportunity with Small Business Server," which is included on the CD-ROM.

Some SBS VAPs are creating password-protected sections on their Web sites or extranets that allow their small business clients to create help desk tickets and track the status of open requests.

Tip

A sample contract for support services, "Support Service Agreement" (a Word document), is also on the CD-ROM. This sample contract is provided courtesy of SBS VAP Dennis Anderson of Net\Works Inc. in Fridley, Minnesota. (*www.net-works-inc.com*).

Regardless of whether you capture service requests using an Outlook and Microsoft Exchange–centric solution or a Microsoft Internet Information Server (IIS) and Microsoft SQL Server browser-based solution, moving beyond simple phone calls, pages, and e-mail service call requests has many advantages. These advantages include:

- **Showcase a sample solution.** Once clients see how easy and beneficial using your service call request system is, they'll start thinking, "Gee, we could use a system like this, too."

- **Obtain more complete information.** By designing the forms that clients are required to submit for service calls, you'll eliminate the need for phone calls back and forth.

- **Provide service call history.** Once stored in either an Exchange public folder or SQL Server database, this history can be made available in a variety of formats to your staff and your clients.

- **Integrate the system with a back-end system.** Especially if you choose the IIS/SQL Server route, consider connecting your service-call tracking system with your accounting system through ODBC hooks.

- **Motivate your clients to use their tools.** As explained in Chapters 21 and 22, small business end users often need a bit of nudging to get them to embrace some of the new client applications on an SBS 4.5 network. With your service call system, they'll have an added incentive to become familiar with Outlook and Internet Explorer.

Pricing Options

In designing a service contract model for your small business clients, one of the most crucial decisions involves how to package and price your firm's services. Why is this so critical? Many new SBS VAPs tend to have significantly more technology experience than business acumen and often consider matters such as billings and collections as an afterthought. Experienced SBS VAPs have learned that getting smart about matters that affect the bottom line isn't an optional part of their daily routine.

You can choose among four basic types of service contracts: fixed-price, time and materials, per incident, and hybrid service.

Fixed-Price Arrangements

A fixed-price service contract essentially gives your client unlimited access to your firm's resources, subject to certain caveats and fine-print restrictions. Think of a fixed-price service contract as an all you can eat Sunday brunch buffet at the local hotel. Just as you can have as many drinks, appetizers, pastries, salads, entrees, and desserts as you wish, your client is entitled to as any many hardware repairs, software upgrades, troubleshooting sessions, informal training questions, and help desk calls as it can possibly digest in a given month—all for one price.

Obviously SBS VAPs who adopt the fixed-price model have major risks. First and foremost, you could easily end up with a disproportionate share of clients with seemingly insatiable appetites for technical support, given that the incremental cost of a service call has been reduced to zero dollars.

Second, if your clients with fixed-price service contracts all have emergencies around the same time each month, do you have the staff capacity to handle the workload?

Tip

For assistance with SBS VAP staffing and partnering challenges, see Chapters 4 and 6 respectively.

While staff capacity becomes an issue even with other types of service contracts, the whole response time concern becomes more of a sticking point with fixed-price agreements. When clients who have paid in advance for fixed-price service contracts can't get their first choice of appointment times, they're likely to become much more militant than those who pay as you go on other types of service contracts.

To mitigate many of these hazards, SBS VAPs tend to offer only fixed-priced agreements at prices high enough to offset the inherent risks. In addition, most SBS VAPs will specifically disclaim certain items (that is, say that these items cost extra).

Fixed-price arrangements have some benefits, however. The small business client gets a predictable cost each month for ongoing service and maintenance, while the SBS VAP has a predictable recurring revenue stream.

Some SBS VAPs will offer fixed-price contracts only when the client has an internal guru who's fairly competent about SBS. Without a guru on site to perform basic level 1 or level 2 types of help desk work, you're likely to field an endless stream of very basic questions on topics like walking end users through rebooting their PCs or power-cycling printers.

Tip

To learn more about internal gurus, see Chapters 1 and 2.

Time and Materials Arrangements

While fixed-price service contracts are certainly a valid choice when their scope is very well defined and their prices are set according to the risk factors discussed above, many experienced SBS VAPs gravitate toward time and materials based service contracts. Often viewed by SBS VAPs as the most equitable, time and materials service contracts require that clients pay for the service hours that they utilize—no more and no less.

Tip

Most SBS VAPs also enforce certain minimums such as a 15-minute minimum for phone support or two hours for an on-site service call.

All service calls, training sessions, phone support, hardware repairs, and upgrades are billed by the hour. In addition, any materials utilized or expenses incurred, whether it be a replacement SCSI ribbon cable for a hard disk drive, a dozen blank CD-Rs, or mileage, are billed as well.

The only real negative for clients is that if you encounter a particularly challenging problem that requires a long time to resolve, individual service calls can sometimes get expensive.

Per Incident Arrangements

Although some ISVs, especially those that can spread or amortize fixed costs over thousands of customers, often price their phone support on a per incident basis, SBS VAPs often shy away from per incident pricing.

Per incident pricing can really be successful with SBS VAPs only if they have a very clearly defined document that specifies what's included in an incident. Even with such details, per incident pricing can lead to a feeling of resentment where one party feels like a winner and the other party feels like the loser. This isn't what being an SBS VAP—that is, the virtual IT department— is all about.

Tip

Chapter 28 shows how you can elevate your firm from service provider to trusted small business advisor status, comparable to an accountant or attorney.

Hybrid Service Contracts

Hybrid service contracts offer SBS VAPs a way to create a best of breed offering that places certain services under fixed-priced or per incident arrangements, while the bulk of services are still provided under a pay by-the-hour model.

For a task that has a very definite beginning, middle, and end, such as upgrading a tape drive or flashing the firmware on a bank of modems, a fixed-price or per incident model might be successful. Some SBS VAPs will also charge a flat fee for items such as the server installation or individual client configurations for SBS. If you're not confident that you've allowed for every possible task, billing by the hour is overwhelmingly the business model of choice for SBS VAP service contracts, subject to the types of budgets you developed in the Chapter 9 project plan.

Service Level Agreements and Response Time

While most seasoned SBS VAPs have their attorney review the document template for service contracts, no amount of documentation will completely protect you against the client who's determined to get into the *Guinness Book of World Records* as the biggest nuisance known to VAP-kind.

Unlike owning a retail computer store or similar transaction-oriented business, being an SBS VAP isn't about one-shot deals. I can't imagine many who'd want to build long-term relationships with a client who's going to cause ulcers or premature hair loss among you or your staff. Keep this in mind as you begin to draft your service level agreements and response time clauses in service contracts.

Although larger VAPs and OEMs commonly advertise certain service level agreements (SLAs) and response times, SBS VAPs often find that providing such arrangements is extremely challenging. Unless you happen to have a relatively large, versatile staff, partnering with other local technology providers is often the only way to prepare yourself for the inevitable day when 90 percent of your clients have emergencies.

Many SBS VAPs also take precautions to make sure they don't promise more than they can deliver. For example, if the client insists on a written service level agreement or response time, you can address this by making the time span lengthy enough to be doable while short enough to satisfy the client.

Managing expectations is important as well. If a client demands and is willing to pay for a 30 minute, two hour, or four hour on-site response time, the service contract either needs to be extremely lucrative for your firm or your client needs to step up to the plate and hire a full-time network administrator. When most small business owners find out what the going salary range is for even junior level IT staff or the annual costs of keeping him or her trained, suddenly the four hour on-site response time that you propose is acceptable.

Which brings us to another related topic—tiering the response times. You have at least three types of support you can offer for typical network emergencies at client sites:

- Phone

- Remote

- On-site

First and foremost is the response time for phone support. In other words, how quickly can you get a trained staff member on the phone who can begin the troubleshooting process. For a typical SBS installation, a returned call within 15 to 30 minutes is an acceptable response to a 911 or server-down emergency.

The next level of tech support is remote support—dialing or RASing into the SBS 4.5 system for remote troubleshooting. Since your staff person would need to have a modem, "dial tone" (whether it be a leased line, a cell phone, or analog line), PC, and remote control or remote access software, this usually rules out handling the call while in transit.

Most SBS VAPs typically place the target response time for emergency remote support somewhere in between phone and on-site support. For example, if the client has a server down issue, you could promise a call back from a system engineer within 30 minutes, who might walk the guru through having everyone log off the network and rebooting the server. This might be followed up by a commitment from the system engineer to have someone from the VAP dial into the SBS 4.5 system for remote diagnostics within the next 60–90 minutes. If necessary, this would be followed by an appointment for on-site service within the next four hours.

If the client insists on on-site support when your staff member feels that phone or remote support would be just as effective, this discrepancy needs to be factored into your pricing model for on-site support. For example, if clients know that an emergency phone support call has a $50 minimum while a remote support call has a $100 minimum, they might be more inclined to opt for one of those options if they know the on-site emergency call has a $350 minimum.

In Scope vs. Out of Scope

Knowing everything about every possible permutation and combination of hardware, applications, and operating systems is impossible. For that reason, most SBS VAPs tend to pick their favored or preferred products and stick with them year in, year out. It can get very expensive to support six different brands of laptops or three different relational databases. Think about all the lab time, training, research, and lab expense associated with achieving expert proficiency on different products and platforms. So VAPs tend to develop their standards, which although modified slightly for each unique client's needs, provide the foundation for their support offerings.

To help the client sort through how the supported standards will apply to each end user on the SBS 4.5 network, Chapter 9 introduced the "Supported Application Matrix," an integral part of the "Network Design Report." Once this document is prepared and then subsequently discussed, revised if necessary, and accepted during your discussions outlined in Chapter 10, the "Supported Application Matrix" becomes the basis for determining what type of support is in scope.

You have at least two ways to handle out of scope hardware, applications, and operating systems. One very simple way is to refuse flat out to support any additional elements that aren't in the "Supported Application Matrix." This, of course, isn't necessarily the most practical way to approach the matter because most clients don't like dictators and needs do change over time.

Often the best way to address this issue is to provide a few sentences in the service contract that allows you and your client to agree mutually to review and add elements to the "Supported Application Matrix." Many SBS VAPs also choose expressly to disclaim liability and responsibility for any elements installed at the client site without the VAP's supervision and shift the financial burden back to the client.

The out of scope addition is often implemented through a rate premium, which gives your clients one more incentive to make sure you're kept in the loop on any changes to the configuration of their systems. For example, if your client has to pay 50 percent more per hour to have your staff support products not on the "Supported Application Matrix," the client has a terrific motivation for talking with you about how this new application or device should be integrated into the client's standard configuration.

The Bottom Line

Once the SBS 4.5 network is installed and the users are trained, the service contract takes over as the guiding force binding you and your small business client. Because this document and what it stands for is so crucial to the long-term harmony of the VAP/client relationship, spend time carefully mapping the various pros and cons of different types of offerings. This chapter introduced you to tools for developing a service contract that fits both your firm and your clients.

Chapter 25

Proactive Maintenance

Chapter 24 looked at how the service contract solidifies the long-term relationship between the small business client and the VAP using Microsoft Small Business Server 4.5.

Small business owners don't always understand the need to plan ahead with technology until it's too late. At that point, members of your staff begin getting urgent messages on their pagers, and they're forced to swing into a reactive, fire fighting mode. However, as any firefighter will tell you, the best way to fight fires is through prevention.

So you need to explain how a network is much more complex, albeit infinitely more powerful, than stand-alone computers. The stakes are much higher if a network is left unchecked because a lot more can go wrong. When an entire company relies on the SBS system, a proactive maintenance plan is *not* optional.

A maintenance plan is a lot like an insurance policy. As you saw at the beginning of Chapter 15, the hourly and daily costs of downtime can devastate small businesses. The costs of proactive maintenance are miniscule in comparison.

Now I turn my attention to some of the more technical and operational tasks that typically go hand in hand with an SBS maintenance plan. Chapter 25 will help you develop consistent service methods for preventing problems.

Server Status Tool

As was detailed in Chapter 15, the Server Status Tool (SST) is new to SBS 4.5. This tool uses the Scheduled Task Wizard and either Microsoft Exchange Server e-mail or the Microsoft Fax Service to send you certain log files at a frequency you specify. In Chapter 15, you also saw how you can leverage the Small Business Server Customization Tool, part of the *Microsoft BackOffice Small Business Server 4.5 Resource Kit*, to easily add more log files to SST report groups. These files include tape backup logs, antivirus logs, accounting application logs, and logs for custom database applications. The chapter concluded with a step-by-step tutorial on how to integrate UPS statistics from the software PowerChute *plus,* made by American Power Conversion (APC).

Tip

If you intend to use SST to keep tabs on the System, Security, or Application log in Event Viewer, check out the dumpel utility in the *Microsoft Windows NT Server 4.0 Resource Kit.*

You can choose to have these log files, or reports if you will, faxed or e-mailed to your firm daily or weekly. The default is daily at 2 A.M. But how can you put them to best use? For starters, if you have more than a handful of small business clients sending you logs daily, you'll need some type of automation to deal with the influx of e-mails. Through the Rules Wizard in Microsoft Outlook 2000, you can have messages from certain senders or bearing certain subject lines automatically moved to a folder set up for each client in your own individual e-mail box. Better yet, you could have the messages moved to a Public Folder to which all Exchange Server users have access in your office.

You should look through the log files daily or weekly for anomalies. For example, if the available space on your client's SBS 4.5 system "c" drive drops from 50 percent to 10 percent in just one day, something is definitely up that requires immediate attention.

Most small business owners would prefer to have their VAP sift through all the log data and decide which items are worthy of follow up (and which aren't). However, many also want to be kept in the loop, at least at the 30,000-foot level.

A brief executive summary document, prepared monthly, can help the small business owner understand the value of your firm gathering and examining routine data. Such a document should summarize the data you find as you monitor daily or weekly log files, give the big picture view of what the data means, and emphasize the importance of spotting trends and catching problems before they fester into emergencies. The CD-ROM for this book includes the "Server Status Tool (SST) Executive Summary," a Word template to organize your SST synopsis, as shown in Figure 25-1.

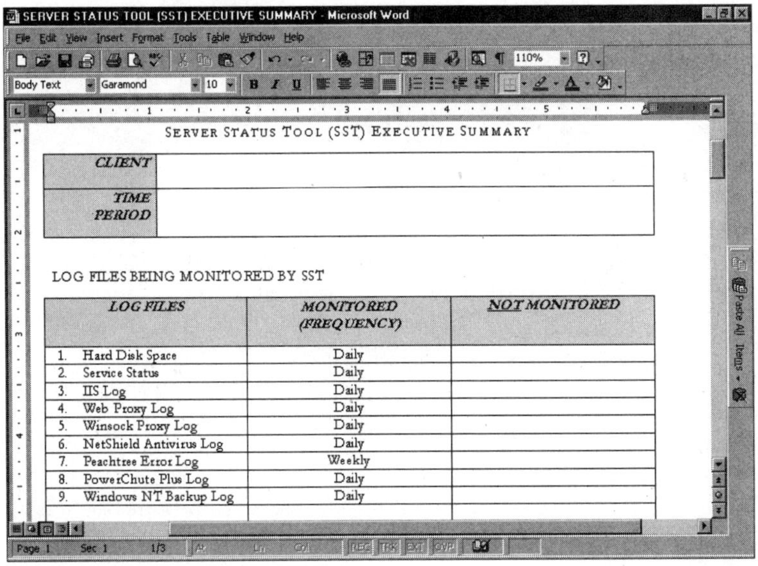

Figure 25-1
"Server Status Tool (SST) Executive Summary."

Licensing and the Client Add Pack

As your small business clients hire more employees, they'll probably need to add client workstations to their SBS 4.5 networks. The basic license for SBS 4.5 covers 5 workstations. Through Client Add Packs, you can increase the number of licenses on an SBS 4.5 network in increments of 5 or 20 to a maximum of 50 workstations. For more details on SBS 4.5 licensing options, see Chapter 2.

Unique among Microsoft NOS products, SBS 4.5 limits the number of users through the License Logging Service. To install a Client Add Pack onto an SBS 4.5 system, choose the Add Client Licenses task on the To Do List of the SBS Console, shown in Figure 25-2 on the next page.

Figure 25-2
Installing a Client Add Pack.

Because installing a Client Add Pack requires you to reboot the server twice, it's important to schedule the installation at a time when all files on the SBS 4.5 system have been closed. Also, if your client requires more than one Client Add Pack, it's critical that you number the disks in the order in which you apply them to the SBS 4.5 system. This sequence becomes relevant if you need to reinstall SBS 4.5 on this system and reapply the Client Add Packs.

Establishing Benchmarks

As you saw in Chapter 1, SBS VAPs, like their small business clients, wear a lot of hats. In a Fortune 1000 IT department, the network manager would likely have a whole slew of server statistics that need constant monitoring. In a small business, your firm is the network manager, help desk representative, desktop support specialist, software trainer, system analyst, integrator, technician, and project manager.

Because you have so many different areas to oversee and a limited resource commitment (in other words, budget) from the small business owner, you need to be extremely judicious in where you recommend they allocate funds. However, it's very difficult to tell if something is wrong with an SBS 4.5 system if you have no framework for normal activity.

Tip

The white papers named "Optimization" and "Capacity Planning" from Microsoft Product Support Services (PSS) are two "don't miss" resources on SBS 4.5. For your convenience, both are included on the CD-ROM with this book.

To help differentiate potential problems from routine behavior, you should gather performance baseline data around the time you test the tape backup, UPS, and firewall solutions (as described in Chapter 23). You should pull this data at least once a quarter, around the same time you repeat the tests outlined in Chapter 23 and meet with your client to discuss the Quarterly Update Report (covered in Chapter 9).

Performance Monitor

Through the Microsoft Windows NT Server 4.0 portion of SBS 4.5, you can use Performance Monitor to take a snapshot of server performance. Launched from the Administrative Tools option under the Start menu, Performance Monitor is a graphical tool you can use to assess the performance of a system running Windows NT.

Tip

Many familiar with Performance Monitor refer it by the name of its underlying executable, Perfmon.

Performance Monitor allows you to monitor different types of objects such as Cache, Paging File, Processor, and Server. Although Windows NT Server 4.0 includes dozens of objects, each BackOffice Server application included with SBS 4.5 brings additional objects. Even Microsoft Fax Service and Microsoft Modem Sharing Service, applications unique to SBS, have associated objects that you can monitor using Performance Monitor.

Tip

Many third-party applications, especially those that carry the Microsoft BackOffice family logo, add their own sets of objects and counters to Performance Monitor.

Each object in Performance Monitor is subdivided into counters. For example, under the Processor object, you can monitor percent processor time or interrupts per second. If, at any time, you need additional information on the function of a specific counter, click the Explain button in the Add To Chart dialog box, shown in Figure 25-3.

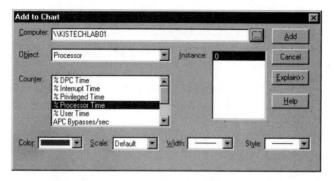

Figure 25-3

Click the Explain button in the Add To Chart dialog box of Performance Monitor to learn the function of a particular counter.

In addition to Chart capabilities, Performance Monitor can be configured to send alerts when certain thresholds are reached and to provide results in a report. Note, however, that because Performance Monitor is *not* a service, it must be running on the SBS 4.5 system in order for it to work.

Performance Monitor's value, at this stage in your SBS rollout engagement, is to establish benchmarks for normal activity on your small business client's SBS 4.5 system. If you suspect a problem, benchmarks allow you to compare results you collect performing preventative maintenance with those collected immediately following deployment.

Tip

Whenever you're at the client site, it's always a good idea to take a quick look through the System, Security, and Application logs in Event Viewer (under Administrative Tools). In particular, be on the lookout for entries with red stop signs.

Some of the more useful SBS 4.5 objects and counters to record, at least at the most basic NOS level, include:

- **% Processor Time (Processor)**—the percentage of time the processor is in use. If this amount consistently exceeds 80 percent, the processor is being overutilized.

- **Interrupts/sec (Processor)**—shows how many interrupts per second the processor receives from devices. A sudden spike might indicate a hardware problem.

- **Page Faults/sec (Memory)**—indicates how often the working set (RAM) fails to satisfy requests, which must be then redirected to the hard drive for retrieval.

- **Queue Length (Server Work Queues)**—the number of processes waiting for the processor. If this number is consistently higher than two, it indicates processor congestion.

To add these four counters to a chart:

1. Click the + button (Add Counter) on the toolbar in the Chart View of Performance Monitor.

2. From the Add To Chart dialog box, select the appropriate object and counter from their respective drop-down lists. Then click the Add button. When complete, click the Done button.

3. The Chart View window then displays real time statistics on each of the four counters you selected, as shown in Figure 25-4 on the next page. A legend at the bottom of the window indicates the scale and corresponding color of each line on the chart.

4. Finally, from the File menu, choose the Export command to save the contents to a .csv (comma separated value) file for further analysis in Microsoft Excel.

Tip

For more information on Performance Monitor, see Chapter 26, "Administrative Tools," in the *Microsoft BackOffice Small Business Server 4.5 Resource Kit*. The *Microsoft Windows NT Workstation 4.0 Resource Kit* and the *Microsoft Windows NT Server 4.0 Resource Kit* also cover Performance Monitor.

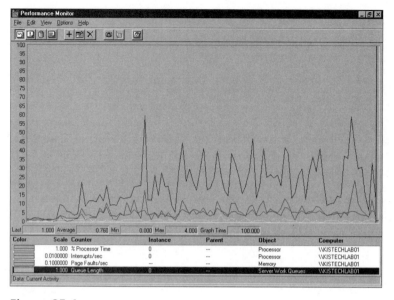

Figure 25-4

Viewing percent processor time, interrupts per second, page faults per second, and queue length in the Performance Monitor chart window.

Windows NT Task Manager

The Windows NT Task Manager is another extremely valuable tool that SBS VAPs use to quickly get a handle on the performance of the Windows NT Server 4.0 NOS portion of SBS 4.5. You can launch the Task Manager by pressing Ctrl+Alt+Delete and then clicking the Task Manager button in the Windows NT Security dialog box.

The Windows NT Task Manager window shows three tabs: Applications, Processes, and Performance. A status bar at the bottom of the window tells you how many processes are running, what the CPU usage is, and how much memory is being used out of the total available memory (physical RAM plus virtual memory). The Applications and Processes tabs provide valuable information. But the Performance tab, shown in Figure 25-5, interests us the most at this point.

From this tab, you can see:

- **CPU Usage**—instantaneous view in upper left-hand corner. A continually high number indicates that your client needs a faster CPU, your client needs an additional CPU, or you should address some other problem.

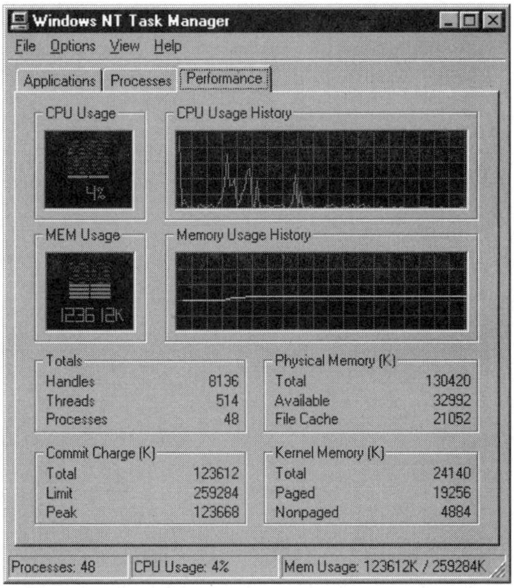

Figure 25-5

The Performance tab of Windows NT Task Manager provides a wealth of easy-to-decipher data.

- **CPU Usage History**—recently charted view in upper right-hand corner. You can adjust the Update Speed on this chart (Normal, High, Low, Paused) by choosing the Update Speed command on the View menu.

- **MEM Usage**—instantaneous view in left-hand center that displays the amount of combined physical and virtual memory in use. This value is the same as the Commit Charge (K) Total as seen near the bottom of the window.

- **Memory Usage History**—recently charted view in right-hand center.

- **Physical Memory (K)** – shows how much RAM is available, relative to the total, and how much RAM is being used for File Cache. If RAM usage approaches its capacity too often, you might recommend that the client either run fewer applications on the SBS 4.5 system or increase the amount of RAM in the system. (Most clients opt for the latter solution.)

Disk Defragmentation

Because SBS 4.5 utilizes the NTFS file system, many SBS VAPs mistakenly believe their client's disk volumes are immune to the type of disk fragmentation seen under the FAT-based file systems in MS-DOS 6.x and Microsoft Windows 95/98. Although NTFS resists fragmentation more than FAT does, an SBS 4.5 system can fragment *very* quickly.

Another widely held misconception is that RAID (short for redundant array of inexpensive drives) systems eliminate fragmentation. This idea is also false because disk volumes based on RAID, whether software or hardware, are just as susceptible to fragmentation as any other volume. As far as NTFS is concerned, a RAID volume is seen as a single disk, and it accordingly gets fragmented just like a single disk does.

One way to stay on top of disk fragmentation is through third-party defragmentation utilities such as Executive Software's Diskeeper. For your convenience, a 30-day trial version of Diskeeper is included on the CD-ROM with this book. To learn why you need to protect your small business client's SBS 4.5 systems from the performance degradation associated with disk fragmentation, visit the Executive Software Web site at *www.executive.com*.

Eliminating 16-bit and MS-DOS Applications

Applications based on MS-DOS or 16-bit architecture can become an enormous performance drain on an SBS 4.5 system. It's not uncommon to see these "legacy" applications cause the CPU utilization to spike to 100 percent on SBS 4.5 systems that use the Windows NT Server 4.0 NOS. This issue affects more small businesses than large organizations because small businesses are more likely to rely on vertical or industry-specific applications that they purchased 5 or 10 years ago and never updated to 32-bit technology.

Older applications usually don't trash network performance if they don't depend on network traffic or a particular network protocol and they don't need to be run on the server (that is, if they can be isolated on a Windows 95/98 client workstation). However, an outdated application often becomes a problem when you need to document disaster recovery procedures, as well as daily data protection concerns such as tape backup, power protection, security, auditing, and antivirus protection. A legacy application often causes small business clients to retain one or two Windows 95/98 PCs, even if they have already committed to standardizing on Windows NT Workstation 4.0.

On the CD-ROM for this book, I've included my VAPvoice column for September 1999, "How to Pull the Plug on Old DOS Apps," which appeared on the Microsoft Direct Access Web site. This column includes strategies for persuading your client to dump outdated software.

Tools for Investigating Questionable Entries

By now, you should be receiving and analyzing daily or weekly log reports from the Server Status Tool, monitoring statistics with Performance Monitor and Task Manager, and tracking results from a defragmentation utility such as Diskeeper. With all this data coming in, you're likely to amass a list of questionable entries. Some of these items might ultimately turn out to be relatively innocuous. Others might foreshadow doom and gloom if left unchecked. However, often the only way to know is by doing some research.

The Microsoft TechNet and Microsoft TechNet Plus CD subscriptions, as discussed in Chapter 22, are great tools for investigating various error messages and irregularities. For example, if I received an error message that referenced vaprpt.exe and I had *no* idea even where to start troubleshooting, I could run a query in Microsoft TechNet on vaprpt.exe, as shown in Figure 25-6.

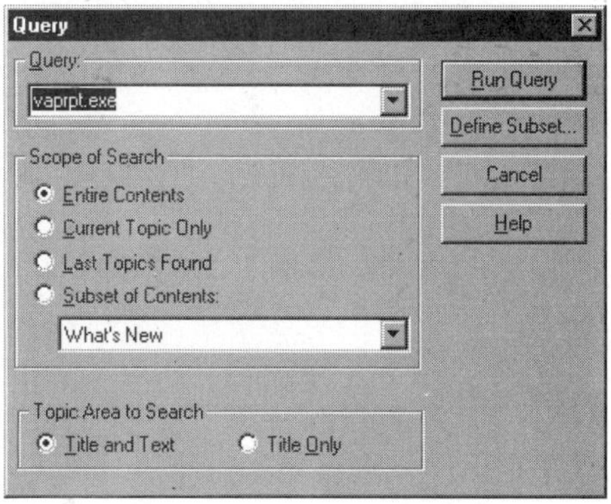

Figure 25-6

Using Microsoft TechNet to investigate an error found at the client site.

Microsoft Certified Solution Providers (MCSPs) pay for subscriptions to TechNet as part of their annual fee. For more information on applying to the MCSP program, see *www.microsoft.com/mcsp*. VAPs can also purchase TechNet subscriptions from a variety of resellers and distributors. For information on TechNet subscriptions, see *www.microsoft.com/technet*.

The Support page of the Microsoft Direct Access Web site (*www.microsoft.com/directaccess*) also has several tools available to jump-start an SBS VAP's efforts at resolving error messages and performance issues discovered at client sites. They include:

- **Newsgroups moderated by Microsoft Product Support Services**
- **Public newsgroups**
- **Business critical phone support**—for business-down emergencies
- **Search support online**—Microsoft TechNet Online knowledge base
- **Service packs and downloads**
- **Deployment guides**

Tracking Service History

After weeks, months, and years of servicing various clients, you'll accumulate a formidable number of service calls, whether they take the form of phone support, remote support, or on-site support. It's important to develop an effective mechanism for logging and tracking your calls so you can efficiently address questions and concerns that clients raise repeatedly.

Some SBS VAPs adapt their tracking mechanisms to a time and billing module in an off-the-shelf package, such as Timeslips or Peachtree's Complete Accounting. As an alternative, many SBS VAPs develop some type of Microsoft Access database that, at the minimum, has fields, queries, and reports that track:

- Client name
- Impacted end user(s)
- Date and time of service request
- Date(s) and time(s) service was rendered and request was closed
- Delivery method (phone, remote, on-site)

- Time spent to resolve the request (This data can be used to generate an invoice.)

- Type of problem (hardware, software, application, operating system, other)

- Analysis of problem (This might be lack of user training or another cause.)

- Problem category (This category approximates the type of project phases listed in the Time Estimate section of the Network Design Report—see Chapter 9 and the CD-ROM for the book.)

- Description of problem

- Resolution of problem

Tip

For help designing an Access database to track your client's service calls, see *Running Microsoft Access 2000*.

Regardless of how you log your calls and generate invoices, it's important to be able to run queries and reports that tell you exactly what each client's biggest needs are. Look for trends and patterns in the types of problems and questions. This data can often become the basis for discussion at your next quarterly update meeting.

For example, if you discover your client has incurred 18 hours of phone support on Microsoft Excel during the past three months, perhaps you should talk about designing a customized training program to address those needs. If your client has incurred 35 hours of on-site support in configuring modems in laptops, perhaps it's time to talk about selecting a laptop and PCMCIA modem that's easier to install.

In evaluating each client's service call history, consider:

- Where are their greatest expenses?

- Who are the highest maintenance users? Why?

- Could hardware or software upgrades have prevented any of these problems? How do the replacement costs compare to the benefits?

- Are there any issues that could be solved by training? (This is an extension of the effort covered in Chapters 21 and 22.)

- How do their service call requests fit into projects, completed or planned, in their most recent Quarterly Update Report? (This report is described in Chapter 9 and included on the CD-ROM for the book.)

Remote Administration Through NetMeeting

Many SBS VAPs have been using Symantec's pcAnywhere (*www.symantec.com*), by itself or in conjunction with RAS, to remotely administer SBS servers and workstations.

New to SBS 4.5, Microsoft NetMeeting is now the preferred method for remote administration. SBS 4.5 ships with NetMeeting 2.11; however, NetMeeting 3.0 provides Remote Desktop Sharing (RDS) and is available as a free download from *www.microsoft.com/netmeeting*.

RDS allows you to connect to the SBS 4.5 system without on-site client intervention. While connected, you can remotely administer the SBS Console or any application on the SBS 4.5 system, whether made by Microsoft or another vendor. This, of course, assumes that permission has been enabled for RDS in general, that you have a valid user account and password for the SBS domain, and that access has been granted specifically for that user account. To configure Remote Desktop Sharing, choose the Remote Desktop Sharing command on the Tools menu of NetMeeting.

Account Creation

To keep a tight rein on remote administration, you should create an account with the right to connect and log on to the SBS 4.5 system. You can accomplish this through the Select Additional Access Rights page of the User Account Wizard, shown in Figure 25-7.

The final page of the User Account Wizard is the Administrative Privileges page, shown in Figure 25-8. This is where you grant the account the right to log on directly at the SBS 4.5 console.

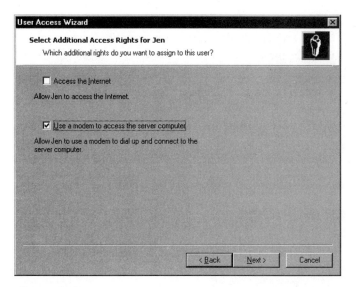

Figure 25-7

Creating an account with rights to connect by modem to the SBS 4.5 system.

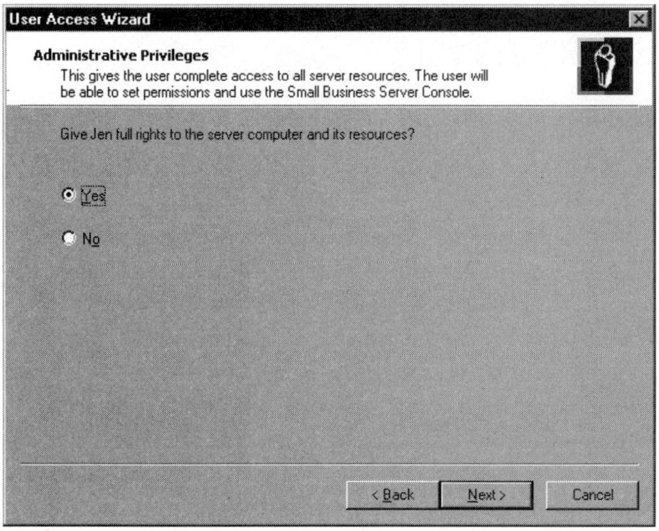

Figure 25-8

Creating an account with rights to log on directly to the SBS 4.5 system.

Now that you have created a user account and granted it both RAS and local logon rights to the SBS 4.5 system, you should enable auditing so you can tell whenever someone is using the account. Although Windows NT Server 4.0 doesn't support auditing of RAS activity, you can audit all user accounts for logon attempts, whether successful or failed. You can do this through the Audit command on the Policies menu of User Manager for Domains. This is one of those rare instances where you'll need to stray from the SBS Console for user account management. Figure 25-9 shows the Audit dialog box, which lets you specify what you want to audit. For more information on this topic, see Microsoft Knowledge Base article Q173634.

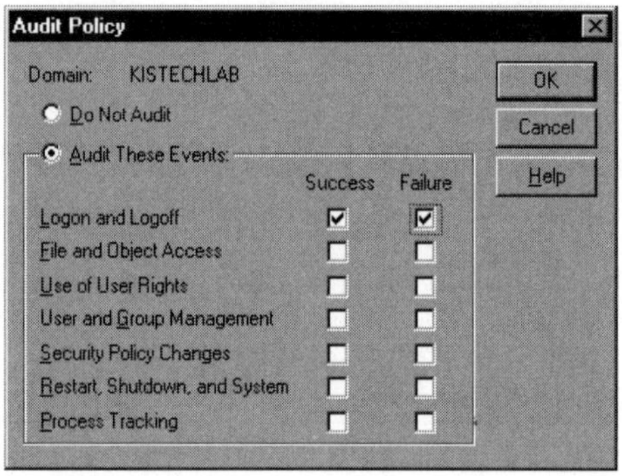

Figure 25-9

Enabling auditing of the success and failure of attempts to log on and log off.

NetMeeting Tips

Because NetMeeting 3.0 sends account credentials in clear text, it's best to dial in directly to the SBS 4.5 system, as opposed to connecting over the Internet.

Both the client and the SBS 4.5 system need to run NetMeeting for that product to work. The client needs to initiate the call, while the server, activated for Remote Desktop Sharing, waits for the connection.

Once the VAP's client workstation connects to the SBS 4.5 system via RAS, they'll get a DHCP-assigned IP address lease. Assuming no defaults have been altered, the dynamic IP address will be on the 10.0.0.x subnet. To connect to the server, click the Place Call button in the NetMeeting window, shown in Figure 25-10. Then enter the DNS name of the SBS 4.5 system or its *internal* IP address, which is usually left as its default of 10.0.0.2.

Figure 25-10

Once connected via RAS, click the Place Call button in NetMeeting to initiate a call to the SBS 4.5 system.

For more information on how NetMeeting works with SBS 4.5, see the Microsoft PSS white paper named "Technical How-To: Managing BackOffice Small Business Server Remotely." For your convenience, this document is included on the CD-ROM with this book.

Tip

To conserve the SBS 4.5 system resources and tighten security, you don't need to have the complete NetMeeting software running. Only the Remote Desktop Sharing (RDS) portion of NetMeeting needs to be running and activated in order for the SBS 4.5 system to accept calls.

The Bottom Line

Once your small business client has committed to the service contract you proposed after reading Chapter 24, you'll need to incorporate a variety of technical tasks into your daily, weekly, and monthly routines. Although the precise steps and methods will vary from client to client, this chapter outlined many of the more common steps you'll need to take to stay proactive about each of your clients' SBS 4.5 networks. This includes summarizing your findings from the Server Status Tool report, adding SBS 4.5 workstation licenses, establishing benchmarks for normal activity, eradicating antiquated applications, investigating anomalies, tracking service calls, and remotely administering the server.

Further Growth Opportunities

Chapter 26

Adding Value to Exchange Server

On the surface, Microsoft Exchange Server might seem to be just an e-mail server. Exchange Server, however, goes beyond e-mail; it's a comprehensive messaging platform that encompasses group scheduling, shared contacts, public folders, company-wide task lists, and custom forms. Microsoft BackOffice Small Business Server 4.5 VAPs can leverage Exchange Server to develop collaborative solutions rapidly and cost-effectively. The best part is that you can develop some very sophisticated Exchange Server solutions without programming.

Before you get started, make sure that you thoroughly understand all of the Internet access issues that affect Exchange Server, such as Microsoft Proxy Server, the Internet Connection Wizard (ICW), and access methods such as dial-up, router-based, and broadband. This material is covered in Chapter 18. In addition, Chapter 13 provides introductory coverage of many of the topics explored in this chapter.

You'll also want to make sure your small business clients are prepared to deploy company-wide Internet access and e-mail. For many of your small business clients, this will be the first time they've ever had more than one person in the company who has Internet access and e-mail. You can add tremendous value donning your virtual CIO hat and helping your clients write a simple, yet effective Internet and e-mail usage policy, as was described in

Chapter 10. The CD-ROM for this book includes "Company E-Mail and Internet Usage Policy Planning Worksheet," a Word template you can use to help your clients write their policy.

Bear in mind that Microsoft has a tremendous wealth of online materials available to help you learn more about what you can do with Exchange Server. Two resources worth adding to your Microsoft Internet Explorer Favorites list are the Microsoft TechNet Exchange Technology Center, which can be found on the TechNet Web site (*www.microsoft.com/technet*) and, for VAPs only, the Microsoft Direct Access Exchange Server Product pages, which can be found on the Direct Access Web site (*www.microsoft.com/directaccess*).

Tip

Chapter 3 and its accompanying CD-ROM white paper "Training Options for Related BackOffice Applications" give you additional pointers for getting Exchange Server training.

Exchange Public Folders

Traditional e-mail is based on one-to-one relationships, even if the e-mail is sent to a distribution list or multiple recipients. The e-mail is delivered to the Inbox of each person who needs the information. Public folders, on the other hand, are designed and optimized around one-to-many group communication. Some popular applications for public folders include:

- Electronic bulletin board
- Threaded discussion forum
- Customer activity tracking
- Help desk ticket management

Public folders can contain just about any conceivable file type, such as contacts; tasks; or Microsoft Word, Microsoft Excel, or Microsoft PowerPoint files. Once the items in a public folder are organized, the information can be made available company-wide, to select individuals or even to anyone with anonymous access over the Internet. These access permissions are quite granular and can be controlled either by the internal guru or the VAP through Exchange Administrator or by individually empowered end users through Microsoft Outlook 2000.

Note

Most of your small business clients' daily Exchange Server administration jobs, such as creating mailboxes and managing distribution lists, can be performed within the SBS Console. The SBS Console, however, only goes so far regarding Exchange Server administration. For many of the tasks in this chapter, you'll need to utilize Exchange Administrator. If your clients can't perform the Exchange Server administration task within the SBS Console, their best bet is to call their VAP because of the complexity involved in configuring Exchange Server.

Creating a Public Folder

To create a public folder in Outlook 2000, follow these steps:

1. From the View menu, select Folder List.

2. In the Folders List pane, expand Public Folders, and select All Public Folders. See Figure 26-1.

3. From the File menu, choose New, followed by Folder.

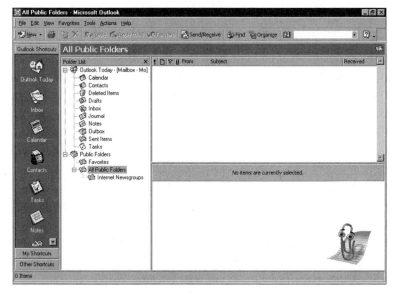

Figure 26-1

To create a public folder, first select the All Public Folders icon in Outlook 2000.

4. In the Create New Folder dialog box, type the name of the public folder in the Name field. (This is the name end users will see in Outlook.)

5. In the Folder Contains drop-down list, select the type of objects the public folder will contain. The default object type for the Folder Contains field is Mail Items, which can also contain files of any type—although you can designate the object type as Appointment Items, Contact Items, Journal Items, Note Items, and Task Items.

6. If you wish to change the location of your folder within All Public Folders, select the new location in the Select Where To Place The Folder box.

7. Click OK.

8. If you intend to utilize this public folder often, click Yes when you're prompted to Add Shortcut To Outlook Bar. Otherwise, click No.

Tip

You can always add a public folder to your Outlook Bar at a later time by simply dragging from the Folder View pane and dropping the folder on the Outlook Bar.

Once you've created a public folder on Exchange Server, you can administer the folder by right-clicking it and choosing Properties. In the Properties dialog box, you can specify the following settings for your folder:

- Forms to be utilized

- Default home page (an HTML page that introduces the folder)

- Whether the folder is available to add to e-mail Address Books

- How the folder is initially viewed (by Conversation Topic, By Subject, or By From)

- Rules that need to be applied to the folder

- Who can access the folder

- Whether the folder is moderated

- Who has permission to perform various functions on the folder

As an example of how to set permissions, I created a public folder called SBS VAPs, which is comprised of contacts. Clicking the Permissions tab in the SBS VAPs Properties dialog box reveals how Outlook and Exchange Server configured the defaults for this public folder. See Figure 26-2. By default, anyone who has a valid logon to the Exchange Server, which in this case are all SBS 4.5 user accounts, can be an author in the SBS VAPs public folder. This means users can see the folder in the list of public folders, can read items in the folder, and can use the contact form to create new items. The SBS VAPs Properties dialog box shows that users can edit and delete their own items. Anonymous users—those without a valid SBS 4.5 user account—have no access to this folder.

Figure 26-2

Set user permissions for a public folder on the Permissions tab in the Properties dialog box.

Mo, the user account I used to log onto the system and create the public folder, is the owner. This means Mo has the ability to see the folder; read, create, edit, and delete all items in the folder; and create subfolders. Mo also serves as both the folder owner and folder contact. Customizing roles and permissions from the Permissions tab is pretty straightforward. For many of your small business clients, however, the defaults Outlook provides for user permissions should be acceptable.

Populating a Public Folder

Once the public folder is created and you've confirmed the default Permissions are acceptable, you need to fill up the public folder with content. You can accomplish this in basically two ways. First, you can drag content (contacts in the example above) from a personal Inbox to a shared public folder. In the example above, Mo, the owner of the SBS VAPs public folder, already had a respectable collection of contacts stashed in his personal VAP Contacts folder, which resided in his mailbox on Exchange Server.

One day, Mo, who is the friendly SBS VAP sales manager, decided that he needed to get others in the company actively involved in working with the company's network of SBS VAPs worldwide. So he decided to transform his personal contacts into company-wide contacts. To do so, he dragged his personal contacts into the newly created SBS VAPs public folder.

If Mo didn't have a folder full of contacts, the contacts in the SBS VAPs public folder could be added by creating new items within the folder. To do this, simply select the SBS VAPs public folder and click the New Contact button on the toolbar. Then complete the blank New Contact form and click the Save And Close button.

The Exchange Administrator View of the Public Folder

You can do most, if not all, of your public folder administration from Outlook. The Exchange Administrator program, however, does provide a different view of the public folder, as well as some additional administrative control. To examine and modify the properties for a public folder, launch the Exchange Administrator program (from the Microsoft Exchange folder under Programs on the Start menu) and connect to the Exchange Server 5.5 site on your SBS 4.5 system, which will have the same name as your Windows NT domain computer name by default. (For instance, the site and domain name is KISTECHLAB and the server name is KISTECHLAB01.) To view or edit the properties of a folder, select the folder and then click the Properties button on the toolbar. See Figure 26-3.

In the Properties dialog box, you can control the same basic permissions as you can from Outlook, as well as several additional attributes. You'll notice three tabs in the Properties dialog box that deal with public folder replication: Replicas, Folder Replication Status, and Replication Schedule. The replication features of Exchange Server 5.5 might not be all that relevant to your small business clients now, but the features protect their investment from thief as they grow.

The features on the Distribution Lists tab, however, can be quite important right away because you can add the content of an entire public folder to an existing e-mail distribution list. You can edit the associated SMTP e-mail address for a public folder on the E-Mail Addresses tab. This feature is relevant if people e-mailed you contents destined for a public folder from the Internet.

For most of your small business clients, you'll use the Limits tab. See Figure 26-4. By default, Deleted Item Retention Time will have the same value

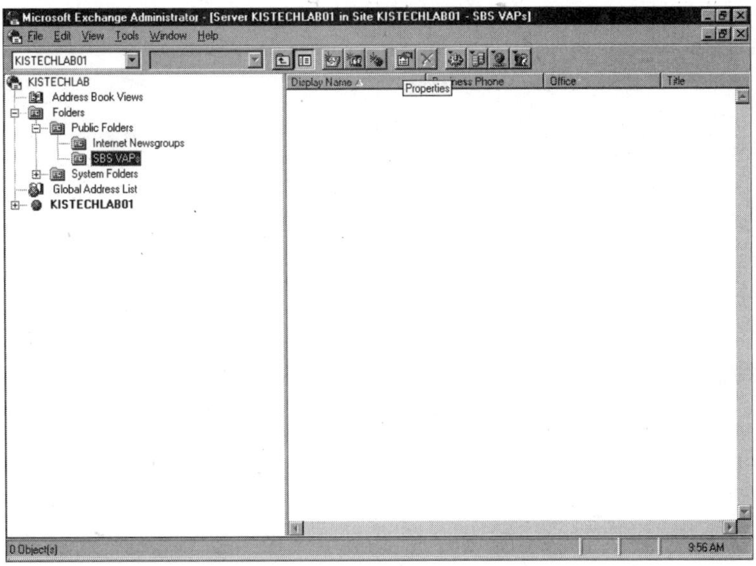

Figure 26-3

Manage properties of a shared public folder from Exchange Administrator.

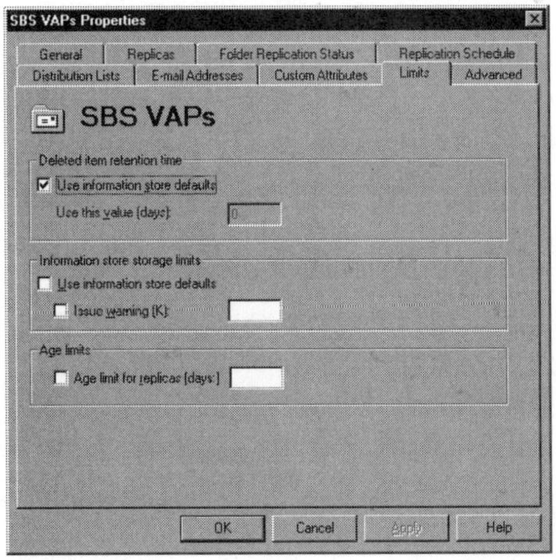

Figure 26-4

Configure storage, age, and time limitations for shared public folders through Exchange Administrator.

as the defaults for the Information Store. For the Public Information Store, zero days is the default. In other words, deleted items in the Public Information Store and the public folder are in fact *deleted*. From the Limits tab, you can set

Exchange Server to retain deleted items for a specified number of days for a public folder by deselecting the Use Information Store Defaults and entering an appropriate number of days in Use This Value (Days) field.

In addition to controlling how long deleted items are retained, you can control through the Limits tab how much space a public folder occupies. For Public Information Store Storage Limits you can rely on the defaults for the Information Store. (The default is no limit.) Or you can set Exchange Server to issue a warning when the public folder exceeds a certain size (in kilobytes).

Configuring Moderated Public Folders

You can configure a public folder in Outlook so it's moderated. Items posted to a moderated folder are first forwarded to a designated recipient or public folder for review. Once the item has been approved, the designated approver moves the approved item into the relevant shared public folder.

To make a shared public folder a moderated folder, follow these steps:

1. Right-click the shared public folder and choose Properties.

2. In the Properties dialog box, click the Administration tab and then click the Moderated Folder button.

3. In the Moderated Folder dialog box, select Set Folder Up As A Moderated Folder.

4. Click the To button under Forward New Items To and then select a user account from the Global Address List (GAL) stored on Exchange Server.

Tip

You can also select another public folder in which to store new items. See below for steps to add a public folder to the GAL.

5. If you wish to send an automated response to users who try to post to the public folder, select Reply To New Items With. Choose either Standard Response or Custom Response. If you select Custom Response, click the Template button and enter in the dialog box the message you wish to send to users.

6. Click the Add button to select one or more Moderators.

7. Click OK. See Figure 26-5.

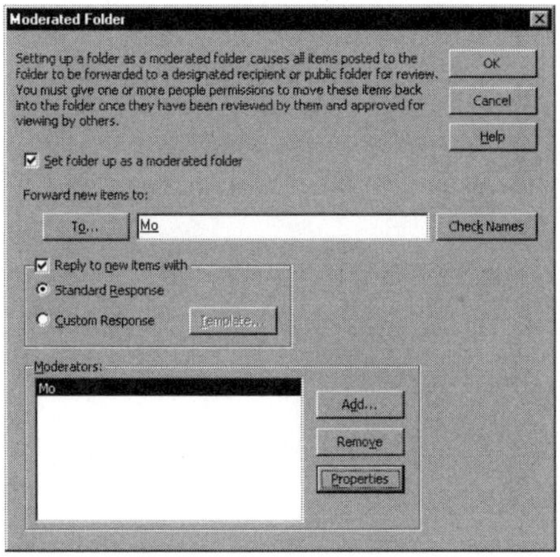

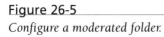

Figure 26-5

Configure a moderated folder.

Tip

Creating a sophisticated shared contact management system is often a very compelling point with which to close the sale on a project. Just ask the small business owner, VP of sales, or sales manager, "How many sales opportunities do you think are falling through the cracks each month because of a lack of shared information and inefficiently handled lead tracking?" Talk about quick return on investment!

Adding Public Folders to the Global Address List

Because public folders are often recipients of e-mail messages, users both on the Internet and on the SBS 4.5 network should know how to reach the public folder. One of the easiest ways to communicate this information to end users who use Outlook is through the Exchange Server GAL.

By default, each user account on an SBS 4.5 network has an Exchange Server mailbox and an entry in the GAL. Each time you create a new message in Outlook, you can select a recipient from the GAL by clicking the To button. If you add the public folder as an entry in the GAL, users on the SBS 4.5 network could choose the e-mail address of the public folder from among the list of other available e-mail aliases on the network. To accomplish this, open Exchange Administrator and follow these steps:

1. Expand Folders And Public Folders.

2. Double-click the appropriate Public Folder to display Properties.

3. Click the Advanced tab and deselect Hide From Address Book. See Figure 26-6.

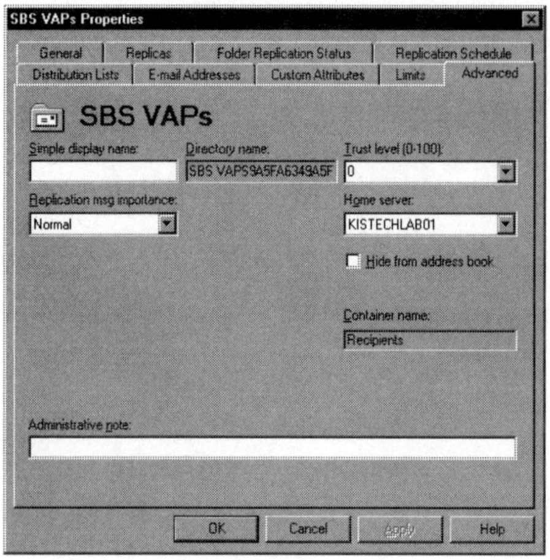

Figure 26-6

To add a public folder to the GAL, deselect Hide From Address Book setting on the Advanced tab in folder's Properties dialog box.

Configuring Threaded Discussions

Setting up a threaded discussion group is often extremely useful for small business clients who have workers that never seem to be in the office at the same time. For example, the bulk of the sales staff may be in the office only one or two days a month. Alternatively, perhaps your client has a 7 × 24 operation where people on different shifts hardly ever see each other. A threaded discussion is a great way to involve a team or an entire company in ongoing discussions about various topics in a much more efficient fashion than individual or group e-mails.

Using the steps described earlier in this chapter, you could create a shared public folder for e-mail through Outlook and use this folder to contain threaded mail items. A post for a threaded discussion looks very similar to a new e-mail. Instead of addressing the e-mail to a recipient, the e-mail is addressed to the name of the public folder.

By default, these postings in the shared public folder look like a bunch of e-mails. In Outlook, when you choose Current View from the View menu and select By Conversation Topic, the folder is transformed into a threaded discussion. See Figure 26-7. By clicking on the + (plus) and – (minus) signs for each conversation topic, you can expand and collapse the level of detail shown.

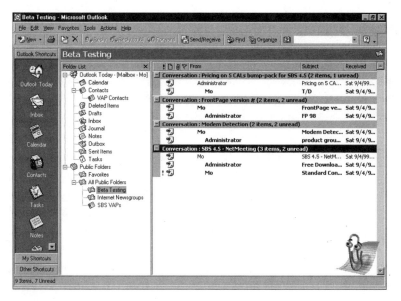

Figure 26-7

Create a threaded discussion in a shared public folder.

Additional Resources

Public folders are an extremely powerful backbone of any SBS 4.5 collaborative solution. This chapter provides an overview of some of the easier to implement features of public folders that are most appropriate for small business clients.

To learn more about the enormous potential of leveraging public folders in a custom solution, check out "Deploying, Managing, and Using Public Folders" and "Managing Microsoft Exchange Public Folder Resources," white papers on the TechNet Web site (*www.microsoft.com/technet*).

You can also extend a public folder solution through the use of Exchange Server–based scripting and routing. To learn more about these topics, see KB articles Q181036, Q183394, and Q180121 in the Microsoft Knowledge Base.

Finally, the Exchange Server Web site (*www.microsoft.com/exchange*) has a white paper, "Collaboration Evaluation Guide," that should prove quite useful if you intend to explore more intermediate to advanced level public folder applications.

Leveraging Outlook 2000

As you've probably already guessed by its inclusion with SBS 4.5, Microsoft Office 2000, and Exchange Server 5.5, Outlook is the preferred messaging client for Exchange Server. Outlook, however, isn't just e-mail. Outlook has integrated and extensible calendar, task, and contact management capabilities.

Setting up Shared Contacts

Once your clients are accustomed to using Outlook for e-mail, Contacts is usually the next logical application for them to use. To help demonstrate the tight integration between Inbox and Contacts, I'll usually show clients how to drag a message from their Inbox to the Contacts icon on the Folder List to create a new contact.

Then I'll show them how to create a new contact from scratch by selecting New from the File menu and choosing Contact. Another method for creating a new contact is by selecting the Contact icon in the Folder List and then clicking the New Contact button on the standard toolbar.

After you've worked with someone to add a dozen or so contacts to Outlook, the natural question is who else needs access to this information. There you have it...a natural lead-in to contacts stored and organized on a shared public folder.

You'll also want to have them utilize a number of more intermediate to advanced level features with an Outlook shared contacts solution, such as importing existing contacts, tracking activity, and categorizing contacts.

Importing Existing Contacts

One of the biggest obstacles or objections you'll hear from small business end users is that they already have all their contact information stored in another application or format, such as Symantec ACT!, GoldMine, Microsoft Works, or a custom dBASE application. Fear not; Outlook 2000 has the very powerful and easy to use Import And Export Wizard.

Tip

Users always have a fear of importing duplicate records into any contacts list. Outlook has a built-in mechanism to protect against this. In the event Outlook detects that you're trying to add a duplicate record, you'll be prompted with a Duplicate Contact Detected dialog box. You'll then be able to add the record as a new contact or update the existing contact with any additional information.

In a small business where each end user has his or her own favorite application, you can use the Import And Export Wizard and its accompanying Map Custom Fields capabilities multiple times to bring all this information together into one centrally stored shared pubic folder. You can launch the Import And Export Wizard from the File menu. Then just follow the Wizard's instructions.

Tip

If the application you need to import files from isn't listed as a supported choice within the Import And Export Wizard, you might be able to work around this by first exporting the files to a supported format from the desired application.

Activity Tracking

A shared contacts system needs to have a mechanism to keep track of activity related to each contact. The tracking mechanism might need to include any mail messages, journal entries, notes, and upcoming tasks, and appointments associated with a contact. The Activities tab on the standard contact form allows you to do just that. Figure 26-8 on the next page shows a contact named S. Mo with five associated items: one appointment or calendar item, one tasks item, one journal entry, and two sent items.

Categorizing Contacts

Sometimes placing contacts into various folders and subfolders works well to organize different types of contacts into logically related groups. For example, if I were an SBS VAP who was designing a shared contact management system for my own business, I might want folders for prospects, clients, and inactive clients. What if I wanted to track what type of work I perform for clients? I might be tempted to sort clients into folders such as network integration, training,

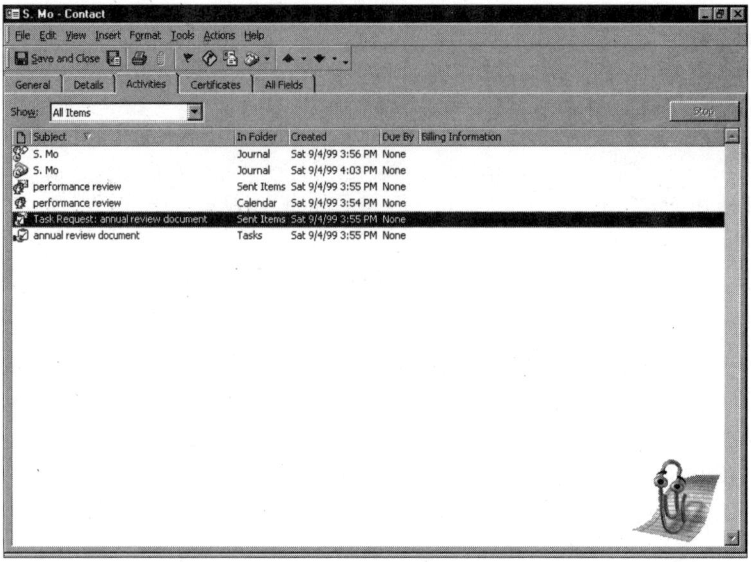

Figure 26-8

Use the Activities tab on a shared contact to keep tabs on which activities have been completed and which are pending with various people in your organization.

Web site design, and applications support. But then what happens when I have one client who needs services from my firm in more than one category? Would I create a copy of the contact for the client in each folder? This seems like an inefficient waste of storage space and time, and it dramatically increases the opportunity for clerical errors. A better way exists.

I can assign each contact one or more categories by clicking the Category button at the bottom of the General tab in the contact form. Available categories include business, competition, hot contacts, and key customer. I can add categories based on my line of business, such as network integration, training, and Web site design, to this list simply by typing the desired entries in the Item(s) Belong To These Categories box and then clicking the Add To List button. See Figure 26-9. When I run an Advanced Find query on the contacts in the shared public folder, I can specifically look for contacts that are categorized for the relevant lines of business.

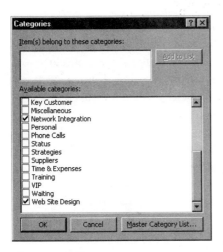

Figure 26-9

Tag a shared contact with default and custom-created Categories.

Tip

For more information on setting up shared contacts, see the Microsoft Office white paper, "Using Microsoft Outlook 2000 for Contact Management" (October 1998), which is available on the Microsoft Office Web site (*www.microsoft.com/office*).

Group Scheduling

Group scheduling is another powerful tool that a small business end user might not discover. Implemented through the contacts portion of Outlook, group scheduling helps your clients make the best use of time.

The seeds for group scheduling are usually planted with end users who utilize individual calendars to keep track of individual appointments. To show these end users how tight the integration is between the various Outlook tools, I'll drag a contact to the Calendar icon in the Folder List. This opens a meeting form and fills in the contact's e-mail address on the To line.

Scheduling a Group Meeting

One of the biggest challenges faced by end users in companies both large and small is coordinating multiple schedules to get everyone together for meetings. Outlook group scheduling provides an easy to use solution for this. To start, let's choose New Meeting Request from the File menu (the process is almost identical for a creating a new appointment). In the meeting form, click the To button to access names of users on the SBS 4.5 network that are stored in the GAL. In this case, I'll invite Mo and Jen. Then I'll add a subject and location. Note that the drop-down list next to Location lists previously entered locations. Next I'll choose a Start Time and an End Time, select Reminder and choose Busy from the Show Time As drop-down list. See Figure 26-10.

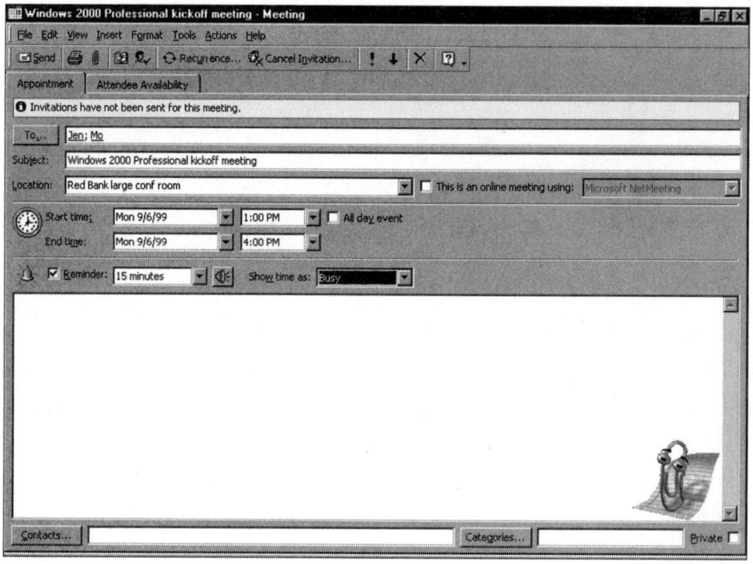

Figure 26-10

Schedule a group meeting using the Appointment tab on the meeting form.

Now comes the magic of using Outlook and Exchange collaboration for scheduling. Click the Attendee Availability tab and you can see the availability of invitees for the proposed time, before even sending the invitation. This information, which shows the availability of individual SBS 4.5 end users who have mailboxes on the Exchange Server, is commonly known as the Free/Busy Connector. When I click Show Attendee Availability, I can see that I need to rethink my initially proposed time. See Figure 26-11.

Tip

You see the sum of the availability of all attendees by looking at the All Attendees line on the meeting request form. The All Attendees line can be quite useful for larger meetings where potentially dozens of availability conflicts exist.

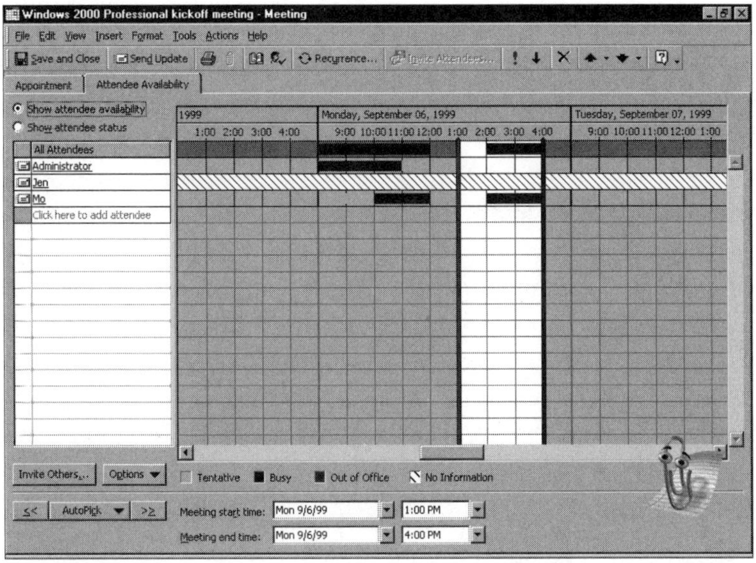

Figure 26-11

The attendee availability information gives me my first inkling that the meeting time isn't mutually acceptable, even before I send out the meeting invitations.

Although Jen is available to attend the meeting, I see that Mo is busy from 2–4 P.M. and as such has a scheduling conflict. I can either manually adjust the meeting time or click the AutoPick button to have Outlook and Exchange Server select a time when all required attendees are available. Then I'll click the Send button to send the actual meeting request.

Caution

Copying individual Calendars to shared public folders isn't generally a good idea. In fact, Microsoft Product Support Services (PSS) goes so far to caution against this practice.

A meeting request appears in Mo's and Jen's Inboxes. All they need to do is to open the request and click the Accept button, which will add the meeting to their calendars, update their Free/Busy Connector information, and send the updated RSVP information back to the meeting originator.

Tip

Meeting invitations are in many ways like an e-mail. A meeting request can have an attachment, body text, and a priority level.

Delegating Calendar Access

End users on a SBS 4.5 network can delegate access to each other's calendars. This can be helpful to the administrative assistant who books appointments for his or her boss. With the appropriate permissions assigned, the administrative assistant can open the manager's calendar and schedule meetings and appointments.

To delegate calendar access to a user, follow these steps:

1. Right-click the Calendar icon in the File List or on the Outlook Bar and choose Properties.

2. In the Properties dialog box, click the Permission tab.

3. Click the Add button and select a user from the GAL.

4. Assign the user a role from the Roles drop-down list. See Figure 26-12. Then click the Apply button.

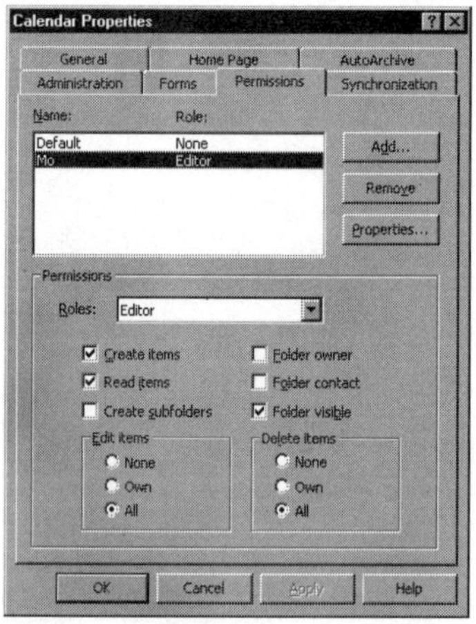

Figure 26-12

The first step in delegating calendar access is to assign permissions in the Calendar Properties dialog box.

Tip

You can grant users granular permissions for a calendar. For example, some people might need read-only access while others required read/write, like the author or editor role.

If I decide to give Mo editor privileges for the administrator calendar, he should have read/write access. To test this, I logged on as Mo and opened Outlook. From the File menu, I chose Open and then Other User's Folder. I clicked the Name button and selected the Administrator Folder from the GAL. Then I selected Calendar from the Folder drop-down list. Voilà, Mo has full editor access to the administrator calendar.

For more information on delegating calendar access, see KB article Q160302 in the Microsoft Knowledge Base. You can also download a very useful white paper titled "Using the Microsoft Outlook 2000 Calendar" (October 1998) from the Microsoft Office Web site.

Tip

Outlook 2000 can easily publish a calendar to a Web site. Simply select the Calendar icon in the Folder List or the Outlook Bar, choose File and then Save As Web Page. A dialog box opens that takes care of every configuration detail required to transform your calendar into a Web page or series of Web pages.

Adding Internet E-Mail Addresses to the GAL

Often your clients will need to send e-mail to Internet e-mail users. One option is for them to maintain a Personal Address Book containing these miscellaneous Internet e-mail addresses. Alternatively, they could store various Internet e-mail addresses in a personal or shared contacts folder.

A third and often preferable way is to integrate commonly used Internet e-mail addresses of vendors and customers into the GAL. You can do this by creating a Custom Recipient through the Exchange Administrator program. Just follow these steps:

1. In Exchange Administrator, click the New Custom Recipient button on the toolbar. See Figure 26-13 on the next page.

2. In the New E-Mail Address dialog box, choose Internet Address and click OK.

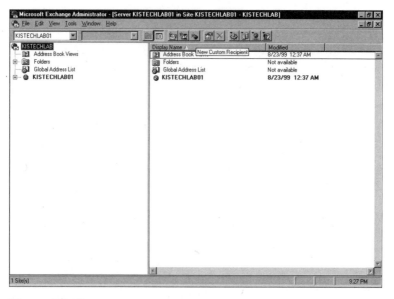

Figure 26-13

Add an Internet e-mail address to the GAL by clicking the New Custom Recipient button in Exchange Administrator.

3.   In the Internet Address Properties dialog box, fill in the desired e-mail address.

In the next Properties dialog box, I'm greeted with the full complement of attributes that come with any standard GAL entry. See Figure 26-14. For example, I can enter full address and telephone information. I can create an alias just for use within the SBS 4.5 domain. I can click the Organization tab and add a Manager and Direct Reports, as well as select the Distribution Lists tab to have this GAL entry join various distribution lists.

To see the effect, I can create a new message in Outlook and click the To button. The alias JoshuaF is now available to select from the GAL. I can also place a globe icon to the left of JoshuaF in the GAL, indicating the unique nature of the entry.

Customizing Outlook Forms

As you've already discovered, every Outlook item is based on forms. Whether you need a message, contact, task, appointment, or journal entry, Outlook has a form to structure the data entry, storage, and retrieval of information.

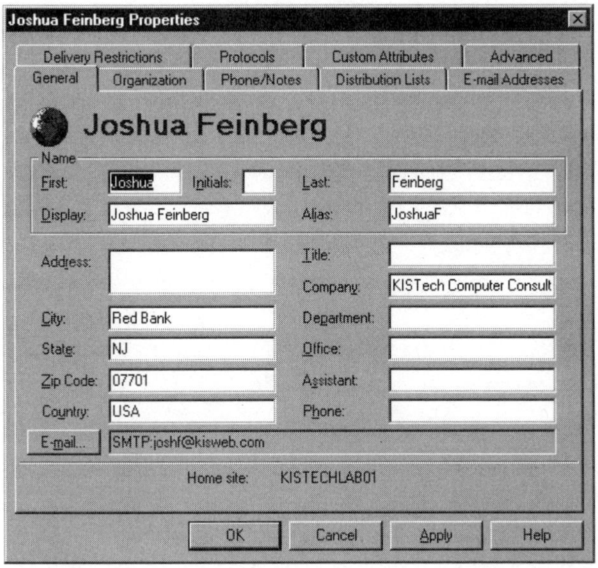

Figure 26-14
Creating a Custom Recipient gives full access to the standard GAL attributes.

In my June 1999 VAPVoice column, "How to Translate Sticky Notes into a Major Outlook Groupware Opportunity with Small Business Server," on the Direct Access Web site, I wrote about how you can design custom forms to streamline your client's communication and collaboration efficiency. The article even includes a walk-through on talking with end users about your planning efforts, as well as a technical how-to part on using Outlook Form Design. For your convenience, the column is included on the CD-ROM for this book.

If you really want to get into the finer points of Outlook Form Design, check out KB article Q146636 in the Microsoft Knowledge Base.

On a related note, you can customize and troubleshoot various facets of Outlook 2000 by using command-line switches. To learn more about supported switches for Outlook 2000, see KB article Q193282 in Microsoft Knowledge Base.

Outlook Web Access

Outlook 2000 is a 32-bit application that requires a relatively modern PC configuration running Windows 95/98 or Windows NT Workstation 4.0. Many of your small business clients might have legacy PCs running Windows 3.x that have slow Pentium or 486 processors. Although these types of PCs are far from optimal clients for an SBS 4.5 network, you can provide a subset of Outlook 2000 functionality for the users of these PCs.

In addition, your client might have some non-Windows computers, perhaps Apple Macintosh systems or UNIX workstations. While the Windows 3.x, Macintosh, and UNIX based systems can't readily run Outlook 2000, these systems can run a relatively recent Web browser. The browser becomes the universal client for Outlook messaging—a plug-and-play way to access your Exchange Server mailbox over the Web, whether over an intranet or the Internet.

You might ask how a Web browser can be used to approximate the functionality of Outlook 2000 on systems that can't run Outlook 2000. Quite simply, three magic words: Outlook Web Access (OWA).

Tip

OWA, when configured on an SBS 4.5 system with a full-time connection to the Internet, can also be used by traveling end users to obtain basic Outlook 2000 functionality without the nuisance and weight of schlepping around a laptop. Even without a full-time Internet access connection from the SBS 4.5 system, SBS 4.5 end users can still run OWA over a conventional RAS connection. (RAS is covered in Chapter 27.)

Understanding the Technology Behind OWA

With the conventional e-mail and messaging applications that this book has covered, end users on the SBS 4.5 network use Outlook 2000 to leverage the Exchange Server 5.5 back-end server. With OWA, on the other hand, users on client workstations use a Web browser with the major functions of Outlook 2000 rendered through Active Server Pages (ASPs). ASPs and Collaborative Data Objects (CDOs), which are important components of Internet Information Server (IIS) 4.0, provide the interface between end users' Web browsers and the Exchange Server mailboxes and folders.

Although OWA was available in SBS 4.0 through Exchange Server 5.0 and IIS 3.0, SBS 4.5 greatly improves upon OWA functionality. Through Exchange Server 5.5 with SP2, OWA now supports e-mail that leverages the GAL, attachments, and hyperlinks. In addition, OWA supports shared public folders, contact management, and calendar management, including both one-time and recurring appointments.

Because of the rich functionality possible through a standard Web browser, such as Internet Explorer 5 (IE 5), you could set up a full-time Internet access connection for your client's SBS 4.5 system to host a prefabricated extranet through Exchange Server. This could include anonymous access or secure logons for clients, vendors, or business partners, so they could use your client's e-mail, threaded discussion groups, calendars, and contact lists.

Installing and Configuring OWA

OWA is strictly a server-side application and isn't installed by default with SBS 4.5. In order to install OWA, you'll need to run the Exchange Server setup program. Take note that the installation program will stop IIS services and then restart them. Make sure your client is aware of this issue if the client hosts a Web site.

To install OWA, follow these steps:

1. Launch the Exchange Server setup program, which is on SBS 4.5 CD-ROM Disk 3 in \ExchSrvr\Server\Setup\i386.

2. In the Microsoft Exchange Server Setup dialog box, click the Add/Remove button.

3. In the Microsoft Exchange Server Setup–Complete/Custom dialog box, select Outlook Web Access, as shown in Figure 26-15, and click

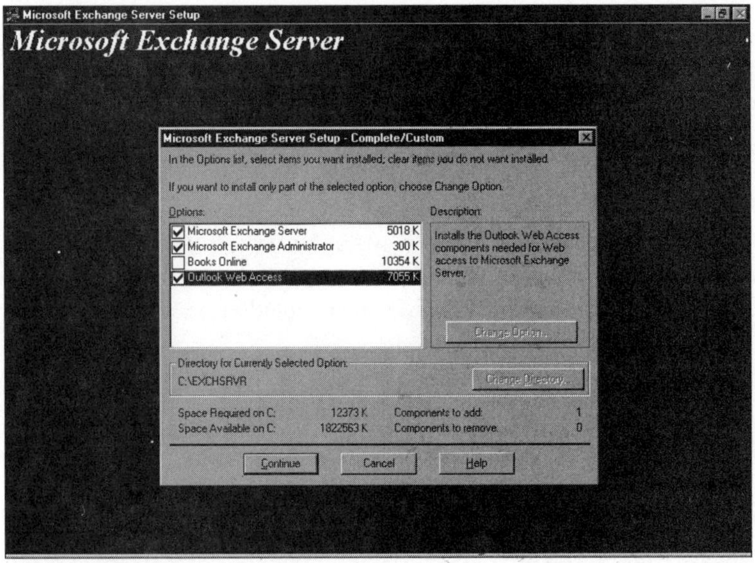

Figure 26-15

Reinstall Exchange Server to add OWA.

the Continue button. A dialog box appears that warns the setup program will temporarily stop the IIS services.

4. Follow the instructions in the rest of the Setup program.

Once the OWA installation is complete, you need to configure two steps manually. First confirm the IUSR_ account (that is, the Internet guest account), which is used by IIS for anonymous access, has the ability to log on locally to the SBS 4.5 system, which contains Exchange Server 5.5 and IIS 4.0. You can verify this through User Manager for Domains, under Administrative Tools. Select User Rights from the Policies menu. In the Right box, select Log On Locally. The IUSR_ account should be listed in the Grant To box. See Figure 26-16.

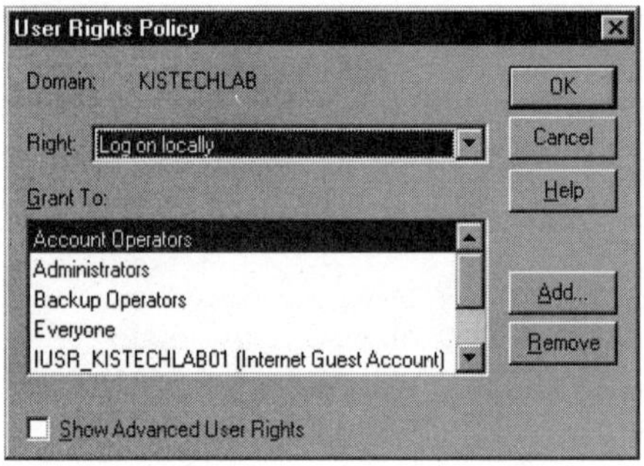

Figure 26-16

In order for OWA to work properly, the IUSR_ account, as well as those accounts of any users wishing to utilize OWA, must have the right to log on locally.

If the IUSR_ account isn't listed in the Grant To box, you can add it by clicking the Add button. In the Add Users And Groups dialog box, click the Show Users button, select the appropriate user or users, and click OK twice. The second manual configuration step is to grant to each user who needs access to OWA the right to log on locally. You can verify and add user accounts in the same fashion as you did the IUSR_ account.

While giving the right to log on the server locally to each user who needs access to OWA does pose certain security risks, you can mitigate the risk. Because Exchange Server 5.5 and IIS 4.0 are running on the same server, you can utilize the strongest supported authentication mechanism: Windows NT Challenge/Response (NTLM). In addition, end users need to be instructed that they must always log off OWA when they've completed their session. In the event you had to utilize Basic Authentication, which sends credentials in clear text, you could always enable the secure sockets layer (SSL) between the Web browser and IIS 4.0 to provide browser-based encryption of authentication credentials and data.

Chapter 18 looked extensively at how to use the Internet Connection Wizard (ICW) to configure various facets of Internet access. OWA does impact one of the ICW dialog box choices. Figure 26-17 shows how the Configure Firewall Settings dialog box should look if your client has Exchange Server 5.5 e-mail connected to Exchange SMTP e-mail either through an Internet service provider (ISP) or with direct DNS queries. In addition, the Configure Firewall Settings dialog box shows that Internet users have access to the Web, which is necessary so that end users can receive the ASP rendering of Outlook generated by IIS.

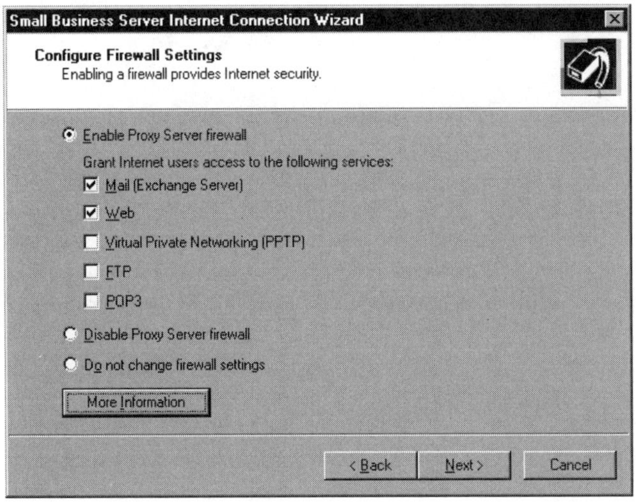

Figure 26-17

The Internet Connection Wizard Configure Firewall Settings dialog box is configured for Exchange SMTP e-mail and OWA.

Browser-Based Sign On to OWA

To access OWA from a Web browser, such as IE 5, follow these steps:

1. In IE 5, enter the DNS host name or externally exposed IP address of the SBS 4.5 system followed by /exchange for the Exchange virtual directory running on IIS 4.0. See Figure 26-18 on the next page. Note that /logon.asp is at the end of the URL because logon.asp is the default Web page in the Exchange virtual directory.

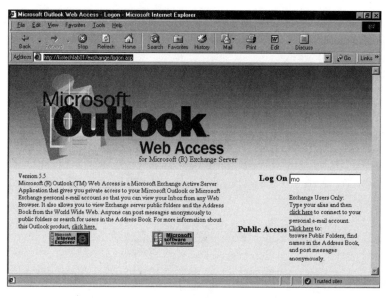

Figure 26-18

You can access the OWA logon page from IE 5.

2. In the Logon dialog box, type the end user's e-mail address or alias, which in most cases will be the same as his or her SBS 4.5 user name.

Tip

Because logon.asp is a standard ASP running on IIS 4.0, you have the ability to customize the logon page for your client, such as adding your client's company name, logo, and security disclaimer.

3. When prompted, enter the network password, which almost always needs the user name entered as well, in the format of DOMAINNAME\username. Then enter the password. Although you can save this password in your password list by enabling the box at the bottom of the Enter Network Password dialog box, I don't advocate this because it has the potential to weaken security.

Because passwords in most SBS 4.5 networks are set to expire every 42 days, OWA users need a way to change an expired password. OWA provides this, using the Internet Service Manager as a conduit, as you see in Figure 26-19.

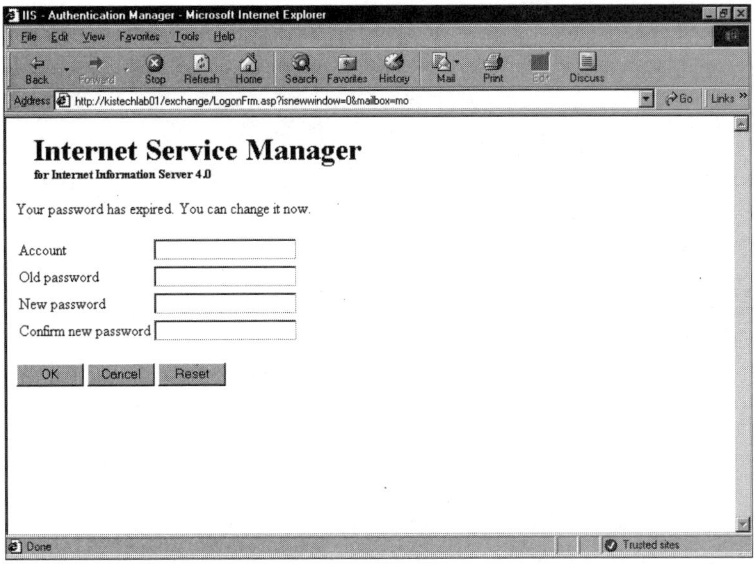

Figure 26-19

OWA has a mechanism to allow end users to change expired passwords.

Tip

For more information on OWA, see the "Troubleshooting Guide for Outlook Web Access" on the Microsoft Personal Online Support Web site (*support.microsoft.com/support*). This white paper includes an invaluable server configuration checklist.

Dealing with Spam

Unless you or your clients have been living under a rock for the past year or two, you're probably all too painfully aware of junk e-mail, commonly known as spam. Sometimes unsolicited e-mail is just a minor annoyance. Sometimes it wastes precious bandwidth and resources. Spam is almost always a productivity drain on end users and administrators alike. And in some cases, such as the infamous Melissa virus in March 1999, unsolicited e-mail can get so out of control that it overloads an entire company's Internet e-mail gateway.

What can you do to help your small business clients battle spam? While spam is virtually impossible to eliminate short of disconnecting their SBS 4.5 network from the Internet, you can implement a few easy strategies to mitigate the impact of spam.

Exchange Server Strategies

An update to the Internet Mail Service (IMS) in Exchange Server 5.5 Service Pack 1 (SP1) provides some very straightforward GUI-based tools to filter and prevent relaying of spam. Under Exchange Server 5.0, these restrictions can still be configured; however, they'd require direct registry manipulation, a practice that's always fraught with risk.

To access the IMS configuration settings, follow these steps:

1. Expand the server or site name in Exchange Administrator.

2. Open the Configuration folder and select Connections. See Figure 26-20.

3. Double-click Internet Mail Service to open the Internet Mail Service Properties.

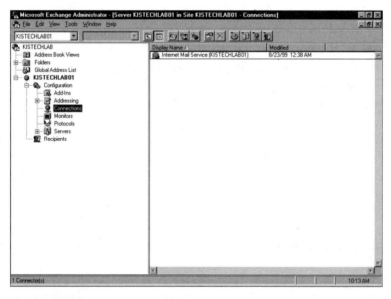

Figure 26-20

Locate IMS in Microsoft Exchange Administrator.

Click the Routing tab to verify that Do Not Reroute Incoming SMTP Mail is selected. See Figure 26-21. This configuration choice prevents Internet e-mail users from using your Exchange Server to reroute e-mail. Once you've enabled this option, only messages addressed to end users in the GAL on the SBS 4.5 system will be delivered, or accepted, into the Exchange Server 5.5 Information Store. All other messages will be returned as nondeliverable.

Figure 26-21

Prevent Exchange Server from serving as SMTP router for incoming e-mail.

In addition, you can explicitly filter out messages originating from specific e-mail aliases and domains. This is accomplished from the Connections tab in the IMS Properties dialog box by clicking the Message Filtering button.

Tip

For more information on basic strategies to secure Exchange Server 5.5 from spam, see KB article Q196626 in the Microsoft Knowledge Base.

Outlook Strategies

In addition to server-side strategies, Outlook 2000 has tools that can help end users control spam.

One such tool can be accessed by clicking the Organize button on the standard toolbar in Outlook. In the Ways To Organize Inbox window, click Junk E-Mail. You can configure Outlook to color code junk and adult content e-mail. Note the disclaimer at the bottom of the Ways To Organize Inbox window, shown in Figure 26-22 on the next page.

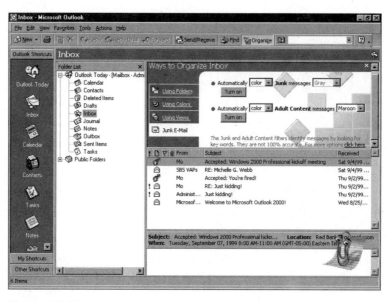

Figure 26-22

Configure Outlook to color code messages it deems to contain junk or adult content.

Another tool in Outlook 2000 that can help users filter spam is the updated Rules Wizard. This wizard features a Run Rules Now command, allowing you to apply rules on demand. To configure the Rules Wizard, choose Rules Wizard from the Tools menu. Then follow the instructions. As shown in Figure 26-23, I configured a rule called Delete Junk And Adult Content Messages. This rule deletes a message after it arrives if Outlook deems the message to be from junk senders or adult content senders—except when the message is directly addressed to me.

Note

When the Rules Wizard is used in an Outlook mailbox that's located on an Exchange Server, the rules actually reside both with the Exchange Server and the mailbox. This is so the rules can run on the server even when the user isn't logged on.

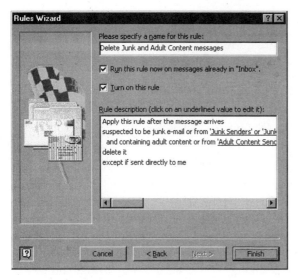

Figure 26-23

Use the Outlook Rules Wizard to block spam.

Comparing Messaging Options

An SBS 4.5 network has at least three different ways for end users to send and receive e-mail. As with most SBS rollout phases discussed in this book, the various options for sending and receiving e-mail have pros and cons in terms of features, security, performance, extensibility, ease of administration, and costs. This section will highlight some of the major differences between SBS 4.5 e-mail based on Exchange Server and POP3 mailboxes or browser-based e-mail on ISP-owned servers and domains.

Exchange Server

When small business clients have a full-time connection to their ISPs (that is, the connection is 7 × 24 with a static IP address), your clients are most likely going to use Exchange Server exclusively for internal and external Internet e-mail. To accomplish this, the Exchange Server IMS uses SMTP, a bidirectional e-mail protocol, for message transfer with other SMTP servers on the Internet. The ISP will also arrange for Network Solutions (*www.networksolutions.com*) or another approved InterNIC domain name registrar to add the SBS 4.5 system's external network card IP address as a mail exchanger (MX) and address (A) record in DNS servers. For more background on DNS, see Chapter 18.

Note

IMS is installed by default during the SBS 4.5 unattended setup.

On the other hand, when small business clients have dial-up connections to their ISPs, they can still utilize Exchange Server SMTP-based e-mail exclusively. Configuration, however, becomes more complicated. Without full-time Internet connections, messages destined for your clients' domains are stored on their ISP e-mail servers. ISPs request that your clients' domain records be configured so that MX and A records point to the ISPs' e-mail servers. This is in sharp contrast to the full-time connection scenario where your clients' e-mail is delivered directly to their SBS 4.5 systems by virtue of their DNS lookup records.

In order to make IMS communicate effectively for Internet e-mail when a dial-up connection is used, Exchange Server needs a way to signal the ISP's e-mail server that the e-mail server should send messages directly to Exchange Server when the Exchange Server is online or connected to the Internet. This signaling is done through a command that dequeues the stored messages. One of the most commonly used dequeueing SMTP commands is called ETRN (pronounced ee-turn), short for extended turn. Like the SBSETRN and ATURN commands, ETRN is used for dial-up and on-demand router-based connections to the ISP to signal that the SBS 4.5 system is ready to dequeue stored messages.

Regardless of whether your clients have full-time or on-demand connections to the Internet, they'll need static IP addresses if they wish to have Exchange Server rely exclusively on SMTP-based e-mail. The only exception to this is the SBSETRN dequeueing command, which can use a dynamically assigned IP address if the ISP supports the creation of a temporary WINS record for the duration of message dequeueing. Since SBSETRN isn't widely implemented by ISPs worldwide, using Exchange Server SMTP e-mail requires a fixed IP address for all practical purposes and intents.

Exchange Server SMTP e-mail is configured and implemented in SBS 4.5 through the ICW Configure Internet Mail Settings page. For the scenarios described in this section, select Use Exchange Server For Internet Mail. This choice in ICW activates IMS. The second choice on this page, Do Not Change My Exchange Server Settings, basically says, "I've figured this out already. I'm not going to change my mind. Leave the Exchange Server IMS settings alone." The third choice, Disable Exchange Server Internet Mail, still allows end users to send and receive e-mail locally on the SBS 4.5 network although IMS is disabled.

The benefits of using Exchange Server based e-mail include:

- Control over account setup, administration, and data protection is complete.

- Creating additional e-mail accounts and aliases doesn't incur incremental costs.

- Message transmission is instantaneous among SBS 4.5 network users.

- A single instance storage model provides most efficient use of server resources.

- End users can send and receive any type of e-mail, including blind carbon copy (BCC) and listserv messages.

- E-mail aliases and the Web-site domain name URL have brand-name recognition because clients own their domain names.

- Collaborative tools, such as group scheduling, shared contacts, and shared tasks, can be integrated with Internet e-mail among Outlook users.

Additional benefits with a full-time connection, as opposed to dial-on-demand, include:

- Accounts have near instantaneous receipt of Internet e-mail messages (real-time sending and delivery of messages, no delay for polling or message dequeueing).

- No busy signals are encountered.

- Most ISPs support this option.

Note

The Exchange Server name, the same as the SBS 4.5 system name, can't be changed without reinstalling SBS. Since this can be an incredibly time-consuming task, take great care in planning naming conventions prior to installing SBS 4.5. For more information, see Chapter 15 in the *Microsoft BackOffice Small Business Server 4.5 Resource Kit*.

POP3

Unlike the SMTP e-mail protocol, POP3 is unidirectional in nature and can be used only to download e-mail stored on an ISP's e-mail server. POP3 is primarily meant to be an e-mail protocol used with stand-alone dial-up accounts, the type of ISP account that your small business clients were likely to have been using before you showed up at their door. With a stand-alone dial-up account, POP3 is typically used to receive incoming messages while SMTP is used to send outgoing messages.

With a POP3 account, the mailbox or mailboxes reside on the ISP's server, not on the SBS 4.5 system. ICW doesn't really help to configure POP3 accounts. In fact, if you select Use POP3 For Internet Mail in the Configure Internet Mail Settings dialog box, all you get when you click the Next button is a dialog box instructing you how to configure Profiles *manually* in each end user's Outlook 2000 configurations.

SBS 4.5 needs to do nothing on Exchange Server 5.5 or Proxy Server 2.0 aside from making sure Winsock applications are enabled to pass through the Proxy Server. On the client workstation, the WSP Client needs to be installed (in the same way that SCW is installed, which was shown in Chapter 17). Then verify that Enable Winsock Proxy Client is selected in the end user's WSP Client applet in Control Panel.

Tip

Outlook POP3 end users typically store their e-mail in a .pst file. Although .pst files can be stored on the SBS 4.5 system to centralize backup and data protection, .pst files are often stored on individual end user's local drives. Under this scenario, you need to develop some way to back up this .pst file regularly. Over time, .pst files can become very large, increasing the risk of data corruption and reinforcing the need to regularly back up the file.

Comparative benefits of POP3-based e-mail include:

- Account setup, administration, quotas, and data protection can be outsourced to the ISP.
- SBS 4.5 system resource usage is minimized, because POP3-based e-mail can be used independently of Exchange Server.
- End users can send and receive any type of e-mail, including BCC and listserv messages.
- E-mail aliases and the Web-site domain name URL have brand-name recognition if clients own their domain names and the ISP supports domain based e-mail.
- Most ISPs support this option.
- The cost is relatively low.

- A single, secure connection to the ISP is all that's needed for end users to send and receive e-mail if they're using the WSP Client on an SBS 4.5 network. This eliminates the need to have several analog lines and dial-up Internet access accounts.

Note

You can combine Exchange Server e-mail that's used strictly for internal messaging with POP3 e-mail that runs through the Winsock Proxy on the Proxy Server for Internet e-mail. Because of Outlook's universal inbox capability, end users can receive both types of messages in the same place. This type of setup also enables one person to have access to POP3 e-mail, who then forwards messages as appropriate to internal users.

Browser-Based

Browser-based e-mail, provided through sites like Microsoft Hotmail (*www.hotmail.com*), is an option but generally not a great option for SBS 4.5 end users. For browser-based e-mail, usually all users need is an Internet access connection and a Web browser. With browser-based e-mail on an SBS 4.5 network, end users would launch IE 5, which would run through a secure Web Proxy connection on Proxy Server 2.0.

Comparative benefits of browser-based based e-mail include:

- Account setup, administration, quotas, and data protection can be outsourced to the e-mail provider.

- The cost for setting up accounts is negligible and in most cases free once the client pays for Internet access.

- No additional cost is incurred to create additional e-mail accounts and aliases.

- End users can send and receive any type of e-mail, including BCC and listserv messages.

- SBS 4.5 system resource usage is minimized because browser-based e-mail can be used independently of Exchange Server.

- End users can use any computer with a Web browser, including those outside the office and those that can't run Outlook 2000, to access e-mail.

Tip

For more information on the differences between an SBS 4.5 implementation of Exchange Server, POP3, and browser-based e-mail, see the "Choosing the Best Internet Messaging Option for Your Small Business" and "Microsoft BackOffice Small Business Server Messaging Solutions" white papers produced by Microsoft PSS, which are included on the CD-ROM with this book for your convenience.

Exchange Connector for POP3 Mailboxes

Prior to SBS 4.5, small businesses had only three choices for connecting their internal mailboxes to Internet e-mail:

- Invest in expensive hardware and installation and incur monthly fees for the telco circuit and ISP to get a full-time Internet access connection. Until very recently, this meant ordering a fractional T1 or frame relay line, supporting always-on bandwidth of 64–256 Kbps at a cost of $500–$1,000 per month plus $1,000–$2,500 for installation fees and hardware. Since broadband and full-time ISDN coverage still isn't available in many geographic areas, full-time Internet access is beyond the reach of many small businesses.

- Locate an ISP that will support an SBS 4.5 e-mail dequeueing command.

- Forgo the benefits of Exchange Server SMTP e-mail and use POP3 mailboxes administered by the ISP and accessed through a shared, secure Proxy Server connection.

Making Exchange Server E-Mail Affordable for Small Businesses

In July 1999, just weeks after the release of SBS 4.5, Microsoft offered a download that added a whole new dimension to the affordability of e-mail for small businesses. The download, Exchange Connector for POP3 Mailboxes, is available free to licensed SBS VAPs. Exchange Connector for POP3 Mailboxes is both a Windows NT Service and an Exchange Server Connector. It allows small business clients to utilize an inexpensive dial-up Internet access account and one or more global POP3 mailboxes while still realizing the tremendous benefits of using Exchange Server exclusively for internal and external e-mail.

A global POP3 mailbox account is configured to take all e-mail messages addressed to anyone in a particular domain and store them in a single mailbox. Although Exchange Connector for POP3 Mailboxes can work with individual POP3 mailboxes, a small business that's interested in the most cost-effective route to providing Internet e-mail to all employees will likely seek to have the ISP create a global POP3 mailbox.

Instead of spending $500–$1,000 per month (or more) for a full-time Internet access connection or searching far and wide for an ISP that fully supports a compatible message dequeueing method, small businesses can sign up for a basic dial-up account and a POP3 account. In most areas of the United States, these ISP services are priced in the neighborhood of $25–$100 per month, making Exchange Server e-mail much more of a budgetary reality for the installed base of small business clients running SBS 4.5. Exchange Connector for POP3 Mailboxes also dramatically increases the number of ISPs worldwide with which SBS VAPs and small business clients can work.

Exchange Connector for POP3 Mailboxes is available to licensed SBS sites as a free download from the SBS Web site at *www.microsoft.com/ smallbusinessserver*.

How the Technology Works

At preconfigured intervals, Exchange Connector for POP3 Mailboxes retrieves messages residing in POP3 mailboxes maintained by the ISP. It then delivers the messages to IMS, which subsequently distributes the Internet POP3 messages based on predetermined alias criteria to internal mailboxes. IMS handles the internal routing by examining the name of the recipient on the To line of the message.

Exchange Connector for POP3 Mailboxes doesn't affect outgoing messages. IMS still takes the outgoing messages, connects to the ISP, and sends messages to the ISP's e-mail server using SMTP. The Exchange Connector for POP3 Mailboxes just handles the receipt of incoming messages and the handoff to IMS.

Note

While Exchange Connector for POP3 Mailboxes can be used with full-time Internet access connections, it's most appealing to those small businesses that can't have a full-time Internet access connection.

Installation

To install Exchange Connector for POP3 Mailboxes, follow these steps:

1. Launch the popsetup.exe program that you downloaded from the SBS Web site.

2. In the first two dialog boxes, confirm the registered Name and Company Name and accept the End-User License Agreement.

3. Confirm that the installation path is correct (the default is \Program Files\POP3 Connector) and that Auto Start is selected.

4. Choose how your SBS 4.5 system connects to the Internet: Modem, Router, or Broadband. (Your choice should match the setting you selected through ICW, which was shown in Chapter 18.) If needed, select the Dial-Up Networking connection and associate its User Name, Password, and Domain (if the Domain is applicable).

5. In the next dialog box, enter the DNS host name of your ISP's Inbound POP3 server and the ISP logon information (account name and password) that corresponds to the POP3 server credentials.

Exchange Connector for POP3 Mailboxes has all the information it needs to complete setup.

Configuration

Once setup is complete, open Microsoft Exchange Administrator, click the server name and then click Configuration. Click Connections and then double-click Connector for POP3 Mailboxes to reveal its properties. The Properties dialog box has four tabs, as shown in Figure 26-24. These tabs include:

- **Connect & Download**—On this tab you can modify the Mail Administrator, the Internet connection type, the dial-up networking connection and its associated account credentials, the schedule behind Connect & Download (the default is once an hour, Monday through Friday), and Global ISP Mail Hosts. In addition, the Deliver Now button forces an immediate connection and download.

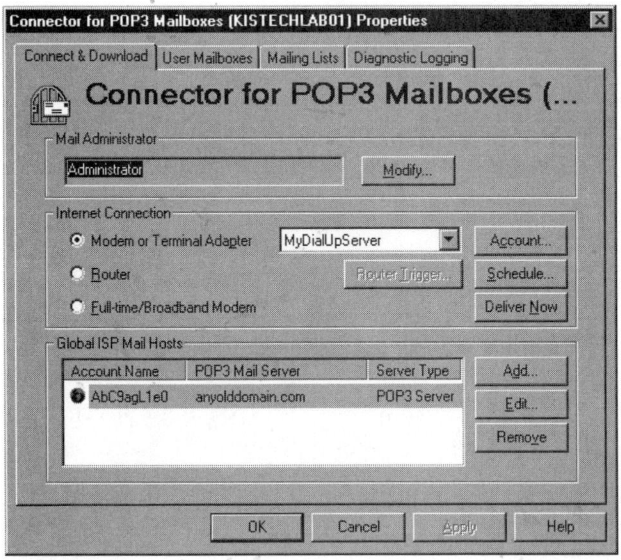

Figure 26-24

The Exchange Connector for POP3 Mailboxes configuration is divided among four tabs.

- **User Mailboxes**—Click the Add button, and the Mail Download Properties dialog box appears. In this box, you can match each POP3 alias to a GAL entry on the SBS 4.5 network.

- **Mailing Lists**—Because the POP3 alias of recipients on mailing lists typically don't appear on the To line of the message, you need to configure a mailing list display name and sender e-mail address to match up with a GAL entry on the SBS 4.5 network.

- **Diagnostic Logging**—This tab determines how event logging is handled for various facets of the Exchange Connector for POP3 Mailboxes.

Note

Mailing list messages become problematic because the recipient isn't shown in the To line of the message. Blind carbon copy (BCC) messages have a similar problem, which unfortunately can't be easily addressed by Exchange Connector for POP3 Mailboxes. If IMS is configured for NDRs, senders of BCC messages will receive one. The only way to get around this is to configure all NDRs to be forwarded to the mail administrator account indicated on the Connect & Download tab. From there, the administrator can attempt to forward to the appropriate GAL recipient in the company.

Data Protection Best Practices

The final section of Chapter 26 covers five topics related to protecting the data residing on an Exchange Server in an SBS 4.5 network: backup and circular logging; individual mailbox recovery; upgrading from SBS 4.0; virus protection; and deleted messages.

Backup and Circular Logging

Exchange Server, because it relies on database files that are perpetually open, has some unique data backup concerns, which were covered in Chapters 13 and 23. Windows NT Backup has a special window for Exchange Server, separate from the windows used to select various drive volumes. If you're using a scripted command-line version of Windows NT Backup, you'll also need a separate set of switches and commands to drive a backup of the Exchange Server Information Store and Directory.

Tip

Fortunately for SBS VAPs and small business clients, the nightly backup procedure can be completely automated. Chapters 13 and 23 showed how to use the Scheduled Task Wizard to schedule unattended tape backup jobs. In addition, third-party tools, such as VERITAS Backup Exec Small Business Server Suite for Windows NT version 7.3, include even more powerful job scheduling capabilities, such as managing the tape sets and rotation schedules.

To provide enhanced performance and fault-tolerance, Exchange Server writes transactions to a series of log files before the transactions are committed to database files. Although each log file has a fixed maximum size of 5 MB, Exchange Server has no limit to the number of log files it'll create. In fact, if left unchecked, Exchange Server will completely fill a disk volume with its log files in a matter of weeks.

Fortunately, Windows NT Backup, as well as nearly all Exchange-aware third-party tape backup solutions, will truncate these log files after the database and log files are backed up. This process removes the log files that have already been committed to the database from the volume.

If backups of Exchange Server aren't being run nightly, examine for how long Exchange Server keeps its database logs. If your small business client backs up the Exchange Server files each night, the logs are cleared out. On the other hand, if the Exchange Server files were never backed up, the logs have the potential to completely fill up disk space.

One way to get around this potential hazard is by enabling Circular Logging. Configured at the server level for both the Information Store and Directory, Circular Logging allows the Exchange Server to begin overwriting log files when existing log files fill up. While this certainly reduces disk space storage requirements, Circular Logging precludes you from incremental and differential backups and restores. Circular Logging can prevent you from recovering your SBS 4.5 system from backup to the exact point of failure. With Circular Logging enabled, the only option is to recover the Information Store and Directory to the point of the last full backup.

Circular Logging also makes it difficult, if not impossible, to perform an individual mailbox restore to a spare server. To check whether Circular Logging is enabled on a given SBS 4.5 system, expand the Configuration And Servers folders in Exchange Administrator. Then look on the Advanced tab of the server properties. Circular Logging is enabled by default for both the Information Store and Directory.

Individual Mailbox Recovery

Windows NT Backup doesn't natively support backup and restore of individual mailboxes. Backing up and restoring the Information Store and Directory through Windows NT Backup is a take it or leave it proposition. Either you back up and restore the entire Exchange Server or you get nothing.

In order to restore an individual mailbox, you'll need a spare server, identically configured, where you can restore the entire Information Store and Directory and then copy the user's mailbox to a .pst file. Although you lose many of the Exchange Server benefits, such as the single instance storage model, rules, views, and security, this often is the only way to recover an individual's mailbox if you aren't using a third-party Exchange-aware tape backup solution.

Tip

Before attempting to perform a full Exchange Server restore, you'll need to have at least twice as much free disk space as the system requirements claim.

Of course, backing up and restoring an individual mailbox is dramatically simplified by the use of a third-party solution such as VERITAS Backup Exec Small Business Server Suite for Windows NT version 7.3.

> ### Tip
>
> A 60-day evaluation version of VERITAS Backup Exec Small Business Server Suite for Windows NT version 7.3 is included on the CD-ROM.

If you're stuck operating without a third-party Exchange-aware tape backup solution, you could always try to use the Exchange Mailbox Merge program (Exmerge.exe). This utility extracts a mailbox from the source server Information Store restore, converts it to an individual .pst file, and then transfers the data back to a personal mailbox on the server Information Store. For more details, see KB article Q174197 in the Microsoft Knowledge Base.

Upgrading from SBS 4.0

In my May 1999 VAPVoice column, "How to Get Ready to Profit from SBS 4.5," on the Microsoft Direct Access Web site I provide a top 10 list for getting ready for an SBS 4.5 version upgrade. The article is included on the CD-ROM for your convenience.

In addition to the tips discussed in that column, some SBS VAPs advocate making an offline file-based backup before the upgrade. This means that you stop all Exchange Server Windows NT services (from the Services applet in Control Panel) while you back up the ExchSrvr folder. Many SBS VAPs also advocate that you copy any shared public folders (especially contacts) to a .pst file on a client workstation prior to the upgrade.

Virus Protection

The boot sector virus used to be the most dangerous type of virus. The most common way for a PC to become infected with this type of virus is by accidentally booting from an infected floppy disk. Although boot sector viruses are still at large today, viruses spread through e-mail attachments can be even more lethal. While a boot sector virus can cripple an individual workstation, viruses propagated through e-mail, such as the now infamous Melissa virus, show how a single virus, disseminated by Exchange Server, can bring an organization's Internet communication to its knees.

Every small business client needs a reliable third-party antivirus solution, which was covered in Chapter 22. Just installing it, however, isn't enough. With new viruses being discovered every day of the year, integrating updates of the core antivirus program engine and pattern files into any maintenance updates is crucial. One product that allows you to stay on top of viruses that can be spread through Exchange Server e-mail attachments is Trend Micro OfficeScan for Microsoft Small Business Server. For your convenience, a 30-day evaluation version of this product is included on the CD-ROM.

Tip

To learn more about "Fifth Annual ICSA Labs Computer Virus Prevalence Survey: 1999," see Chapter 22.

Deleted Messages

If an individual end user's messages seem to have disappeared without so much as a trace, all hope isn't necessarily lost. Exchange Server 5.5 supports something called Item Retention Time, where deleted messages are retained in a hidden area of the Exchange Server database for a certain number of days before being permanently eradicated. If Item Recovery is configured properly, it can be a true lifesaver.

This feature can be configured on the General tab for both the Private and Public Information Stores in Exchange Administrator. The default for Deleted Item Retention Time is 0 days, so the feature is effectively disabled. I'll enter 14 days as shown in Figure 26-25 and enable the option below as well to add an extra control. This additional safety measure prevents items from being deleted until the Information Store has been backed up.

Figure 26-25

Enable Deleted Item Retention to provide an extra cushion against accidentally deleting items in either Private or Public Information Store.

Recommended Reading

For additional background in this area, make sure to check out the following resources:

- *Microsoft BackOffice Small Business Server 4.5 Resource Kit*—Chapter 27, for extensive background on performance benchmarking and tuning of Exchange Server

- *Microsoft Exchange Server 5.5 Resource Guide* (in the *Microsoft BackOffice Resource Kit*)—Chapter 12, for information on disaster recovery

- "Disaster and Recovery Planning," a white paper on the Exchange Web site

- "MS Exchange Disaster Recovery" (Parts I and II), white papers on the TechNet Web site

- "MS Exchange Backup and Restore Basics," a white paper on the TechNet Web site

The Bottom Line

As you can tell by how this chapter just barely scratched surface, Outlook and Exchange Server provide an enormous opportunity for your firm to add value. This chapter showed how you can easily create applications that leverage shared public folders and Outlook contacts and calendars. In addition, you saw how you can extend the reach of Exchange Server–based messaging through OWA. Then the chapter covered easy to implement strategies for blocking unsolicited commercial e-mail. I rounded out the chapter by comparing various SBS 4.5 e-mail options, giving an overview of Exchange Connector for POP3 Mailboxes, and assembling a list of the top 5 Exchange Server best practices for data protection.

Chapter 27

Implementing RAS and Fax Services

Small business end users often need the ability to access files, e-mail, contacts, and schedules while on the road or working from home. Through the Microsoft Windows NT Server 4.0 Remote Access Server (RAS) Service, Microsoft BackOffice Small Business Server VAPs can build an extensible, flexible remote access infrastructure.

In addition to their RAS needs, small business end users are often heavy users of fax machines. Chapter 8 covered how you can show the small business owner how the SBS 4.5 Fax Service can lead to an extremely rapid return on investment (ROI). Once your clients understand what paper-based faxing really costs, you'll need to be prepared to discuss how Fax Service can streamline their flow of outgoing and incoming faxes.

This chapter helps you implement the RAS and fax services in SBS 4.5.

Note

When I cover using RAS or the client-side component dial-up networking (DUN) with SBS in this chapter, I'm primarily looking at inbound RAS, where end users call the SBS 4.5 system from home or on the road. DUN is also used for outbound calling, Modem Sharing Service, and dial-up Internet access connections. This chapter, however, will focus primarily on inbound RAS. For more information on Modem Sharing Service, see Chapter 13 in the *Microsoft BackOffice Small Business Server 4.5 Resource Kit.*

Guidelines for Number of Ports Required

Begin planning your RAS and fax solution by analyzing how many modems or ports are required to accommodate your clients' RAS and fax needs. This becomes an especially tricky issue because small business owners and, to a lesser extent, new SBS VAPs are accustomed to thinking of modems as devices that are installed in stand-alone PCs and that are advertised in the Sunday newspaper for bargain basement prices of $19–$49.

Veteran SBS VAPs, on the other hand, know that being judicious in product selection and meticulous in planning are the keys to RAS and fax modem success. The next section of the chapter focuses on hardware selection.

Understanding the Limitations of a Single Modem Solution

If you're new to SBS, you might wonder why more than one modem is required in the first place. In some unusual circumstances one modem might actually suffice. As an example, suppose your client had a broadband xDSL Internet access connection that utilizes the secondary or external network adapter (see Chapter 18). So a modem wouldn't be required to connect the SBS 4.5 system to the Internet.

The SBS VAP could conceivably use the Point-to-Point Tunneling Protocol (PPTP), explained later in this chapter, to perform remote administration. In addition, individual end users could dial up their local ISP and use PPTP to connect to the server for remote access. Now, let's assume this office is a very light user of the Fax Service, perhaps sending three to five page inbound and outbound faxes 10–15 times a day.

The scenario described above is just about the only time when a single modem can be used to implement both RAS and fax. Even then, the VAPs and end users are better served when a dial-direct RAS connection to the server exists. The VAP's remote administration is more secure, and end users can use the RAS connection as a backup in the event their ISP or the SBS 4.5 system's ISP is down. So now that you know why a single modem solution isn't appealing for many SBS 4.5 networks, let's look at how to allocate modems between the RAS and fax services.

Sharing vs. Dedicated Modems

Once you've gotten your clients to agree that they need more than one modem and analog phone line for their SBS 4.5 systems, you need to figure out what jobs each modem and analog line will have. In determining which modem will be used for which purpose, examine the following:

❑ Inbound faxing

❑ Outbound faxing

❑ Outgoing RAS through dial-up Internet access (see Chapter 18)

❑ Outgoing RAS through Modem Sharing Service

❑ Incoming RAS through direct-dial access (vs. incoming RAS through PPTP)

With multiple usage scenarios, where your client is using the SBS 4.5 system for two or more of the above purposes, consider dedicating a modem and analog line for specific applications. Although the SBS system can share modems for various purposes, this type of configuration can become a bottleneck very quickly and dramatically complicate ongoing support and troubleshooting.

Tip

For more information on planning RAS and Fax Services implementation, see Chapters 12 and 13 of the _Microsoft BackOffice Small Business Server 4.5 Resource Kit._

Pooling modems allows you to have more than one physical device recognized as one logical device, in much the same way that you can pool two or more physical laser printer devices into one logical pooled printer. In the event you do decide to pool modems, be sure to purchase and install the same make, model, and firmware revision so that the same device driver can be used for all physical devices.

> ### Tip
>
> To avoid future compatibility problems and ensure a consistent configuration, install all pooled modems together at the time of SBS 4.5 system installation.

RAS

In order to assess the number of modem ports required for RAS Service and whether modems can be shared across applications, consider the following:

❑ Evaluate how outbound RAS for Internet access is being configured. For example, Chapter 18 looked at the three Internet access methods supported by ICW and how a DUN phone book entry comes into play with analog and ISDN dial-up Internet access.

❑ If your client will be using DUN for Internet access through Proxy Server, consider how often during the day end users will need to be connected for Web browsing or Winsock applications (Microsoft Outlook, Outlook Express, and so on).

> ### Tip
>
> If your client's end users are typical, they might be connected most of day through a Web browser or other Winsock applications. If so, this basically means this modem and analog line won't be available for other purposes.

❑ Look at inbound RAS needs. For example, how often will end users be dialing into the SBS 4.5 system? How many end users will have dial-in capability? How long does a typical DUN session with the server last? For even a small number of RAS/DUN capable end users dialing in from home or on the road, dedicate at least one modem to inbound RAS.

> ### Tip
>
> The goal of any RAS rollout is usually to make end users' on-the-road experience as similar as possible to their in-the-office experience. Although bandwidth will dictate slower speed, the performance still needs to be acceptable. Later, this chapter looks at remote client applications.

❏ Decide whether direct-dial RAS is required or whether some or all of the end users can leverage PPTP to create virtual private network (VPN) connections with the SBS 4.5 system. When fully configured on clients, PPTP end users can run the same dial-up networking applications set up on Microsoft Windows 95/98 and Windows NT Workstation 4.0, just with different phone book entries and Desktop shortcuts. To use PPTP-based RAS, end users first dial into their local ISP. Then using an additional DUN phone book entry and connection, a PPTP connection is initiated through the Internet to the SBS 4.5 system. PPTP is explored later in this chapter.

Note

If most end users will be connecting to RAS through PPTP, your client only needs one or perhaps two direct-dial RAS setups with modems and analog lines. The only reason to have these is for backup and fault tolerance when either the user's or the full-time Internet access connection is down. PPTP doesn't actually require a full-time connection. Most PPTP implementations, however, are based on servers with static IP address, registered DNS domain names, and full-time Internet access connections.

Fax Service

In order to assess the number of modem ports required for Fax Service and whether modems can be shared across applications, consider the following:

❏ If your client is incurring a moderate to heavy daily fax use (over 50 faxes a day), commingling RAS and fax hardware devices is not a good idea. Although optional, this rule should be followed if your client is serious about either application.

❏ If your client utilizes analog DUN to connect to an ISP (as configured by the ICW, shown in Chapter 18), don't mix RAS and fax hardware devices in the same pool.

❏ If your client is a fax power user, consider dedicating up to four phone lines and modems to nothing but fax (that is, the phone lines and modems should be independent of RAS).

❏ Look at inbound fax calls. How will the SBS 4.5 system be able to tell the difference between inbound RAS and fax calls on the same analog line and modem? Unless the selected hardware supports adaptive answer, which can distinguish between inbound RAS and fax calls, dedicate one or more inbound modems for faxing. Even if the modem supports adaptive answer, you can tremendously simplify installation and ongoing support by keeping RAS-allocated devices separate from fax-allocated devices.

❑ Think about outbound fax calls. In the event your client will be sending a large volume of both inbound and outbound faxes (over 50 faxes a day), consider having more than one fax modem. In this scenario, you could also allocate one modem for inbound faxes and one for outbound.

Tip

For more information on justifying the cost of the SBS Fax Service to a prospect or client, see Chapter 8. For more information on planning RAS and fax, see the August 1999 "Microsoft Fax and Modem Services Usage and Troubleshooting" white paper by Microsoft Product Support Services (PSS). This white paper is on the SBS Web site (*www.microsoft.com/ smallbusinessserver*) and for your convenience, is included on the CD-ROM with this book.

Hardware Selection

As mentioned earlier in this chapter, choosing the right hardware (that is, modems and multiport serial adapters) is a crucial part of planning a successful RAS and fax services implementation.

Tip

Both modems and multiport serial adapters have associated device drivers and firmware. To learn more about keeping up with these important files, see Chapter 22.

The Benefits of External Modems

Small business end users might be attracted to price savings of internal modems. Often this ends up being the fool's bargain because the small business client will spend an unusually large amount of money due to the number of billable hours the VAP incurs installing a difficult to configure device.

Although an SBS-friendly modem is almost always more expensive than generic brand internal modems, your client's installation and ongoing support costs are minimized by predictable, easy to configure, standardized hardware. This leaves more money in your clients' budgets for higher-impact, higher-margin services such as training (see Chapters 21 and 22) and creating custom Outlook forms (Chapter 26).

Tip

The 3Com Courier V.Everything and Sportster V.90 external modems tend to be extremely popular among SBS VAPs. For a more complete list of modems, see the Windows NT hardware compatibility List (HCL), which can be reached from the SBS Web site.

So what are the most compelling benefits of external modems? These include:

- External modems can be reset without rebooting the SBS 4.5 system (and forcing all end users to log off their systems).

- LEDs on the outside of the modem help novice end users at the client site participate in over-the-phone diagnosis with SBS VAP.

- Because external modems are modular, they're easier to troubleshoot and replace.

Setup Detection

The SBS unattended setup program needs to be able to detect installed modems in order to install server applications that depend on modems, such as RAS Service, Fax Service, and Modem Sharing Service. As a result, any external modems need to be plugged into a power source (preferably to an uninterruptible power supply or UPS) and the appropriate serial port prior to setup.

If all goes well, the modems should be detected correctly during the Windows NT Server 4.0 portion of setup. If setup sees a modem on a particular COM port but is unable to identify a match between the unimodem ID in the modem's firmware and the unimodem ID of a standard Windows NT Server 4.0 device driver, the modem will be labeled as undetected.

This designation is the same as a standard modem, which is often seen in Windows NT Server 4.0 or Windows NT Workstation 4.0, independent of SBS. The SBS program managers changed the GUI label to undetected to emphasize the potential hazards of ignoring this warning. For more information on the Modem Confirmation Page and how Microsoft built this to help VAPs achieve greater success with SBS 4.5, see Chapter 2.

Note

Make sure the device driver has been revised to accommodate the latest firmware revision. For more background on this topic, see Chapter 22.

Class 1 and Business Class

In order for the modem to properly work with SBS 4.5, especially the Fax Service, the modem should be a Class 1 rated device and designated by the modem manufacturer as business class.

If the documentation or product packaging isn't available to confirm conformance to these requirements or you'd like to verify the OEM's claim of Class 1 compatibility, you can do so through HyperTerminal. Before opening Hyper-Terminal, temporarily stop the three modem-dependent services in SBS 4.5—Fax, Modem Sharing, and RAS—through Control Panel. Then follow these steps:

1. Open HyperTerminal by selecting Programs from the Start menu, choosing Accessories, then choosing the HyperTerminal folder, and clicking HyperTerminal.

2. When prompted to create a New Connection, click Cancel.

3. Type ATZ to reset the modem.

4. Type AT to take the modem off the hook. Assuming the speaker volume is turned up, you should be able to hear dial tone on the modem line.

5. Type AT+FCLASSS=? to see if the device is in fact a Class 1 modem. (One of the responses should include the digit 1, as seen in Figure 27-1.)

Multiport Serial Adapters

When selecting hardware for a RAS and fax solution, consider how the modems will interface with the server hardware, specifically the bus on the motherboard. Most servers, regardless of whether they are white box VAP-assembled systems or servers from top-tier OEMs, have only two serial ports. This is a convention dating back to the original IBM PC design of the early 1980s.

Tip

For more information on the white box PCs and servers, see Chapter 5.

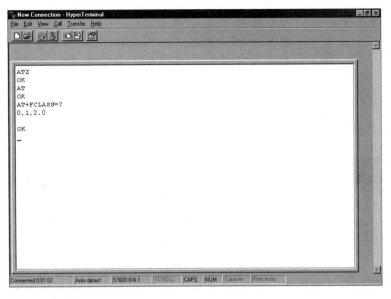

Figure 27-1

Use Hyper Terminal to verify that a modem is in fact a Class 1 compatible device.

I sincerely hope you're sold by this point on why no SBS 4.5 should ever go into production without a UPS connected up to the server through the serial interface. This means you only have one serial port left for all of the modems you've identified that your client needs.

To get around this, you'll need to look at multiport serial adapters. These devices were introduced in Chapter 22. Multiport serial adapters usually add at least four and in many cases eight serial ports to an SBS 4.5 system. Because an SBS 4.5 rollout often needs multiple modems, you should find a multiport serial adapter with which you're comfortable and add this to your standard SBS 4.5 system hardware configuration for most of your clients.

In addition to mitigating the scarcity of serial ports, most multiport serial adapters have built-in processors that off-load overhead to the board. This frees the Pentium class CPU to focus on processor intensive tasks, such as running a Microsoft Exchange Server or Microsoft SQL Server database.

Many vendors who've traditionally offered multiport serial adapters are now also offering multiport modems. These boards actually integrate multiple internal V.90 modems on a single PCI (or in some cases ISA) expansion card. While these products with built-in modems can be useful, bear in mind that you lose many of the advantages of external modems discussed earlier, such as the ability to reset a hung modem easily without rebooting the server.

Tip

One of the leading multiport serial adapter OEMs and one with numerous products on the Windows NT HCL is Digi International (*www.digi.com*).

Understanding Remote Client Applications

Now that you've seen how to figure out how many modems are required, how the modems will be allocated to services, and how to select hardware, I'm shifting gears more toward the end user perspective and looking at client applications.

When installing SBS 4.5 client applications that will be run over RAS, always perform the initial installation while the users' computers are physically connected to the LAN. By having the clients locally connected to the SBS 4.5 system during installation, the clients can leverage the automation and customization of the Setup Computer Wizard (SCW) just like the client workstations that are permanently situated in the office.

Tip

To learn more about SCW, see Chapters 16 and 17.

In the event the desktop or laptop doesn't have an installed network adapter, most SBS clients will find that the minimal cost of a basic 10Base-T Ethernet network adapter (about \$30–\$50) is more than justified by the tremendous time savings offered by SCW. In fact, you might actually be unwittingly performing an additional value-added service for the client because the home PCs for the company's end users are now ready to connect up to a broadband Internet access offering, such as a cable modem or xDSL.

Note

If you've exhausted all possibilities and can't install the client applications using SCW, Chapter 22 of the *Microsoft BackOffice Small Business Server 4.5 Resource Kit* walks you through the manual configuration steps of setting up remote client computers.

File and Printer Sharing

Once a client computer has made a DUN connection to the SBS 4.5 system, end users can act just as if they were sitting at client workstations on the LAN in the office.

For starters, they can map a network drive, restore a persistent drive connection, or open a shortcut to the user or company-shared folders to work with shared files and folders. This means, for example, that end users can launch the copy of Microsoft Word 2000 sitting on their home computers or laptops, issue a standard File Open command, switch from their hard disk drive to a network drive, and retrieve any document that they would normally have access to in the office.

Tip

For information on configuring drive mappings and default file locations for Microsoft Word and Microsoft Excel, see Chapter 17.

In the same way that end users can access their shared folders and files, they can also print to a network printer in the office, although with slower performance.

Outlook and Exchange Server Messaging

Once end users are remotely connected to the SBS 4.5 system, they can perform a variety of messaging functions in addition to accessing shared files, folders, and printers.

For example, end users can launch the copy of Outlook 2000 on their home computers or laptops and access their Exchange Servers to manage group contacts, e-mail, tasks, public folders, calendaring/group scheduling, and custom forms. In addition, the end user could also use Microsoft Internet Explorer 5 (IE 5) to run Outlook Web Access (OWA).

For more information Outlook and Exchange Server messaging applications, see Chapter 26.

Faxing

Just as remote users can print to a shared network printer in the office, those same users can access one of the shared fax printers on the SBS 4.5 system. In many cases, they might be dialing into one modem that is configured for inbound RAS calls, while their faxes are going out on another modem, configured for outbound fax calls.

Note

Both RAS and fax permissions can be granted and revoked on a user-by-user basis through the User Access Wizard.

Regardless of whether the fax client is used in the office on the LAN or through RAS/DUN connection, a fax printer on an SBS 4.5 network looks like just another printer. This means a fax printer is listed in the Printers folder in the end user's Control Panel and is accessible in any Windows application by selecting Print from the File menu.

Web Browsing

Remote users can use IE 5 to browse the Web or run other Winsock applications through the Proxy Server on the SBS 4.5 system. This type of configuration can be particularly useful for saving money because the need to purchase multiple dial-up ISP accounts diminishes if users are a local call to the office. You should note that if end users browse the Web for hours on end from remote locations and tie up limited dial-up RAS resources, your client has effectively become a micro ISP for its remote dial-in users.

On the flip side, because end users are logged onto the network through their RAS/DUN connection just as if they were logged onto their client workstations on the LAN in the office, your client can harness the power of Proxy Server. This means you can explicitly grant or deny user access to browsing the Web through the User Access Wizard. You can also apply domain-filtering rules, logging, and monitoring. For more information on configuring Proxy Server for these features, see Chapter 18.

Note

If end users aren't within local calling range to the office and they need to browse external Web sites for extended periods of time, they should definitely contract with a local ISP for Internet access. This will prove to be much more cost-effective for the end users and the client, even for relatively low-usage end users.

Configuring and Managing the Infrastructure

Now that you've seen how to plan the infrastructure for RAS and fax and learned about some of the more popular client applications that small business end users run remotely, I turn my attention to the SBS 4.5 system. In particular, I'll look at some of the tools and utilities available for administering RAS and fax on an ongoing basis.

RAS Administration

Once the SBS unattended setup program detects an SBS-friendly modem, the RAS service is installed. As you create user accounts following installation, you'll need to decide on a user-by-user basis who gets the right to access the SBS 4.5 system by modem.

Native Tools

By default, RAS isn't enabled in user accounts. Unless you instruct the User Access Wizard otherwise, none of the user accounts created will be able to RAS into the SBS 4.5 system. To enable the right to use a modem to access the server computer, simply select the appropriate box in the Select Additional Access Rights dialog box in User Access Wizard. See Figure 27-2.

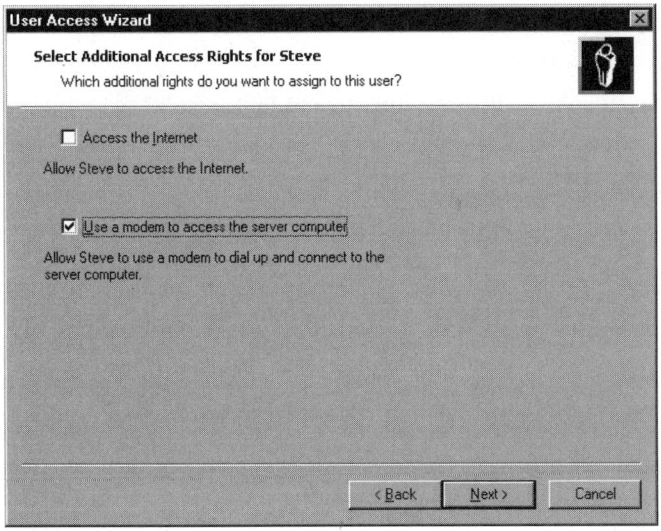

Figure 27-2

Grant a user account the right to connect to the server through RAS/DUN.

Resource Kit Tools

The *Microsoft BackOffice Small Business Server 4.5 Resource Kit* has tools designed for monitoring underlying modems used for RAS, including:

- **TAPI.exe**—Command line utility that displays the status of TAPI lines, such as connected, idle, dialing, and so forth.

- **Timon.exe**—Windows NT 4.0 service that the TAPIstate client can tap into to monitor the state of TAPI lines. Timon needs to be started first (timon.exe /service) before the TAPIstate client can be started.

- **TAPIstate.exe**—GUI-based client of the Timon service that provides status information on the TAPI lines.

Troubleshooting Pointers

In the event you need to troubleshoot an analog phone line for inbound direct-dial RAS, you can ask a number of rudimentary questions to locate the source of trouble, including:

- Is the wiring properly run from the telephone company network interface at your client's office to the inside jack location and terminated?

- Do you get a dial tone when you plug an analog phone into the phone jack?

- Can you dial out on that phone line to place a voice call to a local number? To a long distance number? Are any restrictions in place or dialing codes required?

- Can you receive a voice call through that phone line/jack?

Fax Administration

Fax Service can be administered through various buttons on the SBS Console and tools in the *Microsoft BackOffice Small Business Server 4.5 Resource Kit*.

Native Tools

Just like the RAS service, permission to specific fax printers is granted on a user-by-user basis through the User Access Wizard. See Figure 27-3. Because you can configure multiple fax printers for different fax modems, archive storage locations, and time restrictions, you'll want to configure all fax printers before you create user accounts. This way you can grant permissions to the appropriate fax printers as you create user accounts. Granted, you can always come back later and modify these permission; however, it's often quicker to get these permissions configured at the outset. Also note, all users have access by default to all fax printers. You can modify this by using the Add and Remove buttons.

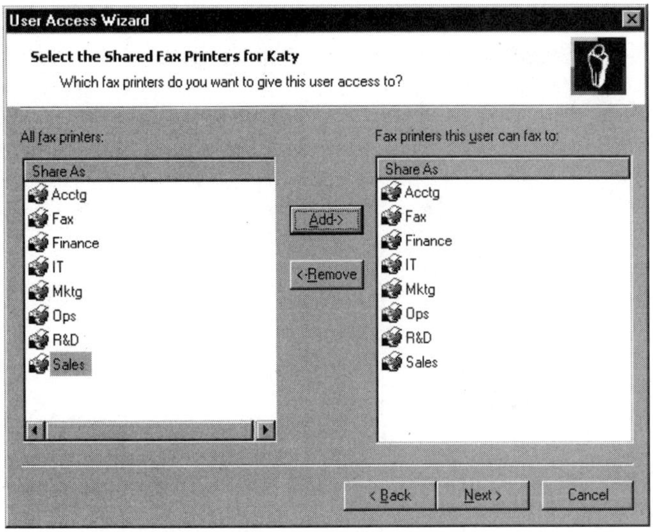

Figure 27-3

Select the shared fax printers from the User Access Wizard.

Note

By default, the unattended setup program configures Fax Service for outbound faxing, but not inbound faxing. If you want to configure one or more fax modems for inbound fax reception options, run Change How Faxes Are Received or Configure Fax Service task from the To Do List on the SBS Console. For more details, see Chapter 13.

Most Fax Service administration tasks can be performed directly on the Manage Faxes page in the SBS Console or be reached through links on that page. See Figure 27-4 on the next page. The eight buttons shown in Figure 27-4 are like mission control for the SBS Fax Service.

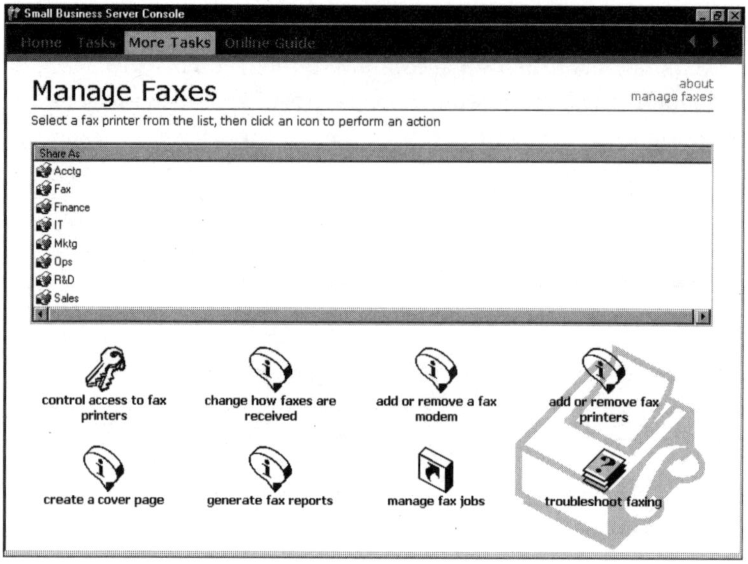

Figure 27-4

Use the Manage Faxes page to perform Fax Service administration tasks.

Most of the buttons are very straightforward. The five buttons with the "i" icon take you to information in the Online Guide, which has links that open the appropriate applet in Control Panel. The bulleted list below shows corresponding ToolTip text for each of these five buttons:

- **Create A Cover Page**—Create and add cover pages for fax printers

- **Change How Faxes Are Received**—Change options for receiving and routing faxes

- **Generate Fax Reports**—Produce reports detailing the use of your fax server

- **Add Or Remove A Fax Modem**—Add or remove a fax modem or change fax modem settings

- **Add Or Remove Fax Printers**—Add or remove a fax printer or change fax printer settings

When an inbound fax is received, Fax Service can do one or more of three functions. First, Fax Service can print to a local or shared printer anywhere on the network.

Next, Fax Service can save faxes in TIFF format to a local or shared drive anywhere on the network. Be advised that these archives can consume space on a server volume very quickly. So you might want to use the Scheduled Task Wizard to set up a job that moves the current months' content to a last month folder.

Tip

For more information on the Scheduled Task Wizard, see Chapters 13 and 15.

Third, the Fax Service can route inbound faxes to the Exchange Server Administrator Inbox. From here the faxes can be forwarded or you can grant users access to the Administrator Inbox. For details on delegating access to user mailboxes, see Chapter 26.

Clicking the Control Access To Fax Printers button on the Manage Faxes page in the SBS Console actually launches the Printer Access Wizard (highlighting the architectural similarities between network printing and network faxing). In reality, this button performs a Fax Service–specific subset of the functions performed by the User Access Wizard.

Clicking the Manage Fax Jobs button opens a console page that lets you cancel and restart jobs. This page is very similar in function to a Printer window view of the fax printer in that you can cancel or restart a stalled print job on any other local or network printer.

Finally, clicking the Troubleshoot Faxing button opens a window with links to various Online Help topics for remedying common Fax Service maladies.

Resource Kit Tools

The *Microsoft BackOffice Small Business Server 4.5 Resource Kit* includes two
tools designed for monitoring and troubleshooting Fax Service:

- **Faxmon.exe**—A GUI-based fax utility that provides real-time
  status of each fax modem, as well as a job history (logged
  to faxhistory.log) and device status history (logged to
  devicehistory.log). Both log files are placed in the folder from where
  faxmon.exe is launched.

- **Faxperf.exe**—A GUI-based fax utility that tracks a number of performance oriented statistics, such as inbound bytes, outbound faxes,
  and outbound failed transmissions, all of which are logged to
  faxperf.log. Data is updated once a minute.

Logs

You have two ways to tap into the native logging and reporting capabilities of
the Fax Service. First, you can configure your log requirements from the Logging tab of Fax Server Properties. See Figure 27-5. By default, all four categories are set to Maximum Logging Level. These results are sent to the Application
Log in Event Viewer. By using the DUMPEL utility, included with the *Microsoft
Windows NT Server 4.0 Resource Kit,* and the Scheduled Job Wizard, you can
configure a job to run nightly that prepares a flat text log file. This log file can
then be incorporated into the SST reports, as discussed in Chapter 15.

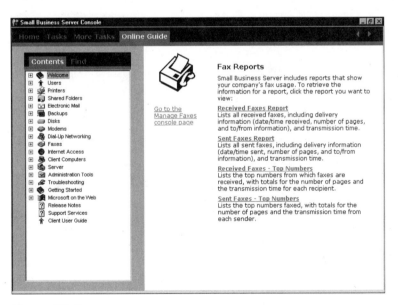

Figure 27-5

Configure Logging for Fax Server in Fax Server Properties.

Second, you can access canned fax reports by clicking the Generate Fax Reports button on the Manage Faxes page in the SBS Console. This opens an Online Guide page with a brief description and hyperlink for each report. See Figure 27-6.

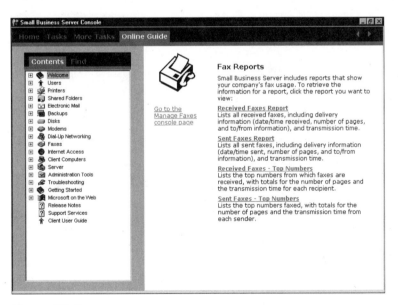

Figure 27-6

Access Fax usage reports from the Online Guide page in the SBS Console.

Cover Sheets

Another important area for configuration and customization are the Cover Sheets For Use With Fax Service. Configured from the Cover Page tab of Fax Server Properties, you can edit any of the four default cover sheets—confdent, fyi, generic, and urgent—by clicking the Open button. Editing is done from an application, Fax Page Cover Editor, which is a cross of WordPad and Paint. See Figure 27-7. Alternatively, by clicking the New button on the Cover Page tab, the Fax Page Cover Editor opens and allows you create a custom cover page.

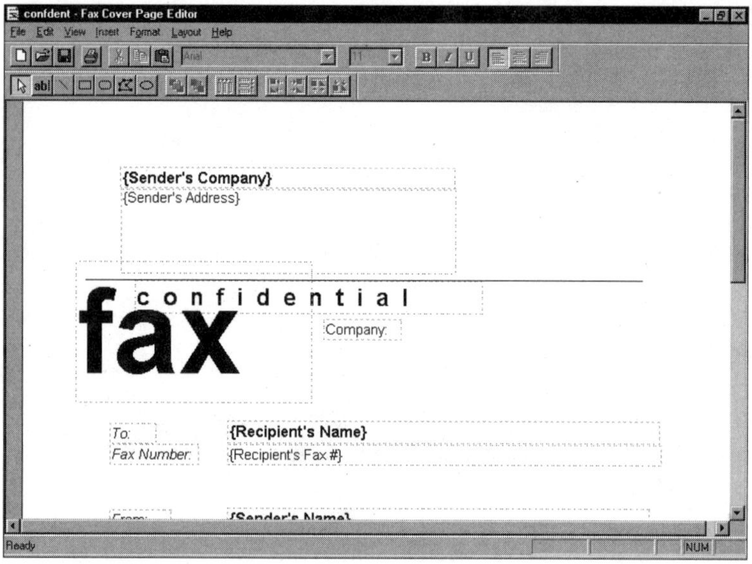

Figure 27-7

Fax Page Cover Editor allows you to create and customize cover pages easily.

Note

The mandated setting, Clients Must User Cover Pages, is enforceable only on Windows NT Workstation 4.0 clients.

Troubleshooting Pointers

This next section will wrap up the Fax Administration section with a listing of miscellaneous tips, hints, and pointers to additional resources:

- Fax Service doesn't work with PBX or DID phone lines; Fax Service is designed to work with only conventional analog phone lines.

- Fax Service can be tailored to your clients' needs for one of three purposes: outbound and inbound faxes, outbound faxes only, and inbound faxes only.

- End users don't need to track down the guru or VAP just to see how their fax jobs are doing. They can monitor their fax jobs by checking the queue of a fax printer, just like they'd check the queue of a local or network printer.

- The fax client included with SBS 4.5 isn't compatible with the Windows 95/98 fax client or any other third-party fax application, such as Symantec WinFax PRO. To prevent clients from causing major problems, remove incompatible, potentially conflicting applications before using SCW to install the fax client.

- KB article Q222532 in the Microsoft Knowledge Base, "SBS: Recommended Practices with Fax Service."

- KB article Q225384 in the Microsoft Knowledge Base: "SBS: Fax Service Does Not Use Second Modem When the First One Is Busy."

- KB article Q225461 in the Microsoft Knowledge Base: "Outlook Contacts Are Not Accessible from Fax Send Utility on the Server."

- KB article Q225374 in the Microsoft Knowledge Base: "Fax E-mail Confirmation May Not Work if You Reinstall Fax Client on a Multiple User Workstation."

- *Microsoft BackOffice Small Business Server 4.5 Resource Kit* Chapter 55, "Fax Service Troubleshooting."

Growing Momentum Behind VPNs

Earlier in this chapter, I alluded to the existence of two types of RAS:

- **Traditional RAS**—Remote users directly dial into the server by modem and private phone lines.

- **VPN RAS**—Remote users connect to their ISP and then connect to the server over the Internet by using PPTP.

RAS and PPTP

In order to use a VPN over PPTP to access the SBS 4.5 system remotely, first install PPTP support on the server. This is done by opening the Network applet in Control Panel and selecting Protocols. See Figure 27-8. Each type of preferred SBS 4.5 client, Windows 95/98 and Windows NT Workstation 4.0, will need PPTP client software installed.

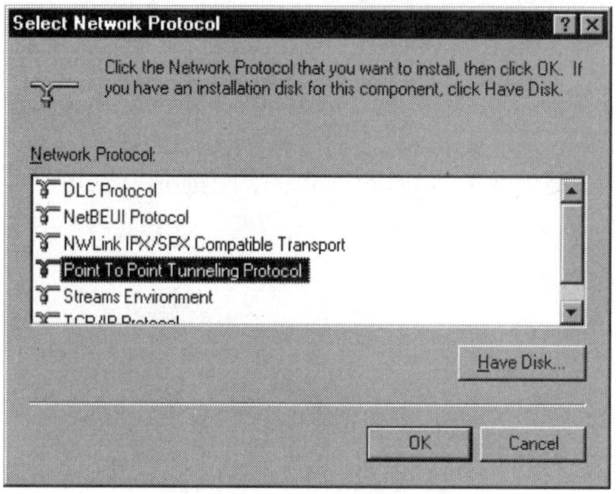

Figure 27-8

Install PPTP on the SBS 4.5 system with the Network applet in Control Panel.

PPTP creates secure connections over the Internet through tunneling encryption. Although most SBS 4.5 systems and clients will run only TCP/IP, PPTP can even provide tunneling for the IPX/SPX (NWLink) and NetBEUI protocol suites. In order to use PPTP, a VPN—a virtual device similar in function to a modem—first needs to be created.

As you can imagine, opening SBS 4.5 for secure remote access over the Internet makes many an SBS VAP and small business owner apprehensive at first. Proxy Sever 2.0's firewall, however, protects the internal network and SBS 4.5 system from non-PPTP traffic. In fact, PPTP traffic is blocked by the firewall by default unless you specifically instruct ICW to enable Virtual Private Networking (PPTP) in the Configure Firewall Settings dialog box. See Figure 27-9. For more details on ICW, see Chapter 18.

Overhead Requirements

To have an SBS 4.5 system serve as a PPTP server, your client doesn't necessarily need a full-time Internet connection. PPTP remote access, however, does tend to be more useful when users know the SBS 4.5 system is available by PPTP 7 × 24 and it has a static IP address, valid on the Internet. Because end users will likely be accessing the SBS 4.5 system through a dial-up connection to their ISP, your SBS 4.5 system can't have a private IP address on its external network card. To minimize training, configuration, and troubleshooting efforts,

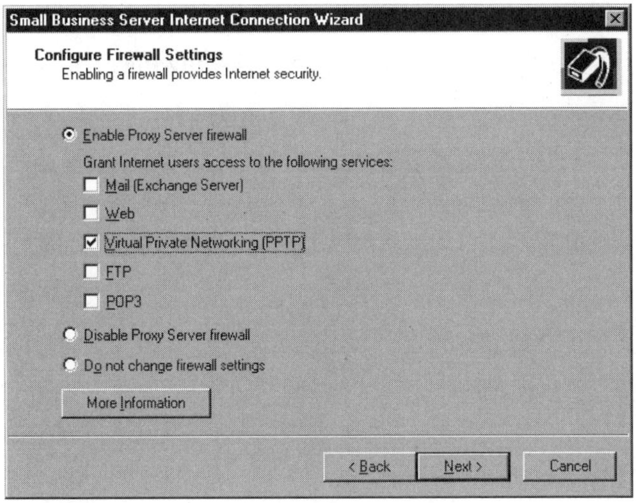

Figure 27-9

Enable PPTP through ICW.

be sure to have your ISP configure a static IP address and an associated registered domain name.

Traditionally, full-time Internet access has been cost-prohibitive for many small businesses. Chapter 18, however, showed how broadband technologies, mainly cable modems and xDSL, are making full-time Internet access connections affordable to even the smallest of small businesses.

End users can generally use a standard ISP dial-up connection to initiate a remote access PPTP session with the SBS 4.5 system. But an even more compelling solution becomes evident when remote end users sign up for broadband Internet access at home for a high bandwidth connection to the office.

Cost Reductions

In addition to providing robust bandwidth possibilities, PPTP is rapidly growing in popularity due to the tremendous potential cost savings. Because users leverage public Internet lines, as opposed to privately constructed network, PPTP has these benefits:

- Multiple analog lines aren't needed, so the client saves the cost of their installation and ongoing monthly fees (and message units).

- Multiple modems and multiport serial adapters aren't needed, so the client doesn't need to buy and maintain (including firmware upgrades) them.

- Assuming end users utilize ISPs that are in local calling range, the client doesn't need to pay for long-distance charges on either the server or client side.

Tip

For more information on PPTP, see Chapter 23 of the *Microsoft BackOffice Small Business Server 4.5 Resource Kit*. Also check out the Microsoft TechNet Networking & RAS Technology Center at *www.microsoft.com/technet*.

The Bottom Line

RAS and Fax Service solutions provide a great opportunity for your clients to make better use of their technology investments. This chapter showed how the RAS service can help your small business end users to access network resources from home or on the road. In addition, the chapter showed how Fax Service can be deployed to help your client get a better handle on high volumes of inbound and outbound faxing.

Chapter 28

Elevating Yourself from Service Provider to Strategic Partner

As an SBS VAP, you need to constantly reevaluate your competitive position as you strive to provide comprehensive virtual IT services to your small business clients. In Part 2, you looked at how to plan your firm's strategy around training, recruiting, margins, and partnering. Then in Part 3, you saw how to begin architecting long-term relationships with your clients by thoroughly analyzing their needs, developing a plan of attack, and building consensus.

Now that you've completed the rollout, configuration, customization, training, and testing, you need to concentrate on nurturing your long-term VAP/client relationships. In Chapters 24 and 25, I talked about setting up *mutually* beneficial service contracts and proactive maintenance programs. The service contract sets the tone for your intermediate time-horizon: the next four quarters. In order to rise from service provider to trusted business advisor status, however, you need to go even further and incorporate your clients' goals into your firm's goals. This chapter will help you build this mindset into your daily activities.

Building Your Clients' Goals into Every Project

As you've seen throughout earlier chapters, many small business owners, and even internal gurus to a lesser extent, think about technology planning as nothing more than assembling a shopping list of hardware and software. Chapters 7, 9, 10, and 11, however, showed why you and your clients really must have a meeting of the minds on several issues before you can make sound asset purchase decisions.

This involves an initial consultation to identify their business problems and define their goals and objectives, while developing a few concise bullet points that describe how technology could provide a solution. In Chapter 7, I introduced several tools, included on the CD-ROM, to jump-start your efforts in this area. These include the following:

- "30-Point PC Security Check-Up" (Microsoft Word template)

- "IT Audit Opportunity," which is the Microsoft Direct Access VAPVoice column, "Elevating a Microsoft Windows NT Server Sales Call into an IT Audit Opportunity" (HTML document)

- "Letter of Engagement for Initial Consultation" (Word template)

- "Roadmap Template for SBS Network" (Microsoft Excel worksheet)

- "Summary of Findings from Initial Consultation Meeting" (Word template)

Then, after you've defined their goals and problems, you can begin to transform the "Letter of Engagement for Initial Consultation" and "Roadmap Template for SBS Network" into a more concrete network design report. In Chapter 9, you learned how to build this project-plan document, leveraging an Excel workbook on the CD-ROM titled "Network Design Report."

Next in Chapter 10, you reviewed, recapped, and refined the information gathered during the exploratory fact-finding meetings and other on-site visits. When you return to the client, the objective for this meeting, or series of meetings, is to explain what each element of your network design report means to the client's business and how it supports their business goals. As you reach some definitive conclusions on how the engagement will proceed during these discussions, you need to make sure all key parties are on the same page with respect to the findings and analysis.

Reevaluating the Technology Roadmap

The documents you prepared for your client with the tools presented in Chapters 7, 9, 10, and 11 comprise their technology roadmap. Regardless of how you present these documents—whether they are stapled together, assembled in a plastic report cover, inserted into a binder, or uploaded onto a password-protected extranet site—the technology roadmap will evolve over time. For this reason, the "Roadmap Template for SBS Network" on the CD-ROM for this book has three columns: "Current," "Needs," and "Future." After the initial consultation meeting, you'll be able to categorize your new client's needs and wants relative to their current installed base of technology, what they need right away, and what solutions they'll need within the next six to twelve months.

In Chapter 7, I also introduced the "Quarterly Update Report," a Word template on the CD-ROM for this book, that's used to document your clients' existing OS, applications, and hardware standards. In addition, this report summarizes the projects that have been recently completed by the client, those currently in progress, and those scheduled to start within the next three months. Keeping this document current, continuing the best practices for the quarterly maintenance described in Chapters 24 and 25 *and* sitting down to revise this document with your client four times a year, are crucial steps. By utilizing the "Quarterly Update Report" as a living, breathing blueprint, you and your client can continually assess how their various technology investments and projects are progressing against the technology roadmap.

Managing the Life Cycle and TCO

Another assumption, often found among small business owners, is that they can *buy* a particular system and it will last their company ten years. Under this logic, your clients' investments in a custom MS-DOS-based Clipper relational database application and a fleet of 33 MHz 386 PCs, 2400-baud modems, and Hewlett-Packard LaserJet II printers should be ready to be retired in early 2000. While this example might be a tad exaggerated, veteran SBS VAPs are always amazed when they walk into meetings with new prospects and hear accounts of how data is still being passed around the office solely by virtue of 3.5-inch—and sometimes even 5.25-inch—floppy disks. Some clients insist they're running a 32-bit Windows-based application, even when it's MS-DOS-based, just because it has a nifty looking icon on their Windows 95/98 Desktop.

So getting your clients thinking about the big picture is extremely important. While they certainly don't need to replace major technology investments every year just for the sake of having the latest and greatest toys, small business owners do need to be cognizant of what their business goals are, how technology will get them there faster, and what this means in terms of hardware, software, and OS requirements.

One way to make this hit home with your clients is to explain technology investments in the framework of PC hardware leasing. Most veteran SBS VAPs, myself included, tend to be pack rats when it comes to saving old installation media, software documentation, and trade magazines. C'mon admit it…you must have at least one set of DOS 6.x and Windows 3.1 disks still lying around in your office.

To that end, dig up an old computer magazine from around 1992 to1994, such as *PC World*, *PC Week*, or *PC Magazine*. Look for ads from top-tier OEMs advertising leasing on desktop, server, and laptop purchases. Chances are, any leases are quoted in terms of a *five-year* time horizon.

Now, go back to the same magazines or the OEM's Web site and print out a current price quote with a lease option, based on a *three-year* time horizon. Since small business owners are often cash starved and love to lease everything from cars, to desks, to copy machines, they should be able to relate very well to the PC industry shift in shortening leases from five years to three years. This is indicative of how the obsolescence cycle has changed dramatically, even within the past five years. These trends necessitate a fundamental shift in how you'll need to guide your client's thought processes on the life cycle planning and timely retirement of technology assets.

Life cycle planning isn't a function of obsolescence so much, but rather relative value. This gets to the very heart of the need to go beyond the shopping-list approach to planning hardware and software purchases and make sure that *all* purchases support the business *and* technology goals, identified your clients' technology roadmap. Once you've elevated your client's understanding of technology to this new level— one of the main goals of this book—your client will consider the acquisition of adequate hardware and software as just a necessary cost of doing business to support their big picture technology investments.

When you and your client have solidified this understanding, you can begin to talk about how planning PC purchases and retirements, in the context of meeting system requirements, can actually minimize their total cost of ownership (TCO).

A very typical example: You've just landed a new account with a small public relations firm that's far behind the curve technologically. Your new client is starting to land some rather prestigious accounts, and they're growing so rapidly that their old systems (hardware, applications, and information management) just can't keep up. You've been called in to assess where they stand and to develop a plan to get them where the company president thinks they need to be.

There are 14 staff members currently sharing eight PCs. All of these desktop computers were purchased about four years ago. They all have Pentium 90-MHz CPUs, 16 MB of RAM, and 800-MB hard disk drives. Your technology roadmap identifies that they need SBS 4.5 with Windows NT Workstation 4.0 and Office 2000 Professional running on each client PC. The small business owner asks the guru and controller to sit in on an early meeting.

Much to your surprise, these two staff members have gotten a half-dozen quotes from local retail stores on the cost of RAM upgrades. They think that they can just add more memory to these desktop computers and be all set to install their new network. Their point of view changes as you begin to pull all the upgrade data together. This is what they will need:

- RAM upgrades: 16-MB module and 32-MB module to upgrade to 64 MB—$125 per PC

- Hard disk drive replacements: 6.4-GB IDE hard disk drive—$150 per PC

- 10/100 network adapters—$75 per PC

- Windows NT Workstation 4.0 licenses—$275 per PC

So the guru and controller, looking to come off as cost-saving heroes in front of the boss, are now 110 percent behind this idea of sinking $625 into each computer to extend its life. Then you remind everyone present that you'll have about 90 minutes to two hours of billable labor per PC to install and test all four of these upgrades. Again, the guru and controller shrug your concerns off as no big deal, thinking that it's still much less than the cost of the new PCs that you're recommending. But is it really?

Bear in mind these old PCs are long out of the manufacturer's warranty and have a relatively slow CPU and an antiquated video system. So by the time your client is done, it'll sink what amounts to just shy of $800 into eight PCs that barely support minimum hardware requirements, if they do at all. Or your client can think of the big picture and TCO and recognize that new desktops, for just a few hundred dollars more per PC, will provide substantially greater value in the long term. The new PCs will also likely have CPUs that operate at a minimum of four times the speed of their existing desktop PCs.

Tip

If your client is concerned about investment protection, another huge part of TCO, be sure to point out that the Windows 2000 Ready hardware requirements specify a minimum of a 300-MHz Pentium-class CPU.

Using the Technology Roadmap for Budgeting and Cash Flow Analysis

Because small business owners tend to keep a very close eye on their company checkbook and daily cash flow, your clients' technology investments and related asset acquisition patterns often are driven by ebbs and flows in their business cycles. This might manifest itself in any of the following ways:

- "I know we've been talking about upgrading from dial-up to xDSL Internet access, but we just hired three new employees. This puts all our nonemergency technology projects on hold."

- "It's our slow time of the year, so we have no budget left to train our staff. We'll just have to wait until next year to train the staff on the new applications on the SBS 4.5 network."

- "We were hoping to land a big deal last month to pay for the new RAID array in the SBS 4.5 system. But it was just an average month, so we'll have to keep our fingers crossed that the server hard disk drive doesn't crash before we can afford to install fault tolerance."

These types of situations are all too common among small business owners when they take an entirely reactive approach to technology. Another major theme of this book, however, has been to give you the tools to show how a proactive approach provides an infinitely more reliable, sound, and cost-effective strategy for both the SBS VAP and client.

By developing a technology roadmap that considers the big picture and supplementing this with a quarterly update report and accompanying meetings, your client will be able to budget for various projects and their associated time and materials costs, at least three to six months in advance. For example, if six months from now, you and your client have slated an extranet development project calling for an estimated 120 billable hours, your client has at least a ballpark idea of what needs to be in the budget and accounted for in the cash flow forecast in the months preceding the project.

Communicating with Your Client's External Advisors: Legal, Accounting, Marketing

This book has developed tools to help you and your clients build a close, long-term relationship. If you have such a rapport with your clients, they shouldn't call your firm only when something breaks or the day before a new hire is starting and needs a new fully configured laptop. As their virtual IT director, you and your firm assume a role that places you in the same category as other trusted advisors, such as their attorney, their accountant, or their marketing consultant.

Because you're taking such an approach to assessing business needs and how technology will provide solutions to existing problems, sooner or later your clients will likely want to get you and one or more of their other trusted advisors together to proceed jointly on some task or project.

Some typical discussions with your client's attorney might include:

- Developing a policy for company e-mail and Internet usage (See Chapter 10, as well as the accompanying Word template, "Company E-Mail and Internet Usage Policy Planning Worksheet," on the CD-ROM for this book.)

- Adding a disclaimer to your client's Web site

- Gathering evidence from Proxy Server logs to file a civil suit against a hacker

- Retrieving messages from Exchange Server mailboxes to support your client's termination of an employee sending adult-oriented, racist, or other grossly inappropriate e-mail

- Preparing a logon disclaimer that pops up on the SBS 4.5 system and Windows NT Workstation 4.0 clients each time someone presses Ctrl+Alt+Delete to log on

Some typical discussions with your client's accountant might include:

- Refining the hardware, software, and OS standards to accommodate an upgrade to your client's accounting package

- Configuring auditing through Windows NT Server 4.0 to track usage of certain sensitive files

- Developing a security-planning matrix to ensure that file and object permissions and rights are configured consistently and appropriately for your client's needs (The goal is usually to keep unauthorized users away from sensitive data and expensive resources.)

Tip

For more information on this topic, see my September 1999 Microsoft Direct Access VAPVoice column, "How to Sell the Security Features in Windows NT Server 4.0," which is included on the CD-ROM for your convenience.

- Testing and selecting a vertical industry application for your client

Some typical discussions with your client's marketing consultant might include:

- Designing collateral materials in such a way that they can be easily converted from paper-based glossies or brochures to the client's Web site or other electronic formats or vice versa

- Refining corporate identity, color schemes, and logos to be consistent across printed materials and Web sites

- Preparing Web-based qualification forms—the type of form a Web site visitor fills out online to indicate an interest in your client's products or services

- Analyzing Web site statistics to plan advertising budgets and develop more focused banner advertising campaigns

Staying Flexible and Adapting to Change

Now that you've been armed with the best practices, tools, and strategies in this book, you're in a much better position to survive and thrive in the future. After all, the demand for small business networking services is red hot. There are not nearly enough skilled IT workers to fill open IT positions at Fortune 1000 companies, which have substantially greater hiring budgets than SBS VAPs, let alone SBS VAP positions. From 1998 to 1999 alone, the number of unfilled IT jobs in the United States doubled from 180,000 to 360,000. So the future is very bright for you and your firm.

As the early chapters in this book discussed, however, the only constant in our business is change. This change encompasses the hot skills that your small business clients are demanding, how your small business clients' needs evolve on an ongoing basis. Take time to plan and strategize, but you also need to stay flexible.

Despite your and your clients' best-laid plans and most thorough network design report, their needs will change. If you and your staff want to satisfy and delight these clients, you need to be prepared to adapt as well. Make sure, however, their changes don't derail your firm's reputation for sticking within the guidelines of the budget and project timeline.

To that end, getting sign off on any client-initiated changes to project plans is crucial. In Chapter 11, I introduced "Change Order," a Word template included on the CD-ROM with the book. Don't be afraid to customize this template to your firm's unique needs and use it often.

But don't let the paperwork get in the way, either. After all, 28 chapters later, you're now ready to go out there, discover an enviable crop of small business client opportunities, and build a highly successful and profitable business as an SBS VAP.

The Bottom Line

In the earlier chapters of this book, I talked about how many small business clients and new SBS VAPs tend to see technology purchases and the services your firm provides as commodities, which they can shop for as they do photocopy machines, cases of paper, and toner cartridges. This probably isn't the kind of business you want to be in. You're really after the type of accounts that are looking to build long-term relationships, not ones who go out for bid and select the VAP who can provide technicians with the lowest possible hourly rates.

Throughout the chapters, you looked at how your clients will gradually come to the conclusion that they are best served by hiring your firm to serve as their virtual IT department and you as the virtual CIO. Over time however, you'll know you've arrived at an even more desirable status when your small business clients think of you as a trusted business advisor, in much the same way they call on their attorney, accountant, or marketing consultant.

Afterword

Computer books don't usually have a beginning, middle, and end. Often the material earlier in a book tends to be more basic and introductory, while chapters toward the later part of the book tend to be more advanced, and less universally applicable.

But then again, this isn't a typical computer book. In fact, this entire project was conceptualized from day one as a "how to build your business" guide—like a franchise start-up kit—leveraging SBS 4.5. This book recognizes that the overwhelming majority of SBS installations involve a reseller or consultant. And I knew the advice in the book would need to be easily accessible, tangible, and hard hitting.

I hope you've enjoyed reading this book as much as I and all of the terrific folks at Microsoft Press, the SBS product group, the book's SBS VAP focus group, and the Microsoft Direct Access team have enjoyed assembling all of various elements.

I also hope that you use the advice and tools in this volume to take your SBS VAP business to even more successful levels than you ever could've imagined.

Best of luck and keep in touch! Like you, I'm an SBS VAP and I'd love to hear from you. Drop me a line at buildingsbs@kisweb.com and let me know how *your* SBS VAP business is doing.

Index

References in italics refer to information contained in tables or illustrations.

Josh Feinberg is president of KISTech

Computer Consulting in Red Bank, New Jersey, where he specializes in implementing and supporting Microsoft BackOffice Small Business Server (SBS).

Prior to shifting his focus to the small business arena in 1996, Josh consulted for Merrill Lynch, Compucom Systems, Bear Stearns, Bankers Trust, and IBM. Josh has written for *Selling Windows NT Solutions*, *Windows NT Magazine*, and *Microsoft Certified Professional Magazine*, including print and online columns, features, and reviews. In addition to writing *Building Profitable Solutions with Microsoft BackOffice Small Business Server 4.5*, Josh writes monthly columns for the SBS and Windows NT Server Microsoft Direct Access Sales Centers.

An MCP+Internet and MCSE, Josh helped launch the New Jersey Windows NT User Group and is on the Board of Directors of the Monmouth Ocean Development Council (MODC). Josh has a BA in Economics from Rutgers College and has attended the Stern Graduate School of Business at New York University.

The manuscript for this book was prepared and submitted to Microsoft Press in electronic form. Text files were prepared using Microsoft Word 2000. Pages were composed by Siechert & Wood Professional Documentation using Adobe PageMaker 6.52 for Windows, with text in Berkeley and display type in Frutiger. Composed pages were delivered to the printer as electronic prepress files.

Cover Designer and Illustrator
Tom Draper Design

Interior Designer
James D. Kramer

Technical Editors
Blake Wesley Whittington
Thomas Williams

Principal Compositor
Paula Jeanne Kausch

Principal Proofreader
Carl Siechert

Indexer
Dan Connolly

About the CD-ROM

The companion CD-ROM for this book contains a wealth of information that will help you work with SBS systems and your small business clients more effectively. You'll find all the documents, templates, and spreadsheets covered in the book; copies of third-party evaluation software that can supplement your SBS installations; white papers on SBS written by Microsoft Product Support Services; copies of my VAPVoice columns, which contain more advice on working with SBS; and white papers written exclusively for this book.

CD-ROM Contents

To access the files on the CD-ROM, open the CD-ROM home page. To do this, select Run from the Start menu and type d:\building.htm (where d: is the letter of your CD-ROM drive). If you don't have a Web browser with which to view this page, I've provided a copy of Microsoft Internet Explorer 5 on the CD-ROM for your convenience.

If you wish to copy the documents from the CD-ROM to your hard disk drive, the setup program on the CD-ROM will do that. Please note that this setup program won't install the evaluation software or Internet Explorer on your system. To install copies of the software on the CD-ROM, click the appropriate link on the CD-ROM home page or refer to the readme.txt.

Evaluation Software

The \eval folder contains trial versions of the following programs:

- Executive Software Diskeeper 5.0 for Windows NT Server 4.0
- Executive Software Diskeeper 5.0 for Windows NT Workstation 4.0
- Executive Software Undelete 1.2 for Windows NT Server 4.0
- Executive Software Undelete 1.2 for Windows NT Workstation 4.0
- Trend Micro OfficeScan for Microsoft Small Business Server
- VERITAS Backup Exec Microsoft BackOffice Small Business Server Suite version 7.3

Excel Workbooks and Worksheets

The \excel folder contains the following Microsoft Excel workbooks and worksheets:

- Company Shared Folders Organizational Structure
- Courseware Comparison Matrix
- Guru Documentation Pack
- Internal Skills Inventory
- ISP Selection Matrix
- Network Design Report
- Roadmap Template for SBS Network
- Site Survey Inventory (Excel)

Exclusive White Papers

The \exclusive folder contains the following white papers, which I've written exclusively for this book:

- History of the SBS VAP Roundtables
- Roots of SBS
- Training Options for Related BackOffice Applications

Microsoft Direct Access VAPVoice Columns

The \vapvoice folder contains the following columns, which I originally wrote for the Microsoft Direct Access Web site:

- Be the Hero
- Elevating Small Business Server from an Expense to an Investment
- How to Get Ready to Profit from SBS 4.5
- How to Pull the Plug on Old DOS Apps
- How to Sell the Security Features in Windows NT Server 4.0
- How to Translate Sticky Notes into a Major Outlook Groupware Opportunity with Small Business Server
- IT Audit Opportunity
- Mining the Intranet Opportunity in Windows NT Server 4.0
- Overcoming the I'm Too Small to Need Windows NT Server 4.0 Argument

- Ten Ways to Help Your Clients Overcome Windows 2000 Upgrade Paralysis
- The Portal to More Value-Added Services
- The Top Ten Ways to Position Windows NT Server 4.0 Against Peer-to-Peer Windows 9x

Microsoft Product Support Services White Papers

The \pss folder contains the following white papers, which were provided by Microsoft Product Support Services:

- Choosing the Best Internet Messaging Option for Your Small Business
- Internet Connectivity and the Small Business Server Internet Connection Wizard
- Microsoft BackOffice Small Business Server 4.5 Administrative Console
- Microsoft BackOffice Small Business Server 4.5 Capacity Planning
- Microsoft BackOffice Small Business Server 4.5 Client Setup
- Microsoft BackOffice Small Business Server Messaging Solutions
- Microsoft BackOffice Small Business Server—Server Setup
- Microsoft Fax and Modem Services
- Microsoft Small Business Server Deployment Guide
- Optimization
- Technical How-to: Managing BackOffice Small Business Server Remotely

Microsoft Software

The \ie5 folder contains the setup files for Microsoft Internet Explorer 5.

Word Documents and Templates

The \word folder contains the following Microsoft Word documents and templates:

- 30-Point PC Security Check-Up
- Change Order
- Company E-Mail and Internet Usage Policy Planning Worksheet

- Credit Application
- Interviewing Checklist
- Job Description
- Letter of Engagement for Initial Consultation
- Letter of Engagement for Network Design
- Letter of Engagement for SBS Rollout
- Network Design Cover Sheet
- Quarterly Update Report
- SBS 4.5 Disaster Recovery Planning Template
- SBS VAP Partnership Planning Worksheet
- Server Status Tool (SST) Executive Summary
- Service Contract Planning Worksheet
- Site Survey Inventory (Word)
- Summary of Findings from Initial Consultation Meeting
- Support Service Agreement

System Requirements for Evaluation Software

Executive Software Diskeeper 5.0 for Windows NT Server 4.0

The system requirements for this 30-day evaluation copy are as follows:

- x86-based or Alpha-based computer running Windows NT Server 4.0, Service Pack 3 or higher
- 6 MB of hard disk drive space

Executive Software Diskeeper 5.0 for Windows NT Workstation 4.0

The system requirements for this 30-day evaluation copy are as follows:

- x86-based or Alpha-based computer running Windows NT Workstation 4.0, Service Pack 3 or higher
- 6 MB of hard disk drive space

Executive Software Undelete 1.2 for Windows NT Server 4.0

The system requirements for this 30-day evaluation copy are as follows:

- x86-based computer running Windows NT Server 4.0, Service Pack 3 or higher
- 4 MB of hard disk drive space

Executive Software Undelete 1.2 for Windows NT Workstation 4.0

The system requirements for this 30-day evaluation copy are as follows:

- x86-based computer running Windows NT Workstation 4.0, Service Pack 3 or higher
- 4 MB of hard disk drive space

Trend Micro OfficeScan for Microsoft Small Business Server

The system requirements for this 30-day evaluation copy are as follows:

- x86-based computer running Microsoft BackOffice Small Business Server version 4.0 or 4.5

VERITAS Backup Exec Microsoft BackOffice Small Business Server Suite version 7.3

The system requirements for this 60-day evaluation copy are as follows:

- Intel P166 or higher compatible processor running Microsoft BackOffice Small Business Server version 4.0 or 4.5
- 40 MB hard disk drive space
- 96 MB RAM required
- CD ROM drive
- Any host adapter supported by Microsoft Windows NT
- A compatible tape drive:
  - Most DC6000, 4mm, 8mm, and DLT SCSI tape drives, including those branded by Archive, Compaq, Conner, DEC, Exabyte, HP, IBM, Mountain, Quantum, Seagate, Sony, Tandberg, Tecmar, WangDAT, and Wangtek

- Most SCSI/IDE DC2000 tape drives, including those branded by Archive, Conner, CMS, Exabyte, HP, IBM, Iomega, Irwin, Mountain, Seagate, Summit and Wangtek

System Requirements for Microsoft Internet Explorer 5

The system requirements for Internet Explorer 5 are as follows:

- 486DX/66 MHz or higher processor that is running Windows 95, Windows 98, or Windows NT 4.0 with Service Pack 3 or higher
- For Windows 95 and Windows 98: 16 MB of RAM minimum
- For Windows NT: 32 MB of RAM minimum
- Minimal install (browser only): 45 MB hard disk drive space required for install and 27 MB hard disk drive space required after restart
- Typical install: 70 MB required for install and 55 MB required after restart
- Full install: 111 MB required for install and 80 MB required after restart
- Mouse
- Modem or Internet connection
- CD-ROM drive

Some components may require additional systems resources not outlined above.

MICROSOFT LICENSE AGREEMENT

Book Companion CD

IMPORTANT—READ CAREFULLY: This Microsoft End-User License Agreement ("EULA") is a legal agreement between you (either an individual or an entity) and Microsoft Corporation for the Microsoft product identified above, which includes computer software and may include associated media, printed materials, and "on-line" or electronic documentation ("SOFTWARE PRODUCT"). Any component included within the SOFTWARE PRODUCT that is accompanied by a separate End-User License Agreement shall be governed by such agreement and not the terms set forth below. By installing, copying, or otherwise using the SOFTWARE PRODUCT, you agree to be bound by the terms of this EULA. If you do not agree to the terms of this EULA, you are not authorized to install, copy, or otherwise use the SOFTWARE PRODUCT; you may, however, return the SOFTWARE PRODUCT, along with all printed materials and other items that form a part of the Microsoft product that includes the SOFTWARE PRODUCT, to the place you obtained them for a full refund.

SOFTWARE PRODUCT LICENSE

The SOFTWARE PRODUCT is protected by United States copyright laws and international copyright treaties, as well as other intellectual property laws and treaties. The SOFTWARE PRODUCT is licensed, not sold.

1. GRANT OF LICENSE. This EULA grants you the following rights:

a. **Software Product.** You may install and use one copy of the SOFTWARE PRODUCT on a single computer. The primary user of the computer on which the SOFTWARE PRODUCT is installed may make a second copy for his or her exclusive use on a portable computer.

b. **Storage/Network Use.** You may also store or install a copy of the SOFTWARE PRODUCT on a storage device, such as a network server, used only to install or run the SOFTWARE PRODUCT on your other computers over an internal network; however, you must acquire and dedicate a license for each separate computer on which the SOFTWARE PRODUCT is installed or run from the storage device. A license for the SOFTWARE PRODUCT may not be shared or used concurrently on different computers.

c. **License Pak.** If you have acquired this EULA in a Microsoft License Pak, you may make the number of additional copies of the computer software portion of the SOFTWARE PRODUCT authorized on the printed copy of this EULA, and you may use each copy in the manner specified above. You are also entitled to make a corresponding number of secondary copies for portable computer use as specified above.

d. **Sample Code.** Solely with respect to portions, if any, of the SOFTWARE PRODUCT that are identified within the SOFTWARE PRODUCT as sample code (the "SAMPLE CODE"):

   i. **Use and Modification.** Microsoft grants you the right to use and modify the source code version of the SAMPLE CODE, *provided* you comply with subsection (d)(iii) below. You may not distribute the SAMPLE CODE, or any modified version of the SAMPLE CODE, in source code form.

   ii. **Redistributable Files.** Provided you comply with subsection (d)(iii) below, Microsoft grants you a nonexclusive, royalty-free right to reproduce and distribute the object code version of the SAMPLE CODE and of any modified SAMPLE CODE, other than SAMPLE CODE (or any modified version thereof) designated as not redistributable in the Readme file that forms a part of the SOFTWARE PRODUCT (the "Non-Redistributable Sample Code"). All SAMPLE CODE other than the Non-Redistributable Sample Code is collectively referred to as the "REDISTRIBUTABLES."

   iii. **Redistribution Requirements.** If you redistribute the REDISTRIBUTABLES, you agree to: (i) distribute the REDISTRIBUTABLES in object code form only in conjunction with and as a part of your software application product; (ii) not use Microsoft's name, logo, or trademarks to market your software application product; (iii) include a valid copyright notice on your software application product; (iv) indemnify, hold harmless, and defend Microsoft from and against any claims or lawsuits, including attorney's fees, that arise or result from the use or distribution of your software application product; and (v) not permit further distribution of the REDISTRIBUTABLES by your end user. Contact Microsoft for the applicable royalties due and other licensing terms for all other uses and/or distribution of the REDISTRIBUTABLES.

2. DESCRIPTION OF OTHER RIGHTS AND LIMITATIONS.

- **Limitations on Reverse Engineering, Decompilation, and Disassembly.** You may not reverse engineer, decompile, or disassemble the SOFTWARE PRODUCT, except and only to the extent that such activity is expressly permitted by applicable law notwithstanding this limitation.

- **Separation of Components.** The SOFTWARE PRODUCT is licensed as a single product. Its component parts may not be separated for use on more than one computer.

- **Rental.** You may not rent, lease, or lend the SOFTWARE PRODUCT.

- **Support Services.** Microsoft may, but is not obligated to, provide you with support services related to the SOFTWARE PRODUCT ("Support Services"). Use of Support Services is governed by the Microsoft policies and programs described in the user manual, in "on-line" documentation, and/or in other Microsoft-provided materials. Any supplemental software code provided to you as part of the Support Services shall be considered part of the SOFTWARE PRODUCT and subject to the terms and conditions of this EULA. With respect to technical information you provide to Microsoft as part of the Support Services, Microsoft may use such information for its business purposes, including for product support and development. Microsoft will not utilize such technical information in a form that personally identifies you.

- **Software Transfer.** You may permanently transfer all of your rights under this EULA, provided you retain no copies, you transfer all of the SOFTWARE PRODUCT (including all component parts, the media and printed materials, any upgrades, this EULA, and, if applicable, the Certificate of Authenticity), **and** the recipient agrees to the terms of this EULA.

- **Termination.** Without prejudice to any other rights, Microsoft may terminate this EULA if you fail to comply with the terms and conditions of this EULA. In such event, you must destroy all copies of the SOFTWARE PRODUCT and all of its component parts.

3. **COPYRIGHT.** All title and copyrights in and to the SOFTWARE PRODUCT (including but not limited to any images, photographs, animations, video, audio, music, text, SAMPLE CODE, REDISTRIBUTABLES, and "applets" incorporated into the SOFTWARE PRODUCT) and any copies of the SOFTWARE PRODUCT are owned by Microsoft or its suppliers. The SOFTWARE PRODUCT is protected by copyright laws and international treaty provisions. Therefore, you must treat the SOFTWARE PRODUCT like any other copyrighted material **except** that you may install the SOFTWARE PRODUCT on a single computer provided you keep the original solely for backup or archival purposes. You may not copy the printed materials accompanying the SOFTWARE PRODUCT.

4. **U.S. GOVERNMENT RESTRICTED RIGHTS.** The SOFTWARE PRODUCT and documentation are provided with RESTRICTED RIGHTS. Use, duplication, or disclosure by the Government is subject to restrictions as set forth in subparagraph (c)(1)(ii) of the Rights in Technical Data and Computer Software clause at DFARS 252.227-7013 or subparagraphs (c)(1) and (2) of the Commercial Computer Software—Restricted Rights at 48 CFR 52.227-19, as applicable. Manufacturer is Microsoft Corporation/One Microsoft Way/Redmond, WA 98052-6399.

5. **EXPORT RESTRICTIONS.** You agree that you will not export or re-export the SOFTWARE PRODUCT, any part thereof, or any process or service that is the direct product of the SOFTWARE PRODUCT (the foregoing collectively referred to as the "Restricted Components"), to any country, person, entity, or end user subject to U.S. export restrictions. You specifically agree not to export or re-export any of the Restricted Components (i) to any country to which the U.S. has embargoed or restricted the export of goods or services, which currently include, but are not necessarily limited to, Cuba, Iran, Iraq, Libya, North Korea, Sudan, and Syria, or to any national of any such country, wherever located, who intends to transmit or transport the Restricted Components back to such country; (ii) to any end user who you know or have reason to know will utilize the Restricted Components in the design, development, or production of nuclear, chemical, or biological weapons; or (iii) to any end user who has been prohibited from participating in U.S. export transactions by any federal agency of the U.S. government. You warrant and represent that neither the BXA nor any other U.S. federal agency has suspended, revoked, or denied your export privileges.

6. **NOTE ON JAVA SUPPORT.** THE SOFTWARE PRODUCT MAY CONTAIN SUPPORT FOR PROGRAMS WRITTEN IN JAVA. JAVA TECHNOLOGY IS NOT FAULT TOLERANT AND IS NOT DESIGNED, MANUFACTURED, OR INTENDED FOR USE OR RESALE AS ON-LINE CONTROL EQUIPMENT IN HAZARDOUS ENVIRONMENTS REQUIRING FAIL-SAFE PERFORMANCE, SUCH AS IN THE OPERATION OF NUCLEAR FACILITIES, AIRCRAFT NAVIGATION OR COMMUNICATION SYSTEMS, AIR TRAFFIC CONTROL, DIRECT LIFE SUPPORT MACHINES, OR WEAPONS SYSTEMS, IN WHICH THE FAILURE OF JAVA TECHNOLOGY COULD LEAD DIRECTLY TO DEATH, PERSONAL INJURY, OR SEVERE PHYSICAL OR ENVIRONMENTAL DAMAGE. SUN MICROSYSTEMS, INC. HAS CONTRACTUALLY OBLIGATED MICROSOFT TO MAKE THIS DISCLAIMER.

DISCLAIMER OF WARRANTY

NO WARRANTIES OR CONDITIONS. MICROSOFT EXPRESSLY DISCLAIMS ANY WARRANTY OR CONDITION FOR THE SOFTWARE PRODUCT. THE SOFTWARE PRODUCT AND ANY RELATED DOCUMENTATION ARE PROVIDED "AS IS" WITHOUT WARRANTY OR CONDITION OF ANY KIND, EITHER EXPRESS OR IMPLIED, INCLUDING, WITHOUT LIMITATION, THE IMPLIED WARRANTIES OF MERCHANTABILITY, FITNESS FOR A PARTICULAR PURPOSE, OR NONINFRINGEMENT. THE ENTIRE RISK ARISING OUT OF USE OR PERFORMANCE OF THE SOFTWARE PRODUCT REMAINS WITH YOU.

LIMITATION OF LIABILITY. TO THE MAXIMUM EXTENT PERMITTED BY APPLICABLE LAW, IN NO EVENT SHALL MICROSOFT OR ITS SUPPLIERS BE LIABLE FOR ANY SPECIAL, INCIDENTAL, INDIRECT, OR CONSEQUENTIAL DAMAGES WHATSOEVER (INCLUDING, WITHOUT LIMITATION, DAMAGES FOR LOSS OF BUSINESS PROFITS, BUSINESS INTERRUPTION, LOSS OF BUSINESS INFORMATION, OR ANY OTHER PECUNIARY LOSS) ARISING OUT OF THE USE OF OR INABILITY TO USE THE SOFTWARE PRODUCT OR THE PROVISION OF OR FAILURE TO PROVIDE SUPPORT SERVICES, EVEN IF MICROSOFT HAS BEEN ADVISED OF THE POSSIBILITY OF SUCH DAMAGES. IN ANY CASE, MICROSOFT'S ENTIRE LIABILITY UNDER ANY PROVISION OF THIS EULA SHALL BE LIMITED TO THE GREATER OF THE AMOUNT ACTUALLY PAID BY YOU FOR THE SOFTWARE PRODUCT OR US$5.00; PROVIDED, HOWEVER, IF YOU HAVE ENTERED INTO A MICROSOFT SUPPORT SERVICES AGREEMENT, MICROSOFT'S ENTIRE LIABILITY REGARDING SUPPORT SERVICES SHALL BE GOVERNED BY THE TERMS OF THAT AGREEMENT. BECAUSE SOME STATES AND JURISDICTIONS DO NOT ALLOW THE EXCLUSION OR LIMITATION OF LIABILITY, THE ABOVE LIMITATION MAY NOT APPLY TO YOU.

MISCELLANEOUS

This EULA is governed by the laws of the State of Washington USA, except and only to the extent that applicable law mandates governing law of a different jurisdiction.

Should you have any questions concerning this EULA, or if you desire to contact Microsoft for any reason, please contact the Microsoft subsidiary serving your country, or write: Microsoft Sales Information Center/One Microsoft Way/Redmond, WA 98052-6399.